The Hotel and Restaurant Business

338.476   Lundberg, Donald E.
L   The hotel and restaurant business / Donald
          E. Lundberg. -- 4th ed. -- New York, N.Y. :
          Van Nostrand Reinhold Co., c1984.

              vii, 352 p. : ill. ; 28 cm.

              Includes index.
              ISBN 0-8436-2271-7(pbk.) : $21.95

                          24794

                                        SEP 87

              1. Hotels, taverns, etc.   2. Restaurants,
          lunch rooms, etc.   I. Title.

The Hotel and Restaurant Business

Fourth Edition

Donald E. Lundberg

A CBI Book
Published by Van Nostrand Reinhold Company
New York

A CBI Book
(CBI is an imprint of Van Nostrand Reinhold Company Inc.)
DEC 21 1987

Copyright © 1971, 1974, 1976, 1979, 1984 by Van Nostrand Reinhold Company Inc.

Library of Congress Catalog Card Number 83-23561

ISBN 0-8436-2271-7

Printed in United States of America

Designed by TKM Productions, Peabody, Massachusetts

Published by Van Nostrand Reinhold Company Inc.
115 Fifth Avenue
New York, New York 10003

Van Nostrand Reinhold Company Limited
Molly Millars Lane
Wokingham, Berkshire RG11 2PY, England

Van Nostrand Reinhold
480 La Trobe Street
Melbourne, Victoria 3000, Australia

Macmillan of Canada
Division of Canada Publishing Corporation
164 Commander Boulevard
Agincourt, Ontario M1S 3C7, Canada

16 15 14 13 12 11 10 9 8 7 6 5 4

Library of Congress Cataloging in Publication Data

Lundberg, Donald E.
    The hotel and restaurant business.

    "A CBI book."
    Bibliography: p.
    Includes index.
    1. Hotels, taverns, etc. 2. Restaurants, lunch
rooms, etc. I. Title.
TX911.L785 1984   338.4'76479   83-23561
ISBN 0-8436-2271-7

Contents

Preface

The fourth edition of *The Hotel and Restaurant Business* continues in the same stream as previous editions—delineating the development of the hospitality business from early inn to present-day megahotel, from the family restaurant to the billion-dollar restaurant corporations.

Emphasis is on the market dynamics of change, market forces, human motivation, and innovation. Biosketches of industry leaders are contained in each chapter. Ellsworth Statler, Conrad Hilton, and J. Willard Marriott have appeared in previous editions; this edition has added some of the current industry leaders, including Jim Collins of Collins Food International, and Louis Szathmary, restaurant industry personality.

Computerization, video conferencing, time-sharing, and condominium growth are current forces of change in the business and are discussed in this new edition. Other topics include: point-of-sales terminals actuated by computers; hotels within hotels, chains within chains, and new definitions of luxury; hotel security and safety from fires; the new job titles of concierge and director of tours; club management; and foreign investment in hotels and restaurant chains.

The entire book has been updated—a never-ending task in a book that since its first edition represents an overview of one of the most dynamic of businesses.

Introduction

What is the field of hotel and restaurant administration? It is an area of work and study that applies principles and information from a number of disciplines to the problems of selling food, beverages, and lodging to persons away from home. It includes a number of practices and techniques that have been developed, mostly from experience, for accomplishing these purposes.

A closely related extension of the field of serving the public is the area covered by foodservice in institutions: food served in schools, colleges, hospitals, and industries. The management of city and country clubs is also within the purview of the broader field of hotel and restaurant management.

Inextricably bound together with the hotel and restaurant business is that amorphous business called travel and tourism. Airlines, rental cars, travel agencies, parks, and attractions are woven into the fabric of what, for lack of a better name, can be called the hospitality business.

The field of restaurant and hotel management is interdisciplinary. It draws upon economics, psychology, management, food technology, food chemistry, microbiology, physics, engineering, architecture, accounting, marketing, and law. From these disciplines are formulated approaches, systems, and analytical tools designed to make lodging and foodservice satisfying emotional experiences for people when they are away from home.

Much of hotel and restaurant supervision is an art and will remain so in the future. The relations with people—guests, patrons, employees, purveyors, and the community at large—are closer and often more sensitive than in most fields. Retailers are concerned with customer relations but they do not have their customers eating, drinking, and often sleeping under the same roof.

Hotel, restaurant, and club managers often deal with a wide range of personalities. A patron or guest may be exhilarated, and on his or her best behavior. On the other hand, the guest may be depressed, drunk, or expressing latent feelings of deficiency in many ways.

THE ART IS COMPLEX

Systems and practices make the job of managing a hotel or restaurant much simpler, but the human element is difficult to systematize. Sinclair Lewis, who worked in a hotel for a number of years and knew the business well, expressed some of the complexities of the hotel business when he had one of his characters, a traveling salesman, say to the hero of the story:

Look here, son! Somebody been ribbing you about hotelkeeping not being a dignified and highfalutin' line of business? You tell 'em to go soak their head! Dignified! Why, say, a fellow was telling me, he was a college professor or something, I met him on a train, and he showed me where in the olden days surgeons were barbers, too, and folks didn't think much of them. They about ranked with the third assistant hired girl. But now, good Lord, when a surgeon agrees to cut you up, you'd think he was the King of France! Hotelkeeping—well, up till now it hasn't

1

been so good because the hotels—taverns they used to call 'em, and inns, and so on—and they weren't so good. But that's all changing. I tell you, way I figure it, some day there's going to be even bigger and sweller hotels than the Waldorf, and then, as the hotels get bigger, the hotelmen are going to be more important. Lots of swagger folks will get sick of housekeeping and go live in hotels. It will be one of the most important lines of business in the country, with some of the biggest folks in it.

And as for the usefulness of hotels, well, say, it takes a traveling man to appreciate a hotel—come in all tired and wet and sick of day coaches and cinders, and get a good hot cup o' coffee like Mother Weagle makes, and a good clean bed like here —though you might have some of the mattresses made of straight-grained pine, next time, and not all this knotty stuff. But I'm just joking. Nothing you could do more important—or interesting—meet all kinds of people, and see 'em with their shirts off, you might say; see the Senator soused and the up-state banker meeting a peacherino. And you belong to the hotel; you've got the start. Nobody, hardly ever, learned hotelkeeping right down to the ground unless he was born under the kitchen sink and did his teething on a file of overdue bills! Go to it, boy! You've got to learn a lot. You'll have to get into a lot bigger hotels than this—say, like in Bridgeport—biggest city of its size in the U.S.A.! You'll have to learn accounting and purchasing; not just run out and pick up a beefsteak, like you do here, but deal with big supply houses for maybe a thousand knives and forks, a hundred turkeys, five kegs of oysters—how to bargain and how to stand in with 'em. You'll have to learn manners—learn to be poker-faced with guys that would take advantage of you. Now, of course, you're only a kid, but even so, you're too doggone open-hearted; I can tell right away when you're pleased or kind of hurt. You'll have to know all about china and silver and glass and linen and brocade and the best woods for flooring and furniture. A hotel manager has to be a combination of a hausfrau, a chef, a bar-room bouncer, a doctor for emergencies, a wet nurse, a lawyer that knows more about the rights and wrongs of guests and how far he dast go in holding the baggage of skippers than Old Man Supreme P. Court himself, an upholsterer, a walking directory that knows right offhand, without looking it up, just where the Hardshell Baptist Church is and what time the marriage license bureau opens and what time the local starts for Hick Junction. He's got to be a certified public accountant, a professor of languages, a quick-action laundryman, a plumber, a heating engineer, a carpenter, a swell speechmaker, an authority on the importance of every tinhorn state senator or one-night stand lecturer that blows in and expects to have the red carpet already hauled out for

him, a fly cop that can tell from looking at a girl's ears whether she's sure-enough married to the guy or not, a money-lender—only he doesn't get any interest or have any security. He's got to dress better'n a Twenty-third Street actor, even if he's only got a thin dime in his pocket. He's got to be able just from hearing a cow's moo to tell whether she'll make good steaks. He's got to know more about wine and cigars than the fellows that make 'em—they can fool around and try experiments, but he's got to sell 'em. And all the time he's got to be a diplomat that would make Thomas F. Bayard look like John L. Sullivan on a spree. He's got to set a table like a Vanderbilt and yet watch the pennies. . . . If you can do all this, you'll have a good time. Go to it, Cap'n. Well, I think I'll go in and feed.[1]

Sinclair Lewis overstated some aspects of hotel management and tended to give the impression that a hotel manager must be a slave to the job and a master of everything to be successful. It is true that most people do not have the temperament to stand the pace, sometimes the intensity, and very often the long hours required of the successful hotel manager or restaurateur. This is changing, however; now there are many management positions in the field that require only forty hours a week of work when the manager has the necessary skills and organizational ability.

On the other hand, many people revel in long hours of work, finding it not work but "great fun" much of the time. Generally speaking, however, hotel or restaurant managers should have a high level of energy and be able to live with long hours and a multitude of demands on their nervous systems.

DIVERSE PERSONALITY REQUIREMENTS

Studies have shown that successful entrepreneurs who start their own businesses may be quite different personalities than successful professional managers. In many cases, entrepreneurs become successful businesspeople, not because they have particular gifts not possessed by the bureaucrats or because they are more daring, but because they do not fit into a bureaucratic system. In other instances, entrepreneurs are not content to be a part of a larger

---

1. Sinclair Lewis, *Work of Art* (New York: Doubleday, 1934). Reprinted with permission.

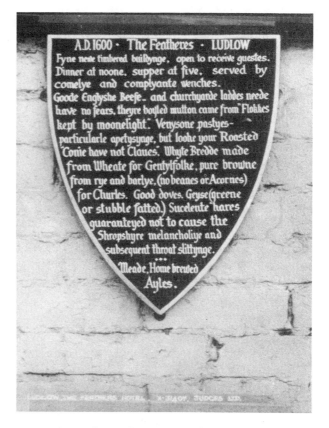

Figure I-1 *The Feathers Hotel of Ludlow, Shropshire, England. The hotel first opened for business in 1600.*

Figure I-2 *This welcoming sign lists a most appetizing bill of fare, as well as an unusual invitation: "Fyne newe timbered buildynge, open to receive guestes. Dinner at noone, supper at five, served by comelye and complyante wenches."*

organization or they may be strongly motivated for money and feel that opportunities will be greater if they go into business for themselves.

A greater range of skills and knowledge is usually required of the independent operator than of the person who is part of a chain organization. The stresses are usually also greater for the independent operator who often stakes everything on the business venture for the possibility of greater financial return. It is not unusual to find an independent restaurant operator making considerably more money than the president of a large chain organization. On the other hand, the independent usually does not have the perquisites and prestige that go with the corporate office.

The owner of a hotel or restaurant is usually profit-minded, thus concern with profit dominates his or her thinking until the business is sold or the person retires. The professional manager has somewhat different motivations. After about the age of forty, the professional manager tends to settle down into a particular area of hotel or restaurant management. The individual thinks of himself or herself as a club manager, resort manager, chain commercial house manager, manager of a luxury restaurant, quantity food producer, or whatever niche he or she fills.

MANAGING THE LARGE HOTEL

The 400 or so managers of the really large hotels throughout the country tend to be a fraternity among themselves. They march to a different drummer than the hundreds of innkeepers of the Holiday Inns. The large hotel managers usually start their careers in a major hotel, whether as recent college graduates, dishwashers, or front desk clerks. Rarely is the progression of jobs from motelkeeper to medium-sized hotel to large hotel management. These hotelpeople may be known primarily for their promotional skill or for their knowledge of good food, because there is need for much specialization in the field of large hotel management.

With the growth of the large hotel and restaurant chains, there is less need for "mein host," the well-rounded hotelperson or restaurateur, the suave conversationalist, diplomat, and personality. "Mein host" was likely to be associated with a particular property over a long period of years.

Such an association is more the exception than the rule today. The Sheraton chain and Saga Food administration have a definite policy of shifting managers every year or so. It is believed that such a policy prevents the manager from getting into a rut, offering the individual fresh challenges in a new scene of activity at regular intervals.

Other personality types needed in foodservice/lodging are the comptroller/accountant, the personnel, and the clerical types. Each of these personalities tends to have certain values and to be motivated in a particular way. The accountant personality places much value on precision and order, often tending to be compulsive about the need for a structured environment. He or she is likely to place excessive value on rules, procedures, control, and restraints. Cashiers are likely to have similar personalities. Every organization has need for a few such people.

"Personnel" is another staff job that requires the helpful, but not necessarily the managerial, type of personality. The employee in personnel is likely to be highly intelligent and people-oriented, rather than profit-oriented as the manager must be. He or she is usually not willing to take great risks and sometimes has less confidence than the typical manager-entrepreneur is inclined to have.

The independent operator must rely on personal resources, experience, and judgment, while the manager in the chain organization is likely to be guided by a detailed policy manual. The chain or franchise manager makes few of the policy-level decisions, and almost no financial, merchandising, or basic economic decisions. He or she works within the policy framework laid down by top management or the franchisor.

The innkeeper in a Holiday Inn unit or a Howard Johnson Motor Lodge unit is primarily concerned with day-to-day operations, especially those relating to the employees. He or she engages in little competitive buying and is not concerned with site, decor, or even menu planning decisions to any extent. What the innkeeper can and cannot do is carefully spelled out in manuals or in discussions with the area supervisor, and his or her salary reflects these limited responsibilities. The franchise holder's position is similar to the chain manager, but since the individual has risked some personal capital, his or her rewards are usually greater. The franchisee must also conform to franchise policy. Variations between independent ownership and professional management exist. Some companies give their unit managers partial membership and require only limited investment from them.

Glamor Assignments

Whether or not a job is glamorous depends on the individual viewing it, especially the person's social aspirations, values, and the level of excitement he or she enjoys. What could be more glamorous than being a manager of a luxurious resort hotel in the Caribbean? For many people the job holds no glamor at all; for others, it is the ultimate glamor.

Many people would find the job of foodservice director for a college to be demanding, exacting, and monotonous. Others are thrilled at the challenges offered by the students, the excitement of being in authority over perhaps hundreds of employees, the novelty of continually searching for new ways to prepare and present food, control costs, and satisfy thousands of student patrons.

The introspective person who places high value on time to reflect and withdraw from business life is usually not happy in a hotel or restaurant job. Characteristically, the person who is stimulated by working for and with people and who enjoys a relatively exciting atmosphere gets "the hotel or food business in his blood."

For the average employee in the business, wages are relatively low, but the intrinsic rewards from the job are such that the individual would not trade for a job on an assembly line, for example, with twice the pay. For those whose egos are enhanced by rubbing shoulders with persons of fame and fortune, life in a better class hotel or motel can be thrilling. As is true in any field, when competence and knowledge are gained, a person becomes more secure and confident.

Many of the careerists in hotel and restaurant management might have been just as satisfied in other fields. However, once they have started in the hotel and restaurant field, they feel comfortable in it, build friendships, attend meetings and conventions for the fraternity, and are hesitant to try another field.

Entertainment usually centers around banqueting, and this is another "reward" for being in the field. A special loyalty is likely to develop among the individuals, compounded with their emotional reactions—both favorable and unfavorable. This peculiar loyalty is not found in many other fields; the community of feeling that develops is unusual.

Nearly all managers in a foodservice/lodging operation receive meals at no cost while on the job. In some jobs, such as front desk responsibilities in a hotel, a uniform-type of coat is provided. The managers of most hotels are granted, or take, the privilege of not paying for their drinks. In some of the larger operations, an entertainment account is set up for the manager which may run into several hundred dollars a month.

In resort properties, as well as in many other hotels and motels, managers are expected to live on the premises and are given complete maintenance; that is, food, beverages, and rooms for themselves and their families. This practice has declined considerably in the last twenty years because many managers prefer to live away from the hotel or motel. A similar circumstance exists in country clubs.

The Hazards of Management

The ready availability of food and beverages has its liabilities. There is the tendency to overeat and to drink too much coffee. The manager of a resort hotel must be continually on guard to avoid visiting the bar too frequently with the guests.

Some managers are thrust into their positions before they have been tempered with experience, and their new power "goes to their heads." Finding that they are now the center of attention, at least to their employees, some managers are carried away with their importance. Suddenly, managers, even though only moderately attractive in appearance, find they have great appeal to members of the opposite sex who are interested in the advantages of associating with people of influence.

Ready access to cash is also a temptation that has been the downfall of some managers. As the old saying goes, "fast women, slow race horses, and alcohol" are ever-present temptations. The long hours and consequent stresses that are almost inevitable at times in the business weaken the defenses against such pursuits.

A well-organized personality and efficient planning can make the life of an innkeeper or restaurant keeper fairly routine and can keep stress at a minimum. However, generally speaking, the field is not one in which to grow old gracefully.

Managers in this field are much more mobile than in most fields, and necessarily so. The assistant manager or manager usually has to move on if he or she wants to move up, to acquire more responsibility and income.

Long Work Hours

Long hours and work during the evenings and weekends are the rule rather than the exception in the hotel and restaurant business. This looms as a disadvantage to the person who prizes a weekend of leisure, long hours with the family, or a routine that fits in with the habits of neighbors. To many people, the unusual hours are no handicap at all. The excitement of the job more than compensates for what might be considered disadvantages by others.

In taking over a new position, it is not unusual for a manager to stay on the job sixty or seventy hours a week; in larger hotels the manager may not leave the property for days at a time. In the seasonal resort the first few weeks of opening the property are particularly exhausting. All time and effort must be focused on the problem of getting the hotel open in time, usually with a large number of inexperienced personnel.

Strangely enough, many hotel and restaurant managers speak with pride of the excessive number of hours they work, perhaps considering it evidence of their stamina. Unfortunately, they often see the long hours as a model for others to follow and justify it in terms of economic necessity.

The work week, however, is getting shorter in hotels and restaurants. It has been found repeatedly that reducing a work week from fifty to forty-four hours, or from forty-eight hours to forty hours, increases the efficiency per hour worked. In most cases, total productivity is not markedly reduced.

For the average managers, efficiency drops after forty-four or forty-eight hours of work a week. Decision-making ability suffers with the longer hours. The person who works extremely long hours is handicapping the enterprise. The forty-hour week is becoming standard in hospital, industrial, and school foodservice.

The managers of hotels and restaurants usually work with a large percentage of employees who are relatively unskilled, uneducated, and disadvantaged. For well over a hundred years a large portion of the employees in hotels and restaurants in the East have been recent immigrants; in the last few years the majority have been from Puerto Rico and Cuba.

In New York City over 40 percent of the employees in the industry are Spanish-speaking. The southern kitchen is typically manned by black men and women. In the Southeast the majority of employees are black or Mexican-American; in the Southwest the kitchen staff will most likely be Hispanic.

At one time the better kitchens around New York City were almost completely French, but few Frenchmen are coming to this country now. In the 1960s, many of the food and beverage directors of New York City hotels were of Hungarian extraction. Working with newly arrived or disadvantaged groups can be a challenge and a problem.

According to results of the Wonderlic Personnel Test, the average waitress, cook, baker, and maid score well below the high school level of intelligence, although there are exceptions to this statement. It should be pointed out that academic intelligence as such is not as important in the jobs mentioned as is emotional stability, personal organization, energy, and

tact. Even so, hotel and restaurant managers should realize that, by and large, they are working with employees who require more training and supervision than is true in many other fields.

The status of the manager varies widely depending on the status of the establishment and his or her own personal wealth and education. Ellsworth Statler, the famous hotelman, envisaged the hotelman as being an owner-manager, a pillar of the community. Some hoteliers have achieved such status and recognition.

Generally speaking, the managers of the larger, more luxurious establishments have the most status, while the small restaurant operator, even though he or she may have an income superior to the morning-coated hotel manager, has little status. The owner of a roadside diner may have an income in excess of $50,000 while the manager of a large city hotel may be in about the same income bracket. The status gulf is considerable.

Restaurant operators are particularly sensitive about status and with good reason. In large sections of this country restaurant ownership has not been held in high repute. A few restaurant chains existed before the turn of the century, but the rapid chain growth took place after World War II. Before then, most of the restaurants were relatively small and many were family enterprises, often operated by immigrants.

Club management as a recognized field of work is also of recent origin; as late as 1912 the steward of the Harvard club had to insist upon a contract in which he was named as manager, not steward.

Despite the sacredness of our belief in democracy, there have always been elements of the master-servant relationship between those who own and those who do not, between those with status and those who lack it. This goes back to our colonial period and is still very much present in the East and South.

It was not so long ago in some parts of the country that respectable families would not allow their daughters to work in hotels or restaurants. Fortunately, such attitudes have almost disappeared. Summer work in hotels and restaurants for college students apparently has never carried any stigma.

The range and style of operation within the hotel and restaurant arena is tremendous. It is not realistic to think that a "hotelman" or a "restaurateur" can step in and manage any hostelry or foodservice operation well. The skills and social poise needed to manage an elite club are fairly rare. The person who might be highly successful in such a club might not do well at all as a director of a college foodservice.

The manager of a large urban hotel must necessarily rely on department heads who are specialists in their own right. Such a manager is primarily an administrator and coordinator; he or she does not need to be particularly knowledgeable in any one of the specialties found within the hotel. This same manager might not do well at all as a country innkeeper with no expert department heads to call upon.

Manager Needs "Nuts and Bolts"

Oddly enough, the manager of a small operation must know more "nuts and bolts" than the manager of a large operation. Similarly, the owner-operator of a highly successful restaurant may find it impossible to work within the confines of an organization of which he or she is not the boss.

Many restaurants are the reflection of the personalities of the owners, while the personalities of some chain enterprises are the result of the thinking of a number of specialists—site experts, food specialists, architects, decorators, and financial planners.

In some cases, presidents of large and successful hotel operations have been failures when they struck out on their own as owners. Ralph Hitz, the well-known hotel operator of the 1930s, was able to make impressive profits when he operated for other owners. According to his son, Ralph Hitz, Jr., he was never able to make a profit in the hotels he owned himself. He seemed to cast aside caution when it came to investing his own money in a property or in an idea.

It is only necessary to attend a meeting of a group of hotelmen, to observe their dress and manner, and then compare them with a group of motel owner-operators to see that their motivation is different. Restaurant owners also tend to differ from professional restaurant managers.

Hotel managers, characteristically, are not owners and, as might be expected, place high value on maintaining friendships with the accounting firms and with individuals who can help them into better positions. The investor is usually keenly interested in improving his or her operation to increase profits, the professional manager is much less so.

This book is an attempt to present an overall view of the hotel and restaurant business. The view is necessarily selective. Only enough background information is given to provide a feeling for the place of the inn, and later the hotel and restaurant, in history. When possible, the emphasis is on interpretation rather than fact.

IT'S A PEOPLE BUSINESS

All business reflects people, but the hotel and restaurant business is primarily a people business. It is especially important to look at the men who have shaped this business. We can learn from their experiences. Unfortunately, we can learn little from their mistakes because successful people usually succeed in hiding most of their weaknesses and mistakes.

You should get a feel for the history of the industry and an understanding of the scope and variety of technology, skill, and temperament that can be put to use in hotel and restaurant management. You should also get an idea of the vast opportunities that await the energetic and capable individuals who pursue foodservice/lodging careers.

A major appeal of the entire hospitality field is the sociability factor, which may partially explain why people in it say "it gets in your blood." It is hard to be lonely working face to face with customers. Add to this the fact that much of the personal interaction takes place in pleasant surroundings, much of it with people who are enjoying themselves, and it becomes clear that loneliness, that bugaboo of a competitive society, is less likely to be around in the hotel and restaurant business.

THE ROUND PEG IN THE ROUND HOLE

The skills and personality traits that make for success in the hotel business have much in common with those needed to do well in the restaurant business. The club field also requires qual-

TABLE I-1   Comparative Requirements, Advantages, and Disadvantages
for a Manager of a Hotel, Restaurant, or Club

Manager	Hotel/Motel	Restaurant	Club

People Relations	Supervisor/owner
	
	Department Heads
	Large numbers of
	   employees
	Guest Relations
	Public Relations
		Patron Relations
		
		Employee Relations:
		high turnover
		large percent teenagers
		   and women
			Chairman of House
			   Committee
			
			Member Relations
			Department Heads
			Employee
			Public Relations

Time Demands	High
	(can be seasonal)
		Very High
		(weekends highest; can be
		   seasonal)
			Moderate
			(high on weekends and
			   during club events; can
			   be seasonal)

Energy Level Required	High	Very High	Moderate
Personal Qualities	Determination/Confidence Personal organization Cost consciousness Imagination	Determination/Per- severance Personal organization Cost consciousness	Affability Personal organization Good taste
Special Skills	People skills (leadership) Marketing Food and Beverage (F&B) Front Desk Accounting	People skills (drive) Food and Beverage Financial (if owner)	Social poise Diplomacy/Tact Good taste Food and Beverage

Toughest Problems	Owner/Supervision rela-
	   tions
	Marketing
	Department Head Relations
	Employee Relations
	Food and Beverage
		Cost Controls
		Employee Relations
		Maintenance of Food and
		   Beverage Standards
			Board Relations
			Member Relations
			Department Head Relations
			Financial

Advantages	Status
	Several fringe benefits for
	   owner or manager
	Social/Cultural opportuni-
	   ties
	Sports in a resort
		Large profits possible on
		   investment
			Comfortable life
			Low stress
			Sports availability

Disadvantages	Can feel imprisoned Can be stressful Nontenured	Less social/cultural time Constant attention required High risk of owner High tension for some Odd and long hours Nontenured if not owner	500 bosses Unconventional hours of work Nontenured

ities in common with those of the hotel and restaurant fields. Condominium management, cruise ship "hotel" operations, and attractions management are not far away in requiring similar qualities.

Table I-1 is intended to be informative and provocative. It compares the demands placed on the manager of the hotel, restaurant, and club, and suggests some of the advantages and disadvantages of each field. All of the hospitality fields place an emphasis on people relations, and some are more demanding than others in time and energy. Personal qualities required in each field are somewhat different, as are the special skills needed.

The accountant/auditor personality, for example, is supposed to be of a separate mold —trained to be somewhat suspicious and withholding. In a facetious note, Albert Hubbard, in 1922, described an auditor as

... a man passed middle life, tall, spare, wrinkled, intelligent, cold, passive, noncommittal, with eyes like a codfish, polite in contact but at the same time unresponsive, cool, calm, and as damnably composed as a concrete post or a plaster-of-paris cast: a human petrification with a heart of feldspar and without charm of the friendly germ; minus bowels, passion or a sense of humor. Happily they never reproduce, and all of them finally go to hell.[2]

THE HOTEL/MOTEL MANAGER'S VALUES

An analysis of personal values shows the hotel/motel manager placing high value on leadership activities. He or she must be able to direct staff employees, sometimes quite large in number, and have final responsibility for their performance.

Variety, too, ranks high in the hotel manager's hierarchy of values. There can be considerable variety in the type of people problems confronted; on the other hand, there is little variety in the place of work. The manager is confined to the hotel or motel during most of the working hours.

For the manager who owns his or her own place, there is a great deal of independence.

For the person who is keenly interested in a large salary, hotel management may not be as good a career choice as some of the other pro-

fessions, although the range of salary is great, usually depending upon the size of the hotel.

For the person who likes routine and regular hours, the hotel/motel field of work is not a good choice.

The hotel/motel manager must have initiative, self-discipline, and the ability to organize and direct the work of others, build employee morale, solve problems, and handle details. The manager combines good business sense with good people sense, and must get along with guests and employees. The manager solves problems, administers the operation, and coordinates and budgets profits and expenses.

To match up your own traits and values with particular jobs within the hospitality field, complete the inventory form in Figure I-3. Give each item a number from 1 to 10, 1 being of little personal value, 10 being very significant. Place the numbers of those items in which you marked high value (8 to 10) under the jobs you think most require such high-scoring traits or values. For example, tact is a trait much called for in club management. Placing a high value on routine favors a job in accounting/control. A high value placed on variety of work suggests hotel management as a career. If high income is a primary goal, the person who is willing to take risks should aim toward becoming an owner. High energy is particularly important for restaurant managers. Salespeople generally score high in the need for social approval and the desire to be with other people. All managers need to be high in self-discipline and organization. Owners need a lot of determination, as do managers. Salespersons enjoy being around fun people. Managers have needs for responsibility, some power, and challenge. They also should bear a high tolerance for frustration.

Paid managers usually have more need for security than do those who are ready for risks and want to do their own thing in business.

If you have an urge to be around prestige people, a job in a prestige hotel, restaurant, or club may be more important and satisfying than a job that may produce more income but have less status.

It turns out that a majority of club managers do not want employment contracts and usually move from one club to another after about three years. Apparently, job security is not a strong need for them.

---

2. Quoted in *Cornell Hotel and Restaurant Administration Quarterly* (May 1977): 4.

Figure I-3 *Trait and Value Inventory*

1. 1 _____ New Experiences _____ 10

2. 1 _____ Job Security _____ 10

3. 1 _____ Desire for Responsibility _____ 10

4. 1 _____ Desire for Power _____ 10

5. 1 _____ Desire for Social Approval _____ 10

6. 1 _____ Desire to Do My Own Thing _____ 10

7. 1 _____ Opportunity to Travel _____ 10

8. 1 _____ Variety of Work _____ 10

9. 1 _____ Association with Fun People _____ 10

10. 1 _____ Association with Prestige People _____ 10

11. 1 _____ Predictable Associates and Environment _____ 10

12. 1 _____ High Income _____ 10

13. 1 _____ Need for Continuous Challenge _____ 10

14. 1 _____ Tolerance for Frustration _____ 10

15. 1 _____ Energy Level _____ 10

16. 1 _____ Readiness for Risk _____ 10

17. 1 _____ Perseverance/Determination _____ 10

18. 1 _____ Self-Discipline/Personal Organization _____ 10

19. 1 _____ Concern with Detail _____ 10

20. 1 _____ Desire for Routine; Regular Hours _____ 10

21. 1 _____ Desire to Be with Other People _____ 10

22. 1 _____ Tact _____ 10

Travel Agency Owner/ Operator	Restaurant Owner	Restaurant Operator	Hotel Manager	Club Manager	Accounting & Control	Personnel Manager	Hotel Sales

UNIVERSITY EDUCATION FOR
THE HOTEL AND RESTAURANT BUSINESS

Until the 1920s, education for the hotel manager was largely through experience. Most managers, like the managers of other enterprises at that time, did not have the advantage of a university education. The American Hotel Association was responsible for initiating a program of instruction for hotel management at the college level.

Frank Dudley, who became president of the American Hotel Association in 1917 when it became a truly national trade association, was president of the United Hotel Corporation, a company that was building hotels in the cities. J. Leslie Kincaid, chairman of the board of the American Hotels Corporation, was interested in building hotels in smaller communities. As their hotels grew in number, each man became painfully aware of the shortage of trained managers and department heads.

Maitre d's and chefs had been coming from Switzerland and France, but the demand exceeded the supply. Hotel managers, trained in the European tradition, did not understand the American commercial and family hotel. Dudley, as president of the AHMA, appointed Lucius Boomer, president of the Waldorf-Astoria, to chair an Education Committee to study educational needs.

First Courses at Cornell

One of the committee's recommendations was to establish a School of Hotel Management at Cornell University, in Ithaca, N.Y. The late Howard B. Meek, who had taught a course in resort management at Boston University beginning in 1918, was appointed to head the school which was started in 1922. Financial support, pledged by AHMA members, did not materialize; Ellsworth Statler then stepped in to underwrite $70,000 of the association's indebtedness, if the other members would pay off the remaining $30,000 of their debt.

Statler, who did not favor college education for hotel managers, visited Cornell in 1925 as a personal favor to an old friend. At one of the classes on the first day of his visit, he was asked to say a few words and dropped this bomb, "Boys, you're wasting your time here.

You don't have to learn this stuff to be a hotelman. When I have an engineering problem, I hire an engineer. I don't know a damn thing about the British thermal units, and there's no reason for you to, either. Go on home and get a job."[3]

By the end of his second day on the campus, however, Statler had changed his mind, and at a banquet that marked the end of the two-day "Hotel Ezra Cornell," he was asked to speak again. His second speech was as startling as the first: "I am converted. Meek can have any damn thing he wants." The words were prophetic. In his will, he left 10,000 shares of Statler common stock (then worth $10 a share) to set up a Statler Foundation. By 1975, the Cornell Hotel School had received more than $10 million for the construction of teaching facilities, faculty salaries, research projects, and student scholarships. Since then, additional millions have been given the school by the foundation.

The Cornell Hotel School under Professor Meek, and later Robert Beck, became the best-known of the hotel schools. Its Statler Hall, completed in 1950, pointed the way for hotel training facilities. With Statler Foundation sponsorship, a number of research projects were begun at Cornell in the early 1960s.

A number of other universities ventured into hotel management education, with varying degrees of enthusiasm and persistence. In 1928, Michigan State University started a hotel program under Bernard "Bunny" Proulx. Later, the school was headed by such well-known administrators as Leslie Scott and Donald Greenaway.

The M.S. and Ph.D. degrees were offered at Cornell, beginning in 1927, but were open only to those who completed the undergraduate program there. An active Master of Business Administration program with a hotel and restaurant major was offered at Michigan State in 1962. In the late 1930s, the University of Massachusetts, Pennsylvania State University, the University of New Hampshire, and Washington State University began hotel programs. After World War II, Florida State University and Denver University undertook similar programs of study.

3. Floyd Miller, *Statler, America's Extraordinary Hotelman* (Ithaca, N.Y.: The Statler Foundation, 1968).

Programs Begun at Other Universities

More recently, programs were begun at the University of Hawaii and the University of Las Vegas in Nevada. Two universities in Britain, Strathclyde in Glasgow and Surrey in Guildford, also established four-year degree programs in hotel administration. Three more universities added programs in 1969: the University of Houston, Stout State University in Wisconsin, and the University of Guelph, the first such university program in Canada. In 1972, the first classes in hotel, food, and travel services began at Florida International University in Miami. In 1973, California, the largest state in tourism, got its first four-year degree program at California State Polytechnic University, Pomona.

A directory of baccalaureate programs in hotel, restaurant, and institutional management in the United States, published in 1982, listed 75 institutions offering such programs.[4] More than 300 junior and community colleges offer programs in hotel and food management, two of the more prominent being the City College of San Francisco and Paul Smith College in upstate New York.

As a new discipline, hotel management has received only sporadic support from university and college administrators. Most of the programs have too few faculty members and insufficient financial support. Several universities have started programs only to allow them to lapse. The curricula in most of the four-year schools include blocks of instruction in food preparation and service, accounting, hotel engineering, management, finance, marketing, and business law; these are in addition to the usual university-required blocks in the basic sciences, humanities, mathematics, and English. More recently, courses involving data processing have been added.

Hotel and restaurant management is an eclectic discipline drawing upon numerous other disciplines, especially economics, nutrition, psychology, marketing, engineering, insurance and real estate, law, accounting, statistics, and data processing.

Closely related to the general business field, many of the skills useful in hotel and restaurant management are transferable to any management field. Signal evidence of the transferability of hotel management skills to another field was seen in the career of Edward Carlson, who grew up in the hotel business and became president of Western International Hotels, then president of United Airlines of which Western International (now called Westin) is a subsidiary. Mr. Carlson did an outstanding job of management in both presidential positions.

To be successful in any business requires that a person has highly developed skills in time management, social management, money management, and strategic planning. These are transferable skills, useful in a bureaucracy as well as in a business enterprise. The hotel and restaurant manager requires some numerical skills such as those in accounting, statistics, and data processing. Business law, insurance and real estate, and marketing principles are invaluable, and most programs in hotel and restaurant management require that those majoring in the field take these subjects in the school of business. But hotel and restaurant management requires specific technical skills as well: professional background knowledge, some understanding of nutrition, a great deal of skill in food preparation and service, particular skills in food and beverage cost controls, knowledge of wines and spirits, specialized information about hotel management, restaurant management, travel management, and property management. The manager must also take marketing principles and adapt them to the specialized hotel and restaurant field.

In looking at the four-year degree program as offered in most universities in the United States, one finds that the programs can be broken down into three parts: two years are devoted to general education as required by the university at large, one year of business subjects offered by the school of business, and one year of specialized hotel and restaurant courses.

It took almost 50 years for university administration and the field itself to recognize hotel management as a separate discipline, one complicated enough and broad enough to be offered at the university undergraduate and graduate level. In 1969, about 700 degrees were granted to students completing the four-year courses, and about thirty-five graduate degrees were granted. The numbers involved have increased sharply since then.

4. National Restaurant Association, 1982.

THE CERTIFIED HOTEL ADMINISTRATOR

The American Hotel and Motel Association has established a certificate program, Certified Hotel Administrator (CHA). Details are handled by the Educational Institute of the American Hotel and Motel Association headquartered at East Lansing, Michigan. Among the qualifications for the certificate is work experience of at least three years in a staff operational or educational phase of the lodging industry, completion of ten courses in the Institute's Diploma Program, or passing of the Educational Institute's Diploma Challenge Examination. In addition, the candidate must complete five other Educational Institute courses. Other individuals who, because of their leadership positions in the industry, feel they qualify for the certificate may take a comprehensive examination without completing the formal Institute courses.

GROWTH OF SERVICES
RELATED TO HOSPITALITY BUSINESS

Forecasts bode well for the hospitality business: more spending in hotels, restaurants, and for travel; more hospitality employment; and more hospitality managers.

Economists divide the economy into four sectors or types of activities: primary (extractive), secondary (industrial), tertiary (services to primary and secondary), and quaternary (services for their own sake). The primary sector comprises agriculture, forestry, fisheries, and mining. The secondary sector involves contract construction and manufacturing, whereas services deals with transportation, communication and public utilities, wholesale and retail trade, finance, insurance and real estate, and services in government. As an economy develops, it moves from the primary sector (largely agriculture) to the other phases. As industrialization increases and moves through a postindustrial era, the primary and secondary sectors become relatively small compared with the third and fourth sectors.

In the United States, for example, services by 1972 accounted for 67.5 percent of the employment and 56.4 percent of the gross national product. It is estimated that services will climb to 71 percent of employment by 1985 and constitute almost 60 percent of the GNP.[5]

5. Kahn, Brown, and Martel, *The Next 200 Years* (New York: Morrow & Co., 1976), p. 52.

Questions

1. The hotel and restaurant business is fast becoming a science. What parts are likely to remain an art?

2. Name at least three personality requirements of a successful hotel or restaurant manager.

3. In what way does the large chain partially eliminate the need for "mein host"?

4. Owning and operating a hotel or restaurant calls for several skills not required of the nonowner-manager. Name three of them.

5. It is often said that the hotel and restaurant business gets into your blood. Analyze the statement and name the factors that could make this true.

6. What are some of the temptations for a hotel or restaurant manager that can lead to failure?

7. What qualities would be necessary to successfully manage an elite country club that would not be necessary in a small hotel?

8. Who would need more detailed technical knowledge—the manager of a 150-room hotel or a manager of a 500-room hotel?

9. The qualities of affability and good taste would probably be more important in which of these operations: a private club, a restaurant, or a medium-sized hotel?

10. Tight cost controls are probably more important for which of these: hotel, restaurant, or club?

11. If you are seeking high status, you would probably aim toward managing which of these: large hotel, prestige restaurant, or country club?

12. Which of these operations would probably demand the least personal energy: country club, large hotel, or highly successful restaurant?

13. Which of these would require the most personal time: highly successful restaurant, hotel, or club?

14. The financial return would probably be greatest in which of these: a 150-room hotel, a highly successful restaurant, or a name club?

Discussion Questions

1. In the future what subjects will take on greater importance for success in the hospitality field?

2. How important is it for a student of hospitality management to have a basic course in chemistry? In physics? In psychology? Substantiate your arguments with examples and reasons.

ELLSWORTH STATLER (1863–1928)*

* Information adapted from Donald E. Lundberg, *Inside Innkeeping,* Brown Publishing, 1956, and from Floyd Miller, *Statler, America's Extraordinary Hotelman* (The Statler Foundation, 1968).

Ellsworth Milton Statler is considered by many to be the premier hotelman of all time. He brought luxury, or at least a higher standard of comfort and convenience, to the middle-class traveler at an affordable price.

His life story is that of a man overcoming adversity. At age fifteen, with two years of experience as bellboy at a leading hotel in Wheeling, West Virginia, Statler became head bellman. Noting the oversized profits gained from the hotel's billiard room and railroad ticket concession, he persuaded the owner to lease him these concessions. A studious promoter, he billed special exhibition games, and brought in the crowds.

Soon he had launched out into a bowling alley, then into a restaurant—The Pie House. It was the best in town. Mother Statler's chicken sandwiches and pie were served on the finest china and with quadruple-plate silver. By 1894, at the age of only thirty-one, Statler was making $10,000 a year and was ready for new fields to conquer.

Buffalo, New York, was the setting for his next venture, one that almost proved his undoing. Underwritten by a friend and the equipment house that had furnished his Pie House, Statler opened a restaurant in the basement of the Ellicott Square Building—a new office building billed as the "largest in the world." But there were no large restaurant crowds; Statler found that Buffalo was an eat-at-home town. Despite a brass band and an efficient operation, his creditors closed in.

Undaunted and with incredible imagination and energy, Statler changed the eating habits of Buffalo's downtown businesspeople. He advertised "All you can eat for twenty-five cents." Six meals were sold for the price of four, and prizes were given to lucky ticket holders. He tightened his operations, bought on a day-to-day basis, fired his expensive chef, and when beans were cheaper than peas on a certain day, beans appeared on the menu. Always efficiency-minded, he developed a service table for the dining room where waitresses could pick up napkins, glasses, butter chips, ice, silver, and linen without making a trip to the kitchen. The service table had running ice water—the first on record. To seat more people, he designed octagonal dining tables. In three short years the tide had turned. Statler was in the black and ready for bigger and better things.

He opened a 2,100-room hotel—the "Outside Inn"—a temporary hotel built to house visitors to the 1901 Pan American Exposition in Buffalo. The Exposition was a dismal failure, but fortunately, Statler had learned from his restaurant venture to buy with cash so he was not in debt.

Three years later, he plunged again, this time at the World's Fair in St. Louis. The "Inside Inn" of 2,257 rooms was described as the biggest exhibit at the World's Fair. At the end of the season, Statler found himself with $300,000 net profit and a yearning for a "big hotel."

In 1908, he opened a 300-room, 300-bathroom hotel in Buffalo. Statler's genius was seen in many details: Back-to-back rooms used common shafts for plumbing (which were later known as the "Statler plumbing shaft") and electrical conduits. He brought circulating ice water into every guest room. (According to Statler, "90 percent of the calls for a bellboy are to bring ice water. With ice water already in their room, we can cut down on the service staff. Also the guest avoids the annoyance of having to tip the bellboy.") A telephone in every room was another innovation. Also, every guest room included a full-size closet with a light in each closet. A towel hook beside each bathroom mirror made it easy for the guest to hang up a used towel rather than throw it on the floor—the result: a saving in linen and laundry. Little wonder the place made $30,000 profit the first year of operation. From then on the Statler story was one of successive successes.

Simplification and control were ever on his mind. He installed a food cost control system in 1907, and, in 1915, he hired C. B. Stoner, a professor of business administration at Carnegie Institute of Technology, to sharpen standards and controls. Stoner found a lack of uniform auditing systems. The resultant cost accounting methods became standard for the industry.

Anticipating the coming expansion of the convention business, Statler built the Cleveland Statler in 1912. Here it was that the Statler policy of "a free newspaper every morning" began. This policy necessitated another one—that of cutting one inch off the bottom of each guest room door so that the newspaper could be shoved underneath it.

The kitchens at the Cleveland Statler were planned for unhindered traffic flow of food and personnel. The dining rooms were located around the kitchen instead of being placed on a lower floor as was the common practice of the day. One kitchen served the dining room, coffee shop, and a cafe, all of them operating off and around the kitchen. Guest rooms were decorated with variety but always with related colors so that draperies, bedspreads, and rugs could be interchanged from room to room throughout the hotel.

The Detroit Statler was built in 1915, followed by the St. Louis Statler in 1918, and the Pennsylvania Statler in 1922. Here, Statler introduced the Servidor, a bulging panel in the guest room door which permitted the guest to hang clothes needing cleaning or pressing. Clothes could be picked up and returned by a bellman without the guest being confronted by the bellman for a tip. The Pennsylvania Statler was also the first hotel to offer complete medical services.

Other Statler innovations included: posted room rates; attached bed-headboard reading lamps; radio reception at no extra charge to the guest; liberal quantity of towels and writing supplies in rooms; and group insurance for employees on no other condition than a year's service.

Statler is credited with being one of the first hotelmen to be concerned with employee relations and benefits. He devised a profit-sharing plan that allowed many a maid and bellboy to eventually retire with dignity and security.

"EM," as Statler signed himself, was a dynamo of energy, and no detail of construction or operation was too small for his attention. He might be found lying down in a bathtub, fully clothed, gazing around the room to see what the guest would see in a similar position. If he spotted plaster smeared on the underside of the washbowl, he invited the manager of the hotel to assume a similar position. The smeared plaster was quickly removed. He could be seen on the top floor of a new hotel, stopwatch in hand, timing to the second how long it took the toilet to flush or a bath to fill.

Statler was continually preaching the theme of service to the public. "The Statler Service Code" was a formal company policy, each employee being required to memorize it and to carry a copy of it on his person during working hours.

The Statler Foundation today has assets of many millions and has made grants totaling well over $14 million. The School of Hotel Administration at Cornell has received more than $10 million for teaching facilities—Statler Hall and the Statler Inn—and for scholarships, faculty salaries,

and research. San Francisco City College has a Statler Library. The Statler Foundation matches funds raised by regional hotel and restaurant educational foundations, funds that have totaled several hundred thousand dollars.

"Life is service. The one who progresses is the one who gives his fellow human being a little more, a little better service." Such a philosophy, public or private, fits the hotel business perfectly and fit Ellsworth Statler in particular. Statler service became world famous, and through the Statler Foundation, his contributions to American hotel development will continue to be effective.

1 The Early Inn/Tavern

Innkeepers have been around for centuries. Necessarily so, because they satisfy basic needs—the need to eat, drink, and sleep. They are one of society's escape valves, offering: (1) a respite from ceaseless competition, (2) the pleasures of the table and the bed, (3) a sanctuary for the weary, and (4) titillation for the bored or frustrated.

Reference to tavernkeeping was made as early as about 1800 B.C. in the code of Hammurabi. The death penalty could be imposed for merely watering the beer. A tavern owner who ignored an order that set the price of six measures of liquor at five measures of corn was put to death by drowning.[1] The Greek tavern keeper, like his modern day counterpart, offered food, drink, and sometimes a bed. The taverns of ancient Athens served both domestic and imported wine. The food served was likely to be based on the Mediterranean triad of grain, olive oil, and wine.

There might have been cheese (made from goat's milk), barley bread, cabbage, peas, broad beans, and lentils. Figs and olives were also available. Cheese cakes, honey buns, cakes of sesame seed were favored.

If there was meat, it was usually goat, pork, or lamb. A banquet might include thrushes, finches, and hares. Stuffed paunch of ass was considered a delicacy in Athens. There might also have been sausages and hog puddings. Fish and eel were common. Coriander was the most popular seasoning, but cumin, fennel, and mint were also used.

AFTER THE SACRIFICE, A FEAST; AFTER THE FEAST, DRINKING

For a very practical reason, the early tavern might be located near a temple. From the temple the sacrificed animals were taken to the tavern and eaten (after the sacrifice, a feast; after the feast, drinking). Each guest lay on a couch with a cushion or bolster under the left arm.

Flute girls were called upon to exercise their talents during the meal. At some of the taverns there might be a small stage for theatrical entertainment. When the meal was finished it was the Athenean custom to pour three libations: one to the gods, one to the departed heroes, and one to Zeus. Garlands and, on occasion, perfumes were handed out, then the drinking began. Some taverns had cubicles into which the worshipers of Aphrodite might retire.[2]

In Egypt, during the same and earlier periods, the menu was based on bread, birds, beef, fish, and fruit. Roast goose was a particular favorite. The poor ate mainly dried fish and whatever bread they could afford. At a banquet, the guests wore wigs, and they might also have a small cone of ointment placed on their

1. *Wall Street Journal* (March 5, 1980): 18.

2. William Younger, *Gods, Men, and Wine* (London, England: The Wine and Food Society, 1966).

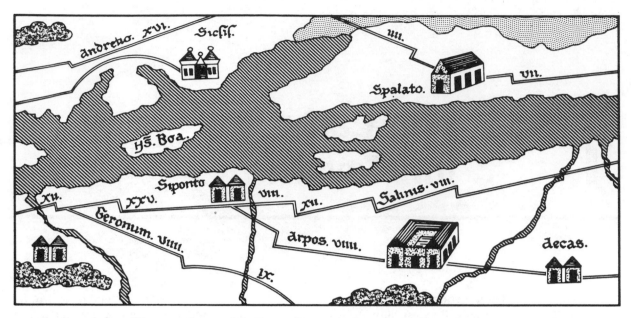

A segment of a military road map of the Roman Empire in the time of Emperor Theodosius Magnus (347–395 A.D.). The symbols on the map indicate types of accommodation:

 1. the simplest roadside accommodations suitable only for rest

 2. better accommodations than the places uninhabited

 3. better quarters for larger units but no service (no live-in slaves or local vassals)

 4. good shelter, a place for longer rest, recuperation, and refurbishing of supplies.

Figure 1-1   *Artist's rendering of a military road map of the Roman Empire (347–395 A.D.).*

Source: Map privately printed in Vienna in 1753. Used here courtesy of Chef Louis Szathmary, The Bakery, Chicago, Illinois.

heads, which melted and ran down over the wigs or hair. The serving girls and the guests were provided collars of flowers.

By the time Rome had conquered the then known world, inns and taverns were well established. An accurate picture of what they were like can be seen at Pompeii and Herculaneum, small resort towns in southern Italy that had the misfortune to be located near Mt. Vesuvius. In 79 A.D., the mountain erupted as a volcano. Ashes, lava, and hot mud smothered these towns, preserving them for modern times.

A segment of a military road map of the Roman Empire in the time of Emperor Theodosius Magnus (347–395 A.D.) is a kind of mobile tour guide of the time. The symbols on the map (Figure 1–1) indicate the kind of accommodation.

The traveler can wander about Pompeii and see the hospiteum, the caupona, the popina, thermopoliums, and the tabernas. They are much as they were, even the graffito "Serena hates Isadore," on a wall in the town.[3] The caupona and hospiteums were inns or hotels providing lodging and, in some cases, a basic menu of wine, bread, and meat.

The reputations of the operators, the caupones or innkeepers, were even worse than those of the tavernkeepers. Apart from being accused of fraudulent or immoral dealings, the female caupones occasionally achieved a reputation for sorcery. Nearly every block of houses had its own bar, in much the same way

3. Howard Luxton, *Pompeii and Herculaneum* (London, England: Spring Books, 1966).

that we find cafes in every downtown block of American cities. In Pompeii alone, a relatively small town in its day, 118 bars or restaurant bars are identifiable.

The thermopoliums, the snack bars of the day, sold wine from a "hot drink and food counter," which faced the street. Pottery jars were set into a marble counter and held snacks such as olives, dried vegetables, and probably pickle appetizers. Some of the counters were fitted with a small furnace used to heat water for the caldum, a hot drink made of wine and boiling water. Some thermopoliums had a room behind the counter which served as a dining area. The popina, predecessor of our modern restaurant, sold hot restaurant food only. Thermopoliums sold only snacks.

Tabernas, forerunners of the bar of modern times, might also sell food and offer such attractions as gambling and prostitutes (not too different from some bars and B-girls of today). In Rome, taverns were identifiable by their pillars, "girt with chained flagons," and the fact that red, thyme-flavored sausages were hung around the walls. Floors were bright with mosaics and the walls were enlivened by paintings, similar to the decor found in the trattorias of modern Italy.

In the country were rustic pubs where the owner might grow his own grapes and make his own wine. Small dried cheeses hanging in rush baskets were also available.

Hospitality terminology owes much to the Romans. The word *hospitality* is derived from the Latin *hospitium*. Related words are *host*, *hospice*, *hostelry*, and *hotel*.

With the decline of the Roman Empire, in about 500 A.D., several hundred years passed during which the inn was largely lost to civilization. Travel was infrequent and trade largely at a standstill. Since there were few travelers, there was little need for innkeeping. Even so, in England, inns for travelers were referred to as early as the middle sixth century by the Laws of Acthelbert of Kent (560–616 A.D.).

CHURCH HAVEN FOR TRAVELERS

The church came to be dominant and the only recognized authority from one country to another. Monasteries and other religious houses took in travelers (and welcomed donations).

Hospices, a form of inn, were operated by religious orders; guest houses were also maintained by some of these orders.

One such religious order, the Knights of St. John of Jerusalem, was founded in 1048 when a hospital was erected in Jerusalem to care for pilgrims making the visit to that city. Later it became a military and religious order of considerable power and was given the responsibility by the Pope of protecting pilgrimages to and from Jerusalem.

Many cathedrals and monasteries made guests welcome, the rich and noble sitting with the head prelate, the poor being housed in separate quarters. There were no room rates. Often the monastery porter, whose primary function was that of gatekeeper, also managed the guest house. It might be said that the church operated the first hotel chain.

The Crusades, beginning in 1095 and lasting over the next 200 years, encompassed a great social revolution, creating trade that led to the rise of a middle class. Indirectly, it revived innkeeping. Northern Italy was the first to feel the effects of the renaissance brought on by the Crusades. Innkeeping there became a solid business and guilds of innkeepers flourished, making regulations for themselves and for their guests.

In Florence, Italy, for example, there were enough innkeepers by the year 1282 to form a guild (a mutual-benefit society). The guild innkeepers of Florence controlled business to the extent that all strangers to the city were interviewed at the gates by city officials who directed them to officers of the guild, who, in turn, assigned foreigners to designated inns; natives of Tuscany, the local province, were assigned to other hostelries.

THE OLD ENGLISH INN

The early English inn followed in the tradition of the ale house or ghildhus of Saxon England, where people gathered to socialize and to express themselves. An evergreen bush attached to a pole was understood by everyone to mean that ale could be had inside. (The custom is still observed in some Austrian villages. A green bough or twig signifies that apple wine is available and for sale in the wine cellar.)

Armies for the Crusades were recruited in pubs and Chaucer's pilgrims quenched their thirst with beer on their way to and from Canterbury.

It was in an inn over a glass of ale, according to one commentator, that the rudiments of self-government evolved; there, also, much of what meager pleasures were to be had could be found. By the thirteenth century, the inn had special significance, at least for one Walter de Map who said, "Die I must, but let me die drinking in an inn. . . ."

Though each parish had its ale house, those that rented rooms were few. Inns were found in the larger towns and at the crossroads and ferries. Buildings were often little more than shelters with a minimum of furnishings. Rushes thrown on an earthen or stone floor acted as a carpet and made a convenient place to throw bones or other food remnants. A main room with mattresses placed along the walls for guests to sleep on was the extent of the appointments. Meals were an individual matter as most guests brought their own.

By the fifteenth century, some of the inns had twenty or thirty rooms. The George Inn, one of the better known, had a wine cellar, a buttery or pantry, a kitchen, and rooms for the host and for the hostler, the caretaker of the horses. The rooms or chambers were named after well-known people, cities, or prominent offices; they included the Earl's chamber, Oxford chamber, the Squire's chamber, London chamber, and the Fitzwarren chamber.

During the Tudor period (1485–1603), and for some time thereafter, the courtyards of some of the inns were used by traveling troupes of players. They declaimed to the audience who sat in the surrounding galleries of the courtyard.

The inns or taverns were identified by simple signs. This was necessary because of the number of people who could not read, but could say, "Meet me at the sign of the Bull." There were many Lions, Golden Fleeces, White Harts, Black Swans, Dolphins, and similar signs.

In the later 1700s some of the names were changed to include the word *Arms,* such as the King's Arms or Dorset Arms, Display of a lord's arms at an inn often meant that the inn was in the territory of a particular noble family and was under its protection. Some heraldic signs

Figure 1–2   *A sign for a local tavern of the Tudor period (1485–1603).*

were related to the original ownership of the land on which the inn stood, or a servant-turned-innkeeper might use the arms (or badge) of his former master. Even today there are said to be 400 pubs with the King's Head name, 300 Queen's Heads, and more than 1000 Crowns.

Some early inns had open galleries that were approached by outside staircases. With time, the galleries were enclosed as a protection against weather. In the courtyards were boxes or stalls, and harness and hostler's rooms. A mounting block in one corner allowed the more portly customer to climb aboard his horse. At the larger inns, above the stables, were quarters for the postboys (boys who carried the mail).

Many old inns had a garden and bowling green, and some had brew houses for making beer. A long room or assembly room contained a fireplace at one end and was the function room for banquets and dances. A partial census of 1577 counted 14,202 alehouses, 1,631 inns, and 329 taverns in England and Wales.[4]

Inns Helped by Henry VIII

Without intending to do so, Henry VIII fostered the growth of innkeeping by suppressing the monasteries in 1539. They had played a major role in travel, maintaining the principal roads for pilgrims to the larger cathedrals. Hostels had been established adjacent to an abbey or monastery where pilgrims could stay for two days, accommodated and fed according to their rank. When church lands were given away or sold, the church's function as host to the traveler disappeared.

Another factor that favored the development of inns was the fact that long before a national postal system was established, selected innkeepers were forced to retain stables and horses to meet the demands of the royal post.

The first stagecoaches in England, first mentioned in 1635, were huge, lumbering vehicles, joyless for the riders, especially since travel began early in the morning, usually before sunrise, and lasted until late at night. Later stagecoaches had such improvements as springs, seats for four inside, and seats for eight or ten on top. Outside passengers were treated as a superior race of Spartans, says one historian, while the interior seats were left for "anaemic spinsters and querulous invalids."

In the period from 1400 to 1800 the dietary regime of the common man hinged on the word *monotony*. According to one historian the common man in Europe ate the same meal, day after day, "bread, more bread, and gruel." Adult males consumed two and three pounds of bread a day; in the East it was rice; in Mexico it was corn. Alcohol was drunk excessively. Men and women drank themselves into insensibility.[5]

Menus in the early English inn relied heavily on meat and ale; the vegetables eaten were relatively few. The vegetables we are fond of today were not eaten because they were not available until the sixteenth century. Tomatoes, sweet and white potatoes, pumpkin and squash, string beans, kidney beans, lima beans, peppers, cocoa, tapioca, corn, cranberries, blueberries, and strawberries are all products of the New World. Potatoes were not known to Europe until Pizarro found them in Peru and Chile.

In the middle 1600s some inns even issued unofficial coins which the innkeepers, men of repute, guaranteed to redeem in coin of the realm. The fact that an innkeeper issued such tokens meant that the inn was of considerable importance at the time.

The English inn was headquarters for a variety of sports, both indoors and outdoors. A variety of dart and dice games, dominoes (going by such odd names as Hazard, Strutt, and Shove-groat), billiards, and bagatelle were played; cockfighting was also common, both indoors and out. The bloodthirsty could enjoy bull and bear baiting—putting dogs on the animals—and throwing at cocks. Those who liked the active sports used the inns as headquarters for fishing, shooting, coursing, hunting, and falconry. Dogfights and prizefighting practiced on rough grounds were popular. Of course the main pastime was drinking beer, ale, wine, and later gin.

The word *hotel*, used by the French to refer to a mansion or public building, was borrowed by the Fifth Duke of Devonshire and applied to a crescent-shaped building in London about 1760. It housed the Grand, the Centre, and St. Anne's Hotels. In France large houses in which apartments were let by the day, week, or month were called *hotel garni*.

Old Inns Still Operate

English common law early declared the inn to be a public house and imposed on the innkeeper social responsibilities for the well-being of travelers. The innkeeper had not only the right to receive travelers, but the duty as well. He was required to receive all travelers who presented themselves in reasonable condition and were willing to pay a reasonable price for accommodations.

---

4. Michael Brander, *The Life and Sport of the Inn* (New York: St. Martin's Press, 1973).

5. *The Structures of Everyday Life*, Volume I, 15–18th century, Fernand Braudel, Harper and Row, 1982.

Figure 1–3   *The Swan, Lavenham, England. This half-timbered inn grew from three houses built in 1425. In its early day, it had stabling for fifty horses. Here, traveling apothecaries invited sufferers of diverse diseases to come to the inn to be cured. In 1607, John Girling, the innkeeper, issued a trader's token—a sure sign of a good reputation.*
Source: Courtesy of Trust Houses, Limited.

Approximately 200 of the old coaching and posting inns, together with some hotels, are operating today in England and Wales as part of the Trust Houses, Limited. Some of these date back more than 400 years.

The Trust Houses began in 1903 under a group that wished to prevent the old inns from becoming merely local taverns. The majority of these old inns are now managed by husband and wife teams, much as they were originally. The standard of cleanliness and the quality of food and service are excellent. Rates are quite low compared with the usual city hotel rate. Trust Houses, Limited, has become the largest hotel company in Great Britain.

The image we are likely to have of the old English inn is that of the coaching inn, which

flourished during the eighteenth and early nineteenth centuries. The coaching era in Great Britain began in earnest in 1784 when Parliament commissioned government mail delivery by coach. Until then, mail had been carried by postboys riding horseback over the poor roads of the time.

Mail coaches soon made their appearance and were easily identified by scarlet wheels and underbody with the upper part of the coach painted black. At one time there were fifty-nine of the large mail coaches in England and Wales, each pulled by four horses. Scotland had sixteen mail coaches, and Ireland had twenty-nine. Attesting to the size of the operation, more than 30,000 men and 150,000 horses were employed primarily in moving the mail.

The mail coaches carried a maximum of seven passengers: four inside, and three up in front with the coachman; only the guard rode in the rear. At the height of the coaching era, seventeen mail coaches assembled each evening at the General Post Office in London. Nine others left inns in Piccadilly and the West End of London each day of the week.

The traveler paid a little more for riding in the mail coach, with its security and the limita- tion on the number of passengers. Private stage- coach companies had their own coaches and took as many passengers as could be squeezed in on top of the coach. Sometimes as many as thirteen people rode in and on a coach, four in- side, four up front, and five in back, with lug- gage piled on the roof.

A traveler with the money and the desire for prestige and privacy could ride a post chaise. This was drawn by two horses, one of

Figure 1–4   *The Black Swan Hotel, Helmsley, North of York, England. This inn has been added to and renovated many times in 400 years. The rough stone walls are more than two feet thick. For many years the Earl of Feversham held his annual Rent Dinner here, entertaining over seventy ten- ants. Venison from the Earl's deer park has been served here at least once a week in season.*
Source: Courtesy of Trust Houses, Limited.

which was ridden by a youngster called a post-boy. Although costs for such elegant travel were twice as much as for the usual tallyho, many people used the post chaises. A nationwide posting system was established with many inns used exclusively as posting inns.

Speeding the Stagecoach

Speed was the challenge; the coach company that could cut travel time got the business. The mails averaged about ten miles per hour and the stages or inns where the horses were changed were ten miles apart. Competition to decrease travel time was fierce. One way was to cut the time required to change horses, and this was finally reduced to forty-five seconds. In 1830, the Birmingham Independent Tallyho averaged 14½ miles per hour on the trip from London to Birmingham.

The coachmen were the athletic heroes of the day, many of them driving four horses and averaging sixty miles a day, three stages out and three stages back. Young gentlemen often bribed the coachmen to let them take the reins. So intense was the interest in driving that a few noblemen set up their own stagecoach companies to insure their participation in the sport of driving.

The country inns were largely dependent on the travel habits of their customers, and a large part of their business came from providing horses for the coaches. Several inns maintained as many as 50 horses, while the Bow and Mouth in London kept 400 horses. However, travel was still slow and it required something like 34 stages and 42 hours to cover 400 miles.

When the railroad appeared in 1825 in England, most people were not aware of its implications for innkeeping; the innkeepers were no exception. Travel time from London to Bath, a distance of 110 miles, was reduced from the 11 hours required by coach to only 2½ hours by steam locomotive. The choice of travel was obvious.

In 1838, when Parliament permitted carrying of mail by railroad, the coaching era was over. It was not until the 1900s, when the country inns were rediscovered by cyclists and then later by motorists, that the beautiful inns of the countryside of England, Wales, and Scotland returned to their former position.

Today in Britain some pubs claim to date back nearly a thousand years to earlier taverns on the same site. Others have been in business in the same building for several centuries and are protected as national landmarks.

THE EARLY AMERICAN TAVERN

"With a heart full of love and gratitude, I now take leave of you. I most devoutly wish that your later days may be as prosperous and happy as your former ones have been glorious and honorable." It was General George Washington saying farewell to his top-ranking officers on December 4, 1783.

Washington spoke with difficulty, "I cannot—I cannot come to each of you but shall feel obliged if each of you will come and take me by the hands."[6] The place was the old DeLancey mansion, The Fraunces Tavern, at the corner of Pearl and Broad Streets in New York City. The black proprietor was Samuel Fraunces, known as Black Sam.

The Fraunces Tavern was an appropriate place for Washington to say farewell to his officers since it had been a meeting place of the Sons of the Revolution. Samuel Fraunces, a former West Indian, was later to be voted cash grants for his services to American prisoners of war and for "other acts." When British officers occupied New York and frequented the tavern, they apparently were unaware that Fraunces' sympathies remained unchanged and that he was one of our first intelligence agents. He later became the first chief steward of the Executive Mansion, again serving Washington, this time when he was president.

Patrick Henry called the taverns "the cradle of liberty." In Boston, The Green Dragon and the Bunch of Grapes had been the meeting places of the Sons of Liberty during the Revolution. The Boston Tea Party was planned in The Green Dragon.

Buckman Tavern had been the rallying point for the Lexington militiamen. Catamount Tavern was where Ethan Allen and the Green Mountain Boys met to plot their strategy against the New York Staters and against Gentleman Johnny Burgoyne. Generals Israel

---

6. *American Heritage Book of the Revolution* (New York: Simon & Schuster, 1958).

Figure 1-5   *Table setting of an early American tavern (Ordinary at the Hall Tavern, Charlemont, Massachusetts, 1700). Note the use of the wooden serving ware and the horn drinking cups. Dinner was served family style. In some taverns along the Eastern seaboard, the menu was fairly long. At the more primitive inland taverns, the menu might include corn (in some form), bread, bacon, and whiskey.*
Source: Courtesy of the Heritage Foundation. Photograph by Samuel Chamberlain.

Putnam, Jethro Sumner, and George Weeden were former tavernkeepers. John Adams, our second President, owned and managed his own tavern between 1783 and 1789.

Coles Ordinary: First Inn in the Colonies

The first tavern in Boston, and probably the first in the Colonies, was opened by Samuel Coles in 1634 and known as Coles Ordinary. Coles, who had been a comfit-maker in England, came with the first shipload of Puritans in 1630. (A short-lived tavern was part of the ill-fated Jamestown Settlement earlier.) His place was later to be called the Ship Tavern. Coles be-

came one of Boston's first citizens, a deacon of the First Church, a steward of Harvard University, and a leading businessman.

The ordinaries closely followed the establishment of churches. The courts at first recommended, and later required, that some kind of public house be set up in each community. Sometimes land was granted and tax exemptions or other inducements were offered to encourage the keeping of an ordinary. The term comes from England where it was customary for eating places to have a daily "ordinary," a midday meal or supper, often consisting of a particular dish in which the host specialized, served at a common table at a fixed time.

The principal meal of the day was served at two o'clock in the afternoon. Guests were called together by ringing a bell in the street. Customary fare was salmon in season and veal, beef, mutton, fowl, ham, vegetables, and pudding. Each guest had a pint of madeira at his or her place. The carving was done at the table in the old English way, each guest helping oneself to what he or she liked best.

The early New England taverns were under the strict guardianship of the Puritan fathers. Prices were well regulated. In 1634, when the first taverns were built, sixpence was the legal charge for a meal and a penny for a quart of ale or beer in a tavern.

If a man were clocked at his beer tankard on a weekday for more than a half hour, he was guilty of idleness and could be fined. In 1633, a Robert Coles of Boston was fined ten shillings and enjoined to stand with a white sheet of paper pinned to his back which read "Drunkard."

Happier Days with the Huguenots

Luckily for us today, the Puritans were followed by Huguenots in 1685. The Huguenots came to escape religious persecution following the revocation of the Edict of Nantes. They were everything that the Puritans were not—merry, buoyant, cheerful, and music-loving. They loved dancing, theatricals, and entertainment. They even went so far as to bus their wives and other men's wives on Sunday, or any other day, for that matter.

Although French cuisine was never widely popular in the United States, it has influenced our hotel and restaurant menus. Thomas Jefferson was especially fond of French cooking and wines, and frequently entertained (far beyond his means) as president, and later at his home, Monticello.

A well-known hostelry of the colonial period was the City Tavern. Built on the docks of New York City in 1642 by the West India Company, it was primarily for the English traveling from New England to Virginia. The Blue Anchor, on the Delaware, in what is now Philadelphia, was where William Penn first stopped on his arrival in the New World.

In Colonial Williamsburg some thirty inns, taverns, and ordinaries welcomed guests. The King's Arms in Williamsburg offered a meal of some fifteen courses. Four well-known taverns of the period have been reconstructed on their original foundations and reopened as distinctive colonial eating places: Christina Campbell's Tavern, the King's Arms Tavern, Chownings, and The Raleigh Tavern.

It was in The Raleigh Tavern that Phi Beta Kappa, the honor society, was founded. The tavern's motto "Hilaritas, Sapientiae et Bonae Vitae Proles" "Jollity, the offspring of wisdom and good living") is appropriate to any good hostelry, then or now. The Williamsburg taverns have been modernized to an extent and the menus are not completely authentic pre-Revolutionary, but the overall flavor is there.

On the Bill of Fare in Early Plymouth

Meals in a colonial tavern were simple but plentiful. Here is a bill of fare from an early Plymouth, Massachusetts, tavern:

A large baked Indian whortleberry pudding

A dish of saughetach (corn and peas)

A dish of clams

A dish of oysters and a dish of codfish

A haunch of venison, roasted by the first Jack brought into the Colony

A dish of sea fowl

A dish of frost-fish and eels

An apple pie

A course of cranberry tarts and cheese made in the Old Colony

Beverages flowed freely. At first the only choice was between poor beer and rum. Later, these were combined to make the most popular drink—flip, which consists of rum, beer, cream, beaten eggs, and spices, heated by plunging a hot loggerhead into the mixture. It was said to be both food and drink, and if you had enough, it was also lodging for the night. There were also bounce and sling, punch and shrub, eggnog, and Tom and Jerry, some hot, some cold, but all basically rum.

Travel was on the rugged side. Travelers were called at 3:00 A.M. and rode until 10:00 P.M. One pair of horses usually carried the stage twelve to eighteen miles. The first regular stagecoach inn was established in 1760, between New York City and Philadelphia. Later, between Boston and Providence as many as forty coaches were on the road at one time.

In populous sections like Pennsylvania, where the sixty-six-mile Lancaster Turnpike was located, there were sixty taverns of varying social acceptability. Wagon drivers slept on bags of hay and oats on the taproom floor. Cattle drovers stopped at drover stands (taverns that had lots into which the livestock could be turned and fed). These taverns were also known by their signboards, some of which were imaginative, such as "The Jolly Tar."

The word *turnpike* came from the practice of placing a pike or staff across the toll road. One side was embedded with spikes. When the toll was paid, the pike was turned, spikes down, so the traveler could pass. The first turnpike was built between Philadelphia and Lancaster in 1792. By 1838 Pennsylvania had 2,500 miles of turnpike.

Accommodations follow travel. In the late 1820s, Pennsylvania began the development of what eventually became 1,200 miles of canals. Canal taverns sprang up every 10 or 12 miles. The state of New York also had a fairly extensive canal system with taverns, and later hotels, edging the canals.

Old Taverns Open for Inspection

Many a New England village and town today contains a home that was previously a tavern, for most of the taverns were originally constructed as large homes and were used as homes by the tavernkeeper. The furnishings and the equipment of these old taverns is not a matter of speculation since considerable effort has been taken to preserve a few of them.

In Old Deerfield, Massachusetts, one can tour the Hall Tavern and see the long tavern table set for guests with "treen," wooden dishes, horn spoons, and cups. Pewter plates replaced the wooden ones in later Colonial America. The barroom stands ready to serve the traveler and one can almost hear the tavernkeeper call out, "Mind your p's and q's" (pints and quarts), to permit another round of drinks before closing time.

The family of the tavernkeeper was kept busy making souse (boiled pig's feet, ears, and skins pickled in vinegar) sausage; filling pork and corned beef barrels; preparing lard and tallows for candles; and making mince, apple, and cranberry pies. If this was not enough to keep the innkeeper's wife busy, she could make clothes for her family. In the cellar were barrels of cider, vegetables in bins, seed, and the apples of the time—golden pippins, greenings, russets, seek-no-furthers, and pumpkin sweets.

FACTORS IN THE GROWTH OF THE HOTEL AND RESTAURANT BUSINESS

Innkeeping, and later the hotel and restaurant business, has paralleled the growth of trade, travel, and industry, and in modern times correlates highly with disposable income and the cost and convenience of travel. The ancient period, 500 B.C. to about 500 A.D., saw the growth of inns in Ancient Greece and in Ancient Rome, inns, snack bars, and military messes. During the medieval period, from about 500 A.D. to about 1300 A.D., trade and travel was severely limited; and much of the travel had to do with pilgrimages, the travelers being fed and sheltered at various religious houses. The Crusades had the effect of spurring trade and travel, and the Renaissance, from about the fourteenth century in Northern Italy to the seventeenth century in England and Northern Europe, saw the rebirth of tavern and innkeeping. The suppression of the monasteries in England by Henry VIII in 1536 forced the growth of innkeeping in England.

Prior to 1775, all societies were preindustrial. In the period 1775–1875, Northwestern Europe, Japan, and North America became industrialized; and in the period 1875–1950, mass-consumption societies developed in those places. Beginning about 1950 there was rapid world-wide economic and population growth, and industrial societies made disposable income available for the masses to travel and to frequent hotels and restaurants.

Invention in travel modes has also been a determinant in the growth of the hotel and restaurant business. As each new form of transportation brought down the cost of travel and increased its convenience—the steamship, the railroad, and the automobile—travel became possible for those other than the elite. The commercial jet airplane in 1959 ushered in the era of international travel.

The time chart in Figure 1–6 provides some perspective to the modern period of the growth and development of the hotel and the restaurant.

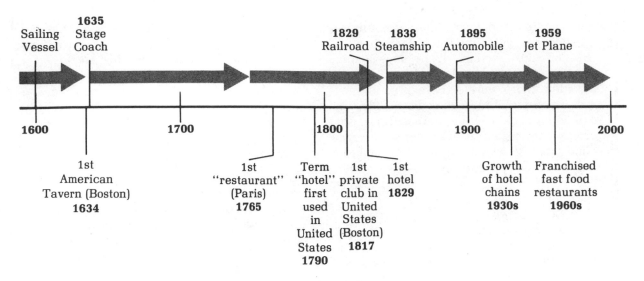

Figure 1-6   *Hotel and Restaurant Time Chart, 1600–2000* A.D.

Chronology of Hotel and Restaurant Business to 1900

ANCIENT PERIOD, 500 B.C. to 500 A.D.

Greek symposiums, Spartan and Roman military mess the forerunner of the private club.

Greek inns close to temples "after the sacrifice, a feast . . . after the feast, drinking."

In the Middle East the travelers stopped with their caravans at caravanseries and kahns, primitive types of inns.

Roman inns, caupona, and hospiteum provided rooms, and sometimes a restaurant. Served limited menu of bread, meat, wine, and perhaps figs and honey. First limited menu (not from choice but by necessity).

Popinas sold wine and restaurant food; thermopoliums sold wine and snacks; tabernas were essentially bars.

Nearly every block of houses in Roman times had its own bar.

MEDIEVAL PERIOD, 500 A.D. to 1300 A.D.

Monasteries and other religious houses took in travelers; donations were welcome.

Inns were primitive. In England, beer was the beverage and could be had at the sign of the bush, any green bough, or bunch of leaves. (In Austrian villages today a green bough over a wine cellar means apple wine is available and for sale.)

1095. First crusade preached by Pope Urban. The crusades stimulated trade and travel.

During the period of the crusades, hospices operated by the Knights Hospitalers (founded in 1048) in Jerusalem primarily for pilgrimages to and from the Holy Land.

About 1183. Public cookhouses on London's river bank offered "dishes of roast, fried and boiled fish, great and small, venison and byrds."

RENAISSANCE PERIOD, 14th and 15th centuries [Italy]; 15th and 16th centuries [Northern Europe].

1400. Food sold at Westminster Gate in London included "bread, ale, wyne, ribs of beefe, hot peascod, hot sheppes feet, macherel and oysters."

Inns in northern Italy as trade revived.

In Tudor England (1485–1603), selected innkeepers forced to retain stables by Royal Act.

Some innkeepers acted as unofficial postmasters and kept stables for the royal post.

1533. Catherine de Medici (from Florence) married the future Henry II of France (both at the age of 14) and is credited with initiating a concern with things gastronomic; brought brigade of chefs with her.

1536. Henry VIII suppressed the monasteries, forcing the growth of inns.

Inns served meat, poultry, ale, bread. New World foods (turkey, cranberries, tomatoes, corn, potatoes, cocoa, and coffee) were not yet available.

Mermaid Tavern, scene of the first English Club, founded by Sir Walter Raleigh; frequented by Shakespeare.

Catering established in France. There were few inns, but private homes could be rented for the occasion.

Henry III of France (reigned 1574 to 1589) made the fork fashionable.

EARLY MODERN, 17th and 18th centuries [Europe]

Louis de Bechamel, Marshal Mirepoix, and Cardinal Richelieu were food-minded; invented or had sauces and other culinary items named for them.

1645. First coffee house in Venice.

1650. First coffee house established at Oxford. Coffee houses reached great popularity in late 17th and early 18th centuries. More than 200 coffee houses in London by 1700.

1653–1658. Cromwell in power in England suppressed culinary and other pleasures.

1658. Stagecoaches introduced in England; gave taverns further prominence.

Louis XIV (reigned 1643–1715), glutton with a tapeworm, made dining a state occasion, and focused attention on food; Hated water (did not bathe) but loved food.

1669. Coffee introduced to Paris by Turkish ambassador; served by beautiful slave girls.

Louis XV (reigned 1715–1774) showed interest in love and food, in that order.

Large houses in which apartments were let by the day, week, or month were called *hotel garni.*

1760. Word *hotel* introduced in London about 1760 when Fifth Duke of Devonshire constructed a crescent-shaped building which housed the Grand, The Centre, and St. Anne's.

1765. The first restaurant (as distinct from an inn, tavern, or food specialty house) opened by Boulanger in Paris.

1784. Coaching era in England with first government mail routes.

About 1790. Count Rumford, born Benjamin Thompson in Woburn, Massachusetts, invented the drip coffee maker, the kitchen range, and learned much about heat transfer. He invented portable steamers for cooking army food; invented Rumford soups (boiled combinations of peas, barley, and potatoes); added croutons; helped make potatoes popular in Europe.

1792. Louis XVI, after being condemned to death, was able to sup on six veal cutlets, a chicken, eggs, and three glasses of wine.

In France, hotels, the residences of nobility, were made available as public houses because of the absence of their owners, some of whom lost their heads.

In England, posting and other inns became plentiful, usually built around a central courtyard (unlike American taverns). Many of these English inns are still operating.

MODERN, 19th and 20th centuries [Europe]

1800–1833. Careme fashioned "La Grande Cuisine."

1825. *La Physiologie Du Gout* published by the world's best known gourmet, Brillat-Savarin.

1825–1858. Alexis Soyer gained culinary eminence. He wrote *Gastronomic Regeneration,* and introduced steam cooking at Reform Club, London, in 1840s; only chef to be mentioned in Britain's *Dictionary of National Biography.*

(continued)

1841. Thomas Cook began the travel agency business in England.

1880–1900. Cesar Ritz enticed the elite from their homes to hotels for entertaining; managed the Claridge, the Carlton, and the Savoy.

1907. Ritz Development Company franchises the Ritz name to the Ritz-Carlton Hotel, New York City. Later the franchise was used in Montreal, Boston, Lisbon, Barcelona.

1880–1935. Auguste Escoffier, known as "chef to kings and king of chefs," worked with Ritz, and published *Le Guide Culinaire* (1907); considered by many to be the New Testament of Cookery.

INNKEEPING IN THE UNITED STATES [from Tavern to Motel]

1634. Ships Tavern, Boston, opened by Samuel Cole who had arrived with the Puritans in 1630.

1642. City Tavern, New York City, built by West India Company.

1670. First coffee house in Boston, served coffee and chocolate.

American Plan in use, although not called by that term. It was similar to table d'hote, the French plan in which the traveler or guest sat with other such people, with the host at the head of the table. The meal was called the ordinary, and some of the taverns were called ordinaries.

Menu favorites: Journey cake (johnny cake) dunked in cider, suppawn (cornmeal in milk or butter—the cornmeal was sometimes boiled in molasses), and Tipsy cake (cake with wine or liquor added).

Beverages were rum and beer and variations of the two, such as flip—strong beer and rum sweetened with dried pumpkin; cherry bounce—rum and cherries sealed in a keg for at least a year, and other whimseys such as "Whistle Belley Vengeance," sour beer and molasses.

1775. The Green Dragon in Boston was the meeting place of American revolutionists. Patrick Henry called the taverns of colonial America the "cradles of liberty."

Most taverns were named for their proprietors, but there were many "Red Lions," "Golden Bowls," "White Horses," and "Black Horses." After the Revolution, a number quickly became "George Washington's," Washington's visage being painted over that of the British monarch, George III.

1785. Jefferson was American minister to France, which began his interest in French cookery and wines; served French wines and crepes while President.

1790s. Word *hotel* began being used in United States. (1790: Carre's Hotel, 24 Broadway, New York City)

1794. The City Hotel (first known as the Burns Coffee House), 115 Broadway, New York City (had population of 30,000).

1794. The first canal opened, a modest affair; circumnavigated the falls of the Connecticut River, South Hadley, Massachusetts.

1794. French refugee opened a restorator in Boston; served truffles, cheese fondue, and delicious soups.

1801. Francis Union Hotel, Philadelphia; made from the former presidential mansion and later an inn.

1801–1820. Taverns rechristened "hotels," following a surge of popularity for all things French. The tavern then became a place with emphasis on drinking.

A typical tavern of the early 1800s was a large home-style building painted white with green blinds and trim. It contained about twenty-five rooms and a combination dining room and bar.

1806. The Exchange Coffee House in Boston, seven stories tall, contained 200 apartments; largest building in America.

1817. Forerunner of the Somerset Club formed in Boston.

1824. The Mountain House, first of the large resort hotels in the Catskills, opened; eventually had 300 rooms and accommodated 500 persons; American neo-classical architecture.

1825. First record of gas stove.

1825. Erie Canal opened; linked New York Harbor via the Hudson and Mohawk Rivers with the Great Lakes; hotels built fronting on the Canal.

1826. City Hotel of Baltimore (Barnum's) became the first "first-class" hotel; 200 apartments.

1827. Concord Coach appears; makes travel more bearable.

1829. America's first restaurant opened, Delmonico's in New York City; served lunch and had a lady cashier. First of more than a dozen eating establishments that brought the name "Delmonico's" to preeminence in the service of fine food.

1829. The Tremont House in Boston appeared with (1) first bellboys (rotunda men); (2) first inside water closets; (3) first hotel clerk, complete with standard smile; (4) French cuisine on Yankee menu; (5) first menu card in this country; (6) annunciators in guest rooms; and (7) room keys given to the guests. Designed from cellar to eaves to be a hotel; three stories, 170 rooms.

1830. "American Plan" established itself when "Americans were churning around the West"; resembled the French "table d'hote."

Tipping had, theretofore, been considered undignified by the "help," but because of immigration of persons accustomed to receiving tips, tipping became part of the business.

1834. Boston and Worcester railroad opened.

New England-trained hotel managers were in demand in the nation.

1834. The Astor House, New York City, first palatial hotel; rooms furnished in black walnut and Brussels carpeting.

1836. First private membership club with rooms of its own in New York City, established in the City Hotel.

1846. First centrally heated hotel, the Eastern Exchange Hotel in Boston.

1848. Safety deposit boxes provided for commercial guests by New England Hotel, Boston.

1855. Original Parker House of Boston opened; offered the "European Plan."

1856. Baking powder sold commercially.

1859. First passenger elevator ("verticle railway") in a hotel; upper rooms could have a higher rate than those on lower floors.

1868. Commercial yeast available.

1870s. Sporting country and city clubs formed in United States.

1875. The Palace Hotel, San Francisco, "World's largest hotel"; floor clerks installed.

1875. *The Hotel World*, trade magazine, started; *The Hotel Red Book* first published.

1876. Fred Harvey founded the company that in the 1880s established Harvey Houses every 100 miles along the Sante Fe Railway.

1881. Louis Sherry opened his first restaurant; developed the art of catering.

1882. Electric lights dazzled the guests of New York City's Hotel Everett.

1880 to 1890s. Resort boom in Florida, New England, Virginia, Pennsylvania, and Atlantic City; Fred Harvey and John R. Thompson were first to develop the large restaurant chains.

1884. First co-op apartment in New York City (now Chelsea Hotel); forerunner of condominiums in this country.

1887. *Stewards Handbook and Dictionary*, Jessup Whitehead.

1887. Ponce de Leon, St. Augustine, built; first luxury hotel in Florida.

1888. Del Coronado built; first luxury resort in California.

1890s. The John R. Thompson Company operated first extensive commissary system (Chicago).

1894. *The Epicurean*, cookbook by Charles Ranhofer, chef at Delmonico's; "gave away Delmonico's secrets."

Questions

1. Tavernkeeping is an old business going back as early as _____ B.C.

2. The early Greek tavern was often located near a temple for a very practical reason. What was that?

3. Fastfood services were seen in what ancient culture?

4. In Ancient Rome taverns were identifiable on the outside in that their pillars were hung with what?

5. In what way was a hospice similar to a hotel of today?

6. How would a passerby of an early English tavern know that ale was served inside?

7. The early inns and taverns of England had tavern signs, such as a white hart or a black swan, for a very good reason. What was it?

8. Besides being a place offering food and lodging, the early English inn had other functions. Can you name two or three of them?

9. Why were stagecoaches called by that name?

10. Henry VIII had an influence on the development of the early English inn. In what way?

11. In 1825 something happened in England that drastically changed the hospitality business. What was it?

12. In what way did the Huguenots leave an imprint on the hospitality business of this country?

13. The Crusades in the Renaissance had what impact on the development of the hospitality business?

14. The Roman military roads were used by the military and what other group of people during the Roman period?

Discussion Questions

1. Henry Ford at one point in his life said, "History is bunk." Do you agree or disagree? Why?

2. As a professional hotel or restaurant person, do you feel that knowing what innkeeping was like in the medieval period has any value or relevance? Defend your viewpoint.

CESAR RITZ (1850–1918)*

Cesar Ritz's beginnings in life were anything but ritzy. When he was 15, he was apprenticed to a hotelkeeper in the town of Brig, Switzerland. He later headed for Paris, hub of the hotel universe at the time, and worked as a handyman in a small, undistinguished hotel. At the age of nineteen, he became a restaurant manager, no small accomplishment in the Paris of the 1860s.

The Voisin Restaurant was the most famous restaurant of the era, and it was to the Voisin that Cesar went, starting over again as an assistant waiter so that he could learn the best methods and have the opportunity to serve the famous and the wealthy. He learned to deal with people so well and was so responsive to their wishes that before long customers were insisting on being served by him. It was the beginning of his rise to fame and influence. By serving the elite and the powerful, he learned their likes and dislikes, their habits, their vanities, and, eventually, how to influence them. To cultivate fashionable society and to make an impression on its leaders was for Ritz purely a career decision.

To be near the top of the social pyramid, Ritz traveled to Vienna to work in a restaurant close by

*Information concerning Ritz was adapted from Marie Louise Ritz, *Cesar Ritz, Host to the World* (Philadelphia: Lippincott, 1938), and Stephen Watts, *The Ritz* (London: The Bodley Head, 1963).

the Imperial Pavillion; at the Pavillion Emperor Franz Josef entertained on a grand scale. His waiters were employed from the restaurant where Ritz worked.

It was here that Ritz secured himself a most important and lifelong patron, the Prince of Wales. Ritz studied the Prince and learned his tastes. The Prince told Ritz at one time, "You know better than I do what I like; arrange a dinner to my taste."

At the age of twenty-seven, Ritz was offered the managership of the largest and most luxurious hotel in Switzerland, the Grand National at Lucerne. Even though the Grand National was the most luxurious hotel in the world when it was built in 1870, it was losing money. Ritz sent out a large number of personal letters to former patrons and to the social elite of Italy to whom the name of the owner, Colonel Pfyffer, meant something. Ritz's diligence and imagination paid off. Before long, dukes and duchesses, Morgans and Vanderbilts came to the Grand National. If honors and pomp were dear to a person, he received them at the Grand National.

Ritz did not hesitate to spend money when necessary to achieve an effect. On one occasion, 10,000 candles were lighted to show off a beautiful mountain. A huge bonfire was built on a mountain peak. Later in his career, he was not daunted by the suggestion that he flood the lower dining room of the Savoy, turning it into a Venetian scene complete with gondolas and singing gondoliers.

For eleven seasons, Ritz reigned at Lucerne in the summer. The Grand Hotel became the center of continental social life. Winters were spent managing or operating hotels and restaurants in France.

Much of Ritz's success can be attributed to his association with Auguste Escoffier. Both knew the importance of pleasing the rich. Ritz catered to them in furnishings and decor and saw to it that Ritz-operated hotels were to their social liking; Escoffier catered to their palates and to their egos.

In 1887, at the age of thirty-seven, Ritz married the daughter of a hotelkeeper. Soon after, Ritz reached the apogee of his career. The Savoy Hotel of London had opened and, after six months of operation, things were not going well. Ritz had previously been paid to go to London for the opening of the Savoy and to make recommendations. He was now asked to take over the management on his own terms.

According to some commentators of the period, Ritz revolutionized dining out in London. He was even accused of breaking up home life by making dining out fashionable. London club life changed; men who previously dined in their men-only clubs now took their wives out to dinner or supper at the Savoy.

How did he do it? He introduced orchestras to play during dinner, starting with Johann Strauss. Music extended the dining period and the sale of beverages. He made evening dress compulsory in the dining rooms and banned unaccompanied ladies. For the first time, the glamorous coquettes of the day dined in the company of the aristocracy and their families.

Ritz understood the power of women and that they wanted to be beautiful. He decided to help them be so. Lighting can be glaring and functional, or it can be soft and romantic. Ritz experimented with light and shadows, colors, and their effects on the skin.

He spent weeks experimenting with the effects of various colors and intensity of light on the clothing and complexion of his wife. Apricot peach, he decided, most complimented the skin. In the Paris Ritz, alabaster urns were hung from the ceiling, lights in them being reflected upwards onto tinted ceilings. In the bedrooms, bowls suspended from the ceiling created similar indirect lighting effects. Rich, fashionable women traveled with many clothes; therefore, Ritz planned king-sized closet and drawer spaces in the Paris Ritz.

Ritz "stayed on top" of new projects, checking out details that many of today's executives would delegate to others. In March, 1898, three months before the opening of the Paris Ritz, Cesar and his family moved into one of the top-floor apartments to be on hand to supervise the finishing details in person.

Each day after the workers had gone, Ritz walked through the hotel, noting what had been done that day and planning for the next day. Elaborate notes were taken: a new lamp needed here; a tapestry for a wall was too thin; sheerer curtains for a window with a fine view; a room with a north light must have the pale blue curtains lined with pale rose. He personally taught the housekeeping staff the art of bedmaking.

While hotels in America were being built with bigger and more plush lobbies, Ritz built a small lobby to discourage idlers. To reduce maintenance costs he painted the walls rather than paper them. Ritz believed that the style of decoration was not as important as how well the decorations and furnishings were done. If the furniture was the best, harmonized perfectly, and was arranged with a view to maximum comfort, it created in Ritz's opinion a good room. With the changing fashions in decor, his view has been proved correct: subdued elegance and absolute comfort are goals to strive for in any hotel decor.

The service was dignified; the servants served in silence, but were always at hand when needed. In short, it was the Ritz, and the term was used throughout the English-speaking world to mean the ultimate in hotelkeeping. Guests were escorted to their apartments by an attendant. They could lay out their wrinkled clothes and go to breakfast. Returning in the early evening to dress for dinner, they would find their clothes freshly pressed and hung ready for use. The food was epicurean, prepared by Escoffier or his disciples.

Once the Paris Ritz was successful, the master turned his attention to the Carlton in London. The house was renovated, and the Carlton became the first London hotel to have a bath in every room. The Carlton opened one year after the Paris Ritz and was an immediate success. A 7-percent dividend was paid to the stockholders the first year.

Ritz placed the handling of people as being the most important of all qualities for the hotelier. His son says that he would have made a great general because he was logical, intuitive, and decisive. He thought quickly and devoted himself completely to the job at hand. His imagination and sensitivity to people and their wants contributed to a new standard of hotelkeeping. Ritz was a driven man, driving himself to the point of exhaustion.

Though Ritz suffered a nervous breakdown in 1902, the Ritz name has been carried on by the Ritz Development Company.* In 1907 the company franchised the Ritz name to The Ritz-Carlton Hotel in New York City. Later other franchises were sold to hotel companies in Montreal, Lisbon, Boston, and elsewhere. The Ritz-Carlton in New York City is no more, but the Boston Ritz-Carlton remains active and is considered to be one of the "great hotels" of the world. The Chicago Ritz, the most impressive of all, was completed in 1975.

---

*Page and Kingsford, *The Master Chefs* (New York: St. Martins Press, 1971), p. 200.

2 The Developing Hotel/Motel

The hotel emerged from the tavern by the simple expedient of a name change; the term *tavern* was changed to that of *hotel*. The word *hotel* had a more glamorous ring, since in France it was the city residence of a wealthy or prominent person, or referred to a public building such as the "hotel de ville," the town hall, or, better yet, the "Hotel de la Monnaie," the mint.

During the French Revolution, many private places in France were converted into public houses and naturally called hotels. Country houses which served as inns were known then, and are still known, by the term *auberge*. French items were popular about 1790 because of French aid to us during the American Revolution and because the early days of the French Revolution were looked upon as a great democratic upsurge.

The term *hotel* has a common root with the words *hospitality, hostelry, hospital, hospice,* and *host*. The Spanish word, *huesped* (guest) probably goes back to the same Latin origin.

Colonial taverns and taverns-turned-hotel were originally designed as private homes where the innkeeper lived with his family. The term *hotel* was well known in America at least as early as 1791, and the city directories of the 1790s show that many a tavern became a hotel.[1]

About 1800, the terms *tavern, hotel,* and *coffee house* were being used, but by 1820 the word *hotel* was the generally accepted term. From this point on, the tavern became more of an eating and drinking place with emphasis on the drinking.

SPECIAL STATUS FOR HOTELKEEPERS IN THE UNITED STATES

From the outset in America, tavernkeeping and, later, hotelkeeping were usually in the hands of respected members of the community and enjoyed a status not found in Europe. George Washington owned several small public houses, and, later, Abraham Lincoln was part-owner of a tavern in Springfield, Illinois.

In the thirty years before the Civil War, hotelkeeping came to be referred to as a "profession." Many managers strove to be hosts rather than proprietors, which puzzled the British visitor no end. Charles A. Stetson, manager of the Astor House in New York City, put the difference like this, "A tavernkeeper knows how to get to market and how to feed so many people at a public table. A hotelkeeper is a gentleman who stands on a level with his guests."[2]

The early hotels continued the tavern custom of serving an "ordinary," a set meal served at a given hour and at a fixed price. Hotels from the beginning were known for their good tables, or lack of them.

1. Doris Elizabeth King, "Early Hotel Entrepreneurs and Promoters, 1793–1860," *Explanations in Entrepreneurial History* (Harvard Research Center in Entrepreneurial History, VIII, February 1956).

2. Thomas Lately, *Delmonico's, A Century of Splendor* (Boston, Mass.: Houghton Mifflin Co., 1967).

Figure 2-1 *The Nicolett House was a structure that Minneapolis could well boast of in 1858—five floors and seventy spacious rooms. The first floor was rented to a bank and several stores, which gave the House an assured income. Ladies had a private entrance and separate "parlors." Speaking tubes led from the front desk to all floors, and bell pulls for service were in all rooms, a practice borrowed from the early inns. Cooks and porters stoked the hotel's ranges with cordwood. Three complete meals and a room cost $2.00. The building was used until 1923 when a new thirteen-story Pick-Nicollett was built on the same site.*

Source: Courtesy of Albert Pick Hotels.

Hotels proliferated as the cities grew. New York City had only 8 in 1818; by 1836 there were 28; and ten years later, in 1846, there were 108.

THE IMPACT OF THE HOTEL ON AMERICAN CULTURE

Until recently, historians had little to say about the effect of the hotel in shaping our culture. Daniel J. Boorstin fortunately has much to say on the subject in his book, *The American National Experience.*[3] He titles his chapter on hotels "Palaces of the Public." In his book, *The American Hotel,* Williamson calls the hotel "the most distinctively American of all our institutions."[4]

An English barrister, Alexander McKay, who traveled in this country in 1846, observed the differences between English and American hotels. He pointed out that in England hotels were regarded as purely private property, in appearance very much like the private houses that surrounded them. In America, hotels were looked upon as public concerns and even looked like public buildings. Often, they were the most impressive and grandest buildings in the town or city.

AMERICAN HOTELS DIFFERED FROM ENGLISH INNS

Indeed, the American hotel served a different purpose than the inn or the railroad hotel in England. The class system was not firmly rooted in the country, and the hotel was a place where all classes of people stopped and all classes of people tended to mingle, the wealthy together with the workingman or the frontiersman.

3. Daniel J. Boorstin, *The American National Experience* (New York: Random House, 1965).

4. Jefferson Williamson, *The American Hotel: An Anecdoted History* (New York: Alfred Knopf, 1930).

Tipping, so much a part of the hotel today, was considered un-American until the flood of Irish and German immigration appeared in the 1830s and 1840s. It did not become widespread until an even greater flood of immigration took place at the end of the century.[5]

In England, the upper classes had enormous homes and large staffs of servants. When they traveled they were likely to stop with friends. When they entertained it was in their homes. It was not until the turn of the century that they were enticed away from their homes to dine out with Cesar Ritz and Auguste Escoffier in such places as the Savoy and the Claridge.

In America, the hotel was a place for businessmen to gather. In fact, many of the hotels were called exchange houses and operated somewhat as a stock exchange. Some secured bank privileges and issued paper currency. As late as the 1860s the Burnet House in Cincinnati issued $5 bills authenticated by its cashier, and carrying an engraved likeness of the building. In New Orleans, the lobby of the St. Charles Hotel was used for public slave auctions. Hotels were the usual meeting places of civic committees, associations of businessmen and, in the frontier communities, were the meeting places for the city council and other government agencies.

Quite logically, the promoters of the new towns recognized the values of a good hotel, and, in several instances, the hotel was built before the town even existed. As Daniel Boorstin says, the hotels were both the creature and the creator of communities, as well as symptoms of the frenetic quest for community.

Origin of the American Plan

The American Plan, the arrangement by which one charge covers both room and meals, was probably the extension of the practice of tavernkeepers of offering room and board (also beer in many taverns) for a single all-inclusive price. The European Plan (first introduced in France) was first offered in the United States in the 1830s. A New Englander visiting New York City reported three hotels in that city were operating under the new system—food, beverage, and room being priced separately.[6] The American Plan especially suited the resort where families might stay for the season, and many resorts even today operate on the American Plan.

Even in the early nineteenth century, Americans gathered to do their politicking and conventioneering. The first national nominating convention of a major party met in 1831 to name Henry Clay for president, and where did it meet? Quite naturally, in a hotel—Barnum's City Hotel in Baltimore, a six-story building with 200 apartments, reputed to be one of the best in the country. The custom of group meetings has been with us for a long time but it reached its full blossom in the 1950s, and today conventions account for over one-third of the occupancy in our hotels. In some properties, convention sales constitute 90 percent or more of the business.

Another way in which the nineteenth-century American hotelkeeper was different from his counterpart "mein host" in Europe was his self-concept and his social standing. The innkeeper in England was supposed to be a genial, deferential individual, one cut above a servant.

SIZE AND SCOPE OF THE INNKEEPING INDUSTRY

There are about 100,000 hotel and motel properties in the world (about 45,000 are in the United States). Hotels having more than 200 rooms number about 3,000 in the United States and about 6,000 to 7,000 in the rest of the world. In 1979 the United States had about 2.03 million hotel rooms, more than one-fourth of the world total of 8 million rooms. Projections suggest that by 1989 the world will have 9.2 million rooms, with the United States having 2.29 million.

According to the American Hotel & Motel Association (AH & MA), U.S. hotel and motel chain operations account for 31 percent of total U.S. properties, but some 69 percent of total rooms. Of the motels, about half of the business was done by motor hotels, the larger motels that combine the luxury and comfort of the hotel with the convenience of the motel.

5. Doris Elizabeth King, *The Community Hotel* (SFA Economist, Dept. of Business Administration, Austin State College, Vol. 4, No. 2, Spring, 1960).

6. Dorsey and Devine, *Fare Thee Well* (New York: Crown Publishers, 1964), p. 33.

For the United States as a whole, there are about 13 hotel-motel rooms with private baths per 1,000 persons. This ratio, probably the highest in the world for any large country, has remained constant since 1948 and earlier. Australia, a contrasting example, has a ratio of only 4.4 rooms with private baths per 1,000 persons.[7]

Five Major Classifications for Hotels

The 6,060 members of the American Hotel and Motel Association (AH & MA) in 1977 classified themselves as follows:

Transient hotels	5,224
All-year resort hotels	364
Seasonal resorts	314
Residential hotels	116
Condominium hotels	25

The most common transient hotel had between 76 and 200 rooms; the model resort hotel had between 76 and 125 rooms. The same was true for the residential hotel.[8]

The larger, newer motel, "the motor hotel" as it is called, became popular in the 1950s. An industry newsletter, produced by the Helmsley-Spear Company of New York City since 1965, has published an annual census of these properties. Their definition of a motor hotel is "a property with transient lodging facilities, built or completely modernized since 1945, open more than half the year, and containing at least fifty guest units, plus adequate on-premise free parking."

Perhaps another useful classification is the "convention hotel," the hotel that builds its occupancy around group business. Such hotels include what would ordinarily be called commercial hotels or resort hotels.

A "budget motel" has been defined as one with rates 20 to 40 percent below the area's Holiday Inn. So defined, in 1983 there were fourteen chains with at least twenty-five budget motel properties each, about 210,000 rooms. The largest of these chains, Days Inn, is headquartered in Atlanta, with 311 properties. Motel 6, with offices in Santa Barbara, has 304, Econo Lodge and Econo-Travel has 180, and

Super 8 has 155. The numbers change daily. Most do not offer foodservice; Days Inn is an exception. Its attached restaurants offer free meals to children twelve and under when accompanied by an adult guest.

Many of the larger hostelries that carry the name *motor hotel* are also convention-oriented. Recognition of the convention hotel and motel as a separate classification was seen in 1968 when the *Hotel Red Book* first published a separate listing of properties with business meeting facilities, nearly 700 of them in the United States.

The resort hotel might also be called a vacation hotel or motel. Until about 1950, most resort hotels were seasonal, open either in the winter or summer. Many still are, but most resorts in Florida, California, Hawaii, and the Caribbean remain open the year around, with low seasons in the spring and fall.

The residential hotel is essentially an apartment building, offering maid service, a dining room, room foodservice, and possibly a cocktail lounge. Some of the better-known hotels, such as the Hotel Pierre and the Plaza in New York City, rent a large number of suites on a permanent basis, which makes them at least partially residential in character. The Waldorf Towers, a part of the Waldorf-Astoria Hotel, is also residential in character.

The Hometel

Catering to the transient traveler, the Hometel offers the guest a suite of two rooms plus a small kitchen. An added attraction is a complimentary full American breakfast and a daily two-hour cocktail hour. The concept is a variation of the resort motel that offers a housekeeping unit and resembles the condo rental.

Expansion has been rapid via limited partnerships with investors. The parent corporation, Hometel, is the general and managing partner. Investors are limited partners, their risk being limited to what they invest. Earnings are paid out quarterly and have been much higher than from the usual hotel or motel.

Reasons for the high earnings include a low labor cost, running between 12 and 20 percent of sales. This is possible because food service, except for breakfast, is provided by a separately leased restaurant. Administrative personnel are kept to a minimum, usually employing only a general manager and a sales director. Employee motivation is high because of a profit-

---

7. *The Accountant, LKHH,* Vol. 48, No. 3, 1969.

8. American Hotel and Motel Association, 1977 membership.

sharing plan that distributes sizeable profits quarterly. Costs of the complimentary breakfast and cocktail hour run at less than 5 percent of sales. (In a 260-room Hometel, breakfast is offered for a three-hour period by two cooks. Foodservice ware is disposable. Only well (less expensive) drinks are available during the cocktail hour.)

Rental Condominiums

Thousands of rooms have been added to the public accommodations inventory by the construction of rental condominiums in resort areas. A typical owner of a vacation condominium has an annual income of an upper middle-class or higher level and looks upon the vacation condominiums as an investment as well as a vacation facility. The rule of thumb is that the annual income of the condo buyer is about the same as the price of the condominium. In other words, the buyer of a $100,000 condominium would probably have an annual income of at least $100,000. (The rule, however, is not followed by many buyers.) The big appeal of the condominium is that in the past it may have appreciated two to three times in value over a five-year period.

Condo experts point out that the owners should not expect cash flow from rentals to reach the amount necessary to carry the mortgage and maintenance charges on the condominium.

The usual owner who rents a condominium does not occupy it for more than two or three weeks of the year. Under the federal income tax regulations, if the condo is occupied for a longer period the owner is not eligible for tax deductions resulting from maintenance and repair costs, interest cost, or for depreciation allowances. Owners can avoid this restriction to a certain extent if, while they are occupying the condominium, they engage in maintaining and repairing it.

Condo Management

The management of condominiums for owners has become a business unto itself. In some ways it is more difficult and in other ways less difficult than resort hotel management. Since most condominiums have no restaurants, the food and beverage problems associated with restaurants are not present. On the other hand, condo management is similar to club management in that the manager has numerous bosses rather than one or a few. A one hundred-room condominium resort may have eighty or ninety owners who participate in a rental pool. Each owner is concerned with getting the maximum return from rental income and in maintaining the individual apartment in the best possible manner. Furniture and equipment may not be uniform, and owners often install personal items that are sometimes a problem to care for and keep in place. Housekeeping takes on added importance since owners are much more critical than renters.

Under a management contract agreement, a management company or individual arranges a separate contract for each owner. Management is then directly responsible to the owner. Continuous communication between management and owner is necessary to maintain good relations. Owners are particularly keen on having current financial information.

When a strike against an airline that serves a particular destination takes place, occupancy can drop sharply. When United Airlines employees struck in 1979, occupancy dropped sharply in hotel and rental condominiums in Hawaii. Cost of jet fuel reflects itself in air fares and occupancy, which are of immediate interest to owners since they are reflected in occupancy levels.

Condo management in resort destinations such as Mexico, Hawaii, and the Caribbean confront peculiar personnel problems, and in high-cost areas like Maui, scarcity of employees because of the lack of living quarters is a major problem. Condo managers must live in as residents, which proves to be highly confining after a period of time. Many persons who think condo management would be a fun job find it to be otherwise.

Reserving space in a condominium may be particularly difficult in that owners often do not specify long enough in advance the time that they wish to occupy their units. Management must then schedule around the owner's schedule of occupancy which is often difficult when blocks of rooms are needed for groups.

Hotel Classification by Number of Rooms

Although the typical hotel is small, the large hotel does the lion's share of the business. The 700 properties that are included in the Harris, Kerr, Forster Annual Survey have revenue equal to more than 25 percent of the receipts of all the nation's hotels and motels. It is a far cry from the "Mom and Pop" motel, operated largely by husband and wife, to the new megahotels of 1000 and more rooms and 900 and more employees.

The average number of rooms per hotel jumped from 62 in 1948 to 72 in 1974. From 1948 to 1974, motels and motor hotels with payrolls increased from 11,302 to 27,625; and the number of motel rooms from 304,000 to about 1.5 million—an increase of close to 500 percent.

Quite naturally, the older, less well-located properties are in their declining years, many of them only marginal operations. Competitive obsolescence forces hundreds of them out of business each year while the newer and brighter operations are usually quite profitable.

The hotel business can be seen as a four-tier business in terms of rates, service, and prestige. At the top are the luxury hotels with room rates of $100 a day and up. The next level down, the first-class hotel, has rates of $50 to $100. The next level down is the up-scale motor hotel—Ramadas, Holiday Inns, Rodeways, and the like. On the bottom tier is the budget property with rates of $15 to $25.

Another way of dividing the hotel business is to view it from the level of service offered. At the bottom is the budget property and many small motels—the "Mom and Pops." Then come the motels that offer only rooms. The La Quinta chain is an example. Rooms offer the largest profit potential. Restaurants can be a loss operation. Condominium operation is another no-food-and-beverage service style.

The hometel is another service style: free breakfast and free cocktails in the evening, and rooms the size of a suite. But there is no restaurant as an integral part of the service.

Bed and breakfast, homes converted into small hotels by owners, is a rapidly growing hospitality business segment. Unlike the Irish and British B&B's, many of these in the United States charge substantial prices and offer an abundance of amenities, plus wine and cheese, and a luxury breakfast.

The current ultimate in service is the club within a hotel. Many of the first-class hotels in this country are allocating their top one or two floors for a hotel within a hotel. Private elevators, private check-in and check-out, and a concierge on hand to take care of hospitality and travel problems are offered. The rate for these executive floors may be one-third higher than on the regular floors. Expense account travelers are the biggest market.

HOTEL CITIES

Where is the hotel business concentrated? The greatest concentration of hotel rooms is in the cities that are heavily populated trade centers. Population alone is not a guide to the number of hotel rooms expected in a city.

Institutional cities, such as Washington, D.C., have a larger concentration of hotel rooms. Market cities, for example, New York, Los Angeles, Chicago, Atlanta, Boston, and San Francisco, require a number of hotel rooms for the large number of buyers and other business-people visiting the cities.

Cities that are primarily industrial centers have fewer hotel rooms because their populations are stable, and there are fewer reasons for travelers to visit them. Cleveland, Pittsburgh, and Detroit are examples of such cities.

New York City has the greatest concentration of rooms. In 1980 some 6,000 new rooms were built—all in the high-rate category. Boston has a total of 10,000 rooms; Miami Beach, about 38,000 (forty-eight hotels per square mile). Las Vegas, Miami Beach, and Atlantic City are hotel centers, convention, and resort cities, with probably the highest concentration of hotel rooms per capita in the world. (Small areas such as Monaco, in southern France, may have an even higher ratio of hotel rooms to resident rates.)

LEADERS IN LODGING

A few hotel chains existed before the turn of the century. The Statler chain dominated the hotel world until the 1930s when Conrad Hilton began building the Hilton chain and Ernest Henderson began the Sheraton chain. On the West Coast, headquartered in Seattle, Westin Hotels grew slowly but surely.

Probably the best indicator of the concentration of the hotel business is seen in the wage and salary disbursements made by hotels and other lodging places. These figures, compiled by the U.S. Department of Commerce each year, show the number of millions of dollars paid to employees of hotels and other lodging places by state.

The top twenty-five lodging organizations are seen in Table 2–1. The chart includes the promotion/referral chains, those whose membership is voluntary and ownership rests with the individual members. In the chart, a referral group, such as Best Western, is called a *consortium*.

TABLE 2–1 Top Twenty-Five World Hotel Chains

Rank	Organization	Rooms '81	Hotels '81
1	**Holiday Inns** **Memphis, TN, USA**	**311,697**	**1,759**
(1)	New intl properties opened in '81 in Hong Kong (the Harbour View), Pakistan, Japan, Taiwan, Chile, Egypt, the UK and Canada. In USA, hotels opened near airport in San Antonio, TX, and in Nashville, TN.		
2	**The Sheraton Corp.** **Boston, MA, USA**	**113,000**	**430**
(2)	USA expansion continues with hotels in '82 in Dallas, Houston, LA, New Orleans & Seattle. Expansion elsewhere includes New Zealand, Baghdad, Qatar, Pakistan, Canada, Jamaica, the Seychelles, Australia & Tegucigalpa (Honduras).		
3	**Ramada Inns** **Phoenix, AZ, USA**	**94,000**	**616**
(3)	Larger more luxurious hotels, named Ramada Renaissance Hotels, have opened in major markets around the world, including London, Hamburg, West Germany and Washington, DC. Chain targets Central, South Am. for franchises.		
4	**Hilton Hotels Corp.** **Los Angeles, CA, USA**	**77,437**	**221**
(5)	Hilton's growth continues. Tapa Tower adds 1,056 rooms in Hilton Hawaii Village. Construction underway for 1,300-room Los Angeles Intl airport. Corp. acquired hotels in Reno, Nevada, and Phoenix, Arizona.		
5	**Trusthouse Forte** **London, England**	**73,324**	**805**
(4)	Acquisitions include Ritz in Madrid and Alrae in NY. Chain continues to push presence in USA where its profits are up with contracts for hotels in Washington, DC; Provo, Utah; Charleston, West Va; Miami; New Orleans; NY.		
6	**Balkantourist** **Sofia, Bulgaria**	**61,207**	**658**
(7)	Luxury property division of state tourism agency plans additions to Balkan Hotel in Sofia and Bulgaria Hotel in Burgas in near future. This division also runs restaurants that served 5.2 million meals in '81 and plans 6 new facilities in 5 years.		
7	**Howard Johnson Co.** **Braintree, MA, USA**	**60,600**	**520**
(6)	Despite its acquisition by Britain's Imperial Group in 1979, Howard Johnson has confined itself, for now, to properties in Canada, USA and Puerto Rico.		
8	**Quality Intl.** **Silver Springs MD, USA**	**51,170**	**423**
(9)	Dynamic new executive team moving fast added 10,000 rooms, 100 properties in '82 via franchise route. Internationally, link-up with European Crest for marketing.		
9	**Club Mediterranee** **Paris, France**	**45,921**	**167**
(10)	Orient beckons top holiday club company: 700-bed Club Deifu near Canton in China to open in 1985, plus vacation villages planned for Thailand, Philippines, Fiji and New Guinea.		

(continued)

Rank	Organization	Rooms '81	Hotels '81
10 (8)	**Days Inns of America** Atlanta, GA, USA	45,726	315

When it completes the 12 inns now under construction, the Days Inn system will be in 33 states in USA and in Canada. The chain made its mark with budget hotels. Inns are 40% company owned; 60% franchised.

Rank	Organization	Rooms '81	Hotels '81
11 (11)	**Novotel SIEH** Evry, France	45,029	353

Meteoric growth (fueled by Jacques Borel Hotels acquisition last year and continued new construction) plus diversification (Borel's industrial catering acquired in '82) makes Novotel formidable hotel/catering group on continent.

Rank	Organization	Rooms '81	Hotels '81
12 (13)	**Marriott Corp.** Washington DC, USA	41,909	102

20,000 additional rooms in '81 & '82 for fast-track Marriott. Internationally, 300-room Amman, Jordan, Marriott opened last year.

Rank	Organization	Rooms '81	Hotels '81
13 (12)	**Hyatt Hotels Corporation** Chicago, IL, USA	36,000	65

Renovations amounting to over US$1.6 mil. are underway at 1,100-room Hyatt Regency O'Hare near O'Hare Intl Airport, Chicago. Hyatt hotels operate only in USA but have close ties with Hyatt Intl, a separate company.

Rank	Organization	Rooms '81	Hotels '81
14 (14)	**Motel 6, Inc.** Los Angeles, CA, USA	34,960	325

One of top budget chains in USA, Motel 6 built network on strictly no-frills philosophy. It promises single room for $14.45 nationwide. Rate is up $1.60 from '81. Chain took name from its original $6-a-night charge.

Rank	Organization	Rooms '81	Hotels '81
15 (16)	**Hilton International Co.** New York, NY, USA	31,949	86

Hilton Intl began operating more hotels in Malaysia in '82. Chain plans hotels in Australia, Pakistan, Germany, Canada and USA. Manages Vista Intl in NY's World Trade Center.

Rank	Organization	Rooms '81	Hotels '81
16 (15)	**Intercontinental Hotels** New York, NY, USA	31,900	85

Grand Metropolitan bought InterC from Pan American in '81. As a result, some Grand Met hotels have been incorporated into InterC div. New InterC hotels will open in Athens; Singapore; Abu Dhabi, UAE; and Jeddah, Saudi Arabia.

Rank	Organization	Rooms '81	Hotels '81
17 (18)	**Intourist** Moscow, USSR	30,243	101

Tourism minister Nikitin calls tourism "a major branch of Soviet economy," and state company seems well on the way to meeting 5 year goal of 40,000-bed increase by '85.

Rank	Organization	Rooms '81	Hotels '81
18 (17)	**Westin** Seattle, WA, USA	24,652	50

This United Airlines subsidiary, formerly known as Western International, plans future openings in Boston; Dallas; Vail, Colorado (hotel and condominium apts.); St. Louis, Missouri; Ontario, Canada; Mexico and Raffles City, Singapore.

Rank	Organization	Rooms '81	Hotels '81
19 (20)	**Hoteles Agrupados S.A.** Madrid, Spain	18,669	36

Recent acquisitions include three five-star hotels in Spain (Los Bardinos in Las Palmas, Gran Canaria; San Felipe in Tenerife and Corona de Aragon in Zaragoza). The Corona was redecorated and reopened in March '82.

Rank	Organization	Rooms '81	Hotels '81
20	**Rodeway Inns** **Dallas, TX, USA**	18,321	151
(19)	1981 was a year of realignment as Rodeway closed or sold off 9 hotels and added only 1.		
21	**Meridien** **Paris, France**	16,623	41
(38)	Air France subsidiary opens 2 hotels in Hong Kong and 1 in Bagdad in '82. Started in '72, Meridien adds French touch to local tradition in its hotels worldwide.		
22	**CEDOK** **Prague, Czechoslovakia**	14,000	132
(21)	In the past three years CEDOK has been active in new construction opening 6 hotels including center city and resort properties.		
23	**Crest Hotels** **Oxfordshire, England**	13,545	106
(22)	Crest in refurbishing many of the Centre Hotels it acquired in '81 as well as the holiday centers in its Pontin's group. Has new reservation link with Quality Inns USA. Crest is subsidiary of brewing giant, Bass.		
24	**Grand Metropolitan** **London, England**	12,975	67
(23)	Currently in process of full-scale merger with Intercontinental. Future of Grand Met's London hotels uncertain; 3 have been sold; others put in InterC group. Country hotels sold.		
25	**Hyatt International** **Chicago, IL, USA**	12,877	38
(24)	Hyatt adds Carlton Tower in London to its group, gaining a firm foothold in Europe where it plans to build 10 hotels in the next few years, including ones in Hungary and Switzerland. It will also build in Mexico, Jerusalem, and Bangkok.		

Source: Hotels & Restaurants International, 1982.

AMERICANS ABROAD

Until the late 1940s, few Americans went abroad to manage hotels. The American Hotel Corporation managed two hotels in Panama and one in the Dominican Republic, and Eugene Eppley managed hotels in Panama before World War II. The English and the Swiss were about the only national groups that went abroad to manage hotels in any number, and their overseas hotels were relatively few. True, the several Ritz Hotels relied for advice on the Ritz Management Company, but they were not controlled by that company. American hoteliers were reluctant to invest money in hotels abroad; most had their hands full keeping pace with the changes going on in this country. In 1948 this changed.

The U.S. government, casting about for ways of improving the economy of Latin American countries, asked several hotel companies if they would be willing to build properties in these countries. Only Pan American Airways under Juan Trippe agreed to do so.

Inter-Continental Hotels Corporation was set up as a completely owned subsidiary of Pan American Airways, and hotels were built in several Latin American countries. Management leases were taken on other hotels, and, by the late 1950s, IHC had properties in Venezuela, Brazil, Uruguay, Chile, Colombia, Mexico, Curacao, Cuba, and the Dominican Republic. By 1981, IHC had 81 hotels in about fifty countries.

In 1948 Conrad Hilton secured the contract to operate the Caribe Hilton in San Juan, touching off a tourism boom for that island and setting the pattern for Hilton International, which by 1974 operated sixty-one hotels (23,263 rooms) in thirty-nine countries outside the continental United States.

Hilton International Company was spun off from Hilton hotels to operate as a separate company in 1964. In 1967 Hilton International was bought by Trans World Airlines. By 1970 nearly every major airline was in, or planning to enter, the hotel business. See Table 2–2 for a list of airlines in the hotel business.

Partly as a result of Hilton's and IHC's successful overseas operations, Sheraton Hotel Corporation of America, Westin Hotels, Knott Hotels, and Hyatt International have gone abroad. It may be that Holiday Inns will be the largest innkeeper internationally as well as domestically.

HOTELIERS EXPORT MANAGEMENT CONCEPTS

The American hoteliers abroad have brought a new sense of management to international hotelkeeping: a huge referral system in many cases, a flair for promotion and advertising, and a willingness to spend money (a trait found only rarely outside of the United States). Of course, they would much rather spend somebody else's money—a local investor's or the local government's—in building the hotel abroad. Preferably, they would operate on a management contract, which removes more of the risks and tends to insure better treatment within the country.

Some hotel corporations are going abroad simply because profits are higher than those in the United States. Where room rates charged in the United States can be charged—and they usually are—and a reasonable occupancy maintained, the hotel can make considerably more profit than in the United States because of the scarcity of first-class hotels and the desire of North Americans to stay in American-operated hotels. In the past, one reason was clear: cheap labor. Even though more employees are needed, labor costs abroad seldom exceed 30 percent of the gross sales. In the United States, labor costs are between 35 and 40 percent of gross sales. In some areas abroad, occupancy runs much higher than in the United States.

Americans travel abroad in greater numbers and spend more money than other national groups. In 1980 they spent $14.57 billion in international travel. Many of these travelers want to go first-class and feel reassured if they can stay in a Hilton, IHC, or other American-managed property.

The economic consequences of American-managed hotels abroad are much greater than would be indicated by the 60,000 or 70,000 rooms involved. The Istanbul Hilton, for example, realized a $13 million profit during its first year of operation in 1955 and played an important part in the 60 percent increase in tourism in Turkey that year. The Caribe-Hilton is said to be one of the greatest profit makers in hoteldom, after the casino/hotels located in the continental United States.

In many countries the American-managed hotel is the only hotel of any consequence, and it is almost always the newest, the biggest, and the best in the country. For example, in Caracas, capital of Venezuela, the Tamanaco Hotel

TABLE 2-2 Airline Hotels and Ownership

Airline	Country	Airline	Country
Aer Lingus	**Ireland**	**Garuda Indonesian**	
Dunfey Family hotels subsidiary slated to expand in southwestern USA, Canada, Europe. Jurys hotels in Ireland also a subsidiary.		**Airways**	**Indonesia**
		Newly-created subsidiary Aerowista Hotels & Catering to operate a chain of domestic hotels. One 450-room property being constructed.	
Alitalia	**Italy**		
Italian carrier has investments in CIGA group of luxury hotels and the international Aerhotel chain.		**Gulf Air**	**Bahrain**
		Gulf operates 3 hotels in Qatar, Oman and Bahrain and invests in others. Also a major gulf area industrial and airline caterer.	
Air France	**France**		
Air France hotel partner Meridien to open nine new properties during 1981 in USA, Mid-E, Pacific. Meridien activities include airline catering.		**Japan Air Lines**	**Japan**
		Linked to the JAL system: a chain of 10 properties and more than 60 reservations affiliates. Building in Singapore, Mexico City.	
Air India	**India**		
Air India involved in hotel business through partnership with the Hotel Corp of India. Currently scouting for sites in London.		**Loftleidir**	**Iceland**
		Icelandic airline is investor in Loftleidir Hotel, by far the largest in this island nation.	
Air New Zealand	**New Zealand**		
Two properties in Polynesian Cook Islands are owned jointly by Tourist Hotel Corp. and Air New Zealand.		**Lufthansa**	**Germany**
		German carrier boasts large catering revenues. Invests in hotels; does not operate. Shareholder in German Intercontinentals.	
All Nippon Airways	**Japan**		
Diversification of Japan's national airline: chain of 8 ANA hotels, and hotel/leisure/real estate development arm. 1 Hawaii hotel.		**Pakistan Int'l Airlines**	**Pakistan**
		PIA and Novotel are partners in new Minhal chain. Two Minhals with 1,300 rooms open now in NYC, Paris; Riyadh, Karachi coming soon.	
Ansett	**Australia**		
Six hotels under the Gateway Inns trademark in Australian cities are operated by Ansett, which also owns one resort.		**Swissair**	**Switzerland**
		Joint company set up with Nestle to launch an international chain of 10–15 hotels. Among investments: Penta, Prohotel.	
British Airways	**England**		
Holds investment in more than 40 BA Associates Hotels operated by others. Also offering travelers direct-book London apartments.		**SAS**	**Denmark/Norway/ Sweden**
		SAS subsidiary SAS Catering & Hotels operates 15 hotels with 1,900 rooms plus 84 catering facilities. Big airline catering biz.	
British Caledonian	**England**		
Addition of a 2,000-room hotel pushes sister co. Caledonian Hotel Mgmt. up to 7,000 rooms. Blue Sky Holidays also part of group.		**United Airlines**	**USA**
		UAL, Inc. runs both United Airlines and Westin Hotels (formerly Western International) in addition to airline catering service.	
Canadian Pacific	**Canada**		
CP's hotel affiliate operates in Canada, USA and W. Germany. Other CP interests: a restaurant chain and a major airline feeder.		**TWA**	**USA**
		TWA and its sister corp., Hilton Int'l Hotels, are both subsidiaries of Trans World Corp., along with Canteen and Spartan catering co's.	
Cathay Pacific	**Hong Kong**		
Owned by the Swire group, which also has holdings in restaurants, airline catering services, and the Peninsula hotel group.		**Varig**	**Brazil**
		Varig's Tropical Hotels chain serves Brazil's hotel-short secondary cities, such as Manaus, Santrem or Boa Vista	
Continental Airlines	**USA**		
Continental trying to dump its four hotels on Guam, Saipan, Palau and Truk. No takers thus far at US $25 million for the lot.			

Source: Hotels and Restaurants International, 1981.

and Hilton Hotel stand out as the leading hotels in several ways. Before their construction there was only one first-class hotel in the city, the Avila, and this was a Rockefeller hotel. There are only a few first-class hotels in Panama, one of which has been managed at different times by Hilton and IHC. Some of the developing nations have but one first-class hotel; some none.

In 1973 American hotel companies moved into London in force: 9,500 new rooms were added. Of these, 4,100—or 43 percent—were being built by American firms. The Esso Company built a chain of motor hotels through Europe, from Scandinavia into Italy.

American management abroad does not mean any considerable number of American hotel management personnel abroad. In most countries, an agreement is reached between the management company and the local government to restrict the number of Americans who will be employed. Except for a few top-level personnel, the rest of the employees must be nationals. In Mexico, for example, only personnel with special skills unavailable in that country can get work permits, and arrangements for training nationals within three years must be made.

However, the few American personnel are enough to install American business enterprise and methods and, most important, American merchandising methods. Nearly all of the American-managed hotels abroad are impressive, large, and beautifully designed. The local country usually sees them as a symbol of national prestige and builds accordingly.

THE HOTEL GUEST

Who stays at a hotel or motel? The answer varies according to the location, rate structure, and image that has been created for a hotel or motel. A number of studies have been done in an attempt to identify the hotel-motel guest. One of the more recent of these studies brought out the following facts:

> Tourists make up about one-third of the typical hotels' business. Larger hotels have added specialized staff to work with tour groups. The Los Angeles Hilton, for example, has six personnel assigned to this responsibility. Most of these Tourist specialists are attractive ladies who relate to tour

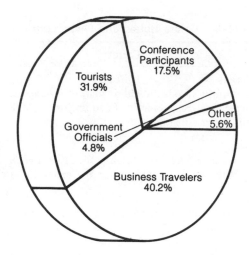

Figure 2-2   *Composition of the U.S. Hotel Market, 1980*

Source: Worldwide Lodging Industry 1981.

operators and see to it that once a tour arrives at the hotel, registration and luggage distribution to guest rooms are expedited.

Conference participants seem to grow in number each year and comprise nearly one-fifth of the typical hotels' house count.

Government officials add up to about 5 percent of total guest registration.

The mainstay of the hotel business, however, continues to be the business traveler. In some hotels 80 to 90 percent of the total registration are businesspeople. In the United States as a whole the business traveler is 40 percent of the average hotel's occupancy. Figure 2-2 shows the various components of the hotel market.[9]

CHOICE OF HOTELS

According to a Gallup Poll of travelers stopping at major hotel and motel chains, the most important factors bearing on the selection of a chain hotel or motel were cleanliness, reasonable prices, and comfort.[10]

9. Worldwide Lodging Industry, 1981.

10. *The American Hotel and Motel Association News* (July 1969).

A different method of questioning and different questions might have brought out such other factors as convenience, prestige, the effect of advertising, etc. Several surveys have shown the conventioneer to be the biggest per-day spender, followed by the businessperson and the person traveling for pleasure. This is easy to understand when the question is asked, "Who is paying—the individual traveling or someone else?"

THE MOTEL EMERGES

When Henry Ford put the Model T in reach of the average pocketbook, travel from town to town and into the city became a peculiarly American diversion and preoccupation—almost a way of life. Travelers needing to stop overnight were pleased to find four walls, one dangling lightbulb, a bare floor, and an outside privy when away from the towns and cities.

Some of these accommodations had been built and rented the same day. Rates were low—$1 a night was the prevailing rate in the early 1920s—and it was all part of the sport of travel. The word *motel* was first used in 1926 in California. The motel became a quick stopping-over place for the traveler, and no attempt was made to provide food and beverage. The motel met an obvious need.

Spectacular Growth Rate for Motels

The growth of the motel business was spectacular in number and in nature. In 1935, the U.S. Bureau of Census listed 9,848 motels. The figure increased to 13,521 in 1939. World War II placed a definite brake on expansion and for a time, with the shortage of tires and gasoline, many motels were hard-pressed to survive.

Following the war, a pent-up urge to travel burst forth and motels sprang up to help in the satisfaction of that urge. Husband and wife teams invested their savings and borrowed to build ten- to twenty-unit motels—and were quite successful. Many of them made enough to pay back the entire cost of the motel in five years or less. By 1951, the *American Motel Magazine* estimated that there were 43,356 motels in operation.

About this time a significant change took place in the character of the building and the operation. Investors with several hundred thousand dollars available moved into the field, and the small motel, operated by "Mom and Pop," was no longer the typical operation. Many motel operators kept up with the times by offering indoor plumbing, radio, TV, enclosed showers, carpeted floors, and tiled bathrooms.

As the competition forced the issue, however, a new style and pace was introduced. Large motels were built, requiring investments running well over $1 million. A sizable swimming pool, a luxurious lobby, and a restaurant of some size were an integral part of the luxury motel.

By 1962, the 100-unit motor hotel had become a standard. The typical new motel of today, other than the budget motel, has over 125 rooms, a restaurant that seats more than one hundred people, and an average of eighteen employees who work full-time in the restaurant. It has a large swimming pool—heated the year round—and television.

Telephone and optional room service are standard services in what is called the "motor hotel." It is also usual for the motel to be located within five minutes of the city's downtown area, with free transportation available to and from the business district. The downtown motel is taking on the atmosphere of a resort. More recreation facilities, such as children's playgrounds, putting greens, swimming pools, shuffleboard, and badminton courts are being built into the motel. "Pleasure domes," central areas with a pool and a transparent roof, are often seen.

Multiple-unit organizations have influenced the business significantly. There are about 130 multiple-unit companies operating motels.

Motels Offer High Profit Performance

One reason for the rapid growth of motels and motor hotels was that in 1969 they produced an average profit of about $1,500 per available room after real estate taxes, but before other capital expenses. The same figure for hotels was about $1,200. By working long hours, the small motel operators—usually husband and wife teams—could pay off their mortgages in five to ten years.

For the traveling family, the motel is more informal, tipping is likely to be less, restaurant prices are usually lower, and there is a swimming pool. No need to travel into the heart of the city to get to the accommodations; the newer motel is probably located near a super highway on the periphery of the city or town. The newer motor hotel is also apt to be chain-affiliated, and the traveler can make a reservation the evening before at another unit of the chain-affiliated operation. The traveler is reassured by the affiliation, relatively certain that the place will be clean, safe, and attractive. The same can be said of most of the new budget motels that came in large numbers in the 1970s.

THE HOTEL AND MOTOR HOTEL COME TOGETHER

From the 1920s to 1940s, the motel operator had little in common with the hotel owner and operator. The motel was small; its owners were amateurs. It usually lacked food and beverage facilities. The motel operators' life savings were tied up in the motel. They wanted to hold what they had and to expand their business.

Hotel managers, quite differently, had a tradition going back at least to hotels in the 1830s. They had status. The complexity of their job called for professional expertise. Managers of the larger hotels looked upon hotel management as a career field and they were constantly on the lookout for bigger and better jobs.

In the eyes of the hotel owner and manager, the motel owners were small potatoes, sometimes an object of fun. As one wit put it, "The motel was sired by the tourist camp and damned by the hotel." Motels were sometimes referred to as "hot pillow joints." Hoteliers did not associate with motel people; they had separate trade journals and separate trade associations.

By the early 1960s, the motels were an accepted part of the hotel business. The American Hotel Association changed its name to the American Hotel and Motel Association. The larger motels, especially the chain-affiliated, became members of the AH&MA and were listed in the *Hotel and Motel Red Book*. The leading hotel trade journal, *Hotel Management,* became the *Hotel/Motel Management Review.* The larger motor hotels, similar in operation to hotels, were glad to join forces with the hotel fraternity.

This was not true of the small motel operators who saw themselves as small businesspeople largely selling rooms along the highways. They continued to maintain their own state and national trade associations.

The larger motor hotels or motels—whatever the descriptive term—are hotel operations and include most of the services offered by the large hotel. The atmosphere tends to be more relaxed, and less emphasis is placed on group business. Foodservice in the motor hotel or motel is likely to be less formal, more often than not a coffee shop-style of operation.

For large hotels, those of about 300 or more rooms, the target markets fall into these major categories:

Business and Corporate Groups

Meetings and Convention Groups

Tour and Travel, domestic and international

International and Incentive Groups

Hotels catering to the business and corporate markets tend to provide at least some suites that will appeal to top-level executives or can be used as hospitality suites for corporate entertainment, public relations, and sales. These hotels are likely to include a health club in their facilities, including an exercise room and sauna.

Some hotels specifically go after tour groups and employ a tour director who solicits such business and coordinates tour groups once they have arrived at the hotel.

Some of the larger hotels employ a director of public relations who coordinates with or is part of the market department. That position may be assigned all of the in-house advertising and work with an advertising agency. Special promotions such as holiday promotions can be part of the public relations role. The public relations person may prepare routine letters of response to guest complaints for the manager's signature, conduct tours of the hotel, and work with photographers and travel writers.

GROUP BUSINESS GROWS

By 1975, package tours were an important part of group business; packages including travel, food, and lodging are sold largely by travel agencies. Nearly every large hotel has a marketing department headed by a director of sales, regional salespersons, and often a director of conventions and tours.

"The Americans of all ages, all conditions, and all dispositions constantly form associations." The writer, Alexis de Tocqueville, a widely quoted commentator about the American scene, made this remark in 1831. The judgment is as valid today as it was then.

The real impact of group business did not hit American hotels until the 1950s. By the late 1960s, most of the large downtown hotels were getting at least 40 percent of their business from conventions and corporate meetings. Some hotels get as much as 90 percent of their business from conventions and other groups. The gregarious American character, jet travel, and the desire to keep abreast of one's field in a pleasurable setting are responsible for the "multibillion dollar American ritual."[11]

New York City attracts the most conventioneers; the New York Hilton and the Americana were built expressly for the convention market. Jet travel and tax deductions for business purposes make it easy for Americans to express their desire to get together with others or exchange information, look for a new job, buy new merchandise for their businesses, and have fun doing it. In 1980, about 22 million travelers attended conventions, trade shows, exhibitions, and business meetings.[12]

Conventioneering means big money to hotels. As many as 100,000 delegates attend some national gatherings—enough to fill rooms for miles around. The average delegate to a national convention, says the International Association of Convention Bureaus, spends about $367 per convention. What makes conventioning even more interesting to hotel managers is that conventions can often be scheduled to fill low-occupancy periods, weekends, and off-seasons. Also, once a convention has checked in, most of the guests take most of their meals in the hotel.

Much of the convention business has quietly merged into the vacation business. The independent businessperson may have his or her spouse as an officer in the company; both travel to a business meeting at business expense, which is tax deductible. The executive going to a business meeting has expenses paid; the small extra cost for double occupancy of a room makes the trip relatively inexpensive for the spouse.

With group air fares, today's convention is likely to be a family affair. Spouses accompany over half of the conventioneers to New York City, while about 75 percent of the convention-goers to Florida bring their spouses.

Group meetings for salespeople of a company are likely to be a combination of entertainment and sales pitch. Philco-Ford charters thirty jets to carry 5,000 appliance and electronic dealers and their spouses to such places as Puerto Rico, Hawaii, Las Vegas, and Paradise Island in the Bahamas. The entertainment may cost $300,000 for the group. A resort hotel like the Princess in Acapulco may rely on groups for more than half of its sales.

THE ROLE OF THE TRADE SHOW

Trade shows and exhibitions are closely related to the convention business. Many of the trade associations get the bulk of their income from conducting a convention-trade show each year. The National Restaurant Association receives much of its budget from this source.

Space for most shows can be rented for less than $1 per square foot and sold for up to $9 per square foot. The difference is largely profit for the associations. Convention bureaus join with hotel associations to build up convention business. Municipalities also join in to promote convention sales.

CONVENTION AND VISITOR BUREAUS

More than 125 Convention and Visitor Bureaus have been established in cities around the country, 30 in California alone. The bureaus have the primary purpose of attracting visitors to the area they represent. Those representing larger cities with several thousand guest rooms compete for the large conventions and group meetings: groups representing professions such as teaching, medicine, and law; governmental groups such as city councilmen or tax collectors; trade groups such as plumbers or junk dealers; and union groups. Political conventions, especially on the national level, bring thousands of visitors to an area.

Convention bureaus often act as housing bureaus, assuming the complete responsibility for accommodating a large group, allocating rooms among various properties in an area. A bureau may also manage a Convention Center, selling exhibit space, arranging for registration

11. *Forbes Magazine* (February 15, 1969).
12. *New York Times* (October 1980).

and side trips, providing for buses between hotels and the Convention Center, helping with the news releases, and working with the media of the area.

Within a convention bureau, such as the Anaheim Convention and Visitors' Bureau, a number of salespersons are employed, each responsible for up to 1,000 groups, keeping files, information as to meeting dates, names of association executives, and other information of value in soliciting the groups to come to an area. Convention bureau work is closely related to hotel sales work and calls for an alertness, a pleasant personality, and the ability to relate easily to association executives. It is also an asset to be able to type so that the necessity of employing a secretary to work with an account executive is avoided. Convention bureau work can be highly rewarding financially and otherwise, and can offer a more stable career than hotel management. A large convention bureau often may employ thirty to fifty persons full-time and double that number part-time.

Cities that formerly were not considered convention towns have gotten into the act. Houston is one of the new convention centers. Its Astrodomain includes a 52,000-seat Astrodome, the 57-acre Astroworld amusement park, the 16-acre Astrohall, and a 1,500-room hotel-motel complex. The Astrohall is said to be the world's largest exhibition and convention center.

Acapulco has perhaps the most spectacular of all convention centers. Other large convention cities are Chicago, New York City, Anaheim, Las Vegas, Los Angeles, San Francisco, Dallas, Atlanta, Honolulu, Detroit, Houston, New Orleans, Denver, and Washington, D.C. The top convention states (convention activity) are California, Texas, Florida, New York, and Illinois, in that order. Attracting conventions is a specialized business; to further it, the larger cities have set up specialized convention and visitors' bureaus. Competition for business is keen. In southern California, convention bureaus in Palm Springs, Anaheim, Los Angeles, Long Beach, and San Diego often vie to serve the same groups. Funding for conventions and visitors often comes from a tax on hotel rooms, typically 6 percent. Bureau budgets can exceed $1 million a year, as does that of the San Diego Convention and Visitors' Bureau. The Las Vegas Convention and Visitor's Authority has a budget of $13 million a year generated by a 6 percent tax on the 43,000 guest rooms in the city. Of the sixty principal convention centers, reports show that most have operated at a financial loss made up by public funds—local, state, or federal.

IN-HOTEL CONVENTION MANAGEMENT

Within the hotel, the sales department personnel not only have the responsibility for attracting a convention but for seeing to it that the convention runs smoothly once it has checked in. This is a full-time job for at least one person and, in the large hotels, for several people. Within a large hotel there may be a Director of Sales (DOS), three more national sales managers, and a Director of Tours and Conventions. This latter person is the first-line liaison between a group and the hotel, seeing to it that all functions move as planned and all facilities and services within the hotel work to satisfy the group guests.

Rooms assigned to the officers of a large convention are often complimented by the hotel; sometimes meeting rooms also are made available without charge. The convention group can then rent to purveyors and others if they wish.

While more and more manufactured goods can be produced by fewer and fewer people, the number of persons engaged in management, finance, sales, higher education, and a variety of technical positions has grown steadily. Sales meetings, conferences, technical seminars, training sessions, and educational meetings have made Americans "the meetingest people in the world."

We have a special eagerness to exchange information and pass on, even to our competitors, ideas which in other countries are retained entirely for the benefit of the person who has them. Many industries formerly located in downtown sections are now on the outskirts of the metropolitan areas, making it necessary for their management and technical people to travel to a meeting to do business and exchange information. Large corporations with plants scattered all over the country must bring their technical and managerial personnel together frequently, which is another source of group business.

CHAIN HOTEL CONTROL OF CONVENTIONS

A sizable part of the convention business is controlled by the larger chains, those with large hotels in the principal cities. Hilton, Hyatt, Ramada, Loews, Sheraton, and a few of the other larger chains can afford a big convention sales staff—specialists whose principal business it is to cultivate and sell key people in the large national associations.

Conventions for some of the large national groups, such as the National Education Association and the American Medical Association, are planned at least five years in advance, some even earlier. The American Chemical Society selects its convention sites ten years in advance. Most of these associations move the annual meeting from place to place to equalize travel distance for members from all parts of the country. Some go abroad to Canada, Mexico, or the Caribbean. Another reason for moving conventions is to add interest and fun to the national meeting by holding it in a new place each year.

Only the larger hotel chains have the budgets necessary to make and continue the contacts needed to influence the location decisions of these associations. In this sense, the chains have a real competitive advantage over the independents. It should be pointed out that the very large hotels that can accommodate large national groups are mostly managed by the chains; because this is so, the chains are not competing with the smaller or independent hotels as much as they are with each other.

Convention Service Organizations

Convention business has grown to such an extent that a number of companies serving conventions have been established. These organizations handle many of the details of a convention other than lodging or those that take place within the hotel. In Los Angeles, for example, some 700,000 people attend conventions and spend close to $300 million a year. A large portion of this goes to convention planning services, the people who work behind the scenes to see that everything runs smoothly, providing practical services—transportation, tours, activities for traveling companions, delegate registration, and, in general, arranging for free time activities. Tours to Disneyland, Beverly Hills, and golf or tennis tournaments, are part of the arrangements. Some companies are geared to the "incentive market"—those visitors being sent by their companies as bonuses, usually for sales efforts. One company alone hires some seventy part-time tour guides and staff people to obtain tickets for theatre or sporting events, set up sightseeing tours, and arrange special parties. Service personnel are often dressed in distinctive costume for better recognition. The planning service may arrange for parties of all sorts. Some of the convention service companies have an office within a leading hotel and work closely with hotel personnel. Many large corporations have their own convention planning staffs.

Video Teleconferencing

Teleconferencing, largely arranged through Bell Telephone, may have a significant impact on conventions, conferences, and meetings. Video signals plus phone lines originate at one hotel, and can be sent to numerous other hotels. Conferees can gather at locations around the country and see and hear speakers at the originating property. Communications can be carried on between the groups. Where travel to gather at a convention is great, teleconferencing can reduce total costs drastically.

Holiday Inns has set up a subsidiary, Hi Net, that delivers first-run movies after 4 P.M. to their hotels via satellite. After that time the system can be switched into each hotel's meeting rooms for teleconferencing.

A permanently installed commercial satellite receiving station is needed for each property.

What are the effects on the hotel business? The jury is still out. Teleconferencing reduces travel and total guest room sales, but it probably increases conference room and food and beverage sales.

A Sixty-Year Occupancy Curve, 1920–1979

Laventhol & Horwath, the international accounting and consulting firm, has compiled occupancy rates for American hotels for the sixty-year period from 1920 to 1979. For those who like to take the long view of events, the curve of the occupancy rates (Figure 2–3) makes for a few philosophical comments.

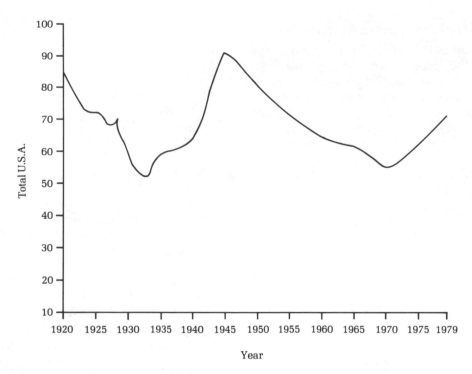

Figure 2-3   *Percentages of Occupancy 1920–1979*

Source: Adapted from *U.S. Lodging Industry*, Laventhol & Horwath, 1980. Prior to October 1927, no systematic monthly study was made of the trend of business in hotels. The only figures available are those compiled by Horwath & Horwath in 1928, covering the years 1920–1926. They were based on the records of a relatively few hotels that did, however, include two of the largest chains of hotels existing at that time.

Following World War I, the hotel business boomed. In 1920, hotel occupancy peaked at 85 percent, then, as numerous hotels were built, occupancy fell off through the 1920s. With the beginning of the Great Depression in 1929, occupancy dropped sharply and bottomed at 51 percent during 1932 and 1933. Chicago commercial hotels had a 35 percent occupancy rate in 1932. It was said that some 80 percent of the hotels were in receivership.

With the National Recovery Act, business (and occupancy) picked up gradually through the rest of the 1930s. Our entrance into World War II brought a surge in business that carried through the war years and peaked in terms of hotel occupancy in 1946. The 93 percent occupancy figure for that year has never been topped. In fact, following 1946, occupancy trailed downward year after year to 60 percent in 1963. Another low, 54 percent, was experienced in 1971. Since then, occupancy climbed gradually and in 1982 was around 69 percent nationwide.

The hotel occupancy figures are merely suggestive of what happened in the hotel busi-

ness. Highway hotels/motels were dealt a severe blow immediately following the 1974 OPEC oil embargo and the five-fold increase in gasoline prices.

Those little percentage numbers, with their lows during the 1930s and mid-1960s only intimate the rise and fall of the well being of thousands of hotel employees and investors. These numbers point to a central fact of American business: it never goes up continuously. And individual hotels, even cities, may prosper mightily while other hotels and whole areas fade away economically.

Hotels in large cities have an average occupancy about ten points higher than hotels in smaller cities. Large hotels usually have higher occupancies than smaller ones. Some of the national chains are running in the 70 to 80 percent range, with many of the newer and bigger hotels booked to capacity much of the year.

Occupancy varies from place to place and with rate structure. In 1980, Philadelphia experienced a 60 percent occupancy, whereas San Francisco had an 80 percent occupancy. Within the greater Los Angeles area, occupancy rates differ by as much as 25 points from one district to another.

The annual occupancy rate, or even the weekly occupancy rate, can be very misleading. The majority of commercial/transient hotels are likely to be filled Monday night through Thursday night with weekend occupancy dropping to 55 percent or less. Resort hotels near cities usually fill up on weekends. A beach resort hotel in a warm climate may be filled around Christmas and again from about January 15 to March 15. The "shoulder" periods, early spring and early fall, can evidence very low occupancy rates with a summer season somewhere in between. Every hotel experiences a different weekly, monthly, and annual occupancy rate, which when averaged may seem inordinately low.

Rapid Rise in Room Rates

Table 2–3 provides the key ratios for the hotel business of this country during the twenty-year period from 1961 to 1980. The chart is based on data from 800 hotels and motels. The occupancy rate for these properties remained in the range 66 percent to 70 percent while the average room climbed steadily, even faster than inflation, tripling in amount from $14.06 to $45.55.

Food cost in the hotel/motel restaurants remained at a steady rate, about 33 percent of sales. Beverage costs went down, from 27.8 percent of sales to 21.4 percent, suggesting that customers were paying more and getting less for their drinks.

Payroll as a percent of sales also remained surprisingly constant, between 33 percent and 35 percent of sales.

As might be expected, occupancy rates rise and fall with the economy. Pannell Kerr Forster, an international hotel accounting firm, plotted the curves seen in Figure 2–5. During the period from 1962 to 1981, a close correlation is seen between the real gross national product and the hotel occupancy rate.

TABLE 2–3 Selected Revenue and Expense Items—20-Year Trend

	Year							
	1963	**1968**	**1973**	**1978**	**1979**	**1980**	**1981**	**1982**
Ratios to Total Revenues								
Revenues								
Rooms	50.4%	53.5%	54.1%	57.3%	59.2%	59.9%	60.4%	60.5%
Food	30.5	28.2	27.9	26.0	25.1	24.0	23.7	23.5
Beverages	11.5	11.1	11.0	9.6	9.4	9.1	9.0	8.9
Other Revenues and Income	7.6	7.2	7.0	7.1	6.3	7.0	6.9	7.1
Total Operated Departments' Income	47.0	50.4	48.1	51.7	52.6	53.9	54.0	53.4
Income After Property Taxes and Insurance*	22.0	25.9	21.1	23.9	25.5	25.8	25.2	23.6
Property Taxes and Insurance	4.1	4.3	4.6	3.8	3.2	3.0	3.1	2.9
Payroll and Related Costs	34.9	32.9	35.7	34.2	33.0	32.8	33.0	34.1
Dollars Per Available Room								
Total Revenues	$ 6,961	$ 8,607	$10,278	$15,929	$17,678	$19,258	$20,853	$21,152
Income After Property Taxes and Insurance*	1,534	2,231	2,164	3,811	4,516	4,962	5,261	4,989
Cost Per Dollar of Sales								
Food	34.8¢	33.6¢	35.6¢	33.8¢	34.7¢	33.7¢	33.1¢	32.8¢
Beverages	27.2	24.3	22.9	21.5	21.6	21.5	21.4	21.3
Combined Food and Beverages	32.7	31.0	31.9	30.4	31.0	30.3	29.7	29.5
Percentage of Occupancy	67.8%	72.9%	69.2%	72.7%	72.8%	69.5%	67.5%	64.8%
Average Room Rate	$ 14.30	$ 17.41	$ 22.07	$ 34.69	$ 39.26	$ 45.38	$ 51.09	$ 54.08

*The Income After Property Taxes and Insurance, wherever it appears in this study, is before deducting Depreciation, Rent, Interest, Amortization and Income Taxes.

Source: Trends in The Hotel Industry, Pannell Kerr Forster, NYC., 1983.

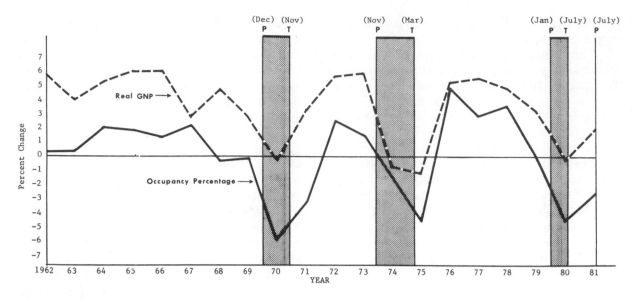

Figure 2-4 *Percent Change in Real GNP and Occupancy Percentage between 1962 and 1981*
Sources: Pannell Kerr Forster, Department of Commerce, Bureau of Economic Analysis, January 1983.

HOTELS ALSO FADE AWAY

Most hotels in this country, unlike those in Britain and Europe, do not acquire charm and patina with age. They become less competitive, room rates go down, the furnishings become shabby and threadbare, and the clientele changes. The hotel passes through the hands of a number of owners and leases, finally ending on the auction block. Hundreds of hotels have gone this route.

STRUGGLING TO SURVIVE

In 1974, the oil embargo by the OPEC nations sent shudders through the hotel industry; these were increased by an economic recession. Highway hotels were most sharply hit, and many of the new ones with heavy debt loads were unwillingly foreclosed by the lenders and the banks. Several real estate investment trusts became reluctant owners of motor hotels. Shades of the experiences of the 1930s were around. Commitments for new construction almost stopped. By 1978, however, travel and occupancies were up, and a few new hotels and motels were being built.

The hotel industry of 1980 saw its highest occupancy rate in twenty years. Hotel rates escalated sharply. The $100 room rate, once only spoken of as a possibility, became a real-

ity in a number of hotels. Spurred on by a weakened U.S. dollar abroad, visitors to the United States reached a new high and accounted for as much as one-fourth of the occupancy in some properties.

An economic recession beginning in 1981 saw occupancies decline and the real income per room drop off. Rack rates, the published rates, remained high, but sizable discounts brought the average room rate down.

INDUSTRY ANALYSES
MADE BY ACCOUNTING FIRMS

Statler led the way in establishing controls and comprehensive accounting procedures for his hotels.

In 1931, the firm of Horwath and Horwath (later to become Laventhol and Horwath) began publishing annual studies of hotels; today these cover one hundred hotels.

In 1936, Harris Kerr Forster & Co. (later to become Pannell Kerr Forster) published their first study of the operating results for one hundred hotels. Each year since then a similar study has been done by the firm, the studies growing more comprehensive with time.

These annual studies by the two firms, plus their other publications, have been invaluable to the student of the accommodations industry.[13] These two international accounting firms, by placing resident auditors in larger hotels, and in other ways, have helped to standardize accounting and control practices in the hotels of this country and of the world.

TRADE, ENDORSING, AND REFERRAL ORGANIZATION

Hoteliers began banding together for mutual benefit and protection toward the latter part of the nineteenth century. The Michigan Hotel Association was started in 1886, and other state organizations were formed later. In 1912, the American Hotel Protective Association of the United States and Canada was incorporated in Illinois. It was the forerunner of the American Hotel and Motel Association which took its present form in 1919.

The American Hotel and Motel Association is an association of state hotel and motel associations. It publishes *The Red Book,* a widely used, respected travel directory in the travel field. Only members of the AH&MA are listed in it.[14]

Best Western, largest of the hotel/motel referral and promotion-type chains, was established in 1948 in Long Beach, California, as a referral organization. The company, now headquartered in Phoenix, Arizona, dropped its "referral" organization image in 1974 and began competing with other chains on a full-service basis. In 1981 some 2000 lodging establishments were part of a chain that is nonprofit, promotional oriented.

Its headquarters offices are located adjacent to the Arizona Biltmore Resort and employs about 400 reservation sales agents who are contacted through an 800 phone number. Best Western provides marketing programs for its members and has an educational division for developing training programs to increase employee productivity among member properties. The company offers a credit card program and has negotiated master contracts with major

credit card companies, such as Exxon, Master Charge, Cart Blanche, and American Express. A Tour Marketing Department has the purpose of developing additional group/tour, travel agent, fly-drive, and corporate meeting business.

The American Automobile Association is the largest of all organizations for travelers. Each of its twenty million members receives a guide book that lists the better lodging places within an area. Hotels and motels may purchase the AAA sign if they meet the standards set up by AAA.

CENTRALIZED RESERVATION SYSTEM

Travelers, especially automobile travelers, want assurance that they have a reservation for the night ahead. The chain referral systems have central reservation offices to arrange such accommodations and also for making reservations for future dates. Until the 1950s, the travelers who stopped at a Quality Court, Holiday Inn, or similar referral system called long distance to the place of their choice and received a confirmed reservation. They paid for the call. Now prospective guests can call any of the larger chains and a reservation will be made in any of their establishments, whether located in this country or abroad.

Today, TraveLodge has a central office served by WATS (Wide Area Telephone Service). Prospective guests need only to dial 800-255-3050, and they are connected without charge to the TraveLodge central reservations office. Room reservations are confirmed at once or if there are no TraveLodge rooms available, the reservationist suggests an alternate hostelry in the immediate area.

Best Western International connects over 150,000 rooms by means of its reservations system, "Star." During the busy season some 900 reservation sales agents are employed in the Phoenix headquarters offices.

First Electronic Computer System

One of the great advantages of belonging to any referral or franchise system is the fact that the property is tied into the centralized reservation system. Western International Hotels, using teletype equipment, installed a reservation system in the 1950s. Sheraton Hotels installed the

13. Pannell Kerr Forster and Co. publishes "The Transcript" monthly (420 Lexington Avenue, New York City 10017). "The Accountant" is published quarterly by Laventhol and Horwath (866 Third Avenue, New York City 10022).

14. *Hotel and Motel Red Book,* American Hotel Association Directory Corporation.

first electronic computer system, the Reserva-tron. In 1964, Holiday Inns initiated their computerized reservation system, the Holidex. Quality Courts followed with Qualimax in 1967. By the end of 1968, all of the eight largest hotel and motel groups had similar reservations systems.[15]

Holiday Inns Holidex system consists of twin IBM 360 computers, interconnected with regional offices and inns by 50,000 miles of leased wires and by communication satellite. The cost was $12 million. Holidex II was being installed in 1980. The total cost was $2.5 million. Terminals include the CRT scope viewer, which eliminates the need for printing out facts. Advanced reservations can be recalled along with a printed list if desired. Guest registrations can be preprinted from information stored in the computer.

Intercontinental Hotels is hooked into Panamac Reservation Network owned by Pan American. Intercontinental bedrooms are sold together with aircraft seats from the same system.

Pre-Check-In and Check-Out

Responding to a major complaint voiced by travelers that they must wait in line to be registered, then wait again in line to check-out, some hotel/motel chains have offered pre-registration and check-out by mail. The individual or group merely picks up the room key(s) at the front desk. Tour groups have their luggage delivered to their rooms without face-to-face contact with a bellperson. On leaving the place, the guests merely drop off their keys, and their company is billed by mail for the guests' purchases. Such service assumes a favorable credit rating by the travelers concerned.

In 1975, Howard Johnson announced a Gold Key Service, a reservation and pre-registration system by phone. The Gold Key credit card, which is issued to the traveler, carries a code number that is used in making the reservation—name, address, name of credit card, and affiliation. To check in, the traveler merely signs in and picks up his or her key.

American Express offers an "Assured Room Reservation Plan" to innkeepers and cardholders. Card members give their AM-EX

15. Thomas F. Powers, "The Competitive Structure of the Hotel/Motel Market." Paper presented to the Council on Hotel, Restaurant, and Institutional Education, 1969.

card number when making reservations and rooms are held until check-out time of the day following arrival date. If the card member does not arrive and does not cancel, he or she is charged for one night. If the person arrives and finds no room, the property involved must supply the individual with a free room at a comparable inn and pay for transportation there and for a phone call advising business or family of change of address. The plan may set a pattern and help to reduce the number of complaints involving overbooking.

COMMENTARIES ON HOTELS AND HOTEL LIFE

Life in a hotel has excited writers and a sizable segment of the general public for centuries. The English inn was seen by many observers as a place of good cheer, comfort, respite from the workaday world, and a place where the good things of life were assembled.

Samuel Johnson, famous English lexicographer and author, made the widely quoted comment, "There is nothing that has been contrived by man by which so much happiness is produced as a good tavern." One can still relish steak and kidney pie in the very seat occupied by Johnson in The Cheshire Cheese Inn in London.

Modern-day writers have frequently set their plots in hotels, probably because the hotel is a natural place for things to happen, for strangers to meet, for passion to erupt, and generally a place of excitement and ferment where deals are made, jobs lined up, and "contacts" made and reinforced.

The hotel is a scene of high excitement and great despair, a place where you celebrate, and a place where the four walls close in on you, the location of a well-attended banquet, and a place of loneliness. The rich and the powerful can be observed. There is glitter and the sound of laughter.

The hotel is many things, for it is life in a capsule: the place of the handshake, the quick smile, the setting for marital bliss and for illicit love. It is a place where deference can be bought, where a phone call brings food and drink. It can be a sanctuary from discouragement or a room relieved only by a TV; a place to flaunt one's ego or have it deflated; a place where a hotel employee may subtly dominate a guest or be dominated.

Stopping at a prestige hotel supports the ego and adds luster to one's social cachet. The price tag of the room reflects the affluence of the person. The hotel world is a microcosm of the larger world, the larger world compressed into a building where the hopes and fears of people can be more readily observed. No wonder writers have used it as a setting for their novels.

Imperial Palace concerns life in The Savoy of London.[16] Vicki Baum had two best-sellers whose plots unfolded in hotels, *Grand Hotel*[17] (The Adlon) and *Hotel Berlin*.[18] Ludwig Bemelmans, who had worked in a hotel restaurant as a waiter, presented the foibles of hotel people in a friendly but satirical manner. His books are particularly humorous.[19]

As seen by John Portman, the hotel of the future is an integral part of a living complex. The site model, shown in Chapter 3, of the new Bonaventure Hotel in downtown Los Angeles dramatizes this relationship.

A best-seller that gives insight into hotel life as seen from management's viewpoint is the book, *Hotel*.[20] Its popularity can be judged by the fact that more than 2 million copies were sold by 1969. *Hotel* made the author a small fortune from sales and movie rights.

Interestingly, the excellent and apparently authentic hotel scenes in the movie "Hotel" were Hollywood sets, for the movie was filmed almost entirely in Hollywood; the hotel lobby was constructed specifically for the movie. The setting was New Orleans, but according to E. Lysle Aschaffenburg, owner of the Pontchartrain Hotel in New Orleans, the fictional hotel was a composite of hotels in New Orleans, reminiscent of the Royal Orleans, the Roosevelt, the Sheraton-Charles, and the Pontchartrain. Mr. Aschaffenburg feels that the leading character was a combination of Seymour Weiss, late owner of the Roosevelt, and of the late Captain Michael Leary of the Sheraton-Charles. The banquet scene was very much the Roosevelt.

16. Arnold Bennett, *Imperial Palace* (New York: Doubleday, 1931).
17. Vicki Baum, *Grand Hotel* (New York: Doubleday, 1931).
18. Vicki Baum, *Hotel Berlin* (New York: Doubleday, 1944).
19. Ludwig Bemelmans, *Hotel Splendide* (New York: Macmillan, 1941).
20. Arthur Hailey, *Hotel* (New York: Doubleday, 1965).

Figure 2-5 *The lobby of the Crown Center Hotel of Kansas City. This lobby contains a water fall, four stories high.*

Naming the "Greatest"

From time to time, various writers take it upon themselves to nominate hotels as being "the greatest." The mantle of "greatest" usually falls upon European hostelries of age and reputation. Attention to the individual guest is a prime criterion. The ratio of staff to guest must be high. The Savoy of London, for example, has four employees per guest room. One unusual duty of the staff is to make notations on 120,000 cards in the central reservation office that lists the regular clientele's whims, wishes, and needs. "Remember a basket for a guest dog," says one card. Another records that a certain countess cannot sleep with flowered curtains. American hotels do with less than one staff member per room, more like eighty people per one hundred rooms. Spaciousness and character are important. The nominators are not a little snobbish.

Richard Joseph named his three greatest hotels as being the ninety-nine room Gritti Palace in Venice, The Plaza of New York City, and the Mauna Kea Beach Hotel on the island of Hawaii. The Plaza Hotel with 1,000 rooms and 1,400 employees seems to make everybody's great list. Joseph does not care for Hilton Hotels because of the Hilton philosophy of mak-ing every square foot of space revenue-producing. Overseas, Joseph says, the Hilton International Hotels are much better, since they are built by local investors and designed with an eye to national prestige.

Of all the books about hotels only one attempts to convey the charm and romance of some fifty hotels, mostly in Europe, while also

Figure 2-6 *The Plaza Hotel seen from the vantage point of the picturesque duck pond in Central Park, which is directly across from the hotel on 59th Street in New York City. Considered by many to be the queen of hotels, the Plaza displays no sign. There is a belief that if a patron does not recognize the Plaza, he should not be going to the hotel.*

describing the appointments and delineating the characters of the managers, chefs, and concierges. Christopher Matthew, an Englishman who wrote the book, *A Different World,* is more than slightly biased in favor of European hotel-keeping: "... since the art of hotel-keeping originated in Europe toward the end of the Nineteenth Century and practically all the great hoteliers of the world since have been Europeans by training if not by birth, it is almost inevitable that most of the finest examples of that art should still be found on this side of the Atlantic."[21] A magnificent writer, Mr. Matthew almost convinces us that a hotel cannot be great without a history of famous guests, numerous art objects, luxury in abundance, and the personal attention of the manager and staff. Who could disagree with the last criterion?

Only four properties in the United States receive Mr. Matthew's imprimatur: the Stanford Court in San Francisco, the Cloister on Sea Island off Georgia, the Greenbrier in White Sulphur Springs, West Virginia, and the Ritz Carlton in Boston. Perhaps Mr. Matthew's standards for guest concern are out of "sync" with the American scene, or even the American traveler. His guests are "people who care passionately about being looked after hand and foot by a devoted army of servants who are capable of interpreting every slightest wish before it has been expressed or even thought of, and who are prepared to pay handsomely for the privilege." It may come as a surprise that staying at the "great" hotels of Europe is seldom more costly than staying at any of the leading hotels in the United States, where the European elites who place their shoes outside the door expecting them to be shined during the night may open the door to find no shoes at all.

Hoteliers and those who love travel will find Mr. Matthews a fascinating raconteur, breathing magic into the hotels he loves and stirring desires to walk through their corridors, eat in their dining rooms, and talk with their personnel.

An American writing about hotels might be expected to take a different view. Brian McGinty finds American hotels to be not only first rate but loaded with history and romance.

In his book, *The Palace Inns,* he claims that America invented the hotel and goes on to talk about such famous hostelries as The Parker House in Boston; The Greenbrier, White Sulphur Springs; and The Palmer House in Chicago. The Palace of San Francisco he calls a dream of gold and silver. The Del Monte Lodge of Pebble Beach on the Monterey Peninsula in California he labels a treat for the nabobs. The history of the first major hotels in Hawaii, The Moana and The Royal Hawaiian, is detailed, as is that of The Hotel del Coronado near San Diego. He finds The Brown Palace of Denver and The Broadmoor of Colorado Springs loaded with Western romance. He traces the development of The Grand Hotel on Mackinac Island in Michigan, and waxes poetic about The Breakers Hotel in Palm Beach. In Pennsylvania there is The Mohonk Mountain House, and in New York City, The Plaza and The Waldorf-Astoria. All of the properties he finds to meet his criterion of operating today building on a legendary past.[22]

What makes for an elegant hotel? First and foremost, elegant people stay there. If the right people choose a hotel it automatically gains status. The Brown Hotel in London is an example. Unless you like a dowdy Victorian style, the place is not particularly attractive. But since bonafide aristocrats choose it, the place has luster.

Next, the hotel must offer service—an abundance of service personnel. While commercial and convention hotels almost always have less than one employee per room, the luxury hotel may have two and even three employees per room. (Hotels in India don't count. Labor is so cheap that in addition to the regular staff a servant may be found outside each guest room.)

We still look to the British for defining what is posh, and the afternoon tea is becoming *de rigueur* in the elegant American hotel. High tea is as much ritual as refreshment, as are cucumber and watercress sandwiches, scones with Devonshire-style cream (extra heavy with butterfat), strawberry preserves and French pastries, and tea or coffee, of course. It helps if somewhere in the background a dignified per-

21. Christopher Matthew, *A Different World* (London, England: Paddington Press, Ltd.).

22. Brian McGinty, *The Palace Inns, A Connoisseur's Guide to Historic American Hotels,* Harrisburg, Penn.: Stackpole Books, 1978.

son is caressing a baby grand piano or plucking a harp.

At the elegant hotel the guest is seated while registering, then escorted to the room by an assistant manager. A porter follows, bags in hand, ready for the tip.

Another nice European touch is once the guest is ensconced in the room a knock on the door announces the floor maid or a valet who inquires if "the gentleman (or lady) requires his (or her) bags to be unpacked."

Guest room amenities become part of the steeplechase—which elegant hotel can come up with something a little more posh in the way of amenities: eiderdown comforters, velour robes, scented soaps, name bottled waters, sachets, shower caps, a small box of chocolates, splits of champagne, fruit, bathroom scales.

The ultimate in guest room amenities may have been reached in the penthouse suite of the Park Hyatt, Chicago: thirteen telephones, five TVs, fourteen bedside switches in the master bedroom, personalized stationery, a sunken marble tub, an 1898 Steinway piano, and an open bar with a butler completes the package. Now top that one if you can!

Turn-down service is a must at the elegant hotel. The maid (not the "room cleaner") taps discreetly on the door and, if invited in, turns down the covers at the top of the bed. The elegant guest must not stoop to such indignities. It helps if the maid is an elegant Finnish beauty or speaks with a decided French or English accent. A would-be snob once informed the writer that he would never stop at a hotel without turn-down service.

Some little favor like a chocolate mint or an orchid should be placed on the pillows, especially if the hotel is in Hawaii.

Posh hotels almost invariably come equipped with a team of concierges, those urbane ladies or gentlemen who can arrange almost anything a guest desires: a tuxedo, a seat at the opera, or a plane reservation. The concierge at the Imperial Hotel in Vienna will get you into the Spanish Riding School. In Rome the concierge may get you an audience with the Pope or a seat in a sold-out performance of Tosca. In Dallas it may be a seat on the fifty-yard line for a Cowboys football game. In New York the concierge can arrange to have you met by the maitre d' hotel of a famous restaurant and the bill sent to the hotel. In Paris the concierge may arrange a complete trip around the continent for you. On the Riviera you may desire a fully staffed yacht. Just ask the concierge. You'll recognize the European concierge by the golden crossed-keys—clefs d'or—on his lapel. In this country many concierges are women.

Robert Morley, the well-known British actor, comments on his list of "great" hotels insisting that room service should be rushed to the guest room, the breakfast tray received in two minutes. The simple secret, he says, is to have a kitchen on each floor. This is no secret, but it is expensive.

Morley declares the greatest hotel in the world to be the Ritz in Paris. He loves the golden clocks that he found in each Ritz establishment. At the Ritz, the guest is a guest, and nobody forgets it for a single moment. He does not care for hotels that conserve space, likening them to batteries for hens or humans. He hates to be attacked by the fast-moving doors of the modern elevators. Too bad; slow-moving elevator doors mean slow elevators.

Morley graciously includes an American hotel, The Century Plaza of Beverly Hills, in his list of greats. Designed by Minoru Yamasaki, the hotel is part of a "city within a city—a place to work, to live, to shop, and to participate in leisure activities." The hotel has 800 rooms, including 67 suites, each with private balcony, lanai, and color TV. It has the largest hotel ballroom in the West, seating up to 3,000.

I would include the Warwick Hotel of Houston on any list of great hotels. The owner, an oil multimillionaire, has refurbished an old hotel into something special. Among other things, he dismantled two French chateaux and installed their paneling and furnishings in his hotel. The lobby is spacious, gracious, and charming. The rooms are large and beautifully furnished. The rooftop club is reached by an outside elevator; the ride in it is an experience in itself.

Aesthetically one of the great hotels of the world is the Caneel Bay Plantation in the U.S. Virgin Islands. Mexico has Las Brisas and The Princess in Acapulco. Both are architecturally unique. Las Brisas, built up the side of a small mountain, has 200 villas with private pools. The Acapulco Princess, part of the Princess chain, headquartered in New York City, is probably the most beautiful high-rise resort ever built.

With 770 rooms, it employs about 1,500 people, 70 of whom keep its magnificient landscaping and plants beautiful. Twenty flower-bedecked floors center on a breeze-swept patio. The floors are stepped to resemble a Mayan temple.

Many a person's secret desire is to run a small hotel like the sixteen antique-filled rooms of The Mansion in San Francisco. Robert C. Pritikin, The Mansion's owner, bought a three-story house for $100,000, and spent $45,000 on Victorian-era furnishings, oriental rugs, and fresh flowers. Mr. Pritikin has tried to create an Edwardian fantasy world in his Queen Anne-style building, which was built by a Gold Rush millionaire. Breakfast is served in bed: coffee, orange juice, warm croissants, butter, and strawberry jam. The owner, dressed in striped trousers, greets the guest at the door and escorts them in for a glass of chablis while taped strains of Bach play in the parlor.

GREAT ROOM SERVICE

Some luxury hotels go all out for room service. Table tents are placed in every guest room. A few hotels advertise room service on TV. Most popular of all breakfasts, of course, is the continental breakfast—choice of juice, beverage, and breads. At the medium-priced property, room service comes via a tray. In the luxury hotels, it is wheeled in on a cart that is made into a table and is covered with fine linen. Coffee is served from a heated pot. Marmalade and berry preserves have their individual jars. The eggs may be served in egg holders. The silver is spotless and the meal becomes an experience.

At a few hotels, a room number guest list is kept by the room service order taker so that the guest can immediately be addressed by name. Room service waiters in the posher places become room service stewards, and each floor may be equipped with its own pantry, manned round-the-clock. This enables the steward to reply quickly at the door of the guest room after being summoned by a special room-service button.

Feelings about room service vary among general managers. Holiday Inn managers may offer it on a limited-hour basis and only as a necessity; they prefer guests to eat in their dining rooms. Some luxury hotel operators charge high prices, offer service around the clock, and

make a profit in doing so. A few hotels have a separate room service department. Most operate as an adjunct of the main kitchen.

SOCIAL PRESTIGE DETERMINES RATING

The social prestige of the clientele of a hotel determines its overall rating. The Claridge of London gets high points for exclusivity as does The Paris Ritz and The Beverly Wilshire in Beverly Hills, California.

The posh hotel, it is reported, should be ready for any occasion. Claridge's in London has a story that one evening an elderly, titled lady marched out of the lift on her way to an important dinner, dressed only in her jewelry. She had simply forgotten to put any clothes on, a mistake that was instantly rectified by the manager. He at once stepped forward, covered the lady with his own coat and accompanied her back into the lift as though nothing had happened.[23]

That hotel also ran into another problem when two kings arrived, both intent on staying in the Royal Suite. The solution: the manager ordered the workmen to pull down half the ceiling in the Royal Suite, showed the unfortunate damage to the ambassadors of both countries in question, and arranged for two smaller royal suites immediately. The Claridge, incidentally, isn't much to look at from the outside but arranges for no fewer than six waiters, six chambermaids, two valets, a house porter, and three bathroom cleaners to be ready at the ring of the appropriate bell to come springing along the corridor to administer to the guest's slightest need. It is said that even a simple whiskey and soda arrives on a trolley covered with a white linen tablecloth, together with "crisps," black and green olives, and hot salted almonds. That hotel is also one of a very few that has a number of "courier" rooms set aside for the personal servants of guests.

A good press must be maintained if a hotel is to be recognized for its name and "greatness." Of course, the greater the prestige of the evaluator, the better for the hotel. Cesar Ritz could do no wrong after the Prince of Wales, later Edward VII, said, "Where Ritz goes, I go."

23. Christopher Matthew, A Different World (London, England: Paddington Press, 1976.)

Figure 2-7 *The Waldorf-Astoria is probably the best known hotel in the world. It was completed in 1931 and carries the name of the older, now demolished Waldorf-Astoria, built in the 1890s.*

Opened in 1975, The Ritz Hotel in Chicago represents the luxury hotel in the Ritz tradition as seen in America. The hotel, reported to cost $80,000 a room (about twice the cost of the first-class urban hotel built in 1975) is located on floors eleven through thirty-one of the seventy-four-story Water Tower Place on fashionable North Michigan Avenue. Like many hotels, it is part of a condominium building which also contains offices and a seven-story shopping center containing such prestigious stores as Marshall Field and Company, and Lord & Taylor.

The Chicago Ritz makes food and beverage catering, secretarial, and maid service available to condominium owners who also have access to the health club, which has a swimming pool, exercise rooms, saunas, and masseurs.

The twelfth floor is the main lobby, a three-acre, glass-walled expanse of dining rooms, bars, and a 210-foot promenade. A sky-lighted garden terrace is part of the hotel's showcase, and a ballroom with 400,000 gem-quality crystals adorning the ceiling is part of the food-service.

Much larger than The Paris Ritz in France, as well as most of the other five Ritz hotels in existence around the world now, this one has 450 guest rooms and twenty apartments for permanent residents. The larger suites have two floors, connected by spiral staircases. Some have such deluxe appointments as oriental rugs and dressing rooms with mirrors on all four walls. Employees will number three for every two guests. The guests in any of the rooms may summon a waiter by pushing a bed-side button, and each floor contains a food pantry.

According to a former general manager, service is elegant: "No staff member will commit the unpardonable sin of asking the guest if everything is all right." Discriminating guests who are used to excellent service will complain if they do not like the service.

Details of equipment have been carefully considered. Extra-thin china, which costs twice the price usually paid for china, is used. China teapots, especially made to be dripless, were imported. The place opened with an inventory of 25,000 bottles of French wine.

The hotel has been equipped to reduce noise. Walls of guest rooms are twice the thickness of most new hotel rooms. Air conditioning equipment has been specified with oversized fan coils.

To instill the "Ritz Mystique" in new employees, each was invited to spend a night in the hotel prior to the opening. With all of its ritzy appointments and service, the hotel got off to a shaky start; occupancy the first year ran at 50 percent. Because the hotel lost about $4 million the first year, its general manager was let go and service was cut (one waiter for two floors). Marketing policy was changed to attract small groups.[24]

The Chicago Ritz is now a part of the Four Seasons Hotel chain headquartered in Toronto. The company also operates The Pierre in New York City.

24. Wall Street Journal, Sept. 14, 1947.

The Paris Ritz Hotel, probably the best known prestigious hotel in the world, as well as one of the highest tariffed hotels, makes very little profit.[25] The Ritz philosophy of hotel operation places profit as secondary to maintaining standards and service. According to Bernard Penche, general manager of The Paris Ritz, Cesar Ritz's only interest in making money was to enable him to make more and better hotels, "to maintain the atmosphere of a private home" in the hotel. Guests should be offered the ultimate in comfort and the best staff available. The Paris Ritz offers twenty-four-hour room service but no self-dialing because it would constitute a "decrease in personal service." While the gross operating profit in a 1975 study done of French hotels profits amounted to 16.4 percent, the Ritz showed only a 3.1 percent profit. Food costs and liquor costs were high—45 percent of sales for food and 29 percent for liquor, even though menu and beverage prices were comparatively high.

By 1980, The Ritz was taken over by a mid-Eastern investment group.

Hotel ratings vary around the world but can generally be classified into three categories: deluxe, first class and tourist/standard/economy/budget.

The term *deluxe* is little used in the United States, but it is used widely in Europe and it means the best, Five Star, A, or Number 1. Hotels so rated are exclusive and expensive and are supposed to offer the ultimate in service, accommodations, facilities, and location.

First-class hotels are also labeled Four Star in some countries, Three Star in others, B in others, and number 2 or 3 in still others. In the United States, a luxury class hotel could be the same as a deluxe hotel elsewhere.

The lower category of *tourist* could be labeled One or Two Star, standard, budget, economy, or inexpensive. At the lower end, most American travelers would not appreciate the quality.

European hotels are likely to be rated by the national tourist office. France, for example, has 82 deluxe hotels, 311 Four Star, 1738 Three Star, 4,978 Two Star, and about 10,000 One

Star Hotels. Spain also has a rating system imposed by its national tourist office. In Italy the Ciga Hotels management characterizes their deluxe hotels as having wide corridors, high ceilings, and spaciousness. The look is said to be luxurious: crystal chandeliers, veined marble, frescos, tapestry, silk and velvet draperies, period furniture, and fine art in baroque frames. According to Ciga sales literature, little things count too—hand-milled soap, fresh flowers, thick bath towels, engraved stationery, plenty of personal service, your robe laid out every night on your turned-down bed, and buttons to summon chambermaid, valet, hall porter, or waiter from stations on each floor.

The editors of the *Mobil Travel Guide* each year select a number of hotels, motels, and resorts to receive its 5 Star Awards each "One of the Best in the Country." In the 1977 list of resorts was The Arizona Biltmore in Phoenix, honored for eighteen consecutive years with the 5 Star designation; The Broadmoor Hotel in Colorado Springs (seventeen years); Greenbrier in White Sulphur Springs, West Virginia (sixteen years), and The Boca Raton Hotel and Club in Florida.

Among the city properties so honored were The Fairmont Hotel and Tower of San Francisco, The Stanford Court in the same city, and The Beverly Wilshire in Beverly Hills. Opposing the notion that only small- or medium-sized hotels can achieve ratings of distinction, the *Mobil Guide* lists the enormous Waldorf-Astoria in New York City and The Century Plaza near Los Angeles in its top classification.

Most major cities around the world have at least one or two outstanding hotels: in Paris, The Crillon and the Ritz; in Lisbon, The Ritz; in Madrid, The Ritz and The Palace; in Vienna, The Sacher and The Imperial; and in New York City, the Plaza and The Pierre, chateau-like, have long enjoyed outstanding reputations.

The AAA Tour books include ratings of some 15,000 properties that are graded on a scale of one to five diamonds.

Mobil Travel Guide awards One to Five Star ratings of 4,000 restaurants, 15,000 motels, 1,000 hotels, and 400 resorts.

In considering hotel glamour, it must be said that there are at least two hotel worlds. The one is the glamour hotel that covers the luxury resort hotel and the prestigious city

25. Lothar A. Kreck, "The Effects of Differences in Hospitality Management Philosophy as Measured by Operational Achievement in Two Parisian Hotels," *The Journal of Hospitality Education* (July 1978).

hotel. Together, these hotels may constitute less than 20 percent of the innkeeping industry.

The tendency may also exist to think of the hotel world in terms of the giant hotels, those like The Statler and The Waldorf-Astoria in New York City, The Hilton in Las Vegas, and The Sheraton Waikiki. In reality there are fewer than seventy hotels in the world with 1,000 or more rooms. Japan has nine of the fourteen such hotels in all of Asia. Europe, including Russia, has eleven; Africa has one. The rest are in North America.

A good share of the spending at the prestigious city hotel is by people on expense accounts. The $100 single rate means little to them since they are not spending their own money. Some guests are probably invited to hospitality suites maintained by a company that would like to sell them something or influence them in some way. The tabs for several of the guests' meals are picked up by somebody else, or they go on the expense account.

Then there are the people of wealth who can well afford the prestigious hotel, or the people on the way up who cannot afford to stop at other than a prestige hotel. The glamour resorts are frequented by the wealthy in season, by the not-so-wealthy out of season.

HOTELS FOR THE MAJORITY

The other 80 percent of the hotel world is prosaic; it is the one where the vast majority of people stay when they travel. The hotel is likely to be smaller, and the rates may be one-half or less than those in the glamour places. The hotel can be located in just about any community.

The newer motor hotels, including Holiday Inn, Ramada Inn, Rodeway, TraveLodge, Hilton Inn, Howard Johnson Motor Lodge, and other chain operations, are the stopping places for families of moderate income, businesspeople, and the other technical and professional people of the vast middle class.

The motor hotel or the average hotel that has been well maintained is a pleasant place in which they spend the night or several nights. One room, however, looks pretty much like another. People who travel a great deal say that sometimes, before they are wide awake in the morning, they look around the room and wonder which city they are in.

Hotel restaurant fare is fairly standard throughout the country; the menu is selected to appeal to the great American taste that thrives on meat and potatoes. There are no French chefs in the kitchen, only the local cooks who learned their trade by looking over the shoulder of the cooks ahead of them.

Despite all this, the "leading hotel" in town manages to convey a certain sense of excitement. It probably has a lively bar and a certain amount of gaiety prevails. Hotels on the way out, however, are sad places, indeed, where the desperate hopes of the owners are mingled with the stoicism of the guest.

WHAT HOTEL GUESTS WANT

Ernest Dichter, the founder of Motivation Research, has a great deal to say about the way people really feel about hotels and hotel rooms.[26] By conducting in-depth interviews with a number of people, Dichter reaches down into their subconscious and exposes how they really feel about things.

Dichter says hotel guests want a "live-in" feeling. They want reassurance and ways of avoiding that old devil—loneliness. They want to take possession of the hotel room by inspecting, feeling, trying out the lights, and performing various rituals to reassure themselves. A call from the front desk or VIP treatment from an assistant manager goes a long way.

Once guests are in the room they resent intrusion on their privacy (such things as the maid checking the room). The room should reflect the city where the hotel is located. Too many hotel rooms, Dichter observes, have paintings or pictures of faraway places like Paris, Greece, or London. Guests want local scenes on the walls. They also want to be needed and to meet other people. Make the hotel a social center where guests can mingle and meet, and satisfy the craving for companionship. The hotel should be more like a club, not just a cold empty room.

The average guest, according to Dichter, is searching for adventure and would welcome the feeling of independence derived from finding a pantry in the room where one could help

26. Ernest Dichter, Address before the American Hotel and Motel Association, October 20, 1967.

oneself. In Sweden some of the hotels have breakfast bars where guests help themselves, then carry their trays to their rooms or into a snack room.

He advises hotel operators to try to avoid giving the guest the feeling of being anonymous. Piles of luggage in the lobbies look as though the people are being evicted. Set up hospitality rooms such as is done by the airlines. Add Tower Suites, like the ones in The Palmer House in Chicago, where there is a small kitchen from which guests can help themselves to cookies, crackers, sandwiches, and fresh fruit with payment by the honor system. The corridors of the modern hotel, says Dichter, look very much like a cell block. To avoid this, he suggests circular floors.

Whit Hobbs, speaking at the same meeting, said that hotel guests have changed dramatically: "Guests want more. And every move is a move up . . . Out of economy and into luxury . . . Always wanting more . . . More style, more quality, more flair. More originality and surprise. Today there has to be a very personal, one-at-a-time, customized approach."

A quick survey of 200 of Hobbs' friends revealed their appraisal of the hotel today as too cold, too impersonal, sterile, tasteless, and lacking personality. Their comments include these remarks: "Sears Roebuck decor. No atmosphere. No special favors. Nobody really cares. All motels are plastic. They all look the same—tacky, tacky, tacky."

When these people were asked what they would do for a guest if they were running a hotel, the list was long: a comfortable easy chair, disposable paper slippers, a really good map of the city, a good clock in the room, a radio in the bathroom, more mirrors, larger pieces of soap, larger towels, longer beds, and better insulation between the rooms. "You sneeze and the guy in the next room says 'Gezundheit,' " was a common criticism.

NO TIPPING

Mr. Hobbs' friends hate tipping. "I dread driving up to the front door, and out comes the bucket brigade to handle the luggage: doorman to bellboy, to desk, to bellboy, to room. I hate to have to worry about it, to have change ready. Whatever it is, add it to the bill."

Another universal gripe is: "Those spooky women who knock on the door—or don't knock on it—at ungodly hours—and stick their heads in. Just checking. On what? It's none of their business."

The survey showed that nearly everyone was in favor of an optional buffet breakfast. "There it is. To eat or not to eat. No waiting. No tipping. No fuss."

Another universal gripe was the checkout line. "Isn't there an easier, faster way of getting out of there?" In answer to the gripe, Sheraton and Hilton have arrangements by which there need be no checkout, if the guest sees an assistant manager or the credit manager some time before leaving. Oddly, only about 15 to 20 percent of the guests use this "instant checkout" service.

Mr. Hobbs' friends wanted the same kind of shoeshine service found in European hotels where guests can place their shoes outside the door at night to be shined. The respondents wanted to be treated as someone special. "Don't always do it for money; sometimes do it for love." "Put a piece of chocolate on my pillow with a note that says 'sweet dreams.' " (The Warwick in Houston puts the chocolate on the bedstand.) They like what they find in Japan. "A small refrigerator in each room that's stocked with beer, cola, liquor, and snacks—with the price list on the door, and I pay for what I use."

Do Hobbs' friends steal? About half of them do. "I never take anything myself, but my wife usually does." Or, "Ho hum, what's to steal?" (Paintings or pictures are bolted to the hotel room walls to discourage guests from taking them.) Of course, most people would be very pleased with something free like a continental breakfast, a free phone call home, a free drink, or a free paperback.

Hobbs was more than critical of hotel advertising. The one hotel ad he liked was a tiny one in The New Yorker for The Ritz-Carlton: "The only things we overlook are the Charles River . . . Back Bay . . . and the Boston Public Garden."

COMMON COMPLAINTS

In prosperous times, the biggest complaint had to do with being turned away while holding confirmed reservations. A 1975 American Express survey showed that over one-quarter of their cardmembers had a supposedly guaranteed hotel reservation not honored. At least half said they would not stay at the hotel involved again.

Hotel managers explain that large numbers of persons making reservations are no-shows. The Regency-Hyatt House of Atlanta reported that eighteen of every one hundred persons making reservations there did not show up. Naturally, the hotel overbooked, and once in a while almost everyone appeared "and you're in a bucket," since hotels typically overbook 15 percent, especially if they can direct the overflow elsewhere.

One reason for going overboard is that many guests overstay their scheduled visits, meaning that patrons with reservations arriving later sometimes cannot be honored. Miami hoteliers complained that this often happened when a cold snap up north spurred patrons to linger a while longer in Florida. The hotel manager tries to ease the overstayers out, sometimes locking them out of their room.

Another complaint relates to high prices. One patron said he was charged a high price at a new hotel and found his room so small "I had to go out in the corridor to change my mind." Hotels often either tried to raise their quoted prices when conventioneers started showing up or put them in the worst rooms.

Travelers were generally displeased with slip-ups on the part of inexperienced hotel personnel. One gentleman said that telephone operators at a major hotel in Los Angeles had, on three occasions, told people calling for him that the hotel had never heard of him and that he was not registered. Actually, he was a convention manager of a medical organization and had been in the hotel for three days.

Complaints about banquet foodservice are common, but understandable, since many banquet waiters are moonlighters who are postal workers, taxi drivers, or police officers sent over for the evening by the union and who have little or no interest in, or knowledge of, proper table service.

A survey of travelers conducted by *Market Facts* found that though first-time guests mentioned convenience (location) as a prime reason for staying at a hotel/motel for the first time, repeat guests placed cleanliness/appearance in first place and moved service up to a strong second place. The overwhelming reason for guests going elsewhere was lack of service. The major offender was the "don't-give-a-damn" front office treatment; another was inadequately made-up guest rooms.

What infuriates a number of travelers is to be moved from one room to another because of an error or deficiency in the room. James J. Kilpatrick, a syndicated newspaper columnist, reported on one of his trips to a hotel in Las Vegas—the experience proved a disaster and received a host of sympathetic reaction from readers:

A hostile desk clerk assigned my wife and me to Room 2379, which was already occupied; then to 2307, which was intolerably small; then 2361, where the television didn't work. The housekeepers' office couldn't say when the TV might be repaired—maybe today, maybe tomorrow, maybe never; and no, it wouldn't be possible to send up a spare TV set because there weren't any. An assistant manager exuded hauteur and hostility; he could not have cared less. After a modest uproar, a fourth room assignment was attempted, no. 2641; the prior guest had left it in a shambles, and by 3 o'clock in the afternoon no maid had put a hand to it. We wound up in Room 1375 and my exhausted wife turned back the bedspread to take a nap: the sheets were dirty.

The writer complained bitterly about the snippy, snappy clerks giving the guest the kind of cold eye reserved for deadbeats and bill collectors. When he is carrying a two-pound briefcase a bellman appears as if by magic, eager to assume the dreadful burden, but on the other hand when the guest is carrying something heavy the bellman can be hard to come by. On the way to the room were dirty breakfast trays still languishing on the floors outside guest doors, another common complaint. The TV set—that indispensable friend of the lonesome traveler—is on the fritz one time in five.

At checkout time the traveler often discovers that the casher's window offers the least courtesy and the least efficiency in the whole establishment. According to Kilpatrick it has not occurred to the manager that as many as five or six guests might want to check out at the same hour. "The idea has not crossed his mind."

Said Kilpatrick:

At bottom, the guest wants a little tender loving care, to be treated as a guest, as a tired human being who asks little more than a clean room, a firm mattress, some ice down the hall, and a TV set that works. He wants prompt room service, cheerful telephone operators, a cashier who speeds the guest cheerfully on his way. The difference between a poor hotel/motel and a good one lies in the experience, the attitude, and the personal attention of the man or woman who runs the place. If the manager does a good job in training the maids and pays them tolerable wages, and treats them with dignity, and praises them for doing well, that manager's rooms will be comfortable rooms where the maids will have checked the light bulbs and tried the TV before they leave. If the manager insists upon friendly courtesy on the part of his desk clerks, he can get it—or he can get some new desk clerks.[27]

WOMEN TRAVELERS

Women traveling alone have probably always had certain problems revolving around sexism, amorous males, and fear for personal safety. Businesswomen claim that they are often treated like second-class citizens on planes and in restaurants. Some businesswomen get upset if a male insists on carrying their briefcase or in any way patronizes them. One lady executive recalls an executive who called her "honey." She retaliated by calling him "sonny." Bars can be intimidating, and some women travelers just don't go to bars alone. Western International Hotels teaches its bar employees to judge whether a woman is being harrassed in a bar and to help "discreetly." Ramada Inns has turned its hotel lobbies into well-lighted areas where a woman can feel comfortable over a drink.

---

27. *"Nation's Business,"* December, 1977.

In the matter of who gets the check when a woman is entertaining a man in a restaurant, Ramada Inns tells its waiters to place the dinner check half way between the man and woman dining together.

Women often feel they have to be just as aggressive and demanding as men if they are going to get the kind of service that is offered to men. This is especially true, they say, when making an airport car rental.

As for personal safety, a number of hotels place women on the same floor and increase the security on that floor. Hilton Hotels introduced the Lady Hilton program in 1966 that included "women only" floors. The Radisson Hotels provide extra security on its women-only floors, paint the rooms in pastels, and include feminine amenities such as blow dryers, skirt hangers, makeup mirrors, shampoo, and complexion soap.

Hyatt Hotels believe that women make up 25 percent of the transient business market and are "high-end-of-the-market" travelers. Hyatt adds women's magazines and perfumes to rooms reserved by women. Concierges contact women guests to ask if they would like reservations in the hotel's restaurants. Sheraton adds bath crystals, hand lotion, needle/thread packs, and cream rinse to rooms reserved by women. Films on the right and wrong ways to deal with particular situations involving women guests are part of the employee training program.

CHRONOLOGY OF HOTEL/MOTELKEEPING, 1900–1982

1904. Statler built the Inside Inn, a temporary hotel for the St. Louis World's Fair with 2,257 rooms, largest building of the time. The hamburger, as Americans know it, was first served at the same fair.

1907. Buffalo Statler opened. Each of the 300 rooms had a bathroom: "A room and a bath for a dollar and a half." The name changed to Buffalo Hotel when a new Buffalo Statler was built in 1923. Some Statler firsts:

1. Access plumbing shafts that served two bathrooms and ran from first floor to top floor
2. Posting of room rates
3. Built-in "free" radios
4. Free newspaper under the door each morning
5. Circulating ice water in guest rooms
6. "Servidors" in doors that eliminated tipping for cleaning and pressing service
7. Free stationery for all guests
8. Mail chutes connecting all floors

1907. The Plaza on Central Park opened for the elite. Pincushions and room telephones were provided in each of the 1,000 rooms.

(continued)

1910. American Hotel Protective Association of the United States and Canada incorporated in Illinois. Forerunner of the American Hotel and Motel Association.

1912. McAlpin in New York City, 1,700 rooms, twenty-five stories opened. "World's Largest" (at that time).

1913. Miami Beach is reached by causeway from Miami.

1918. Pitco fry kettle marketed.

1919. The National Restaurant and Hotel Associations take on their present form.

Frank Lloyd Wright first to electrify a hotel kitchen (The Imperial Hotel in Tokyo).

Hotel Pennsylvania opened, 2,200 rooms, "World's Largest."

1920s. The "drive-in" and "motel" appear on the edge of town.

1921. The Pig Stand, outside Dallas, became one of the first drive-in restaurants.

Child's Restaurants becomes the largest restaurant chain.

1922. Cornell University offers first degree-course in hotel administration.

1925. *Hotel Management*, by Lucius Boomer. First substantial book on hotel management.

1926. First motel in San Luis Obispo, California. First fast-food franchise: A & W in California.

1928. The Stevens Hotel (now The Conrad Hilton) was built at a cost of $35 million.

1928. John Courtney, Cornell Hotel School student, initiated the exchange of accountancy information among fifty hotels. Picked up by Harris Kerr Forster and by Horwath and Horwath.

1929. Hotel New Yorker built: forty-three stories, 2,500 rooms.

1929. First airport hotels go up at Croyden, England; Templehof, Berlin; Oakland, California.

1932. The new Waldorf-Astoria opens, best-known hotel in the world and until 1967 the largest in cubic space; forty-seven stories, 2,150 rooms.

1940s. Sheraton and Hilton became major chains.

From 1942 to 1945 (World War II). Number of meals eaten in restaurants climbed from 20 to 60 million per day.

1947. Intercontinental Hotels, a subsidiary of Pan American Airways, began operations in Latin America and became first large international hotel chain.

1948. Raytheon introduces the first microwave oven, Radarange.

1949. Shamrock Hotel, Houston opened. First large hotel built since early 1930s.

1949. Hilton goes international with management contract to operate the Caribe-Hilton in Puerto Rico.

1952. Holiday Inns started in Memphis. Franchising plans become popular for motels and restaurants.

1950s. Howard Johnson demonstrates profitability of large-scale commissary and long-distance distribution of frozen foods.

Convention business grows in importance. Many hotels become convention-oriented.

Beginning of computer applications made to hotels and restaurants.

Beginning of the travel and entertainment credit card boom.

Large hotels developed specialty restaurants, HCA, later Sheraton, Hilton, and others.

Large motor hotels built by hundreds. Older hotels razed. Number of hotels declines but number of hotel rooms remains constant.

1954. Federal tax law permits rapid depreciation that encourages hotel construction.

1959. Gas-fired convection oven introduced.

United States Airlines begin shift to jet planes.

United States Supreme Court rules to include many hotels and restaurants under jurisdiction of National Labor Relations Board (declared to be interstate commerce).

1960s. Era of mergers and franchising.

Transportation companies enter the hotel and motel field.

Cruise business takes over trans-oceanic liners by becoming floating resort hotels.

Frozen entrees begin to be used in restaurants. Swing to convenience foods.

1962. Budget motel industry began with Motel 6 in Santa Barbara.

1964. Supreme Court ruling strengthens prohibition against racial discrimination in hotels and restaurants.

1967. TWA purchases Hilton International. Offers travel club plans in competition with travel agents. Forty or more other airlines enter accommodations business.

Federal minimum wage law applied to hotels, motels, resorts, and restaurants grossing $500,000 or more in sales annually.

1967. Hilton permits guest to check out when they check in.

1967. Hotel Rossiya in Moscow opens, took over title of "world's largest hotel." 3,182 rooms accommodating 5,890 guests; can serve food to 4,500 persons simultaneously. Really three adjoining properties, each with own manager.

Food manufacturers enter the restaurant business.

Del Monte—Service Systems
General Foods—Burger Chef
United Fruit—A & W Root Beer
Ogden Corporation—ABC Consolidated
Pillsbury—Burger King
Pet, Inc.—Schrafft's
General Hosts—Uncle John's

The Hyatt Regency of Atlanta opens and sets style for multistoried hotel lobbies.

1968. Twelve franchise food companies have sales exceeding $50 million: Big Boy (Marriott), Burger Chef, Burger King, Castle Franchise, Denny's, Frisch's, McDonald's, Shakey's, A & W Root Beer, Howard Johnson, ITT, International House of Pancakes, Orange Julius.

1969. About 2.5 million public guest rooms available. 270,000 public eating places.

The value of meals eaten away from home exceeds $24 billion.

Federal minimum wage law applied to hotels, motels, resorts, and restaurants grossing $250,000 or more in sales annually.

1967-1969. The number of junior colleges offering hotel and restaurant courses of study increases from forty to ninety-eight.

Hotel and restaurant stocks boom. Price/earnings ratios of 35 to 50 become common.

1969. Holiday Inns of America merge with TCO (second largest inner-city bus line and Delta Steamship Lines). Becomes the largest of the travel-accommodations conglomerates with twenty-five subsidiaries.

McDonald's initiates a 4½-day work week for all office personnel.

Travel to Caribbean exceeds 4 million tourists.

1970. Serious fall-off in hotel and luxury food business.

Puerto Rico and Virgin Islands suffer drop in tourists.

Several franchise food operations fail.

United States Airlines suffer over $100 million in losses.

1971. Edward Carlson, President, Western International Hotels, made president of United Air Lines, first hotel man to head a major airline. Demonstrated the interchangeability of hotel know-how with airline management.

AMTRAK formed to upgrade and increase efficiency of passenger rail service.

1970s. The management contract for hotels supplants the franchise: risk-free enterprising. Grew out of the lease—why lease when you can contract?

Real Estate Investment Trusts (REITS) loaned more than $1 billion for hotel and motel construction—becoming owners by default.

In the middle 1970s a revitalization of central business districts included new hotels funded in part with government money.

(continued)

Hotels added facilities and services to attract pleasure travelers.

Hotels provide added security and amenities for women traveling alone, including floors for women only. "Hotels within hotels" provided by setting aside top floors with concierge and other special services at premium rates.

Sharp increase in consumer and employee litigation against hotels, restaurants, and travel companies.

Numerous health, diet, and weight-reducing restaurants begin operation.

1976. Eighteen of twenty largest hotel chains use data processing for at least part of their corporate accounting and reporting. Five of the eighteen use outside computer services; the others have their own computer installations.

Timesharing plans, interval ownership, and right-to-use plans become popular in the vacation business. Condominium purchasers acquire a fee interest in a unit for a week or more (interval ownership). Resort hotels offer the right to use a specified type of accommodation for a week or more over a period of twelve to forty years.

Condominiums built in large numbers in a number of resort destinations and rented out as hotel/apartments.

Proprietary health-care chains have made big inroads in the health-care field. Many hospital and senior citizen facilities have become both owned and managed by investor-owned companies. Government insurance pays much of the bill.

The hotel guestroom becomes an entertainment center; by 1981, 500,000 guestrooms provide in-room movies.

1980. Hotels can install their own satellite earth stations communicating directly with satellites hovering 22,300 miles above earth and receive up to twenty-four programming channels.

Some 300 Holiday Inns offer teleconferencing facilities.

Questions

1. The early hostelries of the United States were known as taverns, but later the name of many of them was changed to hotel. Can you explain how this came about?

2. Why have the larger city hotels been called the "palaces of the public"?

3. If someone says, "Tipping has always been a part of American hotel and restaurant keeping," what is your reply?

4. After about 1840 and until the 1940s the best location for a downtown hotel was likely to be close to what?

5. How does the early American hotelkeeper compare in social status with the innkeeper of England?

6. Hotels can be classified in a number of ways: commercial or transient hotel, resort hotel, residential hotel, and what other major classification?

7. By all odds the largest number of any particular classification of hotels are: transient, resort, residential, or condominium?

8. Can you name two organizations that rate hotels in this country?

9. Name five major "hotel" cities.

10. Which hotel chain has the most hotel rooms?

11. Chain properties control what percentage of the total number of hotel/motel rooms in this country?

12. In the late 1940s, which hotel chain made a major commitment in Latin America and really started Americans in the international hotel business?

13. Which hotel in Puerto Rico acted as a model for large hotels in the Caribbean when it was built in 1948?

14. Numerous hotel companies operate abroad today. Why is it that U.S. companies seem to have an edge in international hotelkeeping?

15. Kemmons Wilson has had a major impact on hotelkeeping in this country by forging the Holiday Inn system. Name three factors that may account for the spectacular success of that company.

16. In observing the growth of hotels would it be safe to say that there are more hotels today than there were thirty years ago? Why or why not?

17. Which city is the biggest convention city in the world?

18. What does a person with the title "tours director" do in a hotel?

19. Why is it that the major hotel chains get the lion's share of the convention business?

20. While the national occupancy may be 70 percent, does this occupancy level hold generally around the country?

21. Generally speaking, the highest hotel occupancy and the lowest occupancy are experienced in which two months?

22. Name the two international accounting firms that are the source of most of the statistics available on hotel operation.

23. Who publishes the *Red Book* and what is its purpose?

24. Several of the referral groups use an 800 number in relation to the reservation system. How does this work?

25. Travelers have complained about arriving at a hotel with reservations and finding no room available. Some of the major chains are now doing something about this problem. Explain.

26. Travel writers and other writers like to pick "great" hotels. What are some of the criteria used in making these nominations?

27. Name five "great" hotels in this country or abroad.

28. The "great" hotels always provide excellent room service. From the point of view of the hotelier, what is wrong with offering such splendid room service?

29. In Europe the term "deluxe hotel" is used widely. Who decides whether a hotel is in the deluxe category?

Discussion Questions

1. Why should we care that a British writer does not feel that our service is up to standard?

2. Many students studying hotel and restaurant management aspire to working abroad. Will opportunities for such work increase or decrease over the next ten years? Identify the forces that helped determine your answer.

RALPH HITZ (1891–1940)

Hitz does not rank with the other great hotelmen in the sense that he built an empire or left an estate. He did neither. His period in the limelight lasted only ten years—a period when the hotel business was at its low ebb in American history. Hitz was a sales and promotion phenomenon, who was able to take ailing hotels and predict within a few dollars what their sales and profits would be, then produce the sales he had forecast. During the 1930s his was the largest chain of hotels, The National Hotel Company. In New York it included The New Yorker, The Lexington, and The Belmont Plaza. He had The Adolphus in Dallas, The Netherland Plaza in Cincinnati, The Nicollet in Minneapolis, The Van Cleve in Dayton, and one in Chicago.

Ralph Hitz had early struggles similar to Statler's. In his teens he ran away from home in Austria to the United States and worked at any job he could get, as a busboy, waiter, and cook. He learned rapidly and at the age of thirty became manager of Cleveland's sedate Fenway Hall and of the Tilson.

He spent $20,000 (a large sum in the depression year of 1930) in changing a delicatessen into a coffee shop. The coffee shop was an instant success. Against the owner's wishes, name bands were brought to the Cleveland hotel. Ice

shows were also a favorite with Hitz. He saw to it that his shows and performances were well attended even if 30 to 40 percent of the guests at first night performances were "dead heads" (nonpaying guests). His explanation: "Business brings business."

According to his son, Ralph Hitz, Jr., Hitz was the first to air-condition a hotel dining room. Again a simple explanation: "People eat more when they are cool."

By 1932 he was able to sign a contract for the operation of the 1,200-room Book-Cadillac (now Sheraton-Cadillac) in Detroit. It was the beginning of the National Hotel Company, which grew rapidly as word of the Hitz service and promotional skills spread.

During the registration procedure the word loved most by the guest, his or her name, was used at least three times. The bellman continued to use it. This "strange music" of one's name did not stop until the guest was cozily settled in his or her room.

First-stay guests could expect even more of the red-carpet treatment: a few moments after settling down in their room, they were called by the "Hospitality Desk" and a solicitous inquiry was made to see if "anything further can be done to make your stay comfortable."

Statler started the idea of slipping the daily newspaper under the guest room door, "compliments of the management." Hitz went a step further and provided a hometown newspaper for the guest (provided he came from one of the cities from which most of the hotel's business was derived).

Tall people were given rooms with seven-foot beds. Parents with children were sent a special children's letter soon after registering. Sick patrons were personally visited by the floor managers. Guests leaving on an ocean trip were sent bon voyage messages. While most hotels were requiring guests without luggage to pay in advance, a no-luggage guest at a Hitz hotel was provided with an overnight kit containing pajamas, toothbrush, toothpaste, and shaving gear.

Everyone in the Hitz hotels was trained and expected to be a supersalesperson. Room clerks were sent out over the country for one or more months each year to pick up business and get acquainted with their customers firsthand. A Hitz man was supposed to give his all for the hotel, and room clerks were expected to make calls within their own city during their off-hours. To insure compliance, each salesperson kept a file card on each prospect and noted the time of the contact. Hitz hired a seven-passenger plane to sales-blitz all cities of 100,000 and more in population.

Selling went on all the time the guests were in the hotel. If they opened a closet door, there staring them in the face was a placard advertising one of the hotel services or a dining room. Even the mirrors in the bathroom medicine cabinets held advertisements. Should the guests settle down on the bed to listen to the radio they were still within the master-seller's voice range. The radio was interrupted at set intervals so that the hotel services might be extolled and called to the guests' attention.

Hitz is credited with being the first to develop and exploit a guest history. Before the turn of the century, Ritz had sent private letters to his hotels describing the idiosyncracies and special likes and dislikes of his guests. Hitz systematically collected the information he wanted on each guest and set up a guest history department. This department, manned by a separate staff, kept guest records and followed the Hitz system of bringing the guest back to the hotel.

The system also kept track of each guest's birthday and wedding anniversary date, his or her credit standing, and other information of value to the hotel. It was also routine to send a letter to all first-time guests, to each guest who had stopped with the hotel twenty-five times, fifty times, and one hundred times.

On the fiftieth visit the guest received a complimentary suite. With the hundredth visit an appropriate gift with a letter was sent, and the guest became a member of the Century Club and had his or her name engraved in gold on a gift notebook. Birthday greetings and wedding anniversary felicitations went to all regular guests. Color signals on the record showed if there was to be no publicity, if the person was undesirable and not to be welcomed, or if the address given was questionable.

Any complaints made were also recorded, and personal explanations were made by one of the hotel's traveling representatives. When guests returned, they would be given the same room they occupied on their last visit—another personal touch to increase one's ego. Special credit cards for people important to the hotel were developed by Hitz management.

To insure that guest rooms were really clean and in immaculate order, a full-time room inspector went from room to room checking on everything in the room. His inspection was over and above the "O.K." placed on the room by the regular inspector.

Hitz demanded much from his employees, and, because he was a leader and because it was a time of economic depression, he got superior performance. He also paid higher wages. The prevailing wage was $85 a month for a room clerk; Hitz paid $135. His department heads were the highest paid in the business because he knew it was through them that his systems would be effected.

Promotion was a part of the Hitz personality, and he used it to promote himself as well as hotels. In 1927 he was offered the management of The Cincinnati Gibson Hotel, which was having financial difficulties. No one was more surprised than the board of directors when Hitz promised to earn $150,000 in profit during his first year of operation. The directors were more astounded than surprised when his first year's profits were $158,389.17.

Not one to hide his light, Hitz publicized his methods and cost accounting system to the entire hotel industry. In 1929 The Hotel New Yorker made its debut, along with the great depression. Undismayed, Hitz went on as its manager, to use The New Yorker as a laboratory where all operations were done by the book.

Because he gave the man or woman paying $3 to $5 deluxe service of a type usually associated only with deluxe rates, his hotels ran high occupancies. During the depression, when hotel occupancies over the nation were at 50 percent and lower, such an operator was in great demand.

Hitz did more than promote; he introduced all-out standardization to hotelkeeping. His kitchens were fine examples of efficiency and uniformity. Controls of all kinds were installed and thorough-going accounting practices followed. Hitz memorized standard operating ratios, then set about to excel them. The income from his restaurants, and such services as valet and guest laundry, were so high as to confound his contemporaries. What others had done, he could do better.

Like others before him, he could make money for other people—but not for himself. With friends, he bought The Belmont Plaza, across the street from The Waldorf-Astoria, ran out the prostitutes, and put in the Hitz systems. Nothing seemed to work. According to his son, if an idea failed, he would not admit failure, as he would have done if spending other people's money. Instead, if an ice show failed to bring in the crowds, Hitz would spend another $50,000 for promotion of the show. This did not prove to be the answer. The Belmont Plaza was one of the causes of his death. He died leaving only a small estate.

A hard-driving man, he was also known for quick thinking and a well-developed sense of humor. It is said that he craved friendship and had a genius for hospitality. To get a true picture of him, one had to see him making daily tours of his house, busily taking copious notes, and later, during the check-in hours, to see him in the lobby, a short, ebullient man, personally greeting new arrivals in an almost incomprehensible Viennese accent. He also had his failings; drinking and gambling were problems. He died in 1940 at the age of forty-nine.

Because he was the driving force of the company that operated ten of the country's largest hotels, his death brought quick disintegration of the system. Hitz owned no hotels and left no institutions as his shadow. Surprisingly, his name is scarcely known to the younger generation; his memory almost lost.

3 Hotel/Motel Finances and Building

People thinking of operating a hotel can go a number of routes if they have the knowledge and an access to money. They can build or buy an existing hotel, then personally operate it. Traditionally, they could lease a hotel and pay the owner a percentage of gross sales—such as 20 to 35 percent—or make some other agreed upon financial arrangement. They can get a group of friends and form a syndicate and perhaps manage a hotel which the syndicate buys or builds. They can purchase a concession from the owner of a concession in one of the state or federal parks, or they can bid for a concession from the state or federal government directly.

With the rapid growth of condominiums, they may—with enough background and knowledge—develop a condominium, sell the units, and manage the rental pool, which they set up for the owners, as well as manage the condominium itself. The hotel/motel business can be thought of as two separate businesses: (1) financing, building, and owning; and (2) managing and operating. The two are often quite different businesses.

The big change in operating practice that has come about since about 1970 has been management by contract. Most of the major chains are divesting themselves of ownership and seeking to manage by contract—a happy arrangement for operators since they invest little or no money, take few or no risks, and receive payment for their services regardless of profitability of the venture, or what happens to the economy and the value of the property itself. To get a contract usually presupposes that the manager or management firm is a well-known, established operator who will have no difficulty in performing well. It helps if the operator has already established a large referral system and has a sizable promotion and advertising program under which the unit can be managed and integrated.

FINANCIAL MANAGEMENT AND PROFITS

The greatest profit connected with the hotel business does not usually come as profit generated by the sale of food, beverages, and lodging to the general public. The great fortunes in the hotel business have come in other ways, largely as a result of looking at the hotel business as requiring as much real estate manipulation as actual innkeeping.

People build hotels for a variety of reasons: pride of ownership; profit from building; profit from promoting and financing; profit from appreciation in value of the property; to increase the value of surrounding property; and for reasons connected with reduction of income taxes. In the 1920s, many hotels were built by promoters who had no intention of operating the properties.

Today, many hotels are being built as a part of large-scale housing or entertainment complexes and as part of the rehabilitation of the downtown area of cities. The great increase in value of the Hilton and Sheraton Companies has not come from operating profits but from buying, selling, tax advantages, and in the appreciation of value of the hotels with time. Financial management is the name of the game, and it is a complex game. (Casino hotels are something else. If popular, they can be veritable mints. The profits come from gaming, not the hotelkeeping.)

Profits reported from hotel operations have always been small, ranging from 0 to about 10 percent of the income of the hotel.

If return on sales and return on investment is so low, why does anybody go into the hotel business? How is it possible that many fortunes have been made in the business?

The answer to this question varies with the economic conditions of the country, especially the price of real estate, the tax laws in effect, and the competitive advantage of particular hotels at the moment. Professor Albert Wrisley at the University of Massachusetts presents his hotel classes with a standard conundrum: how can a hotel worth $10 million break even year after year, and the owner still come up with more than $1 million gain in assets, if he sells at the end of five years?

The answer revolves around the owner's taking the maximum depreciation allowable, and the fact that, over much of U.S. history, real estate has appreciated in value. In selling, he would probably have received $10 million or more. It is quite possible, and even likely, that the hotel built in 1960 for $10 million would have been worth $15 million in 1979.

THE VIRTUES OF GOING INTO DEBT

Get rich by going into debt. This is exactly what happens if money is borrowed at reasonable rates of interest, and the value of money depreciates each year. Borrow $100,000 this year and five years later you may be paying it back with money worth $80,000. Of course, the money borrowed must be returning some income to offset the cost of the interest paid on the loan. Oddly, in our economy, the person who can owe $10 million has usually arrived. God has been on the side of the optimist over the long pull. Over the short pull, many individuals are wiped out.

Even though he lost most of the ownership of his eight hotels in Texas during the depression of the 1930s, Conrad Hilton is a good example of the optimist who came back strong

in the late 1930s and 1940s to create a hotel empire. Ernest Henderson, in 1938, began buying hotels for a fraction of their value in cash. Before his death in 1967, he had created the largest hotel chain the world had known.

Borrow or otherwise acquire as much money as possible, buy properties with as little cash down as possible, take maximum depreciation, and when the depreciation has begun to run out, sell the property. Buy a new property, again with as little cash as possible, and repeat the cycle.

As long as there is a rising economy and the property shows some profit, the entrepreneur can pyramid his or her holdings spectacularly. If the economy falters or some of the properties are losers, it is quite easy for the entrepreneur to become overextended. The system can then collapse. The system has been used many times in other businesses, but it is particularly effective in the hotel business since it is as much real estate as hospitality.

The system works because people have confidence in a particular business and will buy bonds or stock in a business; the economy continues upward; real estate appreciates; and the value of the dollar depreciates.

Conrad Hilton was able to buy controlling interest in The Waldorf-Astoria, the world's best-known hotel, for $3 million in cash. Hilton himself clinched the deal with only $100,000 of his own money. The purchase, he points out in his book *Be My Guest*, did not come off as a coup d'etat, but was the result of four years of delicate negotiation, careful planning, and a lot of prayer.

METHODS OF FINANCING HOTELS

The methods of raising capital for a hotel run a fascinating gamut. Several of the first hotels built in the 1790s were put together by "tontine" associations. Early in the 1790s, a group of New York City merchants built The Tontine Coffee House. The famous City Hotel of New York was another product of the tontine, an arrangement by which the survivors among the investors inherited the interest held by the other investors. The tontine arrangement of survivor-take-all would not seem designed to promote peace and tranquility among the "partners."

As civilization spread westward, the hotel went along, sometimes even preceding the people. Real estate developers, quick to recognize the importance of a hotel for the growth of a community, often built the hotel before the community arrived. (The Gayoso Hotel in Memphis stood alone in a meadow for years.) A few other hotels never acquired a town around them and fell into decay.

The dangers of overextension of credit were experienced early. The most impressive public house erected in America between 1793 and 1825, according to historian Doris King, was The Boston Exchange Coffee House. It was a victim of poor financing.

OVERBUILDING IN THE 1920s

In the early 1920s, hotel investment looked very tempting. Room occupancy had jumped over 72 percent in 1919 to 86 percent in 1920, and up until 1927 the occupancy never dropped below the break-even point for nearly all hotels. The great boom in hotel building resulted. Chicago, for example, had 11,000 hotel rooms in 1920; by June 1926, the figure increased to more than 22,000.

Hotels were built for a variety of reasons other than pure investment. In many towns without a first-class hotel, the hotel was an expression of civic pride and the center for community activity. In some of the larger communities, the hotel was built to boost a particular section of the city. Hotels were also built to satisfy an individual's vanity or as a monument to someone or something.

It also became clear that a valuable piece of land could be made more valuable by the addition of a hotel. Promoters who had a considerable part in creating the boom were able to do well for themselves financially. Investment houses, too, were interested since a new hotel provided an outlet for the sale of securities. In the 1920s, much of the investing public had a mistaken notion about the value of bonds, thinking that the word *bond* denoted a sort of value that would not depreciate. Many were so eager to buy bonds that they bought first and questioned the value of the bond later.

Mr. Charles Moore, who was active at that time as a hotel promoter, relates that the total cost of financing many hotels in the 1920s averaged between 12 and 20 percent, with as much as 88 percent of the total amount borrowed for actual payments on construction. Many hotels had very little actual cash put into them by the owner up to the time the building was completed. If it was a success from the start, well and good; if not, trouble lay ahead.

The idea of buying a large mortgage, dividing it up into small pieces, then selling it to the public was sound in theory, says Mr. Moore, but many people entered the field who did not know the business and too many hotels were built.

Creating a Hotel from "Thin Air"

An example of how a hotel could be created out of thin air (with no equity capital) is based on what happened in Pittsburgh in the late 1920s when a contractor needed a job to keep his organization busy. He purchased a large lot in exchange for a second mortgage, providing an equity behind the purchase in the form of securities or services. He then created a third mortgage, for about twice his legitimate fee as a contractor, sold half of the third mortgage to subcontractors to build a hotel, and retained the other half for his fees.

An apartment house, costing $1.5 million, was built with not one dollar of cash invested in it except what was secured from selling first mortgage bonds to the public, bonds that sold like hot cakes the moment they were announced in the local newspapers throughout the country.

A typical hotel was financed in this period by an owner with an equity equal to about 30 to 40 percent of the total cost of the land, building, and financing expense. He would apply to one of the first mortgage houses for a combined building and permanent loan. If approved, the building would start at once, even though this method of financing was relatively expensive.

Aftermath of Overbuilding

Hotels financed in this way made good investments as long as occupancy was high. High occupancy required the kind of monopoly in location which was hard to come by, since overbuilding was rife. If a 100-room hotel was needed in a community, local enthusiasm often forced the building of a 200-room house.

With the depression of the 1930s, occupancy dropped below 40 percent in many hostelries, and many of the hotel ventures sold for a few pennies on the dollar. It is said that over 80 percent of the country's hotels were in serious financial trouble, many of them taken over by insurance companies and other lending institutions that were forced to foreclose on their mortgages.

Many hotels, however, were successful from the day they opened, especially when they were: (1) in prime locations, (2) financed with cash, and (3) built so that the first floor of the hotel could justify a good share of the value of the land. As always, it was important to build so that not an inch of space or a single dollar was wasted.

THE RISE OF CHAINS

The debacle in hotel values in the 1930s offered a rare opportunity for a few bold entrepreneurs. The story of Sheraton Corporation of America is a case in point. In the 1930s, Ernest Henderson and Robert Moore, of Boston, secured control of three investment trusts and reinvested the money from one of them in The Hotel Continental in Cambridge, Massachusetts. They improved the building and began merchandising the food and rooms. Out of the profits they paid off the mortgage and bought additional property.

At the time, control of hotels and office buildings was easy to get with a small amount of cash. The Park Square building in Boston, which was owned by the First National Bank of that city, had a sale price of $4 million; however, Henderson and Moore acquired control for only $125,000 in cash. The bank was persuaded to give a first mortgage of $3 million, and an individual put up $150,000 for preferred stock. The $125,000 went to buy half of the $250,000 in common stock which was created.

The process was continued by Messrs. Henderson and Moore as they took earnings from properties that they owned to acquire loans against buildings bought from banks and insurance companies. The sellers of the properties were pleased to take back second mortgages from Henderson and Moore, particularly after seeing the success these men were having with other Sheraton properties.

In Detroit, a hotel was taken over for no cash at all because the owner was impressed with what Sheraton had been able to do elsewhere. The Sheraton Corporation took a huge step forward in 1956 when it purchased twenty-two hotels from Eugene Eppley, who had acquired them all in the course of his lifetime.

Conrad Hilton had a similar experience. He purchased his first hotel in Cisco, Texas, in 1919 when the owner, who was doing capacity business, preferred selling his hotel for $50,000 down and going out for oil in the area.

Following World War II, motel construction boomed, but by today's standards these motels were Mom and Pop operations of six to thirty or forty units. The money for construction came from savings, banks, and local savings and loan associations. Many were owned and operated by couples retired from a principal career, such as military or retail trade. The land and buildings were mortgaged as collateral for the construction and development loans. Few hotels were built until the middle 1950s.

From then, and especially during the 1960s, numerous large hotels were built, as were motor hotels with more than one hundred units. Larger properties tended to replace smaller ones which, with time, became obsolete.[1] Typically, motor hotels were built on or near major highways leading to or around towns and cities, bringing obsolescence to the downtown hotel, typically an older property built in the booming 1920s.

In the late 1960s and early 1970s, several cities became overbuilt with hotels. A prime example is the Orlando area where motels and hotels were built in quantity to serve visitors to Disney World and what was expected to be the growing Orlando area.

Major hotel chains expanded rapidly in the cities, at first by constructing and operating. Later, the big chains, such as Hilton and Sheraton, shifted policy from owning to operating under management contracts. It had proved much safer and more profitable to manage than to own and operate. Today, 70% of the hotel rooms in this country are chain operated.

Hotel construction was fostered in the late 1960s by investors who had become discour-

1. Laventhol & Horwath, *Financing the Lodging Industry: A Survey of Lender Attitudes* (Philadelphia, 1975).

aged with the bear stock market and were seeking tax-sheltered investments, investments that produced significant tax losses as a result of allowable tax deductions. The resulting tax losses were used to reduce tax liabilities that were attached to other, unrelated taxable income of the investors. Most tax-sheltered investments were made possible because of tax laws passed by Congress and were not the result of tax loopholes as many people believed. A hotel/motel business seemed an excellent medium for realizing capital gains rather than straight income.

THE REAL ESTATE INVESTMENT TRUSTS

Another major factor in the rapid hotel construction of the period came as a result of a new type of trust made possible by a law in 1968, the Real Estate Investment Trust (REIT), "a mutual fund of real estate loans." Such trusts acquired millions of dollars, which eager investors made available because of two features of the REIT:

1. By law, the REIT must pass 90 percent of its earnings on to its investors. (In the usual public corporation, the Board of Directors decides whether the investor gets anything at all.)
2. The trust, being a trust, was not taxed.

A number of REITs went public, attracting billions of dollars, and were able to borrow additional millions from commercial banks. As an example, a REIT with $10 million might borrow $90 million and invest $100 million in hotels and other real estate. At first, the REITs prospered mightily, loaning money to developers at rates of 15 percent and more; a few REITs had millions of dollars to invest every day, and many rushed into construction and development (C and D) loans for hotels and motels without proper investigation of the borrower's experience or a reasonable feasibility study of the site and the project.

Savings and loan associations, commercial banks, insurance companies, and mortgage bankers were guilty of the same thing, but to a lesser degree. A 1975 study of financing for the lodging industry found that twenty-four lending institutions had made $3 billion in loans and investments in the hospitality business in the previous few years.[2]

REITs had made C and D loans covering 82 properties, and, of these loans, 72 percent were "distressed," which means that the lenders were not being paid according to agreement or had foreclosed on the property. It was nothing like the conditions prevailing in the 1930s, but serious.

Overbuilding, the energy crisis (which hit in late 1973), increases in construction costs, increased interest rates, and reduced demand for all sorts of real estate were principal causes of the problem faced by lenders to the hospitality business. Unemployment increased and travel—both pleasure and business—dropped. Developers, many of whom were highly leveraged and lacked back-up capital, lost some or all of their equity in the hotels or motels they were constructing. Inexperienced operators failed to budget enough money to cover start-up costs, which in a major downtown convention hotel could run up to $1,500 a room before the hotel reached a break-even point in sales.

Lenders pushed up the cost of money to 15 percent and more. Overly optimistic developers paid not only record interest rates for their borrowed money, but also agreed to front-end fees, charges made in addition to interest. Equity kickers were also demanded, the lender receiving 1 or 2 percent of gross room receipts—this on top of the high interest rates on front-end fees.

In 1975, lending institutions and borrowers were a chastened lot. Lenders were extremely cautious in loaning money, investigating borrowers very carefully, and requiring that the operator have at least five to ten years of operational experience. C and D loans were not made unless the borrower had a firm commitment for long-term financing. Many lenders would not get involved unless the borrower agreed to invest in the project and put up as collateral as much as 25 percent of the value in cash or land placed in escrow.

When a property became distressed, the lender was reluctant to foreclose because costs of the hotel and construction continue even

2. Ibid.

though the construction has halted. Capital is tied up in unproductive real estate, taxes continue, and guards must be employed to protect the property. If an operating hotel is closed down, getting the traveler to come back after it opens again is difficult. Bankruptcy of the owner often means loss of liquor licenses, which can cost thousands of dollars to acquire. The lender usually tries to reach a "workout" agreement, perhaps granting a moratorium on the repayment of interest, even advancing money to keep the property operating. In return, the borrower usually agrees to various stipulations, providing monthly financial reports and permitting frequent inspections. In some cases, management is changed and a consulting firm brought in to assist management in turning the property around.

THE BIG HOTEL INVESTORS TODAY

Three insurance companies—Prudential, Equitable Life Assurance Society of the United States, and John Hancock Mutual Life Insurance Company—had investments of over $2 billion in the lodging industry in 1976. Insurance companies invest heavily in lodging because of the ability of hotel management to change rate structures rapidly, one of the few areas of real estate that can rapidly reflect inflation. Another reason for insurance company interest in hotel investment has been the high inflation rates. Although an insurance company may get a 12 percent return on an investment, if the inflation rate is at 10 percent and corporate income taxes are 50 percent of earnings, the company actually loses in purchasing power each time it pays taxes.

WHAT IS A MOTEL WORTH?

What is a property worth? Over the years motels and hotels have been selling for between about four to nine times the average annual operating profit after taxes and insurance, before income taxes. Suppose this amount is $50,000 for a particular motel. The value of the property then would be $400,000, based on a times-earnings ratio of 8. If the motel in question sold for $400,000, the percent return on the equity investment might be arrived at as follows:

Purchase Price[3]		$400,000
Equity Investment		200,000
50% Mortgage Debt		200,000
Projected Income		50,000
Less: Interest @ 7%	$14,000	
Depreciation (Est.)	2,000	$30,000
Taxable Income	$16,000	$20,000
Income Tax—Corporate Rates		7,000
		$13,000
Present Return on Equity Investment		6.5%

In 1977 motels and motor hotels in California were selling for between three times and six times the gross income. The buyer tried to buy for three times the income and sell for six times that amount. Operating costs for the motel were running at about one-third of gross income, not counting the labor of Mr. and Mrs. Operator.

Because of tax considerations, sellers did not want to take more than 30 percent of the sales price as a down payment (including the first year's installment payments). If they took more, the payment was considered straight income and taxed at that level. Under the 30 percent figure, income could be considered capital gain. The vast majority of motels and motor hotels in California from 1975 on were purchased by Koreans, Taiwanese, Thais, and people from India. A motel purchase presents an opportunity to become a legal resident of the United States, provided that the person invests at least $40,000, and at least one U.S. citizen is employed in the operation.

THE BEST USE OF LAND

Fortunes have been made by asking the simple question: "Is a property being used to its maximum advantage?" In other words, what kind of property should be built on a piece of land?

---

3. James L. Robel, "How Much Is Your Motel Worth?" *Transcript* (January 1964). (To update figures, double them.)

Should an office building be erected, or a hotel? In New York City, the answer has often favored the office building over the hotel. In some cases, the hotel should be razed and the land used for an office building. Some of the older motels can be better used as apartments or offices, especially those that have been bypassed by super highways.

The "best use" of some of the older resort hotels may be found by giving them to a charitable or educational institution. By giving them to such organizations, the donor has the right to value the property at its book value, or at a value established by an appraiser. The book value may be much higher than the market value. Usually the appraised value is higher than its real market value. By giving the property away, the donor is able to write off of his or her income taxes the full amount of the appraised value or of the book value. The donor who is in a high-income bracket may "make" money by giving away the resort. This has happened several times in the past.

Fires offer another way of getting maximum value from some hotels. A surprising number of resorts have burned that have been fully insured. The place burns, and the owner is delighted to collect much more from the insurance company than the market value of the hotel.

If the cash sale price of a hotel is $1 million, the seller might increase the sale price to $1.2 million or even $1.5 million. Such financing enables a chain to "own" a property with a relatively small amount of cash as down payment. More is paid in total, but payment extends over a longer period of time. If the hotel "throws off" a good profit, everyone is happy; if not, there are problems.

FRANCHISING AS A MEANS OF FINANCING

Franchising is also a means of financing growth, although it is indirect and not ordinarily thought of as a means of raising capital. The franchisor, in effect, uses the resources of each franchisee to expand the franchisor's business.

Franchising became important in the hotel and restaurant business with the growth of the Howard Johnson restaurants in the 1930s. During World War II it almost came to a halt. In the 1950s, the rapid growth of Holiday Inns of America demonstrated the advantages of franchising, and in the late 1960s franchising spread across the country. Franchising is further discussed in Chapter 4.

GOING PUBLIC

Since 1965, "going public" with a stock offering has been the favorite means of raising capital for foodservice operations and, to a certain extent, for hotels and motels. Hotel and restaurant stocks suddenly became the glamour stocks of the stock market. Public investors were literally swept off their feet by anything that sounded like a hotel or foodservice business. Literally dozens of companies have offered stock to the public. Many companies making public stock offerings have little to offer but a marketing concept, neither tested nor modified by actual operating experience.

Before 1950, only a few hotel and restaurant stocks were listed on the New York Stock Exchange, among them Sheraton Hotels, Hilton Hotels, and the Knott Corporation. By 1979, dozens of stocks that were classified as hotels and motels were listed on the New York and American Stock Exchanges.

Beginning about 1966, dozens of companies were formed. The stocks were sold through brokerage firms, putting the principals well on their way to fortune, if not to fame.

Investors saw quick money and went on to bid up the price-earnings ratios. The average for hotel and motel chains in 1969 was thirty-two times earnings. By comparison, the Dow-Jones Industrial Stocks sold for about nineteen times earnings at the time of the comparison in February of 1969.

TRAVEL CONGLOMERATES

Another means of rapid growth in the hotel and restaurant business has come via the merger or, more precisely in most cases, the buying of control of one company by another.

Airlines bought into the hotel business; hotels and motels bought into free-standing restaurants. Some of the large oil companies began building and operating inns and restaurants. Some of the huge food manufacturers bought into restaurant chains. The conglomerates bought into just about everything. Some of the more notable "mergers" include: Litton Industries (a conglomerate) bought Stouffer's, the largest table service restaurant chain in the country, and later, Canteen; Trans World Airlines bought Hilton International Hotels; International Telephone and Telegraph, another conglomerate, bought Sheraton Hotels, the largest hotel chain in the world; and the Fred Harvey Corporation was bought by a Hawaiian conglomerate, AmFac.

In 1969, Holiday Inns of America merged with T.C.O., a company which owns Trailways, the second largest intercity bus line, and Delta Steamship Lines. Holiday Inns of America became a travel-accommodations conglomerate with some twenty-five subsidiaries.

Closely intertwined with the hotel and restaurant business is the travel business. Companies such as American Express are very much a part of the overall hospitality business. With billions of dollars as a "free loan" from people buying their travelers checks, American Express has vast resources to expand into allied hospitality ventures.

THE CREDIT CARD EVOLUTION

By 1982 more than half of the guest accounts in hotels were settled by credit card charges. The corporate traveler, the lodging industry's most lucrative market, uses one or more credit cards to pay for almost everything bought while away from home. It's easier that way. The credit card issuer provides a neat record for the corporation for which the traveler works or to the individual for record and tax purposes.

The credit card appeared in some auto service stations as early as the 1920s. It spread quickly in the 1950s with the beginnings of Diners Club and the bank credit cards. Billions of dollars are involved each year. Reluctant to accept credit cards at first because of the cost to the hotel, operators today accept them routinely and many refuse personal checks without a credit card back up.

MECHANICS OF TAKE-OVER

The mechanics of take-over of one company by another needs explanation. Suppose two companies are each earning $1 a share each year.

One of the companies is a glamour company whose stock sells for thirty times earnings, or $30 a share. The other is a more conservative firm, whose stock sells at fifteen times earnings, or $15 a share. If the glamour company can take over the conservative company by a stock exchange—one share of the glamour company for two shares of the conservative company—the glamour company's earnings suddenly shoot up.

In the merger the glamour company ends up with every three shares of the merged stock earning $2 instead of the $1 per share it previously earned. The usual investor, unaware of the arithmetic of the transaction, sees only the earnings report of the glamour company and is impressed with the rapid rise in earnings. The stock of the glamour company is bid up further and the glamour company is free to acquire another conservative company.

The company with the high-priced stock buys the company with the low-priced stock. The buying company increases its earnings per share by the acquisition. As long as the price-earnings ratios of the glamour companies remain high, as was the case with Denny's restaurants, Lum's, Loews, and most hotel and restaurant stocks in 1967 to 1969, their most rapid means of expansion was likely to come by acquisition.

Should a take-over attempt fail, the glamour company is not necessarily disappointed. When a glamour company announces a tender offer to buy the stock of another company at a certain price, the stock of the conservative company ordinarily goes up. The glamour company can then sell what stock it owns in the company at a profit. In 1968 Loews Theatres made a profit of $28.5 million before taxes and expenses when dealing in the stock of the Commercial Credit Company.

SYNDICATION

Another way of raising capital for the hotel and motel business is through syndicates. A syndicate is a group of investors who join together as limited partners to own property. Theoretically, the syndicate members own the property and receive rent from it. Part of the rent represents depreciation on the property. This part is tax free and considered as a return of the capital. What a nice way to avoid income taxes.

Several real estate syndicates that owned hotels operated during the 1950s and 1960s. Returns from these investments were largely tax free. Usually the return on the investment was something like 5 to 15 percent, most of it tax free. From a tax viewpoint, owners were taking back what they had put in.

Of course, the owners believed that the property would appreciate to the extent that, when sold, the original investment and more would be gotten back. Meanwhile, over the years they would be receiving nontaxable income. (When the property is sold, the appreciation is taxed at the capital-gains rate.) Two of the better known syndicate managers, William Zeckendorf and Robert Futterman, included a number of hotels in their portfolio of investments. Mr. Zeckendorf overextended himself and his empire collapsed. Futterman drove himself to the point that at times he reportedly had to be slapped awake to sign a contract. Ironically, he choked to death trying to swallow a piece of steak and died before the age of thirty.

How Syndicates Operate

Under a syndicate arrangement, funds are placed in the hands of syndicate organizers and managers. Usually the managers receive 10 to 15 percent of the syndicate shares. The managers obtain a lessee operator, and collect and distribute the rents to the syndicate members. Since the purchase of hotels and motels is left to the judgment of the managers, they have complete command of the syndicate's funds.

The syndicate members have only minor control or supervision of the managers. The syndicators acquire high-leveraged properties with minimum cash down. The rest of the debt is financed through first and junior mortgages or by extended installment purchase contracts. The properties are expected to produce more rent than they are capable of doing. The lessee might pay the rent but at the same time milk the property by eliminating maintenance and repairs. The owners receive the property back in a run-down condition.

A weakness of the plan lies in the fact that the syndicate manager may have little or no money of his or her own invested but has complete authority to invest the syndicate's money.

Since he or she is paid a percentage of the cash flow, the syndicate manager cannot lose (until the system collapses).

LEASING LAND AND FURNISHINGS

Another means of partial financing is to lease the land on which the hotel is built and to lease some or all of the furnishings. In some cases the owner of the land leaves the builder of the hotel no choice but to lease. At other times, the hotel or motel owner leases rather than buys because he or she has neither the cash nor the credit power to buy.

The land on which hotels and motels sit usually constitutes about 10 to 20 percent of the total value of the property. In effect, the owner can finance 10 to 20 percent of the value of the total property by a ground lease. The hotel owner may also decide to lease the furniture and equipment instead of buying them and depreciating the value over their useful life.

A number of hotels and motels lease television sets instead of purchasing them. An advantage in doing this may be that the leasing company provides maintenance on the sets during the life of the lease. This arrangement removes from the management the usual concern for maintaining and repairing the sets. Supposedly, the leasing company will provide trained TV technicians when needed, which may not be possible for, or easily arranged by, the hotel owner. After a period of years, the leasing company turns the equipment and furnishings over to the hotel owner at a nominal charge.

The cost of the lease is considered an operating expense and is written off each year, computed before taxes. This has been the great selling point made by the leasing companies. Fast depreciation allowed by the Internal Revenue Service enables the owner to buy and depreciate furnishings and equipment in five years. Because of the rapid depreciation possible, there may be no real tax advantage in leasing.

USE OF LEVERAGE

The definition of leverage, in its financial sense, is to make a little cash do a lot of work. It is maximum use of credit. The investor gets control of a business or property by paying a minimum of cash. If things go well, a little cash controls a lot of assets. If the business turns down, the person using leverage is in trouble because he or she is carrying a big debt load and paying interest on it.

Ernest Henderson was a master at the use of leverage and, as he tells it in his book, *The World of Mr. Sheraton,* parlayed $1,000 into $400 million.[4] Henderson purchased The Continental, an apartment hotel, in 1933 for one-third of its construction cost of about $1 million. Only $25,000 was offered in cash. A few years later, the Continental was singled out as perhaps the most profitable hotel of its size in the country.

The Copley-Plaza was bought in 1941. In that transaction, shares of stock, originally worth $100 each, were bought at $1 each. The normal return on hotel investments, according to Henderson, if enhanced by "leverage" or mortgage financing, is close to 14 percent per annum, before taxes.

Henderson was always ready to pay a higher price for a hotel than asked, if, in exchange, the down payment was small. The purchase of The Beaconsfield in Brookline, Massachusetts, is an example. The owner wanted to sell but the highest offer he received was $150,000.

Henderson offered $200,000, but only $50,000 as a down payment. The owner of The Beaconsfield began to show interest. He had in mind $330,000 as the price of the hotel. Finally, Henderson offered him the $330,000 as the price of the hotel, with the right to pay only $2,500 in cash. A few years later the hotel was sold for $1.25 million. A Detroit hotel was purchased with no cash changing hands at all. The owner had not operated successfully and was impressed with the Sheraton record.

The "plant investment" in the hotel and motel business is high and continues to increase. It requires about $2 of capital assets to produce $1 of revenue. In 1954, capital assets of $1 produced $1 of income. By 1964, the amount of capital assets needed to produce $1 of revenue had doubled.

---

4. Ernest Henderson, *The World of Mr. Sheraton* (New York: Popular Library, 1962).

BOOK VALUE VS. MARKET VALUE

Book value and market value are two different concepts that are often confused. For example, in 1977 the Hilton Hotels' book value based on cost less depreciation was $371 million, whereas the fair market value placed on the Hilton properties by the management was $717 million. Market value tends to reflect closely the earning power of a property; book value is an accounting concept arrived at by subtracting depreciation allowance over the years since the property was purchased. Book value in no way reflects inflation as does market value. In 1977 Barron Hilton, President of Hilton Hotels, stated that though the Waldorf-Astoria was built in 1927, in 1977 it still had a useful life of twenty-five or thirty years. To replace that hotel in 1977 would cost about $180 million even though its book value was only $45 million.

As Ernest Henderson pointed out in the early 1960s, the real value of any business property is what it will produce in earnings. Both Henderson and Hilton have pointed out to their stockholders that the traditional accounting methods are unrealistic as related to hotel properties. Hotel properties tend to appreciate rather than depreciate because the dollar (which the accountant uses as a basic unit of measure) has not been a stable standard. Therefore, if hotels are well-located and well-managed, their market value will be well in excess of book value.

Whether or not a hotel succeeds depends to a large extent on its initial cost and the rate of interest paid to lenders. Suppose a million dollars could be borrowed at 10 percent versus 20 percent. The higher interest rate costs the borrower $100,000 a year more for the life of the loan. Moral: borrow when interest rates are down. Have patience because in the past interest rates have gone in cycles, up and down.

When buying or building a property at a high cost per room, it must be remembered that the property must be in a market that will support the high rates necessary for profitability. At a particular time some markets will not support high-cost properties; others will.

Some financial hanky-panky has been reported. "Arrangements" between two companies owning hotels would be relatively easy. For example, suppose two companies each own a hotel worth $1 million. Suppose also that they have owned these properties for seven or eight years and that most of the depreciation for tax purposes has been used up. Both companies need a new tax base to take maximum depreciation. It would be an easy matter for each company to buy the other's hotel. Each would then start with a new tax base of $1 million.

Suppose the companies decide between themselves to value their property at $1.4 million, even though the market value is $1 million. Since they are, in effect, trading hotels, the sales figure is not important. But with the higher sales price, the depreciation base is much higher. Such transactions are said to have taken place.

What is a reasonable depreciation figure for the hotel or motel? The answer is highly debatable and differs among experts and even among Internal Revenue people. Some motels have been depreciated over a seven-year period even though the building itself would, no doubt, be in usable condition after thirty years.

Depreciation of Furniture and Fixtures

The depreciation of furniture and fixtures is usually much more rapid than that of the building. Guidelines for depreciating furniture have been established by the Internal Revenue Service. These are only guidelines, since some cocktail lounges and restaurants must be completely redecorated every three to five years. Carpets can be purchased for a planned useful life of three, five, seven, or ten years. Draperies, lamps, and occasional furniture are bought for a useful life of ten, twelve, or fifteen years.

The question of depreciation rates for automatic elevators and air conditioning is cloudy. Some experts maintain that these are costs rather than capital improvements, costs necessary to remedy a loss in economic value already sustained. Repairs to capital equipment are written off as current expenses rather than considered as capital outlays to be depreciated over a period of time.

The selection of a rate of depreciation may be critical in a business, especially when it is first starting out and needs "cash flow" to survive. If one were to follow the practice of some of the most successful hotel and motel operators in this country, one would take maximum depreciation over the shortest time allowed by the Internal Revenue Service. As soon as the fast depreciation factor in the tax base has been exhausted, the individual would sell the property, then acquire another one and start with a new tax base for depreciation purposes.

TAXES INFLUENCE INVESTMENT

Real estate taxes vary considerably around the country and must be considered in any hotel or motel investment. Ernest Henderson was well aware of these differences. At one time Sheraton was probably the biggest taxpayer in Boston, but most of the Sheraton properties were sold and the money was invested in Washington, D.C., One of the reasons for the change was the fact that real estate taxes in Washington, D.C., were about one-fourth of what they were in Boston.

A footnote on spelling: Students have long declared that the ability to spell is no measure of a person's worth. This would seem correct, if a story told about one of the bigger Sheraton deals is true. Sheraton Corporation was being merged with United States Realty and Improvements Corporation of New York. Ernest Henderson was making out a check for $9 million. Surrounded by bankers, insurance people, lawyers, stockholders, and the press, together with photographers, Ernest looked up and inquired, "How do you spell million, with one or two l's?"

THE SALE AND LEASEBACK

The sale and leaseback is a financial gimmick that has been used in hotel financing for some time. A motel owner, for example, who needs cash but does not want to give up the motel operation, can sell the motel and at the same time negotiate a long-term lease with the new owner. The old owner has a large sum of cash with which to do business and add additional units, or the former owner can buy another motel. With the lease, the old owner stays on as the operator.

The new lessee (old owner) pays all operating expenses, real estate taxes, and maintains the property. The new owner pays the mortgage-carrying charges. These leases are usually arranged to last fifteen to twenty-five years, with renewal options. A big reason for the sale and leaseback is the fact that the old owner may need cash or may have used up his or her depreciation. The new owner is assured a good return on the investment, and has the ownership of the motel as equity.

MARKET AND ECONOMIC FEASIBILITY STUDIES

On contemplating a new enterprise, the entrepreneur is well advised to draw up fairly detailed statements of what the enterprise can be expected to produce in income, the anticipated cost of doing business, and the expected profit. Such projected statements are the key parts of a feasibility study, sometimes called a market and economic feasibility study.

Until after World War II, entrepreneurs were likely to be their own feasibility experts, drawing upon their own judgment and experience in analyzing the potential market for their product, determining the desirability of a particular location, and projecting income and expenses. In recent years, most entrepreneurs have turned to a management consulting firm or a feasibility expert to provide them with an independent and, presumably, more objective market analysis and feasibility study.

Entrepreneurs expect from the expert a pro forma statement of income and outgo for a proposed hotel, motel, or restaurant. They also expect advice as to the number of rooms or seats that should be built.

A major reason for making feasibility studies is that the lender requires it. No lending officer of a bank, savings and loan association, or insurance company will loan money without one. They are the lender's hedge insurance in case the facility fails.

In the hotel and restaurant field, feasibility studies are usually done by one of the two major accounting firms: Pannell Kerr Forster and Co., or Laventhol and Horwath. Other consulting firms also engage in such studies for a fee.

Ellsworth Statler made the amusing statement many years ago that the three most important factors in the success of a hotel were: first, location; second, location; and third, location. Just what goes into picking a prime location is something else again. The factors that affect location change with time. The roadside inn

was built along a well-traveled road, preferably in town. The canal hotel was built alongside the canal. The city hotel was built as close as possible to the railroad station.

Most hotels built in the 1920s were built close to a railroad station. In New York City, The Pennsylvania Statler was linked by an underground passage to the Pennsylvania Railroad Station. The Commodore Hotel was built on top of Grand Central Station; some 5,000 rooms were gathered around that station. The Waldorf-Astoria Hotel, built in 1931, was close by Grand Central; The Belmont Plaza was built across the street, piggyback to The Waldorf-Astoria, to take the overflow from The Waldorf-Astoria.

Airport hotels were a logical development of increased air travel, and the huge accommodations and foodservice business around O'Hare Airport in Chicago now makes good sense.

Many desirable locations have not always been recognized. The Top of the Mark, the restaurant at the top of The Mark Hopkins Hotel in San Francisco, pointed the way to a new type of

Figure 3–1 *The Terrace Plaza was built in the 1950s and is located in Cincinnati. The hotel begins on the eighth floor; the glassed-in circle and adjoining structure on top of the hotel was one of the first glassed-in top restaurants.*

restaurant location. Even so, it was many years before others saw the "tops" as good locations for restaurants. Now, nearly every community of any size with a high building has a "top" restaurant. Kemmons Wilson, first chairman of the board of Holiday Inns of America, stated that a "top" restaurant can expect 15 to 20 percent greater sales volume because of its location (see Figure 3.1).

SITE SELECTION

Obviously, each style of operation has different factors bearing on the decision as to whether or not a particular site is a good, medium, or poor location. Severance Lodge, located several miles from the little town of Fryeburg, Maine, turns out to have a good location for its style of operation—rustic hospitality amidst scenic forest splendor and Lake Kezar.

The Caribe Hilton has a good location, as long as there is fast and relatively inexpensive transportation to Puerto Rico from Miami and New York City. A suburban motel has a good location if it is serving the visitors to a nearby university and meeting the demands of food, beverage, and room requirements for a new business complex located in the suburb. In an airport motel, the location is good if there is sufficient volume of traffic and stopovers by passengers who need room accommodations close at hand.

Factors beyond the control of any individual or corporation often determine the value of a particular location. Several hotels in Cuba had good locations before the take-over by the Castro regime, but political changes made the locations worthless for American investors. A motel on a well-traveled highway had 95 percent occupancy until a large and striking Howard Johnson Lodge was built across the street, whereupon the occupancy of the first motel dropped by thirty points.

The construction of a complex of business buildings may increase the value of the location of a motel if it is on the intercept route to this complex. Highway changes of all kinds, of course, affect location value, either for better or worse. Hundreds of motels withdrew from the race after being by-passed by the Interstate Highway System.

What Site Experts Seek

Site or location experts are constantly searching for good locations for their companies. Real estate brokers, some specializing in hotel-motel building sites and in arranging hotel-motel sales, evaluate potential hotel-motel locations. They search out those sites that might be available for the construction of a new property and project the amount of business that could be attracted to the site, given certain facilities. Usually several alternative sites are available but, in some cases, there is only one. The expert site scout does not necessarily look for vacant lots; he or she also looks for sites that have existing buildings that might be replaced by a hotel or motel.

The really prime sites are usually too expensive for the erection of a two- or three-story motel; instead, the building must go straight up in order to return enough income to cover the cost of buying or leasing the land. One chain of hotel-motels allocates 17.5 percent of the total expenditure for a facility to the cost of the land; other have different land cost guidelines.

The cost of a building reflects such features as the type of soil on the site, drainage features of the soil, sewage disposal, water availability, the amount of fill or excavation necessary. These factors are particularly important for sites away from established communities and in the less developed countries. Building costs in the Caribbean, for example, usually exceed estimates by at least 25 percent because of the necessity for importing almost every item to be used in the building, including the cement.

Location experts are much concerned about the factor of compatibility with the neighborhood. A run-down neighborhood, or even one or two businesses within the neighborhood that are unsightly, reflects unfavorably on anything that is new, even though it is completely contemporary and pleasant.

Another factor that is acknowledged by experienced operators is the cumulative attraction of an area where there are similar businesses located. A group of motels becomes known as a motel area in the minds of travelers, and many will head for the motel area rather than stop at an individual property, even though it may be as good as or better than many of the motels in the area. Proximity to well-known restaurants, department stores, or sporting facilities is an asset.

Neighborhood Trends

Another factor that is very much an influence on the matter of location is the trend of the neighborhood. Is it growing and being refurbished, or is it declining? Is the city moving away from the area or toward it?

Fortunes have been made through an awareness of growth patterns, combined with the courage to buy or lease land, when the movement of a community is observed going in a particular direction. Knowing the direction of expansion of a community is extremely valuable information. Sometimes a new hotel or motel will set off a chain reaction, triggering renewal and revitalization of an area.

STEPS IN FEASIBILITY STUDIES

Guidelines for making a feasibility study have been drawn up and are especially useful as a checklist to avoid overlooking important factors.

The market and feasibility study includes these steps:

1. Identification of a potential market: the people who can be expected to patronize the proposed hotel, resort, or restaurant

2. Quantification of the market: how many people can be expected to patronize the hotel, resort, or restaurant if a particular facility is built

3. The kind of facility which will appeal to the market

4. Estimation of the size of the facility needed for the market

5. Estimation of the cost of the facility which will serve the market

6. Estimation of the income and expense of operating the facility, itemized by department

7. Estimated profit as a percentage of sales and as a percentage of investment

These steps are not necessarily undertaken in the order given. Entrepreneurs usually spec-ulate that a certain kind of property or restaurant will be successful in a given location. They ask the consultant to confirm or deny those assumptions. Much of the success of a hospitality venture depends on the competition already existing or that is projected for an area.

COMPETITION CAN BE POSITIVE

Competition is not always negative. Another motel in an area may bring more business to existing motels. A proposed restaurant with a different format and menu may not compete at all with existing restaurants. A lone resort in an area may be strengthened by new resorts.

Parking for restaurants depends on the area. Some of the most profitable restaurants have no parking at all; others cannot exist without it. Distance from a market is not always a clear-cut factor. Distance can be measured in air miles, or road miles, or in travel time. In some restaurants, the entire market may live within the same building. In others, the market may include the area within an hour's driving time. Distance to a resort from a market may be 1,000 or more miles. Witness the New York City market's distance from Florida or the Caribbean, or the distance of Los Angeles from Hawaii. The need for changing planes and cost then become prime considerations. New air service to a resort area can make the place highly feasible.

In making a feasibility study for a motel, first a market study is done. It examines where the travelers originate, what they are doing in the area—whether they will be commercial, convention, or transient patrons. It studies the population trends of the area and the existing hotels and motels. The personnel departments of the major manufacturing plants and other large employers in the area are visited; purchasing agents are interviewed as to where salespeople who visit them stop. If the company maintains a visitors' register, it is an excellent source of information.

For a motel, the highway situation—what it is and what it will be—is critical. State highway departments usually have traffic counts for all major highways in the state; also data on the origin and destination of travelers. Sometimes service stations are canvassed and the operators are questioned about the amount of gasoline pumped. Credit card sales information may also supplement the interviews.

A market and feasibility study, though it be detailed and comprehensive, must rely heavily upon the judgment of the analyst. Witness to the fact that even the experts can be wrong are the many restaurants, opened by experienced operators and by chains, that are not particularly successful. Some of the chains will not consider a location for a restaurant unless it is capable of producing at least $500,000 in sales.

Through trial and error, the chains that have a standard menu and format of operation have pinpointed the factors that make their style of operation successful. For example, companies like Howard Johnson can predict fairly accurately what volume of sales can be expected from a particular location.

Is there a large enough market for a particular hotel, motel, or restaurant? It took more than twenty years for the city of San Francisco to catch up with the original Palace Hotel. The hotel was too large and too expensive to be supported by San Francisco when it was built in 1875. Pittsburgh was oversupplied with first-class hotel rooms for many years. Until gaming was introduced in 1978, the City of Atlanta had more than enough hotel rooms.

The fact that a group of hotel or motel operators in a particular community say that the community is already overbuilt means little, however. The established operators in a community would think there were plenty of hotel rooms unless their occupancy were running at 90 percent the year around. A community may be overbuilt with tired, obsolescent rooms and desperately need a new hostelry. The luxury hotel does not necessarily compete with the commercial hotel, nor does the resort hotel necessarily compete with the commercial hotel.

JUDGMENT OF EXPERTS

Feasibility studies for hotels rely heavily on the judgment of experts and the experience of comparable properties built elsewhere. In 1978 several U.S. cities were overbuilt with hotels, based upon the old rule of thumb that an area should have an occupancy level of 75 percent before new properties are needed. Yet, new hotels—very large ones—were being built in several major cities.

Justifications for their construction were several:

1. A downtown area needed a large attractive hotel to support and be a part of the redevelopment of the area. This was the case for the cities of Long Beach, Los Angeles, and Detroit. As part of the redevelopment, federal government money was available at low interest rates which, when factored into the feasibility study, went a long way toward making the property financially feasible.

2. The new hotels were part of a complex and were architecturally spectacular and exciting. It was believed that they would attract conventions and other group business to the city even though the area had plenty of mediocre accommodations.

3. Being new and of unusual quality, it was believed the new properties would preempt business from the less attractive and often obsolete hotels of the area.

4. The quality and design would attract many residents of the area to frequent the downtown section and would also attract individuals from around the country and elsewhere who otherwise would not be inclined to visit the city.

Market studies for new hotels and resorts are very difficult to conduct and are prohibitively expensive if done in depth. A 1,500-room hotel might well attract guests from all over the United States and from many foreign nations. To conduct a market study based on questioning potential guests in all of the possible places of origin would be impractical.

Instead, the market analyst compares a proposal with the experience of similar properties already constructed. For example, the fact that The Hyatt Regency Hotel of Atlanta was highly successful might influence the decision despite the fact that a market study based on numbers alone, numbers such as occupancy statistics, would produce a negative signal, if it were the only factor taken into consideration.

Taking this approach the analyst asks whether a major hotel that is unusual in architectural design and part of a major new complex would experience the same or similar success as occurred in Atlanta.

COMMUNITY SUPPORT

The feasibility study asks, "Can the community support a particular establishment offering a particular product and service?" Sometimes a new facility can create a market not already existing. For example, O'Hare Airport outside of Chicago serviced the most air travelers in the world. For years, only minimum hotel, motel, and restaurant facilities were located in the O'Hare area. Consequently, air travelers went to downtown Chicago for their conventions, business, meetings, and entertainment. Now, the O'Hare Airport area is a huge accommodations and restaurant complex which is rapidly developing into a convention center.

Air transportation, a super highway from California, and gambling have made Las Vegas, originally an isolated village, into a huge entertainment and convention center. Disney World, developed near Orlando, Florida, is another example of an enterprise that is, to a large extent, creating a location.

HOTEL DESIGN

When the Tremont House in Boston was built in 1829, its architect, Isiah Rogers, designed a Greek Revival property which became the talk of the hotel world, if not the world (see Figure 3–2). The architectural sketches became a popular handbook for hotel promoters and designers everywhere. Rogers was at once established as the hotel architect of the day and was widely employed to design similar well-known hotels in Bangor, New York, Charleston, Richmond, Cincinnati, New Orleans, Mobile, Louisville, and Nashville.

Since America lacked royal palaces as centers for society, community hotels became what the *National Intelligencer* in 1827 called, "Palaces of the Public."[5] The hotel lobby, like the outer rooms of a royal palace, became a

5. Daniel J. Boorstin, *The American National Experience* (New York: Random House, 1965.)

gathering place, a vantage point for a glimpse of the great, the rich, and the powerful.

Hotels have been among the first public buildings to introduce the latest in facilities. The Astor House included plumbing on the upper floors. Each floor had its own water closets and bathrooms, fed from a roof tank to which water was raised by a steam pump.

The passenger elevator, originally known as a "vertical railway," was introduced in Holt's Hotel in New York as early as 1833 for baggage. The passenger elevator was first used in the Fifth Avenue Hotel in New York City in 1859. Elevators changed the room rate structure by making it possible to charge more for the upper level floors than for those on the lower floors.

The Tremont House had gas light in its public rooms, and whale oil lamps in the guest chambers. The American House, opened in Boston in 1835, was gas-lit throughout. The Hotel Everett on Park Row in New York City was the first hotel to light its public rooms with electricity. Soon after, the Palmer House, with its own electrical plant, lighted its two dining rooms with ninety-six incandescent lamps. Room phones were installed at the New York Hotel Netherland in 1894.

RESORTS—BLOCK STRUCTURES WITH PORCHES

Hotels built before the twentieth century were likely to be block structures, as seen in Figure 3–1. The unimaginative block design has continued to the present day. Many hotels are built around an open shaft, the court offering no better view than the window of a guest room on the other side of the court or a view of a dirty roof within the court. Inside, the hotel is one long corridor after another, usually unbroken by color, change of lighting, or architectural feature.

During the resort boom of the 1880s and 1890s, resort hotels built in New England were likely to be block structures to which porches were later added. The porch, extending at least the length of one long side of the building, was a distinctive feature of the summer resort. Here battalions of "rockers" relaxed between meals.

The Moorish or Spanish influence in the design of the resort hotel began with the

Figure 3–2 *Then and Now—The Tremont House, Boston (inset), was generally considered to be the first "modern" hotel. It was built in 1829 by Isiah Rogers, who became an authority on hotel construction and strongly influenced hotel architecture in this country for the next fifty years. If featured private single and double rooms; doors with locks; every room equipped with a bowl and pitcher; and free soap. The Tremont was the first to employ bellboys. The architectural sketches of The Tremont became a popular handbook for hotel promoters and designers everywhere. Now—a contrast in architecture, and bellboys, too, is the picture of The Century Plaza Hotel of Beverly Hills, part of a giant trade-living-entertainment complex. At the present time, the hotel is operated by Western Hotels and is ranked among the best in this country. Bellhops are Chinese, dressed in turn-of the century costumes, and are likely to be college students.*

construction of the Ponce de Leon in 1888 at St. Augustine. The minaret and open court were also seen in The Alcazar, built nearby, and in the giant Tampa Bay Hotel built by Henry Plant in Tampa soon after. Even in far-off California, the minaret and the huge open patio were seen in The Hotel Del Coronado at about the same time.

The original Palace Hotel, built in 1875 in San Francisco, occupied 2.5 acres in the heart of San Francisco. Its interior court was a famous meeting room. When the Palace burned, following the 1906 earthquake, the new Palace incorporated a beautiful inner court which was at first used as a carriage entrance. The present Garden Court of The Sheraton-Palace is a beautiful restaurant and has been declared an official landmark by the Board of Supervisors of San Francisco.

Henry Boldt, who managed William K. Vanderbilt's Waldorf-Astoria, abolished the ladies' entrance, and women arrived on the arms of their escorts. The Waldorf opened in 1893, introducing the idea of a room with a private bath. In 1896 John Jacob Astor IV tore down his mansion next door and a new structure was connected with The Waldorf, giving The Waldorf-Astoria a total of 1,000 rooms.

Figure 3-3 *The Willard Hotel of Washington, D.C., was the prestige hotel of the city for many years. The hotel is now closed.*

Some American hotels were built to be truly "palaces of the people," resembling palaces—Willard Hotel of Washington, D.C. (now defunct) and The Plaza of New York City represent the "palace" tradition, which has existed in the occidental world since about 1900 (see Figure 3-3). Several "palace" hotels in Europe were built originally as palaces, not hotels.

RESIDENTIAL HOTEL, AN AMERICAN DEVELOPMENT

Americans have long resided in hotels for long periods of time, much to the astonishment of Europeans. Until about 1950, there were sizable numbers of hotels known as residential hotels. These hotels often took in a few transient guests but devoted most of their attention to "permanents" who lived in suites or apartments and had access to all services offered by the hotel.

When the Plaza Hotel in New York City opened in 1907, about 88 percent of its occupancy was by permanent guests. Lucius Boomer developed The Sheraton Netherlands (no longer in existence) to combine the best features of hotel life with modern apartment house life. It provided freedom from the care or concern over food, supplies, and the hiring or supervision of servants.

A large percentage of the guests at The Hotel Pierre on Central Park in New York City are still permanents. So too are the residents of The Waldorf Towers in the present Waldorf-Astoria. Managers of residential hotels sometimes find that, even though the permanent rate is high, more profit can often be made by renting to transients, and make some or all of the residential rooms or suites into "transients." On the other hand, transient hotels with low occupancies often become partly residential.

The large hotels of the twentieth century are towns in themselves. The Dallas Statler-Hilton Hotel has a capacity of 10,000 people; The Palmer House, 15,000 and The Conrad Hilton, 20,000. The telephone switchboard in the Conrad Hilton has more equipment than is used in a city with a population of 35,000.

William B. Tabler, architect for many Hilton Hotels, says it takes from two to five years, sometimes even ten years, to put together a large hotel. There is the matter of land acquisition, architectural planning, financing, and finally the construction of the building. Actually planning for the guest rooms is only a minor part of designing a hotel; planning the dining facilities is a particular challenge and calls for a foodservice consultant to lay out the kitchen equipment. Nightclubs, ballrooms, shops, offices, laundry, valet, barber shop, beauty shop, telephone rooms, refrigeration, incineration, and boiler plants are part of the hotel. Some of the larger hotels have medical departments with emergency rooms, isolation rooms, and laboratories.

It is little wonder that there are such major oversights in the planning as happened at The Sheraton-Philadelphia which was planned with insufficient elevator capacity. Although elevators in the larger hotels are likely to be computer-controlled, many hotels have elevator traffic problems. These can occur in the morning, when guests all decide to get up at the same time; in the evening when there is a check-in; and later when they all decide to move from floor to floor to visit friends or the public rooms.

At The New York Hilton, which has had extremely high occupany in recent years, the guest may wait twenty minutes to get on an elevator at certain times of the day.

"RULES OF THUMB" FOR HOTEL PLANNERS

William Tabler, who has designed most of the newer Hilton Hotels in this country, has listed eight "rules of thumb" for planners of commercial hotels. (He does point out that there are exceptions to the "rules.")

1. The cost of construction per room should equal about $1,000 per $1 of average room rate. If the room can be sold for $50 on an average, no more than $50,000 can be spent per room. This includes the cost of the public and service areas. Per room cost in a hotel is total cost divided by the number of rooms.

2. At least 50 percent of the total space in a commercial hotel should be given over to bedrooms. It may seem strange that the hotel may have more public and service space than bedroom space but it is quite possible. Public and service space has been responsible for 60 to 65 percent of the construction cost in some hotels. In downtown areas, land costs and the cost of attendant facilities have forced the reduction of the size of the bedrooms. Bathrooms seem to be getting smaller and smaller. In some, a large person standing in a bathroom can reach from wall to wall.

Of the $10,000 per room cost of the Dallas Statler-Hilton, opened in 1959, about $3,500 was spent for the actual bedroom. The other $6,500 per room cost went for lobbies, banquet and convention rooms, restaurants, kitchens, shops, and "behind the scenes" areas. Even though most of the cost of the hotel went for public and service areas, the bedrooms accounted for a large amount of the profit. Operating profits as a percentage of gross income were: 70 percent from the bedrooms, 50 percent on beverages, and 15 percent on rental areas. Believe it or not, the restaurants brought in no operating profit.

Statler, recognizing the high cost of support facilities, did not build hotels in the secondary cities that could not support a 1,000-room hotel. When he built a hotel of less than 1,000 rooms, he found that the public and service areas were proportionately higher and profits lower. Motels, built on less costly land and including less public space, can have larger bedrooms and a small swimming pool.

3. The hotel should be planned so that it can be operated with less than one employee per room. Some luxury hotels located in countries with low labor costs can have two and even three employees per room. The Savoy of London has three employees per guest room.

American hotels are making do with something like .8 of an employee per room. In other words, a one-hundred-room hotel could employ about eighty people. The layout of the hotel, especially the kitchens and dining rooms, accounts for built-in labor costs which are likely to last the life of the building.

4. The cost of land, in most cases, should not exceed 10 percent of the building cost. Where land costs are exceedingly high, the alternative is to put more rooms one on top of each other, stretching the hotel skyward, thus reducing the per room cost of land. Tabler points out exceptions to the rule, one being The Palmer House in Chicago which has revenues of more than $1 million from ground floor shop rentals. In such a case, land costs can be more.

5. What profit should be expected from each department in a hotel? Tabler says that departmental profit should be 70 percent for rooms and 50 percent from the sale of beverages. Rentals should bring in 20 percent of the hotel's total revenue. No profit at all is expected from the sale of food. This may be the experience of hotels in general, but need not be. Hoteliers are seldom outstanding restaurateurs. The hotel restaurant has traditionally found it difficult to compete with the good restaurant that is located nearby or one that, even though it is some distance from the hotel, has acquired a culinary reputation. Some restaurant operators say that the best location for a restaurant is directly across the street from a major hotel. Specialty or theme restaurants in hotels have been much more profitable than the usual dining room or coffee shop operations. The Hotel Corporation of America (now the Sonesta chain) opened its Rib Rooms starting in 1952. Polynesian restaurants have been favored in Hilton and Sheraton Hotels. Tabler's rule of thumb that the food contributes nothing to the profit of the hotel can be gainsaid by instances where hotel foodservices make fairly sizable profits. In some of the smaller hotels, the food and beverage operation is the major reason for the existence of the hotel, the rooms being secondary to the restaurant business.

6. The hotel must have at least 60 to 65 percent occupancy to break even financially. In designing a hotel, Tabler says that the design should allow for the reduction of operating costs when occupancy drops.

7. If room rates are to differ depending on the size of the bedrooms, to qualify for a higher rate a room must be at least 20 square feet larger than the room being rented at the next lowest rate. A smaller differential is not noticeable to guests; they expect to see an appreciably larger room if they are being charged a higher rate.

8. The minimum size for a bedroom is 90 to 110 square feet for a single room; 130 to 150 square feet for a double room; and 160 to 180 square feet for a twin bedroom.

Hotel lobbies have varied in size and grandeur over the years. Few general statements can be made about them. Resort hotels are likely to have comparatively large lobbies because the lobby is the gathering point for guests.

Motels tend to have lobbies only large enough in which to check guests in and out. Cesar Ritz favored the small lobby to discourage idlers; he viewed the lobby primarily as a corridor to dining room and guest rooms.

Statler, who was very cost- and space-conscious, built a tremendous lobby at The Pennsylvania Statler, perhaps because the hotel was built with Pennsylvania Railroad money and leased by him. Some of his other lobbies are also quite large and impressive.

Hilton, well known for his ability to carve revenue-producing space out of a lobby, did so by adding restaurants and bars in lobby space. In some cases he even lowered the ceiling to produce another floor above the lobby. The New York Hilton Hotel has immense lobby space but very few chairs, and it seems to be designed primarily to move people from floor to floor to function and dining room spaces. The Summit Hotel in New York City has a lobby so small that the front desk space is jammed with patrons during check-in and check-out times.

Resort hotels typically have had large lobbies where the guests can congregate. In Miami Beach some of the lobbies have been grand; in Las Vegas they house slot machines by the score. The Portman-designed hotels, described later, are awesome in scale and appointments, marking a new adventure in hotel design.

DINING ACCESS TO STREET

The formal dining room has been out for some time; the specialty room is in. The specialty room almost always is built with access to the street, since patronage from the hotel guests alone will not make it profitable.

The cost of transforming dining rooms or other spaces into specialty rooms can be remarkably high, often costing $500,000 or more. Usually a remodeled dining room requires about six months to a year of operation before it begins to be profitable.

ALLOCATION STUDIES
GOVERN SPACE ALLOTMENT

The Sonesta Hotel's management has done a number of studies to establish criteria for the allocation of space in a hotel. In foodservice areas they allocate 18 to 20 square feet per seat in a dining room, 15 square feet per seat in a coffee shop, 12 to 15 square feet per seat in lounges and bars, and 10 to 12 square feet per seat in banquet facilities. These figures allow 25 to 33 percent of the space for free circulation of service personnel within the facility.

These studies indicate that the kitchen serving a dining room and coffee shop should be about 60 percent of the total area of the dining room and the coffee shop. This indicates that about 10 to 11 square feet should be allowed per seat in these foodservice areas. If there is a coffee shop only, the kitchen should be about 45 percent of the size of the coffee shop serving area, allowing 6¾ square feet per seat. Space allowed for food and beverage storage should be about half that set aside for the kitchen, or about 5 square feet per seat.

Figure 3-4 *In the effort to provide the kind of luxury and service offered by the prestige hotels of Europe, a number of American hotels offer "club floors," hotels within hotels. They usually offer concierge service and a number of amenities not found in the rest of the hotel.*

Banquet kitchens, of course, are much smaller; only about one-fifth of the space of the banquet facility is needed for the banquet pantry and only about 8 percent of the banquet area is needed for banquet storage.

Space to be allocated for housekeeping and general storage gets smaller per guest room as the hotel gets larger, ranging from 8 square feet per guest room in a 1,000-room hotel to 15 square feet in a 100-room property. The same relationship is seen in the need for space for administration and rooms department, ranging from 3 feet per guest room in a 1,000-room hotel up to 5 feet per guest room in a 100-room property.

Often overlooked in planning hotel and motor hotels are the needs of the personnel for eating facilities, lockers, lounge, showers, and so on. Approximately 7 square feet should be allotted per guest room in a one-hundred-room property for employee facilities.

The location of towel racks and hooks is a part of the architect's problem. Towel hooks are placed so that the guest will use a towel an average of three times before throwing it into the hamper. Towel shelves are located so that towels can be reached from the tub, thereby cutting the laundering of bath mats by half.

Designers are forever attempting to maximize a "quality experience" in a minimum of space. Once a desirable room layout has been achieved the room is then replicated tens and even hundreds of times in the same hotel or motel or in a chain of properties. The dollar savings can be considerable. (Figure 3–5 shows a sample floor plan.) Guestrooms today tend to run to a standard of about twelve feet wide and twenty-four to twenty-six feet long, including the bathroom. Designers tend to make suites two or three times larger (see Figure 3–6).

In conserving space and "upscaling" the guest rooms, many hotels have substituted the armoire, an ornate wardrobe that is free standing, for the traditional clothes closet. Occupying a fraction of the space of the closet, an attractive armoire adds a note of class and is quite suitable for the guest who travels with one or two suitcases.

Again to save space, combination sofa beds are used; in some cases the old Murphy Bed, which folds up into a wall space, has reappeared.

In 1977 the Sheraton Corporation introduced a room plan that can be used in almost any room which, with the addition of a draw curtain and a sofa bed, changes the typical bedroom/sitting room.

Great care and attention can be devoted to the design and furnishings of a guest room, since a guest room is repeated several hundred times in a large hotel. Savings in space or cost of furnishings is also repeated. For a time, bedrooms got smaller and smaller but the trend now is toward larger and more comfortable bedrooms.

Room size and furnishings necessarily vary with the market being served. In Japan, room sizes are often smaller than elsewhere; in fact, some are merely sleeping cubicles furnished with a small TV (see Figure 3–7). Budget hotel prices usually mean budget-sized rooms with minimal furnishings and smaller beds. Four meters is considered the minimal width of a room in the United States. Luxury rooms take

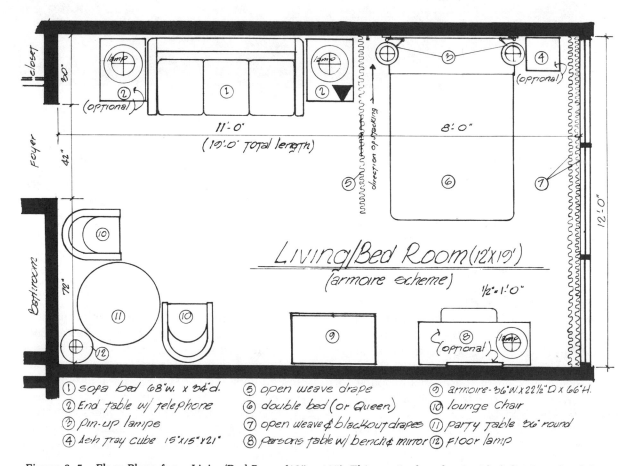

① sofa bed 68"w. x 34"d.   ⑤ open weave drape   ⑨ armoire-36"W.x22½"D x 66"H.
② End table w/ telephone   ⑥ double bed (or Queen)   ⑩ lounge chair
③ pin-up lamps   ⑦ open weave & blackout drapes   ⑪ party table 36" round
④ Ash Tray Cube 15"x15"x21"   ⑧ Parsons table w/ bench & mirror   ⑫ Floor lamp

Figure 3–5   Floor Plans for a Living/Bed Room (12″ x 19″). This particular plan is titled the Armoire Scheme.

Figure 3-6 *The master bedroom of the "Celestial Suite" complete with Roman bath and featured at the Astrodome Hotel. Where else but in Texas and at $2500 per night!*

Figure 3-7 *With the great increase of business interchange with Japan, Japanese investors have bought a number of American hotels and, in the case of The New Otani in Los Angeles, offer the Japanese business traveler similar facilities to those found in first-class hotels in Japan.*

on the character of apartments with artworks, upholstered bed headboards, sunken bathtubs, armoires, phones, and even TVs in the bathrooms. Suites sometimes occupy two and three levels with lots of glass facing choice views.

Beds are a major concern, and more attention is given to firmness than in the past. Guests are often given a choice of orthopedic beds (extra firm). Beds placed on platform, the so-called "sandbox" design, are more expensive, but they eliminate carpet and cleaning beneath the bed.

High energy costs have helped in the return to windows that can be opened by the guest. Some Sheraton properties have sliding glass doors that can be locked in a semi-open position to allow circulation of fresh air without a security risk.

Hotels catering to businesspeople create the multiple-use guest room, one that can be used as bedroom, office, meeting room, and living room.

Gregory Philis states the three categories of guest rooms—economy, first class, and luxury—as seen in Table 3–1. Room widths vary from a little less than 12 feet in the economy property to 16 feet in a luxury hotel. Lengths range from 24½ feet in the economy motel to 28 feet in a luxury hotel. Total square feet may be as little as 290 in a economy motel to 450 in the luxury property.

The use of double-paned glass has permitted "glass walls" to be part of the building; The Flying Carpet Motor Inn, opposite Chicago's O'Hare International Airport, and The Downtown Motor Hotel both have 90 percent of their exterior constructed of glass. The new silent and heat-resistant glass muffles up to 66 percent more of the transmitted noise than plate glass. The sound waves are converted into heat energy by absorption into a treated inner layer

TABLE 3–1

Hotel Type	Width	Length	Total Sq. Ft.
Economy	11′ 9″–12′ 6″	24′ 6″–25′ 0″	290–320
First Class	13′ 0″–13′ 6″	25′ 6″–26′ 0″	330–350
Luxury	14′ 0″–16′ 0″	26′ 6″–28′ 0″	370–450

Gregory Philis, "Hotel Guest Room Design," *Lodging* (July 1983): 8.

between the double glazing. A self-shading glass eliminates glare and heat. Made like a miniature Venetian blind, it is composed of thousands of tiny louvers which are sealed airtight between the two panes of glass.

The new convention hotels usually include an assembly room, a banquet room, smaller meeting and private dining rooms, a registration lobby, and an exhibition hall. Dining rooms and meeting rooms should be near and on the same level as the kitchen, if possible, for reduction in wage costs. The beautiful Beverly Hilton Hotel is built as a "Y" with three wings emanating from a central core which houses the kitchen.

IN-ROOM ENTERTAINMENT

As of 1970, just about every hotel/motel room in this country provided a TV set, and almost all of them are color sets. In-room movies, in connections with a TV set, began being offered in 1971. Relatively new movies without the TV commercials were offered; some are free to guests, others for a fee. By 1981, some 500,000 guest rooms were equipped to provide the movie option, and the technology involved had changed.

Home Box Office (HBO), a satellite/cable subsidiary of Time, Inc., is now one of the largest suppliers. Their programs are on a free-to-the-guest basis. Programming originating in New York City is beamed to an RCA satellite, then picked up on earth by local cable stations. The programs are then carried to the user hotels by cable. The hotels are charged on a per-room-per-month basis. Holiday Inns gets its program direct from a satellite using a pick-up saucer at each participating property. As the TV set has come to be seen as a basic service, many guests now perceive in-room movies and other entertainment as being a standard amenity.

BASIC HOTEL DESIGN

Characteristically, motels and hotels have been built as horizontal slabs with rectangular-shaped buildings. In the beginning they were one or two stories high, then with the development of structural steel and building expertise, hotels shot up into the sky. In 1976 a hotel designed by John Portman as a cylinder reached seventy stories into the sky of Atlanta (Figure 3–8), which was soon followed by another such hotel in Detroit. The downtown hotel in the 1920s was likely to be two to four slabs built around an open court. Later hotels took on all sorts of shapes, L-shaped, Y-shaped and finally, cylindrical (see Figure 3–9). A three-sided motor hotel, the triarc, featured by the Travel Lodge Corporation, favors a view because two blocks of a motel can face an ocean or other scenic view. The elevator is located in the central core.

The hotel built in rectangular form permits orientation along an east-west axis so the rooms face south and north. Such orientation to the sun avoids facing the guest rooms to the west where the heat of the afternoon sun can drive up the cost of air conditioning in a warm climate. Balconies can be built to project four to six feet from the guest room and provide a partial sunscreen. Vertical walls separating each unit are also helpful in excluding direct sunlight.

The rectangle motel, built like a barracks, is probably the least expensive of all designs. Most budget motels are built on the barracks plan. If they are in a moderate climate, most properties omit basements and inside hallways, both which are added costs.

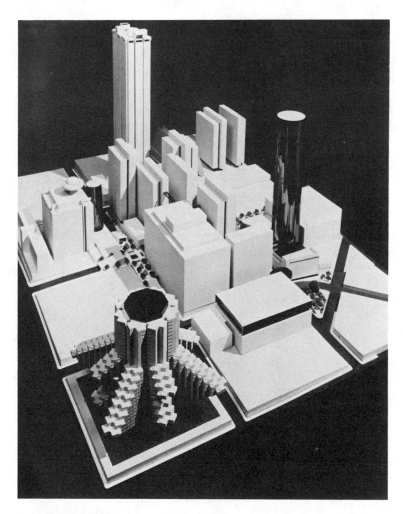

Figure 3–8 *In the Portman view of the new inner-city, the hotel is seen as one habitat among several, an integral part of a living complex where business, entertainment, and residences come together. The cylindrical building in this picture is the hotel in a redevelopment project of downtown Atlanta.*

Figure 3-9   *The new generation of super hotel—glass, concrete, and steel cylinders around a giant atrium—is seen in the Los Angeles Bonaventure Hotel. The principal owners are Japanese.*

A comparison of twenty-seven highrise hotels showed that the circular form plan is the most efficient in terms of surface-to-volume ratio.[6] The guest rooms are necessarily at least partially pie-shaped. The rectangular slab design is more efficient than the more compact, nearly-square tower. The corners of a pure square-shaped hotel are often left void because of the difficulty in providing direct corridor access to them. The floor plans in Figures 3–10 through 3–13 show the circular, slab, square, and a deformed-square-floor plan for hotels.[7]

6. Clark and Benner, "Hotels and Life-Cycle Costing," *Cornell Hotel and Restaurant Administration Quarterly* (February 1977).

7. Ibid.

To avoid a slab-sided, uninteresting exterior, the resort hotel or any hotel that commands a view is likely to have a balcony on each guest room. The balcony adds glamor and architectural interest to the building.

Panel wall construction began in the 1950s. The *Architectural Forum* gives William Tabler credit for using the first true curtain or panel hotel wall in The Hartford Statler. The curtain wall replaces masonry, is lightweight, and has twice the insulating factor of masonry construction, a factor in reducing air conditioning requirements.

The curtain wall is also more watertight than masonry. During the 1955 hurricane, nine inches of rain fell in New York City in twenty-four hours and seventeen ceilings dropped in The New York Statler. Two weeks later about fourteen inches of rain fell on Hartford in the same period of time with no damage. By using panel walls, the heavy columns needed to support masonry are moved from the outside wall to the interior of the building.

Fewer Lobby Pillars with Slab Construction

For The Statler-Hilton in Dallas, William Tabler used cantilevered flat slab construction. These slabs are raised along a central core and are

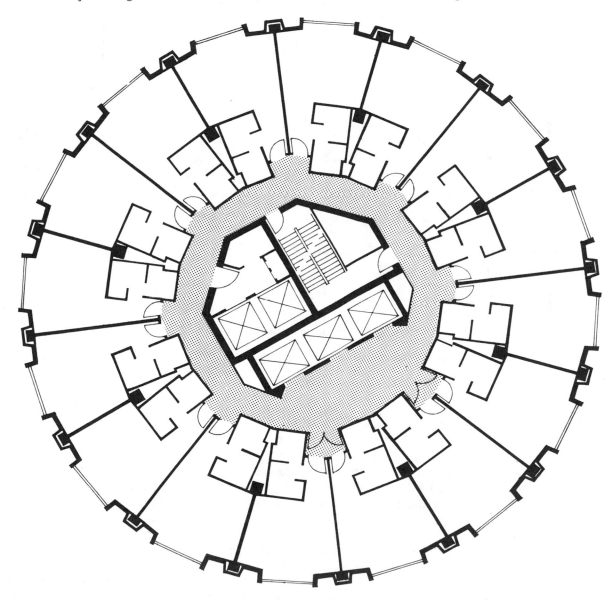

Figure 3-10 *A rendering of a circular hotel plan (Stouffer's Riverfront Towers, St. Louis).*

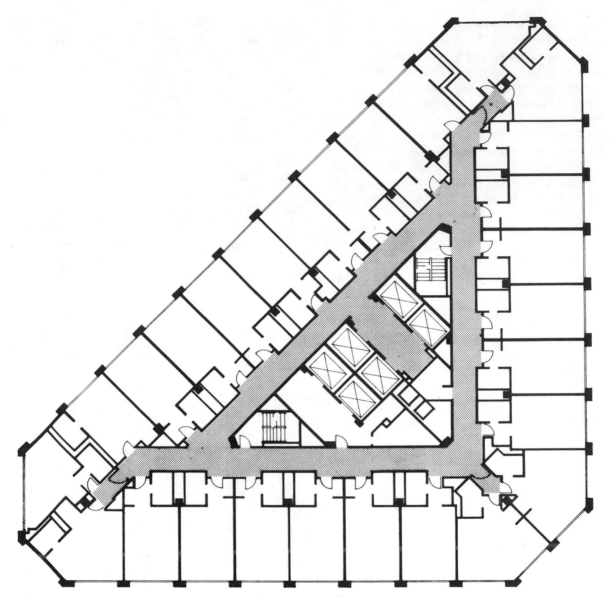

Figure 3-11   *A rendering of a triangular hotel plan with interior corridor (New Otani, Los Angeles).*

held in place by a central support. This reduces the number of columns and the size of the foundation by 50 percent. No beams are required or used, and less reinforcing steel needed. Another advantage in the use of the flat slab construction is the need for only half the usual number of columns in the lobby. These are columns that usually get in the way and have to be covered with expensive marble.

Some hotels are designed with a specific market in mind; it may be the upper-income group, the traveling person, the conventioneer, the corporate training group, the air traveler,

and similar classifications. Hotel markets are not nearly so well defined as restaurant markets. The highway hotel is probably appealing to all possible markets—anyone with the price and the inclination to stop at the hotel.

A motel located in an industrial park area has probably identified its market as being largely people who have business at the park. A resort hotel, located some distance from its market, must be much more highly selective in its clientele and its design must be appropriate to that market. A hotel in the Virgin Islands, for example, necessarily caters to people in the

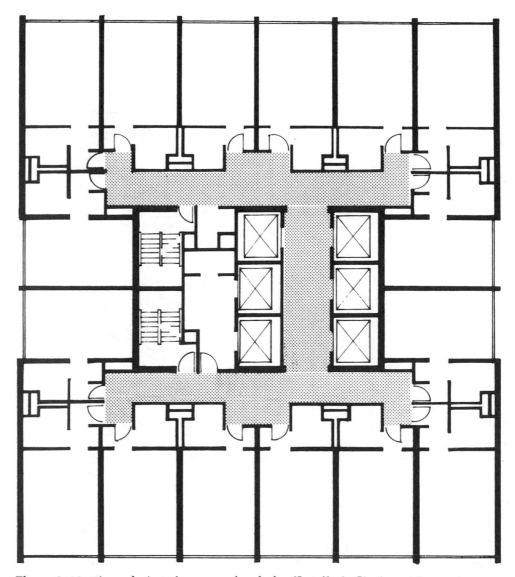

Figure 3-12 *A rendering of a square hotel plan (Stouffer's Cincinnati Towers).*

middle- and upper-income brackets, at least at the height of the season. Only people in those brackets have the discretionary income and freedom to take vacations at that time.

Optimal Size?

What is the optimal size of a hotel or a motel? The answer to this question has not been definitely established. It is probably best arrived at in a series of steps. Most motel experts feel that a motel must be at least 50 rooms in size to be large enough to (1) support a capable manager, and (2) produce enough profit for the motel to be of interest to a big in-

vestor or to a chain operation. A remote resort hotel probably has to have at least 150 to 200 units to stand on its own and be profitable.

If the area can support more rooms, the optimal size of the motel might jump to 100 or 150 rooms. Motels that have 100 rooms and are doing capacity occupancy might well add another 50 rooms. The additional rooms would show a higher percentage of profit on the gross income than the rooms already in existence. The cost of labor for operating the 50 additional rooms is minimal. The only extra personnel needed in the 150-room motel would be two bellmen, one clerk, and four maids. In other words, adding 50 rooms to a 100-room motor

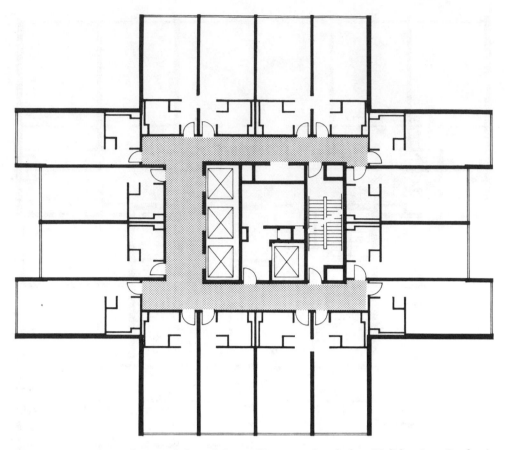

Figure 3-13 *A rendering of the "deformed" square hotel plan (Holiday Inn, Quebec).*

inn increases the basic payroll costs by only $1,200 to $1,500 a month. Computed on an 85 percent room occupancy, the additional labor costs for the added 50 rooms are only 11 to 15 percent of the gross sales. Some experts feel a 225-room hotel is optimal.

At some size the hotel begins to take on a more impersonal character that operates against the personal service expected in a luxury hotel. It is for this reason that the deluxe hotel operator is likely to feel that if maximum personal service is to be offered, the hotel must be under 400 rooms, or perhaps even smaller.

To provide the intimacy of the smaller hotel, operators of large ones often set aside two or more floors, usually the top ones, as luxury hotels-within-hotels. These floors, in effect, are operated separately, reached by a separate elevator. The guest is welcomed by a concierge. Room rates are priced considerably higher and the guest may receive a complimentary breakfast, wine and hors d'oeuvres, and/or afternoon tea including sandwiches, pastries,

and coffee. Other special services are offered, such as the bed turned down at night.

The concept was pioneered in The Waldorf-Astoria in the Waldorf Tower, opened in 1932. Another Hilton property, Chicago's Palmer House, picked up the idea in the mid-1960s. Since 1975 these luxury level rooms have proliferated with names like: Club Floors, Regency Club, Galleria, Executive Rooms, or VIP Floors. They range in size from one floor to eight, 22 rooms to 300. Upper-echelon corporate travelers and, to a lesser degree, affluent leisure travelers constitute the market for these luxury enclaves.

From the point of view of maximum profit on rooms and service areas, the hotel might be any size, depending on the market. An extremely large hotel may be needed to attract the largest conventions. From this viewpoint, anything smaller would not be efficient.

Large ballrooms may require as much as 25 percent of the ballroom space for use as a reception area, space for reception and cocktails before the meal, for use as a registration area, and for coffee service when the ballroom is used for meetings. Additional space of 10 to 15 percent of the ballroom area may be needed for furniture and equipment storage, such as tables, chairs, platforms, and audio-visual equipment.

The cost of land may determine the number of rooms built. The higher the land price, the greater the number of rooms needed to make the hotel financially feasible. Usually the greater the land cost, the higher the hotel must go. In Hong Kong, with its astronomical land costs and limitations on building height, several hotels have floors that go into the ground. In one Hong Kong hotel five floors are underground.

ENERGY MANAGEMENT AND DESIGN

Energy control has become one of the important control aspects of the hotel and restaurant business along with food cost control, labor cost control, time management, financial management, and social management. Energy management necessitates a greater emphasis on "present value analysis," looking at a capital cost from the point of view of not only its present cost but of its cost in years to come—its life cycle cost. From this viewpoint, a building costing $1 million may be a much less desirable investment than one costing $1.5 million, if the added investment will result in lower energy and maintenance costs over the life of the building.

Energy management involves the design of the building, less glass area, the use of solar screens (screens to shut out the sun when not wanted), increased insulation, and perhaps even the consideration of building a hotel into the ground with clerestory windows to let the light into a central well or patio, with guest rooms facing the well.

Equipment is purchased with particular consideration for the life cycle. Controls are installed which permit energy reduction during the peak load hours when the cost of electricity is highest. For example, ice machines can be purchased that will not be operated during the 5 to 8 P.M. period when there is peak load demand on electricity. No hot water need be heated during that period either; instead, it can be stored from times when energy cost is less.

The use of solar collectors to collect heat from the sun and use it in heating the water for the hotel and restaurant began to get serious consideration in 1975. Several hotels, especially resort hotels, added collectors which permitted a large input of BTUs from the sun and a reduction in the amount of oil consumed.

Several hotels and motels are now using solar energy to heat water up to 140°F, and some are using solar energy for air conditioning. Frenchman's Reef, a luxury resort in St. Thomas, U.S. Virgin Islands, uses 13,200 square feet of specially designed solar collectors from Northrup, Inc. The collectors track the sun across the sky and concentrate and focus the rays on copper absorption tubes. Water in the tubes is heated almost to steam and is then pumped to absorption chillers of an air conditioning system.

Most restaurant and hotel owners who have turned to solar energy are installing solar collector panels on the roof aimed at the sun to get maximum sunshine each day. In most systems the piping carries a liquid that is heated by the sun and then moved to a large water tank (heated exchanger) where the heat passes from the pipes into the water. (The liquid in the tubing must contain antifreeze to avoid freezing in temperate climates.) Such systems ordinarily heat the water to about 130°F. If higher temperatures are needed the water is boosted by conventional means, either by electricity or gas.

The heated water can be used in the kitchen or can be pumped by tubes to guest rooms where blowers transfer the heat from the tubes into the rooms for heating.

THE PERENNIAL PARKING PROBLEM

Automobile parking has been a problem for hotels ever since the automobile appeared in number; however, after about 1950 many a hotel succeeded or failed, depending on its parking availability.

The attractive Christopher Inn of Columbus produced a novel approach to the parking problem. The first three floors of the circular inn are a ramp upon which cars can be parked. The inn begins on the fourth floor and extends up ten stories. All guest rooms have a view since they are on the outside circle. The rooms necessarily must be somewhat pie-shaped.

Parking Space Needs

Speculation regarding the number of parking spaces needed in a hotel has been resolved by experience. In their book, *Planning and Operating Motels and Motor Hotels,* Podd and Lesure state the requirements as follows:

One parking space for each guest unit

One parking space for each five restaurant seats

One parking space for every three employees

Two additional parking spaces for service trucks

One unobstructed loading space

An automobile requires between 300 and 400 square feet of space, including the driveway but not including the entrance way. It can be seen that parking requirements add up fast as guest rooms increase.

Since the older hotels had no provisions for parking, most of them had to make arrangements with parking garages to handle guests' automobiles.

A delay in getting a guest's car from the parking garage can sometimes last half an hour or an hour. Such delays are not calculated to soothe the guest who is in a hurry. Sheraton Hotels have instituted a policy of providing free parking for all guests at their hotels, regardless of the cost to the hotel.

Free-standing restaurants require at least one parking space for every two seats; a one-hundred-seat restaurant will need fifty parking spaces. Some municipalities require a greater ratio of parking to seating.

HOTEL DESIGNERS

Design of the modern hotel has been greatly influenced by four men: Morris Lapidus, William Tabler, Emanuel Gran, and John Portman. Tabler did the designs of the new Statler Hotels and Gran has been the consulting

Figure 3-14   *The La Fontaine Room of the Warwick Hotel, Houston. The room is not so large that it loses its charm and feeling of intimacy. This "Top" restaurant and bar is accessible by an outside elevator.*

architect for Hilton Hotel International. Portman is a designer/architect/developer who first teamed up with Hyatt Hotels, and later with Western International Hotels.

Lapidus, originally a retail store designer, thinks of the hotel, and especially its lobby, as a stage that should connote luxury, excitement, and the unexpected. The traditional Grand Hotel achieved an impression of luxury with numerous lounges, thick carpeting, dozens of service personnel, and ornate design and heavy furniture.

The new hotel and motor hotel offer a gala atmosphere that is lighthearted as well as functional. Color is important, and lighting is used for effect as well as for illumination. Lapidus reintroduced the use of hanging lighting fixtures and chandeliers. He also mixed classic design with contemporary, contrasted textures, and made wide use of columns in his lobbies. Whereas the commercial hotel lobby was getting smaller and smaller, Lapidus produced huge lobbies at The Eden Roc and The Fontainebleau in Miami Beach and The Arawak in Jamaica. He is best known for his Fontainebleau design and for the Americana of New York.

According to Lapidus, nobody wants to go to a resort. The average vacationers are not tired and do not need a rest. They do not want peace and quiet. What they do want is a change. Most people, according to Lapidus, are too restless to spend even a week in a hotel. The average stay in a resort area is about four days. He contends that every hotel is a resort; the commercial hotel has been married to the resort hotel.

Nobody, says Lapidus, wants the "home away from home," nor do guests want to do at a hotel what they would normally do at home. Business is conducted in a holiday atmosphere which can hardly be separated from pleasure.

The huge costs of the new downtown hotels, according to Lapidus, are exaggerated. In some cases, publicly stated costs are almost double the real ones.

Confirming Lapidus's idea that the downtown hotel is a kind of a resort, The Palmer House in Chicago built a $10 million "resort within a hotel" by roofing over a twenty-four-story well at the twelfth floor. The Los Angeles Statler, designed by Tabler, introduced reflecting pools and palm trees as part of the lobby of a large downtown hotel.

SPECTACULAR DESIGN

The spectacular in hotel design in recent years has been created in The Mauna Kea, a Western International hotel in Hawaii, The Princess Hotel in Acapulco, and in a series of John Portman hotels.

The 1970s saw a number of hotels that departed radically from the traditionally designed hotels, hotels that better fit the character of a particular location, be it New York, Denver, or Los Angeles. Instead of being built by hoteliers as in the past, the new properties are being built almost exclusively by developers. One reason has been the shortage of money and its high cost. Banks no longer would provide loans for the 60 percent mortgage money for hotel construction. In the 1970s, both banks and insurance companies required a much higher equity by the holder and in many cases demanded participation in the ownership.

In 1967, The Regency Hyatt House in Atlanta with its twenty-one-story open lobby or "atrium," established a new trend in hotel architecture. Designed by John Portman as part

Figure 3-15 *The River Front Inn of St. Louis was built in 1968. It is one of several inns operated by Stouffers, a subsidiary of Litton Industries. An impressive part of its setting is the magnificent arch overlooking the Mississippi River.*

of a renewal project in downtown Atlanta, it paced a series of similar huge-lobbied hotels, most managed by the Hyatt Company. The Atlanta Regency was the first new hotel in years to create a special atmosphere within a large downtown hotel. Probably the most spectacular is The Hyatt Regency, San Francisco. The San Francisco Hyatt with its seventeen-story lobby seems to fit San Francisco, an airy city built on hills.

The Century Plaza Hotel in Los Angeles, designed by Minoru Yamasaki, was also a landmark in hotel construction in that it created its own environment by including a handsome garden, which the lobby overlooks. Its garden restaurant, glass-walled on the garden side, contributes to the garden ambience.

Figure 3-16 *The Prudential Center of Boston has helped to change the face of the city. The center is a trade-educational-entertainment complex. At the top of the fifty-two-story Prudential building is the Top of the Hub restaurant, operated by Stouffer's. The Sheraton-Boston Hotel, opened in 1965, was the first major hotel to be built in Boston since the 1920s. Twenty-nine stories high, it has 1,012 guest rooms and can accommodate meetings of 2,500. The complex also contains the Hynes Auditorium where trade shows and educational meetings of considerable size are held.*

Since the opening of The Atlanta Hyatt Regency, John Portman, who designed that spectacular hotel, has had the greatest impact on hotel design of any architect, possibly of any architect in history. The Regency concept, rooms surrounding an open lobby, is nothing new. The scale, the grandeur, the multi-storied mobiles, glass-sided elevators gliding up and down the lobby, in full view to those in the lobby and in the elevators, are new.

The open lobbies, soaring to the top of the hotel, are called atriums, from the Roman patios of the same name. The lobbies, says Portman, are an explosion of space, an attempt to overcome the tight and cramped space of the central city. Forty-foot trees, lakes, open restaurants, waterfalls, "people spaces"—elevators and people moving on different balcony levels—give the atriums a "live, or kinetic, quality." Birds, trees, reflecting pools, vines trailing down from guest room balconies within the atriums, grounded and hanging sculptures, add interest and warmth. The lobbies are not only filled with guests of the hotels but have become tourist attractions in their own right (Figure 3-17).

What makes the Portman design properties in great demand around the world is that their occupancies were running near capacity in 1975, while the industry as a whole was in the low 60 percent of occupancy.

When The Atlanta Regency was being built, Portman invited the officers of the major chains to Atlanta to discuss possible management contracts. They were not impressed. Portman recalls that Conrad Hilton, after looking down on the hotel construction, announced, "That concrete monster will never fly." When the hotel was offered for sale, the Pritzkers, principals in Hyatt Houses, bought it. Between 1967 and 1972, several Hyatt Regency Hotels —Portman designed—were built and taken on by Hyatt in major cities, an association that helped considerably in making the Hyatt company the fastest growing large-hotel chain in the 1970s.

Unusual for an architect is the fact that Portman is also a developer and an investor in many of the properties he designs. In 1972, he severed relations with Hyatt and later moved to collaborate with Western International Hotels, a subsidiary of United Airlines.

Figure 3–17 *The Regency Hyatt House in Atlanta is one of the most profitable and spectacular of modern hotels. Originally completed in 1967 at a cost of $18 million, it had 600 rooms; 400 rooms were later added. Each room is equipped with color television, carpeted bathroom, and oversized beds. Each room also has an inside and outside balcony made possible by a twenty-one-story center court. La Parasol Lounge has a parasol suspended over it hanging twenty-three stories. The Polaris Revolving Lounge, 327 feet above the ground, revolves at the rate of one revolution every fifty-eight minutes. The hotel also has three speciality restaurants.*

Portman is responsible for a major breakthrough in hotel design, which in effect means hotelkeeping. In the city of over 500,000, Portman sees the hotel as a part of a complex, a rearrangement of inner city living, closing the environment and air conditioning huge blocks of space.

Introducing symbols of rural life into the central city, Portman rearranges space so that it surrounds large areas, producing a new geometry inside of the hotel and in its relation to the other parts of the complex which Portman envisions. Many architects have tried this in the past; Portman is doing it and, in the process, making a fortune for himself and those associated with him.

The problem with enclosing such huge spaces is the rising costs of the energy required to heat and air condition the spaces. Building codes require that fresh air be brought in from the outside for each recirculation, air which usually must be heated or cooled at considerable cost.

THE FUTURE OF THE SUPER HOTEL?

The massive super hotel, represented by The Bonaventure in Los Angeles, is viewed by many as the hotel of the future and has been used in futuristic films as backdrop. People seem to react strongly to these large-space lobbies, either strongly for or against. As a setting for conventions and tour groups—these are prime market targets—these glass, concrete, and steel structures with a large atrium seem to be efficient places for holding conventions and large group meetings, places for an exciting weekend, and an overnight stop for the groups. The super or "mega" hotels are not on a scale to generate

Figure 3–18   *The President's Suite in the Warwick Hotel, Houston. Many of the furnishings were brought from chateaux in France. The Warwick is one of the luxury hotels in the United States.*

warmth and intimacy. Traditionalists have a difficult time identifying with the ambiance. So contrasting are the super hotels to the European personal service luxury hotel that a super hotel may be indeed uncomfortable or downright disorienting to many travelers.

MOTEL/MOTOR HOTEL DESIGN

Today, design of the larger motel is often indistinguishable from that of the hotel. The motor hotel makes the distinction even less easy.

Most of the early motels were designed by the owners. When architects were employed, they were cautioned to keep the structure simple and inexpensive. The early motel could have passed for a long row of boxes in which the tired traveler would enjoy the reverberations of passing traffic throughout the night. Indoor plumbing came as an improvement; the hanging light bulb was changed to a lamp. Every several years progressive owners tore down existing units and replaced them with something more modern and permanent.

The first motels offered no food facilities, recognizing that business from the guests in the dining room was likely to be too small to create a profit. The guests were directed down the road to a good restaurant. Kemmons Wilson, who pioneered Holiday Inns of America, saw the necessity of a restaurant operation in the motel and, beginning in 1952, built one at each of his properties. Gradually the larger motels added food facilities.

The first motels comprised only a few units; for many years the average was less than 20 rooms. Gradually the motel grew larger, and today the usual motel built by the Holiday Inns of America exceeds 130 units.

Because Kemmons Wilson and his partner, Mr. Johnson, were building contractors, they built their Holiday Inns well and efficiently. One of the reasons for the success of Holiday Inns is the fact that the average unit cost in 1969 was $10,000 a room. Even in high-cost Chicago, Holiday Inns built a property for $12,500 a room. In the South, where construction labor is cheaper, the per unit cost may be even less. One of the secrets of keeping building costs in a motel low, according to Wilson, is to omit construction of a basement.

Motel Cost

What is the breakdown of costs in building a new motel? The motel is not likely to have the public space of the hotel and can concentrate more of the investment in bedrooms. Land cost is likely to be less because the motel is usually out of the downtown area with its high land cost. In their book, *Planning and Operating Motels and Motor Hotels*, Podd and Lesure suggest a breakdown for motel costs as follows:

Land	10 to 20 percent
Buildings	65 to 70 percent
Furnishings and Equipment	15 to 20 percent

Since motels are generally built on land that is not as expensive as that used by the hotel, room size is usually bigger, running as high as 20 by 20 feet. Today's motel is very likely to include a swimming pool, even though it may be miniature in size.

Many Motel Shapes

The characteristic motel silhouette of the past was a long line of single, one-story units stretching along the highway. The motel today comes in a variety of shapes and patterns, some exceedingly beautiful. The beach-front motel is likely to be a "U," with the swimming pool in the center of the "U," and the back of the property facing the beach. The high rise motel looks very much like a hotel; it may be a hotel in everything but name.

The better motels have a room size of about 14 feet wide by at least 24 feet long, including bathroom. Because of the cost of land and construction, most good sites require a minimum of sixty rooms for economic feasibility; for absentee management, a one-hundred-room minimum is recommended.

In planning a motel always allow for expansion up or out, if at all possible. As for square footage, at least 650 square feet are needed per room for a two-story motel; this includes the restaurant. The minimum size room averages 12 feet by 24 feet, or 288 square feet. The remaining 362 square feet go outside—for driveways, parking, landscaping, pool, and other facilities. A one-hundred-unit motel then would need a minimum of 60,000 square feet; 100,000 square feet would permit larger rooms and a more attractive "siting." Restaurants need between 40 and 60 square feet per person, including parking space and 100 feet of frontage.

As for motel restaurants, Mariott, a highly experienced chain, recommends having one parking space for every 2.5 seats in the restaurant. A 100-seat restaurant needs about forty parking spaces. Some city building codes require one parking space for every two seats.

A trend in the motor hotel is toward larger lobbies. Where prestige is important, more money must be spent on the lobby, and the lobby should be placed so it is easily seen by the traveler on the highway. Within reason, the larger the lobby, the more people respect the motel. The bigger lobby can usually be paid for by a slight increase in the room rate.

Another trend is to create "fun domes" with swimming pools, miniature golf, pool tables, table tennis, and other recreational facilities that attract the weekend guest, as well as the commercial guest. A major advantage of the motel without foodservice is the reduced need for personnel. A TraveLodge motel of 250 rooms, for example, has only fifty-five employees, with a labor cost of less than 25 percent of total sales.

COMPUTER STANDARDIZING
STRUCTURAL ELEMENTS

A novel use of the computer is being made by William W. Bond, Jr., architect and vice-president of Holiday Inns. Bond has standardized many structural elements in motels and developed optimum sizes for dining rooms and lobbies.

Much of the information is stored in a computer that is linked to a Norwegian-made drafting machine. A rough sketch is made of a proposed new inn and standard bedroom. The information is coded and placed on tape. The tape can be used to activate the drafting machine which in twenty-five minutes provides detailed plans and elevations for an inn accurate to .002 inch.[8]

---

8. "Reveille Sounds for the Hoteliers," *Fortune Magazine* (September 1969).

Use of the computer saves a great deal on interest charges because it is so fast. Each month's delay in building an inn, in effect, raises the cost at a $1 million building site by several thousand dollars.

TraveLodge Corporation has developed an unusual floor plan for reducing costs. Its "tri-arc," 200-room lodge is in the shape of a triangle with concave sides. Because it has no front or back, it can be placed on almost any site. Each lodge requires eight to twelve months to build—about two-thirds the time needed to construct the usual 200-room hotel.

MOTEL LANDSCAPING

In the past, motel experts have recommended that motels be constructed on large plots that can be easily seen for some distance from the highway that passes the motel. The large lot was used for a swimming pool, landscaping, parking, and for possible expansion in the number of guest rooms.

The rising cost of land, however, has forced a change of design on the motel. The swimming pool is frequently located above a terrace or on the roof. Sometimes it is indoors. Landscaping at some motels is also being moved indoors with plants now placed in lobbies. Parking is sometimes underground or on several levels reached by a ramp.

Most motels could do with more and better landscaping. Landscaping, say the experts, should relate to the region. Trees and other plantings should come from the region to make certain they will thrive in the climate where the motel is located.

Stone walls and rambling roses, for example, are perfect for New England; they enhance the appearance of the property and fit the New England image. Trees can be used to screen streets from the buildings and to soften the hard surfaces of the buildings. A few trees, properly placed, effectively "break" or soften harsh horizontal lines of buildings and make them more inviting. Low spreading plants at the base of motel entrance signs "tie them down" to Mother Earth, helping the viewer make the transition from vertical to horizontal.

Lighting can create a romantic glow for a motel, casting shadows on walls, emphasizing beauty spots and adding color at night. A drive past Miami Beach motels after dark should convince anyone of the magic of lighting cast on palms, pools, and other plantings.

Some motels have added pieces of sculpture and reflecting pools to their entrance areas. The Cabana Motor Hotels have beautiful landscaped grounds, including putting greens. A number of pieces of sculpture are set up in front of the motel, reminiscent of the grounds of an Italian villa.

"THE WORLD'S LARGEST"

"The world's largest" anything has an awe-inspiring sound to it. Large hotels are usually among the largest buildings and, in many cases, are the largest buildings in our towns and cities. They constitute landmarks, centers of community activity, and objects of civic pride. The first building in the United States to be built as a hotel, The Tontine City Tavern, created something of a sensation because it had seventy-three rooms. Built in 1794, the name was changed quickly to The City Hotel.

The Fifth Avenue Hotel of New York, finished in 1859, was called the first great modern hotel. It captured the "biggest" title and held on to it until the "Palace" rose in the West in San Francisco. The Palace cost $5 million, a tremendous sum for those days, and had 800 rooms. The Palace burned to the ground following the San Francisco earthquake in 1906.

"BEST KNOWN" TITLE WENT TO WALDORF

The Waldorf-Astoria Hotel is probably the best known hotel in the world. The original Waldorf, completed in 1893, was also probably the best known hotel in the world in its day. When the addition was built in 1897, making it The Waldorf-Astoria, the hotel had 1,000 rooms—the largest hotel in the world at that time. It was estimated that the hotel cost $5 million, a huge sum of money in the 1890s; in addition, 765 of the rooms had private baths, a major innovation in hotelkeeping.

In 1932, the new Waldorf-Astoria was completed, perhaps the largest hotel in cubic space

in the United States. It was the most luxurious hotel of the time, rising forty-seven stories above ground, and at its opening had 2,150 rooms. Its capacity is presently listed in the *Hotel Red Book* as 1,900 rooms. The Waldorf can cater parties up to 6,000 at a time. And for those who care to know, the Waldorf has both a resident gynecologist and mortician. It employs 1,700 people.

"WORLD'S LARGEST" NOW IN RUSSIA

The Conrad Hilton retained the "world's largest" title until 1967, when the Russians took over with the Hotel Rossiya. It has 3,182 rooms, which can accommodate 5,890 guests. As many as 4,500 people can be seated for a banquet at one sitting. Visitors to Moscow report that it is really three adjoining properties, each with its own manager. It employs 3,000 people and has ninety-three elevators.

America still holds the title for the hotel with the most revenue—the MGM Grand in Las Vegas. Its food and beverage sales exceed $35 million a year, more than the total revenue of some large hotels. The hotel was reported as costing $100 million to construct.

LARGE IN-CITY CONVENTION HOTELS: A PART OF THE REVITALIZATION OF CITIES

The early 1970s saw a revival in building large hotels in the downtown areas of the nation's large cities. Nearly every major city has or will have one or several large hotels. These new properties will replace those older hotels that have been replaced by office buildings and will meet the rising demand for hotel rooms, especially in cities that attract conventions—such places as Chicago, Los Angeles, New Orleans, and San Francisco. Because of the large costs per room, frequently $50,000 to $70,000 per room, most of these new properties are owned or were financed by insurance companies and by real estate investment trusts, which have huge amounts of capital available.

Many of the new hotels are enormous, especially in North America and Asia.

Figure 3-19 *An aerial view of Peachtree Center Plaza Hotel in Atlanta, Georgia.*

HOTEL/MOTEL ROOM TERMINOLOGY

Hotel and motel rooms come in a variety of sizes, shapes, and decor. The number of beds and their sizes are important to the guests. Among the various classifications of rooms and bed sizes available in hotels and motels, are the following:

Adjoining Rooms: two or more rooms side by side without a connecting door between them (in other words, rooms can be adjoined without being connected).

Cabana: a room adjacent to a pool area, with or without sleeping facilities; usually separate from hotel's main building.

Double: room with a double or queen-sized bed.

Double-Double: room with two double beds.

Duplex: a two-story suite—parlor and bedroom(s) connected by a stairway.

Efficiency: an accommodation containing some type of kitchen facility.

Hospitality Suite: a parlor with connecting bedroom(s) to be used for entertaining.

Junior Suite: a large room with a partition separating the bedroom furnishings from the sitting area.

King: largest beds available; may be 80 in. by 80 in. or 72 in. by 72 in.; may be formed by putting two twin mattresses crosswise on twin box springs.

Lanai: a room overlooking water or a garden, with a balcony or patio (found in resort hotels mainly).

Parlor: a living or sitting room not used as the bedroom (called a "salon" in some parts of Europe).

Queen: middle-sized bed—larger than double, smaller than a king; dimension 60 in. by 80 in., or 60 in. by 72 in.

Roll-away Bed: a portable, folding single bed that can be moved in and out of a guest room.

Sample: a display room that is used for showing merchandise. It may or may not be provided with sleeping facilities.

Single: a room with one bed for one person.

Studio: a one-room parlor set-up having one or two couches that convert to a bed (sometimes called an executive room).

Suite: a parlor connected to one or more bedrooms.

Twin: a room with twin beds.

Twin-Double: a room with two double beds for two, three, or four people; sometimes called a "family room" or double-double.

Source: Georgina Tucker and Madelin Schneider, *The Professional Housekeeper* (Boston: Cahners Books, 1975).

Questions

1. Give two reasons why people build hotels besides operating them for a profit.

2. Some of the most successful hoteliers have made excellent use of leveraged money in buying hotels. Give an example that will illustrate the term "leveraged money."

3. Ernest Henderson would prefer selling Sheraton bonds to selling Sheraton stock to the general public. What advantage did the bonds have over the common stock for the Sheraton Corporation?

4. In the late 1960s and early 1970s real estate investment trusts owned large numbers of hotels and motels. Was this from choice? Explain how this came about.

5. Why is it that insurance companies have seen fit to invest so heavily in hotels?

6. Large numbers of motels in California and the Southwest are owned by Orientals. Can you explain the reasons for such ownership?

7. At times it is more to the benefit of the hotel owner to give away the hotel than to operate it. Can you explain the circumstances under which this might be true?

8. Oftentimes the company with a high price-earnings ratio buys a company with a low price-earnings ratio, merging the two companies together. The per share earnings of the new company is higher than for the buying company. Can you tell why?

9. Suppose you and four of your friends decide to buy a motel. Could you rightly call yourself a syndicate?

10. What advantages would there be in leasing TV sets for a hotel rather than purchasing them?

11. Suppose a motel has a book value of $20 a share but its market value is $30 a share. How can this be?

12. Very few hotels were built between 1929 and 1954. Why did people become interested in building hotels in 1954?

13. Suppose you owned a million-dollar motel and your financial advisors suggest that you sell it, lease it back, and operate it. What advantage would there be in such an arrangement for you?

14. A motel building might be expected to last forty years, yet the Internal Revenue Service may let you depreciate its complete value in fifteen years. Why would the IRS allow such rapid depreciation?

15. What is an excellent location for a hotel one time may be a very poor one at a later time. Can you give an example where such a change has taken place?

16. In trying to establish whether or not a particular site is a good location for a hotel, is the fact that other hotels are close by necessarily negative? Explain why or why not.

Discussion Questions

1. What do you think the hotel of the year 2000 will look like and how will it differ from the hotel built in the 1980s?

2. Futurists speak of hotels under water, underground, and on the moon. Will these be built within your lifetime? Why or why not?

ERNEST HENDERSON (1897–1967)*

The person who built the largest chain in the world, Sheraton, never took any real interest in designing a hotel or building one, never managed a hotel, and probably never thought of himself as a hotelman. Henderson was forty-four years old before he really took the hotel business seriously. Twenty-six years later at his death, the Sheraton name was on 154 hotels, and Sheraton Corporation grossed about $300 million in sales annually. How did an investor from Boston create the largest hotel system the world has known in the space of about twenty-six years? The answer lies in Henderson's organizational and financial skills, and his hard-bitten New England common sense about investments, operations, and profits. As a person, Mr. Henderson had a strong sense of duty and self-discipline. He was a capitalist in the best sense of the word, believing that there were few virtues greater than those found in ownership and creation of new wealth. Energy, hard work, keen analysis were combined with skepticism and shrewdness. He was also an opportunist—ready to buy or sell a hotel if the right deal could be worked out. Sentiment played little part in whether a hotel was bought or sold; the tax base against which depreciation could be taken was much more important. Some hotels were bought and sold as many as four times by the Sheraton Corporation.

*Information adapted from Ernest Henderson, *The World of Mr. Sheraton* (New York: David McKay Company).

The decalogue that he drew up for the Sheraton Corporation tells something about Henderson. He urged that decisions be made on the basis of facts and knowledge; he commended the merits of self-control, the virtues of probity, and insisted on employees keeping their word. Here is a paraphrase of the Sheraton Ten Commandments:

1. Do not throw thy weight around, however irresistible may be the urge to do so.

2. Thou shalt not take presents from those seeking thy favors; gifts so received must be passed on to a specified vice president for auction and the proceeds used for the employee fund.

3. Suffer not thy wife to gratify a yen to decorate a Sheraton Hotel.

4. Thou shalt not dishonor a confirmed reservation.

5. Thou shalt not give orders to an underling without fully making clear the exact purpose thereof.

6. Thou shalt duly recall that the virtues of those running small hotels may be the vices of those guarding larger establishments (for example, the desirability of delegation of authority and responsibility).

7. Thou shalt not demand the last drop of blood when effecting a business transaction.

8. Thou shalt not permit food to be served cold.

9. Thou shalt make decisions based on facts, calculation, and knowledge, not on a vague feeling.

10. Thou shalt not explode like a firecracker when an underling falleth into error (it may be your fault).

Henderson demonstrated his contributions to hotelkeeping by showing how a hotel organization can rapidly acquire numbers of hotels, rapidly expand its equity ownership in hotels and motels, and yet show only a modest profit for tax purposes. Chain hotelkeeping, as conducted by the Sheraton Corporation, is as much a real estate venture as it is bedmaking, salad making, foodservice, and advertising. Henderson put into practice a theory of minimaxing—minimizing costs and maximizing return on one's investment.

He believed in the use of leveraged money whenever possible and perhaps used it more successfully in the hotel business than anyone else. Leveraging money requires courage, confidence, and judgment. Mr. Henderson apparently had these qualities in abundance. One of the most daring major policies ever set in the hotel business was Mr. Henderson's decision in 1962 to reduce room rates drastically. Net income in that year for the Sheraton Company dropped from sixty cents to seventeen cents per share.

The idea of reducing room rates has been anathema to hotelmen but especially to accountants. Tables have been drawn up showing the impossibility of making a profit when rates are reduced, yet Mr. Henderson, probably over the objection of his advisors, reduced rates in all the Sheraton hotels as much as one-third or more. Reduced rates did increase Sheraton occupancy to about 73 percent (slightly higher than the occupancy rate for Hilton Hotels but much lower than for such chains as Holiday Inns and the Howard Johnson Motor Lodges). Henderson reasoned that if people could be brought into the hotel as guests, they would spend considerable money on food and beverage.

Perhaps equally daring was Henderson's decision to provide free parking at all Sheraton Hotels. The decision was necessary, Mr. Henderson believed, to compete with the free parking of the motor inn. It cost Sheraton Corporation millions of dollars a year. The free parking plan is still in effect, but rates have gradually increased in most Sheraton Hotels so that they are not too different from those charged by competing hotels. Even with the philosophy that life is full of opportunities and that our biggest regrets come from failure to grasp opportunities, some mistakes are inevitably made.

One mistake made by the Sheraton Corporation, according to Ernest Henderson III, was the failure to institute tight controls, budgetary and otherwise, over Sheraton managers during the period of 1961 to 1964. Sheraton earnings fell off sharply in the period 1962 to 1965, and much of the loss was attributed to a loss of control over budgets and operations. Managers are now required to forecast sales and profits for each department for a year in advance. Centralized management with area supervisors is part of Sheraton management policy.

What about Mr. Henderson's feeling about the guest? The hotel-guest relationship in a Sheraton Hotel is more likely to be something like that between a business firm and its customers. The customers are not necessarily right. They may be entirely unreasonable in their expectations. They may want more than they are entitled to.

Henderson felt that one of the most effective management tools was the guest questionnaire. Letters sent to Sheraton headquarters are answered promptly, and compliments and complaints are passed on to the manager concerned. The traveler, said Mr. Henderson, can run hotels better than the management. When the voluntary flow of complaints to the head office ran low, questionnaires were left in hotel bedrooms.

He was no friend of bureaucracy and did not believe in a large headquarters staff. The training department was one man, and the personnel department hardly much larger. Every Sheraton employee—especially staff and executive-level personnel—was expected to contribute, and every day; no prima donnas, please, and no juicy stock options for executives. The top salary before 1967 was $52,000 a year.

Henderson was definitely sales-minded. Though the "sales blitz" idea originated with the advertising department, Henderson strongly favored and encouraged the plan. The sales blitz was a campaign to saturate a city with the promotion of Sheraton Hotels. Salespeople from a wide area converged on a city and in a team effort called upon hundreds of potential Sheraton customers. Sheraton credit cards were distributed in quantity and group business solicited.

He believed in national advertising. Franchising the Sheraton name brought in additional revenue, but of more importance to Henderson was the fact that each franchise added another unit to the Sheraton referral system.

Henderson will probably be remembered largely for his ability to increase the equity value of the Sheraton Corporation from an estimated value of about $50 million in 1947 to close to $400 million in 1967. The increase was brought about with very little speculation in the usual sense of the word. Constant attention was given to avoiding the danger of financial over-extension.

Unlike several of the real estate holding companies of the 1950s and 1960s, Sheraton Corporation never experienced any serious financial uncertainty. Yet, some of his methods of financing and accounting were unorthodox to the point that the stock market took little notice of the company's real worth. Henderson did not hesitate to offer capital income debenture bonds carrying a 7.5 percent interest rate when the going rate was 6 percent.

Sheraton guests might be a little surprised to find an announcement on their bedside table telling them of the merits of buying Sheraton bonds. Henderson explained why in his biography. Interest payments on the debentures were tax deductible to the company; it actually cost Sheraton less in interest payments than if preferred stock had been issued paying 3¾ percent interest. Unlike the bond, interest on preferred stock interest is not tax deductible.

Because the Sheraton Corporation took the maximum depreciation allowable, the equity value of the company increased rapidly while earnings appeared comparatively small. In addition to net income, profits, depreciation, and cash flow, the company reported an "estimated value" of each common share. Also reported were an estimated net asset value and "adjusted earnings." These were theoretical estimates based on the judgment of the Sheraton officers and were presented to show stockholders their real holdings and the value of their stock. Sheraton had the highest cash flow of any hotel chain, taking the maximum allowable depreciation. This practice, of course, made the net profit figure smaller but built equity.

Henderson invested for profit, not prestige. One of his investment rules was that for every dollar added in improving a hotel, the hotel should be expected to increase in value by $2.00. Indicative of the financial orientation of the company is the practice of posting in the corporation office the latest market value of Sheraton stock. What other hotel company would do this?

The financial community never really accepted the financial figures. Although it was obvious that the equity value of a share of Sheraton stock increased year after year, the market value of Sheraton dropped steadily from a high of $22 a share in 1962 to less than $9 in early 1967. The fact that International Telephone and Telegraph Company offered to buy control of the Sheraton Corporation at $35 a share came as a surprise to the "smart money" crowd. The offer from ITT was consummated shortly after Henderson's death in 1967.

How can Henderson's career be summarized? He introduced no major innovations into hotel-keeping as a profession. He bought and sold; he built; he operated well. He gave the public fair value for its money. He was more civic-minded than any major hotel operator before him. His goal was to create a billion-dollar organization, and he worked to that end diligently, quietly, and with amazing insight into the economics of hotel-keeping.

Perhaps it is more than enough to say, "He built the world's largest hotel chain."

4 Hotel/Motel Operations

From the days of the early inn to the modern megahotel, personnel have been and will continue to be the prime ingredient of good hotel/motel operation. The smaller, or budget, motel runs well, or not so well, depending on the know-how and attitudes of the owner. As the motel moves to the larger motor hotel, the hotel and the megahotel, personnel increase in numbers so that finally a few of the very large properties have well over a thousand employees. Even so, the employees, the guest-contact people, combine with the beauty, the reputation, and the equipment of a property to create the end result of a guest stay—pleasure or lack of it.

This chapter only touches the broad subject of hotel/motel operations, brushing over the personnel organization, marketing, technical, and management developments. Only enough will be said to provide a glimpse of what happens and the kinds of information needed for hotel/motel management.

The organization charts for a typical 150-room motor hotel and the organization chart for the Sheraton-Boston Hotel are shown in Figures 4–1 and 4–2 for the purpose of pointing out the wide range in organizational structure within the hotel industry. The usual 150-room hotel has a relatively simple structure; the organization of a large hotel is complex and varies considerably from one property to another.

OPERATING ARRANGEMENTS

Hotels/motels are operated in a number of ways:

Owner operates and manages
Owner sells then leases back and operates
Owner hires professional management

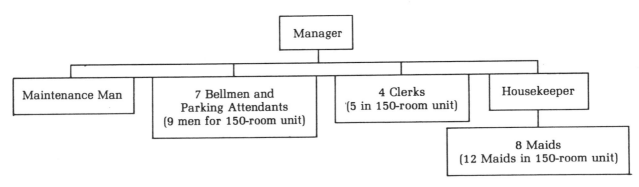

Number of Employees Required
For 100- and 150-Room Downtowner Motor Inn

Figure 4-1 *Organization chart for a 100- to 150-room motor inn—without food and beverage service.*

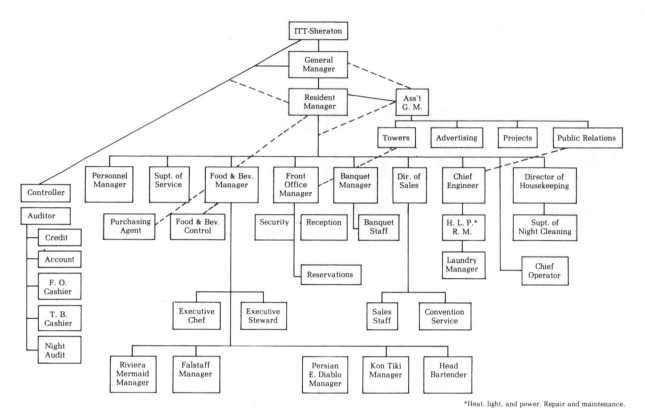

*Heat, light, and power. Repair and maintenance.

Figure 4-2 *Organization chart for Sheraton-Boston Hotel.*

Owner purchases franchise from companies such as Hilton or Holiday Inns and operates under own management

Owner purchases franchise and has franchise company operate

Owner operates but under referral organizational name such as Best Western

Owner leases property to an operating company or individual

Owner employs a management company such as the Hilton or Sheraton to operate

Since about 1960 management contracts have been particularly favored by such companies as Hilton, Sheraton, Hyatt, Marriott, and Westin because such contracts permit them to offer their management expertise without tying up large amounts of capital. In 1975 the ten largest hotel chains in this country were operating some 375 properties under management contract, and a number of newly formed operating companies accounted for several hundred more management contracts.

The large hotels are mostly owned by lending companies-insurance companies and, more recently, real estate investment companies. These companies turn to operating companies for management operating contracts.

Large numbers of hotels were built in the late 1960s and early 1970s as a result of easy money, much of it made available through the new real estate investment trusts. The REITS attracted millions of dollars from investors and REIT managers eagerly loaned out the money. Many of the hotels and motels they financed had to be taken back by the REITS. Since REITS are prohibited by law from managing and operating properties for more than ninety days, they were often desperate to find operators, and signed up reputable hotel operating companies under management contracts with little or no investment by the operator. The large chain operators, however, were not interested in bidding on properties with fewer than 300 to 350 rooms because the smaller properties could not afford their management fees, unless the hotels were experiencing high volume sales.

Basic fees received by the operators were usually 3 to 5 percent of gross revenues or a basic fee plus an incentive fee. Typically the basic fee ran 2 to 4 percent of gross revenue plus 10 percent of the gross operating profit. Other arrangements were made in terms of a fixed amount of dollars plus a percentage of gross operating profit. Still another arrangement was a basic fee paid to the operator or an incentive fee, whichever proved to be greater.

As competition for management contracts grew, operators were forced to make investments in the property as a condition of getting the contract. Investment participation included money for such things as working capital, the purchase of furniture, fixtures and equipment, supplying the preopening expenses, stock purchase, and partnerships.

Contracts usually ran for one year to twenty years. Chain operators were able to negotiate longer initial terms and longer renewal terms because of their reputation and financial stability. Owners of foreclosed properties usually wanted to be able to cancel the management contract quickly since their intent was to sell the property as soon as possible. Experienced operators wanted contracts that were cancelled upon a ninety-day notice.[1]

THE FRANCHISE

Franchising in the hotel and restaurant business goes back at least to 1907 when the Ritz Development Company franchised the Ritz-Carlton name to the hotel of that name in New York City. The franchise was granted by the Ritz Development Company, headed by a group of Englishmen.

In 1927 Howard D. Johnson began franchising his stores and the name Howard Johnson was to become a household word on the East Coast. Later, the company expanded its operation into the Midwest and, in the middle 1960s, into California. In 1973 the Howard Johnson Company included more than 900 restaurants and more than 450 motor lodges.

In 1948 Scott King of San Diego, California, began selling the TraveLodge franchise, an unusual franchise in that the TraveLodge com-

pany and the franchise holder go into partnership in a motel. The franchise holder put up half the cost of the motel; TraveLodge Corporation built the motel with something less than the other half of the investment, since it received the contractor's fee.

The new partners operated the motel and were paid a monthly salary for doing so. All of the accounting was done in San Diego by the central office of TraveLodge, and profits were divided at the end of each month. With the help of TraveLodge, a man and a wife who had $60,000 or $70,000 in cash could get into the motel business on a much bigger scale than if they were to establish the motel themselves.

In 1965 the company began selling franchises of the usual type and had sixty-two such franchised TraveLodges. TraveLodge in 1968 sold some of its stock to TL Management, Inc., a group of English, American, and Australian companies, and an agreement to expand TraveLodge into Australia was reached. Today it is controlled by Trust Houses Forte of England.

Holiday Inns of America

Holiday Inns of America, headquartered in Memphis, Tennessee, is the largest accommodation enterprise the world has known. Franchising made it possible. By 1978 Holiday Inns numbered more than 1,700, varying in size from 100 to 700 rooms, located both in this country and abroad. With more than 275,000 rooms in more than fifty countries, sales exceeded $2.3 billion, about $1.5 million for an average inn.

The standard inn is a one- or two-story brick structure, built in a square or U-shape around a pool, with 100 to 150 rooms, each having large windows covered with heavy drapes. The cost to construct and equip a one-hundred-room inn in 1975 was about $1.25 million, or $12,500 a room. The costs vary with the cost of labor around the country. Holiday Inns helps the owner arrange financing, usually 60 percent of the cost, and suggests an architect and contractor.

One of the reasons for the success of Holiday Inns is that from their beginning in 1952 they were constructed with a sizable number of rooms and contained dining facilities. With time, the average size of the inn had grown larger; by 1969 the average size exceeded 135 rooms.

1. James J. Eyster, *The Negotiation and Administration of Hotel Management Contract* (Ithaca, N.Y.: School of Hotel Administration, Cornell University, 1977).

Figure 4-3 *Major American Hotel and Motel Chains.*

Admiral Benbow Inns
1607 Motor Inn Dr
Girard OH 44420
800-321-2920

Americana Hotels
532 S Michigan Ave
Chicago IL 60605
312-435-8900

American Travel Inns
768 WN Temple
Salt Lake City UT 84116
801-521-0732

Amfac Hotels
111 S Hill Dr
Brisbane CA 94005
415-772-2900

Best Value Inns
2602 Corporate Ave E
Suite 125
Memphis TN 38132
901-398-1841

Best Western
International Inc
Best Western Way
Box 10203
Phoenix AZ 85064
602-957-4200

Budget Host Inns
2601 Jacksboro Hwy
Caravan Suite 202
PO Box 10656
Fort Worth TX 76114
817-626-7064

Days Inns of America Inc
2751 Buford Hwy NE
Atlanta GA 30324
404-325-4000

Doubletree Inns
2345 E University Dr
Phoenix AZ 85034
602-275-4484

Downtowner-Passport
System
5350 Poplar Ave
Suite 518
PO Box 171807
Memphis TN 38119
901-761-3280
Don T Baker

Dunfey Hotels International
Hampton NH 03842
603-926-8911

Econo-Travel Motor Hotels
20 Koger Executive Center
Norfolk VA 23502
804-461-6111

Fairmont Hotel Co
Atop Nob Hill
San Francisco CA 94106
415-772-5000

Four Seasons Hotels
1100 Eglinton Ave E
Toronto ON Canada
M3C 1H8
416-449-1750

Friendship Inns
International
739 S Fourth West St
Salt Lake City UT 84101
801-532-1800

Granada Royale Hometels
3644 E McDowell Rd
Suite 214
Phoenix AZ 85008
602-267-9409
Banks Henward

Guest Quarters Inc
2550 M St NW
Washington DC 20037
202-861-6600

Helmsley Hotels
455 Madison Ave
New York NY 10022
212-860-1624

Hilton Hotels Corp
9880 Wilshire Blvd
PO Box 5567
Beverly Hills CA
90210-3189
213-278-4321

Holiday Inns
3742 Lamar Ave
Memphis TN 38118
901-362-4001

Howard Johnson's Motor
Lodges
222 Forbes Rd
Braintree MA 02184
617-848-2350

Hyatt Hotels Corp
One Hyatt Center
9700 W Bryn Mawr Ave
Rosemont IL 60018
312-860-1234

Inns of the Americas Inc
4099 McEwen
Dallas TX 75234
Joseph N DePalma

Inter-Continental Hotels
Pan Am Bldg
New York NY 10166
212-880-1000

La Quinta Motor Inns Inc
PO Box 32064
Century Bldg
84 NE Loop 410
San Antonio TX 78216
512-349-1221

Marc's Budgetel Inns Div
Marcus Corp
212 W Wisconsin Ave
Milwaukee WI 53203
414-272-6020

Marriott Hotels
One Marriott Dr
Washington DC 20058
301-897-9000

Meridien Hotels
1350 Ave of the Americas
New York NY 10019
212-841-7499

Motel 6 Inc
51 Hitchcock Way
Santa Barbara CA 93105
805-682-6666

Quality Inns International
10750 Columbia Pike
Silver Spring MD 20901
301-593-5600

Radisson Hotel Corp
12805 State Hwy 55
Minneapolis MN 55441
612-540-5526

Ramada Inns Inc
PO Box 590
Phoenix AZ 85001
602-273-4000

Red Carpet/Master Hosts
Inns
Red Carpet Inns
International Inc
2032 Hillview St
Sarasota FL 33579
813-953-7024

Registry Hotel Corp
16250 Dallas North Pkwy
Suite 105
Dallas TX 75248
214-387-5775
Charles W Lanphere

Rodeway Inns
International
2525 Stemmons Frwy
Suite 800
Dallas TX 75207
214-630-9300

Scottish Inns Inc
515 Two Mile Pike
Suite 213
Goodlettsville TN 37072
615-859-6161

Sheraton Hotels & Inns
Worldwide
60 State St
Boston MA 02109
617-367-3600

Stouffer Hotels
29800 Bainbridge Rd
Solon OH 44139
216-248-3600

Summit Hotels
International Inc
2525 Stemmons Fwy
Suite 800
Dallas TX 75207
214-631-5915

Super Eight Motels
224 Sixth Ave SE
Aberdeen SD 57401
605-225-2272
Loren Steele

Surf Resorts
PO Box 8539
Honolulu HI 96815
800-367-5360
Charles McCrary

Thunderbird/Red Lion Inns
4001 Main St Ave
PO Box 1027
Vancouver WA 98666
206-696-0001

TraveLodge International
250 TraveLodge Dr
El Cajon CA 92090
714-442-0311

Treadway Inns Corp
140 Market St
PO Box 2757
Paterson NJ 07509
201-881-7900
Larry T Hines

Trust House Fonte Ltd
810 Seventh Ave
New York NY 10019
212-541-4400

Westin Hotels
The Westin Bldg
Seattle WA 98121
800-228-3000
In Ak & HI 800-228-1212

Innkeepers and restaurant managers (assistant managers) attend a Holiday Inn University at Holiday City in Memphis. Fledgling innkeepers attend the University for five weeks, learning operations, courteous phone manners, and the company philosophy. A separate audiovisual department has developed a series of training film strips.

Several of the Holiday Inn procedures have been incorporated into a teaching machine produced by the Honor Products Company of Cambridge, Massachusetts. The teaching machine, smaller than the size of the average book, is powered by two pencil-size batteries. New employees are given the machine to take home so they can learn such procedures as credit management or waiting.

To help maintain Holiday Inn standards, each inn gets four unannounced inspections a year that cover such things as the condition of the Great Sign, the cleanliness of guest rooms, and the boiler room. The inspector samples the specialty of the day in the restaurant and examines the kitchen. If an inn fails to pass such an inspection, a second inspection is given thirty days later.

A Holiday Inn franchisee pays $15,000 outright for the franchise, plus royalties of 15¢ per room per night, or 3 percent of the gross room revenue, whichever is greater. More about Holiday Inns is covered at the end of this chapter in the material on Kemmons Wilson, founder and Chairman of the Board.

In the accommodations field, the large hotel chains were slow to see the merits of franchising. Perhaps the management was too busy buying, selling, and operating hotels. The phenomenal success of Holiday Inns focused attention on what could be done through franchising, and in the 1960s Hilton and Sheraton began to franchise their names and referral systems to existing hotels and to new inns and motels.

The franchisor can expand business straight across the country by merely signing up hundreds of franchisees. The franchisee is then almost always largely or totally responsible for raising the necessary capital to start the business. The franchisor can expand as rapidly as the franchisees sign. The two principal problems of the franchisor are (1) to maintain the quality and the standard of the product and services being franchised, and (2) to see to it that few if any of the franchisees fail.

Franchise Success

Where the franchise involves primarily the use of a name, as is the case with the Sheraton Hotel franchise, the parent company may quietly nullify the agreement, take back its sign, and remove the hotel or motel from the list of Sheraton Hotels that take part in the Sheraton referral system.

Stephen W. Brenner and A. Carmi Gamoran, writing in the *Cornell Hotel and Restaurant Administration Quarterly,*[2] summarized the costs and benefits of a hotel or motel franchise to a franchisee:

Costs

1. Initial franchise or affiliation fees
2. Royalty fees paid as a percentage of room sales or fees based on number of available rooms
3. Advertising costs
4. Unit cost per reservation or cost for reservation service
5. Sign rentals
6. Other costs, e.g. stationery and other guest supplies, forms, menus, etc., with the trademark or logo of the franchise organization

Benefits

1. More room sales because of a network of reservation outlets within cities and highway locations.
2. National advertising that gives greater exposure to the name of the franchise with which the operator wishes to be identified; also, all groups publish and distribute directories; the distribution of these and their quantity are an important benefit.
3. More sales due to credit card affiliation.
4. Stature that affiliation and identification with a recognized name offers.
5. Group buying—some organizations offer central purchasing advantages; some offer architectural plans, and all generally offer advice on planning, layout, decoration, and other critical areas.

2. Stephen W. Brenner and A. Carmi Gamoran. "The Quest for Identification," *The Cornell Hotel and Restaurant Administration Quarterly,* vol. 8, no. 4 (February 1968).

TABLE 4-1   What It Takes to Join a Chain

	Franchise/membership requirements					Franchise/membership fees
Name of chain	Min. no. rooms	Food facilities	Meeting space	Swimming pool	Laundry	Initial fee
Best Western International	none	•		•		$9,248 on 100 units
Days Inns of America	100	•	•	•		$15,000/100 rooms. $100 for rooms over 100. $5,000 for restaurant.
Downtowner Motor Inns	100	•		•		$50/room minimum $5,000
Econo Lodges of America	50					conversions: $5,000 construction: $10,000
Granada Royale Hometels	160	•	•	•	•	$50,000
Hilton Inns	100	•	•	•		$250/room/first 100 rooms. Over 100, $150/room
Holiday Inns	100	•	•	•		$100/room minimum of $30,000
Howard Johnson	120	•	•	•		$20,000
Quality Inns	none	•	•	•		conversions: $100/unit $9,850 minimum construction: $100/unit $15,000 minimum
Ramada Inns	100	•	•	•		$20,000 on first 150 rooms. $100/each additional room maximum $50,000.
Red Carpet Inns	50			•		$40/room $4,000 minimum
Rodeway Inns	100	•		•	•	conversion: $7,500. construction: $15,000
Sheraton Inns	100	•	•	•		conversions: $15,000 construction: $15,000 + $100/room over 150 rooms, maximum of $40,000
Super 8 Motels	30				•	$15,000
TraveLodge	100					$10,000 or $100/room, whichever is greater

Source: *Lodging Hospitality*, pp. 70 & 72, Cleveland (July 1983).

Royalty	Advertising fee	Reservations fee	Other fees
none	none	none	$24,071/year for 100 units
5% lodging; 3% food, gas & gift	1%	$2.80/room/ month + .8% gross lodging & $1.40/ reservation, less $1/reservation made at another Days Inn	.03% monthly gross lodging for education
2% room gross	1% room gross	$1.50/room/month	none
2% room gross	2% room gross	included in advertising fee	none
4% suite gross	1% suite gross	1% suite gross	none
5% room gross	none	$4.93/reservation	none
4% room gross	1.5% room gross but no less than $.08/room/night	1% room gross but no less than $.06/night	$3.50/room Holidex fee
5% room gross	1% room gross	1% room gross + $2/room/month	none
3% room gross	1% room gross	1% room gross + $.50/system reservation	terminal: $125/ month + phone line costs & installation
3% room gross	3.5% room gross	included in reservation fee	none
2% room gross	$.10/room/month	$1.50/room/month	none
3% room gross	1% room gross	$3.75/room/month + .07 of 1% room gross	sign lease or purchase
5% room gross	none	1.6% room gross, $6/room/month minimum and $12.50/room/ month maximum	none
4% room gross	1% room gross	none	none
2½% room gross	3½% room gross	none	none

6. Training—front office procedure manuals and similar training tools for housekeeping and other departments are available through some franchisors; in addition, some companies hold annual conventions during which members can discuss problems, exchange ideas, and get further help in securing business or in solving operating problems; there are also regional sales and training meetings.

7. Borrowing costs may be lower and mortgage money may be more available if the mortgagor knows that the property will be identified with a nationally recognized franchise organization.

A great benefit of belonging to a nationwide and well-known hotel or motel franchise system is the referral business which membership brings. The same sort of advantage accrues to a restaurant franchisee in terms of increased patronage when the restaurant is a part of a nationally known group that has a favorable public image.

When the Sign Goes Up

Motels have been known to increase their patronage as much as 30 percent the day the franchise sign is erected. The larger the franchise system, the greater the potential benefits to the individual unit. Each unit, if it is favorably received by the public, adds to every other unit.

A Holiday Inn franchise brings to the franchisee membership in a system of motels containing over 1,700 units. Every unit is theoretically tied in to every other via a reservation system. National advertising—impossible for the individual unit—can be carried out by the franchise organization. Most of the contracts of the larger franchisors stipulate that a certain percentage, from 1 to 3 percent of gross sales, be paid by the franchisee into a national advertising fund. Pooling advertising dollars in this manner makes for advertising exposure otherwise impossible by the individual. A franchisee pays $10,000 to $50,000 for a Hilton franchise plus 5 percent of room revenues.

The more successful franchise organizations have arrived at the enviable position of being able to screen and select franchisees carefully. The financial capacity of a franchisee is carefully reviewed; the site for the motel or restaurant must be passed on by the franchisor. In some cases, the franchisee has no voice in the selection of the site but must take the one that has been analyzed by the site expert of the franchising organization.

Disadvantages of a Franchise

From the point of view of the franchisor, the most serious problem is the necessity of continuous control of the product and service standards in every unit. Every customer who frequents a poorly operated unit walks away with a less favorable image of the total organization. The bright orange roof of a Howard Johnson or the Great Sign of Holiday Inns somehow becomes a little tarnished in the mind of the customer. Each unit reflects on all other units. The franchisor cannot afford to allow many units to fall below standard or to fail, otherwise he or she fails.

Franchise Restrictions

From the viewpoint of the franchisee, the agreement is generally restrictive regarding the style of operation, the product, and the services offered. No room is left for imagination or for changes in menu, decor, furnishings, or equipment. Neither is there room for regional differences in taste or other customer preference. Some of the franchise fees add up to 15 percent of the gross sales, and more; this can be a burden, especially during slow periods.

The franchise favors the franchisor. The terms of a franchise agreement are drawn up by the franchisor; the franchisee is free to buy the franchise or reject it. Ordinarily the agreement is fixed. Most franchise agreements contain clauses that permit the franchisor to buy back the franchise, or to cancel it, should the franchisee fail to live up to the terms of the agreement.

Inevitably there are disagreements between franchisor and franchisee. Often the franchisees find that they are not cut out to operate a restaurant or motel. These businesses appear glamorous until the people find that they must live, work, and think their business to remain successful. People who think they can "retire" into a motel or restaurant are usually shocked to find that they have married a business. Baby-sitters for motels or restaurants are hard to find; "mom and pop" find they march to the tune played by the operation.

Not many people have the energy and temperament needed to run a donut shop or many of the variety of franchised restaurants or motels. The operation demands long hours and constant attention. Few restaurant operations do well with absentee ownership. After a few months of being "locked-in" to a motel or restaurant, many franchisees want out.

Getting out without financial loss is not always easy. The bickering between franchisor and franchisee begins. It may go on for months until both parties wish they had never heard of each other. The franchisor usually ends by taking back the unit or installing a company manager to operate it.

When the franchisor acquires capital or when the franchised units are particularly profitable, the franchisor is tempted to buy it back.

In 1975 some 6,463 hotels and motels were franchised and did about one-third of the total sales of all hotels/motels in the United States, some $4.6 billion in sales.[3] In the late 1960s, several economy motel franchisors came into the picture and, by 1975, had several hundred budget motels under franchise. Prominent among them were Days Inns, Motel 6, and Scottish Inns of America. In the late 1960s, campgrounds also began to be franchised.

ELECTRONIC DATA PROCESSING IN HOTELS AND RESTAURANTS

The marvels of EDP (Electronic Data Processing) were dimly felt in the hotel and restaurant business in the early years of the 1960s. The Hilton Hotels were among the first to use the computer to process their payroll. Later, building on the experience of the airlines, hotel chains developed large-scale, computerized reservation systems.[4]

The Midwestern Division of Hilton Hotels, headquartered at The Conrad Hilton in Chicago, utilized an IBM computer to process the payroll of the several hotels within the division. As early as 1962, data concerning wage rates, tax deductions, insurance deductions, and other adjustments were carried by the computer in the central office. Each hotel in the division mailed the number of hours worked for each employee to Chicago. The computer then produced a payroll check within a matter of seconds that was mailed back to the hotel for payment to the employee.

A few other hotels and restaurants began contracting for payroll processing by computer from local banks. Charges for processing each check were about 25¢ to 30¢, less expensive than the amount for which the hotel could handle it.

A few country and city clubs began contracting for a complete service on their accounts receivable. This service was especially useful to a club since statements are usually mailed to club members at the end of the month, and there is a great pile-up of clerical work at that time.

In 1963, The New York Hilton Hotel was opened and considerable publicity was given to the fact that the entire operation would be computerized using IBM equipment. The operation was to be on-line; that is, information about each guest's purchases would be immediately fed into the computer. The guest was given a number, and all charges made by that individual during his or her stay in the hotel would be entered into the computer by that number. When the guest was ready to check out, the computer would produce a complete statement, itemized and totaled. Unfortunately, the programs and the equipment were not capable of the task imposed upon them and part of the system was abandoned.

The Drake Hotel of Chicago uses five programs developed by the Honeywell Corporation. These programs are general programs that can be used for any business. The programs cover the general ledger, accounts receivable, accounts payable, payroll, and inventory reporting and control program.

To use the Honeywell programs, it is necessary to rent a Honeywell computer. Leasing or renting a computer is the preferred arrange-

---

3. *Food and Lodging Hospitality* (Dec. 1975).
4. Ibid., p. 104.

ment because of the expertise needed to maintain and repair computers, and because computers quickly become obsolete.

One of the decisions to make in a computer application is whether or not the computer should be placed on-line with the data input device. If instantaneous retrieval of the information is essential, the on-line arrangement is called for; otherwise, the cost of on-line is excessive.

Several of the companies that have installed EDP have declared that the total cost of EDP is as great as the hand system it replaced, but that information is almost instantaneously available. The availability of information when needed provides the plus factor for the computer installation.

Simulated Decision Making

To familiarize future managers with EDP, several of the hotel schools require students to complete at least one course in data processing. Several schools arrange for students to play management simulation games. The games compress several years of decision making into the space of a few hours. The use of a computer permits the use of a number of variables. The computer produces the results of the various decisions within a few seconds.

The use of EDP to develop a menu has been worked out for hospital menus. The work was done at Tulane University under a government grant. Hospital menus that reflect nutritional balance, color, and cost are being selected by computer. Such menu selection must also reflect the effect of monotony in a diet and regional food preferences as well.

The Century Plaza Hotel of Los Angeles puts the computer to work in a way that should please the guests. When guests have been to the hotel three times, the computer automatically pre-registers them and recalls their room preferences. They need only pick up their key when they arrive.

Undoubtedly, many more uses will be found for the computer. As the cost comes down, wider application can be expected. Time-sharing is likely to be the favorite method of use since banks, insurance companies, and other large companies have sizable amounts of computer time which can be made available for hotels and restaurants on a time-sharing basis at relatively low cost.

Identifying Significant Market Factors by Computer

By using the computer, it is now possible to identify more precisely those factors that bear on the sales volume of a particular hotel or motel. This is done by subjecting occupancy data to analysis. Factors that are thought to be important for sales are correlated with sales figures over a period of time. Correlations between factors are also made. Without the use of the computer, the arithmetic would be too time-consuming to be feasible.

With sufficient information based on past experience, it is possible to identify and weigh each factor that bears on the sales of a particular hotel or motel. It will be possible to predict that if a certain amount of money is spent on advertising, a certain increase can be expected, or that affiliation with a particular chain will result in a predictable increase in occupancy, and so on.

In keeping with the shifting emphasis on the systems approach and the use of the computer, the larger companies are adding new divisions that are responsible for management information systems and computer applications. Saga Food Administration, one of the most progressive foodservice operations, has reorganized top management to include an administrative division headed by an executive vice-president of administration.

Administration is responsible for the broad areas of planning and forecasting. Within the administration division are the departments of personnel, finance, marketing, technical services, and information services. Indicative of the thrust of the Saga Company has been the establishment of a separate division, New Ventures.

The magic words in management today are *computerization, management information systems, linear programming, data processing, input-output analysis, progress evaluation review technique, queuing theory, econometric model, multiple regression analysis,* and a few others. With time, these terms may become a regular part of every manager's jargon.

High Technology Spreading

By 1976 the inter-hotel reservations systems of fourteen of the twenty largest hotel chains were computerized. Eighteen of the twenty used data processing for at least part of their corporate accounting.

The "St*r" computerized reservations terminal used by Best Western hotels/motels, for example, consists of three elements, a Cathode Ray Tube (CRT) display screen, a computerized keyboard for sending reservations, and a hard-copy printer for receiving reservations and messages from other Best Western properties and the chain's marketing and Reservations Center in Phoenix. The St*r computer is programmed so that if no rooms are available at a given property, a display automatically appears showing availabilities at the nearest alternate Best Westerns. Time required: thirty seconds. The St*r terminal is seen in Figure 4–4.

The preparation of financial and operating reports was the most prevalent in-house application of computers. Centralized accounts payable was also computerized widely. Other applications included handling of payroll, budget projections, the consolidation of daily operating reports, and return on investment analysis.

Rather than rush out and learn data processing in depth, the usual hotel manager might take a course in data processing and then learn a particular computer application as one is confronted with it. Computers are now being used in a variety of combinations, including the following:

Figure 4–4 *St*r, Best Western's new computerized reservation system. It features a sophisticated but easy-to-use keyboard and display screen terminal.*

Reservations

Room management, including communication links between front desk and housekeeping

Guest accounting, including both front-office cashiering and night audit

Guest history

Point-of-sale data collection from the hotels and motels, restaurants, bars, and other revenue centers

Telephone circuit board

Marketing analyses

Convention and other function records

Travel agency accounting

Travel agency business analysis

Back-office accounting, or interface with the back office

Data processing is predicted to be widely used in hotels of more than 200 rooms, especially mini-computers as their cost comes down and they are installed on the premises.

LOW-VOLTAGE SYSTEMS

As new hotels are constructed a number of low-voltage systems can be installed in the same conduits. These systems include equipment that will control the peak power demand, room status systems, automatic wake-up systems, electronically controlled guest room access, and electronically controlled storeroom access.

The automatic turn-off or turn-down of heating, ventilation, and air conditioning equipment, and lighting when the guest checks out, and the automatic turn-on when the guest checks in, is likely to become widely used. Energy controlled equipment has a fast pay-off, energy savings equalling the investment within six months or two years.

Room status systems remove the need for constant phone calls between the front desk and housekeeping.

If security continues to be a problem, electronic security systems are likely to be installed with "forced entry" alarms, motion detectors, and metal detectors, for example. Comprehensive security systems have been in use in Las Vegas, Reno, and a few of the larger hotels elsewhere.

Telephone systems owned or leased by the hotel has gained wider acceptance. Automatic transfer of the guest's local charges is made to the appropriate guest folio. This speeds guest check-out and eliminates the manual meters, which count guest's calls.

Larger convention hotels are likely to use other types of low-voltage technology including:

Large-screen TV projection

Paging—audio and visual

Closed-circuit TV

Video recording equipment

Front and rear screen projection equipment

Automatic wake-up systems

HOTELS AND TELECONFERENCES

Teleconferencing has entered the hospitality management scene in a significant way. Holiday Inns offers "teleconferencing" in some 300 of their properties. Hilton Hotels and other chains are moving into conventioning via satellite. Signals from a central conference are beamed (uplinked) to a satellite thousands of miles in the sky, then down to saucers set up on roofs or near the hotel property. The saucer picks up the signal from the satellite and it is displayed on a screen in a conference room or auditorium similar to TV projection. One-way video reception is common. At a greater cost, two-way video reception can be arranged. A corporation can reach literally thousands of its employees, usually sales or corporate staff, at the same time at a number of different locations. Total travel expenses are drastically reduced. Savings in time translated into salary expenses are also sharply cut.

An example of teleconferencing illustrates its advantages and disadvantages. Until 1982 Baskin-Robbins, the ice-cream franchisor, had its top management on the road for as long as five months of the year meeting with franchisee groups. Teleconferencing changed this dramatically. An eight-hour teleconference was originated from a hotel in Dallas. It linked 2,373 franchisees in twenty-five cities across the United States via a satellite traveling 35,000 miles above the earth. The teleconference cost well over $300,000 and took one year to prepare, but it saved money and time.

Western Union contracted to transmit the event. Tele-image, a Dallas-based firm was responsible for operations at the Dallas uplink site. To keep socialization high, participants began the day with a breakfast or lunch and were offered a number of snack breaks. Interaction between franchisees was facilitated by seating them in groups of eight. A cocktail party and dinner climaxed the teleconference.

Participants agreed that the teleconference was less enjoyable and perhaps less effective than the traditional group convention meeting, but that it was efficient and cost-saving.

How will video conferencing affect the hotel business of the future? This question is being pondered by many hotel executives, and no one has a clear answer. Hilton Hotels has arranged for a Hilton Communication Network. Instead of buying the necessary specialized equipment, Hilton relies on the services of an outside company. The system allows video presentation on a big screen plus two-way audio-communication between originator and groups gathered in hotels as needed to serve the originator.

Video conferencing makes it possible to introduce a new program or hold a press conference in numerous locations at the same time. MGM introduced the film "Pennies From Heaven" to sixteen cities in the United States and Canada. The 3M Company, headquartered in Minneapolis, was able to reach 80,000 employees in a relatively short time with a new program. Several cities of origin were used where the program was presented live to as many as 200 people. Many times that number received the program at other locations via the video conference technique.

The Bell Phone Company put the label, *teleconference*, on phone calls with multiple parties sitting in different locations linked by phone. Video conferencing adds the next dimension—the big screen. Next will be the video phone. Will more or fewer hotel rooms come with the technological advances? The chains are taking no chances. Holiday Inn has made video conferencing another hotel feature just as once were the radio, the swimming pool, and the TV set in every guest room.

Video conferencing is seen as increasing the sale of rooms and also of food and beverage by some hotel operators. Travel costs for long-distance meetings and conventions will be reduced, they say, therefore more regional meetings that can be attended by more people will be held. In the past only the top sales, management, and technical people were sent to national meetings; personnel at lower levels attended the regional meetings.

Other operators believe that while food and beverage sales will rise because of an increase in regional meetings, room sales will suffer.

One point of agreement: video conferencing is not revolutionary. It is evolutionary. Its effects on hotel occupancy and food and beverage sales will not be drastic, at least in the near future.

Another point of agreement: video conferencing will never completely substitute for face-to-face meetings where there are one-on-one greetings and exchange of ideas and feelings, people making friends and seeing each other over the years.

Long-distance travel will probably be reduced because of video conferencing. Short-distance travel to locations participating in the video conference should increase.

The video phone, when it becomes widespread, may have much more drastic effects on the hotel business. When it is easy to set up a phone conference around a table with other around-the-table conferees and all involved can see each others' faces, travel and hotel rooms will be less needed.

VIDEO ELECTRONICS ADD REVENUE

As reported by Pannell Kerr Forster, a new source of revenue and another means of guest entertainment has been realized when hotel management has set up coin-operated video games in a game room.

As reported by the *U.S. News and World Report*, a single video game can produce weekly revenues as high as $300 to $400, with a nationwide average of just over $100 per week.

Hotel operators often provide the space and utilities to a concessionaire who then splits the gross revenues on a pre-arranged basis. It is recommended that a revenue breakdown for each machine be made so that machines can be changed as interest declines in older machines.

THE SALES FUNCTION

Hotels have been changing the title of the person in charge of sales to Director of Marketing, a change that implies a much broader role for the individual holding the title. Marketing is concerned not only with selling but with learning more about the product to be sold, the competitor's product, the customer, the customer's motivation and wants, and how the product can best be produced and presented to meet the customer's needs. Marketing implies research. In the case of the hotel it is folio research, carefully identifying who the present customers are, where they come from, what they earn, and what they want in the way of hotel and services. A Los Angeles Hotel may find that its principal "market," its source of customers, is western Canada, San Francisco, and Chicago, or other areas. Promotion and advertising would then be concentrated in those areas.

A motor hotel manager may be surprised to learn that 70 percent of the guests are pleasure travelers, not business travelers. A member of a referral organization may find that less than 30 percent of its customers come as referrals from within their referral system. The Group Marketing Research and Development section of Holiday Inns found Holiday Inns was not as successful as some other chains in attracting families traveling with teenagers simply because the other chains did not charge for teens. As a result a "Teens Free" policy was instituted in 1,300 inns. The same company wondered how business travelers felt about their holidomes (covered courtyards with pools and games). The business traveler thought that they were innovative and impressive, adding to the appeal of the inn. The question was raised among business travelers concerning the chain's policy of "Kids Eat Free." The program was perceived as positive and has influenced the business traveler to stay at a Holiday Inn when traveling with his or her family.

Market analysis can determine where new investment is needed. Should it be spent in redesigning the lobby or improving the restaurant operation? Ask the customer. What effect will a severe winter have on summer business? In Harrisburg, Pennsylvania, for example, a severe winter caused the schools to close three weeks late, a condition that affected the June business for a number of inns that depended on Harrisburg as a summer feeder market. Knowing this, the inns could accept group or meeting business, which they normally would have turned away in June.

Much of hotel market research is not done "in-house" but farmed out to local market research organizations and to business departments in nearby universities.

The Sales Staff

The sales staff of hotels and motels varies in size. In a small motel, the manager performs the sales function. In a megahotel, a director of sales may have a staff of eight or ten persons plus the assistance of the corporate office sales staff. Most of their effort is directed towards group sales.

The Radisson South hotel, a 408-room hotel in Minneapolis, has a staff of five in the sales department with a game plan drawn to determine how to sell, when to sell, and where to sell. Its staff is representative of a medium-sized hotel.

The director of sales is primarily concerned with game planning, setting goals, budgeting, forecasting and supervision. He also spends 20 percent of his time on the road. With the general manager and executive assistant manager, he develops annually a "Rooms Sales Forecast" for every day in the year for group bookings. Day-to-day forecasting is done by the executive assistant manager.[5]

The assistant director of sales spends 20 percent of his time outside primarily on national conventions and assists the director of sales in reporting and record-keeping and in performing analysis and evaluation.

The sales manager spends 35 percent of his time outside and works on convention sales with emphasis on state and regional meetings. A second salesperson spends 70 percent of her time outside promoting corporate bookings of meetings and other multiple reservations. One salesperson spends 90 percent of her time outside visiting corporate offices.

Customarily, hotels provide one complimentary guest room for every one hundred rooms the group fills. Some hotels provide a suite.

PUBLIC RELATIONS

Smaller hotels ordinarily do not employ a full-time salesperson. The owners have the choices of relying heavily on a referral system (such as Best Western) for business, buying the services of an advertising and marketing company periodically, or of doing no marketing and expecting word-of-mouth recommendations or location to attract guests.

Another choice is for the general manager to take on the marketing responsibilities. That person defines market objectives, conducts market research, puts together a sales plan and packages and promotes it. Guest questionnaires can identify the present market. If the property can attract the business traveler, questionnaires (with appropriate rewards for responding) can be sent to secretaries of local businesses.

Current and potential target markets are identified and a promotion plan is then assembled. Promotion is carried out by direct mail, newspaper ads, and travel agent cultivation. All hotels, large and small, are engaged in marketing, whether they know it or not—be it systematic and logical, or haphazard and unplanned.

Travel management is closely related to hotel and restaurant management, both being a part of the broader field of hospitality management. Many hotels are dependent, in part, on travel agents for much of hotel business. Some resort hotels may get 90 to 100 percent of their booking via the 23,000 travel agencies in this country. Others receive as much as 60 percent of their business from tour operators.

Business travelers are increasingly turning to travel agents to book hotel rooms as well as flights.

Several larger hotels have established a new job title in their marketing departments —that of "travel or tour director." This person has direct responsibility for selling the hotel to tour operators and for coordinating group tours once they have arrived at the hotel.

Hotel managers are well aware of the impact of air schedules and fares on their busi-

---

5. "The Radisson South, A Case Study in Hotel Operation," *Lodging* (November 1977).

ness; markets change radically when air services and fares change. For example, West Coast hotels found large new markets developing from Australia and the Orient as Pacific air fares came down.

The larger hotels and hotel chains and theme parks employ public relations personnel whose primary job is to create a favorable image for their properties. This is done by cultivating editors, travel writers, and other media personnel and encouraging them to write about the property concerned. They are encouraged also to send out a series of news releases designed to keep the hotel, theme park, or other attraction in the public eye. The public relations people are usually excellent writers, likable, and often highly imaginative. When the theme park Six Flags Over Texas introduced its new high-speed thrill ride called the "Runaway Mine Train," the ride broke down with a dozen newspaper writers and photographers and four television cameramen on board. The train came to a screeching halt on the high loops and the whole thing could have been a disaster from a public relations viewpoint. The quick-thinking public relations person at Six Flags suggested that the press, TV, and news people treat the incident from a different angle: "Safety Systems on New Run-Away Train Works Perfectly."

Sometimes it takes months to cultivate a good magazine—interesting a good writer by providing accommodations and meals, information, photographs, and background information. The payoff may be an article in a name magazine that would have the effect of tens of thousands of dollars worth of advertising. A giveaway guide book for an area may increase the average stay for a hotel one to three days, the guest having available a number of suggestions of new options for things to do.

NEW SECURITY MEASURES

The Courts and the general public have rising expectations as to what a hotel-motel should provide in the way of security, or perhaps with the rising crime the general public is more conscious of criminal activity and is becoming more wary and demanding.[6]

---

6. *New York Times,* March 20, 1977, p. 13.

Guest security has been a problem in hotels since their beginning. In 1974 a well-known singer, Connie Francis, was raped while staying at the Howard Johnson Motor Lodge in Westbury, Long Island. She sued the restaurant and motel chain for $6 million, charging that the company had failed to provide her with a safe and secure room. The singer was awarded $2.5 million and her husband an additional $25,000 by a Federal District Court in Brooklyn. Howard Johnson's insurance company filed a motion, asking that the award be set aside as excessive. The parties settled out of court in 1977 for $1,475,000. The case alarmed hotel and motel keepers and focused attention on the necessity for providing greater guest security.

Larger hotels have long had security personnel in plain clothes, often off-duty police officers, working the hotel lobby and around the hotel since before the turn of the century. Now hotel operators are strengthening their security forces and looking for new ways of insuring guest security within the room. A number of "security systems" have been introduced.

A system called Lok-a-Wat works in this way: After a hard day a guest unlocks the door, walks into the hotel room, turns on the light and the television, and flops down on the bed to relax. Two and a half minutes later the television goes off, the light goes off, and the air-conditioner shuts down. To activate the electrical system again, the guest must throw a deadbolt in the lock on his or her door. Control for the system is operated from a metal box, eighteen inches by three inches by three inches, fitted under the desk in each room. Wires connect the box to the lock and to the electrical appliances.

Other systems require plastic cards as substitutes for keys. Peepholes are being installed in guest rooms, and stronger locks are being installed. Chain locks have been used in many properties for a number of years: now closed circuit television focuses on corridors and are monitored by security personnel.

Regardless of deadbolts and other systems, it is necessary for hotel personnel to enter the room in case of fire, illness, and other emergencies in which the guest cannot open it.

Security experts state that a principal ingredient in the security program's effectiveness is the ability to respond promptly to a security problem. To this end, one-way beeper systems and two-way walkie talkie systems are widely used in the larger properties. Maintenance personnel can also be equipped with beeper systems and can become a prominent part of the security system if instructed in ways to handle security problems. In a large hotel the security force headquarters itself in a guest room and changes rooms from time to time.

A large hotel like the 1,000-room Marriott at the Los Angeles airport may have a security force of sixteen or more persons plus a number of off-duty regular police officers who shift on an hourly basis. None of the security people wear uniforms and only the regular police officers may make police arrests; the others must make do with a citizen's arrest. Even so they use handcuffs when necessary. This happens sometimes when people are engaged in fights or are drunk and disorderly. By far the largest arrests in downtown hotels are of obvious prostitutes. Guests are also apprehended in carrying off hotel property—although items like stolen towels are overlooked.

One of the most successful security programs utilizes television monitors in all areas where large amounts of money are located. One person can monitor a number of places from one location, and, if a problem arises, can beep security personnel quickly.

WELL-PAID MANAGEMENT

Management personnel are a group apart, almost a caste. Over the years they have been comparatively well paid. The first manager of The Palace in San Francisco received $12,000 a year in gold, an exorbitant salary for 1875. Even during the depression, Ralph Hitz demanded and got a salary of $35,000 a year as manager of The New Yorker. A first-class hotel needs two highly specialized, highly trained executives, the manager and the food and beverage director or the executive chef. The Ritz-Escoffier team illustrates what can be done with the front-of-the-house, headed by the manager, and the back-of-the-house, headed by the executive chef, when both are exceptional people.

As the chains, with their systems, moved into the larger hotels, the importance of having an exceptional individual at the helm dimin-

ished. Staff planning, operation analysts, computers, and systems have partly relieved the necessity of having a person with exceptional planning and organizational skills in the individual hotel. While an exceptional manager sets the mood and creates a tone within the hotel, the design and operational procedures devised by the home office may be even more important.

For some years the Sheraton Company had the policy of moving managers at least every three years, usually more often. Other companies have a similar policy, believing that the manager tends to become too satisfied, or gets into a rut, by remaining very long at the same hotel. With enough system and control imposed upon a manager, the manager acts more as a person who makes the system work than as an innovator or a boniface in the traditional sense.

ACCOUNTING AND CONTROL SEPARATED FROM UNIT MANAGEMENT

In larger hotels the accounting and control function is divorced from everyday management by making the comptroller or finance officer, as the comptroller is sometimes called, separate from line management. In the Hilton Hotels, for example, the finance officer within a large hotel reports directly to the home office rather than being directly responsible to the general manager of the property. Such an arrangement has advantages and disadvantages. The general manager of the hotel may resent losing the responsibility of the control function. In some cases the comptroller and the general manager may clash, and one or the other may have to be moved to another property. The primary advantage is that a specialist is in charge of the cash and accounting within a property, which lessens the possibility of ineffective accounting procedures and speculation on the point of the general manager or the immediate staff. The general manager is also freed from day-to-day concern over accounting and control procedures, hence, more time may be given to concentrate on guest relations, hotel operations, and the marketing function.

MANY DEMANDS ON MANAGER

Regardless of chain affiliation, the manager's job is extremely demanding, and the operation tends to reflect his or her motivation and attitudes. Like the captain of the ship with a structured organization acting as the crew, the manager must remain in command at all times and be responsible for everything that goes on within the hotel or motel.

A perceptive guest can sense something of the personality of the manager without ever seeing the individual. Does the operation run smoothly? How does he or she feel about cleanliness? Courtesy? Attention to detail? What kinds of people does the manager employ? Well-managed hotels have an ambience that is not based on furnishings and design alone. The operation is articulated; things happen when they should, employees are alert and courteous, bedspreads and blankets are clean, and the carpets have no cigarette burns in them.

In a few deluxe hotels, room diagrams are kept for special guests, showing the way they like their suites laid out, the color of draperies they prefer, and the kind of beverage they like to have waiting for them. The repeat guest is addressed by name. An assistant manager may call the newly-arrived guest in his or her room to inquire if everything is all right. The guest need not check out by standing in line at the cashier's desk; the bill is sent later.

WAGES

In the typical 100- to 250-room hotel or motor hotel, only two to four people receive salaries of any size—the manager, the chef, and the food and beverage director. Between them, they are responsible for the complete operation of the hotel, and supposedly their expertise is sufficient to make the property go.

The innkeeper at a Holiday Inn operated by the Holiday Inn Company would typically make a good salary plus receiving food and beverage while on the job. If the innkeeper lives in, then that person and family receive full maintenance, all meals, room service, laundry, and other benefits. The assistant innkeeper of a Holiday Inn-style operation is the restaurant manager, with a salary that approximates that of the innkeeper.

In the independent hotel or motel, the salary is usually higher and the manager would have considerably more responsibility. As the hotel or motel increases in size and complexity,

the manager's salary increases so that in a few of the major hotels, the salary exceeds $60,000 a year plus a number of fringe benefits. Department head salaries also move up. Chefs at some of the prestige hotels may receive a salary of $40,000 a year. Department heads, such as the housekeeper and the engineer, might receive salaries in excess of $25,000 annually.

The reputation of the hotel and restaurant business for the comparatively low wages paid is widespread and of long standing. The reputation is well deserved when applied to the entry and semiskilled positions, but it is not true in reference to wages and salaries paid to technical specialists and supervisory and management personnel.

Since a large number of hotels, motels, and restaurants are small, they are likely to be family enterprises. In 1963, for example, there were almost 4,000 hotels and 16,000 motels and tourist courts that had no paid employees. Wages and salaries in such instances are, in large part, the profit generated by the business. These can be relatively high.

In the larger establishments, 50 to 60 percent of all nonsupervisory personnel are low-paid, unskilled, untipped employees. These include chambermaids, dish machine operators, housemen, washroom attendants, laundry workers, porters, and utility personnel.

Characteristically, such people are from less-advantaged groups who have few other employment options. In New York City, for example, something like 40 to 60 percent of the hotel and restaurant employees are Puerto Ricans. In a twelve-city study, blacks made up 31.6 percent of the hotel labor force, with the great majority in low-paying, back-of-the-house positions. Median age of the hotel employees in 1975 was forty-four, four years older than that for the nation's labor force. Women constituted 53 percent of the employees.

Area differences in hotel wages are large, twice as much being paid in San Francisco, for example, as in Kansas City or the South. With the minimum wage laws, the spread between North and South has narrowed slightly, but it is still great. The wage differentials only partly reflect living costs; union pressures are important.

Skilled and semiskilled workers, such as bartenders, cooks, desk clerks, and pantrymen and women, account for about 10 percent of nonsupervisory hotel employees. Their wages are high relative to those in the unskilled groups.

Productivity and wages are rising together as ways and products are found that reduce labor. No-iron linens, convenience foods, and direct-dial phones eliminate people, as do self-service elevators, vending machines, and shoe-shining equipment in guest rooms.

Tip Employees Often Relatively Overpaid

About 15 percent of hotel employees receive tips. Tipped employees—doormen, bellmen, waiting personnel—are a group unto themselves and are in many cases highly overpaid in relation to their contribution to the enterprise. For the tip employee, the wage may be a relatively small part of total income. The class of restaurant, seat turnover, and average check determine to a large extent the income of the tip employee. It is not unusual for waiting personnel to make as much as $80 a night in tips. A Bureau of Labor Statistics study showed that tipped employees average income was 61 percent higher than their nontipped counterparts.

Tipping practices vary widely throughout the country. The highest rates are in New York City and cities on the West Coast. Tips are less in the Midwest and the South, and are nonexistent in some rural communities. Tipping is reputed to be highest among certain segments of metropolitan New York residents. Well-to-do people are not necessarily big tippers whereas, generally speaking, the nouveaux riches have a reputation for being big spenders, and this includes tipping.

Office personnel account for about 15 percent of the nonsupervisory employment, and their wages are usually determined by the prevailing wage in the community for similar jobs. Front-desk clerks have traditionally been low-paid employees, especially in resort areas. Many people are eager for such jobs since the position has a certain status and is relatively interesting. The job offers psychic income as well as salary.

About 5 percent of the hotel employees are maintenance employees—engineers, firemen, upholsterers, electricians, painters—who are paid at competitive rates for the area. Maintenance people are usually well organized and receive a union scale.

IMPACT OF THE UNION

Unionization has played an important part in hotel management only in the large cities outside the South.

The Hotel and Restaurant Employees and Bartenders Union is the major union in the hotel and restaurant business. Uniformed personnel, such as bellmen and elevator operators, may be members of the Building Service Employees International Union, and other unions also represent some of the technical personnel.

The Hotel and Restaurant Employees Union goes back to 1891 when the Waiters and Bartenders National Union was formed. Even earlier, societies of European national groups were organized to provide mutual financial protection against the hazards of illness, old age, and death. These societies manned the skilled occupations: Germans cooking the food, Italians serving it, the Irish tending bar.[7]

Growth of union membership was slow until about 1937. Between 1940 and 1947, membership doubled to a little over 400,000. The chief barriers to the unionization of service workers in the United States, says Professor Henderson, are employer opposition and worker apathy. Since so many people in the industry are unskilled and constitute a "floating" population, it is difficult for unionism to gain a stable membership base.

Membership in the union is high in northern cities and in the West. In Boston, Chicago, Detroit, New York, St. Louis, and San Francisco, 90 percent or more of nonsupervisory employees, except front desk and office workers, are in establishments with union agreements. In New Orleans, Atlanta, and Memphis, however, the percentage is 20 or below.[8]

As a region, the West is the most strongly unionized with 37 percent of the total union membership; California alone has 25 percent of

7. John P. Henderson, *Labor Market Institutions and Wages in the Lodging Industry* (East Lansing, Mich.: Michigan State University, Bureau of Business and Economic Research).

8. U.S. Dept. of Labor, *Employment Outlook for Hotels*, Bulletin No. 1550-107, 1968.

the total membership in the continental United States. Washington, D.C., and Florida are the only places in the South that have much union representation. Of the total membership, somewhat over 63,000 are found in New York City, another 20,000 in San Francisco.

San Francisco has had one of the strongest union leaderships since the 1930s. In 1934, the separate craft unions joined together into a joint board and began demanding the union shop in all hotels "from the roof down."[9] On May 1, 1937, all of the hotels in the city were struck. "Bartenders took off their coats and aprons; waiters and busboys put down their trays; stenographers left their desks; clerks put on their hats; in fact, every worker just simply walked off."[10] In all, about 10,000 employees were affected.

The strike occurred at a time when San Francisco's famous hotels, such as The Fairmont and Mark Hopkins on Nob Hill, The Palace, and St. Francis were expecting floods of tourists for the Golden Gate Fiesta. Some 4,700 union members, who had been hotel employees, were out on strike. They were helped by 4,000 fellow members in the city restaurants who paid assessments each week so that the strikers might be fed. Some waitresses appeared in costume, on floats mounted on trucks, advertising the strike.

Business losses for the hotels were estimated at $6.5 million for the summer. The strike won the preferential union shop, the eight-hour day, and an elaborate set of work rules. A joint arbitration committee was set up to adjust grievances and wage disputes. In the ten years that followed, membership in the union in San Francisco increased to over 20,000, and wage scales were set, which have remained the highest for the country.

The Labor Management and Relations Act, 1947, otherwise known as the Taft-Hartley Act, encouraged unions to increase organization efforts. In 1955, the union moved in on Miami Beach. In favor of the union was the fact that Miami Beach is one of the most intensely competitive hotel areas anywhere. At the time, it had 350 hotels, with 30,000 hotel and motel

rooms, on a strip of land covering only seven square miles. Hotels were being sold, resold, and often operated by people without previous experience in the industry. Also, many of the Miami Beach employees were loyal union members when they worked in their northern home cities during the off season.

The union spent over $1.5 million on the Miami Beach effort for legal fees, soup kitchens, and other strike costs.[11] The union published ads in other cities warning members that they would be subject to fine and expulsion if they took jobs in struck hotels. Recruiting efforts on lower Manhattan's employment agency row were effectively stymied by pickets placed in front of the employment agencies. Pickets also marched at Idlewild Airport where replacement employees were taken for the flight to Miami. The union was also successful in getting the three television networks—NBC, ABC, and CBS—to stop originating shows in Miami Beach as long as the labor dispute in the hotels continued. An advertising campaign was launched in the North to dissuade travelers from coming to Miami Beach at all.

In 1957, the Hotel Association, represented by only a few hotels, signed an associationwide master contract, bringing to an end the strike that had lasted twenty-one months, the longest and costliest strike in hotel history.

Prior to 1955, the Hotel and Restaurant Employees Union opposed the National Labor Relations Board in taking jurisdiction over hotels and restaurants. Then the union changed its position and favored NLRB jurisdiction. In 1959, the National Labor Relations Board supervised its first election to determine if the union was to be the bargaining representative of the employees.

Restrictive Union Practices

Several restrictive practices imposed by a number of union contracts push up the cost of labor unnecessarily in hotels and restaurants. For example, a contract at The Condado Beach Hotel in San Juan, Puerto Rico, specified that the hotel may never employ fewer than 75 percent of the number of employees employed at the time the contract was negotiated.

9. Matthew Josephson, *Union House, Union Bar* (New York: Random House, 1956).

10. Ibid.

11. Edwin B. Dean, "The Miami Beach Hotel Strike," *Cornell Hotel Administration Quarterly* (May 1962).

Although the unemployment rate in Puerto Rico is above 15 percent and living costs considerably below those in U.S. mainland cities, wages paid to hotel employees are about the same. Labor efficiency is low, 1.5 to 2 employees being needed to accomplish the work done by one employee on the mainland.

Job classifications are zealously guarded by union representatives in many places. A glass washer may not wash dishes. Do not ask a bellman to clean anything, if the union contract does not permit it. A roast cook may not prepare soups, and so it goes.

The ultimate weapon in any union's arsenal—the one weapon that gives any employer or group of employers real pause—is the strike or the threat of a strike.

The union gathers muscle when other non-hotel or restaurant unions back strikes against hospitality businesses. In 1969, in a strike against Seattle restaurants, members of the Teamsters Union refused to deliver supplies.

Learner-Controlled Instruction

Programmed instruction has been developed for a number of jobs in the industry. The first sizable textbook in the hospitality business that was programmed was *Understanding Cooking*, which was an attempt to explain the rationale of the cooking processes and the chemistry and physics involved in those processes.[12] The book has been widely accepted by schools offering courses in food preparation and by a few food-service companies that emphasize employee training. An Anglicized version of the book was published in 1970 in London. The "Holiday Inn University" uses most of the lecture time for discussion and motivation; students are expected to learn the technical material via the programmed instruction materials provided.

The use of the programmed instruction technique is being employed for management education as well as for employee training. J. W. Bottell, a director of Fortes Holdings, Ltd., a British hotel and restaurant chain, has programmed the company's financial control system. The program is considered so valuable

---

12. D. E. Lundberg and Lendal Kotschevar, *Understanding Cooking* (Holyoke, Mass.: Marcus Printing Company, Revised 1976).

that only one copy has been printed. The program has been assembled in one large notebook and is carried personally by a representative of the home office to each of the company's hotels. At the hotel, the manager is asked to go through the program within the next two days. The program is then carried back to the home office and locked in a safe.

EMPLOYEE STOCK OWNERSHIP PLAN

The federal government has encouraged the spreading of ownership via an Employee Stock Ownership Plan (ESOP), under which a company may contribute a percentage of its earnings to a trust, which then buys stock in the company; in effect, a retirement plan funded with the employer's stock. A big appeal of the plan is that the earnings contributed by the company to the trust are not taxed. The maximum that a company can contribute each year is 15 percent of the compensation of the participants in the plan. That amount is treated as a tax deduction for the company. Since a corporation normally pays 50 or more percent of its profits in corporation taxes, the company in effect contributes nothing. The federal government subsidizes the plan. Further encouragement for such plans arises since companies having them are allowed an additional 1 percent investment credit on any new investment, for example, equipment. A 10 percent investment credit is allowed any corporation. Those with ESOPs get an added 1 percent tax credit. The ESOP is designed on the assumption that when employees are part owners of the company, they have added incentive to make it profitable and have a different feeling about the capitalistic system.

Briefly, when a company establishes an ESOP it creates a trust that borrows from outside sources to buy stock from the company at the market price. As the company pays off the loan, the stock is allocated to employees in proportion to their salaries. The employees become stockholders and when they leave, they collect their ESOP stock from a trust fund that has been established. They receive a tax break in that they can use "forward averaging," approved by the IRS and which has the effect of spreading the income over ten years. If the stock has appreciated, it is taxed as a capital gain rather than as straight income—another tax break.

The company itself gets an additional tax break when it establishes an ESOP. A company is allowed to claim an additional 1 percent credit for money used to pay off an ESOP loan.

Each year the company contributes to the trust, which continues to buy the company stock at a price determined by outside experts or by the stock market. If the plan continues, ownership of much of the stock passes to the trust, and from the trust to the employees. The amount of stock distributed to an employee is based on a percentage of his or her earnings and time with the company. The employee is "vested" in ownership at the rate of 10 percent a year. After ten years, the employee is fully vested and has 100 percent ownership of the stock accumulated for him or her by the trust.

As stock is distributed to employees (usually treasury stock), the stock of old stockholders is diluted, and eventually control of the company can pass to the employee stockholders.

The International Restaurant Supply Company of Los Angeles, which introduced an ESOP program in 1973, has found it very effective in stimulating efficiency, cost control, and pride in the company.

Profits that ordinarily would have been paid to the federal government in the form of corporation taxes have been used to purchase company stock. In their experience, earnings have risen sharply since the inception of the ESOP. Ownership that had been closely held is now being shared with employees according to each employee's wage or salary and length of service with the company. The old stockholders expect to pass control of the company to the employees, but since the old owners are also active in management, they, too, receive shares of the stock and have seen the value of their stock increase.

HOSPITALITY BUSINESS
AS LABOR INTENSIVE

The hospitality business is obviously labor intensive, and as industrialized societies raise wages and salaries, the cost of service climbs. In the past, industrially advanced societies have attracted less advantaged groups who are more than willing to work for relatively low wages. As long as these labor streams are available, the costs of hospitality have been kept relatively low. This is a changing condition in the advanced nations.

Consider the fact that one or two persons are needed to service a full-service hotel room, and it is easy to see why the cost of the room has increased so fast. Add to this the fact that the cost of the room itself, the capital investment of a downtown hotel, is anywhere from $20,000 to $70,000 per room; and it is understandable why room rates climb to $50 or $60 a day.

In the restaurant business, low-cost labor has been and hopefully will continue to be available in the form of young folks, teenagers, and students in their twenties, who are quite ready to work at the minimum wage.

As labor costs and capital costs increase in the industrially advanced countries, vacations to those countries are likely to be shortened. Destinations where cheap labor is available increase in appeal because of low cost and the fact that the cost of transportation via air for the pleasure traveler is going down relative to other costs. It is quite possible that it will be cheaper to fly 1,000 persons per plane to Portugal, Spain, Mexico, or Cuba and to live more cheaply than at home. The British have been doing so for years in Spain.

THE RIGHT ROOM RATE

How to determine room rates has been the subject of much discussion and dispute. The idea, of course, is to "optimize" profits by charging a rate that will bring the most profit but is not high enough to discourage the guest from coming or returning in the future. The starting point is to settle on a rate that will cover all costs and still provide a reasonable profit. Once this figure has been determined, the rate can be increased as much "as the traffic will bear," without antagonizing or driving off the guest.

In computing the room rates for a seasonal operation, it must be remembered that about three-fourths of the total revenue of the resort is usually taken in during the peak season, which may last only three or four months. The high season rates must be set accordingly.

Rates Based on Projection of Expenses and Anticipated Profit

One way to determine a room rate is to work backwards: find the total revenue that is needed to break even, add the profit that is expected, and divide by the number of rooms that will be sold in the upcoming year. The Hubbart Formula, developed by the two national accounting firms and named in honor of Roy Hubbart of Chicago, who was the major proponent of the plan, is the best known plan for arriving at a room rate.[13]

It is a formula for estimating the number of rooms that will be sold in the coming year. This number is divided into the amount of money that will be needed for the total operating expenses plus a fair profit. The resulting figure is the room rate that is needed to meet expenses and to make the profit.

As an example, suppose that in a one-hundred-room house the total income needed for expenses and profit is $200,000. On a predicted occupancy of 70 percent, the number of rooms that will be sold in the year is 25,550. Suppose the house costs $2 million and that the owner expects to make 15 percent profit on the investment, or $300,000. The owner needs to take in $700,000 in the course of the year to meet costs and to make a profit. Dividing $700,000 by 25,550 gives him an average room rate of about $27.40.

Recognizing that other factors may be more important than a mathematical computation, the computation is still worthwhile as a guide.

At one time, much attention was paid to developing a proper room mix, the right number of singles, doubles, twins, and suites, that would make it possible to offer a range of room sizes, quality of furnishings, and rates to the hotel guest. It has been found that in the usual transient hotel the suites are the last rooms to be sold. Suites also return the least revenue per square foot.

In convention hotels, however, suites are usually in demand by companies wishing to use them as hospitality suites. The newer convention hotels have a number of suites.

The motels offer a one-size room with two double beds and have demonstrated the value of such an arrangement. Unless a motor hotel is certain that its market will be largely for the single business traveler, most of the rooms will be doubles. A double room can be rented at a single rate to the single traveler and is also available for the couple or for the family.

Rate Cutting

When business is slow the inclination of the motel or hotel owner is to reduce room rates. "There's no business like slow business." A sign goes up outside the motel, "$15 or $20 Monday through Thursday," or some other rate cut. Resorts have always cut rates drastically during their off-season, and transient hotels have a number of special rates: for groups, for commercial people, for students, weekend packages, and so on.

No less a person than Ernest Henderson believed that reducing rates was one way to increase occupancy. In the early 1960s he did just that for all the Sheraton Hotels. Some of the less desirable hotels and blocks of rooms in some of the better Sheraton Hotels were labeled "Sherwyn," and their rates were drastically reduced. He reasoned that by increasing total occupancy the extra profits from increased food and beverage sales would more than compensate for the loss in rates. Later, Sheraton rates were quietly increased.

The accountants have likened the results of rate cutting to the wages of sin, and they can draw up charts to prove it. Laventhol and Horwath, one of the two international accounting firms specializing in hotel and restaurant accounting, drew up Table 4–2 to show how much occupancy must increase to meet various levels of rate cutting.

It is seen that to compensate for cutting room rates by 20 percent when the hotel in question has a 64 percent occupancy, the occupancy level must be raised to 77.2 percent.

Countering these statistics is the fact that "a room not sold tonight is revenue from that room lost forever." What actually happens is the granting of discount rates to all and sundry, the corporate traveler, the weekend getaway, the senior citizen, the AAA member, military personnel, the "package tour" traveler, and so on. Those people who could not plan their trip or is not in a favored category pays the posted (rack) rate.

13. *The Hubbart Formula*, American Hotel and Motel Association.

TABLE 4-2 352-Room Suburban Hotel

Present Occupancy Level	The Price of Rate Cutting Based on 1981 Data*			
	Occupancy Required When There is a Room Rate Reduction of			
	5%	10%	15%	20%
78%	81.6%	85.6%	90.0%	94.9%
76	79.5	83.4	87.6	92.4
74	77.4	81.1	85.3	89.8
72	75.3	78.9	82.9	87.3
70	73.2	76.7	80.5	84.8
68	71.1	74.4	78.1	82.2
66	70.0	72.2	75.8	79.7
64	66.9	70.0	73.4	77.2

*Monthly fixed expenses were $396,349 and variable expenses were $13.46 per occupied room. The percentage of net income to total sales expected at each occupancy level was added to variable expenses.

Source: The U.S. Lodging Industry

Then there is the flexible rate, the rate that is quoted according to the time of day, the current occupancy in the hotel, and how full the general vicinity is at the time. The person who calls from the airport gets one rate, and the "walk-in" gets a higher rate. In times of low occupancy, discounting disguises rate cutting but it amounts to about the same thing.

The $1 per $1,000 Rule

A rule of thumb for determining room rates is that $1 should be charged for each $1,000 invested per room. If a one-hundred-room hotel costs $2 million, the cost per room is $20,000—and the room rate necessary for a fair return on the investment would be $20.

The usual Holiday Inn Motel costs $15,000 to $20,000 a unit, so the rate based on this formula would be $15 to $20. Of course, the actual rate is much higher.

Calculation of the $1 rate per $1,000 building cost assumes a 70 percent occupancy over the life of the hotel and management good enough to show a 55 percent house profit on room sales. House profit is defined as all profits except income from store rentals, and before deduction of insurance, real estate taxes, depreciation, and other capital expenses. It as-

sumes that store rentals are enough to offset real estate taxes and interest charges on the land. Calculation further assumes that the hotel will show a 6 percent return on the total investment.

The average rate being discussed is not the rate advertised by the hotel. Average rate includes double occupancy. As percentage of occupancy increases, so does the average rate. Less expensive rooms sell first and as they are sold out, higher priced rooms are sold, raising the average rate.

By the 1970s, hotel costs—at least in the big city downtown areas—had risen to the extent that the $1 per $1,000 rule no longer applied. When the hotel room cost from $40,000 and up to construct, it was impossible to charge the $40 or more average room rate. A profitable room rate depended on a number of factors: contributions from sub-rentals, the assumption that the food and beverage operations would be profitable (and many were), and the cost of money used to construct them. Several of the large city hotels built in the mid 1970s were part of the urban redevelopment plans of various cities, and the developers were able to secure money at less than the going rate through the Economic Development Administration from the cities involved and elsewhere. In some cases, the land cost them nothing: feasibility studies and the determination of a room rate had to be tailored to the particular property, and the $1 per $1,000 rule of thumb was not relevant. That rule probably still applied to the motor hotels, which could still be constructed at somewhat reasonable cost on the outskirts of cities and towns.

In the last analysis the room rate is what the market will bear, a combination of a number of factors, including general economic conditions, competitive rates, and what is necessary to sustain an acceptable rate of return. The expense account hotel, the hotel that caters to the business traveler, is likely to post much higher rates than the property catering to those who pay their own travel costs.

If a property continues to lose, the owner has the choice of upgrading, selling, or, in a few cases, changing the product or seeking a different market.

The rule of thumb of trying to attain a room rate of $1 per $1,000 invested has been modified to include the cost of land, building, and equipment; and a return of 10 percent on invested capital has been selected as a minimum goal by the firm of Laventhol and Horwath.[14]

A rule of thumb is only a guide since occupancy rate and the ratio of food and beverage sales to room sales vary widely from one hotel to another. Generally speaking, the greater the ratio of restaurant sales to room sales, the higher the occupancy or room rate needed to achieve a desirable return on the investment. The reason for this is that food and beverage sales do not produce the high percentage of profit generated by room sales.

Room Rates Up

Room rates, like taxes, have a history of going up and will probably continue to do so. The average room rate has increased year after year since 1936. In that year the average room rate was $3.03; by 1940 it had increased to $3.29; in 1945 it was $4.00; in 1950, $5.71. Rate increases have occurred month after month until, by 1982, the average room rate as reported by Pannell Kerr and Forster was $54.08 (see page 53).

The traveler may well ask, "Where can I find a $30 room?" Certainly not in the major cities or in the leading hotels. In the new budget motels, yes. Rates are much higher in the convention cities of the north, lower in the south and in the small towns. Many resort hotels have even higher rates but usually include some meals and services in the rate. In 1981 the rate for two persons at the beautiful Mauna Kea hotel in Hawaii ranged from $210 to $280 per day, two meals included.

The Budget Motel

The so-called budget motel appeared on the American highway in 1962. Arbitrarily defined as a fairly new property that has room rates 30 to 50 percent lower than the established nationwide chains—and part of a chain organization, it is either a franchise or owned by a chain.[15]

The definition excludes older or less expensive independents that have low rates because of obsolescence. Growth of the budget motel was slow until about 1970 when it mushroomed across the southern United States, so that by 1974 more than 65,000 rooms existed in such chains as Motel 6, Days Inns, Scottish Inns of America, and Econo-Motor Hotels.[16] The first of such chains, Motel 6, was started in Santa Barbara, is now a subsidiary of City Investment, Inc. of New York City, and is headquartered in Los Angeles.

What starts out to be a spartan, limited operation is often added to with time. The hamburger chains of the 1960s began to add other sandwiches, and the budget inns began to add conveniences and facilities in the 1970s. Days Inns of America, Inc., Atlanta, now offer gasoline stations, a restaurant, gift shop, swimming pool, children's playground, and coin-operated laundries. Of some 250 properties in 1976, 90 percent contained a Tasty World Restaurant, offering a low-priced menu made up of items pre-portioned and vacuum-packed. Purchases are made company-wide and on future contracts, signed months in advance.

The budget properties are usually located near one of the established national chains, such as Holiday Inns, Ramada Inns, or Howard Johnsons, where the budget property attracts the price-sensitive traveler. The lower room rate is possible because of lower construction costs, and, in some cases, the complete absence of public space and restaurants, and a minimum of land and landscaping. Management is often a husband and wife team, the husband having retired from the military or other business in many cases. Management salary is usually supplemented by a bonus plan.

The rooms are quite adequate and well-furnished in most cases. Carpeting is likely to be shag rug; there is likely to be pay television and sometimes a small pool to attract the family trade. Most of the chains are regional in character and have not developed the more costly reservation systems using computers.

Typically, 10 percent of the motel investment is in the land. Television is leased. Cost of

14. "An Updated Formula for Rating Guest Rooms," *Lodging* (January 1977).

15. Hart and Erickson, "Economy Motels—Threat or Opportunity?" *The Cornell Hotel and Restaurant Administration Quarterly* (November 1973).

16. H. Robert Rosenbrough, "A Prospectus on Budget Motels," *The Cornell Hotel and Restaurant Administration Quarterly* (November 1973).

furniture, fixtures, and equipment runs from $750 to $1,000 per room. Modular or prefabricated construction techniques are often used in building the motel, and most of the rooms are slightly smaller than the typical new hotel room of the national chains.

One-piece fiberglass shower stalls with rounded corners to reduce bathroom cleaning time is the rule. Disposable plastic glasses eliminate glass washing. Maintenance teams operating from a regional office visit each property at intervals and do routine repairs and painting. Only emergency work is done by local contractors. On-premise laundries reduce linen cleaning costs. The absence of restaurants further simplifies management and controls.

Using the modular construction permits quick entry into a market and avoids the cost of interim financing. Investment in 1981 was $15,000–$25,000, per room, compared to $35,000–$45,000 for a full service motor hotel. Up to 20 percent higher in the Northeast than in the South and Southeast because of the need in the North for interior corridors and additional insulation.

Occupancy rates usually run higher than the conventional motel and, because of the absence of services, operating expenses were lower.

There is little doubt that the budget motel has intruded on the established motor hotel and motel scene, and will force a leveling or even decrease in room rates in those areas where there are a number of budget properties.

Table 4–3, comparing budget and full-service motor hotels, was prepared by Laventhol Horwath in 1981. As seen, the budget property may cost as little as half that of the full-service motor hotel. Land requirement, two to three acres, for a budget, is one to two acres less than for the motor hotel because lobbies are smaller and there is no restaurant or bar as an integral part of the building. Operating costs are less because of fewer employees in the budget: twenty-two employees as compared with fifty-eight for the full-service motor hotel.

As a consequence, the budget motel average rate in 1981 was $21.21 versus $37.67 for the full-service motor hotel. The end result was that several of the budget motels ran 85 percent occupanies, several points higher than the full-service offering.

TABLE 4–3 Comparison of Budget and Full-Service Motor Hotels

	Budgets versus full-service	
	100-room typical budget property (1)	100-room typical full-service motor hotel (1)
Total construction cost per room	$15,000–$25,000	$35,000–$45,000
Number of acres	2–3	3–4
Total employment (full-time equivalent)	22	58
Gross square footage per room (2)	350–450	550–650

(1) Assumes two-story construction with surface parking
(2) Includes corridors and public space

Year-to-date trend as of May 1981 (Average rate per occupied room)	
Motor hotels	$37.67
Budgets	$21.21

Source: Laventhol and Horwath, 1981.

Special Rates

The price-insensitive traveler prefers the established multiple-serviced motor hotel or motel and is not concerned with the room rate. The same person, though, traveling at personal expense, will often pick a budget property, especially if it is new, clean, and reputable. It is interesting to note the number of expensive automobiles, including Cadillacs, parked in the budget motel parking lot.

The international chains—mostly airline-owned—have also found it necessary to provide less expensive rooms. Room rates in such cities as Tokyo, Paris, and London skyrocketed during the early 1970s and even the affluent traveler began cutting back travel plans or changed to a less expensive destination.

Inter-Continental Hotels introduced their version of a budget hotel—Forum Hotels: self-service is emphasized with vending machines on each floor, buffet breakfasts, and self-service restaurants. Registration and baggage handling is expected to be automated.

European Hotel Corporation—owned by Alitalia, British Airways, Lufthansa, Swissair, and TAP—is a similar chain of moderately priced hotels called Pentas. Room rates of about 30 percent less than that of first-class international are made possible by the absence of bellmen, automated room service, and other cost-cutting practices.

The commercial rate—a reduced rate for regular guests—started sometime before 1915. The traveling individual, usually a salesperson, began asking for the lower rate and usually got one a little lower than was charged the few tourists or other travelers who were in the hotel. The idea prevailed, and still does, that the commercial person, since he or she is a regular patron of the hotel, is entitled to a lower rate than the occasional visitor. Later, during the great depression, many hotels permitted the commercial person to bring his or her spouse along at no extra charge. As is the case with the family plan presently in vogue, cries of "rate-cutting" were heard by those hoteliers not engaging in the practice.

Hotels in resort areas that cater to both commercial people and vacationers have a real problem of separating the sheep from the goats. The goats are those experienced travelers who ask for the commercial rate while traveling as tourists during the peak seasons. The problem can be solved by requiring the person asking for the special rate to have stayed in the hotel at least three times during the off-season.

When the motel first appeared, the practice was to rent the room at a price regardless of the number of people who occupied it. Hotels characteristically rented a room on the basis of the number of people occupying it. The so-called family rate was so popular in the motel that eventually most hotels began offering special rates for family groups. The hotel is more likely to charge a double rate for each room occupied, adding a small charge for setting up roll-away beds.

The "rack" rate, the published room rate, is not the average amount of money received for a room. A number of discounted rates are often offered. The average room rate is the amount actually received, the total amount of room revenue, divided by the number of rooms rented. The average rate reflects double occupancy and the discounted rates.

It is also customary to offer reduced rates to groups and to provide a certain percentage of the rooms on a complimentary basis. Such "comp" rooms are usually occupied by the executive secretary of the group or some of the officers. Seasonal resorts have an off-season rate that may be only half or less than half of the high-season rate.

Hilton, Sheraton, and a number of other chains offer reduced rates to students and faculty, and on many campuses they employ a student representative to publicize the availability of such rates. The Sheraton-Student-Faculty Plan, for example, allows a slight reduction to faculty, administrative personnel, athletic teams, and students during the summer, weekends, and the low period between December 15 and January 1.

Package plan rates, which usually include transportation and lodging, and sometimes meals, are likely to be arranged by a travel agent in cooperation with an airline and hotel or a group of hotels. The rate is often the same as the guests would pay if they had no package plan, but the guests do not know this.

Guaranteed Maximum Rate Plan

Rates for hotel rooms listed in the *Hotel Red Book* range from low to high. But how many rooms are available at the minimum rate? Often, the minimum rate room is an oversized broom closet located next to the elevators or in some other unlikely spot.

One of the biggest headaches of innkeeping is to maximize room sales without "going overboard." Going overboard is selling more rooms than are available in the house. The operator wants to get as close to 100 percent occupancy as possible, and when hotel rooms are in short supply, hotels have operated at 100 plus occupancy, beds being turned over more than once in a twenty-four-hour period. Consequently, the typical hotel manager is likely to take more reservations than he or she has space, anticipating that a certain percentage of the people reserving will be "no-shows."

Many regular travelers, aware of the problem of overbooking, reserve at more than one hotel to be certain of getting into at least one of their choices. Certain reservations are less likely to show than others; for example, MDs are an unsure bet. Weather plays a part. But what happens when a guest with a confirmed reservation appears and has no room at the inn? Quite naturally, the guest is furious; one sure reaction is ill will toward the house.

Various systems have been devised to take care of this emergency. The usual policy is to arrange to get the confirmed guest to another hostelry. Some companies pay the person's cab fare to the other hotel. The Sheraton, for a long time, issued the guest a certificate worth $20 in any Sheraton property.

To assure the guests that they will receive the rate they requested, several chains have established a Guaranteed Maximum Rate Plan. This program guarantees business travelers who qualify a preset maximum rate for accommodations. TraveLodge, for example, has such a plan in effect for more than 1,000 companies.

A flurry of complaints published in the press in the middle 1970s, coming from consumer groups, placed greater emphasis on taking care of the guest with a reservation who appears and finds no room available. Holiday Inns assure such people that if 6 P.M. reservations are not honored, the Inn must secure comparable accommodations, pay any difference in room rate, pay for transportation to the substitute property, and pay for phone calls to family or business to notify them of the change. If the guest has a guaranteed all-night reservation and there is no room, the Inn also pays the full cost of the first night's lodging. The guest must cancel by 6 P.M. to avoid being billed through his or her credit card companies. Those inns that require advance deposits but accept guaranteed reservations by credit card in lieu of a deposit require a seventy-two-hour cancellation notice. Quality Inns International has a similar plan. When a guaranteed reservation is not honored, the Inn must provide and pay for an alternate room elsewhere, pick up the transportation costs to the new location, and pay for one phone call.

When travelers guarantee their room through a credit card and do not show, the credit card company pays the hotel for the first night's lodging regardless of whether or not the guests recognize their responsibility to pay.

THE BREAK-EVEN POINT

Every hotel and motel has a break-even point, the percentage of occupancy necessary to pay all operating expenses including interest on indebtedness. Since the national average on occupancy for hotels and motels is between 60 and 70 percent, the break-even point for the average hotel and motel is obviously lower than 60 percent. The break-even point, of course, changes with wage rates, efficiency of operation, and rise in costs. It also changes with the room rates charged.

A one-hundred-unit motel might have a break-even point as computed here:

Total operating expense	$240,000
Real estate taxes	30,000
Insurance	6,000
Depreciation	40,000
Interest	54,000
Total annual expenses	$370,000
Total daily expenses = $370,000 ÷ 365 days =	$1013.70

In other words, the motel must take in $1013.70 each day to break even. If the motel's average room rate is $20, it must sell at least fifty rooms a day to break even. Its break-even point is 50 percent. The illustration does not consider the food and beverage operation and other revenue departments.

The break-even point is that point at which the income covers both fixed and variable expenses, where no profit is made. Break-even points are difficult to compute, but the concept is valuable. According to the firm of Laventhol and Horwath, the break-even point in 1979 for all hotels and motels in their nationwide sample was a room occupancy of 58.3 percent. The break-even analysis chart for the hotels and motels in the Laventhol and Horwath sample (Figure 4–5) shows that the fixed expenses for that year for the median hotel or motel was $5,938 per available room. In other words the usual hotel or motel in this country for the year 1979 had some $5,938 in expenses, which were fixed for each room, regardless of occupancy level. Total revenue was $254.11 per available room for each 1 percent in occupancy. Variable

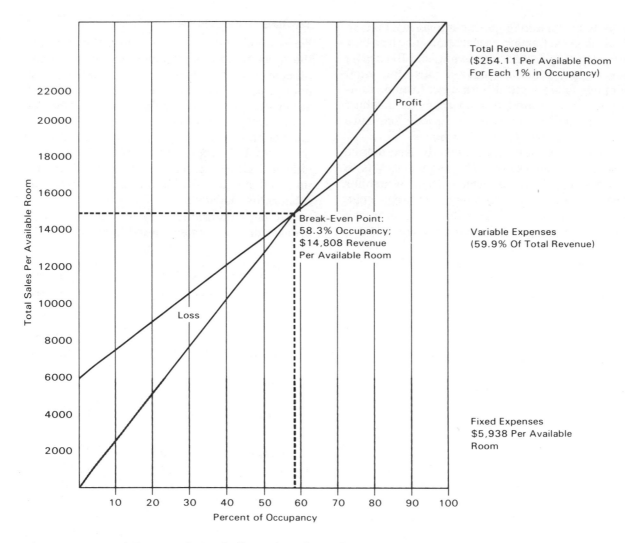

Figure 4-5   *Break-Even Analysis of All Hotels and Motels, 1979*
Source: Laventhol and Horwath, *U.S. Lodging Industry,* 1980.

expenses amount to 59.9 percent of total revenue. The chart shows that $14,808 in sales were needed per available room per year just to break even.

The break-even point analysis is a graphic way of pointing up the fact that once the break-even point is reached, profit rises sharply (the distance between total revenue line and the line representing fixed and variable expenses). In the chart, for example, on a 58.3 percent occupancy there is no profit; but at 100 percent occupancy the profit per available room would exceed $6500 a room.[17]

---

17. Laventhol and Horwath, *The U.S. Lodging Industry,* 1980.

HOTEL MONOPOLY

Can a hotel or group of hotels develop a monopoly and fix prices? A large majority of people staying in first-class hotels are expense-account travelers, many with unlimited expense accounts for hotel bills. Such people will not go to any great effort to stay outside of the area, nor will they stop at a less desirable class of hotel.

Monopoly in the classical sense is not possible in the hotel business over a wide area because of the relative ease of entry into the business by individual corporations. Within a city or small area, and among first-class hotels, however, monopoly or oligopoly (an industry characterized by few sellers) would be possible. In the country as a whole, Thomas Powers has pointed out, only 2 percent of the properties and 4 percent of the rooms are controlled by the eight largest chains.[18] However, in local markets, chains control a very sizable portion of the market. Chains may also have competitive advantages not possessed by independent or smaller operations in their reservation systems, credit arrangements, national advertising programs, and extensive guest services.

According to Horwath and Horwath, "When hotel guests start to economize, first they reduce the amount they spend for cocktails and other alcoholic beverages, then they begin spending less for meals, and their last step is to take more moderately-priced rooms than in the recent past."[19] In effect, if there is a shortage of hotel rooms within a particular trade area, a group of first-class hotels could exercise a limited monopoly. People who are not on expense accounts or unlimited expense accounts—or those who are naturally frugal or parsimonious—will not be affected by the monopoly. They simply stay outside of town or in less expensive hotels or motels.

Indeed hotels have been convicted of price fixing. In 1977 four hotel companies and the Hawaii Hotel Association pleaded "No Contest" to criminal charges of conspiring to fix Hawaii hotel room rates. The Sheraton Hawaii Corporation and the Hilton Hotel Corporation were each fined the maximum $50,000. Cinerama Hawaii Hotels and Flagship International were each fined $25,000, and the Hotel Association was fined $10,000. The price fixing took place during 1971–1972 when visitor totals to Hawaii dropped and many new hotels had opened. Room rates had been cut to below break-even points, while tour operators and travel agents pitted hotels against each other and obtained net room rates that were often 15 percent below rack rates (and lower) for groups. The hotel operators felt some kind of price fixing was necessary to survive.[20]

18. Thomas F. Powers, "The Competitive Structure of the Hotel/Motel Market," paper presented to the Council on Hotel, Restaurant, and Institutional Education, 1969.

19. The Accountant, LKH&H, vol. 42, no. 11 (1962).

20. Travel Weekly (May 1977).

THE LODGING DOLLAR, INCOME AND OUTGO

Each year two international accounting firms, Laventhol, Horwath and the firm of Pannell Kerr Forster, publish an annual survey of the financial results of the lodging business in the United States, providing the most reliable financial statistics for the industry for the preceding year. These studies have been conducted for many years and give a running account of the financial health of the business. Data are collected from the client hotels and motels of the two companies. Therefore, they do not represent the entire industry and are probably biased in favor of the more successful enterprises. Figure 4–6 shows the source of the lodging income and the manner in which most of it was spent. The percentage of income produced by each department is shown below:

Guest room rentals	58.9
Food sales	25.3
Beverage sales	10
Rentals and other income	1.6
Telephone sales	2.6
Minor operated departments	1.6

For the typical property, then, food and beverage sales constituted about 38 percent of the total income; the other departments contributed about 6 percent of the income. Of course, any individual hotel may have a widely different breakdown of income.

Percentages of the income dollar that were spent by each department were as follows:

Payroll and related expense	33.9
Rent, property, taxes and insurance	9.4
Departmental expenses	10.7
Food costs	8.0
Depreciation	5.8
Administrative and general	6.7
Interest	4.7
Energy	4.3
Marketing	3.0
Property operation and maintenance	3.0
Beverage cost	2.2

With these costs net income before taxes was 8.3 percent of sales.

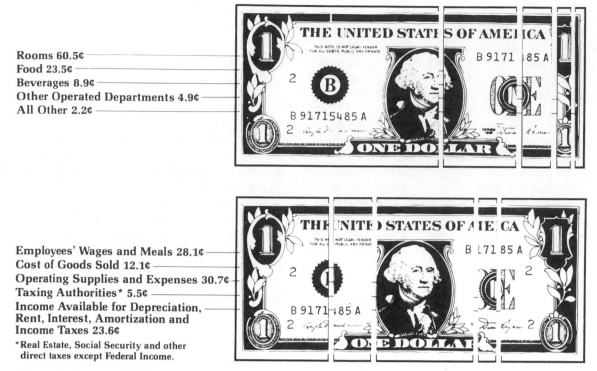

Rooms 60.5¢
Food 23.5¢
Beverages 8.9¢
Other Operated Departments 4.9¢
All Other 2.2¢

Employees' Wages and Meals 28.1¢
Cost of Goods Sold 12.1¢
Operating Supplies and Expenses 30.7¢
Taxing Authorities* 5.5¢
Income Available for Depreciation,
Rent, Interest, Amortization and
Income Taxes 23.6¢

*Real Estate, Social Security and other
 direct taxes except Federal Income.

Figure 4-6 *1000 HOTELS AND MOTELS—Source and Disposition of the Industry Dollar, 1982*
Source: Prepared by Pannell Kerr Forster, 1983.

According to the accountants then, net income before income taxes constituted only 8.3 percent of revenue. It should be remembered that the depreciation, 5.8 percent of the income, was part of the cash flow. Energy costs have almost doubled since about 1972. Marketing costs, constituting 3 percent of the income, would be more representative of the larger property than of the smaller one.

The fact that the depreciation rate is 5.8 percent suggests that most hotels are being depreciated as quickly as possible. If the average hotel took a depreciation of 5.8 percent of its total income, the property would be completely depreciated in about seventeen years. At that time or before, the property would probably change hands so that a new owner could start with a new tax base of 100 percent of the market value of the property.

NEW MANAGEMENT AND PLANNING TECHNIQUES

An emphasis on "management style" is finding its way into the hotel and restaurant field. The style of management refers to the way manage-ment acts in motivating people. In the past, the style of management in a hotel and restaurant business has been, to a large extent, autocratic.

The manager presumably knows what should be done, how it should be done, and when it should be done, and does not hesitate to tell all concerned exactly when and how things should be done. Planning presumably is done only at the top. The boss orders; employees obey. The system works well if the employees are conditioned by their upbringing and temperament to respond to an autocrat. Many of the most successful restaurants and hotels in the world are run largely by an autocratic style of management.

The new style of management, labeled "participative management," involves much more two-way communication between boss and employee. Management is by objective, objectives that presumably are at least partly arrived at jointly by boss and employee. Participative management, however, is not democratic management. The boss must retain the full burden of responsibility for final results. The manager involves most employees in problems and in goal-setting, but his or her is the final determination and the responsibility for profit.

Participative management lends itself to team building where the emphasis is on change, challenge, and group goals. Saga Food Administration, for example, asks each of its unit managers to spend at least an hour each week in group meetings with employees developing team feeling. Participative management conceivably can change the nature of innkeeping for the better.

Recently some hotel and restaurant companies have adopted advanced management training methods and policies. Management by objective, or management by results, is a management system being used by Sonesta. Under this plan each supervisor and his or her superior independently establish, in writing, goals for the next six months. They then meet and together determine the six-month goals for the department. At the end of the six months, the supervisors are asked to itemize—again in writing—what they think their work achievements have been for the previous period. The list is sent to their superior who adds any achievements to the list that the supervisors may have overlooked. The superior at this time assesses the quality of performance by the supervisors. This, too, is placed in writing and given to the supervisors to read.[21]

Sonesta has also developed an interesting management team approach to opening new properties. The team, the six to ten people involved in the opening, go off to a relaxed setting for a two- or three-day session that is led by a skilled consultant. The general manager of the new property and all department heads are asked to describe the assigned role in the new hotel as it appears to the individual. They state their broad areas of responsibility and authority and agree on who is responsible for what. After the opening of the property, follow-up meetings are held to check results and to review the various commitments made at the first meeting. With change taking place at an unprecedented rate, a growing number of companies in the hospitality business are becoming involved in strategic planning (also known as long-range planning).

Typically, companies engaging in long-range planning develop a strategy covering a five-year period. The main purposes of such a plan are to specify the overall objectives of the company, to establish the main courses of action that the company will take to achieve these objectives, and to determine the resource requirements necessary for these courses of action. A five-year horizon (as opposed to four or six years) is commonly used because many security analysts request financial information pertaining to this particular time frame.

These companies also develop short-range plans covering one- and two-year horizons. The one-year plan outlines specific tactics to be carried out during the year and summarizes anticipated financial results. A two-year plan is necessary in some cases because of the eighteen- to twenty-four-month lead time associated with the real estate and construction activities of restaurant and lodging operations. As presented by James Crownover, long-range planner for Saga, the strategic planning process consists of five major steps:[22]

1. Establishing a business definition
2. Setting long-range objectives
3. Diagnosing current company operations
4. Developing strategies for meeting long-range objectives
5. Determining implications of strategies:
   a. Financial resources
   b. Top management resources
   c. Organizational structure

THE BUSINESS DEFINITION

A hotel, restaurant, or foodservice company should be able to state in one sentence the overall purpose of the company. The statement should describe the services or products to be provided and the customer group or groups to be served with these services or products.

Establishing a business definition is particularly important because it provides a foundation upon which the corporate strategy is based. The business definition should not be overly narrow: everyone is familiar with the example of the railroads defining themselves as being in the railroad business rather than the transportation business. Nor should the definition be so broad that it fails to give the company

21. See Lundberg and Armatas, *Management of People in Hotels, Restaurants and Clubs* (Dubuque, Iowa: William C. Brown, 1979).

22. Much of this section is based on a lecture presented by James Crownover, at California State Polytechnic University, 1976.

proper direction in identifying and evaluating alternative strategies.

Examples of business definitions mentioned during the symposium were:

1. "Providing food and feeding services to people who eat away from home."
2. "Providing medium-priced, relatively speedy foodservice to the traveling public on major highways in or near cities of populations of at least 100,000."

3. "Operating major hotels that serve business people and high income travelers in major capitals around the world."

The business definition can be modified if circumstances change dramatically inside or outside the company, but should not be changed on a year-to-year basis.

More on long-range planning is covered in the last part of the chapter on restaurant operations.

ROOM SALES TERMINOLOGY

Like all specialized businesses, the hotel and motel business has coined a number of words and terms peculiar to the business. Among those terms dealing with room rates are the following:

AP (Full American Plan): rate includes three full meals and rooms (full board or full pension).

Bermuda Plan: rate includes room with full American-style breakfast.

Commercial Rate: rate agreed upon by company and hotel for all individual room reservations. Often given to any regular guests who are known to be commercial travelers.

Comp: complimentary, no charges for room.

Confirmed Reservation: an oral or written confirmation by hotel that a reservation has been accepted (written confirmations are preferred). There is usually a 6:00 P.M. (local time) check-in deadline. If guest arrives after 6:00 P.M. and the hotel is filled, the assistant manager makes every effort to secure accommodations in another hotel. (This does not apply to guests with confirmed reservations where "late arrival" has been specified.)

Cut-off Date: designated day when buyer (upon request) must release or add to function room or bedroom commitment. On certain types of groups, rooming lists should be sent to the hotel at least two weeks prior to arrival.

Day Rate: usually one-half regular rate of room, for use by guests during a given day up to 5:00 P.M. Sometimes called a "use rate."

Demi-Pension (European Usage): rate includes room, breakfast, and either lunch or dinner.

Deposit Reservation: a reservation for which hotel has received cash payment for at least first night's lodging in advance and is obligated to hold the room regardless of the guest's arrival time. Guest is preregistered.

Cancellation Procedure: can be cancelled as early as possible but a minimum of forty-eight hours prior to scheduled date of arrival in a commercial-type hotel. For resort hotels, guests should verify cancellation policy at time of making reservations.

EP (European Plan): no meals included in room rate.

Farm-Out (Walk): sending guests who have reservations that cannot be honored to other hotels with vacancies. This is done when there are no rooms available even though guests have reservations.

Flat Rate: specified room rate for group, agreed upon by hotel and group in advance.

Full Comp: no charges for anything taken in hotel including room, meals, telephone, and valet.

Guaranteed Payment Reservation: room set aside by hotel, at request of the customer; payment for room is guaranteed regardless of whether the guest appears unless reservation is properly cancelled.

Guaranteed Reservation: a confirmed reservation with the promise to accommodate, or, if unable, to pay for a room elsewhere, including transportation involved. Guest guarantees to pay if a no-show.

MAP (Modified American Plan): rate includes breakfast, dinner, and room.

Preregistered: no delay check-in, usually provided guests who have stayed in hotel previously; often room assignments based on guest's previous preference.

Rack Rate: current rate charge for each accommodation as established by hotel management.

Run of the House Rate: an agreed-upon rate generally priced at an average figure between minimum and maximum for group accommodations for all available rooms except suites; room assignments usually made on a "best available" basis.

Source: Georgina Tucker and Madelin Schneider, *The Professional Housekeeper,* 2nd edition (Boston: CBI Publishing Company, 1982).

HOTEL/MOTEL OPERATIONS TERMINOLOGY

Daily report a management report prepared daily by the income auditor. The report's content varies, but will usually include: (1) source and summary of sales, (2) room statistics, (3) summary of cash receipts, (4) bank account analysis, and (5) accounts receivable analysis.

Daily room count report a form prepared daily by the night room clerk (from the room rack) that indicates: (1) the occupied rooms, (2) the number of persons in each room, and (3) the rate charged for each room.

Due bill a type of voucher, issued by the hotel in exchange for purchased advertising, that may be used as a credit against specified hotel charges.

Engineer's log a record maintained by the hotel's chief engineer of periodic meter readings, inventories, and consumption of water, electricity, and fuel oil.

Front office the office situated in the lobby, the main functions of which are: (1) control and sale of guest rooms; (2) providing key, mail, and information service for guests; (3) keeping guest accounts, rendering bills and receiving payments; and (4) providing information to other departments.

Front office cash sheet a form used daily by each front office cashier to record all cash receipts and disbursements, itemized as to name, room number, and amount.

Function a prearranged, catered group activity usually held in a private room or area. It may be a cocktail party only, or it may be a banquet, which includes food service.

Function room a special room that is used primarily for private parties, banquets, and meetings; also called banquet room.

General cashier's daily summary a form prepared daily by the general cashier to summarize all cash turned in by the departmental cashiers, which should be reconciled with the day's bank deposit. This report should show, for each cashier and in total: (1) total cash received, (2) paid outs, (3) cash over and short, (4) due backs or exchange, and (5) actual cash turned in. The cash receipts journal may be entered from this report.

Guest account an itemized record of a guest's charges and credits, which is maintained in the front office until departure; also referred to as guest bill, guest folio, and guest statement.

Guest history card a record maintained for each guest who has stayed in the hotel with a separate entry for each visit. Among other things, it can be used as a valuable reference by the reservations and credit departments.

Guest ledger the caption used for trade accounts receivable of guests in the hotel. These accounts are generally maintained in the front office and must be updated throughout the day to avoid undue delay when a guest checks out.

House a synonym for hotel commonly used within the industry. Examples are: full house, house count, house income, house bank, and house charge.

Housekeeper's report a report prepared each morning by the housekeeper based on an inspection of each room by the maids to indicate whether a guest room was occupied or vacant the previous night.

Information rack a visible alphabetical index of guests in the hotel, used at the telephone switchboard and in the front office to facilitate delivery of mail and messages.

Linen control sheet a record kept by the housekeeper of all linen and uniforms sent to and received from the laundry to account for shortages and damages.

Maid's report a form used daily by each maid to report to the housekeeper the status of each guest room based on inspection. The housekeeper's report is prepared from all of the maids' reports.

Mail and key rack a series of pigeonholes numbered to represent each guest room, used to hold room keys and guests' mail. In addition, a series of alphabetized pigeonholes is used to hold mail for expected guests.

Master account the guest account for a particular group or function that will be paid by the sponsoring organization. (*See* **Guest account**)

N.C.R. a commonly used term identifying the National Cash Register Company, a major supplier of mechanical and electronic machines especially designed for hotels, restaurants, and clubs.

Occupancy, percentage of the percentage of available rooms occupied for a given period. It is computed by dividing the number of rooms occupied for a period by the number of rooms available for the same period.

Officer's check a special type of restaurant check used for gratis meals served to hotel staff in a public room.

(continued)

Out-of-order a guest room that is temporarily unsuitable for occupancy and is not to be sold. Generally used to designate rooms being redecorated or in which some maintenance work is being performed.

Overbook accepting reservations for more guest rooms than are available.

Point-of-sale equipment mechanical or electronic devices that, in addition to serving as cash registers, generate sales, control, accounting and management reports; may or may not be part of a computer system.

Pre-cost a food control technique based on forecasts of menu items to be sold and predetermined menu item costs used to establish a potential.

Preregister to register guests before they check into the hotel. This is done to reduce delay and confusion at the registration desk for persons attending conventions and other organized groups expected to arrive at about the same time.

Prime cost the combined cost of food and labor in a food service operation; usually expressed as a percentage of sales.

Public space any area in the hotel that is accessible to the general public, including dining rooms, bars, lobby, and function rooms.

Receiving clerk's daily report a report prepared daily by the receiving clerk listing all merchandise received, and showing cost distribution.

Registration card a form on which arriving guests record their names and addresses and which the room clerk completes as to room number, rate, and length of stay. Some form of guest registration is required by law in each state.

Reservation deposit an advance payment required to obtain a confirmed guest room or function room reservation.

Restaurant cashier's sheet a form used by each cashier in the restaurant on which all guest checks used are recorded. Separate columns for food sales, beverage sales, cover charges, and tips facilitate summarization.

Room change slip a form filled out by the room clerk whenever there is a change in the status of a guest room other than a new registration or a vacated room.

Room rack a special rack with a drop-pocket for each guest room bearing the corresponding room number. Its purpose is to provide a visible index of the exact status of each guest room at all times.

Room rack card a paper card or slip inserted in the appropriate pocket of the room rack when a room is sold. The card should show: (1) room number, (2) guest's name, (3) city of residence, (4) number of persons occupying the room, (5) daily rate, and (6) arrival and expected departure dates.

Room rate and inventory rack card a card for each guest room, which remains permanently in the room rack. It should show the fixed rate structure, bed capacity, and other pertinent information.

Rooming slip a form filled out by the room clerk for each registered guest showing name, room number, and rate. A copy is given to the guest to avoid any subsequent dispute regarding room changes. Other copies are sent to the mail and information desk and telephone switchboard.

Skipper a guest who departs without checking out or paying the bill.

Store rentals revenue derived from the rental of space, usually on the ground level with street access, for businesses that are not ordinarily a part of hotel service.

Telephone traffic sheet a form used by the telephone switchboard operators to record all long-distance telephone calls.

Trade advertising contract an agreement whereby the hotel agrees to purchase advertising space or time in exchange for hotel accommodations and, possibly, restaurant service. (See **Due bill**)

Transcript the daily recapitulation of the guest ledger, prepared by the night auditor in a manual system.

Undistributed operating expenses a group of operating expenses that are not distributed to the operated departments. The general captions for expenses are: (1) Administrative and General, (2) Marketing, (3) Guest Entertainment, and (4) Property Operation, Maintenance, and Energy Costs; also referred to as deductions from income.

Uniform System of Accounts for Hotels a manual outlining and describing a system of uniform classification of accounts for hotels, which has been adopted by the American Hotel & Motel Association.

Waiter's signature sheet a form used by the food checker or cashier to control the issuance of guest checks to service personnel. Each server must sign for checks received (identified by number) and must account for their use.

Source: *A Guide To Terminology in the Leisure Time Industries*, Laventhol & Horwath, Philadelphia. No date.

Questions

1. About how many employees do you expect would be needed in a one hundred-room motor inn without a restaurant?

2. Hotels-motels are often built and operated by the same individual or group. Name three other ways in which a hotel or motel is operated.

3. The large hotel chains today favor which means of operation—ownership, management contract, or franchise? Explain why.

4. The principal owners of the very large hotels in this country turn out to be members of what business?

5. Around the turn of the century the Ritz hotels were highly fashionable in several parts of the world. Were they all owned and operated by the Ritz Company or was there some other arrangement?

6. Be able to name two advantages to the franchisor and two advantages to the franchisee of a franchise arrangement.

7. Name at least two disadvantages for the franchisee and two for the franchisor.

8. By far the largest franchisor of accommodations in the world turns out to be what company?

9. Besides the Holiday Inns franchise arrangement, what other well-known franchises are available in the hotel or motel business?

10. The larger hotel or motel, something over 300 rooms, that installs EDP equipment would probably first put it to use in what two areas of operation?

11. In reservation systems, a cathode ray tube is often used in what way?

12. Explain a room status system and its advantages for a large hotel.

13. In a large hotel catering to businesspeople large numbers of guests want to be awakened at 7 A.M. How can this be done without a large number of hotel personnel being used?

14. In larger hotels a sales staff of several persons are on hand largely to solicit group business. What other functions do they perform?

15. Be able to define these commonly used terms dealing with room sales: Rack Rate, MAP, AP, EP, Commercial Rate, Full Comp.

16. Increased vigilance to insure guests' safety stimulated a number of new security systems including the Lok-A-Wat, plastic cards for keys, beeper systems, and television monitors. Explain the function of each.

17. What is the big advantage of hiring off-duty regular police officers as security personnel in a hotel?

18. Who are likely to be the three highest paid persons in a large hotel?

19. In some hotel chains the auditor or financial officer in each hotel does not report to the general manager of that hotel. Why?

20. What is the name of the most prominent union that deals with hotel employees in the hotel and restaurant business? It is headquartered in what city?

21. What advantages are there for a hotel proprietor to establish an Employee Stock Ownership Plan?

22. As employee costs rise in the hotel and restaurant business what effect does this have on tourism in the less developed countries?

23. In establishing a room rate, the Hubbart Formula factors into the formula all the operating costs, other costs, and one other important factor. What is that other factor?

24. An old rule of thumb for establishing a room rate is the $1.00 per $1,000 rule. Based on this rule a hotel that has cost $40,000 per room to build would charge an average rate of what amount?

25. The dollar per thousand rule of thumb for deriving a room rate can be modified in the light of certain operating experiences. Name some.

26. In the light of experience over the past fifty years, what is the outlook for room rates—up, down, or sideways?

27. Besides the rack rate, hotels offer a number of other rates. Name a few of them.

28. When a guest is "walked," sent to another hotel because of no vacancy, some hotel chains are providing the guest with what to minimize the resentment?

29. How would you explain the meaning of the "break-even point" for a hotel?

30. Is it possible, or has it ever happened, that a group of hotels have exercised hotel monopoly? Explain.

31. Which sector of the economy is most closely tuned to hotel occupancy—wholesale trade, food processing, retail trade, or finance and insurance?

32. What ranks right after guest room rentals as the source of hotel income?

33. The principal cost in operating a hotel turns out to be what?

34. If someone were to say that the net income of a hotel is at least 10 percent of sales, what would be your reply?

35. The allowance made for depreciation in a hotel runs about 7 percent of the income. Where does this 7 percent go?

36. Some of the major hotel chains are setting objectives for a long period of time. Usually the period covers about how many years?

37. Define a budget motel.

38. Is participative management democratic management?

39. Describe "management by objective" as applied to a hotel.

Discussion Questions

1. The Japanese are said to be winning the battle of productivity as compared to us in the United States. Can we expect the Japanese to outcompete us in the world hospitality business and soon control major international hotel and restaurant companies? Give reasons for your answer.

2. As of 1982 the most profitable hotels worldwide were the better Mexican hotels. Why?

KEMMONS WILSON (1913-　　)

Holiday Inns is the largest innkeeping operation the world has known. It incorporates more guest rooms than the Sheraton and Hilton corporations combined. Yet, the man who created the company is little known in hotel circles and probably considers himself more of a promoter, builder, and salesman than an innkeeper, and more an entrepreneur than a professional hotelman.

Kemmons Wilson started Holiday Inns in 1952. In 1976, Holiday Inns had more than 1,700 motels in fifty states and twenty-five foreign countries. (About one-fifth of them are company-owned—the rest are franchised.) Total rooms in 1982 numbered more than 306,312.

Wilson did for the motel business what Statler did for the hotel business. He brought relative luxury to the middle class at prices they could afford. He standardized motel keeping just as Howard Johnson standardized the roadside restaurant. All three men—Wilson, Statler, and Howard Johnson—insisted on cleanliness, relative uniformity, and careful attention to maintenance. Such practices endear a product or service to the middle class who want, above all else, predictability and safety in lodging and food.

Kemmons Wilson was born in 1913 in Osceola, Arkansas. A year later, his father died, and his mother took him to Memphis. He learned business early. At fourteen, he was a delivery boy for a Memphis drug firm and at seventeen set himself up in the popcorn business—with a popcorn popper bought on $50 credit. He sold so much popcorn at a theater that the manager bought him out.

Wilson took the proceeds from the sale of his popcorn business and bought five ancient pinball machines. Later, he purchased an old airplane, prevailed upon the seller to teach him to fly, and sold dollar rides around country towns. Dorothy, his future wife, sold tickets; his mother sold popcorn. Later, he went into the construction business, building homes, and eventually built and operated seven movie houses. He also had a Wurlitzer distributorship. During World War II, in 1943, he sold his businesses for $250,000 and for the next two years served as a flight officer in the Air Transport Command.

The idea for Holiday Inns, he says, came as a result of a vacation trip with his family. It was "the most miserable vacation trip of my life." For poor accommodations he was charged $10 a day plus $2 for each of three children. Here, he thought, was "the greatest untouched industry in the country."

In 1952 Wilson borrowed $300,000 from a bank and built the first Holiday Inn at a cost of $8,000 per room, including the cost of the land. It offered large rooms and two double beds. Most important, it offered a restaurant. Most motels of the day were too small to operate a restaurant. The new owners knew little about foodservice.

The first Holiday Inn was an instant success and still operates with an occupancy exceeding 80 percent. It was so successful that three more were constructed the same year. From the beginning, when he built four Holiday Inns in Memphis, the inns were geared for the family trade and the commercial person. No charge was made for children under twelve. This was more or less a standard practice in the motel business but not the case with hotels.

Every Holiday Inn had to have a swimming pool, another appeal to the family and an added note of luxury. At the time some motels offered free TV; Wilson included free TV, free ice, and a telephone in every room.

In 1952 motels were springing up all over the nation, but most were still relatively small, less than 30 rooms. Wilson built large motels; the structures were imposing and attractive. By 1975 the average Holiday Inn motel exceeded 125 units.

There were 10,000 requests for franchises each year; Holiday Inn accepted 200.

The "Great Sign" used as entrance display by the Holiday Inns is enormous as compared with the usual motel sign, and expensive. The sunburst lighting and a huge lighted space for posting advertising and welcome notices made Holiday Inns stand apart from the many nondescript smaller motels that might be in the neighborhood.

From the outset Wilson realized the tremendous advantage of a referral system. Once a customer stays at a Holiday Inn, he or she is likely to remain in the Holiday Inn system for the rest of the trip. Holiday Inn makes it so simple that the guest follows the path of least resistance. At first, long distance calls were placed by the innkeeper to the other Holiday Innkeepers. The customer paid for the call. Today, the entire reservation and referral system is operated by computer, Holidex, at no charge to the guest.

A referral system increases in value as it enlarges. With each new franchised Holiday Inn, an additional 100 to 200 travelers are fed into the system. Each new Holiday Inn also adds to the attractiveness of this system for the traveler who has one more choice of a motel at which to stop. The more inns in the system, the more valuable it becomes to the traveler and to the individual franchise holder. In peak months 1,000 reservation agents are on duty in the Memphis reservations headquarters.

From the beginning, Holiday Inns has been more of a team effort than most hotel or restaurant chain developments. In 1952, the year Holiday Inns was established, Wilson sought out the active partnership of Wallace Johnson, another Memphis builder, and together they formed what was to become Holiday Inns.

Someone in Holiday Inns, probably Johnson, saw the tremendous advantage of setting up a joint credit card with Gulf Oil Company. Gulf Oil advertises Holiday Inns, Holiday Inns advertises Gulf Oil, to the advantage of both companies. Gulf Oil has also made available large sums of money for Holiday Inns growth. The money has not been used but has permitted Holiday Inns to secure lower interest rates on money it has borrowed. A number of Gulf service stations have opened adjacent to Holiday Inns.[1]

Key to the phenomenal growth of Holiday Inns has been the franchising plan. Franchising permits a company to grow as rapidly as there are people with the money and credit who will buy the franchise. Holiday Inns essentially interests other people in investing and borrowing to become a

---

1. Wallace E. Johnson, *Work Is My Play* (New York: Hawthorn Books, 1973).

part of the Holiday Inns system. Investors of all kinds purchase a franchise to erect a Holiday Inn and to pay the company a daily fee for operating. As long as present franchise holders are successful and make a profit on their investment, more doctors, lawyers, and businesspeople seek to have a motel with the "Great Sign" at the entrance. Franchisees pay the Holiday Inns company about 6 percent on their gross sales.

Holiday Inns is a hospitality conglomerate and has gone over the billion-dollar mark in sales. In 1969 Holiday Inns acquired by merger the TCO Industries, Inc., which controlled Continental Trailways (second largest intercity bus system in the United States) and Delta Steamship Lines, Inc. Operating twenty-five industry-related companies, Holiday Inns with TCO becomes a food, lodging, and transportation system.

By the middle 1970s some of the luster of Holiday Inns was lost as energy costs rose sharply, budget motels attracted some of its market, and inflation and recession cut back travel.

In the period 1975–1980 the Holiday Inns divested itself of some thirty companies, ranging from manufacturing to aircraft sales to food processing and food distribution. Proceeds of the sales were invested into hotels. In 1979, Holiday Inns entered the gaming market by acquiring Harrah's Corporation with a cash and stock deal valued at 300 million dollars. About 100 million dollars was acquired by selling the Trailways subsidiary. The Holiday Inns International Division never made a profit before 1977 and shifted its marketing efforts to localized markets rather than the international market.

The new Holiday Inns of the 1980s are a far cry from the motel company of the 1960s. Most are full-blown hotels; in fact, some are the biggest and best hotels in their area. By 1980 the company had over 1,800 outlets in all fifty of the United States and fifty-six foreign countries. About 350 of them were company owned and managed; the rest were franchised. Total revenues from their Delta Lines (twenty-four vessels), casino hotels (Gaming Group in Reno, Lake Tahoe, Atlantic City, and Las Vegas), and Perkins Cake and Steak restaurants and hotels exceeded $1.5 billion.

In 1974 Roy E. Winegardener was elected Vice-Chairman of the Board of Holiday Inns and Chief Operating Officer. Mr. Winegardener, a pioneer Holiday Inns licensee since 1958, runs the Hospitality Group of Holiday Inns and is directly responsible for the more than 300 company properties which range all the way from two-story roadside inns to highrise hotels and luxury resorts. In 1978, Wilson quietly sold a large percentage of his Holiday Inns stock. In effect, he was no longer in control of the company.

5 Hotel Food and Beverage Operations

In all except the smaller hotels and motels, food and beverage service is expected by the traveling public. For many hotel managers this service presents as much as 80 percent of the problems of managing the property. Much of the hotel's reputation centers around its food and beverage service; much of the appeal of the hotel is in decor, atmosphere, and the service offered in the restaurants and lounges. F & B sales constitute 35 to 45 percent of total sales in the typical larger hotel, but may exceed room revenue in some instances. F & B sales exceeded $5 billion in hotels/motels in 1978 (hotels $3 billion; motel and motor hotels $2.4 billion). Several of the larger hotels experienced F & B income exceeding $10 million annually and the MGM Grand Hotel had F & B sales of more than $35 million.

After the housekeeping department, the food and beverage department employs the most people in the usual hotel. The department is usually headed by a food and beverage director or an executive chef. The department may be divided into restaurants and catering, the catering covering responsibility for banquet sales and service.

The tavern, the predecessor of the hotel in the United States, was the center of community activity and was likely to be the only place where the general public could eat away from home. Service was family-style; food, and sometimes beer or ale, were served as part of the total charge for bed and board. In the South,

some of the larger taverns offered separate dining facilities for ladies. Foodservice became definitely associated with the taverns and later with hotels so that today, by some definitions in some states, a property is not a hotel unless it offers foodservice as well as rooms to the public.

When the hotel, with its larger size, displaced the tavern, it was expected to offer foodservice, and the grander properties in the cities had several dining rooms and at least one ballroom. These "palaces of the people" were the scenes of public and civic entertainment as well as a place where guests could eat and drink.

The "city ledger" was set up to account for sales to other than hotel guests, and much of the success of a larger hotel depended on the promotional skill of the general manager in attracting food and beverage functions into the property. Ceremonial banquets quite naturally were held in the leading hotels of a community, one reason being that there were often no other suitable places to hold them. Famous hotels like The Astor and the old Waldorf-Astoria in New York City became known for their food as well as for their rooms. The hotel dining room of the usual town throughout the United States in the early 1900s and into the 1930s was one of the few first-class eating facilities available. Civic and fraternal clubs held their luncheon and dinner meetings in the hotels, and, except for the private clubs, the hotel became the logical place to meet for entertainment and business

Figure 5-1   *The Garden Court of The Sheraton-Palace Hotel in San Francisco was originally called the Grand Court and was used as a carriage entrance to the hotel. The original Palace Hotel, opened in 1875, was built in the form of a hollow square surrounding a great Sun Court filled with palms and flowers. The original Palace Hotel was destroyed by the fires brought on by the earthquake of 1906. In the Garden Court today there are ten enormous chandeliers, each valued at $50,000. The Gold Service, reputedly one of the oldest and the most complete in the world, adds grandeur when it is used for important functions.*

discussion. Well-known restaurants operating independently of hotels were scarce even in the large cities.

THE BEGINNINGS OF
FOOD COST CONTROL SYSTEMS

Food cost control was pulled together into a system about 1910 by a little-known genius, Fred Baudissin. Hotels, clubs, and restaurants around the country, but especially in the Chicago and San Francisco areas, got Baudissin's Food Control System together with Baudissin for a flat fee or a percentage of the increased profits gained as a result of the system. Getting Baudissin was not always a happy experience, since he was highly temperamental and periodically addicted to the bottle. Some of the chefs were downright hostile to any system, Baudissin or otherwise, which precluded private financial arrangements with purveyors.

One French chef informed Baudissin that he was leaving but that his brigade would remain on the job. After a day or so, during a particularly heavy luncheon, the new chef noted a dreadful silence in the kitchen. Not a cook was in sight. Soon they could all be heard, marching down the street, singing "La Marseillaise." Baudissin had anticipated just such a misadventure and had a roomful of cooks standing by to take over where the dissidents left off.

Baudissin had an uncanny way of studying a food operation, then appearing before the board of directors and predicting within a few dollars the number of dollars he would save. Two books—a Blue Book and a Red Book—were his operating tools. The Blue Book referred to profit figures rather than to red ink figures. Each department in the kitchen—ice cream, pastry, meat, and so on—was kept informed of its progress under the system by monthly slips showing how the department had done. Departmental percentage sheets were kept with the percentage goal placed at the top.

Ellsworth Statler, the hotel genius, instituted a food cost control system before 1915 and later standardized menus as well as controls in all of the Statler Hotels.

Following World War II, independent restaurants and restaurant chains flourished, and by comparison the traditional hotel dining room looked rather unexciting. It was not uncommon to find a large high-ceilinged room in a hotel, well appointed, well staffed, having tables with white tablecloths, and very few customers. The hotel guests wanted to get out of the hotel for a change and to get a quick meal at a moderate price rather than endure elaborate service with the high prices found in the formal dining room.

SPECIALTY RESTAURANTS APPEAR

Hotel management reacted by installing coffee shops, and it was not too long before nearly every hotel of any size in the country had one. Then came the theme restaurant, one of the leaders being Sonesta Hotels with their Rib Rooms, and in the West, Western International Hotels. One of the first Rib Rooms opened in 1952 at The Somerset Hotel in Boston. Rib Rooms followed in other Sonesta properties, with rigid specifications in force regarding the purchase of the rib served in the room. Weight, age, trim, fat marbling, and allowable shrinkage were part of the buying specifications. Steps for cooking, carving, and service were spelled out clearly and in detail.

Larger hotels searched for themes to incorporate into different foodservices within a hotel. Hyatt Hotels, for example, now fill each hotel with up to five different specialty restaurants, ranging from snack to gourmet. Hugo's Rotisserie specializes in roasts and offers a lemon sherbet cone between courses. Hugo's Market features fanciful salad bars and self-service ice cream. There is also an Oyster Kitchen and a Ginsburg and Wong Restaurant. The latter offers the unexpected combination of lox, bagels, and fried rice. Hyatt considers all of its restaurants to be specialty restaurants.

Quite naturally, menus are slanted to fit the theme of specialty; Polynesian food for Polynesian atmosphere, French cuisine for a French

ambience, and roasted items in a rotisserie restaurant. Roast beef continues to be the number one seller in hotel restaurants.

Rules for Hotel Specialty Restaurants

According to Mr. Allen W. Hubsch, the rules for establishing a hotel specialty restaurant are:

1. Establish an easily identifiable image for specialty restaurants.

2. Create atmosphere that appeals to customers' "escapist desires"—period rooms, nationality rooms, steak houses, South Sea Island rooms, garden rooms, hearthside rooms.

3. Manage and promote the specialty rooms in the same manner used for successful street restaurants.

4. Provide direct access to the restaurants from the street or parking area.

5. Merchandise and advertise the specialty rooms separately.

When following these rules, Sonesta has produced departmental profits far and above those usually obtained:

Banquet sales (including beverages)—20 to 25 percent profit.

Beverage sales in bars and cocktail lounges—40 to 50 percent profit.

Specialty restaurants (including beverages)—20 to 30 percent profit.

Outside Management for Hotel Specialty Restaurants

A number of hotels have leased out their specialty restaurant facilities to established foodservice companies. The specialty restaurants that require highly specialized knowledge are often run by persons or companies not directly connected with the hotel.

Hilton Hotels, for example, have contracted with Victor Bergeron, the originator of Trader Vic's, to operate a number of his restaurants in Hilton Hotels. The restaurants are built to Bergeron's specifications and cost from $500,000 to about $750,000. Bergeron receives a management fee for their operation. The first

Trader Vic's was opened in Oakland about 1937. By 1969, there were eighteen such restaurants. The Trader Vic's restaurant needs about $1 million in sales to be really profitable. The food costs run about 32 percent of gross sales; the labor costs about 34 percent.

Not every city is a good market for a Trader Vic's restaurant. The one in The Statler-Hilton in Boston did not break even for almost a year after its opening and required about three years to achieve the $1 million sales figure. The Trader Vic's in The Houston Hilton required a number of years to break even. In other cities, gross sales of $2.5 million a year have been achieved.

Trader Vic's menu is merchandised as being Polynesian. Actually, all Polynesian-style restaurants feature Chinese cookery. The Trader Vic's menu, instead of being reduced as is customary, has been expanded and includes a number of French specialties, such as frogs' legs saute, grenadins of veal, chicken cordon bleu, kidneys saute, scallops mariniere, scrod meuniere, and baby carrots au beurre.

Kon-Tikis, a similar Polynesian-style restaurant group, are found in Sheraton Hotels. They, too, are managed by an outside group —Stephen Crane Restaurants, Inc.

FOOD AND BEVERAGE DEPARTMENT ORGANIZATION

The organization of food and beverage departments varies around the country and with chain policy. Hotels with large group business usually separate the catering function from the regular restaurant operations, the catering function being much more profitable than the restaurants. The organization for The Century Plaza Hotel of Beverly Hills, Calif., an Akstin Hotel, represents the newer thinking in organization (Figure 5-2). The director of food and beverage reports directly to the resident manager and general

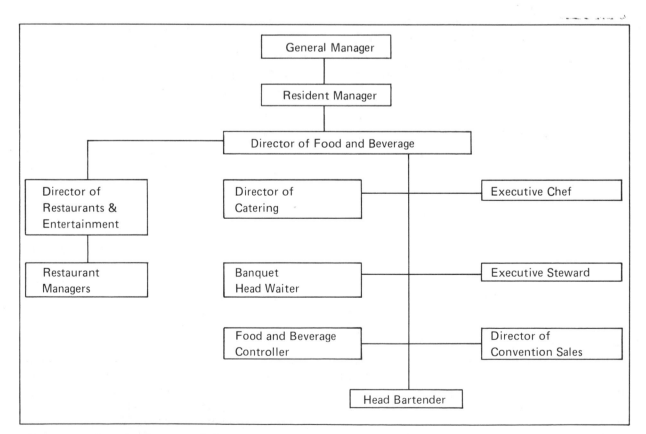

Figure 5-2 *Century Plaza Hotel chart of organization—food and beverage department.*

manager. Responsible to him are the director of restaurants, the director of catering, and the executive chef. (Often the executive chef is responsible to the director of restaurants.)

In the case of The Century Plaza Hotel, the food and beverage controller prices each banquet menu daily and prices the restaurant menus twice a year. He also operates the forecasting system for the food and beverage department. He conducts sales analyses, butcher tests, and can-cutting tests. He makes monthly reports and produces a profit and loss statement for each unit. He also helps in allocating expenses and assists in taking the inventory and making forecasts. The Century Plaza's organization is somewhat unusual in that a director of convention sales lives with a group once they are registered in the property, seeing to it that all of their needs are met. He becomes their "man Friday" and, being completely familiar with the hotel and with the various people involved, can cut across department lines to accomplish whatever is needed for the group.

More than half of the food and beverage business at The Century Plaza is done in catering, about half of the catering being generated by conventions. Half the total revenue of the hotel—about $9 million—is generated by the food and beverage department. The Century Plaza has three restaurants plus a Yamados, a restaurant that is leased to an independent operator. The ballroom seats 2,000 people.

Within the F & B department is an Operations Committee concerned with making suggestions that will help to produce a profit plan. The F & B department in 1976 employed 413 persons.

Food costs for the entire F & B operation of The Century Plaza runs about 30 percent, whereas in the catering department it runs 25 percent. Labor costs in the F & B department of the hotel continued to rise, the fringe benefits going up even faster. In the case of The Century Plaza, fringe benefits added another 35 percent to the wage cost.

A typical hotel, unlike the large properties represented by The Century Plaza, is in the 100- to 300-room category, represented by chains such as Holiday Inns, Roadway Inns, and Ramada Inns. An organization chart of the food and beverage department in such a property is seen in Figure 5-3.

KITCHEN ORGANIZATION

The organization of a traditional kitchen in a large hotel may include a number of specialized craftsmen and women such as an oyster man, a

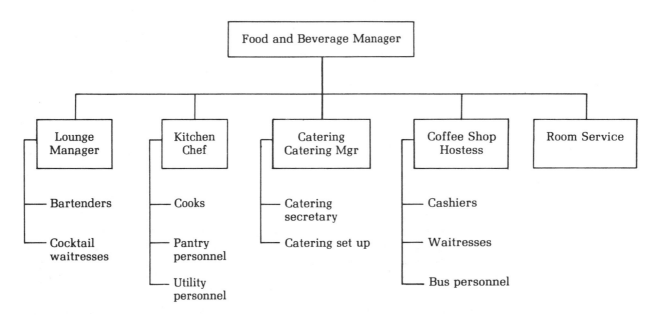

Figure 5-3 *200-room motor hotel—food and beverage department.*

garde manager, a chicken butcher, roast and broiler cooks, vegetable cooks, bakers, sugar workers, ice cream makers, and pastry chefs. The executive chef would have reporting directly to him a night chef, a sous chef, and perhaps a pastry chef.

In traditional kitchens a kitchen steward would be in charge of kitchen sanitation and all the personnel related to performing that function. He or she might also act as purchasing agent for food and other supplies.

In large hotels a resident auditor may be in charge of all bookkeeping and accounting taking place in the property. The night auditor and, in some instances, every cashier in every restaurant reports to the auditor rather than to the restaurant manager. A restaurant cannot even open until the cashier arrives on the scene. All cash and accounting of restaurants' sales goes directly to the auditor's office in such instances. Each restaurant may have a food checker located in the kitchen who prices all food as it leaves the kitchen. That person inspects the food for appearance and whether or not what is taken out of the kitchen corresponds with what is written on the guest check. The practice of having a food checker, however, is fading in this country.

THE CATERING FUNCTION

In a large hotel the catering function is set up as a separate department with a catering manager and special sales personnel reporting to that person. At the operational level a maitre d'hotel may be in charge of the actual banquet setup with head waiters, banquet waiters, and sometimes room-service waiters reporting to him or her.

A catering manager in a hotel, unlike a British manager of the same title, usually deals strictly with group meals and has little to do with the restaurant operations. (In Britain the term *catering manager* is equivalent to restaurant manager or food and beverage manager.)

A catering manager is concerned mainly with working with persons who are arranging for group functions, such as weddings, banquets, bar and bas mitzvahs, anniversary dinners, and so on.

Over the years imaginative hoteliers have produced banquet extravaganzas, as much

drama as meal. History offers plethora of examples, from the Roman orgy to the state dinners of Louis XIV. Louis, who insisted upon centering the attention of France upon himself, used his meals as a public performance. The food was delivered to the Sun King by selected nobility. As it passed the long route from the kitchen across courtyard and into the dining room, the food itself was bowed to by the people as it passed. Before the King would touch it, a marquis tasted it for flavor and, importantly, acted as a guinea pig to ascertain the presence of poison. Anyone could attend the State dinners provided they owned or could rent a hat and a sword.

Some banquets around the turn of the twentieth century were pure theater; one banquet was served with all guests seated on horseback, another served to guests in boats floating in a quickly made lake in the dining room. Today's banquets are much more quietly produced, but some are still presented with fanfare.

ROOM SERVICE

It is agreed that to be a first-class hotel, room service must be available even though that room service may constitute a loss operation. After all, the hotel is a service organization, a convenience. Room service is a hallmark of a first-class hotel and may constitute up to 15 percent of total food and beverage sales. Deluxe hotels may maintain floor pantries from which room service operates. Press a button and in seconds a room service waiter appears.

Successful room service depends on getting the food to the room as quickly as possible. To do a good job, proper equipment is necessary—equipment that will keep hot things hot and cold things cold. Someone must be in charge who is a good organizer, who gets "mise en place" (set up) ready so that the waiter has nothing to do but pick it up and deliver the order.

Breakfast accounts for 70 to 90 percent of room service and perhaps three-fourths of the orders are for the Continental breakfast. "Doorknob" programs—guests check off breakfast items and the delivery time desired on a special card that is hung on the outside of the doorknob—work well. The cards are collected at night so that the service tables can be set up and some of the food prepared, ready for delivery in the morning.

Some hotels allocate a service elevator for exclusive use of room service during the morning rush. The elevator may contain heating and refrigeration units plus space for bread, rolls, linens, and condiments. In some cases Continental breakfast orders are phoned directly to the elevator operator who transports waiters and carts to the designated floors.

Some hotels limit the room service hours; some operate them twenty-four hours a day. Menus are often specialized for room service only; in other cases, guests can order from room service menus or from the menus of any of the hotel's restaurants.

To keep the room service profitable, room service menus are usually priced more highly than the restaurant menus. Some hotels add a service charge.

In the larger properties, captains oversee each room service shift; in the small hotel, the bellman, busboy, or regular waiter makes the room service delivery.

MENU MONOTONY

Hotel banqueting is often the butt of jokes because of menu monotony—"the chicken and pea circuit." After-dinner speakers tell of the "blahs" reaction from having to "stare at the rear end of a rock cornish hen night after night" in hotels around the country. Catering managers reply that actually there are relatively few menu items acceptable to a large group; beef and chicken are favorites because of average taste preferences, cost, and food preparation factors.

Quite naturally when an item such as Beef Wellington proves popular at one hotel it will almost certainly be seen on a number of other hotel menus in the area very soon. Because of the relative ease and brief time to produce a chicken, that product will probably remain inexpensive and a favorite on the banquet table. It is difficult to pick entrees that are acceptable to everyone at a banquet: someone can't stand veal, pork, or fish. Most people will like lobster or crab but are unwilling to pay the price. Veal is also expensive and appears only at a luxury price. Steak is difficult to cook and serve quick-

ly to a large group. The consequence: beef and chicken are the ubiquitous banquet choices. Even so, a multitude of choices in preparation and presentation for beef and chicken can make these items interesting. Buffets are time consuming to prepare and present but can offer something for everyone.

CATERING PROFITABILITY

Banquet sales, or catering sales as they are called in a hotel, can be profitable for several reasons.

1. Banquets can be priced higher than restaurant meals. Banquets are often included in a total package price for a group. For some reason there is less resistance to a higher-priced banquet price than to a restaurant meal price.

2. Income is assured based on a guaranteed number of participants. This permits easy forecasting and less waste in food preparation and in labor.

3. Labor costs are usually comparatively low because waiters are hired for a definite period of time, no longer than needed.

Offsetting these factors are the following:

1. The return on the investment of banquet space is often low and some of the costs connected with banquets are high.

2. Groups holding banquets in the evening usually tie up the banquet space for the entire evening. If banquet space is not used for meetings, that space is idle between meals; often it is occupied only for one meal a day, or not at all.

3. Waiters and waitresses are employed for the four-hour period or at least receive four hours pay if unionized.

4. Compared to a restaurant the seat runover is very low. In a four-hour period a restaurant seat might turnover four to eight times.

BEVERAGE OPERATIONS

While the food business in the usual hotel may not be very profitable, the beverage business usually is. Bar and lounge operations can be highly profitable since "cost of goods sold," and the costs of labor to serve, total a relatively small percentage of the sales dollar. Cost of beverages sold usually runs something under 25 percent of the sales.

In the large convention hotels, beverage costs are often less than 20 percent of sales. In a busy bar or lounge, labor costs are not likely to exceed 15 percent of sales. Profit in a popular bar can be spectacular. The Polaris, the revolving bar at the top of The Regency-Hyatt House in Atlanta, has had sales of close to $100,000 a month with only one bartender on duty. Departmental profit for that bar would have to be at least $50,000 for the month.

The average hotel can expect a departmental profit of 50 percent on the sale of beverages. The sale of beverages in the usual hotel runs about 25 percent of the dollars sold of food. Of course, this figure varies. In family restaurants, beverage sales may run 10 percent of food sales; in some country clubs, beverage sales exceed food sales.

The bar must be located near the heart of the hotel; otherwise, patrons feel left out, which is exactly what they do not want. Robert Sage, president of the Fenway Motor Hotels of Boston, found that moving a bar from the back of one of his motor hotels to the front increased sales 250 percent.

Hotel bar sales as a proportion of total F & B sales are usually much higher than in a non-hotel restaurant. One rule of thumb reads:

Hotel sales—100 percent

Food sales—50 percent

Bar sales—25 percent

In other words, bar sales would run about half of food sales. In many hotels bar sales run a much higher percentage because of the several lounges independent of or semi-dependent on the restaurants. Cocktail parties also increase the proportion of beverage sales to total sales. (In a non-hotel restaurant serving liquor, bar sales tend to run about 25 percent of total sales.)

BREAKING THE FAST

Breakfast, breaking the night-long fast, to many a traveler reigns as the supreme test of a hotel's sensibilities, its speed, and its concern

for its friends (and hang the cost). The veteran, nondieting traveler in some of the really posh hotels will have none of the disembodied voice at the other end of the phone when ordering breakfast. How much better to press a little button on the wall and find a waiter at one's door three minutes later. The newly arrived floor waiter then proceeds to inquire how one wants the coffee brewed, strong or light, and what else the guest needs to be fortified for the day.

Within a few minutes the floor waiter reappears, pushing a trolley over which has been spread a white linen tablecloth and on which are placed croissants, Danish pastry, two types of rolls, Ryvita, two types of brown bread, butter on ice in a dish, and perhaps three individual dishes of such things as jam, honey, and marmalade, each with its own spoon. The single flower in a vase rounds out the morning ensemble.

How different than the room-service breakfast in a large convention hotel where the guest is urged to order breakfast the evening before by checking off a list of foods and then hanging the list on the outside doorknob. Even though one or two elevators have been set aside as mobile pantries, the breakfast may still arrive a half hour late.

The Buffet Breakfast

Hotels are going to buffet breakfasts for the simple reason that a significant number of guests have appointments to keep in the morning and descend en masse on the restaurant in a surprisingly short period of time, everyone in a hurry or at least eager to get black coffee into the system and clear the cobwebs. The breakfast buffet provides the quickest and least expensive method of service. Guests can help themselves and return as often as desired. They are usually quite willing to pay considerably more for the help-yourself-to-all-you-want than for the individual table service.

The buffet permits a display and an assortment of foods that would be almost impossible to manage with complete waitress service. For many people breakfast is the best meal of the day. A theatrically presented buffet with a wide variety of foods has proved the best answer for many large hotels.

TO BE PROFITABLE

The knowledgeable general manager knows that as much as two-thirds of the food and beverage business must come from people who are not guests of the hotel. One study reported that 69 percent of the people questioned ate none of their luncheons in the hotel where they were staying, while 52 percent ate none of their dinners there. Guests are not captive diners; they want to go out of the hotel for some of their meals. Robert Sage, president of Fenway Motor Hotels in Boston, says that in his properties if a guest stays three days, he or she will eat in the hotel the first day, and eat out of the hotel on the other two days. If the hotel has several specialty restaurants, the guest staying a few days may try more than one of them. In addition, each restaurant is merchandised as a separate facility to attract the general public.

In other words, to be profitable, the food and beverage operation of the hotel must usually attract 70 percent or more of its customers from outside the hotel. One gauge of a successful general manager is that something like 50 or 60 percent of total sales is produced by the food and beverage operation. To accomplish this, the hotel and restaurant must compete with numerous independent and chain restaurants unaffiliated with the hotel—places that offer a variety of foods and ambience.

No longer can the general manager turn over the food and beverage operations to an executive chef and hope for the best. Instead, a food and beverage director who is experienced and knowledgeable in food preparation and service, as well as in marketing food and beverages, must be appointed. Much of the hotel's reputation depends on its food and beverage operation. Hotel restaurants add to or detract from a hotel's total image. Hotels become known for their good food, or lack of it. A few hotels cater off-premise parties.

Impressed with the food and ambience of a hotel restaurant, the customer may refer travelers to the hotel. To increase sales, the food and beverage manager works closely with the director of sales and the general manager. The chain hotel can usually expect help from the corporate office. The home office of the hotel chain often has a vice president in charge of food and beverage, a professional who helps establish policy, quality control, and standards for the entire chain. There may also be a corporate level executive chef who is on hand at the hotel openings, is available for consultation, and fills in when needed.

HOTEL FOOD AND BEVERAGE RATIOS

Under the uniform system of accounts for hotels, a number of ratios can be drawn from restaurant statistics, which enable the manager to compare his or her operations with other hotel restaurant operations. The ratios are not comparable to those of independent restaurants because overhead expenses are not allocated in hotel statements. A study by Laventhol and Horwath showed these costs to range from 14.1 to 23.5 percent. Each year the international accounting firms of Pannell Kerr Forster, and Co., and Laventhol and Horwath conduct surveys of the hotel and motel industry and publish the results.

A section of the 1975 HKF survey based on 300 transient hotels, is seen in Figure 5–4. The ratios change little from year to year.

It is seen that the major costs (often called prime costs), food and labor, were high: food cost of about 38 percent of sales, labor cost of about 36 percent of sales. Cost of beverage was about 23 percent of sales. As said elsewhere, the departmental profit, which was 16.4 percent of sales, is misleading because several charges are not made against the food and beverage department. Actually, the food and beverage operations of these hotels probably were very small or nonexistent.

MOTEL RESTAURANTS

The first motels sent their guests down the road to "a good restaurant." One of the reasons for the fantastic success of Holiday Inns was the fact that from their beginning each inn included a restaurant.

During the 1950s and 1960s, 25 percent of the motels were either built with a restaurant or added one. Of the new motels constructed in 1961, 50 percent had restaurants seating about 120 people. Since then, motels with restaurants have done a little better overall than those without, probably because they are bigger and attract more guests because they have restaurants.

By 1969, nearly all of the larger motels being built had restaurants or were in some way connected with them. For example, the Howard Johnson Motor Lodges are built near a Howard Johnson restaurant or in conjunction with one.

Holiday Inns have, for several years, included a number of frozen entrees on their menus. In some of the inns about 25 percent of the sales are of these items. These ready-entrees have been pre-cooked and involve only a few minutes to reheat and serve. Hilton, Sheraton, and a number of other operations also use a number of frozen entrees, but they do not publicize the fact because of possible adverse reaction by the customer.

PROFITS IN A MOTOR
HOTEL F & B DEPARTMENT

A profit and loss statement for the food department of a representative 200-room motor hotel is seen in Table 5–1. The costs and percentages are typical of a Holiday Inn or Ramada Inn type motor hotel. Food costs run about 36 percent of sales. Compared with the independent restaurant, payroll and related expenses are high, which in this case exceed 40 percent of sales.

As stated before, the food department profit, close to 19 percent, is misleading. A number of costs that would be allocated to the food department are not considered. There are no advertising and promotion costs, no administrative overhead, no real estate taxes, and no licenses. Heat, light, and power are not charged to the food department; neither is occupancy cost of the building. The 18.9 percent profit shown probably means a real profit of almost nothing.

When average beverage department profit is considered, the profit picture changes considerably. The beverage department profit and loss statement is seen in Table 5–2. Cost of beverage sold is 20.3 percent and payroll related expenses come to only 22.2 percent of sales. Total department expense was 45 percent of sales, leaving a 55 percent department profit.

CONSTRAINTS ON HOTEL
FOOD AND BEVERAGE OPERATIONS

Several reasons exist to explain why hotel restaurant operations have not been more profitable in the past:

1. Too often the general manager knew too little about menu planning, food purchasing, preparation, and service, and so was happy to turn over the restaurants to an experienced executive chef. The chef, jealous of the general manager's prerogatives and special knowledge, was not interested in educating him or her. The general manager might visit the kitchen periodically but it was more like a tour or state visit. The chef told the manager what he or she wanted to know; the manager's dignity and status remained intact; everybody was happy. Fortunately, this state of affairs has changed as

Figure 5–4   *Hotel/motel expenses.*

Food and Beverages:	
Food Sales	100.0%
Cost of Food Consumed	37.8%
Less: Employees' Meals	3.9
Cost of Food Sold	33.9%
Food Gross Profit	66.1%
Beverage Sales	100.0%
Cost of Beverages Sold	23.4
Beverage Gross Profit	76.6%
Total Food and Beverage Sales	100.0%
Cost of Food and Beverages Sold	30.8
Gross Profit on Combined Sales	69.2%
Cover Charges and Sundry Income	2.9
Total Food and Beverage Gross Profit	72.1%
Departmental Expenses:	
Salaries and Wages, Including Vacation	35.9%
Employees' Meals	2.1
Payroll Taxes and Employee Relations	6.4
Music and Entertainment	3.1
Laundry	1.1
Kitchen Fuel	.3
Linen	.4
China and Glass	1.2
Silver	.5
Menus and Drink Lists	.3
Licenses and Taxes	.2
Other Expenses	4.2
Total Expenses	55.7%
Departmental Profit	16.4%

Source: Trends in the Hotel-Motel Business, 1975 (Chicago: Harris Kerr Forster, and Co., 1975).

TABLE 5-1 ABC Motor Hotel, Profit and Loss in the Beverage Department

	Current	Percent	Year to Date	Percent
Beverage Sales	$ 24,727	100.0	272,000	100.0
Cost of Beverage Sold	4,657	18.8	55,216	20.3
Salaries & Wages	3,398	13.7	40,800	20.0
Employee Meals	142	.6	1,642	.6
Payroll Taxes & Benefits	430	1.7	5,590	2.1
Total Payroll & Related Expenses	3,970	16.1	48,032	22.7
Other Expenses				
Cleaning Supplies	33	.1	398	.1
Guest Supplies	27	.1	358	.1
China, Glass, & Silver	557	2.3	2,785	1.0
Bar Supplies	62	.3	463	.2
Uniforms	29	.1	267	.1
Decorations	85	.3	185	.1
Licenses			600	.2
Miscellaneous	400	1.6	496	.2
Total Departmental Expense	9,820	39.7	108,800	45.0
Beverage Department Profit	14,907	60.3	163,200	55.0

TABLE 5-2 ABC Motor Hotel, Profit and Loss in the Food Department

	Current	Percent	Year to Date	Percent
Food Sales	$ 49,430	100.0	$ 577,600	100.0
Cost of Food Sold	18,903	36.0	207,936	36.0
Salaries & Wages	17,882	34.0	196,710	34.0
Employee Meals	1,179	2.2	12,960	2.2
Payroll Taxes & Benefits	2,260	4.3	27,147	4.7
Total Payroll & Related Expenses	21,321	43.1	236,817	41.0
Other Expenses				
Cleaning Supplies	248	.5	3,466	.6
Guest Supplies	93	.2	1,400	.2
Laundry	27	.1	400	.1
China, Glass, & Silver	670	1.4	8,795	1.5
Kitchen Supplies	54	.1	650	.1
Linen Supplies	211	.4	2,750	.5
Uniforms	107	.2	1,500	.3
Decorations	50	.1	650	.1
Printing & Office Supplies	80	.2	1,200	.2
Telephone	50	.1	600	.1
Miscellaneous			150	
Exterminating & Waste Removal	130	.3	1,560	.3
Contract Cleaning			560	.1
Total Departmental Expense	41,944	84.9	468,434	81.1
Food Department Profit	7,486	15.1	109,166	18.9

chains have taken over much of the business as more trained food and beverage personnel have become available through the universities.

2. Many of the hotels were built in the 1920s with the old-fashioned dining rooms that were unable to keep up with the changing desires of the public. The menu was likely to be high-style, costly, and the service rather slow. To make major changes was expensive, and often the restaurant had to be relocated to have immediate access to an outside street. Hotels reacted by adding coffee shops on a street level, and hoped for the best.

3. Hours of operation of foodservices in hotels must be provided for the hotel room guests even though some of those hours might result in very low volume and unprofitable food and beverage operations.

4. A number of hotels continued to offer room service which has been one of the hallmarks of a first-class hotel. Room service is almost inevitably a loss operation because of the long distances involved in getting food from the kitchen to the guest's room, the labor costs involved in such travel, and the special equipment and space required to offer room service. Guests usually complain about the high cost of room service but fail to recognize its true cost. The deluxe hotel might have a pantry on every floor which, indeed, provides quick room service but obviously is costly.

5. If the hotel is an old one, and has acquired a certian image, it is very difficult to add a fun type of restaurant and expect people to patronize it, since it will still be part of the larger, perhaps gloomy, hotel image.

6. Food and beverage personnel in a hotel may not have the same motivation as found in a conventional restaurant. Profit-sharing and bonus plans are not as likely to be present in a hotel as in a restaurant chain, and the employee lacks the motivation for achievement that is found in the entrepreneur.

7. Because of the higher costs incurred in a hotel restaurant, prices are likely to be higher than in a comparable place outside the hotel, which results in a lower volume of sales than may be required for the hotel restaurant to be profitable.

8. As explained elsewhere, the uniform system of accounts for hotels does not allocate true costs to the food and beverage operation. The restaurant manager may have a false feeling of accomplishment when he or she sees a 15 percent departmental profit. Actually, a 15 percent departmental profit may mean a loss for the restaurant.

9. Banquet sales usually produce a low food and beverage cost, which may be thrown into the overall food and beverage cost for the entire food and beverage operation, which again may mislead management into feeling that they are more successful than is actually true.

10. Older properties are often saddled with inefficient layouts that were designed when labor costs were very low and knowledge of work flow little understood. In fact, a kitchen is sometimes a half a block from the point of service.

11. Restaurants were often located in spots so remote or hard to find that as one food and beverage director said, "A seeing eye dog was needed to find them."

MAJOR COSTS

As with any restaurant, the two prime costs in a hotel restaurant are cost of food and cost of payroll. Other departmental expenses generally make up 12 percent of the total revenue.

Productivity in the restaurants has a tremendously wide range, as found by Laventhol and Horwath. Sales per employee in some establishments are double that of others.

It should be remembered that the hotel restaurant is operated for profit. It is also there as a service to room guests. The independent restaurant can open or close as it pleases; the hotel restaurant is governed by the demands of room guest service. Another factor in the lesser profitability of the hotel restaurant is that many times coffee shops, specialty rooms, and private dining rooms, to say nothing of room service, are located hundreds of feet and often numbers of floors from the preparation kitchen.

JOB DESCRIPTION
FOOD AND BEVERAGE MANAGER
200-ROOM MOTOR HOTEL

Supervise the coffe shop, dining room, banquet service, and lounge operation. Maintain an optimum of good service while assuring maximum profitability of all food and beverage outlets.

SPECIFIC DUTIES AND RESPONSIBILITIES

—Hire, train, and terminate cashiers, waitresses, hostesses, room service, clean up, bar personnel, and kitchen preparation crew.

—Account for the numerical sequence of all checks issued daily.

—Maintain a daily missing check record. Take action, as recommended by the general manager, to correct any accounting problems.

—Test and verify the clerical accuracy on all checks for prices, state and federal taxes, and paid outs of tips.

—Keep a daily payroll record of all food and beverage employees.

—Assist the general manager in preparation of bi-monthly payrolls.

—Assist the secretary to the general manager in preparation of all P-2 forms, on a daily basis, by forwarding all necessary information to keep personnel files up-to-date at all times.

—Assist the general manager in preparation of all F/B daily reports and deposits.

—One week in advance, post a work schedule of all personnel. Schedule coverage of all banquet functions.

—Issue cashier banks for each scheduled shift, including the lounge operation.

—Verify and reconcile the restaurant register machine tapes with total revenue reported.

—Maintain counts of total meals served, comparison of register tapes against reported revenue, etc., as directed by general manager.

—Make sure that a guest check is prepared and posted correctly for each F/B transaction including employee and banquet functions.

—Assist general manager in taking the end-of-the-month inventory of all sundry items.

—Assist the general manager in purchasing sundries and make sure that all items sold are posted on the proper cash register key.

—Responsible for appearance, cleanliness, and proper set up of the coffee shop and dining room. Check the maintenance of all equipment in the dining room, coffee shop, and lounge, and request immediate repair of all damages.

—Make sure that the guests receive immediate and proper attention and endeavor to rectify any complaints, conveying them immediately to the general manager if they cannot be solved on the spot.

—Direct the activities of all service personnel in the dining room, coffee shop, and lounge. Draw their attention to guests newly seated and make sure that orders are promptly and courteously taken; observe when guests are being neglected, and urge employees to give prompt service.

—Ask departing guests if food and service were satisfactory and ask them to come back again.

—Replace, without charge, any unsatisfactory food or beverage item served to a guest.

—Direct pre-meal meetings with dining room coffee shop personnel to relay information, policy changes, and to brief personnel on up-dates of operation.

(continued)

—Call the security officer or general manager for help with disorderly guests or those apparently under the influence of alcohol.

—Insist on full and unprejudiced cooperation of all food and beverage service employees.

—Make sure that established service procedures are adhered to and correct any deviations discreetly, but immediately.

—Make suggestions to the general manager concerning possible improvements in the dining room, coffee shop, and lounge, which would tend to make more satisfied customers, increase volume of business, cut payroll costs, etc.

RELATIONSHIPS

Report to: General manager

Supervise: Hostesses, cashiers, waitresses/waiters, bus help, room service, chef, cooks, preparation and service crew, lounge staff.

Work closely with chef, sales, and catering departments, hotel assistant manager, and front office.

Questions

1. In what way is the "city ledger" related to the food and beverage department operation?

2. The catering department of the hotel is charged with what primary function?

3. Does the hotel management ever turn to outside food service specialists for the operation of any of the restaurants within the hotel? Explain.

4. The cost of beverage in hotel bars is likely to run about what percent of sales?

5. Hotels very often break even or lose money on their food sales. Can you give five reasons why it is difficult to operate hotel restaurants profitably?

6. Why is it that banquet menus tend to be relatively few in number?

7. Why is the banquet department in a hotel likely to be much more profitable than restaurant operation?

8. Generally speaking, bar sales would run about what percentage of food sales in a hotel?

9. Give at least three reasons why large hotels are turning to the buffet breakfast rather than typical sit-down service.

10. Would you guess that room service is a very profitable operation within a hotel? Explain.

Discussion Questions

1. Several of the larger hotel coffee shops are introducing buffet luncheons. Under what circumstances would this arrangement be appropriate? What labor cost percentage could be expected?

2. As a food and beverage director of a 400-room house, you are asked to draw up a marketing plan. How would you go about this and in what sequence?

J. WILLARD MARRIOTT (1900–   )*

Large numbers of innkeepers and restaurateurs have been added to the list of the 200,000 millionaires said to be in the United States. A few have been included in that even more select group of those with "over $100 million"; however, only one in the latter group has also been a bishop and chairman of the inauguration of a President of the United States. He is J. Willard Marriott, chairman of the board of the Marriott Corp.

Responsibility came early for Bill Marriott. At fourteen he was sent on a long railroad trip to San Francisco with several carloads of sheep. At eighteen he had already served two years as a Mormon missionary. Higher education was at Webber College and at the University of Utah. During the summer vacations, he sold woolen underwear to miners and loggers. By his junior year, he had a territory of seven states and forty-five students working for him.

The Marriott Corporation started with root beer. Upon graduation from the University of Utah in 1926, Bill bought a franchise for $2,000 to sell A & W root beer in Washington, D.C. During the first summer in Washington, the chief root beer maker was Bill's new bride, Alice.

"The restaurant business was born of desperation," says Marriott. When, in the fall, root beer sales dropped sharply, Marriott and his partner, Hugh Coulton, tried to sublease their stores.

*See *Mariott* (Salt Lake City: Robert O'Brieny Deseret Book Co., 1977).

No luck, so they added hot food: chili con carne and hot tamales. Hamburgers were not on the menu because at the time they were declasse.

The change from root beer stand to restaurant was made literally overnight. The big orange A & W barrel came out of the front window. Stools went in before the counter. A steam table was placed under the counter, and the name Hot Shoppes went on the front. The name had been suggested by a customer who had jokingly asked: "When are you going to open your hot shops?"

Bill bought out his partner the same year, and when spring came, he opened one of the first drive-in restaurants in the nation. He literally built the restaurant, taking up hammer and nails himself; he had no architect. The design was a simple rectangle, the building painted orange with black trim.

Employees did not just cook or serve food. They painted, washed windows, did carpentry, and, on occasion, acted as bouncers. The drive-in turned into one of the most successful restaurants ever built. Profits from the place were used to finance other restaurants.

In 1930 there were five Hot Shoppes and six years of depression ahead. Profit margins were small, but with full value given to customers, the business prospered. The Marriotts began laying plans for expansion. Characteristically, they had an unshaken belief that prosperity would return.

In 1933 Bill became desperately ill with what was diagnosed as Hodgkins disease. Five doctors were unanimous in telling him that he had but one year to live. Frightened, he took a much-needed vacation trip, and, amazingly, on his return the disease was found to be gone. It was at this time, Marriott states, that he realized the importance of having an organization of people behind him, one that was not dependent upon any single individual.

Diversification came early but was introduced in measured steps. In 1934 the sandwich menu was enlarged to include full-course meals. In 1937 the company became the first airline caterer, putting up meals in cardboard boxes for American and Eastern Airlines passengers out of Washington, D.C. By 1969 Marriott Flite Services was serving fifty airlines from twenty domestic flight kitchens and nineteen overseas airports.

Early in World War II, Marriott moved into in-plant foodservice. Lunch wagons roved around five plants and the cafeteria of the Naval Communications Annex. After the war, the takeout market was tapped with the opening of the Pantry Houses. Their slogan: "Take home food for the family."

In 1957 lodging operations were added to the food business. A 360-room motel was built in Washington, D.C. Because of its design and location, it was an instant success.

To a greater extent than most hotel and restaurant chains, Marriott is family-oriented. Except for periods when her children were small, Alice Marriott continued to be active in the business, serving as an officer. In 1931 brother Paul joined the organization as general manager. Woodrow and Russell, the other two brothers, joined the company in 1933. Woodrow Marriott served as senior vice-president. Today, J. Willard Marriott, Jr., is president of the company.

The company has the largest centralized personnel department of any in the field. Annual employee parties began in 1938. Group insurance, Christmas gifts, length of service gifts, a credit union, and a suggestion system are evidence of the interest in employee relations. Since 1953, when the company stock was offered to the public, employees have been encouraged to buy the stock. Marriott has been an industry leader with the company profit sharing plan. If success in personnel matters is measured by the lack of unionization in a company, Marriott has been eminently successful. In 1982 only a few units in all of the Marriott enterprises were unionized.

Marriott was an early believer in a centralized commissary operation. In 1930 certain food items were prepared centrally for distribution to the other stores. In 1941 production, administration, personnel, and accounting functions were all moved into a new three-story building. In the new commissary, raw food items, such as vegetables, were graded but not cooked. Meat, fish, and poultry were graded and portioned. These items were later cooked at the stores. All baked items, ice cream, and sherbets were made in the commissary. So, too, were soups, stocks, and gravies.

In 1967 all of the service and control functions for the Marriott Company were gathered together into a new central supply and quality control facility known as Fairfield Farm Kitchens. It occupies 285,000 square feet in Prince Georges County, Maryland. Here the procurement offices, warehouses, print shop, butcher shop, kitchen, bakery, and blast-freezing facilities are located. The facility also houses a test kitchen and quality control laboratory.

The Marriott Corporation might be called a conglomerate in that it is a multicompany built around the products, food, and hospitality. It serves food in almost every possible manner: via vending, table service, and counter service. It prepares food, and usually serves it, in industrial plants, business offices, schools and colleges, public cafeterias, and turnpike restaurants. It serves airlines (by 1980 Marriott had sixty flight kitchens operating on four continents) and has specialty restaurants, drive-ins, and coffee shops. It is in the hotel business in a big way, with several of the largest motels in the world (30,000 rooms in 1980). The Essex Hotel of New York City, overlooking Central Park, was purchased in 1969, marking the chain's entrance into the big city hotel business. It also runs cruise ships and two Great America theme parks.

Undoubtedly, many people have grown rich with the Marriott family. The Marriott Company has been one of the industry's biggest winners. Corporate sales fall into five categories: hotels, restaurants, contract food services, theme parks, and Sun Line cruises.

The restaurant group comprises four categories of food service: fast foods, coffee shops, cafeterias, and family-style restaurants.

It will probably be some time before the Marriott Corporation becomes a bureaucracy. Marriott is an entrepreneur in the old style American way, a way that is highly competitive and driving, a way that brutally absorbs the individual engaged in it and moves the organization ahead to whatever goals the person thinks important.

He is not particularly industry-oriented and does not follow some of the traditional practices of the hotel industry. The formal opening of the 433-room Marriott Motor Hotel in Newton, Massachusetts, was an example of the Marriott style in relations with the industry. Instead of inviting a select few hoteliers and prominent people to the opening, 4,000 invitations were sent out. At least 4,000 persons showed up to occupy space that could gracefully accommodate only a fraction of the number. Some of the invited guests who arranged to stay overnight found themselves presented with a bill for payment at full rate.

With son, Bill, Jr., president of Marriott, and Bill, Sr., chairman of the board, the company has moved into a variety of ventures, and the Marriott empire has the thrust for continued expansion. Bill, Jr., has introduced more corporate level staff and spread responsibilities further down the line than did J. Willard. It took a J. Willard, however, to perceive the drive-in and in-flight markets and to have the tenacity and drive to develop those markets—fuzzy and indistinct at the time. Business pioneers somehow foresee markets and dedicate themselves to their development. Marriott is one such person.

6 The Resort Business

The vacation hotel business was originally identified with the resort hotel. The resort hotel most often was a stately, old building surrounded by broad acres of trees, or fronting on a lengthy section of beach or other natural beauty.

Name resorts like The Biltmore in Phoenix, The Boca Raton in South Florida, The Del Coronado near San Diego, The Greenbrier in West Virginia, and The Broadmoor near Colorado Springs represent the grand resort of the early part of the century. They usually have broad acres, sometimes hundreds of acres, large rooms, a multitude of staff, and a bounteous table.

The vacation hotel, which encompasses the bulk of the vacation hotel business today, is more often a high-rise building in an urbanized

Figure 6-1 *One of the salons of the Ritz of Paris, considered by many to be the best hotel in the world. It has no television and does little advertising. Charles Ritz, son of Cesar Ritz, says the place is not "ritzy." Rather, to its patrons, it is a place like home, a townhouse for the wealthy. It has 210 rooms, two restaurants, and three bars. Every guest room has a golden clock and is kept cozy by a wood fire.*

setting, a hotel found among some 400 hotels on Miami Beach, on the Strip in Las Vegas, or in crowded Waikiki. The largest resort hotel in the world happens to be The Las Vegas Hilton with 3120 rooms. The image of the mountain or sea resort hotel is still around but is overlaid in color with the bright new vacation-entertainment complex: the vacation hotel.

Since World War II, business and pleasure traveling have tended to commingle. Much of the convention business takes place in the vacation hotel in Hawaii, Las Vegas, Florida, and the Caribbean. Pleasure travel has become, or will become, bigger business than business travel.

The tourist business is often defined to include the business traveler as well as the pleasure traveler. The distinction between business and pleasure traveling is becoming less easy to define. Much of the travel for business takes on elements of travel for pleasure. The spouse may accompany the businessperson on a business trip; the business trip may be extended a few days to include a vacation. Travel for business purposes is still listed as the number one reason for travel to American hotels. The Sheraton Corporation states that 71 percent of the travel to their hotels is done for business purposes, and 29 percent done for pleasure. Some of the larger airlines have found that the mix is about 50–50. For purposes of this chapter, the tourist will be defined as the pleasure traveler, more specifically the person on vacation.

Strangely, it was not until the middle and late 1960s that the vacation hotel business was recognized as a part of the pleasure travel business. The interlocking nature of the hotel and travel business was underscored in the 1960s when a number of oil companies and airlines bought or built hotel and restaurant chains. Pan American Airways started the pattern in 1947 by setting up International Hotels, Inc., a wholly-owned subsidiary. Until about 1960 its growth was fairly slow and restricted to Latin America and the Caribbean. It then became international with hotels in most major capital cities. Pan Am, unfortunately, because of financial problems, sold International Hotels, Inc., to a British concern.

In 1967 Trans World Airways startled the hotel world by buying Hilton International. Travel and vacationing began to be seen more clearly as two sides of the same coin. Whereas the travel agent, the hotel, and the airline had operated independently, TWA merged the three activities, selling travel and hotel space as a package. International airlines, especially, have moved into the hotel business in a big way, as seen in Table 2–2 of Chapter 2.

CONGLOMERATES BUY HOTELS

The year 1968 saw the vacation business being integrated even further when ITT bought the Sheraton Hotels, linking rent-a-car, airport parking, and the motel and hotel business together.

Another development of importance to the vacation business is the movement of some conglomerates into the hotel business. U.S. Steel, at Disney World in Florida, built the convention complex that contains 5,000 rooms. Alcoa owns The Century-Plaza, the hotel which is part of a living-entertainment-hotel complex in Beverly Hills. MCA owns the Yosemite and Curry Company; Amfac owns the Fred Harvey Company.

The commercial jet plane, which was introduced in the United States in 1959, brought formerly remote resort destinations to within a few hours of population centers.

Larger planes and shorter flying times made air fares less expensive. The result was that tourism surged upward in such resort areas as Hawaii, Puerto Rico, the Bahamas, and Bermuda.

Tourism, formerly a small-scale business in places such as Jamaica and the Virgin Islands, sprang to life, to be reinforced later by cruise ship visitors by the thousands. The southwest coast of Mexico, "the Mexican Riviera," developed rapidly as a resort destination. Tourism became a new major industry in such places as Portugal, Spain, the Canary Islands, and Greece.

International tourism is said to be the second largest single item of world trade, after oil and petroleum products. Most of the international travel, however, is concentrated in Europe and North America. According to the World Tourism Organization (WTO), of the $34 billion in receipts from tourism, 90 percent of it went to fifteen countries in North America and Europe. The number of international travelers visiting Asia, Africa, and the Pacific is only about 7 percent of the total.[1]

1. Som N. Chib, "Measurement of Tourism," *Journal of Travel Research* (Fall 1977), p. 22.

The big reason for the surge in travel was the increased affluence of the Western World. Whereas in 1966 only one family out of twelve had an income of $15,000 a year or more, by 1978 that was the median family income. (Inflation distorts the figures, however.)

How important is travel and tourism to the U.S. economy? The U.S. Travel and Tourism Administration reports that travel and tourism comprise the third largest retail industry. It accounts for $160 billion in domestic and international spending, about 6 percent of the gross national product.

Some 4.5 million persons are directly employed, another 2.2 million have supporting jobs.

Governments benefited handsomely with $14 billion in federal, state, and local tax revenues.

The vacation business is multi-dimensional, a grand mix of business in which nearly every community has a stake. The *New York Times* pointed out that more than half of our states list tourism among their top three industries. Mexico receives 40 percent of its foreign exchange income from tourists.

THE LURE OF STATE AND NATIONAL PARKS

An amazing number of people visit the state and national parks; these visits can be considered part of the vacation business and they generate millions of dollars in the sale of lodgings and in restaurants. The operation of tourist facilities within the parks is big business, sometimes under the direct operation of a governmental unit, and at other times concessioned to a private contractor.

Virginia ranks first in national park visits, followed by Tennessee. New York and California lead the way in numbers of visitors to state parks.

Private campgrounds have surged since the 1960s. In 1975 there were some 800 Kampground of America campgrounds, 50 Holiday

Figure 6-2 *The Ahwahnee Hotel, Yosemite National Park, California, is one of the "grand" old resort hotels.*

Travel Parks, 200 campgrounds in the United Safari International chain, 50 Jellystone Parks, and 18 Ramada Camp Inns.

VULNERABILITY OF THE VACATION BUSINESS

The vacation business is particularly vulnerable to severe economic recession, but is not greatly affected by minor recessions, as experienced during 1972–1975. In August of 1932, during the big depression, a Michigan resort I know of had one paying guest, and some thirty employees. In 1929 when national income was high, resort hotel receipts totaled $76,562,000. By 1932 this figure dropped to $22,237,000.[2]

With the recession years 1971 to 1975, however, travel and vacation spending dropped

only slightly. Longer trips were replaced by shorter ones. Travel to Europe dropped off up to 25 percent, whereas travel within the United States and to places like Canada, Mexico, and Hawaii increased.

CONCENTRATION OF RESORTS

Figure 6–3 shows the concentration of resort hotel rooms within the continental United States. The map is useful in that it shows that resorts are clustered in New England, along the Jersey shore, in Florida, and in the Southwest. Hawaii and Puerto Rico also have heavy concentration of resorts. To be represented, the state must have at least 500 resort rooms, and those rooms must have been listed in *The Hotel Red Book*.

Most resort hotels have one thing in common—seasonal business. New England resorts typically open about June 20 and close on Labor Day, or soon after. Tropical and subtropical resorts have a peak season lasting from about

_____

2. William A. Hayes, *An Economic Analysis of the American Hotel Industry*, Dissertation, The Catholic University of America, Washington, D.C., 1952, p. 139.

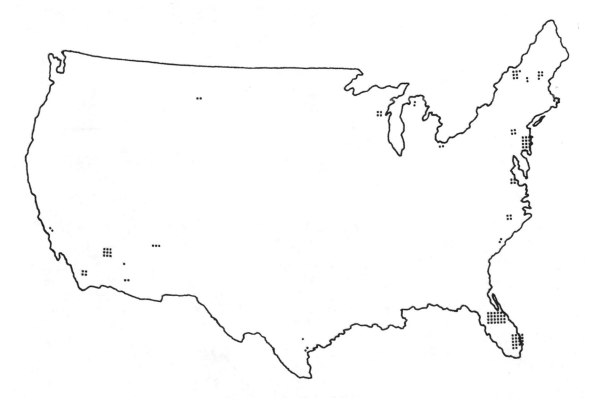

Figure 6–3 *Concentration of resort hotels in the United States.*

Christmas through March and a summer season, with lower occupancies, at reduced rates.

Spring and fall are the low points (so-called "shoulder seasons") in California, Arizona, Florida, and the Caribbean. Atlantic City and the Poconos have year-round occupancy of less than 60 percent. The constant effort on the part of the resort operator is to extend the season, usually by bringing in convention groups at the beginning and the end of the peak seasons.

Until the 1960s, many resort operators could make a profit operating on a 90- to 110-day season. Labor and food costs were comparatively low; the fixed expenses of taxes and insurance were also comparatively low. These expenses are now high; many resorts are surrounded by towns where taxes are up. The resort operator is forced to extend the season and many have done so. October has become a popular month in the Poconos, White Sulphur Springs, and parts of New England.

RESORT MARKETS

Each resort area tends to develop a particular market or markets. New York City is a principal tourist market, and New Yorkers, by all odds, are the biggest resorters in the world. In season, perhaps 90 percent of the guests in Miami Beach are from New York and New Jersey. New Yorkers populate the beachfront hotels of the Caribbean Islands. Californians are the largest group of resorters in Hawaii, Las Vegas, and Mexico.

Figure 6-4 *Wentworth-by-the-Sea, a resort near Portsmouth, New Hampshire, is in the grand style. It opened in 1874, and various owners have spent many millions of dollars in expansion and maintenance. The Wentworth achieved international fame in 1905 when the Russians and the Japanese met there to decide the Treaty of Portsmouth. Many of the greats or near-greats of the world have stopped there over the years. At one time it was only a July to August guest season hotel, then The Wentworth was restyled to take in conventions that now amount to about 60 percent of the total business. The months of July and August are still reserved for seasonal guests. In 1981 the hotel was purchased by a Swiss firm and plans were made to add 300 rooms in New England-style townhouses that were to be sold under a time-share plan. When not occupied by the time-share owners, the rooms were to be part of the hotel room inventory.*

DIFFERENT PLACES FOR DIFFERENT PEOPLE

Obviously, travelers select destinations for different reasons such as climate, historical or cultural appeal, water sports, entertainment, and shopping facilities. The major appeal of England for Americans seems to be historical and cultural. Among a large number of travel customers of American Express to Florida, California, Mexico, Hawaii, the Bahamas, Jamaica, Puerto Rico, the Virgin Islands, and Barbados, the appeals, in descending order of importance, were:

Scenic beauty

Pleasant attitudes of the local people

Suitable accommodations

Rest and relaxation

Air fare cost considerations

Historical and cultural interests

Cuisine

Water sports

Entertainment (e.g., nightlife)

Shopping facilities

Golfing and tennis[3]

In analyzing 230 questionnaires, which had asked respondents to rate various appeals, four basic considerations emerged: entertainment, purchase opportunities, climate for comfort, and cost. These respondents represented a definite sample of persons, a high-income group, almost half of whom were professionals, generally middle-aged, well-educated, middle-to-high income earners, many of them wealthy, and frequent vacation travelers outside the United States. Even within a group, of course, a different constellation of factors would apply. One individual selects a destination primarily because of the golf and tennis, another because he or she likes the local people, and another because the place offers rest and relaxation. Most people are at least somewhat influenced by air fare cost considerations and the convenience of getting to and from the destination.

Many resorts seek to attract only a particular type of guest; others welcome just about anybody who can pay the tab. The larger resort

hotels that rely on conventions may have a medical group one week and the plumbers union the next.

The manager of a resort that relies heavily on social guests is usually concerned about having a fairly homogenous guest list. The manager recognizes that most people enjoy being with people of their own background and social position while in a resort setting, but also recognizes that deep in the heart of most of us lies the urge to be a snob. The origin of the word snob explains a great deal. It comes from the Latin *sine nobilitas*, a term reserved originally for students at Oxford who were "without nobility." Those without nobility, of course, would like to have it and the abbreviation of the two words, "s-nob," refers to the urge to associate with those we consider to be of a higher class and to exclude those considered to be of a lower class. Snobbery is a term to be reckoned with in the nonconvention hotel.

At beach resorts, the pool is the focal point. A tan is a vital part of the experience; it signals evidence that the guest has been on vacation. The tan is sought at all costs, come cold weather, sweltering sun, or sunburn. On with the lotion. Sit in the sun another hour. How else will the folks back home know you have been to Florida, or Arizona, or Nassau? The poolside is the great leveler. The isolated guest cries for friendship. Persons who in everyday life have little in common suddenly develop appreciation for each other. The pool is the body of warmth, the altar of sun worship. Here, the currents of humanity flow, revitalizing the tired, soothing anxieties, and bringing peace of mind.

VACATIONING IS A LONG-TIME URGE

The urge to vacation is deep-seated and expresses itself today in the weekend rush to the beach, the pell-mell trip to the mountains to ski, the ten-day junket to the Caribbean, or the European tour. Vacationing brings change, excitement, and, for some, relaxation. For others, a vacation is a series of slides to show the neighbors. It may be a way of getting a prestige tan during the winter. Going to the "in place," mixing with the best people may be important. For a number of older people, it may be an escape from loneliness. For the young man or woman, it can be a flight to the mating grounds.

---

3. Jonathan N. Goodrich, "Benefit Bundle Analysis: An Empirical Study of International Travelers" *Journal of Travel Research* (Fall 1977).

The urge to vacation has been around a long time. The ancient Romans who had summer villas in Herculaneum and Pompeii were vacationing when Mt. Vesuvius erupted and covered them and their towns completely in lava, hot mud, and volcanic ash. In the United States, resort history does not record exactly when the first resort appeared but many persons who attended the first Continental Congress of 1774 and 1775 "escaped the heat and humidity" of Philadelphia by traveling to Germantown, where they leased homes or stayed with local residents.

The first American resort advertisement, it is said, appeared as a broadside, dated May 20, 1789. It tells of the "genteel and plentiful table" of Gray's Ferry, Pennsylvania. "Guests could expect free concerts weekly and fishing tackle

... to those who may be fond of that amusement." Transportation between Gray's Ferry and the City would be provided twice daily, announced the proprietor, by "a handsome State Waggon mounted on steel springs, with two good horses. . . ."

Resorts as vacation spots satisfy at least four basic human needs: social, recreational, health, and prestige. Different resorts have specialized in satisfying particular needs. Health and therapeutic springs were the vogue before 1850, some of them having been operated since before the Revolution. Before 1900, nearly 2,000 spas (named after a small Belgian village that has bubbling mineral springs) were attracting the health seeker in this country.

The hundreds of sporting camps, built first for fishermen and hunters about 1870, later

Figure 6-5 *The Greenbrier, White Sulphur Springs, West Virginia. The Greenbrier is a mountain spa located at White Sulphur Springs. Surrounded by a 6,500 acre estate, it is a perfect setting for golf, tennis, horseback riding, skeet and trap shooting, hiking, and the numerous other sports available at the resort.*

Figure 6-6   *The lobby of one of the great classical mountain resorts, The Homestead, in Hot Springs, Virginia. The resort sits in 6,000 acres of The Allegheny Mountains. The Homestead is "self-contained," offering golf, tennis, riding, and, of course, hot mineral waters.*

changed into camps and lodges for vacationers. Following the pattern of the lumber camp, these are still built with a central lodge and dining hall with a cabin colony round about. Today, Maine has over 5,000 hotels, camps, and tourist homes where visitors, mostly from the East and from Canada, come to eat, hunt, fish, canoe, climb mountains, and just enjoy the pleasantly cool summers.

In the Alleghenies, just before the Civil War, resorting at the various hot springs became a necessity for both health and social prestige. A grand tour of the springs became the established summer "must" for people of means. The tour covered 170 miles and about a dozen resorts. Colonel Job Fry, proprietor of one of the springs, described the tour when he told his guests, "Go get well charged at the White, well salted at the Salt, well sweetened at the Sweet, well boiled at the Hot, and then return to me and I will Fry you."

Not only were numerous glasses of the usually unpleasant spring water drunk, but at some of the springs mint juleps and food were floated out on trays to the soaking resorters. The mint julep itself was created at the Old White Springs in 1858: French brandy, old-fashioned cut-loaf sugar, limestone water, crushed ice, and young, hand-grown, mountain mint. It was at the Old White that the governor of South Carolina is reported to have said to the governor of North Carolina, "It's a long time between drinks."

Today two famous resorts are left of the dozen that operated there at the turn of the century: The Homestead at Hot Springs, Virginia, and The Greenbrier in West Virginia (see Figures 6-5 and 6-6). The Greenbrier, owned by the Chesapeake and Ohio Railroad, which has invested over $25 million in the resort, is now a grand convention property, a lavish hotel with 650 rooms, no two identical in decor. The prices are in keeping with the style. As one guest reported, "Hand a bellman fifty cents and he'll hand it back to you."

The Effect of the Railroad

The coming of the railroad was as much of a boon for the resort business as it was for the city hotel. People could travel long distances quickly and penetrate areas that formerly were relatively impassable. Where the railroad went into the mountains or other recreational areas, the resorts soon followed.

The Delaware Gap region in Pennsylvania is an example of what happened when the railroads arrived. Around the turn of the nineteenth century, summer visitors to the region braved the trip by stagecoach and canal boat and stayed in the spare rooms rented by the local residents. When the Delaware, Lackawanna, and Western railroad came in, visitors also came in such numbers that hotels were built by the score. Today the area has about 500 hostelries for the summer guest.

One of the oldest tourist establishments in the Gap region, The Swiftwater Inn, took pains to reassure travelers that everything would go well with them while at the inn. The inscription on its sign might well serve as a motto for all good innkeepers (see Figure 6–7).

Romantic Movement of the Nineteenth Century

The romantic movement of the early nineteenth century modified the Puritan tradition of utilitarianism in America. The new religion of nature, as expounded by the romanticists and abetted by Thoreau's "return to simplicity," was hardly needed to get people out of the industrial centers. "Go to the mountains," said the brochures of the time, for "deep reflections, leading to wisdom and happiness."

The Catskills became an early center of American resorting. The Catskill Mountain House opened July 4, 1823. The elite of American society began patronizing the place its very first season. By 1843 one could choose from a selection of burgundies, madeiras, French dishes, and French dances.

The Catskills, romanticized by Washington Irving as being Rip Van Winkle country, became a symbol of the American romantic movement in paintings and literature. Nature paintings by such people as Winslow Homer and Thomas Cole helped to heighten the aura of desirability of a return to nature. Before this time, Americans never thought of going to the mountains and countryside for vacations. Most of them were already there.

In the 1880s and 1890s, converted farmhouses allowed the summer visitor to enjoy the illusion of rural existence without facing its hardships. Farmhouses could accommodate 10 to 25 paying guests. By 1905 there were at least 900 hotels, farmhouses, and boardinghouses accommodating about 25,000 guests in the Catskills.

The Catskills, about one hundred miles north of New York City, are easily reached by highway. The region is an exception to the poor showing of most mountain resort areas. Known as the Borscht Belt, it draws most of its 2 million guests from metropolitan New York. They come to frolic, look for marriage partners, and, as one wit put it, seek exhaustion.

In Sullivan County, where most of the Borscht Belt hotels are located, the first resorts were ramshackle farm buildings of twenty to forty rooms. Each had a communal kitchen for workers from New York's lower East Side who were determined to capture the pleasures of rural life.

The boom 1920s brought Tudor architecture and stuccoed four- or five-story hotels. Most of the 500 Catskill hotels were built at this time. Twenty of them can accommodate 500 or more guests, and there are about 2,000 bungalow colonies, with total space for almost 450,000 people.

Rest ye Bones

Tickle ye Palate

and nae

Rob ye Wallet

Figure 6–7 *Sign at the Swiftwater Inn.*

Grossinger's and the Concord, the largest of the Catskill hotels, have set the pace with something new—a single room with two baths. The larger hotels use big-name entertainers, many of whom started their careers as employee-entertainers at the same place. Celebrities are courted, all expenses free.

Matchmaking is a big business and considered part of management responsibility at Grossinger's. Lists of single persons from the same areas are made, and arrangements made so that they can meet. A prize was once offered to the first couple who met and were engaged while at the resort. No takers. The promotion department became desperate. Finally a couple was located that seemed to be making progress. A canoe trip was arranged—and while the couple believed themselves to be alone—a crew of anxious people played soft music and watched their every move. The program was successful.

Early New England Resorts

New England's resort business had several beginnings: farmers taking in summer tourists; old inns gradually merging into the resort business; and hunting-fishing camps gradually taking on the character of resorts. Big farm families were naturals for the resort business. The big families meant plenty of cheap help, big houses that could accommodate city folks during the summer, and plenty of chickens, eggs, and vegetables to feed the visitors.

The wonderful mountain scenery was free. All that was necessary was a ledger book with a big "Guest Register" scrawled across it and a potato in which to stick a pen for use by the city folks in writing their names and home addresses. As business grew, the family added wings here and there until they finally had a moderate-sized summer resort.

In Maine the first tourists were Indians from inland and Canada who spent their sum-

Figure 6-8 *The Mountain View House, Whitefield, New Hampshire, one of the stately, elegant mountain inns of New England, still survives. The resort is operated by the Dodge family whose forebears began taking summer boarders in 1866. Farmer William Dodge ran the farm that supplied the milk, cream, chickens, eggs, pork, fresh fruits, and vegetables for the table. He also took the "boarders" for rides in his mountain wagon and to church on Sundays. By the 1890s the original farmhouse had disappeared and part of the present building with the cupola had been built. The resort includes some 3,000 acres with a heated swimming pool, a golf course, and an auditorium with a capacity of 450. The Mountain View House is the oldest resort in the country to be in the hands of its original owners.*

mers along the seacoast, fishing and feasting. The first summer boarder came to Old Orchard Beach in 1837 and by 1850 Maine's tourist business was well underway, accompanied by promotion leaflets and handbills.

Mountain Resorts on the Wane

With a few exceptions, mountain resorts in this country and in Canada have not been profitable in recent years. This has not always been the case. Before air conditioning and airplane travel, spending the summer or part of it in the cool mountains was the social thing to do, and a pleasant way to escape the heat of the city. In 1891 the White Mountains of New Hampshire had some sixty resort hotels with more than 11,000 guest rooms. By 1959 the number of guest rooms had dropped to about half as many, and today the number is considerably less. In 1890 the mountain resorts were the center of the summer social season and presented a way of life unique for both the guests and the operator, an aspect of Americana overlooked by most history books (see Figure 6-8).

RAILROAD RESORT OPERATION

During the resort boom beginning in the 1880s, transportation to resorts was by horse-drawn coach, ship and boat, and railroad. Railroad management saw the logic of building and operating resorts that could be reached easily by their railroads. The relationship was clear enough, but railroad management for resorts is almost uniformly lacking in imagination and efficiency. Consequently, the marriages between railroads and resort hotels may have been blissful but costly. The Chesapeake and Ohio railroad was originally involved in The Homestead and now completely owns The Greenbrier, both of which are famous resorts in the Blue Ridge Mountains.

Like most public transportation, railroads are more or less subsidized by the government and not nearly so concerned with costs as are professional hotel groups. The Glacier Park hotels of Glacier National Park, originally owned by the Great Northern Railroad, were a case in point. These hotels regularly lost money until tight management was introduced.

At The Many Glacier Hotel, a 230-room house, the number of personnel was cut from 220 to 165 with no appreciable loss in service. Instead of separate laundries at each location, one central laundry was set up for the four hotels and two motels. A centralized bakery was set up to serve three locations. Gift shops were enlarged, cocktail lounges were added, and beverage sales were promoted by wine carts and room cards. A cycle menu, uniform for the several Park hotels, was introduced and food and beverage costs were reduced, in some instances, by one-third.

The accounting system for the hotels was left in the hands of the railroad, with the result that groups that held conventions in mid-summer were billed as late as the following February. Following typical railroad practice, the hotels had no current operating statistics; hotel managers, paid about half the usual salary appropriate for their jobs, had been content to operate the same way year after year. The old managers were replaced, and a bonus system was installed.

An innovation that proved popular with guests, and a boost for employee morale, was the use of talented college students to provide a series of shows for guest entertainment. Students from Carleton College, Grinnell College, and other schools were employed as waiters, waitresses, bellmen, maids, and housemen. They did an outstanding job for the nightly performances under the guidance of a college music professor. As an outlet for the creative desires of the staff, the shows were in part responsible for the high employee morale that existed in these hotels. A series of questionnaires completed by guests showed that the employee entertainment was the thing they found most enjoyable in the hotels.

The Canadian Pacific Railroad has been a hotel operator of size for a number of years. In 1913 the Banff Springs Hotel in Banff, Alberta, was built for $16 million. From a distance, the 600-room structure resembles a fairy castle.

CANADIAN ROCKY RESORTS

The Chateau Lake Louise, north of Banff in Canada, has one of the most magnificent hotel settings of the world, ranking with Las Brisas in Acapulco, Mexico, The Conquistador in Puerto Rico, and some of the Swiss locations. The Chateau is located at one end of Lake Louise, where a glacier-covered mountain serves as a backdrop for the lake. Some 60,000 oriental poppies blanket one side of the hotel's terrace. As just mentioned, the property is owned by the Canadian Pacific Railroad.

The Canadian National Hotels, a subsidiary of the Canadian National Railroad, operates The Jasper Lake Lodge. The Lodge combines the best of the old cottage-style resort —still popular in Canada—with the modern restaurant and recreational lodge. The central building, built after the old lodge building was destroyed by fire in 1952, is beautiful. The lavish use made of warm colors in furnishings, colored cove lighting reflecting on the dining room ceiling, and a view of Jasper Lake makes for memorable dining (see Figure 6–9).

Both Canadian railroads maintain a continuous chef's training program with each of the hotels committed to train a certain number of trainee cooks. The program provides a steady supply of cooks and precludes the necessity of large salaries for executive chefs and the usual desperate search for chefs in resort hotels. Sun Valley, a year-round resort in a spectacular setting and with incredible ski lifts, was originally owned by the Union Pacific Railroad. Like the other railroad resorts, it probably makes little or no profit after reasonable depreciation is taken.

THE ROLE OF LADY LUCK

Gambling complements vacationing in the minds of many. What would Las Vegas, Reno, and Atlantic City be without the thrill of a brush with Lady Luck? Around the turn of the century one went to Saratoga Springs, New York, for the horses. There were two hotels built and operated in the grand manner: The Grand Union and The United States Hotel.

Saratoga was as famous for its "elegant hells," the gambling casinos, as were its hotels for their "elegant belles." Even so, The Grand Union and The United States Hotel in the 1880s and 1890s locked every entrance at 11 P.M., and no one except registered guests was permitted to come in.

BUILT ALONG THE BOARDWALK

Atlantic City was off to a flying start as a "summer watering spot" when, in 1853, a railroad was built to the shores of Absecon Island. By 1870 the beach, formerly frequented only by

Figure 6–9 *Jasper Lake Lodge in the Canadian Rockies is an example of the resort centered around a lodge with the guests living in cottages, taking their meals and entertainment in the lodge.*

Delaware Indians and "beach-party goers," saw about 5,000 people coming for vacations.

In its heyday, the Boardwalk became a promenade for over 3 million hotel guests a year who strolled for six continuous miles on wood and steel.

By the 1970s Atlantic City had lost its luster and was fading fast. In 1977 the New Jersey State Legislature passed a bill that permitted gambling in Atlantic City, thus giving the resort area a new life expectancy. Industry executives predict Atlantic City will over take Las Vegas in resort gambling revenue. In 1983 some 27 million visitors were expected to leave $1.8 billion while playing with Lady Luck.[4]

Resort areas tend to pass through life cycles—infancy, maturity, and senescence. Each stage attracts a different market. The resort destination can be revived, but the process is difficult and usually very costly.

In California the traveler can still experience the "great and grand" resort by visiting that Victorian/Queen Anne hodgepodge, The Del Coronado, across the bay from San Diego. Built in 1887, it had the first electric lighting system installed in a hotel and in 1971 was listed in the National Register of Historic Places.

Colorado has its own grand resort in The Broadmoor, near Colorado Springs, now an active convention hotel.

THE TOUR AGENT ARRIVES

Thomas Cook started the travel agency business in 1841 when he arranged a railroad trip for a temperance meeting in Leicester, fifteen miles from his home in Market Harborough, England. Soon he was arranging trips for groups all over the British Isles and later into Europe, the United States, and the Near East. In the 1890s, the Pennsylvania Railroad dispatched Pullman excursion trains from New York City to Jacksonville, Florida. This was part of a package plan that included rail fare, hotel room, and meals.

Today, the tour business is said to be the fastest growing segment of air travel. The traveler gets convenience, reservations, and often arrangements for food, drinks, sightseeing, and entertainment. Package tours have had a tre-

mendous effect on the vacation business. Eastern Airlines started the first package tours to Miami in the winter of 1951. Package tours made Miami both a summer and winter resort and have been responsible for filling thousands of empty seats on the airlines.

Package tours are put together by some 200 tour wholesalers in the United States. These wholesalers then turn the tours over to some 23,000 travel agencies who retail them to people who do not want to take the trouble, or do not know how, to arrange their own travel, accommodations, and entertainment.

For their trouble, tour operators get about 20 percent discount on everything they package except the airline fare. If a hotel room rate is $60 a day, the packager may get it for $40 or less. If a tourist attraction charges $5, the tour operator gets it for $4.00. The 20 percent discount is given at restaurants and night clubs as well. The packager keeps about one-half of the discount and passes the other half on to the travel agent.

Resort hotels are usually delighted to be a part of a tour package; some hotels could not survive without being on the regular itinerary of some of the tours. The airlines are pleased; the travel agent is pleased; the restaurant operator is pleased; everybody is pleased—except the traveler who, in some cases, may feel as though he or she is part of a nameless crowd, being herded from one attraction to another; others would not want it otherwise. The sophisticated traveler may join a tour group because of its economy and leave it for part or most of the schedule. Tours can save the traveler tremendous time and effort in making travel arrangements, and in many cases, considerable savings are involved.

THE MARKET VALUE OF A RESORT

What is a resort worth? What is its fair market value? What price will a willing buyer pay and a willing seller sell for, both of whom have the facts, and neither of whom is under pressure to act? Much of resort keeping is tied in with psychic income, pride of ownership, and the pleasure the owner or prospective buyer has or may get from owning a resort on a beautiful lake or a beach.

Tax considerations are often a major factor. Wealthy resort owners may expect operating losses which can be used as tax deductions against other income. Many resorts have been built or bought by such individuals in the past. Special circumstances—estate settlement or partnership disagreement, for example—may also distort the real market value.

According to the Helmsley-Spear Company, the largest of the real estate brokers, the traditional approach to determining fair value has three aspects:

1. Value as compared with comparable properties.

2. Reproduction cost, separating the value of the land from the value of the buildings.

3. The capitalized value of the property, what the property will produce in profit on a free and clear basis.

The approach most commonly used is the one based on the capitalization of earnings: what the property will yield.

From the profit viewpoint, a resort is as valuable as the net income it can generate. For a new property, a *pro forma* profit and loss statement is drawn up which projects revenues, expenses, taxes, depreciation, and expected net profit. For the established property, profit and loss statements for preceding years are a guide to future profits or losses.

ESTIMATING POTENTIAL EARNINGS

The potential earnings of a property may not be the same as what has been produced in the past. The buyer will presumably maximize the use of the property, and may arrive at a value, based on "the highest and best use" of the property, projected over the future period of life. Most large resorts by 1975 were tied in with land development and the sale of condominiums. The hotel itself might be viewed as the activities center of the land development, profits coming from land and condominium sales, not necessarily from operations of the hotel.

Potential earnings of a property take into consideration the land value itself, its setting, environment, and such things as riparian rights, easements, and special circumstances relating to the property.

Potential earnings of many resorts are tied almost directly to the convenience of reaching the place by air or highway. The relations that an owner or prospective owner may have with tour operators and travel agents can be highly important. So, too, is the relationship of the property to present and proposed interstate highways, air routes, and air fares.

Important to the financing of a resort is whether or not the resort can be tied into a nationwide referral system or will be part of a franchise plan. Lending institutions are more favorably disposed to loaning money for a resort operation when it is part of such a referral system.

In the past, a rule of thumb used for arriving at the value of a hotel, motel, or resort has been to multiply the income of the property for one year by seven to eight times. Of course, such a figure is only a starting point to be checked against all of the factors that bear on the net profit figures for the future.

The resort business is a highly specialized business, quite separate from the commercial hotel and restaurant business. There is a body of knowledge and practice that, combined with judgment, makes for expertise. In apparent contradiction to this statement are the numerous entries into the field by outsiders such as conglomerates, airlines, and oil companies. However, the outsiders bring their own financial and managerial know-how, adding it to the specialized management knowledge of the seasoned operator.

The question of "the highest and best use" of the property should always be asked. Many resorts have been "best used" by being torn down and the land sold as building lots. Other resorts have been turned into private clubs; still others, into schools or colleges. In Las Vegas, the hotel is only a setting for the gaming rooms and restaurants to sustain the guests until they can get back to the business at hand—gambling or being entertained.

RESORT PROFITS

What about profits? They vary tremendously, depending on management, location, investment, and, for the summer resort, weather. Some winter resorts also can suffer from weather. Florida's 1958 winter season was shot with cold blasts extending below Miami. Neither guests nor hotels were prepared for the frigid temperatures that shattered orange trees and vacation spirits alike. Guests in a leading Miami hotel slept in their clothes on some nights and paid for the privilege. There were not enough blankets to go around, as the heating system was geared for "Florida weather," not freezing winds.

Rain and cold are the bane of the summer resort manager. Guests soon complain about the food, the personnel, and the management. *Does It Always Rain Here, Mr. Hoyt?* is the title of a book recounting the miseries of a summer resort keeper during poor weather. The title is apt. Most resorts, above all else, are selling their climate and scenery. Bad weather for a season can ruin a lightly financed resort. What is one man's poison is another man's food. While cold, rainy weather may dry up business in the Poconos, the same weather may fill other resort areas to overflowing. "We'll go to the Caribbean to get warm."

Length of season is a critical factor in northern resort hotels. In some areas it gets shorter each year. The day after Labor Day finds most summer resorts everywhere deserted. The Cape Cod season does not get underway until about June 20. The Southeast and Southwest have longer seasons and are developing into year-round resort areas with lulls during May and September.

SEASONAL RESORTS FACE HIGH OPERATING COSTS

With short seasons and many fixed costs, seasonal resorts must charge rates that seem inordinately high to old-time guests. The biggest difficulty faced by resorts is the impracticability of raising rates to meet the rising costs of operation.

Labor rates are surprisingly low in many areas, since college students clamor for jobs as a pleasant way to spend the summer. The Glacier National Park Hotels, as an illustration, received 12,000 applications in one year but had only 600 positions open. College students usually turn out to be excellent employees, but for many the romance of the resort begins to wear thin by early August. A multitude of reasons are found why they must return home—grandmother is dying, mother's demands, necessary shopping for school clothes, and many similar situations. To guard against a mass exodus of employees, nearly all summer resorts pay bonuses to those who remain for the full season.

In reality, many of the bonuses are wages that are withheld to insure compliance with employment agreements.

Many summer resorts were built prior to 1930 and so are in need of constant maintenance and repair. Steam lines leak; water hammers develop in the heating system; boilers explode. Typical of what might be expected was one manager's experience on showing a newly arrived family their room in a Pennsylvania resort. First, the lock on the door to the room would not open; finally, a skeleton key did the trick. The room was cold; no heat was coming in. Just as a matter of checking, an attempt was made to flush the toilet; the float valve was stuck. The commode top was removed and an attempt was made to lift the jammed float valve. It disintegrated in the manager's hands— whereupon he beat a hasty retreat.

Resorts spend roughly 6 to 8 percent of their income on repairs and maintenance. The well-kept ones may expend 10 percent. Without constant rehabilitation, resort hotels are like MacArthur's old soldiers: "They fade away."

RESORT MEAL PLANS

Food—and plenty of it—has long been the hallmark of the American Plan resort. While French wines and French cuisine were offered at a few of the resorts before 1850, and have been since, the American Plan hotel dining room has catered to the typical American appetite. Each hotel has had to have an array of fresh baked goods. The baker might be a professional from the city or, more frequently, one of the local citizens with a flair for baking. The distinctively American food style at a resort can be seen from the menu presented by the Atlantic House of Rye Beach, Rye, New Hampshire, dated July 27, 1859 (Figure 6–10).

Also shown in Figure 6–10 is a breakfast menu, dated January 18, 1887. Note the wide selection of items including pigs' feet, tripe, steak, and liver. Diet be damned. Eat hearty and well.

American Plan resort operators have more or less buried the cost of food in the total daily cost. Suppose the guest pays $100 a day; the operator arbitrarily allocates part of the rate to cover the cost of meals. Many resorts offer meals to nonregistered guests for a flat charge.

ATLANTIC HOUSE
Rye Beach
Rye, New Hampshire

Wednesday, July 27, 1859

Soup
Fish
Leg of Mutton with Capers
Chickens, Pork, Corned Beef, Ham, Tongue
Entrees:
Macaroni, Mutton Cutlets, Corned Veal, Lobsters, Escalloped Oysters
Croquettes of Rice, Chicken Pies
Roast of Veal, Beef, Lamb and Chicken
Vegetables:
Pastry:
Dessert: Almonds, Apples, Fruit, Pecans, Oranges, Blanc Mange
Wines:

The Raymond,

SOUTH PASADENA.   CALIFORNIA.

C. H. MERRILL, MANAGER.

⇥ BREAKFAST. ⇤

—:o:—

FRUIT.

OOLONG TEA.   ENGLISH BREAKFAST TEA.   COFFEE.   CHOCOLATE.   MILK

OATMEAL.   FRIED INDIAN PUDDING   HOMINY.
HOT ROLLS.   GRAHAM ROLLS.   GRAHAM BREAD.
MUFFINS.   DRY TOAST.   DIPPED TOAST.
CREAM TOAST.   CORN CAKE.

FISH.

BROILED BASS.   FRIED COD.
SMOKED SALMON.   FRIED OYSTERS.

BROILED OR FRIED TO ORDER.

SIRLOIN STEAK.   LAMB CHOPS.   MUTTON CHOPS
PORK CHOPS.   HAM.   BEEF LIVER.
BREAKFAST BACON.   TRIPE.   SAUSAGES.   RUMP STEAK
VEAL CUTLETS.   PIG'S FEET.

STEWED KIDNEYS   FRICASSEE OF CHICKEN.

EGGS.

OMELETTES, PLAIN, WITH CHEESE OR ONIONS.
BOILED.   POACHED.   FRIED.   SCRAMBLED.

POTATOES.

BAKED WHITE AND SWEET.   SAUTE.   STEWED.
SARATOGA CHIPS.

BUCKWHEAT CAKES.   GRIDDLE CAKES
MAPLE SYRUP   HONEY.

TUESDAY, January 18th, 1887.

Hotels operate on several meal plans:

EP (European Plan): no meals included in the room rate

AP (American Plan): all meals as part of the room rate

MAP (Modified American Plan): breakfast and dinner as part of the room rate

Continental Plan: the room rate includes a limited breakfast

In the United Kingdom and parts of continental Europe, bed and breakfast (B & B) plans mean that breakfast is included in the rate. In parts of England, Ireland, and Scotland, the breakfast is lavish, including bacon, eggs, cereal, and beverage. In France and Spain, the continental breakfast is likely to be rolls, jam or honey, and a beverage.

Accommodations listed as "garni" mean only breakfast, no regular restaurant service. MAP is growing in popularity. It reduces food cost for the hotel, and is helpful to those guests who are diet conscious. The plan permits the guest to have lunch at some other place than in the hotel, perhaps combining it with sightseeing.

EMPLOYEE SCHEDULING

A continuing problem in operating a resort is feeding the employees. Chefs, eager to hold down food cost or indifferent to employee appetites, are prone to run a few menu items over and over. Few resorts account for employee meals separately. Comparisons between resorts in terms of food costs are usually meaningless because of the numbers of employees being fed and the artificiality of the figure set aside by management for food.

How much of the American Plan rate that is charged should be allocated to income from meals? Usually the prices charged on the menu are the amounts allocated from the income from American Plan rates as food income.

Since employees sometimes came cheap, owners in the past tended to overhire. With analysis and tighter scheduling, the number of resort employees can often be drastically reduced. Each employee, even though he or she may be paid little and does little, eats three meals a day, and requires linen and supervision. Such expenses add up fast.

Another way to reduce payroll costs in resorts is to schedule employees more closely to fit the season. Many resorts open June 15 but have only 20 to 30 percent occupancy until July 1. By contracting for something less than half of the entire crew during the June weeks, payroll is reduced, cost of employees' meals is less, and employee morale is higher. A small crew is easier to train and forms a nucleus of experience on which to build when the rest of the employees arrive in July. Employees are kept busy, which is especially important for tip employees.

Combining jobs is another way of reducing payroll. Strange job combinations are possible: an eighteen-year-old at a resort acted as lifeguard in the morning, switchboard operator during the afternoon, and busboy in the evenings. The boy still found time to ring the fire bell in the wee hours of the morning, causing the guests no small alarm.

What about advertising? Resort operators must be promoters or have an imaginative, alert promoter working for them, either on the staff or in an advertising agency. The best advertising has been, and probably always will be, the enthusiasm of present guests. They, too, must be resold during each visit and between visits.

Nearly every resort has a brochure with copy that often overdoes the superlatives. If the descriptions of what the guest can expect were true, the poor guest would die from pure ecstasy—either that or relax so much that revival would be impossible. Here is the description of the Boom Boom Room in a Miami Beach resort:

Calypso . . . voodoo . . . the cool, cool joy of a jungle cave . . . French-Haitian darkness lit with primitive primary colors and the flickering glimmer from hammered copper oil lamps. Sip a rum and let your pulse respond to the beating drums . . . the offbeat rhythms . . . the dark, glistening movement of Calypso!

DIRECT MAIL

Direct mail, sending letters and literature to former guests and prospects, is a major part of resort promotion. Direct mail can be an art. A

Figure 6-10 *These hearty offerings are typical of the American Plan menus featured in early resort dining rooms.*

few operators rely on it completely, spending nothing on paid advertising. Personal letters, referring to the fact that Mr. James broke par on a certain hole (or says he did), or that it is hoped that little Mary's tooth has grown back in, or that the Van Highnoses were just asking about the Joneses, make wonderful reading and create friends for the resort.

Direct mail must be personalized and, even if the same letter goes to 1,000 people, should always add the cheery closing, "Mary and I are eagerly awaiting your return." Hand signatures are a must, and postage stamps rather than a franking machine help. Direct mail requires skill and knowledge. Guest mailing lists must be kept current. The experts say that mailings should be made to every guest who has been at the resort during the past three years. The value of mailing to those who have not returned after three years becomes marginal. After five years the cost is excessive for the probable return. At least three mailings must be made during the year if the mailings are to be effective for promotion.

Honeymooners are great business for a resort. If the bride is not wearing an orchid, she can still be identified, says a veteran hotelier, by the fact that all of her clothes will be spanking new, especially the shoes. Honeymooners usually keep to themselves but are grateful for any friendliness shown. Certain locations have come to be known as honeymoon spots; for instance, Acapulco, Bermuda, and Hawaii. Guam is a prime honeymoon destination for the Japanese.

ECONOMIC IMPACT OF TOURISM

The vacation business has received increasing attention from local, state, and federal government officials as a spur to a sluggish economy. The federal government, for example, sees tourism as a possible means for developing the economies of such states as Kentucky and West Virginia. The Economic Development Administration, a federal agency, has underwritten millions of dollars worth of resort developments for parks in those states and other millions to foster tourism on Indian lands. States like Nevada, Colorado, Wyoming, Arizona, and Florida are well aware of the value of the tourist dollar.

Many of the islands in the Caribbean may have to turn to tourism as the only realistic way of raising themselves from the poverty level. The tourist dollar, it has been maintained, is more valuable to a local economy than the dollar generated and spent within the economy. Much of the tourist dollar goes to pay for services by people, both in operating, and for the construction of, vacation facilities. It is money that is brought in as fresh—money from outside the economy, triggering several "rounds of spending."

The U.S. Department of Commerce states that the tourist dollar "turns over" an average of 3.27 times during a year. In other words, a tourist dollar is received and spent more than three times in the course of a year. This "multiplier effect" of the tourist dollar varies with the self-sufficiency of the local economy. If food has to be imported, for example, the money that goes to pay for the food is immediately shipped out of the community and does not take part in the multiplier effect.

A study of the multiplier effect of tourism on the economy of the state of New Hampshire showed that within a year, the visitor spending was respent several times. As each "round of spending" took place, additional value accrued to the people of New Hampshire. "Leakages," in the form of savings, federal tax payments, and purchases made outside the state, reduces the amount left for the next round.

In the less developed countries, the multiplier effect is less applicable. Much of the construction materials, furnishings, and equipment, and most of the food must be imported. In the Caribbean, for example, one study showed that for every tourist dollar spent on an island only eighteen cents remained on that island.

The state of Vermont is an example of the change of heart that is taking place among some state officials. In 1969 the Chief of the Promotion and Travel Division of the state announced that, although tourism brought over $200 million into the state, there were dangers ahead. The state decided to place restrictions on land use and to change its advertising theme to restrict the kind and number of tourists who come to the state. The state, he said, wanted quality rather than quantity in tourists. Overbuilding and unwise use of the land, say the officials, will destroy the natural beauty of the state.

The beneficial effect of the vacation business on an area can be great, as seen on the island of Bermuda which is almost completely dependent on tourism. The side effects of tourism, what it does to the psychology of the service people, how residents not connected with tourism react, and how much of the rewards of the venture reach the people at the bottom, vary widely with the area. Several vacation places, including Hawaii, Oregon, and Cape Cod, are having second thoughts about the desirability of unlimited tourist growth in their areas.

THE CARIBBEAN—FLIGHT TO THE SUN

The Caribbean could become one grand vacation lake. It has sun, scenery, and history, and it is the tropical vacation area most accessible to the eastern seaboard of the United States. In 1971, 4.5 million visitors went to the Caribbean

(excluding Cuba).[5] Puerto Rico, the Virgin Islands, and the Bahamas each received about one million visitors, mostly from the United States and Canada. The remaining one million went to the other islands, including Barbados and Trinidad-Tobago. Puerto Rico receives one to two million; the Virgin Islands just over one million. Jamaica had more than 400,000 tourists; Barbados, 236,000. The Bahamas, though not geographically a part of the Caribbean, are very much a part of the Caribbean tourist scene (see Figure 6-11).

Air travel—jet air travel and nonstop flights—was the big change factor in Caribbean tourism. The nonstop flights bring the warm sun of the Caribbean almost as close to New York City as Miami. Once the jet is flying

5. The Caribbean Travel Association, *Report of Tourist Travel to the Caribbean for 1971* (New York City: The Caribbean Travel Assn., 1972).

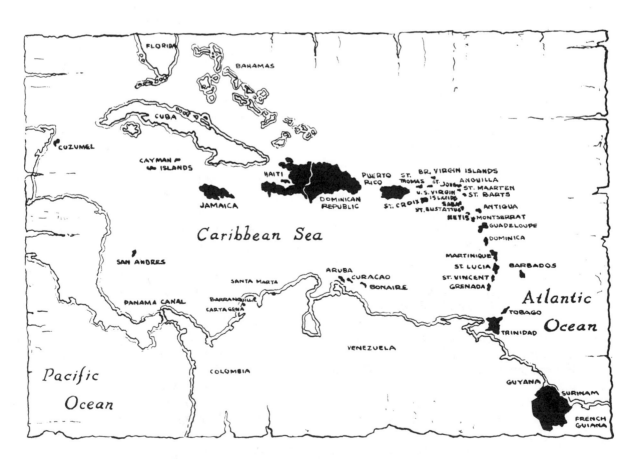

Figure 6-11 *A map of the Caribbean Sea, an area where many of the finest resort hotels are located.*

at an altitude of 35,000 feet, 600 miles is eaten up each hour of flight. The old inconveniences of landing and changing planes are avoided. People who formerly would never consider Curacao, Barbados, and similar islands as vacation spots, now do. Reduced fares opened vast new vacation markets.

Supporting the jet flights are people with the money to afford them, the rising middle-class in North America, both in the United States and Canada. The economists say that travel demand is "income elastic." Travel expenditures increase more rapidly with growth in income than expenditures as a whole. In other words, Mom and Dad, who find themselves in their forties or fifties with an income in excess of $35,000 a year, are likely to place travel near the top of the "most desired thing to do" list.

The Island Travelers

Who are the people who go to such places? First, it is the more venturesome, those who formerly in the 1950s went to such places as Miami Beach. In the early 1950s, Cuba also became the place to go. With Castro, Cuba closed down, and many of these persons tried Puerto Rico and the Virgin Islands.

As soon as an island has been tried by the more venturesome and found desirable, others follow. Airline advertising then takes over as the major factor in tourist travel. College weeks, package tours, and convention sales expose the island to thousands who may become enthusiastic promoters for the island.

Tourism, because of the size of the labor force required to sustain it, brings life and vitality to national economies that have been sick for one hundred years or more. Tourism revenue has replaced sugar revenue on several islands: Antigua, the Virgin Islands, and Jamaica. Barbados' income is about 50 percent from sugar, 50 percent from tourism.

Tourism has replaced salt as the largest share of revenue in the Netherlands Antilles. The Dutch grabbed the dry islands where salt could be evaporated from sea water, and used the salt to preserve fish in the Netherlands. Sugar and slaves made many people wealthy—but fed on the misery of thousands. Tourism on a Caribbean island can benefit most everyone economically, as is the case in Bermuda where there are no shanties, and few unemployed.

It comes as a surprise to most people that many Caribbean beaches are black or non-existent, not expanses of white sand. The islands are volcanic in origin. Several of the islands rise so sharply from the sea that there are no beaches, while many low-lying islands are coral and have not formed sandy beaches.

Tourism had a profound effect on Puerto Rico and on most other Caribbean islands. Land values skyrocketed on most of the islands. None of the islands has a really balanced economy. Several depend largely on bananas as the only cash crop, and this crop is economical only because of preferential sales to the United Kingdom. Tourism cannot help but partially revitalize them, provided politics and prejudice do not interfere.

Jets Encourage Tourism

Direct flight by jets is the most important factor in island tourism. Time and cost of getting to the islands are a primary factor. Advertising then comes into play. Independent hotels cannot afford to reach mass markets through advertising. The airlines can and do; the chains can also; travel articles help. The fact that a friend or neighbor went to St. Martin last year may be critical in making that island next year's vacation choice.

Eastern Airlines was probably the biggest single determinant in the growth of Miami Beach. Eastern Airlines, Pan American, American Airlines, and the other lines serving the Caribbean were of similar importance for the West Indies. United Airlines has been significant in Hawaiian tourism.

Another factor decisive in the growth of island vacationing is the introduction of large management and franchise hotel systems: Hilton, Intercontinental, Sheraton, and Holiday Inns. Their extensive referral systems bring the islands to the attention of hundreds of thousands of people. These faraway and exotic islands suddenly become safe when they have a Holiday Inn or a Hilton Hotel. The food, housekeeping, and safety available can be counted on to be as travelers would find them in the United States.

Cruise ships operating out of Port Everglades and Los Angeles carry thousands of vacationers around the Caribbean, stopping at such places as Nassau, St. Thomas, St. Vincent, Barbados, and San Juan. The passengers file off the ship for sightseeing and shopping. They lunch, observe, and buy, then the ship moves on to another island. Fly/cruise packages enable people from around the country to cover the long distances by plane, then pick up or leave the ship at various ports. Cruise passengers' purchases help the port economies and often stimulate the traveler to return for a longer stay. From Los Angeles, ships cruise up and down the Mexican Riviera and up to Alaska. The ships do not fly the American flag: high costs, especially salaries, have eliminated American shipping and cruise activities.

Other Factors in the Growth of Tourism

Tourism in the Caribbean got off to a slow start. The hotel accommodations that were available before World War I were small and similar to what would be found in an English inn. Since travel to the Caribbean from England and the United States took a long time and was expensive, guests came for the season rather than a week. What tourist business existed before 1930 came to an abrupt halt during the depression of the 1930s and the decline lasted until the end of World War II.

With the end of the war and expanded air travel, guests began coming for shorter stays. They wanted more entertainment and activity than was available. The family-style inn was equipped mainly for rest and relaxation; it was not equipped to attract and entertain people on

Figure 6-12 *The Caribe Hilton, which made its debut in 1949 in San Juan, changed the face of hotelkeeping in the Caribbean, and triggered the tourist industry of Puerto Rico. For its size, this hotel has been most profitable. High room rates, high occupancy, and a gambling casino account for the profit.*

short vacations. Even though the smaller inns added rooms, the scale of operation was usually not economically feasible.

The construction of The Caribe Hilton in San Juan, Puerto Rico, set the style for tourism in the Caribbean. Building design changed: the high-rise resort was introduced in the tropics. The 335-room Hilton hotel was large enough to handle sizable conventions (since enlarged to 707 rooms). The Caribe Hilton is beautifully located on a cove, with rolling surf providing an accompaniment to dining and to swimming in the pool. Gambling is an added attraction. By day, guests can sun at the pool; at night, they can gamble at the gaming tables (see Figure 6–12).

A new dimension to Caribbean resort operations was added in 1958 when The Dorado Beach Hotel was opened by Laurance S. Rockefeller. The Dorado Beach, located about forty miles from San Juan, is a model of luxury and expensive good taste. It was also expensive to build and is expensive to operate. The Cerromar, an 800-room convention hotel, opened in 1972, is now a part of the total operation. (Both have since been sold by Rockresorts.)

An eighteen-hole golf course lies next to the extensive grounds of the main building and cottages. The atmosphere is that of a private and exclusive country club. The larger resorts built since that time in the Caribbean have either been patterned somewhat after The Dorado Beach or have been high rises styled like Miami Beach hotels.

Curacao, the Dutch island off Venezuela, joined those Caribbean islands that saw tourism as an economic savior. Its problems and oportunities in tourism may be typical of those of many Caribbean islands. Over-populated with 138,000 people on a nonagricultural island, Curacao, like most Caribbean islands, has long had an unbalanced economy. Originally the island was valuable only for producing salt to preserve Dutch fish.

Like the Bahamas, the Curacao government provides a tax shelter for foreign capital. Hundreds of companies have incorporated in Curacao.

For political reasons and to insure stability, the Shell Oil Company refines most of its Venezuelan oil at large refineries off shore. The Curacao refinery was built in 1915. Oil tankers, like soldiers in single file, move slowly between Venezuela and Curacao. The island existed to refine and store oil and to serve as a free port for cruise ships.

For the resort operator, Curacao offers problems and opportunities similar to those found in most of the other islands. Low-lying Curacao is almost a desert. Annual rainfall in Curacao is only twenty-two inches. To bring water out of the clouds, a Caribbean island must have mountains that create updrafts to cause clouds to collect and give up their water. In 1928 the island government built the first large water distilling plant in the world.

For the hotel operator, water is expensive. Moreover, pipes carrying the water from the distilling plant to the hotel lie on the surface of the ground. The water is tepid and guests complain that they cannot get cold water from the taps.

On many of the islands the building contractors know little about hotel construction. The Curacao Holiday Inn swimming pool is an example of their lack of expertise. The pool is large and beautiful, the deep and extending below the water line of the nearby ocean. Problem: water pressure from the ocean lifted the pool completely out of its basin. Although the pool is intended to be filled with fresh water, salt water seepage made it partly salty.

Island Operating Problems

The cost of electricity is high on most of the islands. The contractor who built The Curacao Inn, unaware of the relative costs of gas and electricity, installed an all-electric kitchen. To compound the problem, the kitchen equipment that was purchased required a different voltage than what was available on the island.

What looks like cheap labor on an island often turns out to be expensive. More personnel are needed to staff a hotel. Fringe benefits may run as high as 50 percent of the labor cost. Paid holidays exceed those in the United States. Christmas bonuses are obligatory on some islands. Labor relations are not all that they might be. On some islands, once a person is hired or finishes a trial period, he or she is almost assured of tenure. On Barbados and Antigua it is reported that "two people are needed to fill one job." On most of the islands wages are low; so, too, is productivity.

Food is more costly for the hotel operator. None of the islands, including Puerto Rico, produces the quality of food needed to serve the North American guest. Some islands produce only a fraction of their food needs. Even tropical fruits, with the exception of citrus fruits and bananas, must be imported to some of the islands. An operator on one of the Bahamas found he had to send to Miami for shrimp, even though the waters off his island contained plenty of them. The natives were not equipped for catching shrimp regularly.

Quite naturally, spare parts are not stocked on the islands for most of the mechanical equipment. The person who needs a particular screw or nut may wait weeks for it.

The friendliness and readiness to learn of the natives varies considerably from island to island. In 1969 some 5,000 of the islanders on Curacao rioted; tourists were told to remain at their hotels. Many Jamaicans and Puerto Ricans resent North Americans. No doubt such resentment exists on other Caribbean islands.

Resentment expressed as insolence is seen on some of the islands. The hotel operator who recognizes the threat and possible explosive consequences is on the horns of a dilemma. The manager would like to upgrade and give responsibility to the native but, in many cases, finds it almost impossible to do so. The native often lacks the sense of responsibility and urgency required for operating a hotel. More important, the native boss finds it difficult to supervise other natives. "He's just like me. Why should I do what he tells me?" the employee may ask.

Many people, including those in power, are highly suspicious of what tourism will do to the character of the people. They speak of the development of a "servant mentality." We do not want to become a nation of houseboys, they say. They see a danger that the natives will exchange one kind of servitude for another. The new servitude will be comparatively highly paid, but degrading in their eyes. Blacks will still be serving whites, they say, just as they have since Colonial days. The fact that the black is being well paid and is working from choice is not important to such people.

Government officials also find themselves on the horns of a dilemma. They recognize the hard fact that tourism may be the only ready solution to economic depression, yet the masses of tourists are likely to change the expectations and values of the native peoples. They may feel that their island will become a vice palace. They must control the tourist development to gain its benefits and avoid its hazards.

TOURISM, A MIXED BLESSING FOR THE CARIBBEAN

Tourism for the Caribbean is a mixed blessing. It brings change as well as dollars. In the eyes of many, it will spoil the natives. Certainly, the natives will begin to expect and demand the things they see that tourists have. Dissatisfaction, yes; whether it is a healthy dissatisfaction will largely depend on local leadership.

Nationalism and racism can wreck tourism on some of the islands. Jamaica has had rioting and has had much conflict, some of the news of which has been suppressed. Many Puerto Ricans want to be done with tourists. There are signs of growing nationalism.

Most of the islands really have no choice in accepting or rejecting tourism. It is tourism, or else.

The hotel manager or owner who is contemplating the Caribbean should be ready for the paradox of extremely expensive land balanced by low cost for labor (except in Puerto Rico and the U.S. Virgin Islands). He or she should also expect to pay more for just about everything. The owner should anticipate a far different way of life than in the United States, and be prepared to find that the romance of the tropics soon wears thin.

The flight from winter, the hegira to the Caribbean, takes place for hundreds of thousands. Thousands also buy vacation homes; other thousands retire for at least part of the year in the islands. Few North Americans can adjust to living in the Caribbean year around, but a few days vacation in the sun has tremendous appeal.

PUERTO RICO

Tourism is a post-World War II phenomenon in Puerto Rico. In 1949 only 59,000 visitors came to that island. Today the number exceeds one million a year.

Puerto Rico deserves special attention as a resort center.[6] It is a microcosm of the problems and opportunities of a burgeoning vacation center. The story of its growth is fascinating in itself. Before 1949, Puerto Rico had no luxury hotels, nor any tourist business worth mentioning. The island economy, largely dependent on agriculture, was stagnant. Most observers were highly skeptical that Puerto Rico could be made into a tourist center. When The Caribe Hilton made its debut in 1949, it was dubbed "Moscoso's Folly."

Until 1962, the suburb of San Juan, the Isla Verde section, had the only hotel. Other hotels have been built since then in Mayaguez (operated by Hilton), Ponce (Intercontinental Hotel), and Dorado Beach. The Dorado Beach Hotel, as mentioned earlier, was built by Laurance Rockefeller and is one of the most beautifully planned and laid out hotels in the world. It was not designed primarily as a profit-making enterprise, although the company expects to make a profit on all of its properties eventually. It set a tone and a standard of design that influenced resort keeping around the world.

Individuals in higher income brackets can follow the example of the first owners of the Hotel El Conquistador (near Fajardo) and do even better taxwise. During the first unprofitable year of operation, the owners declined the tax relief, and instead applied the hotel's losses against their personal taxes. The law allowed them to postpone the effective date of the tax exemption until the hotel became profitable.

Rising Construction Costs

The cost per room of the newer hotels in Puerto Rico has increased yearly. The figure is arrived at by dividing the total cost of the property by the number of rooms. A large part of the cost has been land price. This forces the construction of high-rise buildings like The Sheraton Hotel and The Ponce de Leon.

Wisely, the Puerto Rico Planning Board has called a halt to all new construction on San Juan's Gold Coast to prevent a "great wall of China" from forming along the beach front. The planning board has tried to distribute hotels around the island so that the hotels with their extensive labor requirements will help the economy of the entire island rather than that of San Juan alone.

The importance of convenient location even to a resort was seen in Puerto Rico. The Dorado Beach Hotel did not make a profit for several years. The Barranquitas Hotel was the island governor's only attempt at building a mountain resort. It proved a failure. The hotel, financed by the government, was taken back by the government and is now operated as a hotel school in Puerto Rico, as is The Racquet Club, near the International Airport.

In the area of labor efficiency, Puerto Rico is probably about the same as other Caribbean operations. Many of the hotels have about two employees per room. The 439-room Americana has close to 800 employees. The Dorado Beach, with 236 rooms, has about 700 employees. At The Holiday Inn in Puerto Rico, an attempt is made to maintain standards of efficiency similar to those found in the States. It has 280 rooms but only 150 employees.

Several hotel operators indicate privately that they are disturbed by the aggressive attack of the union and the lackadaisical attitude of the majority of employees, employees who are well paid by Caribbean standards. For example, the chambermaids receive about the same wages as those in New York City.

Food and beverage cost ratios are low in Puerto Rico because of the high prices charged. Food costs at the beach-front hotels of the San Juan area are about 32 percent of sales. Beverage costs are about 21 percent. For every dollar of food sold at the hotels, 50 cents worth of alcoholic beverages are sold.[7]

Strangely, the island does not produce enough food to feed its own inhabitants. Nearly every item of food, including most vegetables, must be imported. Pineapples, bananas, and plantains are about the only tropical fruits in abundance. With a few exceptions, native Puerto Rican cooks and other culinary employees lack the food tradition found in Europe or North America. Accordingly, most kitchen department heads are Europeans.

---

6. D. E. Lundberg and A. E. Kudrley. "Special Report on Puerto Rico." *Hotel Management Review*, July 1963.

7. "The 1968 Study of Puerto Rico Hotel Operations," *The Accountant*, LKHH, vol. 48, no. 4 (1969).

Profits from Gambling

As in several of the Caribbean resorts, gambling is a big attraction for the hotel guest. At The Dorado Beach about 95 percent of the guests try their hand at gambling, and it has become a form of guest entertainment. Most of the hotels make from 20 to 25 percent on what the guest spends in buying chips.

Gambling is supervised, and a government inspector must be on hand during the hours of play. Television sets are conspicuously absent in guest rooms. Such entertainment might compete with the casinos for the guest's interest.

The big factor in the sudden rise in tourism in Puerto Rico was the extraordinarily low round-trip jet fares between major eastern seaboard cities and San Juan. Most of the vacationers are from New York and New Jersey, with Florida, Pennsylvania, Massachusetts, Illinois, and Connecticut supplying tourists in descending order. The average guest spends about 60 percent of his or her budget for food and lodging, 19 percent for amusements and entertainment, 11 percent for shopping, and 10 percent for miscellaneous items.

In the period from 1970 to 1972, occupancy dropped and profits declined. The Puerto Rican tourism future was clouded by nationalism, unionism, and aggressively rude behavior. As of 1982, twelve hotels that had been in serious financial difficulty were being operated by the Puerto Rican government and were probably not especially profitable.

THE U.S. VIRGIN ISLANDS

The U.S. Virgin Islands, like Bermuda at one time, presented a showcase of what tourism can do for a community. In 1964, income from the tourist trade in the Virgin Islands was $48 million.[8] By 1968, the figure doubled to reach $100 million.

Some 900,000 tourists came, about 700,000 to St. Thomas and St. John; 200,000 to St. Croix. Those who came to St. Croix stayed longer and spent about twice as much per capita compared with visitors to the other two islands. Government jobs were created, free port privileges

were granted, tax advantages were granted to business—tourism growth seemed assured.

The per capita income in the U.S. Virgin Islands was double that of nearby Puerto Rico, and several times that of most of the Caribbean islands. The College of the Virgin Islands, a two-year community college, offers a course in hotel and restaurant management.

All of that changed dramatically with a rise in hostility toward whites. Seven persons were murdered in broad daylight on a St. Croix golf course as part of a robbery. Visitors were insulted, robbed, and mugged while the police often turned away. Residents refused to accept any work they considered menial. Residents of Puerto Rico and other islands came in to do the work, and the groups were resented by the local residents.

Quite naturally, the informed vacationer stayed away, and tourism suffered.

BERMUDA

While Bermuda lies well north of the Caribbean, it is surrounded by the Gulf Stream and for most of the year provides a locale for sun worshipers. It has been referred to as a model of what tourism can do for an island or an area. The island has almost no unemployment. The economy is almost exclusively based on tourism. What little agriculture there was has practically disappeared. Land cannot be set aside for crops; it is too valuable for vacation homes, cottage resorts, and resort hotels. Even so, there has been ugly rioting and race conflict.

THE BAHAMAS

The Bahamas, though geographically not a part of the Caribbean, are really a part of the Caribbean tourist picture. The rise of tourism in the islands was meteoric in the 1960s. In 1949 only 32,000 tourists visited the capital, Nassau. In 1965 the figure had jumped to 495,000 to more than a million in 1968, and to 2 million in 1980, about one-third arriving on cruise ships, mostly from Florida ports. The Ministry of Tourism in 1981 had a budget of $18 million, second only to that of Canada, and spent $11.7 million of it on advertising and promotion. Much of the increase is due to extensive advertising in the United States.

8. Harold Mitchell, *Caribbean Patterns* (London, England: Chamber, Ltd., 1967).

HAWAII

Hawaii's booming tourist industry attracted more than 1.2 million visitors in 1967, up about 500 percent since 1959. The number of visitors hit 2.78 million in 1974, and rose to more than 4 million in 1982.

Virtually every major chain—Sheraton, Hilton, Intercontinental, Western International—has dotted the islands with major resort developments. Hotel rooms number about 50,000, some 23,000 cheek by jowl, in Waikiki.

About one-third of the hotels in Waikiki are Japanese owned. Kenji Osano owns a string of hotels: The Sheraton-Waikiki, The Royal Hawaiian, The Surfrider, and three others.

Hotelkeeping in Hawaii is usually tied in with land development, as a hedge against inflation. As an investment, it has attractive tax advantages. The expenditures are massive. Land prices have soared. In 1975 an acre on Waikiki went for $9 million.

Hawaii is a natural vacation spot for West Coast and Japanese residents. Mark Twain said it best, "The loveliest fleet of islands that lies anchored in any ocean." Its tropical climate—the coldest temperature never drops below the low 50s—offers year-around swimming and tropical foliage found nowhere in the United States except in south Florida. California, with its population of more than 22 million, has been the obvious tourist market for Hawaii. In the late 1960s, direct flights from most of the major U.S. cities made the entire country a market for Hawaii. Jet fares and economy package tours have been reduced to a point where the vast middle class can afford

Figure 6-13 *The curving white beach at Waikiki attracts thousands of visitors monthly. The strand, in Honolulu on Oahu Island, stretches from the Ala Wai Boat Harbor to world-famous Diamond Head. Two lovely spots along the beach area are the grounds of Ft. DeRussy, left, and Kapiolani Park on the right.*
Source: Hawaii Visitors Bureau.

Figure 6-14 *The interior patio of the Mauna Kea Beach Hotel, a Laurance Rockefeller hotel on the island of Hawaii, which opened in 1965. The Mauna Kea is believed by many to be one of the very luxurious hotels in the world. It is currently owned by Western International Hotels.*

the trip. Japanese numbering 600,000 came to Hawaii in 1975. To many people's surprise, Japan is closer than is the United States mainland.

Hawaii has a culture all of its own—a polyglot of races, foods, foliage, and entertainment. A pervading scent of flowers covers most of the islands and seems to say, "This is vacation time." The hotel architecture is often strikingly beautiful. The Mauna Kea, a Westin hotel, is one of the most glamorous and beautiful hotels in the world. Its terraces and striking setting rank it with Las Brisas of Acapulco, The Acapulco Princess, and Caneel Bay Plantation in the Virgin Islands (see Figure 6-14). The Kona Surf Hotel in Hawaii is also spectacular in design and aspect.

The original settlers came to the Hawaiian Islands from the Marquesas Islands in about 1750 A.D. These were followed by other Poly-

nesians from Tahiti many years later. A sturdy race, they were able to travel the 2,500 miles from Tahiti in large double canoes. The social structure was highly defined, feudal in character with priests and chiefs (alii) at the top of the structure, controlling the land and the lives of the commoners by means of force and religious sanctions. The feudal society lasted well into the nineteenth century when American missionaries and their offspring gained control. The natives, susceptible to the new diseases brought in by the white man, were decimated and replaced by successive waves of Chinese, Japanese, Portugese, and Philippinos, who were recruited to do the heavy agricultural work of raising sugar cane and pineapples.

Tourist attractions feature the Hawaiianna of the pre-1890s: the Heiaus, the pre-Christian Hawaiian temples or other places of worship; a City of Refuge on the big island of Hawaii where commoners who had broken the taboos would be forgiven (provided they could make it to the Refuge before being killed); the colorful dress of the chieftains; and the only royal palace in the United States, Iolani Palace, in Honolulu, residence of the last of the native rulers. The early Hawaiian music, chants, songs, and the hula dancing are particularly appealing to visitor and resident alike.

The University of Hawaii has a School of Travel Industry Management, which includes hotel and restaurant management.

Hawaiians are having second thoughts about the desirability of unlimited tourist development. The 15 percent annual growth rate in tourism of the 1960s and part of the 1970s should be reduced, say some of the Island economists. They believe the price paid for the tourist dollar is too high.

The labor market is not everything that the developers would like. Some 60 percent of Hawaii's high school graduates go on to college, which takes most of them out of the hotel employee labor market. Resort operators must constantly search for employees. University students, servicemen's wives, and even vacationers fill jobs as waitresses, buspersons, and bellhops. Military and civil service workers work nights. One hotelman is quoted by The *Wall Street Journal* as saying, "If the Post Office ever made a rule against moonlighting, half the Waikiki bars would close down." The Mauna Kea has a full-time trainer to teach local

Hawaiian women to be waitresses and buspersons.

That the vacation business is delicately balanced was borne out in Hawaii in 1969. In May of that year, room occupancy rates in the major hotels on Oahu dropped to 76.6 percent, compared with 88 percent the year before. Occupancy rates on other islands in Hawaii were even lower, dropping to 63.1 percent on Kauai, compared with 81.4 percent in May, 1968.[9]

LAS VEGAS

"Vegas" is a resort anomaly: it is neither near the sea nor in the mountains; rather, it is in a desert. What makes it all possible is that it has legalized casino gambling, and it is airclose to the population centers of California. Half the visitors are from one city, Los Angeles. Distance is measured in flight time, and the 2,249 miles from New York City becomes 4 hours and 25 minutes by nonstop jet.

The city is really a vast casino with hotel rooms. The gambling casino of The MGM Grand Hotel is 50 percent larger than a football field and contains 1,000 slot machines. The restaurants, night club entertainment, and pools are provided for tourists so they may have something to do when they are not examining a card, throwing dice, or hanging on the turn of a roulette wheel. By 1983 there were about 50,000 hotel and motel rooms in Las Vegas resorts. The climate does its part—at least the skies are not cloudy all day. A sparse 3.7 inches of rain falls annually.

In a way, the Las Vegas phenomenon can be viewed as one huge casino with support facilities consisting of hotel rooms, restaurants, and entertainment. As many as one-third of the guest rooms are complimented to assure that the "premium" gamblers, the big ones, are on hand to add to the "drop," the money that goes from the gambling tables to the management. Entertainment costs to bring the people near the casinos have been huge, as much as $150,000 a week to a name entertainer, such as Frank Sinatra or Johnny Carson. Hotels keep getting larger because only the large hotels can afford the grand-scale entertainment that attracts both gambler and nongaming tourist.

The hotelier, says a veteran observer, looks at three different visitor markets:

1. Those who seek momentary diversion from their regular routine on their days off
2. Those who are on vacation
3. Those who are members of the professional and social groups holding meetings in Las Vegas[10]

Each group is further separated into "grinds," the small bettors, and "premiums," the large bettors. It turns out that junk dealers are one of the best betting groups ever to descend upon Las Vegas. They, like members of other high-risk, speculative businesses that suffer from relatively high rates of bankruptcy, are high rollers. Other groups who produce large casino drops are people in construction, real estate developers, tract home and highway builders, and major contractors.

Income alone is not enough to signify whether a group will be premium gamers. Doctors, dentists, attorneys, bankers, accountants, and insurance salespeople may have incomes well above $50,000 a year but are not premium clients. Womens groups are poor bets for Vegas, and most Strip hotels will not book associations composed of women. What disturbs the pit bosses no end are the "walkers," those who leave the entertainment rooms and walk right through the casino with nary a nod at the alluring extraction devices.

Neither can dress be used as an infallible index of affluence. Pit bosses and others who grant credit have been fooled by sartorial elegance, or lack of it. Once an eccentric millionaire lost $100,000 on a single roll of the dice while wearing worn boots, a torn sweater, and old Levis held up with a knotted rope. The same gentleman left Las Vegas after four months minus $3.2 million.

The vast majority of Nevada's visitors, according to Bill Friedman, who has studied them, are from middle-income groups who can afford the trip to Las Vegas but who are not particularly disposed toward gambling.

The "grinds" seem hypnotized by the slot machines and are overwhelmed by the clanging of large bells and airplane beacons, which go off every time a machine registers a jackpot.

---

9. *The New York Times*, August, 24, 1969.

10. Bill Friedman, *Casino Management* (Secaucus, N.J.: Lyle Stuart, 1974).

Stands on the slot machines that hold the payoff trays are hollowed out so that each tray reverberates with loud thuds as the coins bounce into them on a payoff, and someone screams the amount of every jackpot over a public address system. Since several of the casinos have as many as a thousand machines, a lot of excitement is generated for those who respond to this noise level.

After slots, which women favor, blackjack is most popular, followed by dice, keno, poker, and roulette. Of the dice players, most are men.

Gambling and resorting have an affinity going back a long time. Gambling was a part of the appeal of the watering spots of Europe. Bath and Baden Baden attracted the elite for fun, as well as for health reasons. The "gambling hells" of England predated Vegas in providing free liquor, free food, magnificent rooms in which to gamble, and women—for the big bettors. In the 1700s English club owners figured to keep 25 percent of the money gambled. Las Vegas gives slightly better odds—the casino operators keep 18 to 20 percent.[11]

Monaco, the semi-independent principality on the French Riviera, was largely built around its casino. Horse racing is not only the sport of kings but of everyone who likes to guess which horse will come in first and hope for a profit doing so.

The legalized casino is much a part of the tourist business in several parts of the world but no where more so than in the state of Nevada, especially in Las Vegas and Reno. In no place in the United States is tourism more "dense" than in Nevada (a higher ratio of visitor to resident), largely due to the availability of casino gambling, the massive entertainment, and impressive hotels made available at relatively low cost because of gambling revenues.

Gambling was legalized in Nevada in 1931. Its reputation has not always been the best. One of its early and more notorious developers, Bugsie Siegel, built The Flamingo Hotel on the Strip and named it after his girl friend, Virginia Hill, whom he called his "flamingo." Bugsie was able to build The Flamingo just after World War II when building materials were scarce be-

cause it was considered unhealthy not to deliver them. Bugsie was later shot in the head, reportedly by his associates. Mafia connections in Las Vegas have been reported from time to time. Las Vegas is one of the top five cities in the nation with regard to rate of crime, probably because even though it has one law officer for every 382 permanent residents, it has only one for every 13,000 persons when you count the tourists.

Las Vegas began as a resort in 1941 when Tommy Hull, then of The Hollywood Roosevelt Hotel, had a flat tire a few miles out of town. While his companion went for help, Hull began counting cars, counted for two days, then went back to Hollywood and persuaded the present owners to erect the eighty-room El Rancho Vegas (later renamed The New Frontier). The association of Wilbur Clark with The Desert Inn is well known. One of the early developers of Las Vegas, Clark left San Diego at the age of sixteen, got a job as a bellboy in San Francisco, and later learned the gambling business in Reno.

Many may think that Nevada has a corner on gambling, but there is some form of legalized gambling in more than thirty states. However, in 1977 Nevada, Puerto Rico, and Atlantic City, New Jersey, had the only legalized casino gambling. Gambling is Nevada's chief source of revenue. With 23,000 more cattle than people, the state reported $2.85 billion in gross revenue from gambling in the year ending June 30, 1984. Even though the state collects more than $100 million in gambling taxes, it trails New York and California in tax revenues from gambling. Florida collects about $60 million annually in gambling taxes from its thirty-three legal parimutuel operations for horse and dog racing, but so far has rejected casino gambling.

The Junket Business

The whole idea is to arrange for people to lose money graciously. To that end, airplanes arrive from various parts of the country, loaded with people who are given the illusion that they are getting an all-expense paid vacation to Las Vegas. They pay no air fare, the hotel's rooms and food may be of the best, but only serious gamblers are invited.

Mr. or Ms. Average is reimbursed for his or her fare from Los Angeles or San Francisco.

---

11. Mario Puzo, *Inside Las Vegas* (New York: Grosset & Dunlap, 1976).

Reimbursement quite naturally is in poker chips.

Casinos and jet travel form a happy marriage—the "junket" casino business. A gaming junket is a group put together by a "junket master" who entices a group of persons to fly from such places as Buffalo or San Francisco to a particular casino. Junket members are carefully selected: each player commits himself or herself to gamble a certain sum of money as a minimum; credit is extended to each member depending on credit standing and financial resources; travel costs and the hotel and meals are courtesy of the casino operator. Gambling seems to subsist largely of middle and upper-middle income groups, but there are still some "high rollers" who make gambling a profession or are completely addicted to it and play for high stakes. (And don't overlook the little old ladies mesmerized by the slot machines.) The junket promoter receives a commission based on the quality of the "action" demonstrated by his or her group.[12]

Gaming is a magnet for thousands of people, especially when it is done in pleasant, respectable, and safe surroundings. It offers a sense of adventure usually missing in ordinary life, a small chance for winning money, and a way to ruin one's self, if so inclined.

When money changes hands as quickly as it does over the gaming tables, its value departs. The gambler experiences an exciting, romanticized version of life in the Old West with its flavor of derring-do; and it all takes place in air-conditioned surroundings. The threat of physical violence or hardship is removed.

The MGM Grand Hotel, with 2,100 rooms (until 1979), billed as the world's largest resort hotel, probably is the most profitable hotel in history. (It is reported to have cost $100 million.) A pretentious place, aesthetically barren—it produced $32.6 million in profit in the fiscal year 1975. Its food and beverage sales is said to exceed $50 million a year, topping the total revenues of the largest hotels. It is immense in size, success, and vulgarity. Seven of its suites have a rack rate of $750 a night. They probably are provided complimentary to high rollers. The Grand offers

12. Alberto Caballero and R. B. Taylor, "A Growing of Gaming in America," *L. & H. Perspective* (Spring/Summer 1977).

something new to hotel gambling, jai alai, said to be the fastest of all ball games. The hotel has 3,200 employees.

In the late 1960s, Howard Hughes, "the mystery" billionaire, began buying hotels in Las Vegas and sizable tracts of land in the Las Vegas area. It is speculated that Hughes, who lived in one of the hotels, planned to make Las Vegas a grand world jetport and entertainment complex. In 1970 Hughes owned The Landmark, The Sands, The Desert Inn, The Frontier, The Castaways, and The Silver Slipper Casino; their total value estimated at roughly $200 million.

The other individual owner with extensive holdings in Las Vegas hotels is Kirk Kerkovian, an Armenian-born financier who made his money originally in airlines and in 1969 owned 30 percent of Western Airlines. Mr. Kerkovian owns 51 percent of MGM which, in turn, owns The MGM Grand. Heaviest investment came from the Teamsters Central States Pension Fund, which by 1976 had poured $250 million in loans into the Nevada gaming industry.

For many years the food and beverage operations of the Strip hotels were not expected to make money. They were merely there as adjuncts to the casinos. Beginning in the early 1960s, however, food and beverage operations began to be tightly controlled. Apparently, control is a key word on the part of the casino and hotel operators. Certainly, the odds on the slot machines are controlled in favor of the management. In the game of blackjack, the dealer has a theoretical advantage of 2.5 percent over the player, but most players do not bet wisely, which increases the house odds considerably. In roulette, the casino has a 5.26 percent advantage over the player. Most of the other games offer better odds to the house. The slot machine can be set for practically any odds in favor of the house.

One reason the major hotel chains are so keen on Las Vegas is the tremendous amount of profit possible in an "in" hotel. The expected rate of return on casino income fluctuates between 20 to 30 percent, which means that the players win 70 to 80 percent of the bets placed; the house takes the rest. Of course, costs can be tremendous, costs such as uncollectible accounts, salaries and wages, and the high cost of music and entertainment, which can be exceedingly lavish.

The major hotels spend considerable sums of money in advertising and promotion, decor, and other incidental amenities so as to compete with each other. And each year there seems to be a new, bigger, and better hotel-casino built.

Some hotels are strikingly handsome, some are garish. The nightclub entertainment is the best anywhere in the world and offered at the lowest prices. It does for the middle class what Saratoga Springs once did for the upper class. However, at Saratoga Springs, they at least got outdoors to watch the horses; at Las Vegas, it is all indoors. (A few people brave the weather to sit around the pools and to play tennis.)

Until the late 1950s, Vegas meant gambling, girls, and gangsters, but they were not enough to keep the hotel rooms filled or the dice tables jammed year around. In 1959 the city opened a $10 million convention center on a sixty-seven-acre site, one of the most modern centers in the country. A convention bureau was financed by a tax on hotel rooms. The range of groups picking Las Vegas is wide: from the National Council of Catholic Women to the American Dental Association. Almost every major hotel has also added convention halls and meeting rooms.

The city of Las Vegas is a paradox: 27 percent of the residents are divorced; the city gets most of its income from gambling, yet there are 143 churches and 159 Boy Scout troops. *Time* Magazine calls the place the most vulgar of resorts where an estimated 1,000 whores are at work, while in "the carpeted clockless confines (of the casinos), nothing seems real: time stands still and $100 is just a black gambling chip."[13] The magazine goes on to point out that because of the low rainfall, the water table has gone down so much it has caused the whole town to sink three feet in the past twenty years.

Some Las Vegas Statistics

Some 29 percent of the visitors have a family income in excess of $25,000.

The average stay is four days in which visitors attend 1½ shows.

In 1980 more than 12 million people visited Las Vegas, half from the West.

Junkets and conventions bring in 13 percent of the visitors.

Fridays and Saturdays are the heaviest days; Tuesday is the lightest.

About 30 percent of the visitors are repeaters.

Some 96 percent say they enjoyed their visit.

A number of southern Californians travel to Las Vegas on a regular basis, some as often as once a month. The average visitor to the place makes the trip twice a year.

About 500,000 people come in by plane each month.[14]

The casino/hotel is the most specialized —and most profitable—of hotels. (Harrahs Lake Tahoe Hotel has 535 rooms but grossed an incredible $368 million in 1978.[15])

Hotels host guests but Las Vegas casino hotels offer the professional host—an employee whose job is to get gamblers to come to the hotel and once they are there to make them happy in every way possible. The host arranges show tickets, compliments of the House. He or she arranges special dinners and parties such as golf or gin parties and luxury transportation for sightseeing and shopping trips, and can raise the client's credit limit. The host will even arrange special discounts at hotel gift shops and provide unusual gifts. Some hosts even have "the pencil," the power to sign all expenses at the hotel for the customer.

CAPE COD AND NANTUCKET

Cape Cod, Massachusetts, is a peninsula that in recent years has attracted considerable attention as a summer resort area. Barnstable County, which encompasses Cape Cod, has a population of about 85,000 permanent residents. This number triples and may go even higher during the height of the season. The growth rate has caused considerable dislocation and is not viewed favorably by many of the Cape's residents and by many of the tourists.

13. "Las Vegas: The Game Is Illusion," *Time Magazine*, July 11, 1969.

14. Mario Puzo, *Inside Las Vegas* (New York: Grosset and Dunlap, 1976).

15. *Lodging Hospitality* (August 1979).

For those interested in the vacation business, the stories of Cape Cod and Nantucket can be constructive. Both of these areas were at one time relatively prosperous—Cape Cod from farming, in-shore fishing, and salt-making, while on the island of Nantucket whaling was the all-important business.

Both communities suffered severe economic set-backs and in relatively recent years have turned to tourism as a major source of income. Unplanned and uncontrolled growth of the tourist business has led to serious problems, and now the leaders of the communities are developing new plans for orderly growth. On Cape Cod, the chamber of commerce has decided that growth of tourism should be leveled off and the Cape's economy turned in other directions.

Nantucket seems to be the setting from a movie portraying the happy village life of an early nineteenth century seaport in New England. It hardly seems real. The sea captains' stately homes and the cobbled streets shaded by huge trees provide the setting for what seems the ideal life of the seafarer. Tourism and the ownership of a number of "seasonal" homes by wealthy people have made it all possible. There is no other industry or source of income on the island.

After the Civil War, the 160 whaling vessels that had been actively sailing out of Nantucket were gone. The whales had been exterminated. The natives supported themselves by fishing, raising sheep, and doing small farming. At one time, there were 10,000 sheep feeding on the common land.

Tourism came relatively early. In 1874 there were The Ocean House Hotel and The Springfield House which were open year-around. "Commodious bathing houses" were connected with the hotels for the free use of guests. "The pure sea breezes, unequaled facilities for bathing and fishing, and various other attractions of the island of Nantucket as a seaside resort are too well known by all pleasure seekers to require more than a passing notice.[16] During the summer two boats connected Nantucket with trains coming down to Wood's Hole on the Cape.

Tourism Takes Over

Today, fishing and farming have faded from the scene; the island economy is almost completely dependent on the seasonal residents and the tourists who come to the breezy island to enjoy its particular charm and flavor. A trust has been established for controlling the growth of tourism and for maintaining many of the historical buildings.

Air service to Boston and New York City makes the trip to the island a matter of minutes. The people interested in tourism would rather the day-trippers stayed away. Private clubs and the high cost of real estate help to ensure that Nantucket Island will avoid much of the "razz-matazz" found on parts of Cape Cod.

Cape Cod has a similar economic history; however, it has lacked the control of tourism found on Nantucket Island. Following the Civil War, people moved away from Cape Cod to the Midwest to take advantage of the superior farm land. The in-shore fisheries became depleted, and deep-sea fishing from the Cape was not possible because of the lack of deep harbors. Salt-making was no longer profitable. Jobs and people disappeared in such numbers that by the 1920s and 1930s the population was smaller than it had been in 1860. The Cape became one of the first depressed areas in the country. Even in the 1920s there was no hospital on Cape Cod.

Bestirring themselves, the people formed a chamber of commerce in 1921, but they made the mistake of trying to save the farmer and the fisherman rather than turning to new enterprise. It was not until 1935 that the chamber recognized tourism as a business for the Cape.

Advertising was developed to attract visitors. Since the Cape's greatest appeal to vacationers is as a summer resort, most of the business piles up during late June, July, and August. In 1948 an effort was made to extend the season into October. Any revenue brought in after Labor Day was considered clear profit, since the break-even point for most operations had already been passed. Now, the effort is on extending the season by promoting May and June as a vacation period.

Paralleling the tourist development on the Cape was a rapid growth in the number of retired persons and of people with summer houses on the Cape, but the chamber of commerce was not interested in attracting the people of marginal incomes. In a sense, the tourist

---

16. *Handbook of Nantucket* (Nantucket, Mass.: Island Review Office, 1874).

business complements the business of attracting the retiree. The 40,000 guest accommodations on the island bring people to the Cape, many of whom become interested in the place as a permanent residence.

The chamber decided that guest accommodations should increase to about 50,000 and then level off. Anyone who has been to the Cape during the height of the summer season will agree. Traffic conditions are similar to any urban center, and one can wait for long periods of time merely for the opportunity to move into the traffic flow.

A Balance for Tourism

In the 1970s the basic industries on the Cape were tourism and construction. The once-important fishing industry has dwindled to almost nothing. Farming is confined mostly to the raising of cranberries. Vacationers and construction provided all but about one-third the total.

Future expansion, it was decided, must be carefully planned so that the charm and beauty of the Cape are preserved. Fortunately, this goal was buttressed by the establishment of the National Seashore Park, which spreads over parts of the towns of Provincetown, Truro, Wellfleet, Eastham, Orleans, and Chatham.

The Cape Cod experience demonstrates that a sizable community should not expect high personal income for all of its residents from tourism alone. Tourism must be balanced with other sources of income. It blends well with seasonal homes, retired residents, and some "smokeless industry." Industry, however, must not be allowed to mar the charm and beauty of an area.

The Cape also illustrates the necessity of keeping markets of vacationers well defined. The Cape presently mixes its markets more than is feasible. Cottage colonies can exist alongside motels and hotels. But some of the cottage colonies on the Cape are built so close together, and of such cheap construction, that areas degenerate into vacation slums. Since there are greater profits in renting cottages than there are from other tourist businesses, efforts must be made to insure that cottages are not built too close together and are at least of minimum quality.

FLORIDA

Florida's economy has been likened to a three-legged stool supported by tourism, agriculture, and industry. Tourism is, by far, the largest single business. The increase in tourists has been spectacular: 5 million in 1950, 10 million in 1960, more than 21 million in 1969, and 39 million in 1982. Visitor spending in 1982 was reported at $39.3 billion.

Major appeals of the Florida vacation are "rest and relaxation," the beaches, sports, and the major Florida attractions such as Disney World, Busch Gardens, Sea World, and Cypress Gardens.

Two names stand out in the growth of tourism in Florida: Henry Morrison Flagler, who was responsible for building a railroad from Jacksonville to Key West, and Henry Plant, another railroad tycoon, who pushed a railroad down the west coast to Tampa. Both were self-made men, both were entrepreneurs of the first order, and both made their fortunes prior to the time they went into Florida.

Flagler acquired great wealth as treasurer of Rockefeller's Standard Oil Company. Flagler's first wife died, and later in life he remarried. The honeymoon trip to St. Augustine convinced him of the tourist potential of Florida. He was fifty-three.

In 1887 he built the first luxury hotel in Florida, the 450-apartment Ponce de Leon, in St. Augustine. It cost $1.25 million, at the time a large sum of money. The hotel was authentic Moorish with an imported tile roof and Spanish gardens (now Flagler College). With the success of The Ponce de Leon, another hotel was built nearby, The Alcazar. Its facade is a replica of the celebrated Alcazar in Seville (now a public office building).

Flagler became the rail tycoon of Florida through the Model Land Company which he controlled. Awarded 8,000 acres of land for each mile of railraod built south of Daytona Beach, he eventually owned two million acres of Florida land. As the railroad pushed south from St. Augustine, Flagler built hotels at Ormond Beach, Palm Beach, and Miami. The "winter season" in Florida became not only healthful but a social necessity for the elite of the East.

The present Breakers Hotel in Palm Beach remains. Built in 1926, it copied palaces of Rome, Milan, Geneva, and Venice, and remains the last of the Flagler grand hotels.

Altogether Flagler spent $50 million in Florida, $20 million in pushing his railroad down to Key West. (It was abandoned after hurricane damage in the 1930s, but provided the base for the present U.S. Route 1 to Key West.) In 1900, $50 million was worth several times that amount today.

Flagler's empire reached full tide in 1912: he owned two hotels in Nassau, and a steamship line connecting them to Miami. The Florida East Coast Railroad connected a string of Flagler properties from Jacksonville to Miami. He lived in a marble palace, Whitehall, at Palm Beach, a home which cost $3 million, complete with gold plumbing fixtures, $35,000 worth of throw rugs, and fifty sets of dinner service. Later, Whitehall became a hotel for a short time; it now houses the Flagler Museum.

Though Flagler was unassuming, his political influence in Florida was such that when at the age seventy-one he wanted a divorce from his mentally ill wife, he was able to convince the Florida legislature to pass a special law allowing the separation. His third wife was thirty-four. It was she who urged him to build Whitehall. Ironically, at eighty-three, Flagler died of complications resulting from a fall on the marble staircase of Whitehall.[17] Flagler's dream of extending his railroad/hotel empire to Key West was achieved by the Florida East Coast Hotel Company in 1921, eight years after his death.

On the west coast, Henry Plant built another large Moorish style hotel, The Tampa Bay, now used as a building by the University of Tampa. Plant eventually erected seven hotels.

Through the 1920s, The Belleaire, near Clearwater, one of Plant's hotels, became the winter home of more railroad presidents and industrial tycoons than any other private resort. Private railroad cars by the dozen were parked on the Atlantic coastline spur east of the hotel.

The Florida land boom reached its peak in the summer of 1925, with people swarming into the state in such numbers that railroad tickets were at a premium, and even food was scarce. Shortly after, the boom became bust. But doz-

ens of hotels had been built, many of which faded from the scene during the 1930s.

Miami was opened up in 1896, when the first train chugged into the little community bringing crowds of new settlers and sightseers. Its spectacular growth came later. By 1912, it still counted only 5,000 residents. In 1913 the Collin's Bridge reached Miami Beach. Carl Fisher, one of the founders of Prestolite Company, used millions of his own money and a keen sense of ballyhoo to help make Miami Beach what it is today. One writer claimed that Fisher "rehearsed the mosquitoes so they wouldn't bite until after you bought."

Miami Beach

Miami Beach is one of a kind—it has the most closely packed aggregation of resort rooms in the world. Strangely, only a few of the hotels on the beach are managed by professional hoteliers. Most of the hotels have been owned by a

Figure 6-15 *The Americana, one of the Loews Hotels, on Miami Beach. Note the guest room balconies, so arranged that they all face the Atlantic Ocean. The Americana was one of the first large resort-convention complexes to be built on the Beach. It is truly a resort complex combining guest rooms, food and beverage facilities, convention facilities, and cabanas.*

17. K. C. Tessendorf, "The Lavish Years of Flagler's Florida," *The Travel Agent*, February 15, 1973.

succession of New York City businessmen whose primary interests are not hotelkeeping. Probably nowhere else are there so many partnerships or so many family members involved in the operation of hotels. Each partner gets a title as an officer in the hotel. Hotels are bought and sold regularly.

Hotels are done in lavish and spectacular style. Flood-lit palm trees are standard equipment, as are oversized lobbies. Swimming pools are close to Olympic size, surrounded by sundecks where guests eye other guests, drink, relax, and feel expansive. Most will not consider going into the water.

Large hotels came with the era of conventioning in the 1950s. At the end of the 1940s, a good-sized hotel on the beach had 125 rooms. In the early 1950s a 250-room operation became standard. The Fontainbleau had 1,200 rooms, but in 1977 was in bankruptcy. (In 1978 the hotel was rescued by an arrangement for a twenty-year management contract with Hilton Hotels Corp.)

Figure 6-16 *The Americana—another view. The swimming pool in the subtropical and tropical resort is the center of activity. The Americana's food and beverage business has moved close to the pool, the locale of a large part of the luncheon business at today's resort.*

Financing Miami Beach hotels has been wild in the past. According to Ivan DeNary, a senior member of Horwath and Horwath, most hotels were financed by a combination of methods that represented the equivalent of a financial education at the Harvard Business School. "Interwoven with the financing are the mental gymnastics of income tax planning. It is quite impossible to explain how it is done. One has to see it—and then he probably won't believe it."

Sales promotion is highly prized in Miami Beach. Sales managers often make more in salary and commission than hotel managers. There are many who believe that Miami Beach exists by the grace of the travel agent and the airlines. National Airlines and Eastern Airlines were active promoters of Florida, and especially of Miami Beach. Package plans put together by travel agents and airlines bring thousands of people to Miami during the periods of low occupancy.

Percentages explain a great deal about Miami Beach hotelkeeping. Much of the operation is leased out at a flat rental or a percentage of gross revenue. Some places lease the valet service, shops, parking, cabanas, and even tennis courts.

Resort Concentration

When speaking of Florida as a resort state, we are really speaking of the southern half of the state. Florida is some 500 miles long; northern Florida is not winterized for the resort business. The great concentration of the resort business on the east coast begins at about Ft. Lauderdale and extends down into the Keys. On the west coast, Clearwater is the beginning of Florida's winter resort area.

The west coast is comparatively quiet, largely residential, with relatively small resort hotels and thousands of motels and apartment rentals. Ft. Lauderdale is also relatively reserved and residential in character. Miami Beach is an urbanized resort area thriving on crowds, entertainment, and excitement.

Over 85 percent of Florida's visitors come from east of the Mississippi, with Orlando and Miami the leading destination, followed by Daytona Beach, Jacksonville, and Ft. Lauderdale. Heaviest tourist traffic comes from the

Atlantic seaboard, the southeastern states, and the northern areas of the midwest.

Various sections of Florida attract clientele from specific areas. During the winter season Miami Beach is largely peopled by persons from metropolitan New York. On the west coast—in St. Petersburg, Sarasota, Venice, and Naples—midwesterners predominate. The summer season at Daytona Beach brings guests mostly from states adjoining Florida. Panama City, on the north Gulf Coast, is almost entirely a summer resort peopled by guests from the southeast, as well as Alabama.

Disney World attracts people from all over the world, but predominately residents east of the Mississippi. A number of agencies and people promote Florida. The Florida Power and Light Company has a sizable public relations budget for the promotion of Florida. The Citrus Commission, a quasi-state agency, supported by a tax on citrus sales, ties Florida promotion into its citrus advertising. The State Advertising Commission formed in 1945 advertises Florida widely and has one of the highest state advertising budgets.

Disney World, constructed near Orlando, attracts some 12 million persons a year. The amusement area is five times as large as Disneyland in California. Disney World has become a vast convention and entertainment center with groups vying for the opportunity of scheduling their meetings there (see Figure 6–17). The Orlando area has some 40,000 guest rooms, and has become one of the leading destinations in the world.

Apartments in Florida, to a large extent, are a part of the tourist business. Large numbers of apartments are built primarily for tourist occupancy. The condominium apartment building is set up to be occupied by the owner only during vacations and to be rented during the remainder of the year. This plan helps in financing second or vacation homes as the apartments are largely paid for out of rental fees. Rental management is frequently part of the owners' contract so they do not have to cope

Figure 6–17   *The ultra-modern Contemporary Hotel, Disney World, Florida. The Disney World monorail goes right through the lobby of the hotel.*

with the usual landlord-tenant problems. To attract renters in some locations, foodservice is made available on a catered basis. Florida also has hundreds of licensed mobile home parks, many with swimming pools, tennis courts, and shuffleboard courts. A few have their own post offices. In effect, several are tourist communities with seasonal occupancy and the atmosphere of a resort.

Resorts Rise and Fall

Resort destinations rise and fall. Miami Beach and Atlantic City are excellent examples. Both cities were once meccas for the east coast vacationer. In 1977 both were down at the heels, Miami Beach being supplanted by destinations as far away as Europe, Cancun, Hawaii, Acapulco, and Caribbean resorts. A major factor in the decline of Miami Beach was the bright and shiny new Disney World, located in Orlando in the middle of Florida, cutting off the visitor from the north "at the pass." Things were so bad that the hoteliers went to Washington to seek federal backing for low-cost refurbishment loans refused by South Florida Banks. The number of hotel rooms on the beach dropped to 27,000 in 1976 from 30,000 a decade earlier. *Time* Magazine claimed that only 3,500 of them were first class. In the same ten-year period, Las Vegas added 15,000 rooms for a total of 36,000, and Hawaii's total increased to 44,000 from 16,800. The Mexican resort of Cancun, which did not have a room in 1966, was a fast-growing resort destination.

Miami Beach hopes to survive by attracting as many as 50 percent or more of their visitors as part of conventions. The Fontainbleau Hotel, largest of the beach hotels, thought it had a way out: it advertised a plan for singles that included nude sunbathing in the solarium and video-taped matchmaking services. Outraged citizens in Miami quashed that idea. The once proud Fontainbleau Hotel—largest of the Miami Beach hotels—was sold in 1977 in bankruptcy court. It is now operated by Hilton Hotels.

Miami Beach's problems are said to stem not only from outside problems but by poor management and lack of maintenance. When profits were made, the money was siphoned off without thought for the morrow. Hotels were built close together along the beach, making them invisible from the street and causing beach erosion.

Miami Beach, once the location of a cocoanut plantation, has metamorphized several times, from enclave for the rich in the 1920s and 1930s, a Naval training station during World War II, and then, fading fast, a retirement center, many of the retirees poor. Salvation for the beach appeared in the form of the British working class who are packaged inexpensively for two weeks in south Florida. In 1980 a British Company—Intasun—contracted for 6,000 bed nights for five years. Continental Europeans, Canadians, and Latin Americans are also appearing in number. Dartboards, fish and chips, and barbecues, expected by the British working class, enticed some 200,000 Britishers to Miami Beach in 1980.

THE SKI BUSINESS

Each winter millions of skiers take to the mountain slopes of New England, Pennsylvania, Colorado, California, Nevada, Washington, and wherever else snow falls or can be made for skiing. There is even a ski resort at Gatlinburg, Tennessee, in the Great Smoky Mountains (opened in 1961).[18]

Skiing offers challenging athletics and lively socializing. Skiing also offers opportunity to the resort operators of the area for a two-season operation, summer and winter. Numerous hotels, motels, and an assortment of lodges accumulate around the ski area. The economics of the ski business are not clearcut.[19]

Mt. Snow in Vermont, one of the largest ski areas in the world, is extremely busy on weekends with good snow. Like most ski areas, business drops sharply on weekdays. When there is no snow, the place takes on the air of a ghost town. Mt. Snow is said to be profitable.

Mt. Tom, located within the city limits of Holyoke, Massachusetts, makes its own snow and, since it is available to hundreds of thousands of people within a few minutes, is quite profitable.

Heavy investments and short ski seasons help to account for the financial picture. The number of days of skiing in Wisconsin in 1959 was only 40. Aspen, Colorado, on the other

18. *Wall Street Journal*, March 19, 1981.
19. *Wall Street Journal*, January 7, 1969.

hand, had 147 skiable days in 1964–1965. The 1976–77 season was a disaster in the far west for ski operators because of lack of snow.

Storms and thaws take their toll. Snow-making equipment has added many skiable days, but such equipment cannot prevail against warm weather. In many places, the state involved has helped to finance ski areas. The financing may take several forms, from building access roads to the area to completely building an area, as was done by the state of New Hampshire at Sunapee.

Skiing can bring a great deal of money into an area: construction money, payroll money for lodges, restaurants, and grocery and liquor stores. Ski facilities also stimulate the building of private lodges and year-round homes. Real estate values jump and, to some extent, the community as a whole prospers. A few ski areas are highly profitable and may have seasons running from November into June.

The origins of ski business, as we know it today, are debatable, but it is known that in 1931 the Boston and Maine Railroad sent its first snow train to Warner, New Hampshire, with 197 winter enthusiasts aboard. The skier at that time was regarded as a hardy eccentric who was willing to put up with cold and hardship for a day or a weekend on narrow ski trails.

In 1934 a Model T Ford engine was placed at the base of a hill in Woodstock, Vermont. At the end of a shaft, turned by the engine, was a wheel. Over this wheel, held in position by a flange, a rope was set going; it was the first up-hill tow. In 1938 the skimobile was built at Cranmore Mountain in North Conway, New Hampshire. Later, the aerial passenger tramway was built at Franconia, New Hampshire.

Today, enclosed gondolas travel for miles up mountains. Plush lodges with European cuisine may be scattered around the foot of the slopes. The typical skier, however, does not stop at such lodges. He or she travels by auto from a population center (usually for a weekend), and eats in a cafeteria line or from a vending machine. The usual fare is hot dogs, hamburgers, beef stew, and soups.

As a part of the ski operation, there are usually one or two orthopedists with X-ray machines and plenty of plaster for making casts for broken legs.

The ski business is an adjunct to the hotel and restaurant business; however, for the skiing addict in the business, the lodge can be a sideline to the principal purpose in life, getting onto the slopes.

By the 1960s, skiing had moved into the realm of big business. Much of the ski business and more than 700 ski areas are controlled by big corporations like Twentieth Century Fox, Ralston Purina, Apex Oil, and Solon Automated Services. Many ski areas now cater to the family, offering deluxe accommodations and the American Plan tied in with ski lessons and use of the slopes. Mom and Dad struggle into strange clothes and equipment to join ski classes with their grammar school sons and daughters. Hundreds of thousands of students and young marrieds dash off on Friday afternoon for several hours at a ski area.

The lodge and ski tow operators enjoy it while it lasts. Most are at the whim of the weather. Good snow means big crowds; storms and warm weather and the business collapses. Though snow-making equipment is becoming a must in many places, temperatures above freezing drain away the snow (made during the night), and the profits. Even so, the ski business is likely to continue its mad growth.

Lodges and restaurants in ski areas depend on snow conditions. The lodges at Mt. Snow may be filled to capacity one weekend, and have almost no guests the next. Summer resorts near ski areas have everything to gain, since they can at least do business on skiable weekends. Some of the large summer resorts, of course, do not open during the ski season because of the cost and problems of staffing.

Factors Affecting Ski Operation Profitability

In analyzing profitability—or the lack of it—in ski operations several factors become apparent: the large heavily-invested ski operation with a diversity of activities and attractions has a much greater appeal to the general public than the traditional ski operation with a few tows and a cafeteria style of food service. The large corporation with access to large sums of money can extend the season by introducing indoor tennis courts, a disco, and a variety of restaurants.

Most successful ski operations are part of a larger concept involving land development with condominium and land sales for private homes. Perhaps as much profit or more is made

Figure 6-18 *A heated swimming pool in the midst of a ski resort—this one at Sun Valley, Idaho, is probably the first one to be built. The pool was installed about 1950. Though few people use such pools, they do add glamour, novelty, and decorative value.*

via the land development as in the ski operation itself. The ski operation becomes the focal point and the major appeal of the larger concept. Merely operating ski lifts and hoping for snow is not enough.

The ski operation has a much better chance of success if it is within an hour's travel time of a population center of 50,000 or more people. Mamoth Mountain, said to attract more skiers than any other area, is a little over four hours driving time from Los Angeles.

Climate should be such that there are at least 105 days of snow. The possibility of little or no snow, even in areas where large snowfalls are normal, means that most ski areas should take out insurance in the form of snowmaking equipment.

Summer ski camps are one way of extending the season. Two-week blocks can be sold to groups interested in body conditioning through hiking and skill improvement via movies, professional indoor instruction, and classroom-type lectures. Summer operations can include backpacking tours, fishing camps, health seminars, and related sports and health activities.

Installation of a convention center and emphasis on selling group business during off-peak seasons has long been a means of extending the resort season. Ski resorts enter the convention business to extend the season.

Cluster resorts seem to add to the appeal of the individual resort just as the "restaurant row" is more than the sum of its parts. The avid skier enjoys moving from one ski area to another if they are relatively close together. The cluster resort can also support a greater variety of restaurants and evening entertainment than the individual property.

Larger ski resorts maintain a year-round marketing program, which includes advertising in magazines, newspapers, circulars, radio, and occasional TV. Periodic mailings are made to travel agents, groups, and individuals. Sales calls, ski shows, and ski club councils are contacted and presentations made to them. The primary marketing is done via ski shows.

The ski resort remains a high-risk business requiring heavy capital investment in ski lifts and land (some resorts are on land leased from the National Forest Service). Ski resorts represent a substantial gamble in that they may be highly profitable one year and financially disastrous the next. Generally ski resort profits are reinvested in the property rather than distributed to the owners.

A few ski areas are highly profitable. Mammoth Lakes, California, is one. An average of 220 inches of snow each year permits a long ski season, running from November to or through June. One company there has 1,200 employees and takes in $20 million from ski lift tickets each year.

A major factor in the break-even point of a resort is the uphill ski capacity available—the number of skiers that a resort can move to the top of a mountain.

Typically hotels close to a ski resort run close to 100 percent occupancy on weekends and anywhere from 50 to 80 percent during the midweek.

Ski resorts must continue to innovate, and some are doing so. For example, Squaw Valley maintains an extensive babysitting program. Other resorts sponsor races and exhibitions during slack periods of the ski season.

Skiing historically begins in most ski areas at Thanksgiving where the snow pack is suitable and continues through Easter.

A ski resort could not possibly be profitable without depending heavily on seasonal employees. The free seasonal ski pass is a big inducement for the seasonal employees because the salary range is usually low compared to city pay standards.

VARIETY IN RESORT AREAS

It is misleading to think of the vacation business as confined to the traditional resort areas, such as the mountains of New England, the sea coast of New Jersey, or the ski slopes of Colorado. By far the largest concentrations of the vacation business are in places like New York City, London, Paris, San Francisco, Honolulu, and Las Vegas. The traditional vacation cities such as Paris, Rome, Copenhagen, Salzburg, and Vienna attract many more people than such glamour spots as the Greek Isles or the Canary Islands.

New resort destinations are developing on the southern coast of Spain, the Algarve in Portugal, and several locations in Mexico besides the better known Acapulco (Cancun on the Gulf Coast, Puerto Vallarta, Ixtapa, and Mazatlan on the west coast of Mexico). The island of Maui is second largest in tourism in the Pacific Basin, after Oahu.

THEME PARKS AND RESORT OPERATION

Copenhagen has long had its Tivoli Gardens and Vienna its Prater Entertainment Park, but it took a Walt Disney to demonstrate what can really be done in the way of a major theme park. When well-done and well-operated, a facility becomes a major draw for the area in which it is located and for millions of visitors from hundreds and even thousands of miles away. It becomes a major employer. Disney World employs 23,000 people during its high season. Las Vegas has its gambling, Los Angeles has its Disneyland, Santa Clara has its Great America, and Orlando has its Disney World. Disneyland attracts half of its customers from the Los Angeles area, the rest from "all over." Around these theme parks thousands of hotel rooms and restaurants are grouped as ancillary operations, introducing a new dimension to the hotel and restaurant business.

Since the middle fifties when Walt Disney built Disneyland near Los Angeles, theme parks have become very much a part of the hotel business, magnets for the vacationer, providing entertainment, education, food, and fun for the family. Disneyland was an unqualified financial success to be followed by Disney World, which proved even more successful. Disney World, a 27,400-acre entertainment complex near Orlando, Florida, is said to be the foremost tourist destination in the world.

More than thirteen million visitors came in 1976 and the figure was forecasted to rise year after year. In that year the Disney World complex grossed almost $255 million support for some 40,000 first-class hotel rooms in the Orlando area. The three Disney Hotels within the Park ran occupancy rates of about 97 percent. A Disney World complex in Tokyo opened in April 1983, at a cost exceeding $800 million.

Numerous other theme parks have been developed, with the Marriott Corporation jumping into the field with both feet. Closely related to the theme parks are such attractions as the Polynesian Village on the island of Oahu, operated by the Mormon Church which indeed is an educational experience and adds tremendously to the appeal of Waikiki.

THE VACATION HOTEL
BUSINESS OF THE FUTURE

The vacation hotel business is seen as merging with a number of other businesses or being so related that it becomes a part of them. Perhaps it is better to think of the vacation business as a part of the broader business of tourism. Traveling for pleasure has become one of the world's great businesses, involving vacation planning, the means of travel, accommodations enroute and at the destination, and entertainment during the complete process.

Economic forecasters predict greater discretionary income for the average person, and more interest in travel and vacationing in the future. As airline travel becomes easier and relatively less expensive, its growth will continue.

The vacation business is often inextricably bound with land development, with hotels adding lustre and value to newly developed communities, or in entertainment complexes such as Disney World in Florida, and projects in Hawaii, Spain, Sardinia, the Carribbean, California, and Mexico.

The rapid growth of condominiums that are also rentable as vacation apartments may have a marked effect on the economics of hotelkeeping in resort areas. By 1975 some 300 condo apartment complexes doubled as resort hotels, the owners renting while not in residence. Hawaii had the largest number, but many were in California and Florida. On the island of Maui some 8,000 condo units were for rent as hotel/apartments in 1979 while the island had about half that number of hotel rooms.[20] Others were in Idaho, Maine, Vermont, and Colorado. The condominium owner makes his or her apartment available for rent to a vacationer when the owner is not in residence. About 40 percent of the rental income goes to the owner, the rest to the condominium manager. Foodservice for the condominium renter is available in many areas.

TIMESHARING

Timesharing originated in the French Alps in 1967, and was later imported to the United States to bail out financially troubled, overbuilt condominium developments. The concept spread westward from southeastern states.

San Diego Country Estates, completed in 1979, is said to be the first condominium units in the nation designed specifically for timesharing. Elsewhere, existing properties have been converted from apartment or condominium use to the timeshare and trade concept. In 1980 some 400,000 timesharers and traders worldwide participated in the idea. Business doubled each year between 1975 and 1980. In a sense, timesharing provides an annual vacation at relatively low cost once the original base of the timeshare is paid.

Timesharing, also called interval ownership, has been extended from real estate to houseboats, cruise ships, sailing yachts, ski and beach houses, and even converted railway cars.

There is also the possibility of exchanging ownership or the right-to-use in one property to other properties. At least two organizations have been set up to arrange exchanges. Resort Condominiums International, founded in 1974, is the largest; it uses a "space bank" in which a member "deposits" his or her timeshare and requests an equivalent withdrawal of time at a resort listed in the annual directory. A rival company, Interval International, was started two years later. Both publish annual directories with photographs and descriptions of shared-time resorts.

With Interval International, owners put up their timeshares for exchange and then select a condominium from the ones available, or have their requests put on a waiting list. Exchanges are made on the basis of space, not cost. An efficiency apartment is exchanged for an efficiency apartment although because of building cost differences between areas of the world one may cost double that of another.

Timesharing takes several forms:

1. Time Sharing Ownership (TSO)   Units in a resort are purchased outright, but the unit is shared with other owners, and each may use the apartment, room, or cottage for a specified length of time each year. Title to each undivided interest is conveyed through a warranty deed, including an agreement of use for a particular time period each year. The buyer, in effect, becomes a part owner of a condominium and must pay a pro-rated share of maintenance, taxes, and utilities. The part-owner can sell, transfer, or bequeath his or her interest as in any real property ownership.

---

20. *Los Angeles Times*, Travel Section, September 30, 1979.

The part-owner has the pride of ownership, may participate in a rental pool together with the other owners, and a vacation unit for part of the year. The investment is relatively small, and if the property appreciates, the individual has a profit.

The original owner or developer has his or her money back and perhaps a management contract to operate the establishment. The cost of marketing to the large number of owners, however, is likely to be high.

Part of the resort may be kept as a traditional resort, with units rented to vacationers. TSO units may also be rented when not occupied by the owners.

2. Interval Ownership   This is similar to TSO except that each unit is separate from others, and the ownership is not subject to partition or to tax liens on the interests of other owners. The deed creates an estate—usually for the useful life of the unit—after which it becomes the property of the tenants in common.

3. The Vacation License   The owner buys a leasehold interest in a resort unit for a certain period each year for a specified number of years.

Created by Carribbean International Corporation, the vacation license gives the purchaser the right to use a unit for a certain time period for the useful life of the resort, at least forty years. By 1976 some 6,000 licenses were sold by Caribbean International Corporation for use in their resorts in Ft. Lauderdale, San Juan, St. Thomas, and St. Croix. Buyers have a choice of the resorts for spending their vacations.

The Sea Pines Company, developer of the outstanding resort, Sea Pines Plantation on Hilton Head Island off South Carolina, sells vacation time segments of one or several weeks. According to a company spokesman, the plan enables individuals to invest their vacation dollars, build equity, and, at the same time, have a vacation retreat of outstanding quality in perpetuity for only the amount of time they plan to use it. Corporations can buy TSOs in a resort and use them as employee awards, incentive rewards, and vacation spots for personnel.

A number of hotel groups, including Holiday Inns and Playboy Club International, offer timesharing plans.

4. Vacation Bonds   Like other corporate bonds, the vacation bond represents an unconditional promise of the owner of a resort hotel to pay the face amount of the bond plus interest at a stated rate at maturity. The bonds are secured by either a first or second mortgage on the hotel.

Owners of the bonds may redeem them using them for payment of room rents and receive a 40 to 60 percent discount from the current rack rate.

Time for use of the hotel is specified, one week a year for fifteen to forty years, but the bond holder must reserve sixty to ninety days in advance. Vacation bonds have been sold in California, Hawaii, the Caribbean, and Europe.

Timesharing plans permit resort developers to finance without the need of conventional long-term financing. Owners of existing properties may expand or pay off mortgages.

THE RECENT PAST

As energy prices rose sharply, beginning in 1973, the cost of travel increased as well, causing a rapid change in vacation travel patterns and in the nature of the business itself.

Resort hotels, and others that were big enough, shifted marketing efforts to reach group business. The FITs (Foreign Independent Tour) became fewer; the various tour packages rose in popularity. To reach and motivate group travel, hotels added directors of tours to their marketing departments. The special function of these individuals was to sell group business and to look after the group members while they were guests there.

The package tour took on major importance because of economies possible in selling blocks of airline seats, rooms, sightseeing, and entertainment tickets. On the off season, blocks of hotel rooms would be sold to wholesalers for 25 to 50 percent below the published rate; airlines also discounted their tickets, legally or otherwise. The package hastened what was already a firm trend toward mass travel.

Hotel management and convention and visitor bureaus began to work together much more closely, hotel and bureau representatives traveling together to sell vacations. The San Diego Convention and Visitor Bureau, for example, travels with hotel general managers and sales personnel to major cities in the United States and Canada selling travel agents on San Diego as a destination. The trips are partly underwritten by the airlines. Convention bureaus grew in number and importance, usually partly funded by a hotel room tax of about 6 percent.

Conglomerates such as ITT, MCA, and AMFAC may play an even larger role in the vacation business as they expand around the world. The major chains such as Hilton, Sheraton, and Westin are much involved in vacation destinations such as Hawaii, Las Vegas, San Juan, and Mexico.

The vacation hotel business, until recently the domain of the independent entrepreneur, has changed. It will be interesting to observe the character of the vacation hotel business as it develops over the next several years.

Questions

1. The classic resort hotel of the turn of the century was usually a fairly remote, independently operated mountain or beach resort. How has the resort business of today changed in location and character?

2. Name three prestige resort hotels of the world.

3. Name at least one conglomerate that is active in the resort business.

4. The largest single item in world trade is petroleum and its products. What is the next largest?

5. Of each tourist dollar spent roughly how many cents are realized by federal, state, or local tax agencies?

6. Polls suggest that when there is a recession, people will cut back travel expenditures very quickly. Did this actually happen in the 1972–75 recession?

7. Name two or three major city tourist markets in this country.

8. Regarding seasonality of the resort business, define "shoulder periods."

9. In the early days of the American resort what relationship existed between growth of resorting and the railroad?

10. As a resort destination Atlantic City has been fading but more recently coming back to life because of what legislative change?

11. Thomas Cook is a famous name in the travel business. For what reason?

12. What does the word *garni* signify when used with a European Hotel?

13. What significance does the "multiplier effect" have on the dollar that is spent at a tourist destination?

14. Give three reasons why some states are less enthusiastic about tourism than they have been in the past.

15. Puerto Rico has as many as one million tourists a year. How does this compare with the number of visitors to Hawaii?

16. Give three reasons why the cruise ship business has been growing in recent years.

17. Why is it that cruise and passenger ships do not fly the American flag?

18. Operating a resort in the Caribbean Islands sound romantic; give three reasons why it may not be.

19. Besides Puerto Rico, name three other prominent tourist destinations in the Caribbean or close to it.

20. As a travel manager, what would you recommend people see and do for a two-week period in the Hawaiian Islands?

21. A large proportion of the employees in the hotel and restaurant business are drawn from the so-called disadvantaged groups. Can you explain the reason for this and its effect on society as a whole?

22. Gambling has been a significant inducement for travel. Besides Las Vegas where are citizens of the United States likely to go for casino gambling?

23. Which resort hotel is now the largest?

24. If you were a resident of Cape Cod how would you feel about increasing promotional efforts for tourism to the Cape?

25. Why has Miami Beach declined in popularity?

26. Generally speaking is the ski business a highly profitable one for a ski resort operator? Explain.

27. Contrast Disneyland with Disney World in size and financial objectives.

28. How does employment compare in the service sector of the economy with that of industry generally?

29. Is the service sector of our economy likely to grow in the next twenty or thirty years? Why or why not?

30. How will timesharing affect the hotel business?

31. How does the growth of resort condominiums impact on the hotel business?

Discussion Questions

1. Canada is number one in generating tourism income for the United States. Mexico, the United Kingdom and Japan are next. What factors account for this?

2. Where do you think the next big resort development will take place? Give your reasons.

CONRAD N. HILTON (1887–1979)

Conrad Hilton was the best known hotelman in the world, the first truly international hotelkeeper, and the most durable. At age 90 he was still nominally active as Chairman of the Board of Hilton Hotels Corporation, which owned, managed, or franchised 105 hotels with 46,746 rooms.

According to a Hilton Hotels' release, efficiency in Hilton Hotels is predicated on six factors: time and method studies, job analysis, job standards, safety programs, budgetary control, and pricing programs. Hilton believed that costs must be controlled every day, every week, every month.

With the help of the leading accounting firms, Hilton introduced industrial methods of forecasting and control not previously used in the hotel business.[1] A forecasting committee predicts the number of rooms and covers that will be sold a month in advance, a week in advance, and three days in advance. Forecasts are based on the reservations on hand and the experience for the same month in previous years.

Employees are then scheduled to fit the volume of business forecasted. Deviations from the number of employees allowed under the system must be approved in advance. Department heads are informed if they are over or under in number of employees needed according to the forecast.

Each of the larger Hilton Hotels set up a new position, an operations analyst, a person charged with coordinating the forecasting system. Payroll costs were reduced dramatically because only the number of employees were on hand to service the number of guests in the hotel and in the restaurants that had been forecast. The hotel business fluctuates widely from day to day and between seasons; the forecasting system correlated sales demand and labor needed.

---

1. Donald E. Lundberg and James P. Armatas, *The Management of People in Hotels, Restaurants and Clubs*, see chapter entitled "The Harris, Kerr, and Forster Payroll Cost Control System" (Dubuque, Iowa: William C. Brown, 1978).

Each hotel prepares a detailed daily report summarizing revenues, expenses, profit and loss for the day; the month to date and a comparison of these figures for the preceding month and for the preceding year. Hilton also employs corporate forecasting control. The annual forecast is prepared well before the first of the year.

Though the Hilton organization is decentralized, in the sense that pride is taken in developing a personality for each hotel, accounting and control is highly centralized. Reports reach the Beverly Hills office each day from every hotel and are also funneled into the divisional offices daily so that the top operating executives know exactly what transpires every day.

The Hilton Reservation Service is computerized, with the heart of the system located at The Statler-Hilton Hotel in New York City. The telephone setup and ACD (Automatic Call Distributor) was an innovation in the industry and was designed to accommodate up to 200 incoming lines. In 1972 a computerized communications system (CCS), with private line circuits, linked the office with 160 Hilton and associated hotels around the world. Reservationists handled more than 150,000 reservations monthly.

"Digging for gold" is another Hilton idea. The gold referred to is unused space. Hilton became a master at identifying areas that could be made revenue-producing. He could walk through a hotel and within a few minutes locate new restaurants and bars in the lobby area or project the installation of a lower ceiling in the lobby so that a new floor could be added.

The Waldorf-Astoria is a case in point. The hotel was under the management of Lucius Boomer from the day it opened until Boomer's death. Boomer, a highly respected and knowledgeable hotelman, could never make The Waldorf-Astoria very profitable, even during the war years. Hilton extracted a million dollars in profit from The Waldorf-Astoria the first year that Hilton Hotels operated it. By renting small areas and cases in the lobby, he got $42,000 a year. The laundry was moved from Manhattan to New Jersey, and his "digging for gold" operation produced a number of new revenue-producing bars and restaurants.

The Palmer House in Chicago had always been a money-maker. When Hilton bought it for $19 million, it became a gold mine. The subrentals in the basement of The Palmer House plus the revenue from food and beverage sales are said to pay all the operating expenses of the entire 2,200-room hotel—the first time in history that a bona fide hotel has had a break-even point of zero.

His goal for the Palmer House when he bought it was to increase operating profit by $50,000 a month over the preceding year. Actual

increase during the first year was $1,450,000. All restaurants were converted to seven-day operations; locker room space was converted into sixty additional guest rooms; and nightclubs added photographic departments that yielded $20,000 in profit the first year.

Store rentals at The Palmer House brought in $950,000 per year. Hilton noted that some 4,000 persons passed through the lower arcade every day, with no bar facilities to serve them. He converted a book store (rental of $250 a month) into the successful Town and Country Room, which produced $490,000 in revenue its first year.

When Hilton bought the Statler Hotels, they were among the most efficient of hotel operations. Hilton was able to produce an additional $3 million in profit each year. One way was to remove a million dollars a year in payroll from central office.

One thing most Hilton Hotels have in common—they were bought at bargain prices. The Palmer House cost $25,837,000 to build in 1929. Hilton paid $19,385,000 in 1945. The Stevens was built in 1925 at a cost of $30 million; he got it for $7,500,000. It had been a white elephant, yet Hilton got a net profit from it of $1,730,242 the first year. Since then profits have increased even more.

Hilton's home in Beverly Hills provides an example of his keen sense of a bargain. The home was bought in 1949 for $250,000. In 1979, after his death, the asking price was $15 million, the highest priced private home in California until that date. The furnishings alone, which he got with the home, were worth more than what he paid for the eight-acre estate which was so large that eighteen servants were required to maintain it. Most of the time Hilton lived alone with the servants in this "palace." (Proceeds of the sale were placed in a trust for charitable purposes.)

Perhaps his background explains his character. Hilton was born in San Antonio, New Mexico in 1887, a time when New Mexico was a bona fide frontier with Indians and red-blooded frontiersmen. Conrad's father, Gus, was a plunger, well-fixed part of the time, in bad financial condition at other times.

During one of Gus's lean periods, following the financial panic of 1907, Conrad jumped into the breach and began as a hotel operator. Conrad was up at 3:00 A.M. to meet the train and to rent some of the family rooms in the back of his father's store to traveling salesmen. The tariff was $2.50 for a room and three bountiful meals served by Hilton's mother and sisters.

It was not until 1919, after being a state legislator, a banker in a small way, and having served in the Army during World War I, that Hilton bought his first hotel, almost by chance. It was The Mobley in Cisco, Texas, one of the first of several mints converted into hotels. Hilton went to Cisco intending to buy a bank; he backed out of the deal when the price was raised abruptly. Instead, he bought a hotel when the owner caught the oil fever. Cisco was a boom town short of hotel rooms, and Hilton found himself many nights with the dubious gratification of sleeping in a leather chair in his office, having rented all of his hotel's rooms. Hilton's investment was $5,000.

The Mobley was the first of a Texas chain, which by 1929 included seven properties. Hilton expanded as fast as his profits and credit would allow. His first reverse came during the construction of The Dallas Hotel when he ran out of money. He ended by operating it on a lease.

The depression struck him hard. At one point he was so short of funds that $300 was pressed on him by one of his bellmen for "eatin' money." At one point he was $500,000 in debt. Despite everything that could be done—taking out room telephones, renting out entire floors as storage space, saving on lights and heat, he still could not meet his obligations.

During this phase of his career he learned to operate economically—one of the keys to his future success. He managed to hold on to five of his eight hotels. It was not until 1937 that he was again able to relax, hold up his head, and begin buying hotels again.

With an unshakable faith in the American economy, he acquired the famed Sir Francis Drake and for the first time attracted national attention. Hilton was fifty-one years of age. From this time on, his progress has been steadily up and up. Three times he had had temporary setbacks, but they were minor.

In 1946 Hilton Hotels Corporation was formed. In 1949 controlling interest in The Waldorf-Astoria was acquired, and in 1954 all of the Statler Hotels were purchased in a grand acquisition representing $111 million.

An indication of Hilton's daring and skill was seen in the Statler Hotel purchase. Hilton Hotel Corporation obligated itself to raise about $110 million by a certain date or forfeit $8 million. The $8 million was payable as damages pro rata to each Statler stockholder in case the deal was not closed. The $77.5 million necessary in cash was raised by organizing a new company and offering securities to the stockholders of the existing Hilton Hotels Corporation.

The new company, Statler Hotels Delaware Corporation, was organized, and it was this corporation that raised the money to purchase the Statler Hotels. More than one hundred lawyers in all parts of the country worked on the deal, plus many people in banks, insurance companies, and investment banking houses. The Equitable Life

Assurance Society of the United States loaned $49.5 million, and the First National Bank of Boston loaned $20 million.

With the new company, there was a stepped-up base for the depreciation of the fixed assets, both building and equipment. By adopting a plan of complete liquidation of the old company and distribution of the assets to the stockholders, a capital gains tax was avoided. By using the new corporation, the benefits of the sale-and-lease-back plan were also exploited. After the sale was completed, securities of the Hilton Hotels Corporation in the form of convertible debentures were offered to the stockholders of the Statler Company. Some of the debentures carried a 4½ percent interest rate, others a 4¾ percent rate, and were convertible into Hilton common stock. The warrants for the convertible debentures were oversubscribed.

Hilton International began in 1949 when Hilton was given the contract to operate a hotel that eventually became known as The Caribe Hilton. When the Puerto Rico Industrial Development Company was looking for an operator of the hotel they planned, letters were written to seven hotel executives in the United States asking them if they were interested in the project. Only Hilton was gracious enough to reply in Spanish, starting "Mi estimade amigo." The Caribe Hilton is one of the most successful ventures of all time and has for a number of years made a profit of something like $3 million a year, one-third of it going to the Hilton organization.

The contract between Hilton and the Puerto Rican government set a pattern for later international hotels. The land, buildings, and usually the furnishings and equipment are financed in each country by local capital (government or private), while Hilton International operates the hotels under a long-term percentage rental agreement, with renewal options. Generally two-thirds of the gross operating profits go to the owners, the remaining one-third to Hilton International.

The Hilton International Company cannot lose; the owners are usually pleased because they get the advantage of the Hilton know-how plus becoming a part of the huge international referral and promotion system. The other large U.S. international company, Intercontinental Hotels Corporation, has not been so fortunate. In many cases the company has had to invest at least part of the money for the construction of the hotel.

In 1967 Hilton International Company, owner of thirty-eight hotels, was purchased by Trans World Airlines and merged into the TWA corporate structure as a subsidiary. Hilton International shares were exchanged for TWA securities. As of 1975, Hilton International operated sixty-seven hotels outside the continental United States, including one in Hawaii, The Kahala Hilton. Sales in that year were $143 million. A partly owned reservation system channels business to both hotel empires.

In 1975 Hilton sold a 50 percent interest in six of its larger hotels to the Prudential Insurance Company for $83.3 million, retaining a management contract by which the company receives 3 percent of the gross revenues and one-half of their profits.

The move made Hilton less vulnerable to falling occupancies and enabled the company to reduce its long-term debt to $150 million. By using $26 million of the sum to buy one million shares of its own stock, eighty-seven-year-old Conrad Hilton was left with 29.5 percent of the ownership. Prudential liked the deal because hotel properties tend to be more inflation-proof than other investment properties with long-term leases.

What kind of a man was Hilton? He was energetic, capable, and an incurable optimist. Not one to hide his light under a bushel, Hilton was said to carry around in his pocket a roll of newspaper clippings concerning his own activities. Two biographies have been written about him—*The Man Who Bought the Waldorf*[2] and *Silver Spade*[3]. In addition, he has written an autobiography, *Be My Guest.*[4]

A *Time* article on Hilton noted that he was very conscious of his appearance.[5] The fact that he was 6 feet, 2 inches tall and has the outdoor look made him a handsome man by most standards. He abhored fat men, says *Time,* to the point where he did not even like to do business with them.

His biographer explains that the night life of which he was fond was undertaken upon a prescription of his doctor. Hilton could not forget his work even after working hours. He was told that at

six o'clock he should squire a beautiful woman to a fine restaurant and dance the evening away. This, together with swinging a golf club during office hours, may partly account for his longevity.

Hilton preached the value of God and country. According to his biographer, he prayed regularly and before and after acquiring another property. One public relations ad in *Time* magazine cost $50,000 and was built around the idea of Uncle Sam down on his knees in prayer. Over two million copies of the prayer were distributed. Like most hotel people, Hilton was slow to recognize the value of franchising and only in the middle 1960s began franchising the Hilton name.

The *Time* article had this to say about Hilton's philosophy of innkeeping: "Hiltons are assembly-line hostelries with carefully metered luxuries—convenient, automatic, a bit antiseptic. Conrad Hilton's life is rooted in the belief that people are pretty much equal, and that their taste and desires are, too. His hotels have made the world safe for the middle-class travelers, who need not fear the feeling of being barely tolerated in some of the older European hotels. At a Hilton all they need is a reservation and money." If this is an indictment of Hilton, it is also a commentary on the American traveling public. Many complain about and resent Hilton but continue to patronize his hotels.

In 1969 Hilton joined Statler in having his name closely associated with a school of hotel administration. A gift of $1.5 million made by Hilton to the School of Hotel Management at the University of Houston was used to pay for part of a new Continuing Education and Hotel Administration Building; the name of the Houston School was changed to the Conrad N. Hilton School of Hotel Management. Later the grant was increased by the Hilton Foundation by another $20 million.

By 1977 the Hilton Corporation comprised some 63,000 rooms, 125 of them franchised. The star property is The Las Vegas Hilton, the 3,120 room resort hotel, which in some years, created as much as 40 percent of the corporations total profits. "Each Hilton Hotel and Inn is an individual, a unique and special place, free to do what it does best." That, according to Barron Hilton, is the Hilton difference.

---

2. Thomas E. Dabney, *The Man Who Bought The Waldorf* (Duell, Sloan & Pearce, 1950).

3. Whitney Bolton, *Silver Spade: The Conrad Hilton Story* (Plainview, N.Y.: Books for Libraries, 1974).

4. Conrad N. Hilton, *Be My Guest* (Englewood Cliffs, N.J.: Prentice-Hall, 1957).

5. *Time Magazine,* July 19, 1963.

7 The Restaurant Business

> The pleasures of the Table belong to all times and all ages, to every country and every day; they go hand in hand with all our other pleasures, outlast them, and remain to console us for their loss.
>
> Brillat-Savarin

The restaurant business, says the National Restaurant Association, is the third largest of all businesses in the United States. One of every three meals eaten in this country is eaten away from home. Employees in the industry, including those who work part-time, number more than eight million.

Sales per restaurant increase year after year: average sales for restaurants with a payroll jumped from $66,281 in 1963 to $190,000 in 1975, and continues to increase per restaurant. As sales per unit increase, the necessity of professional management increases. Whereas a few years ago a restaurant with sales of $1 million annually was a rarity, by 1972 about 1,500 had such sales and included coffee shops, cafeterias, and a number of fast-food restaurants that feature the hamburger. By 1981 a considerable number of restaurants with $2 million annual sales were doing business, especially in the larger cities.

The commercial restaurant business prospered greatly following World War II as more people acquired the habit of eating out and had the money to do so. Many aspects of our changing lifestyle (such as more women in the work force) favor restaurant growth. Eating out is tied closely to available disposable income; as disposable income increases, so too do restaurant sales. Food and beverages consumed away from home account for about 5 percent of disposable income of consumers. That percentage holds almost constant.

More than half of the families of households in the United States in 1977 were composed of only one or two persons. The reasons: lower fertility rates, a tendency for young people to postpone marriage, the ease and frequency of divorce, and the ability and desire of young singles and elderly to live alone. The size of households has shrunk from 4.8 persons in 1900 to 3.4 persons in 1950 to 2.9 persons in 1976. Only 65 percent of U.S. households in 1976 were maintained by married couples. What does this mean for the restaurant business? Small households probably encourage eating out in that the dining experience is a social as well as an alimentary experience.

Like hotels, restaurants are becoming fewer but larger. In 1981 total commercial food service (restaurants, fast food, hotels/motels, retail, social caterers, ice cream stores) reached over $100 billion. Table 7–1 shows the breakdown of the total foodservice market for 1981. Keep in mind these figures are not adjusted for inflation.

About 29 percent of the employees in the foodservice business are waiters and waitresses. Cooks and chefs account for 15 percent of the total, counter and fountain workers about 5 percent, and bartenders and clerical workers about 5 percent each. Proprietors and managers constitute about one-fifth of the total employment.[1] In 1975 teenagers occupied about 30 percent of all foodservice occupations; women held 70 percent of all foodservice occu-

---

1. *NRA Washington Report,* April 23, 1973.

TABLE 7-1　Foodservice Industry Sales, 1981, Sales (000)

	1981
Commercial Feeding	$106,118,647
Eating Places	74,896,414
Restaurants, Lunchrooms	39,533,248
Limited Menu Restaurants	30,809,322
Commercial Cafeterias	2,317,606
Social Caterers	806,206
Ice Cream, Frozen Custard Stands	1,430,032
Institutional Feeding	18,938,359
Total Industry	$125,640,280

Sources: Malcolm Knapp, Inc.; National Restaurant Association.

pations.[2] An NRA report (*NRA News*, December, 1976) stated that one-third of the employees in the foodservice business were students, 50 percent in college. The restaurant business thus provides the first job for hundreds of thousands of young people, most at minimum wage.

California leads in restaurant sales. New York is a poor second place, and Texas ranks number three.

HISTORY OF EATING OUT

Eating out has a long history. Taverns existed as early as 1700 B.C. A record of a public dining place in Egypt in 512 B.C. showed a limited menu—only one dish was served, consisting of cereal, wild fowl, and onion. Be that as it may, the ancient Egyptians had a fair selection of foods: peas, lentils, watermelons, artichokes, lettuce, endive, radishes, onions, garlic, leeks, fats—both vegetable and animal—beef, honey, dates, and dairy products, including milk, cheese, and butter.

Women were not permitted in such places then. By 402 B.C., however, women became a part of the tavern atmosphere. Little boys could also be served, if in company with their parents. Girls had to wait until they were married.

Eating Out in Ancient Rome

The ancient Romans were great eaters-out. Evidence can be seen even today in Herculaneum, a resort town near Naples that, in 70 A.D. was buried in some 65 feet of mud lava by the eruption of Mt. Vesuvius.[3] Along its streets were a number of snack bars vending bread, cheese, wine, nuts, dates, figs, and hot foods. The counters were faced with marble fragments and jugs were imbedded in them, which contained wine, kept fresh by the cool stone. Mulled and spiced wines were served, often sweetened with honey.

A number of the snack bars were identical, or nearly so, giving the impression that they were part of a chain under single ownership. Bakeries were nearby, where grain was milled in the courtyard, the mill turned by blindfolded asses. Some bakeries specialized in cakes. One of them had twenty-five bronze baking pans of various sizes from about 4 inches to 1½ feet in diameter.

After the fall of Rome, eating out usually took place in the inn or tavern, but by 1200 there were cook houses in London, Paris, and elsewhere where cooked food could be purchased. The coffee house was also a forerunner of the restuarant of today. It appeared in Oxford in 1650 and seven years later in London.

Coffee, at the time, was considered a cure-all. As one advertisement in 1657 had it: "... coffee closes the orifices of the stomach, fortifies the heat within, helpeth digesting ... is good against eyesores, coughs, or colds ..." Lloyds of London, the international insurance company, was founded in Lloyd's Coffee House. By the eighteenth century, there were about 3,000 of them in London.

Coffee houses were also popular in Colonial America. Boston had many of them, as did Virginia and New York. The words *cafe* and *cafeteria* are from the word *cafe*, French for coffee.

The first restaurant by that name carried this inscription over the door: "Venite ad me omnes qui stomacho laboratoratis et ego restaurabo vos." Few of the Parisians who saw this sign in 1765 could read French, let alone Latin, but if they could, they knew that Monsieur Boulanger, the proprietor, said, "Come to me all whose stomachs cry out in anguish and I shall restore you."

Boulanger called his soup "le restaurant divin." His "divine restorative" was quite an

2. *NRA Washington Report*, November 3, 1975.

3. Joseph J. Deiss, *Herculaneum, Italy's Buried Treasure* (New York: Thomas J. Crowell Co., 1969).

improvement over the bitter herb and vegetable mixtures brewed by the medieval physicians as restoratives. A richly delicious bouillon, it attracted fashionable ladies and gentlemen who would not ordinarily patronize the public taverns where eating ran a poor second place to drinking.

Boulanger's Restaurant Champs d'Oiseau also charged prices sufficiently high to make the place acceptably exclusive and a place where women who were ladies would enjoy being seen. Boulanger lost no time in enlarging his menu, and a new business was born. Soon the word *restaurant* was established, and chefs of repute who had worked only for private families either opened their own restaurants or were employed by a new group of small businessmen—the restaurateurs.

The Restaurant in America

The word *restaurant* came to this country in 1794, via a French refugee from the guillotine, Jean Baptiste Gilbert Paypalt. Paypalt set up what must have been the first French restaurant in this country, Julien's Restorator. Here he served truffles, cheese fondues, and soups. The French influence on American cooking was felt even earlier; both Washington and Jefferson were fond of French cuisine, and several French eating establishments were opened in Boston by French Huguenots who fled from France in the eighteenth century to escape religious persecution.

The restaurant generally credited as being the first in this country was Delmonico's in New York City, begun in 1827.[4] This claim may be disputed by the Union Oyster House in Cambridge, Massachusetts, opened in 1826 by Messrs. Atwood and Bacon and still operating.

The story of Delmonico's and of its proprietors is a fascinating one and it epitomizes much about family-operated restaurants in this country. Few family restaurants last more than a generation, but four generations of the Delmonico family were involved in nine restaurants from 1827 to 1923. The name Delmonico once stood for what was best in the French-American restaurant.

As has happened with most family restaurants, the name and the restaurants fade into

history. The last of the family-owned Delmonico restaurants, at 44th Street and Fifth Avenue, closed its doors in humiliation and bankruptcy during the early prohibition years. The family gathered acclaim and a fortune, but finally the drive for success and the talent for it was missing in the family line.

John Delmonico, the founder, was a Swiss sea captain who retired from ship life in 1825 and opened a tiny shop on the Battery in New York City. At first he sold only French and Spanish wines, but in 1827 with his brother Peter, a confectioner, he opened an establishment serving wines, fancy cakes, and ices that could be enjoyed on the spot.

New Yorkers, apparently bored with plain food, approved the petits gateaux (little cakes), chocolate, and bonbons served by the brothers Delmonico. Success led to the opening of a second-story restaurant in 1832, and brother Lorenzo Delmonico joined the enterprise. Lorenzo proved to be the restaurant genius. New Yorkers were ready to change from a roast-and-boiled bill of fare to la grande cuisine—and Lorenzo was ready for the New Yorkers.

A hard worker—the basic qualification for restaurant success—he was up at 4:00 A.M. and on his way to the public markets. By 8:00 A.M. he appeared at the restaurant, drank a small cup of black coffee, and smoked the third or fourth of his daily thirty cigars. Then home to bed until the dinner hour when he reappeared to direct the restaurant show. He set high standards for himself, Delmonico employees, and for Delmonico patrons. No Delmonico guest could entertain behind closed doors, not even a married couple.

Lavish Banquets

Guests were encouraged to be as profligate with food as they could afford. In the 1870s a yachtsman gave a banquet at Delmonico's that cost $400 a person. Before each guest was a yacht basin, twenty inches in diameter, and in each floated a perfect model of the host's yacht, complete in detail to a tiny gold bar.

At another banquet, a thirty-foot artificial lake was created and in it swam four swans. Golden cages full of birds added to the decor. The most expensive of all Delmonico dinners was one given by a visiting Englishman for one

4. Thomas Lately, *Delmonico's, A Century of Splendor* (Boston, Mass.: Houghton Mifflin, 1967).

hundred New York tea and coffee merchants. The bill was $20,000.

Delmonico's pioneered the idea of printing the menu in both French and English. The menu was enormous, offering twelve soups; thirty-two hors d'oeuvres; twenty-eight different beef entrees; forty-six of veal; twenty of mutton; forty-seven of poultry; twenty-two of game; forty-six of fish, shellfish, turtle, and eels; fifty-one vegetable and egg dishes; nineteen pastries and cakes; plus twenty-eight additional desserts. Some twenty-four liqueurs and sixty-four wines and champagnes were listed. The highest priced entree was canvasback duck, fed on sherry.

What restaurant today could or would offer 371 separate dishes to order? Except for a few items temporarily unobtainable, any dish could be called for at any time, and it would be served promptly, as a matter of routine.

Delmonico's expanded to four locations, each operated by one member of the family. Lorenzo did so well in handling large affairs that he was soon called upon to cater parties all over town. Delmonico's was *the* restaurant. In 1881 Lorenzo died, leaving a $2 million estate. Charles, a nephew, took over but in three years suffered a nervous breakdown, brought on, it was believed, by overindulgence in the stock market. Other members of the family stepped in and kept the good name of Delmonico's alive.

The senior chef, Charles Ranhofer, also acquired a reputation, one of the few chefs in this country to do so. His book, *The Epicurean,*[5] was considered authoritative. Oscar of the Waldorf, whose full name was Oscar Tschirky, got his start at Delmonico's in 1887 as a waiter.

Shortly before the old Waldorf opened, enterprising Oscar composed a letter of recommendation for himself on Delmonico's stationery and collected eight pages of signatures from Delmonico's regular customers. It was sufficiently impressive to win him the job of headwaiter at the Waldorf.

In the 1890s, Delmonico's was given this left-handed tribute by Richard Harding Davis: "Another place where you can get a good square meal, well cooked and fitly served, for about seventeen dollars." In 1910 the last male

member of the Delmonico family to run the restaurants died of a heart attack, and Delmonico's began a slow decline, which ended completely in 1923.

Lobster a la Newburg was invented at a Delmonico's restaurant by Mr. Wenburg. Cruelly, Mr. Wenburg was deprived of gastronomic immortality when, after an altercation with one of the Delmonicos, the first three letters in the dish were transposed.

American Style in Restaurants

Only a few cities in this country could, or would, support the kind of high cuisine and prices offered at Delmonico's. Restaurants in the same tradition, such as Lutec, Antoine's, Ernie's, and the Blue Fox exist only in sophisticated and sizable metropolitan cities. New York City, New Orleans, and San Francisco are the centers of such cookery. Boston has only three such restaurants; Chicago has perhaps the same number; Los Angeles perhaps has ten. Even in New York City there are only about fifteen restaurants that have fulltime sommeliers (wine stewards). These restaurants, of course, influence American cookery but constitute a minute part of the American restaurant business.

The gourmet writers are fond of disparaging the average American restaurant, calling it a vulcanizing plant, and extolling, in contrast, the expensive restaurant in the French tradition. It should be pointed out that there is also an American style in restaurants; in fact, several American adaptations.

These are the coffee shops, fast-food restaurants, cafeterias, and good solid table service restaurants now being copied around the world. They meet the taste, timetable, and pocketbook of the American.

While the Delmonico restaurant is to be admired for its subtlety, grace, and service, it will probably remain more of a novelty on the American scene than the norm. While the Delmonico restaurants won the kudos of the day and were the scene of high-style entertaining, there were hundreds of more typical eating establishments carrying on their business. It has been so ever since.

Louis Sherry was perhaps the best known caterer in the country and, in 1898, he opened a fine restaurant across the street from one of the

---

5. Charles Ranhofer and R. Ranhofer, *The Epicurean* (New York: 1900). The book includes a selection of Delmonico's menus from 1861 to 1894, all French.

Figure 7-1 *The dining room of Le Pavillon in New York City. This was considered by many to have been the finest restaurant in this country, some say in the world. The restaurant was created by Henri Soule who came to this country to manage the French restaurant in the French exhibit area during the first World's Fair in New York City in 1938. House specialities included poached striped bass, duckling aux peches, and plume de veau. Unfortunately, the restaurant closed in 1972.*

Delmonico restaurants. Rector's was the other internationally known restaurant in New York City toward the end of the century. The great and the notorious came to see and be seen. Some thought Rector's was too gay or slightly mad. Some called it Naughty Rector's, which detracted not at all from its glamour. Antoine's, in New Orleans, advertises that it has been operating continuously since 1840, one of the very few that can make such a claim.

Dining for Travelers

After about 1850 much of the fine eating in this country was found on the river boats and in railroad dining cars. Dining car service was among the most elegant and the most expensive, both to the customer and to the railroads. I remember ordering the least expensive item on a cross-country train during the middle of the Depression. The item was three stewed prunes priced at 50¢, very high for that time period.

Railroad dining service on some of the crack trains was indeed deluxe. Yet, on a cost accounting basis, each meal cost the railroad between $1 and $1.50 because of the high labor

costs and the inefficiency of the dining car operation. As on the ocean liners, foodservice on some of the railroads was considered a prestige operation and a promotion cost.

The better known resort hotels and private clubs have always set a fine table, food costs being buried in the cost of the American Plan rate. Many of the finer city hotels were also known for their excellent foodservice.

The public restaurant business grew steadily, but, as late as 1919, there were still only 42,600 restaurants in this country. For the average family in the small cities and towns dining out was an occasion. The workingman's restaurant and the boarding house were strictly meat and potatoes. In 1919 the Volstead Act prohibited the sale of alcoholic beverages and forced many restaurants that depended on their liquor sales for profit out of business. It also forced a new emphasis on food cost control and accounting.

By the 1920s there were enough automobiles to provide a market for a new type of foodservice—the drive-in. Today the drive-in restaurant, with its large parking lot, carhops, and garish entrance sign, has almost vanished, displaced by the fast-food restaurant.

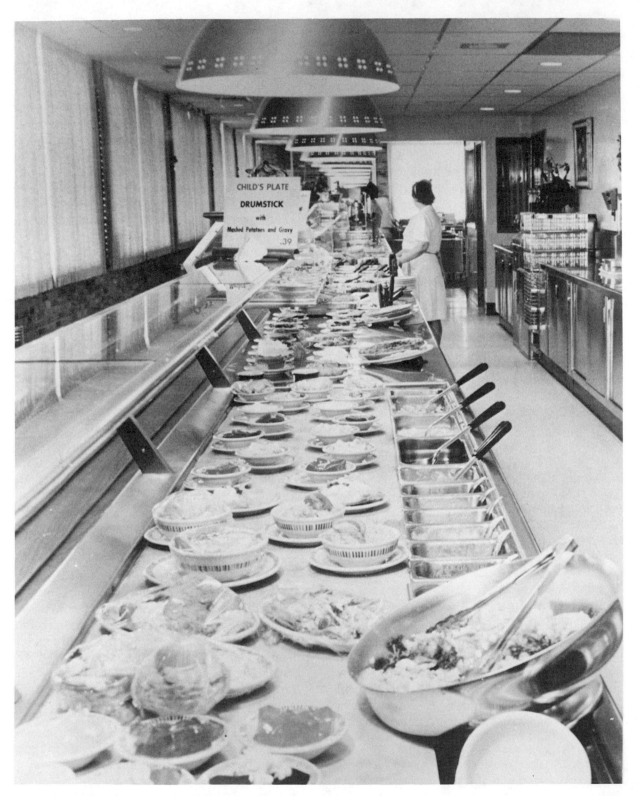

Figure 7–2 *Food display is carefully designed for Pope's Cafeteria counters in the St. Louis area. A bowl of salad and whole desserts are used as highlights on the line. Special merchandising of a Child's Plate speeds selection as children often take extra time when confronted with so many choices.*

Fast-Food Restaurants

Dispensing food on request, fast and hot, is nothing new. The ancient Romans did it at Pompeii and Herculaneum; the roadside diner did it; the automats in New York and Philadelphia did it; but it took the franchise, the automobile, and plenty of parking space to move the fast-food business to become in the 1960s the phenomenon of the restaurant business.

The hamburger sandwich, a meat patty on a bun, has become the cynosure of the fast-food business. The hamburger is pattied, garnished, and eulogized by the smartest advertising people in the business. The hamburger goes to college at Whopper College, training camp for those who aspire to greatness in the Burger King chain. At Hamburger University players are drilled for wealth and status in the McDonald Empire. Little known in the restaurant business until 1930, the hamburger has come a long way.

Indeed it has virtues: most grass-fed animals, including old cows, can be ground up and served. Inexpensive imported boneless beef, raised on grass and containing only 10 to 12 percent fat can be mixed with domestic beef to produce a patty containing 18 to 20 percent fat, which is the desired level. The American public has been conditioned to salivate at the thought of the Mighty Mac, the Whopper, and other anthropomophized forms of the sandwich. McDonald's chain with more than 6,000 outlets and $6 billion in sales, is king over Burger King.

Hamburger history goes back to medieval times when merchants from the town of Hamburg traveling in Baltic areas adopted the Tartar habit of scraping and eating raw meat (Steak a la Tartar is still fancied by some.) Later the meat was browned and the hamburg was brought to this country by immigrants and German sailors.

In England in 1888 a physician, Dr. J. H. Salisbury, promoted a variation of the burger as wonder food, which he was certain would cure an assortment of diseases including colitis, rheumatism, gout, and hardening of the arteries. This was the Salisbury Steak.

The St. Louis Exposition in 1903 served the hamburger in a bun and later, in 1921, the White Castle chain added onions to a flattened meatball and griddled it. The hamburger sold for five cents.

Hundreds of people are examining the hamburger to improve it. No other food item in history has received such minute and enormous attention. Should it be broiled or grilled? Should it be garnished with a tomato? What kind of lettuce should be used with it, shredded or leaf? Should it be dressed with onions, mayonnaise? Should the bun have poppy seeds, caraway seeds, or something else? Should it be prepared and held ready to hand to the customer or made to order? Should it have 20 percent fat or 18 percent? Must the meat come only from the chuck or the whole animal? What percentage of meat trimmings are allowable? Should cheek meat be used? These and other questions have led to the fine tuning of the hamburger.

Although the hamburger itself is king, its courtly accompaniments also bear close scrutiny. Does the crown prince of fast food, the fried chicken, add to or detract from the regal might of Mighty Mac? Fries, shakes, and in some locations even Mexican food, the burrito and the taco, are acceptable at court.

Many entrepreneurs who have flocked to the hamburger banner have been suitably rewarded with millions of dollars. Franchised chains exist within chains, hamburger barons within the hamburger realm. Those who would support king hamburger must not come empty-handed. Something like $500,000 is needed to invest in the Burger King. There are many candidates; few are chosen. To open a McDonald's requires at least $200,000 in cash; the store and property are rented from the parent company.

The fast-food restaurant—with parking lots and walk-up service—surged during the 1960s and into the 1980s. McDonald's and Kentucky Fried Chicken led the way with national limited menus, national TV advertising, and good food. The advertising suggested that the hamburger was love, family, fun, pure ecstasy. Later, fish sandwiches, cheese sandwiches, and other items were added.

Take-Out Service

Not ordinarily thought of as a separate style of service, take-out grows in importance as families become smaller, more people live as singles, and the number of two-income families increase. The fast pace of life makes eating in a car or taking pre-cooked food home more acceptable. Microwave ovens in the home make reheating quick and easy. The take-out meal, purchased at a fast-food restaurant, may be superior to the frozen dinner bought at the supermarket.

Take-out service is nothing new. It is as old as the snack bars of ancient Rome. Certainly the cook houses of twelfth-century London and Paris were examples of take-out. Short-order restaurants—the drive-in and the diner—are all in the take-out tradition. The chicken restaurants—notably Kentucky Fried Chicken—have popularized the take-out, and by the 1980s almost every fast-food hamburger restaurant had installed a drive-through window that increased its total sales without requiring significant additional capital investment. One of the reasons for the popularity of pizza is that it can be ordered by phone and picked up by one person, taken home, and served to any number of people, fairly hot and tasty.

From the operator's viewpoint take-out has a number of advantages:

1. The patrons supply their own seating and dining room space, either in their car or at home.

2. Kitchen space is also minimized because of the characteristic limited menu offering.

3. Labor cost is low compared to offering more service.

4. Few food and beverage skills are required.

5. Because of its simplicity, the restaurant featuring limited take-out menu items is comparatively easy to manage with teen-aged employees.

6. Capital investment required is minimal, as compared with the full-service restaurant.

7. In areas with security risks having only a take-out window reduces the probability of robbery. (Some restaurants close their doors to seating during late evening hours.)

Good take-out locations are not cheap. Mall locations for take-out are not that convenient for the customer and good free-standing locations are expensive.

The customer buying "take-out" sees it as meeting the requirements of economy, speed, and diversion. (The family can sit down to a family meal.) The working wife, it is said, expe-

riences less, or no guilt, in taking home a cooked meal. Take-out, however, is probably more expensive than similar food taken from the frozen-food freezer at the supermarket. Take-out is no substitute for the dining experience, served by attentive and attractive waiters and waitresses. Unless the take-out menu offers more than one or a few items, the food available can quickly become boring. How often do you want fried chicken, spaghetti, or pizza? The major negative for take-out is the fact that once food is cooked, it falls off rapidly in quality. The longer it is held, the less appetizing it becomes.

If take-out is delivered to the apartment or home, one of its merits when served at the restaurant—no tipping—is lost because the delivery person, like the waiter or waitress, expects a tip.

The need for take-out foods need not be debated because its popularity for certain markets is well established. Take-out has moved from being limited to fried chicken and hamburgers to include extensive, expensive meals that can be ordered by an American Express card and includes a variety of ethnic foods such as Japanese sushi and escargot to go.

RESTAURANT CHAINS

Fast-food restaurants, those offering simplified menus and highly standardized service, training, and decor, are dominated by chains. One source estimates that the sale of hamburgers is about 90 percent controlled by large chains. Pizza and ice cream sales are over 80 percent in the hands of the chains. Chain participation in the full menu segment of the market is much less and for a fairly obvious reason. The more complex the menu, the more difficult it is to standardize and control, and the more managerial knowledge and skills are needed. It is comparatively simple to develop a fast-food concept for hamburgers or pizza, lay out the plans and the format of operation, and train relatively inexperienced managers and inexperienced teenagers to operate it. A full-service restaurant is something else—it requires a greater range of knowledge and managerial know-how.

Our first big chain operator was Fred Harvey, an Englishman. His first eating house opened in Topeka, Kansas, in 1876. By 1912 he operated a dozen large hotels, sixty-five railway restaurants, and sixty dining cars.

A man of enterprise and imagination, he sent an envoy to Guaymas and Hermosillo in Mexico to get fruit, green vegetables, shellfish, and other foods. A contract was made with the chief of the Yaqui Indians to supply green turtles and sea celery. The price was right. The Indians were paid $1.50 for each turtle weighing 200 pounds and full of eggs. Turtle steaks and green turtle soup were a house specialty; the sea celery was used for salad.

The Fred Harvey restaurants were models of efficiency: train passengers were served well in minimum time. When patrons disembarked from the train they were immediately asked their choice of beverage. Waitresses used a code in placing the cup on the table and a "drink girl" followed "magically" pouring the patron's preferred beverage without even asking.

The Fred Harvey Company, serving the Santa Fe Railroad, had a major impact in the southwest where Fred Harvey Girls, who were brought to the area as waitresses, married and settled down. The company is now owned by AmFac.

Another early, large chain operator was John R. Thompson. In 1893 Thompson, a young storekeeper, and his wife left the little town of Fithian, Illinois, with $800 to purchase a small restaurant in Chicago. By 1893 there were three units and Thompson, like every successful entrepreneur, cast about for a better way of doing things. He switched from the service-style restaurant to a one-arm dairy lunch, one of the first self-service restaurants. Customers walked up to a serving counter where they picked up their food and carried it back to a school-type chair, the arm being used as a tray.

He was probably the first restaurateur to use a central commissary and delivery by electric truck. Part of his success could be accounted for by the fact that the labor cost of the day was 15 percent of gross sales. By 1926 there were 126 one-armed dairy lunches in the midwest and south. By the 1940s the dairy luncheons were changed over to straight-line cafeterias or sold.

Another chain that was started in the nineteenth century, and is still active, is Horn & Hardart Restaurants in New York City and Philadelphia. The two are separate corporations. Joe Horn, with $1,000 in capital, and Tom Hardart, a luncheon waiter, started the business in 1888. In 1898 they introduced the automat, paying $30,000 for the German invention. The automats, a kind of grand vending machine operation, had their day and are now closed.

Change Constant Factor

Evidence that the restaurant business needs constant revitalization is Child's restaurants, the largest chain in the world during the 1920s. The chain pioneered food cost analysis, breaking down all food purchases into categories and developing standard ratios for each category. Centered in New York City, the chain operated 150 units and did about $28 million in sales.

Then, in the 1930s, the president became fascinated with vegetables because of their presumed health value and because of their low cost. By the 1950s the chain was almost bankrupt and was bought, largely as a tax loss investment, by A. M. Sonnabend, principal owner of Hotel Corporation of America (now called Sonesta).

Stouffer's, probably the best known table service restaurant chain in the country, started in 1924 as a $12,000 lunch counter in Cleveland. Mother Stouffer baked the pies that were sold. Dad and the two sons helped run the restaurant. The chain expanded steadily, going from about $2 million in sales in 1930 to $90 million in 1967.

The company operates "Tops" restaurants sited on the top floor of large buildings in major cities. The company also operates motor inns and a frozen prepared food division. Today it is a subsidiary of Nestle, a Swiss-based corporation, and the Stouffer family is no longer a part of management.

The Marriott Corporation and the Howard Johnson Company, largest of the restaurant chains, both started in the 1920s.

RESTAURANT CHAIN ORGANIZATION

Restaurant chains grow, and when successful they are often acquired by conglomerates such as General Mills, W. R. Grace, and Pillsbury. Typically a restaurant owner builds a small chain, and nearing retirement-age, sells out to a larger company. Some foodservice chains acquire other chains, preferring to buy an established proven restaurant concept.

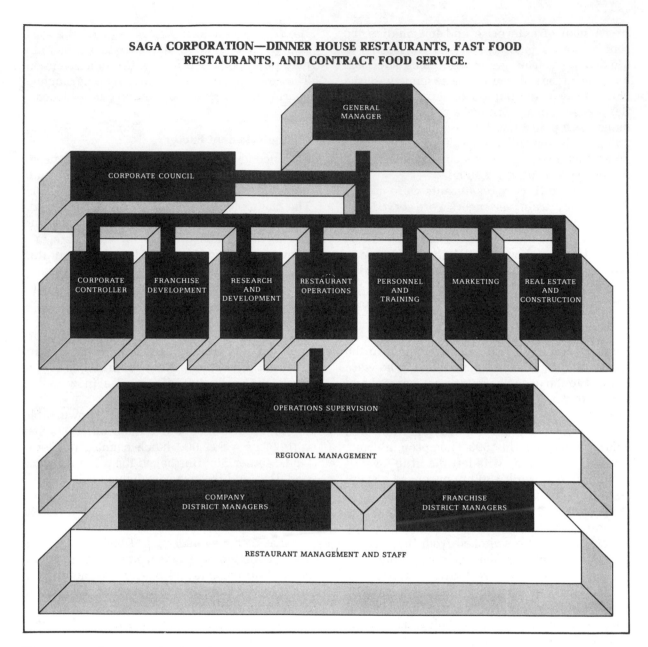

Figure 7-3 *Saga organization chart.*

Saga Corporation has expanded in this way, acquiring other chains, each appealing to a different market. In this way Saga has "positioned" itself in several markets, none of their divisions competing with the other. (The Saga organization chart is seen in Figure 7-3.)

The Saga corporation is the parent organization (headquartered in Menlo Park, California). The company is divided into three principal divisions: Dinner House Restaurants, Fast Food Restaurants, and Contract Food Service.

Straw Hat Pizza, The Velvet Turtle, and Black Angus are restaurant chains within Saga, each with its own format and market. Contract Food Service is another noncompeting division serving schools, colleges, hospitals, and business and industry.

The Mariott Corporation presents a more complicated organization, including separate divisions operating cruise ships, hotels, fast food restaurants, dinner houses, in-flight food services, and most recently, theme parks patterned after Disneyland.

A restaurant chain such as Far West Services is only one company among dozens in the W. R. Grace corporation.

Advantages of the Chain

The restaurant chain, once it has established itself, has several advantages over the independent operator—advantages that chain management often neglects to use. With its larger resources, the chain can more readily establish credit and make long-term leases on land and buildings; in addition, its management can afford to make more mistakes than can the independent. One serious mistake and the independent is likely to go bankrupt.

Nearly every chain has a few restaurants that have never succeeded or have "turned sour." Because of its resources, the chain can afford to experiment with the menu, decor, and design—experiments that the independent is reluctant to try.

Theoretically, a chain can afford to make mistakes through trial and error, eventually developing a highly successful design and format of operation. Once the pattern has been established and is presented to the public—as a Howard Johnson Restaurant or a McDonald's—the chain can replicate the standard by the dozens. This is what has happened. The public, seeing the success of a particular style of operation, is then eager to have part of it, and there is little difficulty in selling either the franchises or stock to the public.

The chain can also afford to employ at least a few people of unusual talents, which cannot be afforded by the independent. The chain can have a top food and beverage director, a far-seeing president, and a few other key executives who may be paid $100,000 a year and up, plus stock options. The chain can afford to employ specialists: an experimental chef, and an advertising and promotion expert. It is also more likely to turn to outside consultants whose fees are sizable.

Chain Dangers

Since the chains have so many built-in advantages, why then are so many restaurants still independents? Part of the answer lies in the development of that insidious disease, "bureaucratitis," hardening of the corporation arteries.

Once the corporation has reached a certain stage of development, it tends to lose its forward motion. Entrepreneurs are replaced by professional managers who are more interested in turning wheels than in making the vehicle go in a particular direction.

Markets change; neighborhoods change; food preferences change; fashions change. The bureaucrats in the large chains are more interested in doing what has been done and preserving their own position than in taking risks and innovating. They have position, power, and status. Why should they exert themselves unduly?

Another disease found in some chains is that of nepotism. The parent, who was a driving, driven, capable person, hands over the reins of the organization to his offspring who often lacks their parent's motivation. The organization begins to lose momentum.

Change in Motivation

The professional manager may be as bright as or brighter than the entrepreneur who formed the chain, but his or her motivation and values are different. The game changes from "Let's be the biggest" to "Let's get accepted into society," "Let's devote our energies to pleasing the powerful." Perquisites of all kinds appear for management. The luncheon begins with cocktails and lasts until 3 P.M. Weekends get longer and factions appear.

The periodic introductions of "operation belt tightening," instituted by men like Ernest Henderson and Howard Johnson, are out of favor. "The company can afford it" becomes the byword. Suggestions for change get lost in committees. No one wants to take responsibility for anything. Why take a chance on something failing?

More secretaries, more assistants, more specialized departments appear to load down the payroll. The company that has been based on a strong tie-in with a particular market rolls along for several years. Profits are good. No changes are necessary, say the new managers. The company has a fine reputation; everybody is happy.

Then symptoms appear; sales hold steady or decline in some units. Really capable people leave for organizations offering more challenge. Those left are the cautious, the well paid, and the complacent. It is about this time that the company goes on the block. An outsider, sensing what is happening inside the company, makes a take-over bid. If the bid is successful, he or she cleans house, and a new entrepreneur is in the saddle.

The restaurant chains actively recruit the graduates of the hotel and restaurant college programs and probably have been the largest employers of hotel and restaurant school graduates.

Some of the chains offer specialized services. Host International concentrates on serving the air traveler. At one time the predecessor company, Interstate Hosts, had contracts with sixty-three different railroad companies. During the 1950s attention was turned to turnpike and airport terminals, and by 1969 Host International had contracts for serving food in some twenty airports. It also operates airport hotels, a chain of Charlie Brown's restaurants, and a number of gift shops. In 1968 it acquired the Church's Chicken of Houston chain of carry-out fried chicken outlets. The chain is now part of Marriott's.

FOOD PROCESSORS AND OTHERS ENTER THE RESTAURANT BUSINESS

Beginning in 1967 a number of large food manufacturers entered the restaurant business. It is only surprising that they had not done so before. By 1973 more than forty major food manufacturers and processors had moved into the restaurant business. Most of the large food manufacturers have separate divisions set up especially to market their products to the institutional food trade, which includes restaurants. They are well aware of the size of the market: at least $20 billion a year is spent on food by restaurants and institutional foodservices.

In 1967 United Fruit purchased the A&W Root Beer chain. United Fruit was in turn purchased by United Brands. General Hosts bought the Uncle John's Restaurants. In 1968 General Foods entered the fast food restaurant field with the acquisition, for $15 million, of the Burger Chef Systems, Inc., an Indianapolis-based, 900-unit, nationwide chain of hamburger specialty restaurants. General Foods also operates the Rix chain of roast beef sandwich shops and, through a Canadian subsidiary, owns the White Spot group of restaurants in

British Columbia, as well as two other restaurant chains in Canada.

The Pillsbury Company bought Burger King Corporation, which had been founded in Miami in 1954. By 1973 it had 854 units. Pet, Inc. bought the Schrafft's Restaurants and Motor Inns. The company also runs the Steak and Ale chains.

General Mills owns about 100 Red Lobster Inns and York Steakhouses. Quaker Oats has a series of Magic Pan Restaurants.

Ralston Purina has more than 300 restaurants known as Jack-in-the-Box, Oscar's Drive-In Hamburger House, and Family Tree Restaurants in southern California.

W. R. Grace, originally a shipping line and now a conglomerate of some 450 companies, owns four restaurant chains, Houlihan's, Del Taco, El Torrito, and Far West Services. In 1977 Pepsi-Cola bought Pizza Hut for $300 million in stock. TWA owns Canteen, one of the largest contract food service operators.

The food manufacturing companies' entrance into foodservice marks a decided change in the character of the restaurant business: these companies bring capital, management know-how, and computer technology with them.

The restaurant business provides these companies with controlled sales outlets for their products. Their restaurants can be used as testing stations for food products. Even more important, the food companies have access to capital for acquiring sites for new restaurants and for buying existing ones. Some of the purchases by food companies, however, have not worked out well; one was a disaster. For a time in 1972, General Foods reported that it had lost $89 million, mostly on Burger Chef since it had been acquired in 1968. The reasons: lack of knowledge about the fast food field, expansion too fast, and excessive prices paid for some Chef locations.

In the 1970s conglomeration grew rapidly. Large multi-companies bought dozens of established restaurant chains.

FOREIGN OWNERSHIP

In the 1970s foreign-owned companies began buying U.S. restaurant chains. Nestle Alementana of Switzerland bought Stouffer's—the well-known table-service chain, the Rusty Scuppers, and the Jaques Borel Group. Trust House Forte bought Colony Kitchens and Hobo Joe's. Howard Johnson's was purchased by the Imperial Group Ltd. of Great Britain. The ice cream chain of Baskin-Robbins was bought by the huge J. Lyon & Co. Ltd. of London.

The W. R. Grace Company that owns several restaurant chains itself acquired a major foreign partner, Friedrich Flick of West Germany. Interstate United Corporation was acquired by Hanson Trust of Great Britain.

In the past a large number of U.S. restaurant companies expanded into Canada. In the 1970s the Canadians returned the favor and about twenty Canadian restaurant firms expanded into the United States. The same can be said for the Japanese.

The Swiss are represented in ownership by Wienerwald Holding, a company that acquired Lums, the International House of Pancakes, Ranch House, and Love's Copper Penny.

A major difference exists between U.S. restaurant representation abroad versus foreign operation in this country. U.S. companies license and rarely invest. Risk to the U.S.-owned company is minimal or nill. Foreign representation here is in the form of investment—and risk can be high.

INSTITUTIONAL FOODSERVICE

Institutional foodservice is usually thought of as being foodservice other than that offered in a commercial restaurant—foodservice in business and industry, schools and colleges, hospitals, nursing homes, and other places of institutional care. It also includes airline catering, the school lunch program, and the foodservices for recreational events such as football and baseball games and race tracks. An indication of the relative size of the institutional foodservice field, as compared with the commercial foodservice field, is the fact that in 1969 about two million persons were employed in commercial foodservices, about one million persons in the institutional foodservices. See Table 7-2.

Contract foodservice for business and industry did not really get underway until World War II when foodservice at numerous war plants became a necessity. Many of the plants were located far from towns and long

TABLE 7-2   Foodservice Market: 1970–1980

Segment	1970	1976	1977*	1980*	Growth Rate 1970–76	Growth Rate 1977–80*
Restaurants	$13,760	$28,490	$31,339	$ 40,650	+ 107.1%	+ 29.7%
Fast Food	6,540	15,240	17,069	25,740	+ 133.0	+ 50.8
Hotels/Motels	1,780	2,990	3,259	4,380	+ 68.0	+ 34.4
Retail	1,480	2,560	2,816	3,750	+ 73.0	+ 33.2
Recreation	1,170	1,890	2,136	2,970	+ 61.5	+ 39.0
Total Commercial	$24,730	$51,170	$56,619	$ 77,490	+ 106.9%	+ 36.9%
Health Care	4,110	6,742	7,281	9,378	+ 64.0	+ 28.8
Colleges/Universities	2,006	3,063	3,337	3,843	+ 52.7	+ 15.2
Schools	4,492	6,600	7,062	8,332	+ 46.9	+ 18.0
Employee Feeding	2,223	4,455	4,856	5,875	+ 100.4	+ 21.0
Transportation	601	931	1,071	1,267	+ 54.9	+ 18.3
Military	2,899	2,836	2,964	3,858	− 2.2	+ 31.0
Total Noncomm'l.	$16,331	$24,627	$26,571	$ 32,553	+ 50.8%	+ 22.5%
Other	1,613	2,436	2,607	3,215	+ 51.0	+ 23.3
TOTAL	$42,674	$78,233	$85,797	$113,258	+ 83.3%	+ 32.0%

*Estimated.

Source: *Institutions/Volume Feeding*, March 15, 1977.

distances from commercial restaurants. The lunch pail, long a symbol of the workingman, gave way to in-plant foodservice, many times offered by the employer at less than cost. Some plants that had cost-plus contracts for government work were pleased to offer luncheons and other meals at reduced cost, or no cost at all, to the employee.

A few contract feeders were operating before the war. Fred Prophet was one of the pioneers. His company later acquired contracts to provide foodservice for a number of the auto plants in the Detroit area.

During the war, persons who had been in the commercial restaurant business were suddenly called upon to take on industrial foodservice, among them Hot Shoppes (now Marriott Corporation) and Howard Johnson. Numerous individuals contracted for industrial foodservice operations since little or no capital was required. In the 1950s and 1960s, dozens of small contract feeders were absorbed by larger companies such as Automatic Retailers of America, Canteen, and Servomation.

Institutional foodservice moves closer to the hotel and restaurant field. Airline catering is managed largely by hotel- and restaurant-trained persons. The Marriotts, in 1937, began putting up meals in cardboard boxes for American and Eastern Airlines out of Washington, D.C. American Airlines, through its subsidiary, Sky Chefs, began providing meals for airplane passengers in about 1941. Later Host International and the Dobbs Houses secured large-scale foodservice contracts for serving a number of airlines.

Hospital Foodservice

Hospital foodservice, or health care food service as it is often called, until about 1950 was typically the responsibility of a dietitian or a person trained in dietetics. In the larger hospitals, the typical foodservice director was a member of the American Dietetic Association. Since about 1960 a number of the larger commercial foodservice companies, including ARA, Stouffer Food Corporation, Servomation, and Saga have moved into the hospital foodservice field, offering contracts for operating the foodservice department.

These companies typically employ a hotel and restaurant university graduate as foodser-

vice director. Under this person, dietitians are in charge of the special diet kitchens, where modified diets are prepared—suitable for patients who must restrict their intake of cholesterol, fat, sodium, or calories, or who have other dietary problems requiring special diets.

Types of Contract

Business and industrial foodservice contracts are usually of two types: either a flat management fee or a "profit and loss" contract. Under the latter plan, the operator agrees on certain menu prices and operating policies, and then gets whatever profit develops. The majority of business and industrial foodservice contracts are of the profit and loss type.

The larger companies maintain test kitchens, separate purchasing departments, personnel departments, and finance and accounting departments.

A food standards supervisor or quality control person is usually employed. The food standards supervisor works with unit managers and district supervisors to develop recipes and specifications for food buying. The specifications are then turned over to the purchasing department.

This leaves the individual unit managers free to concentrate on the operation of their unit. They need not call purveyors for quotations, plan menus, or be personally concerned with accounting, other than to keep records of their own operation. Records are forwarded to the accounting offices for analysis.

As the contract business grew more professional, pro forma budgets were developed for each unit, each district, and the overall company. Costs are computed and the prices for food fixed, so that a predetermined profit can be made.

Where a company has its units in a given geographical area, centralized commissary operations are often established. Servomation Company, for example, has a large commissary operation in Lancaster, Pennsylvania, where an array of foods are prepared and frozen.

Foodservice for business and industry can be classified into three groups.

1. Foodservices for headquarters' offices where the highest quality is demanded. Execu-

tives want the best for themselves, company guests, and customers. Executive dining rooms are often equal to, or more luxurious than, those of the finest private clubs. Such operations are likely to be heavily subsidized by the company.

2. Foodservice for large plants. In these, cafeterias are likely to predominate, backed up by vending operations in remote locations and for evening shifts. These operations are likely to be on a break-even basis.

3. Foodservice for small plants or offices. The manual-vend or complete vend service is more typical here.

The largest of the college foodservice contract companies is Saga Food Administration. It was started at Hobart College, a small private school in New York state, in 1948 when three of the students were asked to serve ninety-nine other students at the college. Their original investment was $1,500. By 1978 the Saga was grossing close to $500 million in sales.

Saga was one of the first to offer students "unlimited seconds" and to include steak and roast beef on the menu each week. The company has an extensive training program for recent hotel and restaurant school graduates, both two- and four-year graduates. Continuous on-the-job training is also offered with technical assistance made available from the home office in Menlo Park, California. Annual food preference surveys among student clientele are made and menus adjusted accordingly. Much of the clerical work is handled in Menlo Park by computer. The company went public in 1968. Saga also owns the Straw Hat Pizza chain, the Velvet Turtles, and the Stuart Anderson Steak Houses.

THE SCHOOL LUNCH PROGRAM

Some 27 million children are fed luncheon and 3.5 million fed breakfast while at school. Subsidized and guided by the federal government, the National School Lunch Program is administered by the U.S. Department of Agriculture. Management at the school level is by a school lunch manager reporting to the school principal.

The manager is beset by the need to hold costs to within budget limits and to follow nutritional standards set up by the Department of Agriculture. Most of the meals are subsidized; many are free to those who cannot afford to pay. Plate waste, food that is rejected by the students, is often high and some program managers are offering food similar to that found in fast-food restaurants. Managers are offered food declared to be surplus at no charge. This is food that the government buys and distributes to maintain prices.

Nutritional standards are changing to keep abreast of the advancing knowledge of what it takes to remain healthy. Reduced amounts of fat, salt, and sugar have been specified for recipes, and many schools have closed out the sale of any food that provides less than 5 percent of the U.S. Recommended Dietary allowances for eight essential nutrients, either per serving or per one hundred calories. This precludes the sale of soft drinks, water ices, chewing gum, and many candies.

There were at least 70,000 unit managers in the various schools around the country. At the level above unit manager are the positions filled by persons supervising a county, district, or several unit managers in a city system. Each state has a state school lunch director and a number of staff personnel, many of whom have had some graduate work and a few who have earned advanced degrees in the field of home economics.

After about 1955, several of the larger foodservice contractors secured contracts to provide school lunches, and even more contractors became interested in school lunch foodservice, both in vending and for manual service.

Food preparation systems vary, but the independent, individual kitchen predominates. The central kitchen is being used successfully by a number of schools; a few use a manufacturing kitchen where bulk food products are processed and then dispatched to individual kitchens for service.

From the central preparation kitchens, food is distributed to the schools in vacuum cans, containers with tight-fitting lids, hot and cold compartment carts, or electrically heated and refrigerated carts.

Where there may be serious delays in making deliveries of food to schools in downtown areas, prepared and frozen meals have an added appeal.

A major advantage of the frozen meals was that deliveries to the school needed to be made only weekly. Some of the food was purchased completely prepared from major food processors. A few of the processors incorporate government commodities, foods that are provided at no cost to the school system, into the frozen meal. In the 1970s a number of school systems expanded the foodservices to include breakfasts and also lunches to the elderly.

ATTRACTIONS OF INSTITUTIONAL FOODSERVICE

A number of hotel and restaurant school graduates have been attracted to institutional foodservice because they are likely to be asked to work a forty-hour week rather than the longer hours characteristic of the commercial foodservice field. Institutional foodservice is also more apt to offer stable employment and more fringe benefits than is usually the case in the commercial field.

Vacation periods are likely to be longer, and most institutions offer their foodservice director participation in a pension plan and medical benefits. There is generally less of the pressure for increasing sales volume and profits found in a commercial foodservice.

In the past, the person entering the institution field recognized that the ceiling on salary would be lower than in a commercial establishment; this has changed. A person joining a contract company and working with an institution has about the same ceiling on salary as a person in the commercial field. It is possible to move into the district supervisor level or into top management, where salaries, stock options, and bonuses are about the same as found in the commercial field.

THE CONVENIENCE FOOD EVOLUTION

As labor costs increase in the kitchen, the trend has been to use more foods that have been completely or partially prepared in the factory—so-called convenience foods. Labor is built into the cost and the operator pays for "the man in the box," as well as for the food itself. The trend is not new; as one wit has put it, "Mother's milk was the first convenience food—and it comes in an attractive package."

What is often meant by the term *convenience food* is the frozen meal that has been precooked and needs only to be heated to serving temperature for service. In the early 1960s Armour & Company and Campbell Soup widely promoted a number of frozen, portioned meals.

Considerable research went into the development of these items, and much money was invested in promoting them. The idea was slow to catch on, and it was not until the mid-1960s that the frozen entree began to be widely used. A number of them are being served on the nation's airlines today.

Convenience Foods Acceptability

A study done at the University of Massachusetts showed that about one-third of the 150 convenience food items examined were acceptable (from the standpoint of quality and cost) for the foodservice at the University. The University Food Service Director wisely introduced the convenience foods in stages. The first stage was to use them for one of two entrees on weekends and to ask the students for their reactions. The response was favorable, and 50 percent of the entrees used were of the frozen convenience type.

The cost of convenience food is a total of the raw food cost, cost of preparation in the factory, cost of marketing and delivery, plus a profit for the manufacturer and distributor. The buyer should expect to pay more for the item, at least as much as or more than it would cost to prepare the item on premise.

The Frozen Entree

The frozen entree comes in a range of quality, from the cheap TV dinner to a high-quality gourmet item. The fact that the entree has been frozen does not in itself degrade the product very much. Fast, low-temperature freezing using liquid nitrogen or carbon dioxide reduces damage done to cell structure in the food. A few foods improve with freezing, especially baked dough products.

Though it is not generally known, the Howard Johnson Company has been serving a large number of frozen foods since the early 1950s. The Dutch Pantry chain began even earlier. Other companies, including Holiday Inns, also do so.

Today restaurant operators have the choice of buying nearly everything ready, or almost ready, to serve, or of making many menu items "from scratch." If they are a Marriott or a Howard Johnson, they may decide to do the processing themselves, producing foods in their own commissaries.

To Make or Buy?

The usual restaurant operator compromises —buying some convenience foods, and preparing other food on the premises.

The concept of producing a meal under industrial conditions, using heavy and expensive equipment, is economically sound. The old kitchen was in itself a processing plant (an inefficient one). Shifting the processing aspect of the restaurant into a modern specialized plant makes good sense. The product that emerges from such plants, however, is not always of desirable quality and may be overpriced.

Effects of Pre-Prepared Foods

As more pre-prepared foods are used, the size of the kitchen and the quantity of kitchen equipment needed is reduced. A restaurant designed to use mostly convenience foods can be small indeed. A "French" restaurant in Chicago has a kitchen about 15 feet by 15 feet. The equipment comprises a freezer and refrigerator for holding frozen foods, and a range top for boiling water used to reheat.

There was no revolution, just evolution. Pemmican—dried meat, fat, and berries—was a form of convenience food carried by the early explorers; it is still used today by campers and explorers. All canned foods are "convenienced" and have been popular since the Civil War. Sliced bread and ice cream are convenience foods, widely used for some time.

RESTAURANT CLASSIFICATION

Restaurants can be classified according to different criteria: types of service, menu price, type of atmosphere, and so on. Variations of older styles of service are constantly appearing. Table service has been the traditional method of service in this country. The coffee shop with its counter or combination counter and table service is widespread today. Self-service pick-up characterizes the fast-food outlets. Fast food, the fastest growing segment of foodservice, features limited menu items like ham-

burgers, pancakes, pizzas, and chicken, "served to teenagers by teenagers." As the term implies, "fast food" means quick service—the food already prepared and being held, or fried or grilled quickly, or reheated by microwave. As distinguished from the coffee shop, its near relative, fast food typically offers no table service and few menu choices. The coffee shop almost always features breakfast items at all hours and offers waitress service. The cafeteria and its sister style of service, buffet/smorgasbord, are popular for special functions and are offered as regular service in many restaurants.

The drive-through restaurant is successful in warmer climates and the carnival/select service, where a group of small booths or small restaurants in an enclosed area offer specialty foods such as fish and chips, sandwiches, Mexican food, and so on, is seen in more cities around the country.

Theater restaurants are still another category. Typically, theater restaurants serve a limited menu, offering a choice of perhaps three entrees. Most owners find buffet style service the most workable—and profitable—format. In general, these establishments use converted buildings rather than new ones and concentrate on offering plays that draw a mass audience. Some hire drama students to wait on tables and double as actors.

Ethnic restaurants, such as French, Chinese, Italian, and Mexican, have existed since before the turn of the century in this country. A 1975 survey found that among the 80 percent of the U.S. population who eat at ethnic restaurants, Italian and Oriental were the most popular foods. Mexican restaurants were moving rapidly in popularity. German restaurants attracted about 6 percent of the group; French restaurants about 4 percent. Specialty restaurants offering a very limited menu, such as seafood or pancakes, or soup and salad, or steak and ale, are growing in popularity. Theme restaurants feature standard food items amidst unusual, oftentimes, funky surroundings. Feedmills, warehouses, barns, hangars, yachts, large old homes, and so on are made into conversation-piece restaurants.

Social catering is yet another type of foodservice: food is typically partly or completely prepared in a restaurant or special kitchen, transported to another location, and served.

Weddings, celebrations, large picnics, and social functions in private homes are often "catered" by professional caterers. (The term in Britain refers to all public foodservice.)

Most American foodservice emphasizes the functional and the utilitarian: efficiency, and speed. Europeans, at first amused and amazed at our emphasis on efficiency and fast service, now are widely copying us in snack bars, coffee shops, and counter service generally. The cafeteria is an American concept, going back to a YWCA foodservice in Kansas City in 1891; so, too, is counter and carhop service.

Table service in some American restaurants has been modified by taking a team approach to serving banquets. The use of intercommunication systems between dining room manager and each waiter or waitress is typically American.

A few restaurants give deluxe service in the form of a modified a la Ritz service, which makes use of the gueridon (cart) and rechaud (heater), captains, and headwaiters. Such places probably constitute less than 1 percent of the total service in American restaurants for two reasons: one, most Americans do not want to take the time for such leisurely dining; two, usually only expense account spenders are willing to pay the high labor cost entailed in this style of service.

Table Service

Most table service is what might be called American service; food is supposedly served from the left and removed from the right of the guest. Typically, the food is plated in the kitchen, then carried to the table on a tray or cart.

In French service food is not plated in the kitchen but, rather, carried on a silver platter to the table for the guest's inspection. Tableside preparation or finishing may take place in view of the customer. A fish may be boned, sauced, and served; a steak, flamed; a dessert or omelet prepared, using the gueridon (cart) and rechaud heater. The service is relatively slow, time consuming, and costly.

At one time, other distinctions in service were made: Russian service and service a la Ritz were identifiable. Today service—especially banquet service—that does not involve plating the food in the kitchen is often called French service. At large banquets, waiters may serve the courses separately—a separate soup course, the meat being served from a tray, vegetables served separately, and so on. Based on its origins, this type of service would more properly be called Russian service.

The food is usually served from the left and removed from the right—but convenience largely determines which side is used. This has come to be called French service as distinct from American service where the food is plated in the kitchen, banquet rings (covers) placed on the plates, and many plates moved to the dining room on carts.

English service, in which the host is presented with a joint of meat which he carves into portions that are then passed by a butler, is a novelty in this country. In fact, it is a novelty in England, except in large private homes.

One of the more interesting and efficient of the modifications of table service was developed at the Tiffin Inn in Denver. The restaurant was purchased by John R. Thompson Company, and the service system used in the Henrici restaurants located in several cities. Under this system, waitresses never leave the dining room. Busboys pick up the food in the kitchen and return the soiled ware to the kitchen. All food and ware is transported by cart. In the dining room, waitresses are hooked into an intercom system with the dining room manager. The manager can request several waitresses to service one table, even though the table is originally assigned to only one waitress.

Fairly elaborate, flaming procedures, and service can be presented in minimum time. In the kitchen, orders are called out by a coordinator. Food is assembled by an assembler and placed on a cart for the busboy to wheel into the dining room. The system is comparatively fast.

A feature of the system is that customers are assigned a number according to their relationship to an anchor point within the dining room. The anchor point might be a clock, or a chandelier, or a door. The patron closest to the anchor point at any table is given number 1. The patron next to number 1, proceeding clockwise, is labeled number 2, and so on. This eliminates the confusion as regards "who ordered what?" Have you ever been asked by a waitress, "Who has the shrimp?" It also permits a waitress other than the person who took the order to serve the food without confusion.

Coffee Shop Service

The California Coffee Shop and much of the drive-in restaurant design originated in California, then moved eastward to be adopted throughout the country. The coffee shop, represented by Dennys, Sambo's, and Bob's Big Boy combines counter service and table service in a bright and gaily decorated atmosphere. It is related to the Howard Johnson restaurants and to most of the highway restaurants found on the turnpikes. The idea has been picked up and used on the M roads in England and the autobahns in Germany.

Cafeteria Service Styles[6]

Commercial cafeteria service is highly popular in the south and midwest. Comparatively little commercial cafeteria service is found in New England, the mid-Atlantic states, and the far west. About 7,500 public cafeterias with payrolls were counted in 1972, about one-third of

6. Adapted from an article in *The Food Service Equipment Dealer*, March 1969.

them a part of chain operations. Cafeteria service is now the typical service found in industrial foodservice and in schools and colleges.

Vending is also widely found in institutional foodservice. A recent trend has been to combine vending with a short cafeteria line to avoid depersonalizing the foodservice. The customers are likely to find a room that contains only vending machines a lonely place to eat.

Straight Line System

The straight line system (Figure 7-4) is the least expensive for a small cafeteria operation, and the slowest. Speed of service is determined by the slowest moving person in line. Attempts have been made to place the customer on a conveyer belt moving past the counter, but the customer resists such mechanization.

When the line is curved or turned at a 90° angle (Figure 7-4), service is slowed, but the design of the room available often requires the straight line to be bent once or several times. The speed of the straight line cafeteria is largely influenced by the speed of the cashier at the end of the line.

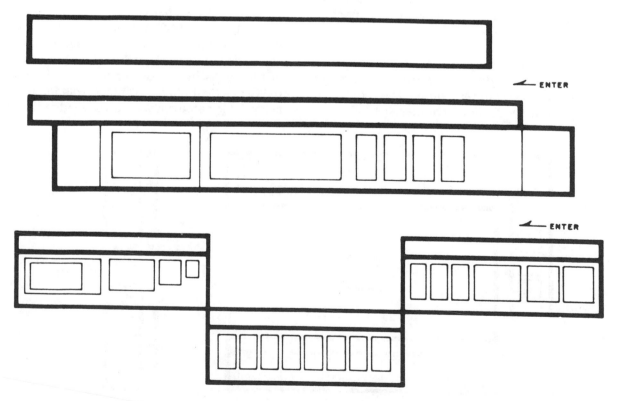

Figure 7-4 *Floor plans.*

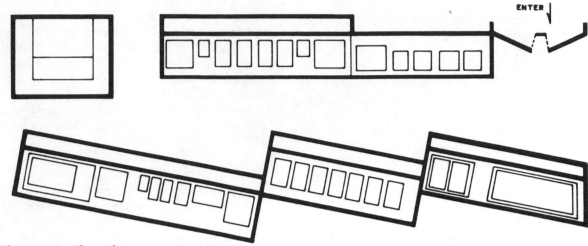

Figure 7-5 *Floor plans.*

By-Pass Line

The serving counter in a by-pass line comprises three sections. The first section may offer salads, cold sandwiches, and relishes. The recessed center section can be devoted to hot foods. The third section may serve desserts and beverages. The by-pass line is a variation of the straight line or the sawtooth and encourages customers from becoming a part of the slow-moving line.

Sawtooth

The sawtooth design (Figure 7–5), a series of diagonally set counters, made its appearance in the middle 1960s. Each counter serves a par-

ticular group of items. The customers can go directly to the counter serving the food of their choice. The sawtooth design is especially good for a long, narrow room. It permits customers to by-pass the line and move directly to the area of their choice. More than one cashier can be used to speed patron flow.

Free-Flow Systems

Before the 1930s cafeterias and counters were all straight line. The shopping center or scramble cafeteria (Figure 7–6) was introduced in the 1930s by the Colonnade Cafeterias and the Grace Smith Restaurants in Toledo. In 1947 a scramble cafeteria was introduced at the Stu-

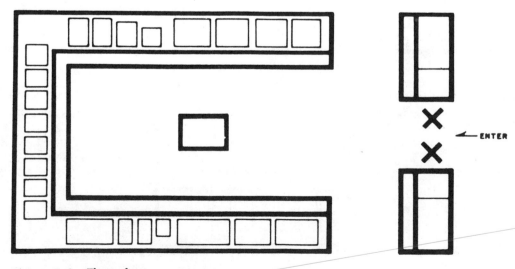

Figure 7-6 *Floor plans.*

dent Union Building of Michigan State University.

The Western Electric plant in Winston-Salem, North Carolina, offered one of the first "shopping center" cafeterias for industrial foodservice in 1951. Since then, the shopping center cafeteria has become widely used. For a given amount of square feet, more people can be served in the shopping center cafeteria than in a straight line operation. The reason for this is that the customers are not forced to travel at the speed of the slowest person in the line. They can move about in the shopping center, going to the counter which is least crowded. Once the patrons get accustomed to the free flow, they usually like it.

The shopping center, or open square, is like a giant U or open square. Three sides of the square are serving counters; hot foods on one side, salads and desserts on the other, and sandwiches and beverages on the third. Snack bars may be included as part of the scramble. Speed of service in a free-flow system is largely determined by the number of cashiers; there should be enough to permit rapid egress of the customer from the system. Total area of the free flow system is greater than that mentioned for other systems.

The speed at which customers move through a cafeteria is also determined by the manner in which cashiering is done. In a commercial cafeteria a cashier can handle a maximum of six to eight transactions per minute, usually fewer. Adding a food checker who totals the bill before the customer arrives at the cashier station may double the number of transactions per minute. Sometimes the line must be slowed so as not to overcrowd the seating area. Free-flow service systems, with duplicate sections serving the same foods, but separated from each other, allow free flow of patrons, moving to the section least crowded, or selecting only the sections from which particular foods are desired.

Cafeterias have been particularly well received by senior citizens who enjoy selecting only a few items from a great array of foods for a particular meal. The fact that many cafeterias avoid tipping by offering complete self-service is an attraction for the low-budget eater.

Successful public cafeterias usually prepare most of their food on the premises, especially those with high sales volume. A number of these cafeterias have sales in excess of $2 million a year. Often the cafeteria does its own baking with a baker who begins baking at 6 A.M., and has the baked goods ready for service at 11 A.M. The key to good food on the cafeteria line is for management to assure that the food is freshly cooked in relatively small quantities so that it does not have to remain in the steam pans on the line long enough to dry out and lose quality. This means that vegetables are often prepared by pressure steamers more or less continuously during the hours of service. Gelatin desserts and salads are not allowed to remain so long on the line that they become rubbery.

The use of frozen entrees has not been especially popular for cafeteria service. One prominent California chain withdrew from the field after trying to prepare meals in a commissary, freeze them, and serve them later in a number of their cafeterias.

FOODSERVICE SYSTEMS

The term *foodservice system* has been applied to the activities involved in purchasing, receiving, storing, preparing, and serving food. Some five different foodservice systems can be identified.

1. *The conventional foodservice system.* This is the traditional restaurant in which food that has been purchased is received, stored, prepared, and served. Most of the food received is raw, or partially prepared. It is prepared in the kitchen and served to the customer immediately or within a short period of time. This system represents a small manufacturing plant, the raw material being food, which is processed and retailed to a restaurant customer.

2. *The ready foods system.* In this type of restaurant some or much of the food is prepared and frozen for later service, the rationale being that some kitchen skills may be available when food is not needed for service and that the food can be prepared in fairly large quantities and stored for use when needed. Food may be packaged in plastic pouches or prepared in quantity in pans. The system assumes that the skills are available in the kitchen to do this type of preparation,

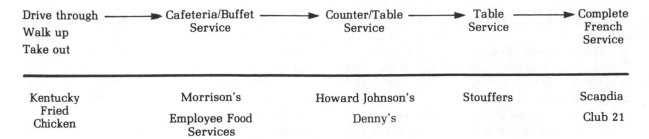

Figure 7-7 *Degree of service offered. Minimal to Full Service is shown here, with examples of each style.*

storage, and service—a dubious assumption for most kitchens.

3. *The centralized kitchen system.* Under this system, food is fully prepared and distributed for service within an area to a number of units. Sizable economies have been achieved in many school districts by preparing the food at a central kitchen and distributing it to the various school lunch rooms within the district, where it is served to the students.

4. *The central commissary foodservice system.* Under this system, food may be partially prepared and distributed within an area or over long distances. The centralized commissary of the Marriott Corporation in Silver Spring, Maryland, is a prime example of a centralized commissary. Food is ordered by code over the phone. The food is prepared in a huge commissary kitchen, using massive steam-jacketed kettles. The food is transported from one place to another via pipes in the form of a slurry and fed into pans. It is then frozen and distributed by trailer truck to dozens of Marriott restaurants on the East Coast. At the restaurants, the food may be finally prepared or finished off. Howard Johnson restaurants operate with a similar system with the commissaries spaced around the country. Under commissary operation, food is not completely plated or ready for service, but most of the preparation is done prior to delivery to the restaurant. Many commissaries prepare only a few items, such as hamburger patties, soups, and sauces.

The "flight kitchen," where meals are prepared for service aboard airplanes, is a kind of commissary operation. Some airlines operate their own flight kitchens: others contract with airline catering companies for the purchase of meals.

5. *The convenience food system.* A convenience food system can be incorporated into any of the other systems. Much or all of the food is purchased pre-prepared and packaged in one form or another, ready for "conditioning" for service. The quality of convenience frozen foods varies widely. There are those who believe that the best of the frozen food cannot be distinguished from foods prepared from scratch on premise. Every restaurant uses a number of "convenienced" foods. It is a matter of degree as to how much of a convenience food system is incorporated into a foodservice.

HOSPITAL FOODSERVICE DELIVERY SYSTEMS

The larger hospitals with their several floors or wings and several hundred patients to be fed three or more times a day have special problems in preparing and delivering food to the patients in a palatable condition. A number of systems have been tried: centralized kitchens with food delivered by conveyor belts to the various floors or wings; food prepared centrally and delivered by cart, sections of which can be refrigerated and other parts heated; and food prepared frozen or chilled, delivered to the floors and heated there by microwave oven.

The hospital foodservice system is complicated by the necessity of preparing a number of special diets—low fat, low cholesterol, low sodium, and such. When patients are given a choice of menu, the system becomes even more complicated.

Some delivery systems utilize a pellet system (the pellet heated and placed in a specially designed dish unit) to keep the food warm until served. Other units use a dish unit having a cover that when placed over the bottom part of the unit seals it, like a thermos bottle, and retains the heat. Several companies have produced food carts that become heat retainers when plugged in. One system uses an insulated cart that holds up to forty full trays. It can be hooked to a chilled air unit until heating begins within the cart. Computer-operated controls contain five heat selections and various temperatures for each tray. At the same time, refrigerated items remain cold. After thirty-five minutes that meal is cooked and ready. Panel buttons control the heating and permit holding late trays for patients who are not in their rooms when food is served. If computer controlled, it can be interfaced with existing hospital computer terminals. Carts keep food hot while being transported from kitchen to patient floor. Carts are powered by batteries, which are charged during the night.

The computer-controlled hospital delivery system flow diagram seen in Figure 7–8 explains one such delivery system. Starting with the patient (1) the menu choice is placed on a memory tape (2). Using the computer entry board (3), the information is fed into the minicomputer with the memory tape (4). The memory tape is fed into a minicomputer, which is part of the food/beverage cart (5).

The food is taken from the chilled tray assemblies (7) and loaded into the cart (8), and the cart is placed into a chilling/holding unit (9).

The cart is transported to the patient floor and connected to chilled/holding unit (10) and the cooking begins following instructions given by the memory tape (11). After the food is cooked the trays are delivered to the patient (14 and 15); and finally the soiled trays are placed back in a cart (16) ready to be transferred back to the scullery for washing and sanitizing.

One hospital foodservice that incorporated microwave reheating of food uses an oven that permits heating only half of a tray. The other half is shielded from the microwaves so that one tray, half to be heated, the other half to remain chilled, can be placed in the oven. This permits assembling the complete tray in a centralized area and avoids the necessity of adding the cold or chilled items later.

TRADE AND PROFESSIONAL RESTAURANT ORGANIZATIONS

Numerous state and local trade and professional organizations relating to the foodservice industry have been formed over the years. Some are specialized, such as the American Culinary Federation, whose members are primarily chefs. Others are more general in character, such as the Food Service Executives' Association with chapters here and abroad. Membership represents supervision, management, and ownership in the foodservice industry.

Some organizations are concerned primarily with fraternal social functions; others have been formed largely to deal with unions. Still others, such as the National Restaurant Association and the various state associations, are concerned with affecting legislation favorable to the industry and in preventing passage of unfavorable legislation. The National Restaurant Association, headquartered in Washington, D.C., conducts an active educational program, including seminars offered around the country and the operation of an active book department and research library.

The various state restaurant associations are not affiliated directly with the National Restaurant Association. Some are very strong and effective, such as the California Restaurant Association, the Texas Restaurant Association, and the Indiana Restaurant Association. The strength and the effectiveness of the associations depend in a large part on their funds. Those that must rely completely on membership fees are not very effective. The National Restaurant Association with a budget of some $7 million a year receives much of its funding from profits made in conducting an annual trade show in Chicago. The California Restaurant Association receives similar funding from trade shows held in Los Angeles. The trade shows make possible the exhibition of new food products, kitchen equipment, and a vast array of other products of interest to the foodservice operator. The fact that the expenses of attendance can be written off for tax purposes adds to the attractiveness of the shows.

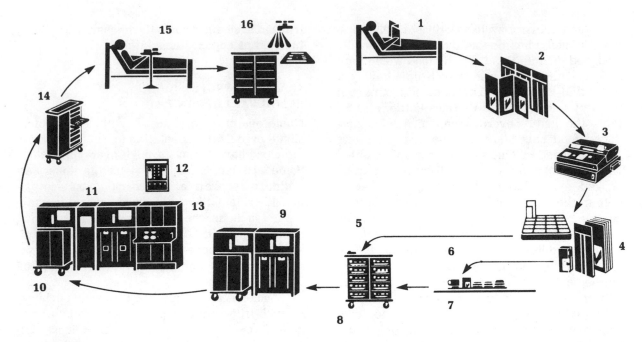

1. Patient Menu.
2. Menus and Memory Tape Worksheet.
3. Computer Entry Board (programs memory tape for cart).
4. Mini Computer with Memory Tape, Worksheet and Menus taken to chilled assembly line.
5. Mini Computer Food/Beverage Cart.
6. Menus.
7. Chilled Tray Assembly.
8. Food/Beverage Cart is loaded with Trays.
9. Food/Beverage Cart is connected to Chilling/Holding Unit.
10. After Food/Beverage Cart is transported to patient floor, it is connected to Chilled/Holding Units. There, hand-sized Mini Computer Pack is inserted into temperature unit.
11. Timed Temperature Control Unit begins scheduled cooking automatically.
12. Computer-operated Controls program non-scheduled meals individually.
13. Additional Unit for hot beverages (also stores undeliverable trays).
14. Meal Service (first time assembled trays are handled).
15. Patient is served.
16. Soiled Trays transferred for washing and sanitizing.

Figure 7-8 *Computer hospital delivery system flow diagram.*
Source: Volume Feeding/Institutions, December 15, 1977.

MOTIVATION RELATED TO EATING OUT

In terms of motivational theory, people eat out for a variety of reasons: to satisfy hunger, social needs, and ego and self-fulfillment needs. People select a particular restaurant because of particular psychological needs at the moment and the way they are feeling about the money they have to spend, the prices of a restaurant, its service, and how the restaurant is perceived in terms of its esthetics, social status, and the kind of people that can be expected to be there (patrons, management, and employees).

Restaurants can be classified according to prices charged, the amount of service offered, and the extent of their menus. Well-known prestige restaurants like Scandia in Los Angeles and Club 21 in New York City project an image of luxury—in price, in menu, and in service.

Moving down the scale a bit, the midpriced restaurants with full menus and "full-service" may be seen in places like Victoria Station and Trader Vics restaurants.

A step down the prestige line and into the moderately priced restaurants, we see such

TABLE 7-3 Restaurant Service, Price, and Menu Related to Needs

Luxury Price, Full Menu	Scandia Club 21	Self-fulfillment
Luxury Service	Four Seasons	Recognition
High Price Full Menu Full Service	Victoria Station Trader Vic	Status Self-esteem
Moderate Price Full Menu	Denny's	Social needs
Moderate Service	Howard Johnson's	
Moderate Price Limited Menu Self-service	Pizza Hut Bonanza	
Low Price Limited Menu Self-service	Wendy's McDonald's	Physiological needs

Source: Based on a concept developed by Dieter H. Buehler.

places as Dennys with a full menu but moderate price and moderate service.

Limited menu restaurants like Pizza Hut and Bonanza are moderately priced with self-service. At the low end of the price spectrum are found the hamburger chains offering limited menus, low prices and self-service, restaurants such as Wendys, McDonalds, and Burger King.

Relating restaurant service, price, and menu size to physiological and psychological needs can be an interesting exercise that provides some insight into why people select particular restaurants. The most popular motivational theory, that proposed by Maslow, states that humans are wanting animals, always wanting. As soon as one need is satisfied another appears to take its place, moving from the safety or security needs up the scale through social, ego, and self-fulfillment needs. People go to restaurants to satisfy not only hunger but self-esteem, self-respect, self-confidence, and prestige needs. Table 7-3 suggests that we may eat at a stand up snack bar to satisfy a hunger or physiological need but will select varying styles of restaurants to meet social needs and will finally go to the high-priced places for self-esteem and self-fulfillment needs.

DISPOSABLE INCOME AND RESTAURANT SALES

Aside from all of the reasons why people find pleasure in eating out or need to eat out, there is the problem of having the money to do so. Discretionary income is the key term here. It is the income that can be used as one sees fit, that is left over from the sum required to meet expenses.

Eating out is usually pleasurable; therefore, the more discretionary income a person has, the more likely he or she is to eat out and to spend more in the process.

As disposable income increases, so, too, does the amount of money spent in eating and drinking places. As with discretionary or disposable income, the greater the family income, the greater the proportion of it is spent in restaurants.

Another interesting correlation between income and eating out: for every 1 percent increase in personal income, expressed in constant dollars, real eating place sales rose .84 percent from 1963 to 1967. Income elasticity rose to .96 percent from 1967 to 1972 and over 1 percent from 1973 to 1975.[7]

THE SMALLER FAMILY AND THE WORKING WIFE INCREASE RESTAURANT SALES

With fewer children, smaller living spaces for the family, and less housework for the wife, the wife and other women have gone to work. The result: more disposable income, a greater desire to eat out, and the money to do so.

In 1950, about 24 percent of wives were in the labor force. This rate increased year by year so that by 1976 the rate was 45 percent.[8] The median family income (what the middle range of families earn) in 1980 rose to more than $19,000, enough so that when the working wife came home at night she felt little guilt about insisting on eating out, or at the very least picking up prepared food from a take-out establishment.

What's more, by 1985 half of the women in the country will be in the labor force. In the twenty- to twenty-four-age bracket, 73 percent will be working—good news for the restaurant business.

7. Economic Report, *NRA*, October 18, 1976.
8. Economic Report, *NRA*, August 8, 1977.

Despite the massive growth of the restaurant chain, the restaurant business is still a stronghold of free enterprise in the United States. Few businesses can be entered so easily with so little capital, and success or failure seen so quickly. Operators who have assessed the market correctly and put together the right menu and format of operation win big; those who are wrong, fail.

Chains and franchisors there are aplenty, but anyone can join them with determination, know-how, and luck. The restaurateur—the small businessperson—is still free to come up with a new design, a new recipe, a new market approach, and must do so periodically to win.

An advertising slogan of Jack-in-the-Box, "Watch out, McDonald's," can be applied to hundreds of restaurant owners. One thing is certain: McDonald's will one day be surpassed by a Wendy's, Carl's Jr., or someone just opening his or her first small restaurant. What goes well in the East may fail in the West, and vice versa. A restaurant flourishes, may proliferate into a chain, become stagnant, and be overtaken by a fresh format, a better market fix, a different sandwich, or a menu mix better tuned to a market. The restaurant business in the United States is challenging and changing—bringing wealth or vast disappointment to its practitioners.

Questions

1. We tend to think of the big restaurants and the small restaurants, but the average restaurant does how many hundred thousand dollars in sales a year?

2. Would you say that restaurants with sales in excess of $1 million a year are a rarity? Explain.

3. List at least three principal reasons why the restaurant business has prospered so greatly since World War II.

4. It has been said that there are fewer restaurants today than there were twenty years ago. Is this true? Explain.

5. About 30 percent of all the employees in the restaurant business are teenagers. What does this imply for restaurant management and for labor costs?

6. To what does the origin of the word *restaurant* refer?

7. In what way is steak "a la tartar" related to hamburg?

8. Fred Harvey, an Englishman, figures in the history of the American restaurant in what way?

9. Name at least three advantages of being part of a chain and three disadvantages.

10. Can you name restaurant chains owned by the following conglomerates: W. R. Grace, United Fruit, and General Foods?

11. Most hotel and restaurant graduates tend to shy away from institutional foodservice immediately following graduation. What advantages does such foodservice offer a graduate over working in a commercial restaurant unit or chain?

12. The term *convenience food* is often misunderstood. Would you describe sliced bread, ice cream, and canned vegetables as convenience foods? Why or why not?

13. Pre-prepared foods have their proponents and outspoken critics. Is there some middle ground regarding the use of such foods?

14. Foodservice is often divided into four types: American, French, Russian and _____.

15. The free-flow system or open cafeteria system has what advantages over other styles of cafeteria service?

16. As more complete service is offered in a restaurant what will happen to the price of the meal?

17. Name at least one highly successful restaurant chain that uses a commissary system.

18. Why is it that hospital foodservice is so much more complicated than that found in a restaurant?

19. Centralized foodservice in a hospital means that food is prepared in a central location and delivered to patients all over the hospital. How is the food transported from the kitchen to the patients?

20. What is the name of the trade association that represents restaurants nationally?

21. All of the various state hotel associations automatically belong to the American Hotel and Motel Association. Do the state restaurant associations automatically belong to the national association?

22. Referring to Maslow's theory of motivation, a person who patronizes a very expensive restaurant does so to satisfy what basic needs?

23. According to the same theory, a person patronizing a coffeeshop does so for what motivational reasons?

24. If you had to identify but one factor that correlates most highly with the number of people eating out in the United States, what would that factor be—disposable income, unemployment rate, or rate of savings?

25. Which of these factors probably accounts for more of the increase in eating out than any other: the working woman, smaller family, smaller living spaces for the family, or more self-indulgence on the part of Americans?

Discussion Questions

1. Relatively few luxury restaurants exist. What is the future of the luxury restaurant? Give your reasons.

2. Of the several types of restaurants, which will be the big money maker of 1990? What will it be like? What menu will it offer?

LOUIS SZATHMARY

Few American chefs have been in the public eye long enough or written extensively enough to leave a lasting mark on the food service industry.

Louis Szathmary, proprietor of The Bakery restaurant in Chicago, is an exception. A bibliophile, he has collected one of the largest culinary libraries, one that will be presented to the College of Hotel and Restaurant Administration at the University of Nevada, Las Vegas. Witty, outspoken, widely informed and a popular lecturer and writer he is the most colorful of the current generation of chef/restaurant operators.

More than 2,000 immigrants aboard the U.S.S. *Hershey* were crossing the Atlantic from Hamburg to New York in mid-December, 1951. They all had one thing in common: a dream of a new world, a new life, a new beginning "over there" on the other side of the unfriendly Atlantic.

During a storm, the *Hershey* collided with an Argentine oil tanker and limped to a port near Lisbon for repairs before continuing to its destination. Because of the unplanned delay, the immigrants had to spend Christmas aboard ship. The ship's chaplain "volunteered" a portly Hungarian with a large handlebar mustache to play Santa Claus. He didn't need too many pillows to fill the makeshift red costume.

Santa Claus was Louis Szathmary, at various times actor, journalist, and psychologist, who had been waiting for the chance to immigrate, meanwhile working in various kitchens in Salzburg, Austria. Most of the time he worked for Hofrat-Bauer, the concessionaire of the Festival House and a brilliant restaurateur who had reached the top from humble beginnings.

The ship finally docked in New York on December 27. After a few futile attempts at getting a job elsewhere, Szathmary accepted an offer from the New England Province of the Jesuit order to cook in a retreat house for semi-retired priests on Manresa Island, off Norwalk, Connecticut. For Szathmary it was a great offer. The salary was low, but room and board came with it. He was the only Hungarian on an island where no one spoke anything but English. He was forced to learn it as quickly as possible. Also, the job enabled him to learn and master the differences between European and American cooking.

His work day began at 6 A.M. and ended at 6 P.M. This enabled him to take an evening job at a nearby diner, where he learned with great admiration something just as foreign as it was new to him: short-order cooking. His European experience had not included automatic gravity-feed, high-speed electric slicers or roll-in, roll-out stainless steel broilers, automatic French fryers, blenders, Osterizers, and such strange items as BLT sandwiches, double cheeseburgers, chicken-fried steak, griddlecakes, flapjacks, banana splits, and Manhattan clam chowder straight from the can.

His greatest fascination from the first day was with frozen foods. During a short stint as a U.S. Army kitchen helper in Austria, he had seen huge blocks of frozen liver being sliced with a power saw into finger-thick portions. In Austria, he had purchased beautiful large frozen tomatoes and green peppers, which, after arriving home, thawed into a wet, runny, soft mess.

But the variety and quality of frozen foods he became acquainted with, both in the Jesuits' kitchen and at the diner on the night shift, impressed him tremendously, and he began serious research with frozen foods.

His first teachers were the salesmen who, as a rule, found great resistance from chefs, especially European chefs, who felt threatened by frozen foods, convenience foods, and ready-to-serve items, and who were reluctant to change their old ways. So, when the salesmen found someone who would listen, and who did not mind trying a frozen item here and there, they gave him all the available information.

As quickly as he learned English, he began to read all the available literature on food freezing and frozen food preparation. When the Jesuits sold their island, Szathmary was delighted to get a job with a company president who had been educated by the Jesuits.

In the mid-1950s, Chef Louis (as he was called by all who couldn't pronounce his Hungar-

ian family name) became the private dining-room chef for Thomas O'Neill, President of the Mutual Broadcasting System, a wholly owned subsidiary of RKO General. His job was to give small, intimate lunches for VIPs from every segment of American society.

Compared with the 6 A.M. to 6 P.M. shift with the Jesuits, coupled with the night job at the diner, this five-day-a-week, six-hour-a-day job preparing lunch for four or six people seemed like heaven. It also gave Szathmary a great opportunity to roam the streets of Manhattan and read the menus on every restaurant door; to browse through the frozen food sections of all the supermarkets; and to talk to hundreds of salesmen and other chefs as well as anyone who could offer any information on food processing, canning, freezing, or foodservice.

Chef Szathmary still had ample time on his hands. Thanks to the recommendations of top Mutual Broadcasting executives, he began catering in homes from the most elegant Manhattan apartments to rambling estates in Connecticut and New Jersey owned by the giants of entertainment and broadcasting, writers, actors, and politicians.

Still, the dream of owning his own restaurant lingered in Chef Louis' mind. When a management decision closed the executive dining room at the Mutual Broadcasting System, Tom O'Neill offered him another opportunity. O'Neill had recently bought the well-known Humpty Dumpty Restaurant in Old Greenwich, Connecticut. It was one of the original "hamburger places" that became the prototype of many later copies. The hamburgers were eight ounces, ground from fresh beef in front of the customer, and served on a toasted, freshly baked bun in a paper bag.

This was the daytime format. Millionaires' kids flocked from nearby Westchester County and Connecticut to jam the place. However, the general manager had other great ideas. At night, he projected a completely different image. Candlelight, soft music, the best standing rib roast money could buy—U.S. Grade "Prime" only—and tremendous U.S. Prime butt steaks—cut by Chef Louis in front of the customers.

They installed a twenty-four-foot charbroiler-grill and expanded the menu with lamb chops, veal steaks, barbecued ribs, and broiled chicken. Chef Louis, who manned the large grill alone, served as many as 600 to 700 people on a Saturday night as well as Sunday noon and Sunday night.

Chef Louis' younger brother, Geza Szathmary, who for years was bartender at the legendary Innis Arden golf club in Old Greenwich, tended bar on Saturday and Sunday at the other end of the room. It wasn't unusual for him to serve 2,000 drinks a night.

Everything went well until one night squirrels, chewing through wires in the main building of Humpty Dumpty, started a fire. The venerable restaurant burned to the ground. Despite an insurance income, Chef Louis couldn't stand his idleness after two months. He took a job in a small Italian restaurant that enabled him to try actual "field tests" in what he was planning to do with frozen foods.

After a few months of experimenting, by sheer chance he met a wealthy young socialite who thought it would be an interesting experiment to fill the catering needs of affluent young suburbanites by offering single or double portions and casseroles for four or six, of entrees such as beef Burgundy, beef Stroganoff, and coq au vin rouge.

After tasting some of the dishes Chef Louis had developed, the young socialite quickly hired him as plant superintendent and partner in his company, Reddy-Fox Catering.

Shortly after the Reddy-Fox new plant and retail store opened in Darien, Connecticut, a customer introduced himself as Harve Hearl, director of packaging development for Continental Can. He asked Chef Szathmary if he would be interested in packing his frozen dishes in special aluminum trays with aluminum coated cardboard covers developed by Continental for the restaurant industry.

This proposal turned into a mutually-beneficial contract. Very soon, Reddy-Fox was selling large batches of institutional frozen food. At the urging of Harve Hearl, Szathmary developed numerous dishes for companies that were pioneering in the field of frozen prepared entrees—Dulany, Seabrook Farm, Stouffer, to name a few. Chef Louis met with Mrs. Stouffer and her son, Vern, and developed formulas for the first Stouffer line of frozen food.

Meanwhile, the packaging industry was undergoing tremendous changes. New types of experimental plastic containers began to appear on the market. Heat sealers became standard equipment. Soon Chef Louis was packaging food in plastic manufactured by the Shalimar Bentley Division of Continental Can.

New starches were developed at his suggestion. Among the first was a rice flour, Waxy Rice, by the California Ricegrowers Association. As sample introductory dishes for his clients, Louis packed frozen chicken paprikash with spaetzels, Hungarian goulash with egg barley, Hawaiian chicken breast with fried rice. The first experiments didn't work out. The starch soaked up all the sauces. The dishes had little shelf life, and, after reconstitution, turned into a sad mess.

To counter this, Louis applied heat seals to the middle of these flexible pouches. He packed the noodles, rice, egg barley, or potatoes on one side, then, after sealing, filled the other end with the sauce and meat. The double pouch was born, making it possible to heat from freezer to serving platter, in twelve to fourteen minutes, individual portions of some forty items.

During a demonstration of this revolutionary concept, William Wood Prince, then president of Armour and Company, offered Chef Szathmary and Harve Hearl jobs in the large foods and chemicals corporation. That is where, in the late 1950s, Chef Louis developed Armour's Continental Cuisine, American Fare, Hospital Fare, and several other lines of institutional products.

In 1960, Chef Louis became product-development manager and continued the job of product-development in that capacity until the end of 1963.

Having more and more contact nationwide with restaurants, lecturing at Cornell University and at industry seminars, and learning more and more about the hospitality industry, Chef Szathmary felt the urge to demonstrate the validity of his ideas in a restaurant of his own.

He firmly believed in certain principles. He felt that gimmicks, promotions, and decor can lure people into a restaurant, but only good food and good service would bring them back. He believed that location is not of primary importance if the product is desirable and of high quality. He felt that it wasn't necessary to have wall-to-wall carpet, huge plastic menus, or sparsely-clad waitresses selling drinks.

Now, almost a quarter of a century after opening his storefront restaurant on Chicago's Near North Side—The "Bakery" Restaurant—in a building whose three street-level stores had been vacant twenty-two years, he feels he did the right thing at the right time in the right way.

The basic "Bakery" concept is unusual in this country: A table d'hote dinner of appetizer, soup, salad, main course with side dishes, dessert, beverage, and bread and butter, for a fixed price—$3.95 in 1963; $22 at the time this article goes to press.

Working for a leading diversified international corporation was a great help to Chef Louis in developing his analytical skills. At Armour he learned the importance of sampling, collecting, and processing statistical data. He applied these techniques in directing The "Bakery" Restaurant. During its first year of operation, The "Bakery" Restaurant added 131 main-course items to its menu. From the very first day, a daily accounting was analyzed on every single item sold. More than half the items were dropped in the second year; some of them for which Louis and his wife Sada (an equal partner in management decisions) originally had high hopes.

When The "Bakery" Restaurant opened, Chef Louis thought that sweetbread dishes, high-quality shrimp items, and veal creations would be bestsellers, but they never moved. From the sixth month on, it became increasingly evident that individual filet of Beef Wellington in the form created by Chef Louis Szathmary at Armour would be the star of the menu. From the seventh month on, Beef Wellington was, and is today, after two decades, not only the No. 1 seller, but accounts for more than 50 percent of all main-course items ordered. Szathmary uses a five- to seven-pound U.S. Choice untrimmed beef tenderloin.

Instead of guarding the secret of this successful dish, he published the recipe in the 1965 issue of *The Cornell Hotel and Restaurant Administration Quarterly.* The article was the most frequently requested reprint in the history of the *Quarterly.* John Sexton & Company ordered 10,000 reprints from Cornell to distribute to its white-tablecloth restaurant customers throughout the United States.

After the beef tenderloin duck is No. 2 in total sales.

News media quickly became aware of the new restaurant. In the first two years, more than 200 articles were printed. Guests came to the establishment from London, Tokyo, and Sydney, as well as from New York, New Orleans, and Montreal.

Of the original three storefronts, he set up one as a small banquet room for private parties for twenty to sixty guests. The "kitchen" is a small room that seats about twenty people. While guests dine there, salads are prepared and glassware is washed. From the beginning, it became the fashion to dine in this room while Chef Louis deboned a lamb or cut tenderloins for Beef Wellington, created fancy pastries, or decorated cold salmon.

A news column, entitled "Chef Louis" by Louis Szathmary, is carried by more than one hundred daily papers throughout the United States. Chef Louis is also a frequent guest on Chicago-area radio shows.

These are not his only extra-curricular activities. He also writes a regular feature, "International Chef," for *Travel/Holiday Magazine,* the oldest travel publication in the United States. Chef Szathmary is very involved in the educational activities of the NRA and is a frequent speaker or demonstrator at the annual shows, as well as all over the United States at regional conventions, shows, exhibits, and educational meetings. The book department of NRA has sold thousands of Chef Szathmary's books over the years through its mail-order catalogue.

Despite all these activities, Chef Szathmary feels that his basic occupation and main concern is being the chef/owner of The "Bakery" Restaurant.

With a keen personal interest in anticipating the future Chef Louis established the Parmenius Foundation at California State Polytechnic University, Pomona. The Foundation funds projects that look into the future of the hospitality business. Chef Szathmary is scheduled to join the faculty of the College of Hotel Management at the University of Nevada, Las Vegas.

8

Restaurant Operations

A person considering the restaurant business has several career and investment options:

Manage a restaurant for someone else (individual or a chain).

Purchase a franchise and operate the franchise restaurant.

Buy an existing restaurant.

Build a new restaurant and operate it.

In considering which way to go, an individual can analyze the advantages and disadvantages of each style of operation and consider the potential risks and rewards of each option.

In comparing the advantages and disadvantages of buying, building, franchising, or managing, the individual should assess his or her own temperament, ambitions, and ability to cope with frustrations (see Table 8–1). Buying a restaurant may satisfy an aesthetic personal desire; if the restaurant is a success, the re-

wards can be very high. If it fails, the financial risk is also high but usually not as high as if the investment were made in a new building. Franchising a restaurant reduces risk all along the line and may also reduce the potential reward because of franchise fees. No financial risks are ordinarily attached to being a manager, but the psychic cost of failure can be high.

Examples can be given of people who have gone into the restaurant business with almost no experience, built a restaurant, and been successful from day one. Such examples are relatively rare. In buying an existing restaurant that has failed or is for sale for some other reason, the purchaser has some information that the builder lacks. The buyer may know that the previous style of restaurant was not successful in that location or that a certain menu or style of management was unsuccessful. Such information could cut risks somewhat. On the other hand, the buyer may find it difficult to over-

TABLE 8–1 Buy, build, franchise, or manage—Advantages and disadvantages

	Original Investment Needed	Experience Needed	Potential— Personal Stress	Psychic Cost— Failure	Financial Risk	Potential Reward
Buy	medium	high	high	high	high	high
Build	highest	high	high	highest	highest	high
Franchise	low to medium	low	medium	medium	medium	medium to high
Manage	none	medium to high	medium	medium	none	medium

come a poor reputation acquired over a period of time by the previous operator.

As a general rule, it is best to learn a format of operation thoroughly before buying or building a restaurant. The franchisee is protected by the fact that he or she usually completes a management training course before opening a franchised restaurant. The franchise parent should be just as eager to avoid failure in any unit as is the franchisee, a plus factor for a franchisee. Of course, franchised restaurants also fail, and the prospective franchisee must be careful to select a reputable franchisor who has an excellent track record.

RESTAURANT LOCATION

Generalizations about restaurant location are must more difficult to make than those relating to hotels and motels. Perhaps these statements are valid:

1. Restaurants catering to the luncheon trade must be reasonably convenient to the clientele. Other than the expense-account restaurants, the luncheon restaurant must be within a few minutes' walk or drive of the clientele. In this country, most luncheons eaten away from home are consumed during a specified lunch time break that may last from thirty minutes to one hour. The business luncheon usually lasts much longer and includes liquor. The quickie luncheon, necessarily, must be close to the place of work, preferably in the same building. The expense-account luncheon can be farther away, but must be conveniently reached by taxi or private car.

2. The highway restaurants, on the main thoroughfares, are placed for convenience to the traveler. The restaurant catering to the highway traveler must be readily accessible. Even a five-minute drive from the highway may be disastrous for the restaurant.

3. Fast-food restaurants are most successfully located adjacent to a main thoroughfare, in a busy shopping mall, or in an apartment condominium area.

4. Locations for the atmosphere, theme, or special-occasion restaurants can be less convenient. The clientele will search them out. One of the most successful in the world, in terms of sales volume, is Anthony's Pier 4 Restaurant in Boston. It is relatively difficult to reach, but its harborside location adds glamour.

5. Restaurants located in a restaurant/entertainment area draw a good number of people. In Marina del Rey, near Los Angeles, for example, some thirty-five restaurants are concentrated. The public comes to think of the area as a place to go for fun and eating out.

Some leading restaurants are found in highly unlikely locations. The Bakery, in Chicago, is found in a run-down part of the city. Commander's Palace in New Orleans is a long cab ride from the heart of town. This is not to say that such restaurants might not be even more successful if more conveniently and pleasantly located.

THE "TOPS"

Restaurants that are on the top of something have a special appeal. "Top" as a location did not become popular until the 1960s. Stouffer's now has thirteen "Tops," all of them successful. The Top of the Prudential Center in Boston, fifty-two stories in the sky, grosses more than $3 million a year in sales. The diner gets not only good food and drink but a marvelous view of Boston Harbor and metropolitan Boston. The top restaurant in the John Hancock Building in Chicago is ninety-five stories in the air; the World Trade Center in New York serves food on an even higher level.

The Germans were the first to revolve a restaurant, one built in 1959 atop a television tower in Stuttgart. La Ronde was our first revolving cocktail lounge and restaurant, perched on top of the La Moana office building in Honolulu. The Space Needle at Seattle's World's Fair brought wide publicity for the revolving restaurant. Currently, they exist around the world: in London, Brussels, Rotterdam, Frankfurt, Montreal, Cairo, Tokyo, and Hong Kong, among the many. Naturally, Russia has the highest, one called Seventh Heaven, an unexpected choice of name in an atheistic nation. It is perched on top of a television tower, 1,085 feet above the ground.

The revolving restaurants turn on donut-shaped turntables around a stationary core. Turntables may have a diameter as large as

Figure 8-1 *Indicative of a trend to luxurious appointments in cafeterias is the Holiday House, a John R. Thompson Cafeteria in St. Louis. Note the wall to wall carpeting, the rich leather upholstered chairs, and decorative lighting fixtures. Note also the fact that the dining area has been broken up into several rooms.*

132 feet. Believe it or not, only two ¾ horsepower motors are needed to revolve a restaurant weighing some 200,000 pounds and filled with over 300 diners.[1]

Obviously, revolving restaurants are expensive. However, since the supporting structure is usually built for some other reason, the restaurant itself may not be excessive. Some problems in operating revolving restaurants exist: lingering customers, trouble finding one's seat after going to the restrooms, and motion sickness.

Kemmons Wilson, chairman of the board of Holiday Inns, who favored the revolving restaurant, is quoted as saying, "At a revolving res-

taurant the food is terrible, the price is high and the service low, but the people are lined up to get in." Wilson estimates that revolving restaurants attract more than twice the business of ground-level restaurants.

The fact that the restaurants revolve makes them about 10 percent more attractive than the nonrevolving rooftop restaurants. Most of the restaurants give the diners one complete turn around the building in the course of an hour. They can buy a drink or two, look down upon the little people, sit eye-level with a passing airplane, and become detached from it all. At the end of the hour's merry-go-round, the restaurant hopes the guests will depart contented, relaxed, and minus $15 or more.

The character of the restaurant—its tempo, decor, noise level, and personnel—must fit a location. In a downtown congested area, people do not seem to mind being processed rather than served. Otherwise, how could the success of such chains as Chock Full O'Nuts and the foodservice of Kresge's, Woolworth's, and Nedick's be explained?

Often customers are required to push their way to the serving counter and stand while eating, and are then expected to leave in about ten minutes. Young people especially seem to relish this type of eating behavior. They will spend little more than a few minutes eating in college and university dining halls that are luxuriously equipped, carpeted, and lighted.

Dinner, however, is something else, especially for the middle-aged and older. The person who is satisfied to sit on a stool just inches away from somebody else at lunch wants a chair with arms on it and at least 15 square feet per customer while eating dinner.

Menu price goes with location. A luxury restaurant in a high seat-turnover location would fail, and the opposite would also be true.

THE USE OF ECONOMETRIC MODELS

The construction of mathematical models for site evaluation and diagnostic simulation, using the computer, is being done for foodservice operations. Econometric (combining economics and mathematics) modeling began in the 1930s and has been used for some years in other businesses. These models have been devised for restaurants by Professor Francis R. Cella at the University of Oklahoma.

1. "Keeping the Diners Going in Circles," *Business Week*, July 13, 1968.

Professor Cella was given a contract in 1966 by the Oklahoma Restaurant Association for the development of models of restaurant operations. These were to be used to simulate a restaurant operation, using a computer, and to determine the potential sales of the restaurants. According to Cella, his models can predict the sales of the restaurant within 5 percent, plus or minus, 95 percent of the time.

Initially, models were built for five types of foodservice operations: general, cafeteria, drive-in, specialty, and hamburger. Information used in building the models was developed from the various experiences of Oklahoma residents.

The theory behind the construction of a model is that if the importance of the various factors that determine the sales of a restaurant can be pinpointed and weighted, according to their effect on sales, then by using the computer it is a matter of a few minutes to derive a forecast of what sales should be produced by that restaurant. The more obvious factors that bear on restaurant sales are: the population in the vicinity of the proposed or operating restaurant, the income of that population, the number of competitors in the area, the volume of traffic passing the location, the ability of the manager of the restaurant, the amount of advertising that is done, and the appearance and kind of structure which houses the restaurant.

Some restaurant developers have a very simple plan for site selection. They go where McDonalds go. Others stick with the mall developers, believing that if a developer believes enough in a location to invest several millions of dollars in a regional center the location would also be desirable for a restaurant.

Carl Karcher Enterprises has come up with a model for site selection. It is a multiple-regression formula for evaluating a potential site by predicting sales on the site. The model compares the characteristics of the site with existing successful restaurants. The information needed for the model, which is important for the Carl's Junior restaurants (fast food), includes:

Daily traffic count on surrounding streets

Total number of existing seats in comparable restaurants in the area

Proportion of the population in the area who are in blue-collar households

Estimated number of office workers within a ten-minute drive of the site

Number of single-member households in a ten-mile radius

Total population within a ten-mile radius

Mean age of area population

The company has found from experience that their most successful restaurants have these factors in common:

The area has less than 1200 fast-food seats.

Some 75 percent of the area's population are in blue-collar households.

Mean age of the area's population is between twenty-six to thirty-two years old.

Some 10,000 office workers are within ten minutes of the site.

This information was put together in a mathematical equation. This theoretical equation considers four key pieces of information and weights them based on the experience of existing restaurants.

$$Y = a - XA + XB + XC + XD$$

where

Y = estimated sales of new unit

A = total number of seats in area's existing fastfood restaurants

B = proportion of area's population in blue-collar households

C = mean age of area's population

D = number of office workers within ten minutes of site

a = coefficient

X = coefficients for weighing four factors

The model is only theoretical since the coefficients used in weighting the four factors are not given.

Up to Thirty Factors Affect Sales

According to Professor Cella, a minimum of sixteen factors affect sales volume, a number that rises to thirty for some kinds of restaurant operations. Subsequently, models for other restaurants have been developed and numerous models built for chain operations. Over 1,000 site evaluations were made between the period of 1966 to 1969.

In addition to being able to predict the volume of business for a potential site, the models can be used for determining whether a particular location is being put to its best use. A location on which an unsuccessful drive-in had been operating was found to be a good location for a hamburger stand. The change was made and, after a shakedown period, the business made more money in one month as a hamburger stand than it had in the previous twelve months operating as a drive-in restaurant.[2] (The Oklahoma Restaurant Association has taken over Professor Cella's computer analysis program and has sharply reduced the claims for what can be done using the program.)

In addition to projecting total business, the models can be used for making management decisions. Each projected course of action can be tested by simulation. If the advertising budget is increased by 5 percent, a forecast of the additional sales it would generate can be made. How much additional business can be expected if the restaurant is refurbished? Would it be better to divide an investment among a combination of factors or to concentrate it on a single factor? How much additional business can be expected if a more experienced manager is employed?

Without the use of computers, the mathematics of correlating the effects of the factors upon the gross sales and upon each other would be very time-consuming. According to Cella, without a computer it would take forty clerks six months to manually make the calculations necessary for one model. Using an IBM 360, these calculations are made in less than five minutes.

The construction of the model cannot be done by a beginner, since some of the factors involved that affect restaurant sales are negative and some are nonlinear. Decisions as to whether a factor is important enough to warrant inclusion in the model requires judgment as well as reference to the experience of a number of operations.

In the past, each expert has been able to prove that his or her specialty is the all-important factor affecting total sales. The sales manager feels that advertising is the all-important factor; the production person feels sure that the quality of the product is most important; the designer feels that the building structure is the thing that brings people in. With an econometric model, the size of each factor's contribution can be determined with a greater degree of accuracy.

Weighing the various factors affecting sales also requires judgment, some trial and error, and reference to the experience of established restaurants. A critical factor in the location of a restaurant is the minimal size of the market needed, what size population is required to support a particular kind of restaurant.

The Kentucky Fried Chicken people say that their restaurants can do about $200,000 in sales in a community of 10,000 people. Population requirements for a McDonald's were once stated by the company at 30,000. Later the company found that in heavily urbanized communities McDonald's restaurants could be located three miles apart. A Polynesian restaurant, serving food that is relatively exotic for the average American palate, may require a market of 500,000. Fried chicken and hamburgers are considered a regular part of the diet; sweet and sour pork is not.

The factor of "competition" also requires close scrutiny. Three restaurants, side by side, may complement each other rather than compete with each other. Numerous "restaurant rows" have experienced added business for each restaurant as other restaurants are added. A fried chicken, a hamburger, and a steak house may not compete with each other if the total market available is large enough. Three hamburger restaurants in the same block almost certainly will compete with each other. An additional hamburger restaurant will necessarily reduce the market of the established ones.

Is a Restaurant Feasible?

Making a major investment in a restaurant is a very risky proposition and requires as much planning as possible. Some of the major ac-

2. Francis R. Cella, *Retail Site Selection*. Printed privately, 1970.

SALES VOLUME

	Number of Seats	Average Turnover Per Seat	Possible Daily Volume	Average Check Per Seat	Highest Daily Sales	Vacant Seat Factor	Total Sales Per Meal	Days Open Weekly	Weekly Sales	Weeks Open Yearly	Yearly Sales
Meals											
Breakfast	___ X	___ =	___ X	___ =	___	X ⅔ =	___ X	___ =	___ X	___ =	___
Lunch	___ X	___ =	___ X	___ =	___	X ⅔ =	___ X	___ =	___ X	___ =	___
Dinner	___ X	___ =	___ X	___ =	___	X ⅔ =	___ X	___ =	___ X	___ =	___
					TOTAL SALES DAILY ___		WEEKLY ___		YEARLY ___		

FOOD COSTS

		Days Open Weekly	Weekly Food Costs	Weeks Open Yearly	Yearly Food Costs
Total Daily Sales ___	X ⅓ = DAILY FOOD COSTS ___	X ___ = ___	X ___ = ___		

PAYROLL

		Average No. Workers Per Shift	Pay Per Worker	Number of Shifts	Daily Payroll	Days Per Week	Weekly Payroll	Weeks Per Year	Yearly Payroll
Manager	Monthly pay ___ X 12 = Yearly Pay ___								
Serving Staff									
Waiters/ Waitresses		___ X	___ X	___ = ___	X	___ = ___	X	___ = ___	
Busboys/ Busgirls		___ X	___ X	___ = ___	X	___ = ___	X	___ = ___	
Kitchen Staff									
Chief Cook		___ X	___ X	___ = ___	X	___ = ___	X	___ = ___	
Other Cooks		___ X	___ X	___ = ___	X	___ = ___	X	___ = ___	
Helpers		___ X	___ X	___ = ___	X	___ = ___	X	___ = ___	
Other Employees									
Bartenders		___ X	___ X	___ = ___	X	___ = ___	X	___ = ___	
Cocktail Waitresses		___ X	___ X	___ = ___	X	___ = ___	X	___ = ___	
Cleanup Staff		___ X	___ X	___ = ___	X	___ = ___	X	___ = ___	
Others		___ X	___ X	___ = ___	X	___ = ___	X	___ = ___	
				DAILY PAYROLL ___		WEEKLY PAYROLL ___		YEARLY PAYROLL ___	

TOTALS

	Daily	Weekly	Yearly
Sales	___	___	___
Food Costs	___	___	___
Payroll	___	___	___

Figure 8-2 Feasibility projection worksheet.
Source: Figures compiled by Small Business Reporter in California.

counting firms stand ready to conduct feasibility studies, and the results can be used in procuring necessary loans.

The feasibility study follows this suggested pattern.

The proposed restaurant will cost $4,000 per seat.

Return on the investment should be at least 15 percent.

What projected sales would be necessary?
$400,000 \times 15\% = \$60,000$
Estimated operating profit—10%
Sales needed, $60,000 divided by 10% = $600,000

Suppose the restaurant has one hundred seats. The feasibility projection worksheet as seen in Figure 8-2 (taken from a Bank of America study) is a worksheet for what can be expected in the way of volume of sales, food and labor costs, and major costs encountered in the restaurant.

THE MENU

The selection of the menu and method of presentation to reach a particular market is critical. The menu, to a large extent, determines what market can be reached. The hamburger-fried chicken-milkshake menu reaches the teenagers and the young marrieds. The steak menu is for the more affluent middle-aged market. The Polynesian menu must be aimed at the "special occasion" market and those people who want to experience a different atmosphere. The meat and potatoes menu may be right for the "have-to" eating out market (the people who eat out day after day and expect to eat more or less the same things that they would have eaten at home). The French menu, indeed individual French menu items, are for the more sophisticated markets, the more widely traveled, and the affluent. The sandwich menu apparently reaches just about everyone, at least for lunch, from the club member to the vacationer on the throughway.

The American restaurant public likes beef. Of the 600 pounds of food that the average American eats each year, more than 100 pounds will be beef. Consumption of pork is going down; chicken is rising, as is turkey; cheese is going up fast; lamb and mutton consumption

is down, and veal is going down. Fish and game are about holding their own.

Ham or bacon and eggs are most preferred at breakfast, but after these Gallup poll results showed that for breakfast young people would like fancy pancakes and sweet or Danish rolls.

Among foreign and specialty foods served in restaurants, the same poll found that Italian food was the leader, followed by seafood. Fried shrimp and lobster tail were the favorites among the seafood choices. Coffee is still the most popular restaurant beverage, but, especially among young people, the cold drinks are gaining.

Tampering with Tastes Unwise

The restaurant operator is not wise to try to change tastes. He or she may discover that a market exists for tacos and other Mexican food. If so, well and good, but the operator must not try to force tacos, or anything else, down anybody's throat. Liver may be an excellent item nutritionally, but it cannot be served more than about once a month in a college foodservice.

It is quite possible, however, to modify existing tastes—to add a fillip to a basic, popular food. For example, Lum's steams its hot dogs in beer. Wurst is a modified hot dog and appeals to a more sophisticated market than the usual hot dog eater.

Nearly everyone likes roast beef and steak. There seems to be a growing preference for foods that are more acid, probably because of the vast amount of carbonated drinks being consumed, most of which are on the acid side. Almost all kinds of snacks are increasing in popularity. The popularity of seafood has gone up; witness the number of successful seafood restaurants.

Some of the most popular new menu items are those that stimulate a number of senses—smell, taste, feeling—all at once.

A hot fudge sundae sets off sensory responses for hot, cold, sweet, and bitter. Add nuts and get a desirable chewiness. Even pain elicited by red pepper has a role in the favorable response to foods. One reason for the popularity of Creole cookery is the bite in the liquid hot pepper sauce used. The gas in carbonated beverages acts on the pressure senses in the mouth. Noise, in the form of the "snap, crackle, and pop" of some foods, is appreciated.

Preference for that old Italian favorite, tomato sauce, is growing, as seen in the rapid growth of the consumption of pizza, spaghetti, and other tomato-sauced foods. There are 300 pizza operators in Milwaukee alone. Kids like hamburgers, hot dogs, french fries, fried chicken, and spaghetti. They like french fries, high in fat (about 18 percent fat).

A severely limited menu may be satisfactory in a new market until competition moves in. Then other items may have to be added to reach additional people. McDonald's has added the fish sandwich, the twin-patty hamburger, breakfast, and continues to add other food items in its operations.

The menu determines the kitchen equipment needed: broiled items on the menu require a broiler or a grooved griddle; fried items need a deep fat fryer. One successful group of fish and chips restaurants has no other equipment in its kitchens except deep fat fryers.

Fried foods are growing in popularity, especially among younger people. And why not? Most foods that are fried are low in fat to begin with—potatoes, young chickens, onions, and veal. The frying process adds about 10 to 15 percent fat to them, which brings the total fat content up to what is found in a good hamburger.

WHAT MAKES FOR PRESTIGE

What constitutes a prestige food for a menu changes with time. Brillat-Savarin, the famous gourmet of the early nineteenth century, ranked truffles and turkeys as the twin jewels of gastronomy. Truffles and caviar are still high status, probably because of cost.

Terrapin turtle, once on nearly every important menu, disappeared almost completely when sherry and Madeira, needed for cooking it properly, were outlawed by prohibition. Canvasback duck was largely eliminated when Army Ordnance took over the bird's favorite feeding grounds in Chesapeake Bay. Not being able to eat their favorite wild celery, they lost their distinctive flavor and, thus, popularity. Hamburgers, before 1930, were low status.

High-status dishes today, at least those served in the prestige restaurants in New York City, include Duck a l'Orange (duckling in an orange and wine sauce), Truffled Fresh Foie Gras (truffled goose liver pate), Veal Cordon Bleu (thin slices of veal stuffed with ham and cheese), and Chateaubriand (thick tenderloin usually served with Bordelaise sauce). Lobster and crab are other prestige items, largely because of their cost. One reason lobster is acclaimed at the moment is because of its high price. Go to any area where lobster is in plentiful supply and low in cost and it is not a prestige food. Chicken is losing its culinary status because of its low price.

Much of wine snobbery has a flimsy basis; the "authority" happens to know a little more about the subject than somebody else. One thing that gives a wine a reputation as being extremely good is its price; the higher the price, the better the wine. Tests of taste preference conducted so that the taster does not know the brand name, price, and origin often produce startling results. Less expensive beverages are frequently selected as best. The same wine placed in different bottles sets off arguments as to which wine is better. Of course, much of dining is romance, and who is the nasty fellow who would destroy romance?

Among the status wines today are: Romanee-Conti, considered by many to be the greatest red wine of Burgundy; Le Montrachet, usually conceded to be the greatest white wine of Burgundy; and Chateau Y'quem, the "great" sauterne.

Food Habits Change

Food habits and food preparation methods change with time, despite the efforts of purists to sanctify certain recipes and culinary practices. A good many people still refer to Escoffier's *Le Guide Culinaire* as the "Bible." The "Bible," it turns out, was written in 1902 and, as Escoffier said, was merely a collection of the best culinary information then available. Before Escoffier, Careme was the culinary arbiter.

In about 1958, the Hotel and Restaurant Catering Institute of Great Britain decided to establish once and for all what was right and wrong in the culinary world. A committee of twelve top chefs in Great Britain was appointed to the task. The committee set about diligently to develop a *Codex Culinaris*.

After 2½ years of weekly meetings, endless debates, and much controversy, the project quietly died. The chefs, representing a number of national cuisines, found it difficult to arrive at any particular standard, since what is good food is largely a matter of what is considered good by a particular social group, at a particular point in time. "One man's meat is another man's poison."

Name almost any food eaten by almost any group and you will find that somewhere in the world another group despises it. The fact that the French are more likely to use potato starch as a thickener than cornstarch only means that potato starch is more readily available in France and that cornstarch is cheap and handy in the United States. The wide use of veal in Europe may mean that farmers are not so likely to raise their cattle to maturity as is done in the United States. Culinary sacrilege usually implies that whoever is committing it is not performing according to the rules or value systems held by the accuser.

VARIATION IN RESTAURANT COSTS BY RESTAURANT TYPE AND SALES VOLUME

Some costs vary with the style of the restaurant. The fast-food restaurants typically have lower food and labor costs than table service restaurants, while occupancy costs with the fast-food places are usually higher than for the table service restaurant. As might be expected, as restaurant sales increase the percentage of gross profit also increases. In other words, the large volume restaurants generate higher profits and a higher percentage of profit as well. Restaurant costs and profits, of course, vary around the country. Labor costs in California run higher than they do for the country as a whole. Profits in California coffee shops and dinner houses are higher than for table service restaurants generally around the country.[3]

Occupancy costs vary widely depending on the arrangement between the operator and the owner of the land and/or restaurant. Many restaurateurs try for a five-year lease to avoid being tied to a location that could prove unsuitable. Leases are paid in several ways:

1. Minimum sum plus, or against, a specified percentage of the gross

2. Straight percentage of gross (usually 5 to 8 percent)

3. Percentage of gross sales that can slide up or down (the more or less the lessee makes, the more or less the landlord gets)

4. A flat monthly sum

Various other arrangements are common, such as the lease trade-off: the more improvements the landlord makes, the higher the rent. The more improvements the operator makes, the lower the rent. Trade-offs are important when the operator is beginning a new restaurant or plans extensive remodeling.

A turn-key lease is one where the restaurant, completely furnished, is turned over to an operator for a flat sum.

A restaurant grossing $1 million needs about eighty employees. These average figures mean little, however, since in very efficient restaurants the productivity per employee may exceed $40,000 a year in sales.

As sales increase, the cost of food consumed tends to go down. In one study, the cost of food and beverages, including employees' meals, ran 40.2 percent in establishments doing less than $100,000 a year in sales. Food cost was reduced as sales increased, until finally, in those restaurants doing between $500,000 and $1 million in sales, food cost dropped to 36 percent.

RESTAURANT PROFITABILITY

Handsome profits have been made in the restaurant business: also many failures have taken place over the years. Amateurs have "made it big," but not often. Even the professionals make mistakes in projecting a style of restaurant for a particular market, and most of the larger chains have had their share of losers. The chain can afford to lose on a few places; the individual cannot.

Consider the profits that are possible with a big winner. Some restaurants gross $12,000 to $16,000 per seat each year while the national average is less than $4,000 per seat. Seat turnover can be as high as seven per hour, or sixty customers per day. In dinner houses, seat turnover is more like one per hour or more, while the average restaurant gets less than two or three per hour.

3. *California Restaurant Operations,* 1977. Laventhol and Horwath, Los Angeles, California.

TABLE 8-2   The Restaurant Industry Dollar

Where It Came From

Food Sales	76.2
Beverage Sales	23.2
Other Income	.6

Where It Went

Cost of Merchandise Sold		
Food		31.6
Beverage		6.1
Total		37.7
Payroll and Related Expenses		
Payroll		26.6
Employee Benefits		3.8
Total		30.4
Direct Operating Expenses		5.4
Music and Entertainment		.7
Advertising and Promotion		1.8
Utilities		2.2
Administrative and General		4.7
Repairs and Maintenance		1.7
Occupation Costs		
Rent, Property Taxes, and Insurance		5.7
Interest		.7
Depreciation		2.2
Other Deductions		.6
Net Income Before Income Tax		6.2

In the United States, if $200,000 is invested in a restaurant, it grosses about $500,000 in sales. Of course, such ratios, investment to sales, vary widely. In recent years many restaurants represent million-dollar investments and expect $1 to $3 million in sales per year. Seats in the dining rooms of The Marriott Motor Hotels are expected to produce about $5,000 per seat per year.

At the other end of the service scale, as it runs from fast food to elegant service, were La Fonda del Sol and the Four Seasons, at that time also operated by Restaurant Associates Industries. These restaurants were known over the country as high check average, deluxe service restaurants, yet neither of these restaurants was particularly profitable. The Four Seasons is now operated by Paul Kovi and Tom Margittai, and is doing well.

Restaurant corporations seldom report net profit, as a percent of sales, exceeding 12 percent. Nationally, the figure is below 5 percent. Corporations are not eager to show high profits on which they must pay corporation taxes. Of course, many restaurant operations are pleased to show any profits.

When a restaurant is successful, it is likely to be successful in a big way. Anthony's Pier 4 Restaurant in Boston, independently owned by Anthony Athanas, has sales exceeding $8 million a year, the largest for any independent single restaurant. With this kind of volume, net profit would probably approach somewhere around 20 percent of sales before taxes, or something like $1.6 million a year in profit before taxes.

Restaurant profits vary widely, depending on a number of factors: check average, seat turnover, cost of food, labor costs, occupancy costs, costs of advertising, and other costs. The fast food outlet, such as McDonald's, has a relatively low labor cost because of employing mostly teenagers and paying minimum wages. Some table service restaurants reduce occupancy costs by remodeling old stores, barns, and houses. Food costs are considerably lower in a Mexican restaurant than in a steak house, though both may be highly successful. The coffee shop may have a check average of $1.70, as compared with one of $20 for a gourmet restaurant, yet the coffee shop may be much more profitable because of greater seat turnover and lower food and labor costs.

Table 8-3, compiled by the *Small Business Reporter, Bank of America,* 1975, compares expenses among various styles of restaurants: table service, drive-in, fast food/carry out, coffee shop, and cafeteria. The fast food/carry out service comes out the winner in profit because of lower food and labor costs. Other styles of service can be highly profitable. Of course, fast food units, as well as other styles of service can fail.

By contrast, in an individually owned business or partnership, the profit includes the owner's return from the operation. Corporation profits of necessity will be lower than profits of other legal forms; this is so because of the differences in accounting methods.

TABLE 8-3   Operating Ratios

	Table Service 100%	Drive-In 100%	Fast Food/ Carry Out 100%	Coffee Shop 100%	Cafeteria 100%
SALES	[food 70–80%] [beverage 20–30%]				
COST OF SALES	35.0 –44.0	35.0 –40.0	30.0 –40.0	33.0 –38.0	35.0 –42.0
GROSS PROFIT	56.0 –65.0	60.0 –65.0	60.0 –70.0	62.0 –67.0	58.0 –65.0
OPERATING EXPENSES					
Controllable Expenses					
Payroll	30.0 –35.0	25.0– 35.0	20.0 –30.0	30.0 –35.0	27.0 –35.0
Employee Benefits	3.0 – 5.0	3.0 – 6.0	2.0 – 4.0	3.0 – 8.0	2.5 – 6.0
Employee Meals	1.0 – 2.0	1.0 – 2.0	0.5 – 1.0	1.0 – 2.0	1.0 – 2.0
Laundry, Linen, Uniforms	1.5 – 2.0	0.3 – 1.0	0.3 – 0.8	0.5 – 1.5	0.5 – 1.5
Replacements	.5 – 1.0			0.5 – 0.75	0.5 – 0.75
Supplies (guest)	1.0 – 1.5	2.0 – 6.0	4.0 –10.0	1.0 – 0.7	1.0 – 2.0
Menus and Printing	.25– .5			0.2 – 0.7	
Misc. Contract Expense (cleaning, garbage, extermination, equip. rental)	1.0 – 2.0	0.75– 1.5	0.5 – 2.0	0.1 – 0.3	0.5 – 1.5
Music and Entertainment (where applicable)	.5 – 1.0			0.1 – 0.3	
Advertising and Promotion	.75– 2.0	1.0 – 2.0	0.5 – 2.0	0.75– 1.5	0.5 – 1.5
Utilities	1.0 – 2.0	2.0 – 4.0	1.0 – 2.0	1.5 – 3.0	1.5 – 3.0
Management Salary	2.0 – 6.0	3.0 –10.0	5.0 –10.0	7.0 –15.0	3.0 – 6.0
Administrative Expense (including legal and accounting)	.75– 2.0	0.5 – 1.0	.25– .75	0.5 – 1.0	1.0 – 2.0
Repairs and Maintenance	1.0 – 2.0	1.0 – 2.0	0.5 – 1.5	1.0 – 2.0	1.5 – 2.5
Occupation Expense					
Rent	4.5 – 9.0	4.5 – 8.0	3.5 – 7.0	4.0 – 7.0	4.0 – 5.0
Taxes (real estate and personal property)	.5 – 1.5	2.0 – 3.0	0.5 – 1.0	1.0 – 2.0	0.5 – 1.5
Insurance	.75– 1.0	0.5 – 1.0	0.5 – 1.0	1.0 – 2.0	0.75– 1.0
Interest	.3 – 1.0	1.0 – 2.0	0.2 – 0.8	0.5 – 2.0	0.5 – 1.5
Depreciation	2.0 – 4.0	1.5 – 4.0	3.5 – 7.0	2.0 – 3.0	2.0 – 3.0
Franchise Royalties (where applicable)	3.0 – 6.0	3.0 – 6.0	3.0 – 6.0	3.0 – 6.0	3.0 – 6.0
TOTAL OPERATING EXPENSES	55.0 –65.0	53.0 –60.0	47.0 –57.0	57.0 –65.0	51.0 –61.0
NET PROFIT BEFORE INCOME TAX	0.5 – 9.0	6.0 –12.0	10.0 –20.0	2.0 –10.0	3.0 – 7.0

Source: Figures developed by Small Business Reporter.

As an ideal, one might set up a model restaurant that costs $3,000 per seat. With one hundred seats, the restaurant's total cost could be $300,000. Ideally, we would want $10,000 per seat in sales per year, or $1 million. Ideally, we would also want a net profit before taxes of 20 percent or $200,000 a year.

RESTAURANT IDEAL

Capital Cost	$300,000
100 seats @ $3,000 per seat	
Sales per Year	$1,000,000
100 seats @ $10,000 per seat	
Profit Before Taxes	
20% of sales ($1,000,000)	$200,000

Of course, only a handful of restaurants, placed in high-income, high-density locations, have such a record. Average sales per seat in successful restaurants in 1975 were about $4,000.[4] As might be expected, restaurants serving liquor usually have slower turnover of seats and fewer sales per seat. The higher profit on liquor tends to compensate for the lower total sales.

Sales Per Seat May Mislead

Sales per seat, of course, is only one way of measuring efficiency and can be misleading. In Valle's Steak Houses, a New England-based

4. *Tableservice Restaurants Operation Report 1976*, NRA, 1977.

chain, each seats about 1,000 persons. Each restaurant costs about $1 million, or $1,000 per seat. Income before taxes was $2.5 million, or a little over 15 percent of sales. Part of the high profit comes from liquor sales.

Chain restaurants and franchise restaurants usually gross at least $400,000 annually and to be really profitable usually gross more than $500,000 annually. These operations are growing in number each year.

If a restaurant is a winner, the return on investment can be very high. A restaurant doing sales of $1 million a year may make as much as $200,000 net profit, before taxes. Such a restaurant might cost $1 million to build. Return on investment (ROI) could be 20 percent. A good restaurant today costs between $2,000 and $5,000 per seat to build and equip, depending

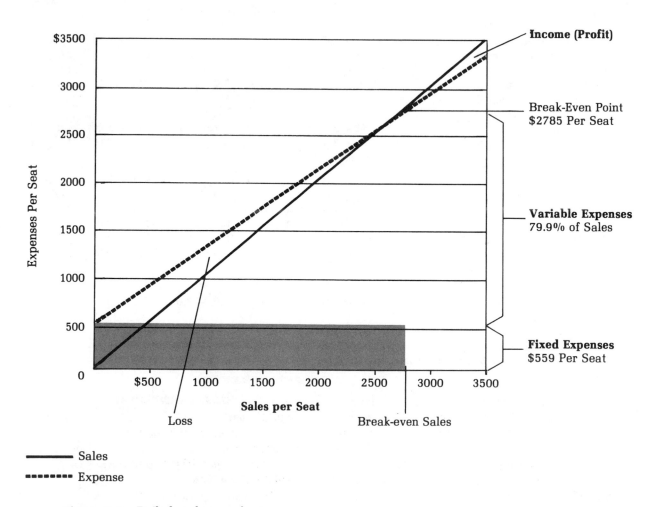

Figure 8-3 *Daily break-even chart.*

on size, cost of land, and appointments. A one hundred-seat restaurant would run between $200,000 and $500,000 in cost. Such a restaurant should gross between $400,000 and $600,000 in sales per year. If it nets 8 percent before taxes, profits would be $32,000 to $50,000 a year.

A few years ago, a restaurant that grossed $1 million in sales a year was a phenomenon; not so today. In 1969 a McDonald's drive-in restaurant took in $1 million; in 1976 more than 100 McDonald's in Canada grossed $1 million in sales. One McDonald's exceeds $3 million. In 1975, dozens of restaurants exceeded the $1 million figure. A number do in excess of $3 million in annual sales. The really financially successful restaurant grosses at least $500,000 a year. At this figure, food cost is likely to be about 36 percent of sales, and labor cost below 30 percent of sales (not always). A winner in a restaurant is likely to be a winner indeed.

Like most businesses, profits are not a direct straight-line percentage of sales. Each restaurant has a break-even point in sales, a point at which the income just pays for all of the operating costs and fixed costs. Until the restaurant reaches the break-even point in sales, no profit at all has been made.

Once the break-even point in sales has been passed, profits may rise on an accelerated scale. For example, the break-even point for a restaurant might be $1,000 in sales a day. If the restaurant does $1,500 in sales, profit may be 10 percent on every dollar of sales beyond $1,000. The profit may jump to 20 percent as sales pass the $1,500 mark. When sales go beyond a certain figure, the operation reaches the point of diminishing returns. When sales go beyond that point, profit begins to fall off.

The break-even point for restaurants varies widely. The family-operated restaurant may have a break-even point of only $50 or so a

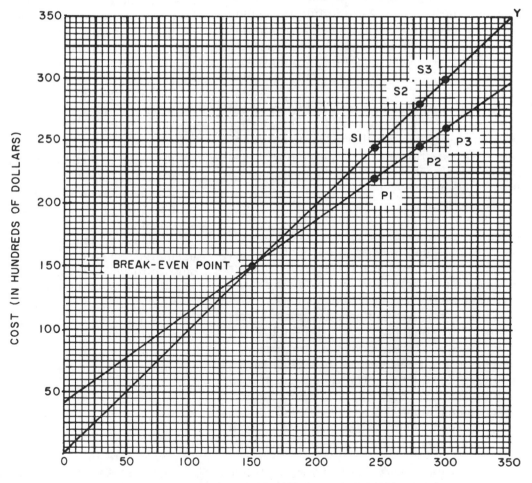

Figure 8-4 *The break-even point.*

day. If there is little business, one family member merely retires from the scene. Taxes, insurance, utilities, depreciation, and other fixed costs, however, go on. Large and expensive restaurants have high break-even points. The Four Seasons, a luxury restaurant in New York City, at one time was said to have a break-even point of $6,000 a day. The Kon Tiki and Trader Vic type of restaurant are said to need sales of about $500,000 per year to break even.

In Figure 8–3 the break-even point is $150 in sales per day.[5] If sales rise to $250 a day, profit would be the difference between S1 and P1, or about $25. If sales go $350 in one day, profit would be $50. The point of diminishing returns would be reached when a line representing cost began trending upward and paralleled the sales line.

No Magic Formula

A survey of table service restaurants done in 1976 for the National Restaurant Association showed a break-even point for the restaurants covered of $2,785 per seat. That volume of sales could have been achieved by a daily seat turnover of 1.24 and an average check (food) of $4.69.

Fixed expenses in that study ran about $560 per seat, expenses which go on whether the restaurant has any business or not. Variable expenses ran about 80 percent of sales. Figure 8–4 shows the break-even point in terms of expenses per seat.

A wide variety in menu format has been successfully merchandised in this country. The upgraded railroad diner, serving foods right off the grill, has been favored in parts of the East by the highway traveler. It is especially popular in New Jersey where most of the "dining cars" have been built. Originally, the diner was a railroad dining car that had been taken out of service or a structure patterned after such a car. New diners are lavish indeed, and expensive.

Nondescript restaurants have been known to succeed for a time, perhaps because of good location and the personality of the operator. Funky restaurants with oddly assorted themes often succeed, whereas the more traditional restaurant does not. Deluxe restaurants come

and go. Fashions in decor change. The specialty restaurant, which has spread widely since World War II, has had a greater chance of success because of its specialization.

If a restaurant meets a need or evokes excitement, glamour, or adventure, the restaurant will succeed, if it is well managed. The big money-makers in restaurants seem to be those restaurants (1) offering a menu that is familiar to a market, or (2) that glamourize a familiar menu. The menu should be offered in an impressive, pleasing, or exciting milieu. For the teenager and patrons in their twenties, the noise level must be much higher than in the restaurant catering to older persons. Loud, rhythmic music—even noise—is pleasing to the teenager and the person in his or her twenties. The "tension level" must be higher for them. A buffet served in a country club will be a failure, if it has the same tension level.

The decor must be pleasing or impressive to a particular market. Something that is known to be expensive, or has status, impresses most people. Americans and Germans have stood in line to stay overnight at Woburn Abbey and breakfast with the Duke and Duchess of Bedford. The tariff was $200 per person.

Charles Creighton has put together some of the most attractive and beautiful restaurants in the world in South Florida. Instead of charging luxury prices, he caters to the great mass of people with a moderately priced menu. His profits are considerable. What is impressive or exciting changes with time. It is a format that usually wins: modestly priced food in luxury surroundings.

Food is only one aspect of a restaurant. All hamburger chains sell hamburgers, one not much different from the other. Why then are McDonald's and Burger Chef so large? The setting and the advertising account for much of the success of one hamburger operation versus another.

If there is a formula for success in the restaurant business it goes something like this:

1. Identify a potential market.

2. Develop a menu that will appeal to that market.

3. Build a restaurant around the menu that will also appeal to the market.

4. Locate the restaurant as conveniently to the market as possible.

5. "Using Break-Even Analysis in Food Service Establishments," *Food Management Program Leaflet No. 13* (Amherst, Mass.: College of Agriculture, University of Massachusetts).

5. Merchandise the total restaurant to the market.

6. Cater to the mass market.

7. Be ready to modify the menu or the restaurant concept as the market calls for such changes.

8. Design the restaurant with style, or to meet a fashion.

9. Set moderate menu prices.

THE RESTAURANT FAILURE RATE

The restaurant business has acquired a reputation, over the years, as having one of the highest, if not the highest, failure rates of retail businesses. The statistics are not in, but it is probable that the failure rate is not so high as believed.

Robert M. Riley, former general manager of the California Restaurant Association, think these figures are grossly misleading. He points out that there are twelve other lines of business that have failure rates higher than restaurants, and that the rate of failure of eating and drinking places has been about the same for the past twenty-six years.

What constitutes a failure must be defined also. The fact that a family continues to operate a restaurant even though their income is low might well be construed as failure. Hundreds, perhaps thousands, of such restaurants exist. Most of these are too small to be very profitable. Hundreds are in old homes. Some are on ferry boats, yachts, old barns, and similar unlikely locations. It would be surprising if the discontinuance rate were not high.

Unlike the European restaurant business, most restaurant operators in this country have had little or no formal training for the occupation. Behind every person who likes to cook, likes to be with people, and wants to make money, lurks a would-be restaurateur. The roads all over the United States are dotted with little restaurants, or the remains of them, holding the hopes and aspirations, and sometimes fortunes, of such people.

Little Chance for Small Restaurant

Most small restaurants never have a chance. They are too isolated from their markets, too small, too unimpressive to compete with the established restaurants. On the other hand, most of the successful restaurant operators of today started in very modest establishments, lacked formal training, and had little financial backing. A comprehensive study of "failure" in the restaurant business would be enlightening and valuable to the industry.

Too often a would-be restaurateur allows optimism to override financial resources and acumen. Too little capital investment, too little working capital, too little market analysis, or too little experience make for too much disappointment when profits fail to appear.

While several millionaire restaurant operators started with small restaurants and were successful from the day they opened, most

TABLE 8-4 Initial Investment Requirements for a Hypothetical Table Service Restaurant

Annual Gross Sales: $200,000–$350,000
Floor Space: About 3,000 sq. ft.
Seats: 100

OPENING COSTS	Range
Leasehold Improvements (wiring, plumbing, air conditioning, painting, labor and materials at $25 to $45 a sq. ft.)	$ 75,000–$135,000
Fixtures and Equipment dining area	2,400– 3,000
kitchen (500 sq. ft. at $20 to $45 a sq. ft.)	10,000– 22,500
Lease Deposit (1st and last month)	2,000– 4,200
Food Inventory (at opening)	1,000– 4,000
Subtotal	$ 90,400–$168,700
OPERATING COSTS	
(first three months) Payroll	
manager's salary	$ 3,000–$ 4,200
employees (4 servers, 2 cooking staff, 1 part-time cleanup)	11,600– 12,800
Food Supplies	26,500– 28,300
Taxes and Licenses	240– 390
Professional Services (legal and accounting)	240– 690
Insurance	290– 400
2 Months' Rent	1,000– 4,200
Cash Reserve	900– 1,500
Subtotal	$ 44,770–$ 52,480
TOTAL	$135,170–$221,180

Source: Figures compiled by *Small Business Reporter* in California.

SCATTER SHEET

SALES PRICE	MENU ITEM	TIMES SOLD	TOTAL	SALES VALUE
	25% Cost			
$ 1.25	Hamburger	~~THL THL THL THL - THL I~~	26	$ 32.50
1.00	Cheese Sandwich	~~THL - I~~	6	6.00
1.50	Egg Salad Sandwich	~~THL - THL~~	10	15.00
1.00	Jello Salad	~~THL~~	5	5.00
	30% Cost			
1.25	Pie, Cherry & Apple	~~THL - THL - III~~	13	16.25
1.00	Ice Cream	~~THL - THL - THL~~	15	15.00
1.75	Cheeseburger	~~THL - THL - THL - THL - THL - THL~~	30	52.50
2.00	Ham Sandwich	~~THL - THL - THL~~	15	30.00
1.50	Waldorf Salad	~~THL - THL - II~~	12	18.00
7.00	Baked Ham Dinner	~~THL - THL - THL - THL - THL~~	25	350.00
5.75	Fried Chicken Dinner	~~THL - THL - THL - THL~~	20	115.00
	35% Cost			
2.75	Pork Sandwich, Hot	~~THL - THL~~	10	27.50
2.75	Beef Sandwich, Hot	~~THL - THL - THL - THL~~	20	55.00
4.50	Shrimp Salad	~~THL - THL - THL - THL - THL - THL~~	30	135.00
6.00	Turkey Dinner	~~THL - THL - THL - THL - THL~~	25	150.00
6.50	Pork Chop Dinner	~~THL~~	5	32.50
1.30	Ice Cream, Sundae	~~THL - THL - THL - THL - THL~~	25	37.50
	40% Cost			
6.00	Lobster Cocktail	~~THL - THL - THL - THL~~	20	120.00
3.75	Club Sandwich	~~THL - THL - THL - THL - THL - THL - THL~~	35	131.25
6.50	Pork Tender, Dinner	~~THL - THL - II~~	12	78.00
8.50	Filet Mignon, Dinner	~~THL - THL - THL - THL - THL~~	25	212.50
2.00	French Pastry	~~THL - THL - THL~~	15	30.00
	45% Cost			
6.00	Oyster Cocktail	~~THL - THL - THL - THL~~	20	120.00
4.50	Fruit Salad, Plate	~~THL - THL - THL - THL - III~~	23	103.50
7.00	Rib Steak, Dinner	~~THL - THL~~	10	70.00
7.25	Rainbow Trout, Dinner	~~THL - THL - THL - THL - THL - THL - I~~	31	224.75
9.75	Prime Rib, Dinner	~~THL - II~~	7	68.25
.50	Coffee	~~THL - THL - THL - THL - THL - THL - THL - THL - THL - I~~	46	23.00
.50	Milk	~~THL - THL - THL - THL - THL - THL - THL~~	35	17.50
	50% Cost			
2.00	Asparagus Tip Salad	~~THL - THL - THL - THL - THL - THL~~	30	60.00
5.00	Prime Rib Sandwich	~~THL - THL - THL - IIII~~	19	95.00
13.50	T-Bone Steak, 16 oz.	~~THL - THL - THL - THL - THL - THL - THL~~	35	472.50
12.50	New York Cut Steak, 12 oz	~~THL - THL - THL - II~~	17	212.50
2.25	Strawberry Shortcake	~~THL - THL - THL - THL - THL - THL - THL~~	35	78.75
	55% Cost			
3.50	Chef's Salad Bowl	~~THL - THL - THL - THL - THL~~	25	87.50
6.25	Calf's Liver Dinner	~~THL - THL - THL - THL - THL - I~~	26	162.50
12.50	Lobster Tails	~~THL - II~~	7	87.50
				$3550.75

A "SCATTER-SHEET" IS A VALUABLE MANAGEMENT TOOL.

"Scatter Sheet"
RECAP

ITEMS	25% Cost	30% Cost	35% Cost	40% Cost	45% Cost	50% Cost	55% Cost	TOTALS
Cost % to Sales	0.4%	4.1%	4.4%	6.4%	9.8%	13.7%	3.9%	42.7%
% of Food Cost	1 %	10%	10%	15%	23%	32%	9 %	100%

Figure 8-5 *Scatter sheet.*

restaurant operators have a rough time financially for the first several months. Many lose all of their investment because of lack of working capital. The time period required to break even in a restaurant is usually much longer than anticipated by the owners.

The initial investment requirements of a hypothetical table service restaurant have been developed by the *Small Business Reporter* in California and are seen in Table 8–4.

Staffing a restaurant and conducting a feasibility study is a fairly complicated project. Figure 8–2 suggests some of the factors to be considered in arriving at three important numbers: sales, food costs, and payroll.

MENU ANALYSIS

Restaurateurs are forever examining their menu to see if it fits their clientele and to determine if each item is profitable. Menu items might be classified as being:

1. Popular and profitable
2. Popular and unprofitable
3. Unpopular but profitable
4. Unpopular and unprofitable

The unprofitable items are usually dropped unless there is some good reason for retaining them. At times, the menu may include a few prestige items that are seldom sold and when sold are not profitable. The items may be retained as window dressing for the menu. Chain restaurants will have none of this kind of thinking and stay with the items that are fast movers and, preferably, long profit.

The Air Force Manual for Operating Clubs recommends careful analysis of the menu to determine exactly what each item contributes in the way of profit to the enterprise. Figure 8–5 is the analytical device used to identify the cost of each item and the contribution it makes to the total sales of the restaurant. (Prices have been updated and the percentages below are illustrative only).

In the example given, the total food cost percentage is 43 percent, but, as the menu is broken down, it is seen that different items have widely different costs:

1 percent of the menu items had a food cost of 25 percent.

10 percent of the menu items had 30 percent food cost.

10 percent of the menu items had 35 percent food cost.

15 percent of the menu items had 40 percent food cost.

23 percent of the menu items had 45 percent food cost.

32 percent of the menu items had 50 percent food cost.

9 percent of the menu items had 55 percent food cost.

Which items should be changed? Which dropped completely? Many restaurant experts urge that menus be severely limited to those items which are highly profitable and that can be done well and quickly by the restaurant. In some styles of restaurant this is not possible. Where possible and where the market exists for the limited menu, it should be used since it permits the highest profits.

What Do Items Contribute?

In Figure 8–5 we see that T-bone steak, selling for $13.50 an order, contributes $472.50. It has a high food cost of 50 percent. Never mind the high food cost, the contribution is the thing. The T-bone steak is a star on this menu.

The chef's salad bowl is something else again. It is time-consuming to prepare and is probably a loss item when the labor cost is added to the food cost. Lobster tails might well be retained, since there is little preparation involved other than broiling them, and they can easily be stored in the frozen state.

The cherry or apple pie might look like a good item to retain or promote since it has only a 30 percent food cost. Yet, the item probably might be dropped, unless the pie has been purchased from a baker and entails little labor cost in serving. Labor cost in making such a pie would be considerable. Ice cream, on the other hand, has almost no labor cost. On the other hand cherry pie may be a menu leader and should be retained. Strawberry pie, freshly made daily, has proved to be a leader in a number of coffee shops.

Menu-making is often considered an art, but it is becoming a science. Research done at Tulane University, under a grant from the National Institute of Health, has pointed the way for menu construction using the computer. Several hospitals now plan menus using the computer. The problem is to select items which are popular, low cost, and together form a nutritious meal. The variables are staggering and cannot be handled efficiently without a computer.

The first step is to place into the computer's memory all the relevant data concerning available foodstuffs. One hospital, for example, has on file 800 recipes and nineteen nutritional factors for each of 2,500 foodstuffs. The cost of these foodstuffs must be included, and the computer must be programmed so that the combinations of foods selected are eye appealing. The computer has been known to turn out menus all bland, all soft, and all white. Restraints must also be placed on the computer so that items do not appear too often on the menu.

PROPER FOOD COST?

What constitutes a proper food cost depends on the amount of service, the cost of the atmosphere, and other factors that are offered together with the food. In an expensive, luxury style restaurant, the food cost may be only 28 percent, but the cost of labor may more than offset the low food cost, running as high as 35 percent or 40 percent depending on what part of the country the restaurant is located in.

In city and country clubs, food costs run 40 to 55 percent. The members want it that way; dues paid make up the deficits. A drive-in restaurant might have a high food cost, 40 percent or more, but its labor cost could be 20 percent or less.

Patterned like a teeter-totter, as labor costs go up, food costs go down. In other words, customers get less food for their money. In atmosphere restaurants, customers necessarily pay for the atmosphere and, in most cases, are willing to do so.

A fast-turnover steak house might run a food cost as high as 45 percent of sales and still make a good profit, if labor cost is 20 percent or less of sales.

In fast-food restaurants, the cost of paper goods is often figured as part of the food cost.

One hamburger chain has a food cost of 37 percent. The reason: the chain features a roast beef sandwich, a 3-oz. portion of roasted knuckle on a roll, selling for 69 cents. Though the food cost of the sandwich is about 43 percent, the cost of labor in preparing the sandwich is low, about 15 percent. One cost balances the other.

How can a hamburger chain sell a hamburger for only $1.20? Easy. If hamburger sells for $1.28 a pound and a two-ounce patty is served, food cost for the patty is about 16¢. The bun costs 8¢. Garnish might add another 4¢, for a total cost of 30¢. The selling price, $1.20, is divided by the cost, 30¢, which gives a food cost percentage on the hamburger of about 25 percent.

Beverages such as coke and orange drink have a food and paper cost of 20 percent or less, which, added into the overall food cost, brings it down.

An odd accounting practice in the foodservice business comes in computing food cost. Usually food cost is expressed as the cost of food consumed divided into the food sales. Cost of food consumed includes the cost of the food eaten by the employees. Other businesses would compute employee meals separately or include them as part of the cost of labor.

Food cost cannot be considered apart from labor cost. As noted previously, if one goes up, the other must inevitably come down. When labor costs rise, the food cost must come down, and the customers pay a little more for a little less. The only way to avoid raising menu prices is to become more efficient or to have the customers help in serving themselves. This is what happened in the rapidly expanding fast-food and cafeteria restaurants.

Combined Food and Labor Costs

It helps to look at food and labor costs as interacting variables, one necessarily affecting the other, if a profit is to be made. Ordinarily, costs other than food and labor costs do not exceed 20 percent of sales. If the combined food and labor costs can be kept below 65 percent, a 15 percent profit in sales can be made. In other words, par for the course is 65. If food and labor can be kept below 65, as is often the case, then 15 percent profit should be forthcoming.

Exceptions exist. Turnpike and airport contracts for foodservice are let to the highest bidder. The successful bidder may pay 15 percent, or even more, "off the top" to the authority operating the turnpike or airport. To meet such fees, the operator must raise food and beverage prices. Food costs come down to below 30 percent; beverage costs drop to below 25 percent.

Food costs in specialty restaurants are likely to vary widely, depending on the menu, atmosphere, and prices offered. Polynesian restaurants—actually Chinese restaurants in a Polynesian setting—have low food costs, usually under 34 percent. The reason: lots of rice. Beverage costs are also low: lots of rum at high prices. Mexican restaurants run food costs of about 30 percent, or less, because of the plenitude of corn, rice, and beans served.

Some rather amazing food and labor cost combinations exist, as reported by *Institutions Magazine* in 1969. The Village Inn Pizza chain had a food cost of 25 percent, a labor cost of 25 percent, for a combined total of 50 percent. The Little Red Hen, Inc., surprisingly, had a combined total of 52 percent: 43 percent food and 9 percent labor.

Lawry's, a roast beef full-service restaurant chain, had a food cost of 43.3 percent, labor cost of 25.4 percent.

Ramada Inns reported food costs of 34 percent in its restaurants, labor cost of 37 percent, indicating the relative inefficiency of the usual motel dining room. Food and labor cost in the Marriott Corporation ran 41.4 percent food cost, 31 percent labor cost.

Cost Combinations That Work

It is common practice in the restaurant business to establish food and labor cost targets that if not exceeded will ordinarily result in profit for the operation. In the old-style table service restaurant a typical cost combination might be:

Food cost as a percentage of sales:	40
Labor cost as a percentage of sales:	25
Balance	65

If other costs did not exceed about 15 percent the operation would produce a 20 percent profit before income taxes.

The combination of food cost percentage and labor cost percentage has come to be known as *Prime Cost*. If the prime cost does not exceed 70 percent, the restaurant ordinarily produces a 10 to 15 percent net profit on sales.

The usual "Other Costs" would not exceed about 15 percent. There are exceptions. Occupancy costs ordinarily run 5 to 10 percent but can go as high as 15 percent in some choice locations such as found in an airport, or a choice location on a turnpike.

On the other hand, occupancy cost can run as low as 2 percent of sales if in a low-rent area or if the owner has taken over an old building and remodeled it. Sometimes also a restaurant location will have failed several times in succession and the owner is quite ready to offer a very low cost lease.

TABLE 8-5 Operating Statement of Midwest Family Restaurant

	January 1978
Total Sales—Food and Soft Drinks	100.0%
Cost of Sales	42.2
Gross Profit on Sales	57.8
Operating Expenses	
Salaries	22.1
Rent	5.3
Supplies	4.3
Utilities	2.2
Telephone	.1
Office Supplies	.2
Laundry	.3
Advertising	.6
Insurance	1.7
Trash Hauling	.2
Taxes and Licenses	.8
Car & Travel Expenses	.6
Repairs and Maintenance	1.1
Legal and Accounting	.8
Interest and Bank Charges	.2
Dues and Subscriptions	.3
Total Operating Expenses	40.8%
Net Profit before Depreciation	17.0
Depreciation	1.6
Net Profit	15.4

This restaurant seats 160 in the family-type dining room and three private party rooms. Serves lunch and dinner and operates daily.

TABLE 8-6 Operating Statement of Midwest Fast Food Shop

	Year to Date September 1977
Sales	100.0%
Cost of Sales	34.5
Gross Margin	65.5%
Expenses	
Salary, Wage	20.2%
Payroll Taxes	2.3
Supplies & Service	.5
Repair & Cleaning	1.6
Advertising	5.9
Rent Expense	5.5
Utilities	2.5
Insurance & Taxes	1.1
Interest	.1
Royalties	3.5
Depreciation	1.2
Operating Margin	21.1%

Fast-food restaurant open 7 days a week. Average check $1.79. 86 seats.

Food and labor costs can vary widely as long as the total does not exceed 70 percent. Some possible combinations in percentages:

A steak house:

Food costs	50
Labor costs	20
Total	70

A mexican fast-food restaurant:

Food costs	30
Labor costs	20
Total	50

Coffee shop:

Food costs	38
Labor costs	26
Total	64

A dinner house featuring roast beef while beef is low in cost:

Food costs	48
Labor costs	20
Total	68

Restaurants that have sizeable bar sales sometimes are less concerned about food and labor costs as long as the average of the food cost/labor cost/ and bar cost comes out to be less than 40. For example, these are the costs of

TABLE 8-7 Operating Statement of a Midwestern Atmosphere Restaurant

	Year to Date 1976
Sales and Revenues	%
Beer	4.63
Liquor	19.25
Wine	2.17
Food	72.65
Subtotal	98.70
Cigarettes	.56
Miscellaneous	.75
Total Sales and Revenues	100.00
Cost of Sales	
Beer	26.94
Liquor	18.60
Wine	46.37
Food	41.23
Subtotal	36.26
Cigarettes	81.91
Total Cost of Sales	36.52
Gross Profit	63.48
Operating Expenses	
Payroll	22.81
Employee Benefits	3.62
Direct Operating	9.47
Advertising and Promotion	3.86
Administrative and General	1.47
Repairs and Maintenance	.79
Total Operating Expenses	42.02
Net Profit Before Fixed	21.46
Less: Fixed Expenses	6.32
Net Profit Before Depreciation	15.14
Less: Depreciation	2.01
Net Profit	13.13
Less: Admin. Fees	8.20
Net Profit	4.93

*Located downtown, this restaurant is open 7 days a week, serving lunch and dinner meals. There is seating for 200 people, with parking facilities available. The guest check averages $2.95 at lunch, $9.75 at dinner. The limited menu features steaks, ribs, seafood, and teriyaki.

Source: National Restaurant Association, November 1976.

a fine dinner house with the sales volume of 1.8 million dollars a year:

Food costs	46
Labor costs	32
Bar costs	22
Total	100
Average	33 percent

TABLE 8-8 Operating Statement of 150-seat Western Pancake Restaurant

	Year to Date 1976		Year to Date 1976
Sales		Administrative expenses	
Food sales	99.4	Bonuses & commissions	.7
Counter sales	.6	Supervisors expenses	.5
Total Sales	**100.0**	Bonus—Manager	.9
		Insurance—General	.6
Cost of sales			
Food costs	30.1	Workman's Comp. ins.	.2
Counter costs	.4	Group insurance	.4
		Interest expense	.4
Total cost of sales	**30.5**	Other	.3
		Professional services—legal	—
Gross profit on sales	**69.5**	Personal property and real estate	.2
Labor costs	27.7	Miscellaneous business taxes	.2
Indirect labor costs	3.5	Rent	3.2
		Maintenance expense—home office	.5
Controllable & variable expenses		Royalty expense	5.0
Advertising	1.1	Home office service fee	—
Bad debts & short checks	—	Home office promotion	.1
Bank or data proc. payroll expense	—	Home office expense	—
Bank service charge	—		
Cash, over and short	—	**Total administrative expense**	**13.2**
Cleaning supplies	.2		
Dishwasher soap	.5	**Total profit before fixed expenses**	**16.0**
Dues and subscriptions	—		
Laundry and dry cleaning	.5	Fixed expenses	
Dry cleaning allowance	—	Depreciation—kitchen equipment	.2
Licenses and permits	—	Depreciation—dining room	
Menus	.1	furniture	.1
Miscellaneous services	.5	Depreciation—auto and truck	—
Office supplies and postage	.1	Office and miscellaneous	
Paper—sundry supplies	1.0	equipment	.1
Promotion and entertainment	.4	Depreciation—leasehold	
Repairs and maintenance—Bldg.	.3	improvements	.5
Repairs and maintenance—Eqpt.	.3	Other fixed expenses	1.0
Replacement—china, glass & silver	.7		
Replacement—kitchen utensils	.1	**Total fixed expenses**	**1.9**
Sign rentals	.3		
Telephone	.1	**Net operating profit**	**14.1**
Uniforms	.1		
Utilities	2.7	Other income and expense	
Unclassified general expense	.1	Vending machine—net	.3
		Interest income	—
Total controllable & variable		Miscellaneous	.5
expenses	**9.1**	Controllable adjustments	(.4)
Total 4 area costs	**70.8**		
Total profit after labor &		**Total other income and expense**	**.4**
controllables	**29.2**	**Net profit before income taxes**	**14.5**

*Family type-sit-down restaurant, specializing in pancakes, eggs, and omelets.

Average no. of employees, part time and full time: 45

Hours open: 6 A.M. to 2 A.M.

Parking spaces: 70

Average guest check: $1.85

Source: National Restaurant Association, December, 1976.

To illustrate the range of costs that can be experienced in various styles of restaurants while each of the restaurants remain profitable, four profit and loss statements from four different kinds of restaurants are seen in Tables 8–5 through 8–8.[6]

It is interesting to note the wide differences in expenditure for advertising and promotion: fast food, almost 6 percent; pancake house 1.1 percent; the atmosphere restaurant about 4 percent.

In the examples above it is seen that the fast-food shop ends up with the highest profit, largely because of food costs of 34.5 percent and labor costs of about 22.5 percent of sales. The pancake restaurant produced an exceptionally low food cost of 30.5 percent and a labor cost of close to 32 percent; administrative expenses ran 13.2, together the principal ingredients in the mix which produced an operating profit of 14.1 percent. The atmosphere restaurant showed a profit of less than 5 percent of gross sales; food cost was comparatively high (41 percent) because the place featured steaks, ribs, seafood and teriyaki, eleven points higher than that of the western pancake restaurant and about 7 percent higher than the fast food shop.

Of course, what really counts is the net profit in dollars, and it is possible that the atmosphere restaurant is the most profitable of the three restaurants because of large sales volume.

SERVICE SETS LABOR COST

Restaurant labor costs are largely influenced by the style of service and the amount of food preparation done on premise. The fast-food restaurant, with its limited menu and minimal food preparation, has a lower labor cost than the table service restaurant. Frisch's, one of the better known drive-in groups, has a labor cost of 24.2 percent, a food cost of 34.3 percent.

Bonanza, a franchise chain, has a labor cost of only 18 percent that permits higher food cost; in this case, 42 percent. Cafeterias might be expected to have a somewhat lower labor cost than table service restaurants because the customers largely serve themselves. However, in table service restaurants most of the labor

6. Taken from NRA NEWS bulletins.

cost of the serving personnel is borne by the customer in the form of tips. Forum Cafeterias, a large midwest chain, has a food cost of 33 percent and a labor cost of 35 percent, not much different than would be expected in a table service restaurant.

The food and labor equation also varies regionally. Where wages are high—in northern cities and the Far West—food costs necessarily must be lower. If labor costs in California average 34 percent, food cost is 34 percent or lower. In the South, with its low labor costs, food costs are higher. If labor cost in a Mississippi restaurant is 20 percent, food costs may be 40 percent or higher.

As has been pointed out, "You don't bank percentages." This means that over-emphasis on maintaining a particular food cost or labor cost percentage may divert management's attention away from its true purpose: maximizing profits.

One way to maximize profits is to sell high-priced items, if patrons will buy them. Steak may have a food cost of 50 percent and sell for $8. A half-chicken might be sold for $1.50 and have a food cost of 33 percent. The profit on the steak would be $4, compared to only 53¢ for the chicken. Increasing the average check is a fast way of increasing profit because ordinarily the higher priced item will bring a disproportionately large contribution of profit, even though the food cost may be higher.

The cost of preparing any individual menu item must be considered in pricing. Those items with a high labor cost might better be omitted from the menu. Harry Pope of Pope's Cafeterias, headquartered in St. Louis, has pioneered the concept of "prime cost," the combination of labor and food cost of a menu item.

He has pointed out that many menu items may have a low food cost but a high labor cost. Ingredients for soup, for example, may cost only 3¢ a portion, but the cost of making the soup is 10 or 12¢. Most establishments today buy soup in canned or dehydrated form. Some of the canned soups are superior, those that are less affected by the high heat required for canning.

Most colleges and universities that offer hotel and restaurant management courses offer at least one quarter or a semester of work in food and beverage cost control, either as a separate course or as part of another. Restaurant

FOODSERVICE PROPRIETOR

	LOSING MONEY	AVERAGE PROFIT	A GOOD DEAL (EXTRA MARKUP)
GOOD DEAL (SOMETHING FOR NOTHING)			
A FAIR VALUE			
RIPPED OFF			

C U S T O M E R

XYZ RESTAURANT
INCOME STATEMENT FOR THE MONTH

3,000 CUSTOMERS
JANUARY 31, 1974

SALES	$15,000	100%
LESS COST OF FOOD SOLD	5,400	36%
GROSS PROFIT	$ 9,600	64%
LESS OTHER EXPENSES		
LABOR COST	$ 4,800	32%
SUPPLIES	600	4%
OCCUPATION	1,500	10%
OTHER	900	6%
PROFIT BEFORE TAX	$1,800	12%

PERCENTAGE MARKUP SYSTEM

ADVANTAGES:
1. PROVIDES A CLOSE RELATIONSHIP—OBVIOUS TO THE CUSTOMER—BETWEEN THE COST OF EACH MENU ITEM AND THE SELLING PRICE.
2. OFFERS A WIDER PRICE RANGE AND ALLOWS THE RESTAURATEUR TO SERVICE A BROADER PRICE MARKET.
3. PERIODIC FINANCIAL STATEMENTS ACCURATELY REFLECT THE EFFICIENCY OF THE OPERATION.
4. RELATIVELY SIMPLE TO ADMINISTER.

DISADVANTAGES:
1. DOES NOT REFLECT THE RISK (HIGH WASTE) INHERENT IN SOME MENU ITEMS.
2. DOES NOT REFLECT THE AMOUNT OF DIRECT LABOR INVOLVED IN PREPARATION.

Figure 8–6 *Pricing Decision Guide Foodservice Proprietor.*

menu pricing policy and the mechanics of pricing are integral parts of such courses.

Traditionally, restaurant menu pricing has been based on rules of thumb passed along from operator to operator. Pricing is a controversial subject, with various operators using different pricing systems to arrive at the selling price of their menu items. The National Restaurant Association has published a summary of three of these systems: the "good deal" philosophy, the percentage markup system, and the gross markup system. The three systems appear in Figure 8–6. Also included are explanations of three analytical tools which bear on pricing policy: average check, frequency distribution of checks, and further discussions of menu analysis.

THE "GOOD DEAL" PHILOSOPHY OF PRICING

For any foodservice establishment to be successful, the customers must believe they are receiving a fair value. The customers' concept of a value will vary. The key to success is to provide what most of your customers see as a value most of the time.

Just as the customer wants a good deal, the proprietor is entitled to at least a fair return. The proprietor has invested money and time and is taking a risk. To remain in business, he or she requires a fair profit.

Successful foodservice operators find ways to satisfy customers and maintain a fair profit. In any pricing work, both customer satisfaction and a fair return must be maintained.

Some methods of pricing are described in the following pages. While there will be a temptation to use one or another system, most operators will adapt one or more of the systems to fit their particular operation, customers, and competition. The concepts and systems are valid, but no concept can take the place of a foodservice professional's judgment and experience.

Percentage Markup System

The basic philosophy of this system is that customers should pay a share of the overhead and nonfood expenses based on the value of the food they buy. This is expressed by using a percentage. If we use the financial statements (see XYZ Restaurant Income Statement in Figure 8–6) as

PRICING SYSTEM   MENU ITEMS

	CHICKEN	STEAK	LOBSTER
DINNER COST	$1.01	$2.26	$ 4.46
"GUT FEEL"	?	?	?
COMPETITOR A	?	?	?
COMPETITOR B	?	?	?
PERCENTAGE MARKUP—36%	$2.80	$6.28	$12.39
GROSS PROFIT MARKUP	$4.21	$5.46	$ 7.66
TEXAS RESTAURANT ASSN.			

STEAK DINNER		CHICKEN DINNER 1/2 chicken—2-1/2 lb. chx @ .45/lb. = 55¢		LOBSTER DINNER	
STEAK	$1.80	CHICKEN	$ .55	MAINE LOBSTER	$4.00
SALAD	.15	BAKED POTATO	.15	BAKED POTATO	.15
BAKED POTATO	.15	SALAD	.15	SALAD	.15
ROLLS & BUTTER	.10	ROLLS & BUTTER	.10	ROLLS & BUTTER	.10
BEVERAGE	.06	BEVERAGE	.06	BEVERAGE	.06
TOTAL MEAL COST	$2.26	TOTAL MEAL COST	$1.01	TOTAL MEAL COST	$4.46

Figure 8–7 *Price*

basis, we see that the food cost for the period was 36 percent and the gross profit was 64 percent. If we are satisfied with these figures, we can set future prices by dividing the cost of the food by the 36 percent figure. If we take the steak dinner example, the computation would be as follows:

$$\frac{\text{Actual Cost } \$2.26}{\text{Food Cost Percentage Desired 36 percent}} = \$6.28 \text{ Selling Price}$$

A second method of computation is to divide the food cost percentage into 100, which produces a factor. Multiply the factor by the cost of the menu price to give a selling price. Example: Divide the 36 percent into 100 = 2.8. Multiply 2.8 × $2.26 (cost of dinner) = $6.33.

GROSS MARKUP SYSTEM

Advantages

1. A restaurateur banks dollars, not percentages.
2. Once a price market has been determined, a restaurateur can compete very strongly in that market. Under this system, the expensive items become very attractive.
3. High costs of entertainment or other special features can be more easily passed along.

Disadvantages

1. Periodic financial statements do not accurately reflect the business's efficiency, since a change in the combination of items sold will change the potential food cost percentage.
2. If the price market is poorly identified, the restaurant can be priced out of the market more quickly, due to the narrower price range.
3. This system does not reflect any high risks inherent in some menu items.
4. This system does not reflect the direct labor involved in some menu items.

Gross Markup System

Gross markup pricing differs substantially from the percentage markup system. The basic idea here is that each customer should share equally the cost in terms of dollars of serving a meal. The cost of serving a chicken dinner is equal to the cost of serving a steak dinner once the raw food is paid for. For example, a customer uses the same tablecloth and napkins, silverware, heat, light, and power, etc., regardless of his or her choice of menu items. Therefore, the customer should pay for what he or she uses.

This is computed as follows: First, we examine the Income Statement (see sample). Let us assume that you are content with the figures as presented and want to base your future prices upon them.

Calculating the Gross Markup

To calculate the gross markup, divide the

$$\frac{\text{Gross Profit } (\$9,600)}{\text{Number of Customers } (3,000)} = \$3.20/\text{customer}$$

This figure is added to the cost of the food to determine the selling price.

For example, take a steak dinner with the following items:

Item	Cost
Steak	$1.80
Salad	.15
Baked potato	.15
Rolls and butter	.10
Beverage	.06
TOTAL meal cost	2.26
Add Markup	3.20
	$5.46 Selling Price

Three Tools to Help You Decide on Prices

How much does the average person spend in your restaurant? Three measures of this important question follow.

1. *Average check* This is a tried and true, but only superficial, measure of what the average guest spends in a restaurant. Average check is computed by dividing total sales by the number of customers served.

Example from the XYZ Restaurant Financial Statement:

$$\frac{\text{Total Sales } (15,000)}{\text{Total Number of Customers } (3,000)} = \$5.00 \text{ average check}$$

Average check figures or, more importantly, changes in the average check can signal problems, such as declining sales efforts or shifting markets. This is a simple computation and offers some help in pricing. The second technique is almost as easy and offers a lot more insight into your market.

2. *Frequency Distribution of Guest Checks* Like the average check, the frequency distribution analyzes what guests spend in a restaurant. Basically this involves a graph (see example). Each guest's charge is plotted at the appropriate place.

For example: to record a party of four with a $22.50 guest check before tip and tax, divide $22.50 by four to obtain an average check of $5.63 for the party. At the $5.50 line on the left scale, indicate that four guests spent in this range by marking off four places on the lower scale.

Once this is completed for all of the checks for a meal, a pattern of spending will emerge. This figure can be used as a guideline in selecting and pricing new menu items and promoting old items.

One note of caution: frequency distributions of guest checks lose some of their value if one menu item accounts for more than 33 to 44 percent of the sales, since the popularity of the item may overshadow the pricing decision.

3. *Menu Counts or Menu Tallies* To obtain a menu tally, count the number of each item sold. Some operators identify each appetizer, entree, dessert, and beverage sold, but most identify each entree and count only the total number of appetizers, desserts, and beverages.

What can a menu count tell you? If one item attracts a major share of sales (for example, more than 20 percent of the total), it should be checked to be sure you are making your predetermined markup. If an item is attracting 40 to 50 percent of the total sales, it may be possible to raise the price. In any event, that item must meet your predetermined markup.

If a menu item sells poorly (less than 2 percent of the total, for example), why does it remain on the menu?

Some Good Reasons
1. Highly profitable
2. No waste
3. Menu variety without waste for regular customers (do they choose it?)

Some Poor Reasons
1. Menu variety
2. The manager likes it for dinner
3. The chef likes to cook it

WAGES AND SALARIES

The public image of the restaurant business is not good, or at least the leaders of the industry, as represented by the National Restaurant Association, do not believe the image is good. Part of the reason can be traced to the fact that many of the jobs in a restaurant are entry positions, those requiring little or no previous experience or training. These positions are filled by the unskilled and, very often, by people disadvantaged in one way or another. In the cities, the dishwashing jobs are often filled by alcoholics or other unstable people who may work for only a day or a few days at a time. At least 30 percent of the employees in the restaurant business work part time, a factor leading to instability in the labor force and contributing to the poor image of the industry.

Perhaps more important as a factor influencing the image are the low hourly wages paid in the industry, usually hovering near the minimum allowable by law.

Salaries paid cooks in the northern cities are largely controlled by union contract; the chef in a southern restaurant receives much less and works longer hours. Salaries of top chefs range from about $25 to $40 thousand a year. The really experienced and knowledgeable chefs are found in private clubs; some leave the restaurant industry to work as research chefs for food manufacturers.

Management salaries, as might be expected, also show a wide range. Management trainees just out of college, in 1982 started at $13,000 a year when employed by the large restaurant chains. The salaries paid managers by unit restaurants, parts of a chain, range from about $12,000 a year to about $40,000 a year in a larger restaurant.

Wages and salaries in hotels and restaurants will increase, probably faster than in other retail trades.

The chains will continue to grow, bringing in more employees to be covered by collective bargaining agreements.

Tipped and Nontipped Employees

The two-thirds of all restaurant employees who are nontipped can be considered low paid in our society, even though they might be well paid by worldwide standards. It should be remembered that 30 percent of all foodservice employees are teenagers working in entry level jobs. The other third of the industry employees, those who are tipped, in many cases are well paid for the level of skill and training required by their jobs.

As noted before, tipping practices vary tremendously around the country. In New York City, a customer buying a 25¢ food item is likely to tip an equal amount; in the Midwest or the South—or in almost any small town or rural community—the tip would be small or nonexistent.

For many jobs in the restaurant business the wages paid constitute only a small part of the employee's income. Wine stewards in some of the well-known New York City restaurants receive $100 a week or less. Their tips may be several times that. In some establishments, the wine steward receives 5 or 10 percent of the income from the sale of wine. In a luxury restaurant, the tip is usually 20 percent of the tab.

If a waiter or waitress can serve twenty persons in the course of an evening, and the average check is $10, tip income should be at least $40 for the evening. Cocktail waitresses make much more.

Aside from the value of the tip in monetary terms, the tip is also seen as a measure of a waitress or waiter's performance, shrewdness, or cunning. For some, the tip is a mark of gratitude freely given by the customer. To others, the tip is a form of blackmail or extortion, extracted by the shrewd waiter or waitress from a reluctant patron. Among waiting personnel, competition to excel in the amount of tips received can generate jealousy and friction.

To promote teamwork, many restaurants insist that tips be pooled, all tips collected and divided equally. In other restaurants, agreements are reached between waiters or waitresses and busboys as to the division of tips, the busboy receiving a percentage taken in by the workers he assists.

Where there are frequent banquets, especially in hotels, the division of tips can be a source of contention. The food and beverage director may unilaterally decide how the 15 percent service charge should be divided; so much to the kitchen, so much to the dining room, so much to the maitre d' and headwaiters. In some cases "so much" goes to the food and beverage director, especially if he or she is of the European school and has been accustomed to the tronc system by which tips are divided according to seniority and position.

Private clubs usually insist that there be no tipping directly to personnel. Often a service charge of 10 or 15 percent is added to all restaurant and bar checks. In other clubs the only "tips" forthcoming are made in the form of a Christmas bonus to which all club members are expected to contribute.

As noted before, there are regional differences in tipping practices; there are also variations among individuals within the regions. Pipe smokers are usually identified as "stiffs": nontippers. Women are usually considered poor tippers. Some wealthy persons are highly conservative in tipping; others quite generous. A "Tippers Form Chart" was put together by a reporter who interviewed a number of Las Vegas waitresses. The chart rates various groups as to their tipping potential:

Classification	Rating
Men with their wives	Forget 'em
Men with their girl friends	Showoffs; good
Man alone	Good, but move carefully
Woman alone	Lock the door; terrible
Women in groups	Worse; move on
Touchers	Generous (if allowed)
Pinchers	Generous (if not slugged)
Craps winners	Tops
Slot winners	Fair
Keno winners	Cautious
Older men with ideas	Real good

Tips, of course, are considered part of wages by the Internal Revenue Service. As such, they are supposed to be reported by the receiver. This presents a problem for the IRS and for the receiver. The IRS has difficulty in determining the amount of tip income; the receiver must wrestle with his or her conscience in deciding what portion of the tips, if not all, he or she should report as earnings.

Each employee in the restaurant business in 1982 was able to produce about $20,000 in sales. In a few cases, productivity reached $40,000 a year. Productivity per employee determines in large part what wage can be paid. The restaurant business is a service business; much of the work is still "two hands and the feet." If a worker produces only $20,000 in sales, the wages paid cannot exceed much over $6,000 a year—small in today's economy.

COST CONTROL

Few businesses exact the kind of attention needed for controlling costs as does a restaurant. Cost control is a never-ending, demanding exercise in operating a restaurant. To put costs in perspective, various expenses and costs are divided into those that are controllable, those that are fixed, and those that are relatively variable.

Fixed costs include:

Taxes

Occupancy costs (rent, lease costs, amortization)

Licenses

Insurance

Of course, no costs are immutable. Rents can be renegotiated, real estate taxes questioned, insurance policies changed.

Some expenses are semi-variable or semi-fixed:

Repairs and maintenance

Utilities (heat, light, power, water)

Telephone charges

Phone companies charge a fixed minimum for having a phone in operation. Long distance charges are additional and variable. A certain amount of utility charges are fixed also.

Other expenses usually considered variable and controllable:

Cost of food and beverage consumed

Administrative and general payroll

Employee benefits

Bookkeeping expenses

Advertising and promotion

Music and entertainment

Laundry and linen

China, glassware, and silver

Cleaning and cleaning supplies

Paper and guest supplies

Service contracts

Even with these "controllable" costs and expenses, part of each is likely to be fixed. A cadre of key employees must remain on the payroll even though business is slow, constituting a fixed cost. Parts of most of the other costs are also fixed if the restaurant opens at all. But by separating costs into those that can be at least partially controlled, management focuses its attention on them and keeps them in line. Food and beverage costs are the perennial problem children, costs that can wreck a restaurant in a short time if not controlled. Other costs can be disastrous as well. Suppose, for example, that utility costs suddenly jump to 10 percent of gross sales when they should be running about 2 percent of sales. The eight points that are being lost could wipe out any and all profit.

Without a knowledge of what each expense item should be as a ratio of gross sales, the manager is at a distinct disadvantage. The manager should know, for example, that utilities ordinarily do not run more than 4 percent of sales in most restaurants; that the cost of beverage for a dinner house ordinarily should not exceed 25 percent and could be much less; and that occupancy cost should not exceed 6 to 8 percent of gross sales in most cases. Of course ratio analysis must be in terms of what is appropriate for a particular style of restaurant: coffee shop, fast food, club, or hotel. Moreover, the ratios must be appropriate for the area. Restaurant labor costs, for example, are usually comparatively low in the South, high in the northern cities, while restaurant food costs are comparatively low in the northern cities. (In other words, restaurant patrons get more food for their money in the South than in the North because of the lower wages paid restaurant personnel in the South.)

REDUCING THEFT AND ACCIDENTAL LOSS

A number of systems have been installed to reduce theft, among them being:

1. *Storerooms are kept under lock and key* Supplies are issued to each station only at the beginning of a watch according to a par stock needed for the day at the station.

2. *Tight key control* All keys are signed out by name and must be returned by name. If an employee leaves, the paycheck is withheld until keys are returned. When a manager leaves all locks are changed.

3. *Shopping reports* An independent shopping company is employed to "shop" the restaurant, to observe and report on every employee at regular intervals. Among the factors observed are whether or not all sales are recorded on sales slips. At the cash register items like candy bars are purchased by the shopper to see if the sale is rung up. Questions such as the following are completed by the shopper:

Was your guest check added correctly?

As you approached the cash stand how many patrons were ahead of you? Was payment taken in a reasonable length of time? How long?

Was the cashier working with cash drawer opened?

Were numerals on cash register window plainly visible?

Did the cashier call back the amount of sale and the amount tendered?

Was change correct?

Some restaurants are in locations where robberies have occurred repeatedly. To reduce such temptation some restaurants often have a policy that no more than $150 in cash is ever in a cash register. As cash in excess of that amount is accumulated, it is placed in an envelope and slotted into a safe, which is impossible to get into without a special key.

A record is kept of each deposit of the envelope into the safe including the day, date, time, amount, and person making the deposit.

Guest Check Accountability

A great temptation by wait personnel exists if guest checks are not strictly accounted for. If they are not, the waiter or waitress may bring in his or her own checks, present them to the customer, and pocket the payment. Guest checks can be altered and substitutions made if the checks are not numbered.

To avoid such temptations, most restaurants require that the wait personnel sign for checks as received and return unused ones at the end of the shift.

Other restaurants issue checks by book, 150 to a book. For tight control, every guest check is audited, additions checked, and every check accounted for by number. Guest check auditing is often done in a central office in the case of a restaurant chain, in someone's home for an independent restaurant.

Many restaurants use a duplicate check system. The second copy of the check is handed to the cook in return for the food. No check, no food. Every food item ordered is recorded on a guest check, even though the order is for only a cup of coffee.

DEPRECIATION AND CASH FLOW

As a business generates income and pays its immediate expenses, including taxes, there is money left over, all of which is not profit. In a restaurant, the building, kitchen and dining room equipment, and furnishings depreciate year after year until finally they have no value or only a salvage value. Theoretically at least, money is set aside for replacing these items—a depreciation allowance. Actually this money is seldom set aside and very often the building appreciates rather than depreciates in value. Even so, for tax purposes the depreciation allowance is a deductible item and can be used by the owner-operator. The money taken in before considering the depreciation allowance is called "cash flow." The restaurateur is much concerned to keep cash flow more than enough to meet current obligations.

The owner of a restaurant gets the depreciation allowance. The owner of the equipment gets a depreciation allowance. The owner of the land on which the restaurant sits gets none, for land is a nondepreciable item whereas other tangible assets that have a life span are depreciable. The matter of depreciation can be quite important in the success of a restaurant and is especially important to whoever owns the building. Restaurants are often owned by a corporation which in turn owns another corporation which owns the land. Still another corporation owns the restaurant building and equipment. The idea is to maximize depreciation so as to pay the least amount of taxes possible, especially during the first several years of operation. Some successful restaurant chains buy land, build a building on it, and sell the restaurant and the land to an investor. Then the chain leases it back from the individual, a sales-lease arrangement which has tax advantages for the investor and permits the operator to expand rapidly with a minimal amount of capital investment.

TAX CONSIDERATIONS

Everyone in business has a partner: Uncle Sam. That gentleman is represented by the tax collector, the Internal Revenue Service, who is interested in every dollar transaction, interested in waiting to skim off a portion of the transaction for the good of the nation. The businessperson operates knowing that the Internal Revenue Service is looking over his or her shoulder. Being a good citizen, the businessperson wants to pay his or her fair share of the taxes collected. What is fair is interpreted differently by the way the business is set up. Some pay a great deal more than their fair share; others pay little or nothing because they have been shrewd enough to have a tax consultant structure the business so as to avoid much or all of the taxes.

Tax laws and their interpretation continually change so that what is said here can only be suggestive. Tax experts recommend putting all real estate and equipment into an asset company. This company should be retained. It owns the building and the land and the operating equipment.

Another company is the operating company, which has as few assets in it as possible. The tax experts recommend always keeping the real estate separate from the operating company. Machinery and equipment can be depreciated and so can the building. In buying a business, buy the building and allocate as much as possible to any item that can be legally depreciated: carpets, trees, fences, roses, garbage cans, dust pans, brooms, vacuum cleaners, dishmachines, stoves. The idea is to build as big a tax base, a depreciable tax base, as possible. Then, say the experts, depreciate it all as fast as possible. Those depreciation dollars are essentially tax-free dollars.

The operating company, quite distinct from the asset company, can carry a great load of expenses, which again are tax free: a company automobile, a medical/dental plan for the officers, travel expenses, life insurance, entertainment expenses. Costs often borne by the individual become tax free.

Restaurant owners with families should seriously consider setting up trusts for their children. Each trust has a tax exemption. In one instance a restaurant owner has twenty-seven legal exemptions, including twelve children.

Always consider that eventually the business will do one of three things: fail, be sold, or merge. Consider the tax consequences when forming the business. Here is another tax avoidance plan:

A corporation owned by you and maybe one or two others leases a piece of land to you, the principal owner. You in turn erect a restaurant on the leased land, then lease the building back to the corporation (of which you are the principal owner). This makes you in effect both a lessee and a lessor. You, the individual, have leased the land from the corporation. You, the individual, have then erected the building and leased it back to the corporation. And you, the individual, own the restaurant and are able to take advantage of the depreciation on the building and to draw money from the corporation in the form of lease payments.

LONG-RANGE OBJECTIVES*

In setting long-range objectives, companies should consider both financial and nonfinancial objectives, as well as risk constraints. The most common types of financial objectives are those that deal with profitability, growth, and shareholder well-being.

Hospitality companies typically use return on equity or capital as their profitability measure and annual earnings per share increase as their growth measure. An objective of a 15 to 20 percent annual growth in earnings per share

---

*Much of this section is courtesy of James Crownover, formerly corporate planner, Saga Corporation.

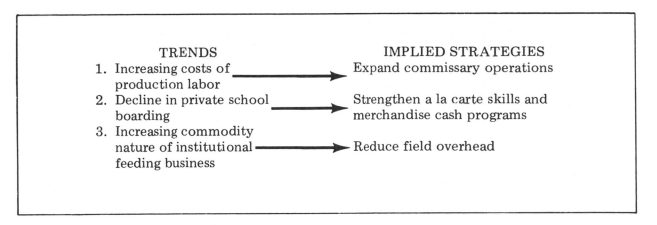

Figure 8-8

has been a fairly common target for companies involved in lodging, restaurants, and institutional foodservice—and many have achieved this target over a number of years.

As a measure of shareholder well-being, companies traditionally have used the market value of their common stock. Gyrations in the stock market and the overall downward price trends have raised questions in the minds of many as to the practicality of this measure.

Some believe that dividend pay-out could be used as a measure of shareholder well-being and as a financial objective together with profitability and growth targets.

Two types of nonfinancial objectives are increasingly being used. First, companies are making specific statements regarding their role with respect to employees. Saga, for example, has a bill of rights for employees. Other companies state objectives in the area of maximizing personal development for employees.

Companies are also establishing objectives regarding their role with respect to society. In recent years, manufacturing companies have been closely examining the area of pollution. Some hospitality companies have begun to define their role with respect to the conservation of resources.

Companies should consider risk at the same time they are establishing financial objectives. Typically, a company may be able to achieve higher financial objectives if it is willing to assume greater risk. For example, by borrowing larger sums of money or by acquiring greater numbers of businesses, a company might achieve relatively higher financial objectives; however, greater risk is involved.

Setting Risk Limits

Some companies set specific risk limits beyond which they will not go to achieve financial objectives. In limiting the dependence on borrowed funds, a company sometimes uses a debt ceiling based on a minimum ratio between after-tax earnings and fixed interest requirements. For example, if a company required that fixed interest requirements would remain less than one-half of current after-tax earnings, this would insure that a 50 percent drop in company earnings would not leave the company unable to meet its debt requirements.

Some companies specify maximum numbers of new businesses that they can become involved in during the year. This limitation is based on the belief that the top management structure of a company can handle only so many new businesses per year before the current business suffers from a lack of management attention.

Guidelines for Business Mix

Finally, a company may set guidelines on the mix of businesses in which they will be involved. For example, a company with institutional foodservice and restaurant foodservice businesses may set a limit on the size of the restaurant foodservice business as a percentage of the total business.

Little Capital Required

The institutional foodservice business requires little capital and, consequently, has little risk associated with it, but its growth rate is rela-

TABLE 8-9

MARKETS	VOLUME	×	PRICE	–	COST	÷	INVESTMENT
College Feeding	1% annual enrollment decline 20 net new accounts per year		No increase due to competitive pressures		5% increase per year More extensive unionization		Minimal
Hospital Feeding	2% annual increase in hospital census 15 net new accounts per year		etc.		etc.		etc.
B. & I. Feeding	4% annual increase in HQ populations 15 net new accounts per year		etc.		etc.		$100 K per year for vending

tively slow. In contrast, restaurants require considerable financial exposure as a result of long-term lease commitments, but the potential growth is large. By setting a limit on the overall size of the restaurant foodservice business as a percent of the total, a company can limit its overall risks. Most of the larger hotel chains are limiting risk by foregoing investment and seeking management contracts.

The third step in the strategic planning process is to estimate the long-range financial results that a company can produce, assuming "business as usual." In developing this "base case" financial projection, a company should make a thorough evaluation of each market currently served by the company and should analyze trends in each aspect of the profitability equation: volume, price, cost, and investment.

The company then makes its base case projection, assuming current levels of efficiency and the continuation of current market trends. The difference between the base case projection and the objective in each financial area is called the *performance gap*. For example, the earnings performance gap is a measure of those additional earnings that will have to be produced, either through better performance in current businesses or through entry into new business areas in order to meet the long-range earnings objectives.

At this stage of the strategic planning process, a check should be made to be sure that the risk contraints developed in conjunction with long-range objectives have not been violated by our base case projection.

Product/Market Strategies

Product/market strategies are brief statements indicating overall courses of action that a company will take in various product and market areas. A company probably should not have more than four or five long-range strategies per business. Strategies should first be developed for improving the results of current businesses. In general, these strategies grow directly from the trends developed earlier and an assessment of the company's strengths and weaknesses.

After these strategies have been developed, another financial projection is made that is based on the likely results of these strategies. Again, the new financial projection is compared with the company's financial objectives.

A company will typically have to evaluate several different sets of strategies for the current business before becoming satisfied with the projected results. If a gap still remains between financial projections and objectives, the companies must look to new business development as a means of reaching these objectives.

TABLE 8-10   California Restaurants

Where It Came From	Coffee Shops	Dinner Houses	Table-Service Restaurants, United States
Food sales	94.4¢	65.3¢	75.7¢
Beverage sales	5.4	33.3	23.5
Other income	.2	1.4	.8
Where It Went			
Food cost	29.4¢	28.1¢	31.2¢
Beverage cost	1.4	9.7	6.4
Payroll and related expenses	34.0	28.8	30.6
Direct operating expenses	4.3	6.3	5.5
Music and entertainment	.1	.7	.8
Advertising and promotion	.7	1.2	1.7
Utilities	2.9	1.5	2.3
Administrative and general	4.7	5.4	5.4
Repairs and maintenance	1.4	1.4	1.6
Rent, property taxes, and insurance	9.0	6.3	5.8
Interest	.3	.3	.8
Depreciation	1.7	2.4	2.2
Other deductions	1.3	.1	.3
Net income before income taxes	8.8	7.8	5.4

Source: California Restaurant Operations 1977, Laventhol and Horwath, Los Angeles, CA 1978.

In Saga's institutional foodservice business, a number of development strategies were evaluated. Saga considered selling new products in current markets (for example, selling vended products to B and I customers in order to complement the existing manual foodservice). They also examined selling the current line of products (for example, manual foodservice) into new markets (for example, public secondary schools). Finally, they evaluated entirely new product/market combinations such as wilderness feeding (for example, feeding workers in construction camps and on offshore drilling rigs).

If, after evaluating a number of its strategies for current and new business, a company still cannot close the gap without violating its risk constraints, the financial objectives would have to be lowered, and the process repeated.

Implications of Strategies

The product/market strategies selected will undoubtedly have a number of implications for the company as a whole. These implications generally fall into three categories: financial, organizational, and administrative. A restaurant or lodging company with an aggressive expansion strategy will require considerable thinking about alternatives for financing its growth. Another hospitality company that chooses to pursue a strategy of actively acquiring companies in different industries may need to hire a top-flight acquisition specialist and redefine organizational responsibilities among top executives to make sure the newly acquired companies obtain sufficient management attention. Finally, a fast-food company that is pursuing a strategy of re-orienting its product line away from mature dishes may need to develop special controls to determine in which location a particular dish is slipping and why.

These are all very good examples of the important financial, organizational, and administrative implications that a set of long range strategies might have. This is the final step of the strategic planning process. In some cases, if the implications identified above are undesirable to the planners, the planning process may have to be carried out again.

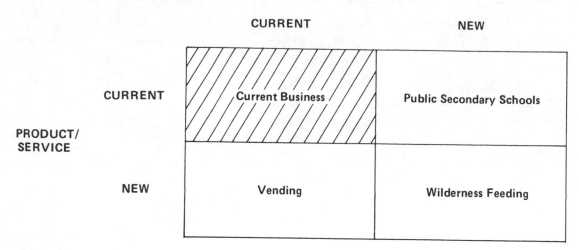

Figure 8–9

Questions

1. According to the textbook, which kind of operation represents the highest financial risk: buying an existing restaurant, building one, franchising one, or managing one?

2. Of the various kinds of restaurants, which one of these could be less conveniently located to the clientele: luncheon restaurant, highway restaurant, fast-food restaurant, or atmosphere/theme restaurant?

3. The econometric model, one combining economics and mathematics, can be used in picking the location for a particular style of restaurant. Can you explain what is involved?

4. Restaurants of the same chain and type should not be too closely located together; management of the McDonald Company feels that there needs to be how many miles between each McDonald's Restaurant?

5. Suppose someone says that there are universal food preferences; some foods will always be liked. What kind of a response do you have to that statement?

6. Give three reasons why certain foods are prestigious at a given time in history.

7. About how many thousand dollars can be expected in sales per seat in a successful restaurant during the course of a year?

8. In what way does seat turnover affect sales and profit? (Consider the seat turnover ratio in relation to average check.)

9. Some cost ratios are worth memorizing as bench marks. About what percentage of sales are these costs in a tableservice restaurant:

   Payroll

   Utilities

   Advertising and promotion

   Occupation costs

   Food costs

   Beverage costs

10. Although the usual restaurant probably makes a profit as percentage of sales of about 5 percent, how high can profitability go in terms of percentage of sales?

11. Why is it important to know the breakeven point of sales per day?

12. In terms of a break-even chart, profit is measured by the distance between what two lines?

13. Which is better to sell, a steak at $4.00 with a food cost of 40 percent or chicken at $2.00 with a food cost of 33⅓ percent?

14. Why is it that the prices are so high at an airport restaurant?

15. Why is it that menu prices are likely to be lower in Alabama than they are in California or New York?

16. Which of these foodservices would you expect to spend the most for advertising and promotion: fast food, pancake house, atmosphere restaurant, coffeeshop?

17. Which of these restaurants would you expect to have the lowest food cost as a percentage of sales: Mexican, coffeeshop, dining restaurant, fast food?

18. The term *prime costs* as related to a restaurant include what two costs?

19. Can you think of some good reasons to retain an item on the menu even though its sales account for less than 2 percent of the total?

20. Part-time employees in the restaurant business are in a large part responsible for keeping labor costs down. Of the total number of employees what percentage constitutes part-timers?

21. Give two reasons why making a frequency distribution of guest checks is valuable.

22. The tronc system of dividing tips used in Europe has certain advantages and disadvantages. Can you name two of each?

23. Are tips considered a part of income by the Internal Revenue Service?

24. Give three examples of fixed costs in a restaurant and three expenses that are usually considered to be variable and controllable.

25. In setting up a restaurant you note that the occupancy cost will run 10 percent of sales. Is this about right?

26. Labor costs are likely to run less in the Deep South than in other parts of the country. What way will this affect the food cost?

27. List at least five items that would be observed by a "shopper" in a restaurant.

28. Why is it so important to issue guest checks by number and to control the number given to a wait person at any one time?

29. Theoretically the depreciation allowance is set aside to replace a building as it decreases in value with age. In actuality what usually happens to the depreciation allowance?

30. According to the tax experts the restaurant should be split up so that there are at least two companies, one that owns the buildings and the equipment, and the other that operates it. Why is this?

31. In buying a business, separate the land value from anything that can be depreciated such as the building and equipment, the trees, fences, roses, even garbage cans and dust pans. Why is this desirable?

32. Suppose you have three children. Tax experts suggest a separate trust for each. Why?

33. Is it possible for a person to own a piece of land on which a restaurant sits and lease the restaurant on that land from himself or herself? Explain.

34. Larger companies are likely to set up long-range plans; a typical one to establish a plan for how many years in the future?

35. In considering an investment the higher the risk, the higher the _____ that should be expected.

36. Diversify the corporation. Is it possible to diversify too much within a given period of time? What are the factors involved?

37. Some food service companies diversified widely, others almost none at all. In looking at companies like Saga and McDonalds what are your thoughts regarding the merits of diversification in the food service field?

38. Strategic planning permits a company to envision a number of projects and to evaluate their results organizationally, administratively, and _____.

Discussion Questions

1. Under what circumstances would it be possible to have a 10 percent labor cost in a restaurant?

2. The subject of employing undocumented aliens is highly controversial. Why or why not would you employ them in your restaurant?

HOWARD DEARING JOHNSON (1898–1972)

Howard Johnson is one of the best-known names to appear in the restaurant business. The name appears on some 1,000 bright and shiny restaurants (including Red Coach Grills and Ground Rounds in forty-one states), strategically located on most of the major highways in the United States. Over 500 motor lodges carry the name. Supermarkets display a variety of Howard Johnson frozen foods and beverages. Road signs, newspaper ads, and TV commercials broadcast the name. The white brick buildings with the orange roof are one of the symbols of modern America.

The Howard Johnson name reflects the driving ambition of an individual, a desire for excellence of a kind, and the perception that the American public would be auto-borne, and would want ice cream, sandwiches, and relatively simple meals while traveling. The name evokes images of white buildings, orange roofs, and rich ice cream. The name is synonymous with restaurants that offer a choice of counter or table seating, quick service of hamburgers, hot dogs, fried clams, chicken, and steaks. To the traveling public, a Howard Johnson restaurant is often a respite from the superhighway—a clean restroom, a quick cup of coffee, an ice cream cone, or sandwich.

Originally, Johnson was a tobacco salesman for his father, preferring business to staying in school. In 1925, after his father died, Johnson took over a small drug store in Wollaston, Massachusetts, borrowing $500 to start it. The principal business was a newspaper distributorship. Though it was highly profitable, Johnson feared that he might lose the newspaper franchise and decided to sell ice cream as well.

It was ice cream with a difference; at first the only flavor was chocolate. Instead of using synthetic vanilla, he used the true vanilla bean. He called on an expert to help produce a quality ice cream, and soon he had ten hand-turned freezers of the ice and salt variety making flavors of ice cream no one had heard of before. When he got to twenty-eight flavors, he felt that he had them all and developed the trademark, "28 Flavors," something like Heinz's "57 Varieties." The "28 Flavors" is still a trademark, though fifty or sixty flavors are produced today.

At the outset, Johnson recognized the value of quality control. From his father he learned the dangers of tampering with quality in cigars. Johnson vowed to make good quality and to control that quality. In the summer he built little shacks along the Massachusetts beaches and hired boys to sell big ice cream cones and frankfurters for a dime.

The idea was new. Customers came streaming in at all hours of the day. As Mr. Johnson put it, "If I was at all bright, it was the fact that I realized that I had an idea that worked, and I followed it and kept following it; and I follow the same pattern today, except that we have improved a lot."

Johnson was a franchise pioneer who franchised many restaurants in the 1930s, legally insisting that the franchisee purchase and sell only specified food items. By 1935 there were twenty-five Howard Johnson restaurants; by 1940 there were one hundred.

In the 1950s and 1960s, the company bought many of the franchises back, arguing that the franchise holders were not maintaining Howard Johnson standards. The franchise enabled Howard Johnson to expand rapidly. In effect, the franchise purchasers were his bankers, providing money to build restaurants to merchandise the Howard Johnson name and products. Highway location, cleanliness, high-quality ice cream, and sandwiches served in clean, attractive, and easily identifiable buildings were keys to the Howard Johnson success story in the 1930s.

With the coming of World War II, the highway restaurant business collapsed; ninety of the one hundred Howard Johnson stores were closed. The war brought gasoline and tire rationing, and, without gasoline, people would not go fifty feet from the center of town.

It is a tribute to Johnson's drive and ingenuity that he came out of the war in better financial condition than he had at the beginning of the war. Part of this was possible because of his prewar production of ice cream, which gave him large quotas of sugar and cream. These quotas were valuable since sugar and cream were strictly rationed and in short supply. He made ice cream for the Louis Sherry firm in New York and for a number of other companies.

He contracted to serve food in colleges that were training the military, to shipyards, and to other military units. When the war ended, he returned to the highway restaurant, refurbished the ones that he had, and built more.

In the 1950s, Johnson pioneered convenience frozen foods. Quietly and without publicity, he built companies in Boston and Miami where many of the Howard Johnson menu items were produced on a production line basis and frozen. Huge refrigerated trucks left the Miami commissary, carrying frozen turkey pies and other preportioned and precooked foods as far west as Texas and as far north as North Carolina. At the time (and even today, to some extent), it was wiser to say nothing about such commissary and frozen food operations. Frozen foods were considered by many to be inferior to freshly prepared ones.

Johnson went quietly about distributing and reheating his frozen foods, while at meetings of professional foodservice organizations debates were conducted about the merits, the economics, and the feasibility of serving frozen meals. Ironically, the most successful restaurant chain in the world was doing just what those experts were debating. He froze entrees years before the idea of the frozen entree was accepted to any degree.

Commissary freezing was a milestone in large restaurant operations. It permitted impressive economies in restaurant labor. As early as 1953, Howard Johnson supervisors were being told that it was no longer necessary to hire cooks; only "food warmers" were needed. In fact, food preparation in Johnson restaurants has been restricted to grilling, frying, and baking.

Teenagers have been griddle and fry cooks. No intricate recipes need be followed for preparing food. No chef salaries, just the minimum wage is paid for a kitchen preparation staff. If a "food warmer" decides to leave, another person can be trained in a few days to take his or her place.

The company continually sought to simplify equipment, standaradize preparation methods, and control portions. When Clyde "Sam" Weithe put together a continuous conveyor belt dishmachine in his garage in Newton, Massachusetts,

he took it to the Howard Johnson Company. It was not long before all new Howard Johnson restaurants were installing the Adamation machine.

One person could operate the machine, both loading and unloading. Waitresses could rack soiled ware in the racks from the dining room. A teenager could operate the machine, keep the restrooms clean, and, if necessary, fill in on the food preparation station. In the New England Division, all of the coffee-making machines were leased from one individual who also contracted to maintain them.

The Howard Johnson menu was aimed directly at the American middle-class traveling public. Ice cream has been a principal appeal, also meat in the form of hamburgers, hot dogs, and steaks. No frills, just solid American food. The food is served in comparative luxury, with decor that is gay and contemporary in the fountain area, and carpeted and chandeliered in the table-service area. In 1972 the usual Howard Johnson restaurant was capitalized at about $250,000.

Later in his career, Johnson developed the Red Coach Grills, designed to satisfy the American nostalgia for early America. The decor is heavy oak and substantial, reminiscent of colonial New England coach stops. The menu features Maine lobster and prime steaks. The average check in the Red Coach Grill is several times that of the Howard Johnson restaurant.

The Red Coach Grills were set apart. The general public was not informed that they were part of the Howard Johnson organization. The Red Coach managers receive salaries that are more than double those of Johnson store managers and are given much more responsibility in buying and operating.

What kind of a manager was Johnson? What made him tick? How was he able to accomplish so much in one lifetime? As Mr. Johnson himself said, his business was his life. He had no hobbies and participated in no sports; when he was at a party he ended up talking business. He drove himself and others. His method of motivation was to needle, to constantly check, and to forever urge people to greater effort.

Stores were open from seven in the morning to midnight and, at any of these hours, he might be found driving up to a store, observing it from a distance, then inspecting it closely inside. He observed everything—the smudge on the front door, the piece of paper in the parking lot, or the stain on the wall. He did not wait to send a memo telling of the discrepancies he found.

The Howard Johnson Company developmental stage was not one for the young graduate of hotel schools, even less for the Harvard Business School graduate. Johnson hired those people who would do what he told them, and would do it with energy, persistence, and without attention to the number of hours worked. Johnson believed in certain things, wanted certain other things, and bent all of his energies and those of the people around him to getting those things.

Few college graduates were happy in the Howard Johnson organization while Howard D. Johnson ran the show. Little stock was placed in theory or in the need for staff personnel. All managers were their own personnel manager, and the ideas they carried out were those laid down by Johnson and a few people close to him at the top.

Managers could not be distinguished from workers. They wore the same little hat and white coat as the fountain personnel and could be found dishing up ice cream, unloading supplies, or operating the cash register. The press was forever on to cut labor cost. The working manager was one way to achieve a lower labor cost. Bonuses were paid on the basis of labor and food cost, little else. Managers were expected to work until the job was done; the six- and seven-day week were commonplace for them.

Salaries for Howard Johnson store managers were not particularly good as compared with salaries paid unit managers of other chains. Supervisors who had responsibility for several stores were expected to step in and relieve unit managers whenever necessary. Most of the higher echelon unabashedly stood in some fear of Johnson. All respected him. All executives knew that, regardless of rank or salary, they could expect to hear from Johnson by telephone, and frequently. When abroad, Johnson called his executives daily to check on operations, costs, and new developments.

Johnson continually worked at standardizing his operations, and he probably standardized foodservice to a greater extent than had ever been done before on a large scale. Statler standardized the foodservices of Statler Hotels long before Johnson was active, but Johnson produced a menu, commissary-prepared food, and a method of reheating and serving food, which was followed almost exactly in all Howard Johnson restaurants.

In about 1955, a hotel student at Florida State University did a study that showed the average ice cream cone being served in Howard Johnson restaurants in Florida cost the company eight and one-half cents. The fact that they were being sold for ten cents meant that the ten-cent cone was a loss leader. Cone prices were raised shortly thereafter, and the dippers used were of a size that made it difficult to serve a larger-than-called-for portion.

The number of seats in a Howard Johnson restaurant varied as new stores were built, but gradually there evolved a standard building with standard seating and equipment. The method of operation became more and more standardized so that each Howard Johnson store might have rolled off an assembly line. Each could have been operated by a system of signals in which each manager was the signal caller.

In 1954 the company opened its first motor lodge. Early ones were small but were built at strategic locations and with an architectural style that allowed for easy expansion. Johnson credits the idea of the motor lodge to his son who at the time was only twenty-one.

In about 1953 Johnson underwent a serious operation and decided to begin phasing out of the day-to-day management of the company. In 1959 he installed his son, Howard Brennen Johnson, as president and told him to "make it grow."

Howard B. Johnson was twenty-eight years old and in many ways the opposite of his father. The new president surrounded himself with experts to whom he gave responsibility and from whom he expected expert advice. The company was divisionalized and a large number of people added at staff levels.

When Howard D. Johnson stepped down from the presidency of the company in 1959, sales were $89 million and profits were $3 million. The company was located primarily on the East Coast and listed 550 restaurants and 75 motor lodges. Perhaps it is fair to say that it took a Howard D. Johnson to build and shape the company and a Howard B. to bring it to maturity. In 1974 there were over 1,000 restaurants—and some 500 motor lodges.

Johnson died at the age of seventy-five in New York City in June 1972. He was a pioneer in restaurant franchising, the person who saw the need for the highway restaurant and set about meeting that need so that his name became a household word. In 1980 the Howard Johnson Company was bought by the Imperial Group, headquartered in England.

9 The Kitchen

What is the commercial kitchen? The definition depends on a number of factors and who describes it. Over the years, it has been likened to hell on earth, stashed away in the nether regions of a hotel or tacked on to a free-standing restaurant; a hot, humid place best forgotten; a place of long working hours, hard floors, and puddles of dirty water; a place where youths are tyrannized by the chef, and workers grow old before their time, burned out by the flames of their stoves and the pressures of their environment.

The kitchen also has been likened to an orderly processing plant with controlled temperature, well managed by people of expertise and compassion; a place of spotless stainless steel with great machines to wash kettles and serving ware, huge kettles that cook food by a mere turn of a valve; a place of respect, and a joy in which to work. Perhaps both descriptions are correct.

In 1526 Henry VIII found it necessary to decree that scullions, the kitchen helpers of the day, "shall not goe naked or in garments of such vileness as they doe . . . nor lie in the nights and dayes in the kitchens . . . by the fireside. . . ."

George Orwell describes the French kitchen of the 1920s as a sort of purgatory, where the plongeur, the dishwasher, was placed in a room without windows and without ventilation to wash dishes. Any fresh air would have cooled the washwater. Life expectancy of the plongeur, according to Mr. Orwell, was three years. Probably the life expectancy of some of our Skid Row dishwashers of today is not much longer.

The modern kitchen can be, and often is, air-conditioned, well ventilated, spotless, and a pleasant place in which to work. In other kitchens, however, the temperature may reach 120°F., and they are anything but pleasant.

The history of the kitchen reflects the social history of the period under scrutiny; it reveals the esteem with which a society held the cook and the other people in the kitchen. When the large hotels in New York City were opened, before 1930, it was customary to recruit the entire kitchen brigade from France. Communication with the kitchen personnel was through the chef, and very often he controlled the lives and destinies of those under him.

A dispute with the chef might mean loss of the entire brigade, and the chef was almost certain to time his departure with the midpoint in service of an important meal. The social standing of the chef has waxed and waned through time, as has that of the kitchen staff. Their position has largely depended on the availability of labor and the class of the kitchen.

A few chefs have achieved a degree of fame—men like Careme who is credited with founding classical cookery; Soyer, chef to the Reform Club of London, and the only chef included in the Dictionary of National Biography, the British equivalent of Who's Who; and Escoffier, "Chef to kings and king of chefs." Their fame came largely because of their writing or affiliations. The millions of cooks and kitchen helpers throughout history who have also served are largely forgotten.

In the past, persons disadvantaged in one way or another have usually filled the ranks of the unskilled jobs of the kitchen. Newly arrived immigrant groups have manned the kitchens along the eastern seaboard and the West Coast.

Hotels and restaurants of today are being called upon to take in and train the hardcore unemployed and the retarded. In New York City kitchens, the language is likely to be Spanish; a majority of the semiskilled and unskilled jobs of the kitchen are filled by Puerto Ricans. The cook, who formerly grew up in the business and was probably of European extraction, is being replaced by native-born Americans who have learned their skills on the job or who have attended a vocational school.

The Culinary Institute of America, the largest of these schools, enrolls over 1,800 students. The management personnel in the kitchen formerly was likely to be drawn from people who had learned on the job, but more recently from those who have attended two-year technical schools or community colleges offering hotel and restaurant courses.

DEVELOPMENT OF KITCHEN EQUIPMENT

Kitchen equipment reflects the materials, the state of technology, and the kind of fuel available. The first cooking equipment was probably a stick held over a fire. The meat on it was cooked by convection currents and radiated infrared energy from the flames of the fire. A more sophisticated form of cooking came along when rocks were heated and food, wrapped in damp leaves or other material, was placed on the rocks and covered, so that the food was steamed. Birds might be wrapped in wet clay and left in the ashes, again cooking by a steaming action. With metal utensils, simmering and boiling were possible and grills could be made to be placed over fire or glowing charcoal.

Kitchen equipment has had an interesting history of development. The Roman tavern-keeper used round and oval frying pans, service pans with handles for serving hot foods in the dining room, saucepans resembling our modern chafing dishes, stewpots with covers, and colanders.

The open hearth served as a range but there was also a *craticula,* a combination broiler and stove. A movable apparatus, it usually rested on top of a brick oven fueled by charcoal. Pans rested over the coals on sliding rods, and special openings at the rear held stewpots.

Then there was the *thermospodium,* a hot drink urn similar to a coffee urn. Heated by charcoal, it was used in the dining room and in snack bars specializing in hot drinks.

The Medieval Kitchen

Step into the Medieval kitchen, if you can. The place is cluttered with fowl lying on the floor, vegetables in baskets, a half bag on the table. It is smoky. The fireplace lacks draft. The place has plenty of cooks, scullions, and serving maids—and maybe a small dog.

The dog is used to turn the spit over the fire. He runs in a wicker cage with a hot coal in it to insure his interest. (Basset hounds were particularly favored in England, and at Oxford there are the remains of basset hound cages.) If the dog caught on, a small boy would do nicely as a substitute turnspit.

Over in one corner is a crew of people grinding up food with mortars and pestles. Everything had to be mashed, hashed, or mixed. Without refrigeration, spices were a necessity for the rich. When sugar became available from the West Indies, it was used with abandon—no chefs' uniforms here and no stainless steel. The kitchen helpers were low men on the social totem pole.

The Colonial Kitchen

The Colonial kitchen was a room with a hearth and a few spot-blackened iron pots and kettles. Until late in the seventeenth century, cooking pots were a scarce and precious item. Handed down from generation to generation, iron pots were commonly listed with the valuables in wills.

A crude spit—a short iron rod, with a handle on one end, resting on crossed iron uprights—some stewpans, iron skillets, and mortars and pestles of copper were the principal cooking tools. The Dutch oven, a shallow iron pot with iron cover designed so that it could be covered with coals, was also used.

In some of the taverns and larger homes a surprising array of handmade gadgets was found: cheese presses, sausage stuffers, butter presses, cabbage shredders, waffle and wafer irons, grinders, warmers, and mechanically turned spits. Hot dishes had hollow pewter bases that could be filled with hot water to keep the contents hot.

Count Rumford, Kitchen Equipment Genius

Most of those in the foodservice field have never heard of Count Rumford, even though he was born an American and is credited with being the first person to study kitchen equipment scientifically. Born Benjamin Thompson, in Woburn, Massachusetts, in 1753, he lived a full life as a military man, an inventor, and an administrator.

Perhaps he is so little known because he picked the wrong side in the American Revolution. He married for money, and when the war came he was appointed a Tory colonel, fighting Washington's troops. After the war he headed for England and then on to Bavaria where he was made inspector general of the artillery and aide-de-camp to mad King Ludwig. Soon he had Bavaria on a regimen calculated to put everyone to work. Beggars were rounded up and placed in jobs in workhouses. He invented several cheap, nutritious soups for the poor, some of which are still served in Europe.

Stoves, Roasters, and Pans

Rumford studied the ways of combustion and designed stoves, roasters, and pots and pans to transfer the maximum amount of heat from the fuel. Until his invention of a kitchen stove, the open ranges in use were installed in an ordinary fireplace. His stove was a complete cooking unit set into the kitchen with only the back used as a flue. With its lids and covers, it was much like the old-fashioned coal range of Grandma's kitchen. His Rumford roasters, with two levels of cooking, are still found in some old New England houses.

Steam-jacketed kettles were also "invented" by Rumford, as well as the double boiler. The first to make a "drip" coffeepot, he designed a single cup device for those who could not afford the pot. He was the first to build a fireplace with a smoke-shelf and throat which separated the warm and cool air into orderly convection currents. Before Rumford, chimneys were merely large holes or flues connecting a fireplace to the roof above.

Rumford also anticipated kitchen planning. His large ranges for military hospitals were oval in shape; the cook did not have to walk around his pots but watched them from the center work area.

Refrigerators

The ice refrigerator made great changes in both the home and commercial kitchen. Thomas Moore, a Maryland farmer, is credited with the first ice refrigerator, which he patented in 1803. It was simplicity itself: two boxes of wood, one inside the other, with the space between the two filled with charcoal or ashes for insulation. The top of the inner box held a tin container of ice.

By 1838 the ice refrigerator was in common use, and in this country salted or spiced meats were no longer the staple diet during the winter. In 1846 an ice-making machine was invented, and by the 1880s ice-making plants had spread throughout the United States. This did not eliminate the old meat safe (garde manger) which is still used abroad.

The iceman cometh and the iceman fadeth away. Nearly everyone of middle age has seen the iceman carrying ice with a pair of tongs on his broad back. Most city-dwelling teenagers have never seen an iceman, at least delivering ice into a home or a restaurant. The iceman, much a part of the restaurant business for one hundred years, had his day and departed. In a generation the iceman has almost disappeared.

Ice cube machines, freezers, and refrigerators are mechanically operated. Compressors to operate them get smaller and less noisy. We can expect miniaturization and perhaps thermo-electric cooking devices, already available, to become widespread, at least for special uses.

Kitchens at the Turn of the Century

By the turn of the century some of the new hotels had large, airy, well-equipped kitchens. The original Waldorf in New York, most prestigious of the new hotels, had a kitchen where "everything was spick-and-span, fixtures

Figure 9-1   *This dishwashing machine probably graced the kitchen of one of the larger hotels about 1890.*

gleaming, rooms spacious, light, and airy, walls spotless with fresh paint, equipment up-to-the-minute.''

Delmonico's, one of the two or three prestige restaurants in New York at the time, was of a different order, more picturesque; in fact, not much different from several of the kitchens of well-known restaurants today in New York City and elsewhere. The kitchen was reached by a flight of shabby stairs and a narrow, dimly lit passage into

a big, low ceiling underground room, so divided by partitions and so blocked off by innumerable tables and refrigerators and storage closets as to be a veritable labyrinth to the stranger. The ranges extend the length of the room, and opposite them are stoves, for the vegetables, leaving an aisle sacred to the use of the forty-five cooks in caps and aprons upon whose final efforts depends Delmonico's fame. . . . When this gloomy, crowded, busy kitchen, dark with smoke, and brilliant with polished copper pots hanging from every rafter, is assailed by a swarm of eager waiters, wonderful indeed is the

Figure 9-2   *The kitchen of the Old Palmer House Hotel, Chicago, about 1890. The kitchen is departmentalized and not too different from some of the kitchens seen in old resorts today. Women cooks were very much in evidence by that time.*

clash of tongues and orders and clash of dishes. . . . The pen into which the waiters are allowed to come is necessarily very small and is accessible to the kitchen proper only through two openings in the wire gratings that separate. In this the hubbub of waiters is appalling. The crowd pushes and jostles each other, in a mighty scramble for the best attention of the cooks. Here and there, rush the chef's assistants, giving orders; and the chef himself, with his thoughtful, kindly face, emerging from the tiny closet office where he concocts his menus and invents his masterpieces of cookery, walks up and down, and keeps all moving smoothly.[1]

Electricity in the Kitchen

Electricity in the kitchen appeared about the turn of the century. At first, skeptics noted that food cooked by electricity had an "electric flavor." The egg takes the honor of being the first food cooked by electricity—in 1877 as a part of an experiment. An "all-electric" kitchen was displayed at the Columbian Exhibition in Chicago in 1893. Saucepans, water heaters, broilers, and boilers were each heated by an individual outlet.

Electric Ranges. George Hughes made the first successful electric range in 1910. In the same year, at Estes Park, Colorado, there were electrically operated ranges, broilers, toasters, and food warmers—the first all-electric kitchen. All-electric galleys in some of the U.S. Navy's vessels were in operation as early as 1912.

The calrod, a heavy-duty heating unit, introduced in 1919, made electric cooking practical by reducing the need for replacing heating elements, formerly a frequent occurrence. Frank Lloyd Wright, as architect, electrified a complete hotel kitchen, that of The Imperial Hotel in Tokyo, in 1919.

During the 1920s a host of electrical cooking equipment was developed: multiple deck ovens, fry kettles, waffle bakers, grills, griddles, and broilers.

---

1. Thomas Lately, *Delmonicos, A Century of Splendor* (Boston: Houghton Mifflin Co., 1967).

The Modern Kitchen

A kitchen can be anything from a one-burner stove to a complex, elaborate food processing plant. Richard Flambert, a kitchen consultant, points out that a kitchen is a warehouse, a factory, a distribution point, a processing plant, a testing laboratory, an artists' studio, a sanitation establishment, a waste treatment plant, sometimes a retailer and bank, a place of diverse skills and trades, and often a boulevard of broken dishes and dreams.

According to Flambert, it is the only kind of establishment where a product is purchased, received, stored, processed, served, and consumed every day. Foodstuffs arrive at the back door, whether fresh, chilled, canned, boxed, or frozen, and then are placed in some form of holding. Vegetables are placed on dry slatted racks a few inches above the floor; dairy products are refrigerated at a temperature between 38° and 40°F. Fresh fish and meat are placed under slightly colder refrigeration. Fresh fruits and vegetables are refrigerated at a slightly higher temperature. Flour, cereals, and pasta products are placed in a cool room at a temperature between 50° and 65°F, off the floor. Frozen foods are sent to freezers between minus 10° and plus 5° Fahrenheit, while canned and boxed foods are placed in a dry storeroom on shelves stored on a first-in, first-out arrangement.

Perhaps a kitchen can be better visualized via the flow chart as seen in Figure 9–3.

MODERN KITCHEN EQUIPMENT

Kitchen equipment can be anything from a pot of water boiling on a one-burner stove to a multimillion dollar, highly engineered food production factory. A fast-food operation may need only deep fryers and use only disposable serviceware. A large dinner house with an extensive menu may use an array of cooking equipment plus a sizeable ware washing facility. A commissory can be like a small food processing plant.

The restaurateur has a choice of cooking equipment, largely determined by the menu: ovens, broilers, fryers, griddles, ranges, steam cookers, and warmers. He or she also needs a ware washing facility, refrigerators, and

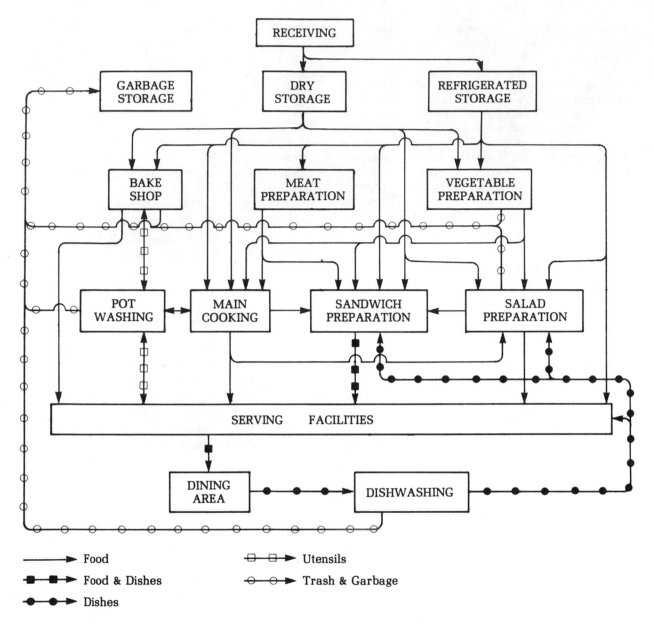

Figure 9–3 *Kitchen flow chart.*

Source: Commercial Kitchens, The American Gas Association, 1962 Edition, page 134.

freezers. Typically, a kitchen has one or several range tops, griddles, and broilers. Range tops and griddles are similar in that they transfer heat from a heating element through a cooking surface to food. The range top can be open, individually-controlled burners or hot plates; a heavy-duty open-top range equipped with tubular coils can be used to cook quantities of up to forty quarts of food.

Enclosed or solid top ranges and griddles have the gas burners or electric coils positioned beneath solid cast iron or stainless steel tops. Controls permit either heating the entire top or one or more sections. Griddles and range tops are used to fry and to sauté. Following is a catalog and brief description of standard items of kitchen equipment commonly used in the American commercial kitchen.

Deep Frying Equipment

Deep Fat (French) Fryers. These are electric or gas-fired kettles for holding fat or oil in which baskets can be immersed for frying food. Temperature usually can be controlled in a range of 325° to 400°F.

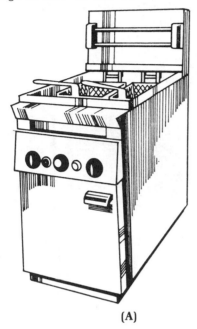

(A)

Figure 9-4 (A-M) *Kitchen equipment*

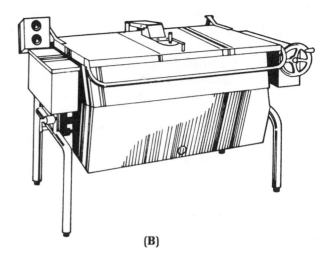

(B)

Deep fat frying has been done in kettles for many years, but in 1918 an integral unit, kettle and gas-fired burner, was marketed by Pitco of Boston for commercial use. Hotpoint introduced its portable electric fryer in 1930. John Welch, later a professor at the University of Missouri, sold ten of these units in Chicago only to have all returned. As with most new equipment, a "bug" appeared that was not anticipated. The electric cord had been tested for withstanding grease that might drip on it. It also met the test

Pressure Fryers. These deepfat fryers have lids that, when closed, act to create pressure within the fry kettle. Increased pressure reduces the cooking time by as much as one half, mainly because there is less evaporative cooling taking place in the cooking process. Some pressure fryers include moisture injection systems. The water injected turns to steam.

Tilting Skillets. Essentially these are large frying pans that can be tilted. They are also called braising pans or griddle skillets. As with any frying pan with a cover they can be used to stew, saute, simmer, and even roast. Because the temperature can be reduced and held at as little as 150°F, the tilting skillet can be used for holding already prepared foods. This is a highly versatile piece of equipment which, because of the temperature control, can be used to braise or roast meat, cook pancakes, scramble or fry eggs, simmer, cook roux, and fry chicken. It can serve as a grill, a hot top, a range, or an oven; with a lid it can become a steamer.

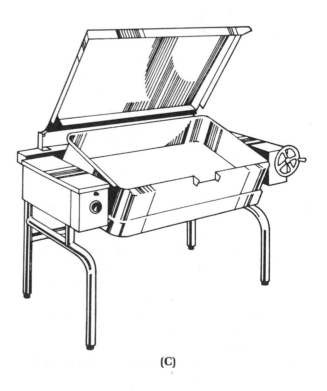

(C)

of not deteriorating when detergent was spilled on it. But when the kettle was in operation and the cord was exposed to both grease and detergent, it deteriorated.

The popularity of deep fat frying became widespread following World War II after thermostats were designed that controlled the fat temperature and prevented fat from reaching the flash point. The taste of slightly browned fat is irresistible to many of us. New kettles are available with self-cleaning coils, cool spots in which food particles can collect, gravity-feed grease strainers, and rapid heat recovery.

Frying under pressure was introduced with the Henny Penny fryer and the Broaster in the 1950s. With a lid on a fry kettle some pressure soon builds up, created by steam produced from the food being fried. If the lid is tight, high pressures are soon created, and some of the steam must be released to avoid dangerous pressures. The Broaster introduces some water into the fry kettle; the Henny Penny uses only the water in the food. Pressure in the Henny Penny is held at nine pounds per square inch; the Broaster goes higher. With pressure, frying time is cut in about half.

The higher pressure prevents as much steam forming in the food and reduces the amount of evaporative cooling that ordinarily takes place when water turns to steam. Colonel Sander's Kentucky Fried Chicken, the franchise operation, at one point used a pressure cooker similar to the home-style pressure cooker.

The frying operation has long been associated with kitchen and hotel fires. More fires are started in kitchens by burning fat than from any other cause. The flash point of fat is 625°F; combustion is sustained at 675°F. Most foods are fried at a temperature of 350°F. Should the cook turn away from the frying pan for a few minutes, or the thermostat on a fry kettle fail, flames are soon soaring to the ceiling. Should the flames reach the exhaust hood, the building may soon be on fire, for most exhaust hoods have an accumulated layer of grease lining them, which also catches fire. Exhaust ducts may extend for several stories and carry the flames to the top of the building.

Throwing water on a fat fire spreads the fire; the water forms steam pockets which explode, spewing burning fat around the kitchen. Cover the fire with a sheet pan to de-prive the flame of oxygen or use a CO_2 extinguisher.

Ovens

Conventional Ovens. Standard or range ovens heat food by heating the air in a chamber. This air surrounds food and cooks it.

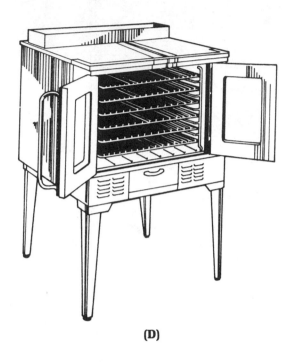

(D)

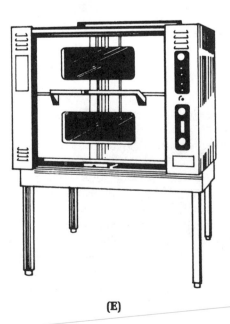

(E)

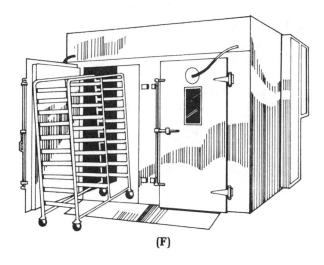

(F)

Deck Ovens. This is the same as the conventional oven except that the chambers are long, deep, and usually rectangular. Constructed in sections, each "deck" is stacked on top of another. Each section can be operated separately and at a different temperature.

(G)

Slow Roasting Ovens. These ovens permit steady, low temperatures and are used primarily for roasting meats. Some of these ovens can be preset to roast for two or three hours, say 300°F, then turn themselves down to 140°F and maintain that temperature until the meat is needed. A cook can place a roast in such an oven at eleven o'clock at night, allow it to cook for three hours at 250°F, and then remain at 140°F until needed for the next day's

lunch. Shrinkage of 10 percent or less is commonplace when using these ovens for roasting beef.

Forced Convection Ovens. These are similar to conventional ovens except that a fan or rotor, usually located in the back, makes for rapid circulation of the air and quicker heating of the food. Preheating times and cooking times are considerably less than with the conventional oven. Directions for baking with a convection oven must be followed exactly, otherwise some foods, such as sheet cakes, will dry out excessively on top. A pan of water is placed in the oven in baking some foods to humidify the oven air and reduce moisture loss in the food being baked.

Microwave Ovens. The cooking chamber is usually small and the capacity much less than that of larger conventional or other types of ovens. Magnetrons, usually in the top of the oven, emit microwaves. These penetrate foods in the chamber, agitating the water and fat molecules to produce heat, which is conducted to other kinds of molecules surrounding them. There is no preheating time since once the microwaves are produced they travel at the speed of light and enter the food material almost instantaneously. Microwave ovens produce relatively small quantities of cooked food, as compared to standard ovens. However, they are excellent for reheating small quantities of food.

Cooking by microwave is a revolutionary form of cooking, relying completely upon radiated energy to penetrate food materials

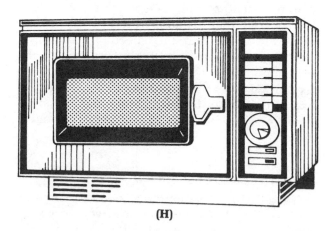

(H)

and set up intermolecular friction, which heats the food. The microwave oven developed from the use of radar during World War II. Electromagnetic waves were used to detect objects at a distance that cannot be seen visually, to see objects at night, and those behind clouds.

In 1947 the Raytheon Company began marketing a microwave oven known commercially as the RadaRange. Electromagnetic waves of 915 megacycles and 2,450 megacycles penetrate, and are absorbed by, food materials containing water. Strangely, some materials are transparent to the waves and are not heated by them. Glass, china, and paper containers do not absorb the waves. Any metal reflects the waves so that metal containers are not used in microwave ovens.

Such a revolutionary form of cooking was certain to stir the imagination and also the hope that the microwave ovens would replace conventional kitchen cooking equipment. Hundreds of microwave ovens were sold and later discarded because the owners did not realize the limitations of the ovens. The ovens available were excellent for heating single or small numbers of portions of food but were not as effective as conventional equipment for large quantity food production.

Since microwaves are absorbed preferentially by water, cooking is not uniform. Instead of heat being applied to the surface of the food, then being conducted slowly into the interior of the food, microwave energy heats the food under the surface. The surface is left unbrowned and relatively cool.

Advantages of Microwave Cooking. Microwave cooking has several advantages over conventional methods of cooking. The energy can be directed; there is no heat loss to the kitchen from the oven, and the speed of cooking is amazingly fast for small quantities of food. Its principal use will probably be for reheating frozen foods that have already been cooked. It has little value for producing baked dough items or any food that involves a leavening action.

Infrared Cooking Equipment

Infrared cooking equipment made its appearance in the 1950s. Like microwave energy, infrared waves, transmitted at the speed of light, can penetrate the vapor blanket that surrounds moist food when heated. Infrared wave lengths used for cooking are only microns in length. Wave lengths of about 1.4 to 5 microns are said to be the most effective for cooking foods.

Temperatures of about 1750° Fahrenheit are created by heating lava rock, human-made ceramics, cast iron, or stainless steel. These or quartz crystal and calrod units emit the proper wavelengths to be classified as infrared. Glowing charcoal also gives off infrared waves.

Broilers

Char-broilers have briquettes, which when heated, give off heat for broiling food.

Ceramic broilers use ceramic chips that are heated to high temperatures and give off heat.

Open-hearth broilers produce heat from gas flames or electric rods that focus heat directly onto meats from below.

Oven-fired broilers produce heat from over the racks holding the meat. Infrared models produce infrared rays once temperatures of 160°F and more are reached. The time to preheat a broiler is a consideration; infrared broilers require no preheating at all. An oven-fired broiler may be part of a griddle so that food can be heated from above and below simultaneously.

Salamander or back-shelf broilers are usually used in conjunction with an oven to hold or finish cooking food. They are sometimes used to create a crust on food or to apply quick heat to a sauced food.

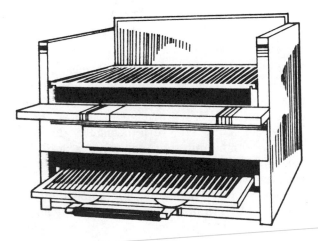

(I)

Griddles

Griddles, the heated flat surfaces used for fast cooking of such items as hamburgers, eggs, and pancakes have been a principal cooking device for fast-food restaurants. Some can be heated by section.

More recently the grooved griddle has been widely used for cooking steaks and in many fast-food restaurants has replaced the broiler. The ridges in the griddle produce marks on the steak similar to a broiler and the grooves allow fat and juices to drain off avoiding the smoke created by the conventional broiler. The grooved griddle cooks faster than a broiler because the food is in direct contact with the griddle. Another important consideration: the grooved griddle uses less fuel than a broiler. Hamburgers cooked by grooved griddle are less likely to be burned. With a hot broiler, the cook looks away for a minute or two and the hamburger becomes a charburger.

Steam Cooking Equipment

Steam-Jacketed Kettles. Kettles ranging from about 1 gallon to 500 gallons are surrounded by an enclosed shell into which steam is introduced. The steam does not come into contact with the food in the kettle but as it condenses it gives up its latent energy. The heat passes through the shell into the food inside the kettle. If the steam is under pressure the steam temperatures increase above 212°F.

Steam-jacketed kettles were on the scene as early as 1874. In fact, the "copper jacket" and seamless cast-iron jacket kettles of the 1870s would not look too much out of place in today's kitchen. The John Van and Company in 1879 (later the John Van Range Company) was urging multiple use of steam kettles and sold "any size" for coffee-making "for large public institutions."

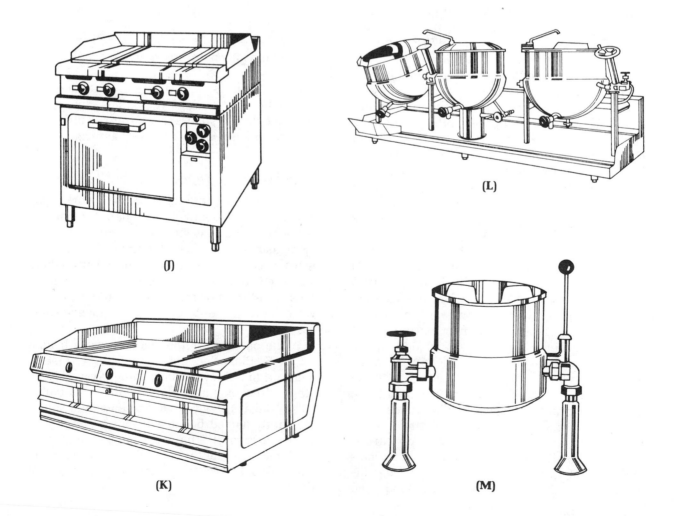

(J)

(L)

(K)

(M)

Steam Tables. These are large rectangular tables into which tanks are placed and filled with about three inches of water. The water is heated with steam, gas, or electricity. Steam table pans are held slightly above the water.

Some so-called "dry" steam tables do not use water at all, but heat air in the manner similar to an oven that keeps the inserted steam table pans hot. Steam tables are intended to hold food rather than to cook it, although cooking takes place whenever temperatures rise much above 140°F.

Bain Marie. Literally "Marie's Bath," the forerunner of the steam table, is a table containing hot water. Pots, crocks, and pans containing food are inserted directly into the water, which forms a warm water bath and keeps the food warm.

Advantages of Steam Cooking

Cooking devices using steam have the advantage of being able to transfer more BTUs of heat to a food material than can be done with hot air. Each pound of steam contains 970 more BTUs than the same pound of boiling water. This "latent energy" contained in the steam is given off when the steam condenses back into water. If the steam is under pressure, the temperature is raised, which also increases the speed of the cooking action. In kitchens where large quantities of soups, sauces, or anything cooked in a liquid must be prepared, steam cooking equipment is likely to be found.

Institutional kitchens, those in hospitals, schools, colleges, and correctional institutions, make wide use of steam-jacketed kettles for soups, stews, puddings, meats, and vegetables. Pressure steamers are also being used in cafeterias and restaurants. Stouffer's pioneered the use of the pressure steamer for cooking small batches of vegetables. Because of the speed of cooking, the pressure steamer permits "progressive cookery," cooking small quantities of vegetables as needed. This method is a big improvement over cooking vegetables in the large steam-jacketed kettles which resulted in overcooking and excessive holding times.

Steamers, steam-jacketed kettles, steam frying pans, and steam pressure cookers are almost universally used in large-quantity kitchens and commissary operations. Their big disadvantage is that the surface of the food is not dried to produce the surface texture and flavor found in foods that are cooked in ovens and broilers.

Mechanical Food Mixers

High-Speed Blenders. These electrically driven blenders come in a variety of sizes. In a few seconds they can cut food materials into minute sizes or into liquid if water is present.

Vertical Mixers. So-called vertical mixers act as large blenders that can chop vegetables and other foods into small sizes or blend them into liquid form. They can be used for chopping vegetables into salad size materials. First made in Germany, the vertical mixer was originally called the Schnell (quick) cutter.

Dough Mixers. These are used for mixing flour, water, and other materials to form doughs. Special pie dough mixers are available.

Other Equipment

Dough Rollers. These machines roll out dough for making loaves of bread or pie dough.

Slicing Machines. A variety of machines are available for slicing vegetables by hand. Machine-driven slicers using rotary knives are used to slice almost every food material.

DISHWASHING MACHINES

Build a machine and let it do your work. Why not also avoid dishwater hands? A tenacious gentleman, Haskins by name, started making dishwashing machines. A few of his machines were used in hotels, but hand dishwashers struggled both with the dishes and the machine. Finally, after several failures, the machines were thrown out and hand dishwashing resumed.

The patents for the machine were bought by G. S. Blakeslee about 1890, and Haskins went on to achieve dishwashing glory. At one stage of development the machine was called "The Niagara," but when one hotelman said it was aptly named because it took a Niagara of water to run it, the name was changed to "Columbia." Another machine did perfect washing but wore the enamel off the edges of the dishes.

The first machines were merely baskets that could be lowered and raised into tubs or tanks of water by means of hand-operated cranks. Their circulating pumps were large and cumbersome, driven by steam or gasoline engines. Because of the large size of the machines—one used 4- by 4-inch supporting beams and stood 10 feet high—remodeling the kitchen was often necessary to install them at all.

Finally water sprays were introduced, with the dishes being placed under them. Electric motors and specific design for various sizes of food operations came by 1910. By the 1920s nickel-bearing chromium steel (stainless steel) was used for hoods, doors, and tanks. The new metal, called ascoloy, was the forerunner of the stainless steel of today. It took until the 1930s for the equipment manufacturers to learn how to weld it, bend it, draw it, or break it.

Dishwashing Machine Improvements

Improvements in dishwashing machines have come along with the years—and well they might for most foodservice operators agree that the biggest problem area of the foodservice is the scullery. In the volume operation, even though there may be an inventory of china amounting to three times the place settings needed, a breakdown of the dishmachine throws the entire operation into a panic. It is not long before there are no clean dishes. A power failure, lack of hot water, or breakdown of the dishmachine has happened to most everyone in the business.

It is the wise operator who knows his dishmachine in detail, how to operate it, and how to train others to operate it. The individual is usually called on at one time or another to replace a part, tighten a valve, or to do other repairs to the machine. Few people are interested in making a career of dishwashing; even fewer can be found who are willing to stand over a hot sink washing pots and pans by hand.

One-Person Machines

In an attempt to make dishwashing simpler and to reduce the number of employees needed, Clyde R. Weithe experimented in his garage for several years during the 1950s to produce a machine that could be operated by one person. The Adamation machine that emerged (named after Adams St. in Newton, Massachusetts, where it was first manufactured) makes possible one-person operation and is widely used by the Howard Johnson Company and many others today. The machine has a circular table attached to it which permits a merry-go-round of racks of dishes to move in and out of the machine.

The circular, horizontal table permits one person to load soiled dishes onto the rack and to wait for the rack to return with the clean ware which can be unloaded by the same person. The table can be extended into the dining room and the machine operated from the dining room by a waitress, if necessary. At first the larger dishmachine builders were not impressed by the machine but later developed similar "rotary table" machines and are marketing them.

In 1969 the G. S. Blakeslee Company of Chicago produced a rotary table dishmachine with a conveyor that carries either racks or can be random-loaded with plates, glasses, or cups. Random loading eliminates the need for pre-sorting soiled ware as it is done for racking. By only racking hollow ware, handling of the other ware is less, and breakage is reduced. Leftover food is dumped in a trough in front and under the conveyor where a rubber-covered spiral screw pushes the refuse along the trough and into a garbage can.

The machine has "sensors" built into the final rinse tank that activate and turn off the hot final rinse water. The water is on only when dishes are passing through the machine, thereby saving hot water, rinse additive, and reducing the detergent dilution in the wash tank.

Today, huge dishwashing machines are in service that can sanitize dishes for thousands of persons each day. Cushioned conveyors carry the dishes between four top and bottom sprays and then through an air drier. Machines come in one, two, three, and four tank sizes and cost can exceed $35,000 in cost for a large one.

Low-Temperature Dishwashing Machines

With costs of heating water increasing, new dishmachines have come on the market that eliminate the need for 180°F water for sanitization. By adding a chemical bactericide to the rinse water, 95°F water can be used for the sanitization process. In some instances, restaurant operators have reported cutting their dishwashing cost in half by using the chemical agents to sanitize rather than the 180° water. In bars where hot-water hookups are not very practical, sanitization is completely done by chemical agents and only cold water is used.

Low-temperature dishwashers rely on the introduction of a chlorine sanitizer (sodium hypochlorite) in addition to detergent to sanitize serving ware. A well-engineered device is necessary to add fifty parts per million of chlorine into the rinse. If there is too much chlorine some remains on the ware and can be tasted by the patron. Water pressure during the wash cycle must be high to clean effectively.

In most machines not only are BTUs saved but the consumption of water is reduced as well. Some machines recycle the wash water. The low-temperature dishwashers can be rented; a counter on the machine counts the number of racks cleaned, and the operator pays a few cents per rack. (The rented machines are single tank and the machine operator is more likely to wash only full racks. Operators using large machines often keep them running without dishes or send partially filled racks through.)

Another advantage of the low-temperature machine is that no steam is produced, hence no exhaust or ventilating system is necessary. Original cost is less than the conventional hot-water dishwasher. The machines have been available for several years but were relatively unnoticed until energy and water costs increased.

KITCHEN ORGANIZATION AND PLANNING

The old prints of kitchens in the royal palaces show huge, high-ceilinged rooms, unpartitioned or sectioned. Some organization was essential. During the time of Napoleon the French chef was seen wearing a long, floppy cap, on the order of a nightcap, as a symbol of his authority. At the other end of the status spectrum came the lowly scullion. Careme is credited with the tall starched chef hat that identified the chef or chief. The height of the "toque blanc" is supposed to correlate with his rank in the kitchen.

Though the large French kitchen had been departmentalized into sections (partis), Auguste Escoffier is credited with synchronizing their operation.

Under the old system, Eggs Meyerbeer, a dish consisting of eggs, lamb, kidneys, and truffle sauce, required fifteen minutes to prepare. With a chef at each station, the dish was prepared in a fraction of the time. An entremetier baked eggs in butter. A rotisseur grilled the kidney while a saucier prepared the truffle sauce. The work of the three specialists was combined and the eggs were hurried to the table.

At the turn of the century, and for some time after that, most hotel builders placed their kitchens in the basement where space was considered less valuable. Kitchens were large. The Astor Hotel of New York City opened in 1904 and had a kitchen 231 feet long with an average width of 150 feet.

Of course, the planners had not reckoned with the cost of operating the kitchens, of moving people, food, and ware from one level to another and within a kitchen. These are built-in costs that continue for the life of the building.

Ellsworth Statler was one of the first to see the merits of placing the hotel kitchen on the same level as the dining areas. In 1917 The St. Louis Statler was built with the kitchen placed on the same floor as all of the dining facilities, which were built around three sides of the kitchen. This layout made it possible for one kitchen to serve the dining room, the coffee shop, and a cafe. The plan has been used several times since, one of the most dramatic examples being The Beverly Hilton Hotel where the kitchen is round with the various dining facilities surrounding it.

Many high-rise buildings, especially where land is a major cost, cannot afford to place kitchen and serving areas on the same level. At The New York Hilton, for example, the kitchen and warewashing facilities are located in a central core of the building, on several floors, connected by elevator to each other and to the restaurants.

The practice of placing a number of preparation stations side-by-side behind a pick-up counter is used by most commercial kitchens preparing food for a large and complicated menu. The Waldorf-Astoria kitchen, for example, stretches a long distance with station after station placed side-by-side. The waiter enters the kitchen and drops off his order at each station, returning later to pick up the prepared food.

Some kitchens in the larger hotels are immense, the distances walked by the waiters in placing and picking up orders prodigious. Waiters and waitresses in huge American Plan resort hotels before the end of the season develop into track athletes from the constant running and walking required, and the distances involved.

Space Controls Planning

In most cases, kitchen planning revolves around the amount of space allocated or available for the kitchen. In downtown, expensive locations, the kitchens are often miniscule, one kitchen employee working almost on the back of another. Surprisingly, small kitchens turn out to be more efficient than the large ones because of the necessity of planning each work station in detail and the elimination of steps formerly required as foodservice workers moved from station to station, station to storeroom, and within a station. In most cases, reducing the size of the menu also improves efficiency.

When the kitchen is the shape of a square, the kitchen equipment is frequently placed around three walls, forming an open square or U. The first station, as the waiter enters the

EDDYS' RESTAURANT   KANSAS CITY, MISSOURI
ARCHITECTS: GENTRY & VOSKAMP
FABRICATED & INSTALLATION:
GREENWOOD'S, INC.   SOUTHERN EQUIPMENT CO.

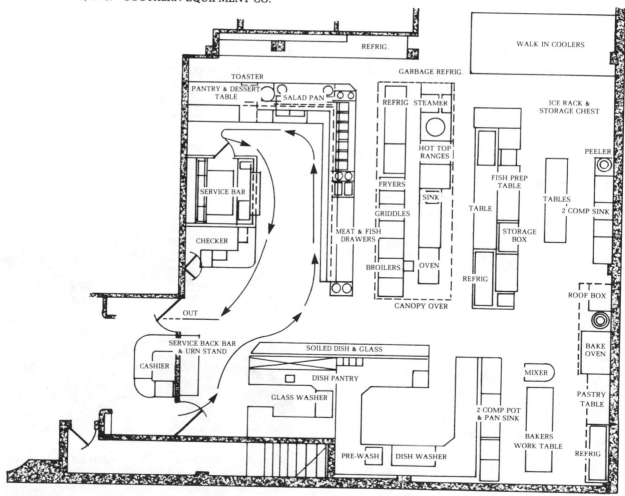

Figure 9-5 A "Custom-built by Southern" Award of Merit winning installation.

Source: Institutions/Volume Feeding magazine.

kitchen, is apt to be the dish room, and the last station before entering the dining room is the pantry, or coffee and dessert station.

An example of a restaurant kitchen designed for function and speed of operation is the prize-winning kitchen of Eddy's Restaurant in Kansas City, shown in Figure 9-5.

Waitress flow is a loop that starts with the dish pantry just six steps inside the door from the dining room. The loop continues past the meat and fish station, vegetable station, salad station, and on to the pantry station. From there it passes the service bar and the food checker. There is no cross-traffic, nor long distances between stations.

Preparation units buttress the serving stations and are so set up that food passes from one department to the next on its way to the serving line. Each employee is trained in two jobs; as work runs out at one station, he or she moves to another point of service.

Multicolored lights signal waiters when orders are ready.

Refrigerated drawers directly opposite the broilers and ranges keep food at the chef's elbow.

All equipment, including ranges, is elevated eight inches above the floor for easy cleaning. Interiors and shelves are removable for complete cleaning. Self leveling plate coolers and warmers are used. Ledges that accommodate two tiers of trays facilitate the assembling of orders.

Here is a case where the kitchen was planned and the building put up around it. Most kitchens must conform to the building with resulting poor layout, making process flow analysis all the more needed.

Institutional kitchens are often larger than necessary and have more cooking and other equipment than needed. Institutional kitchen planners are prone to specify extra equipment recognizing that, once money has been allocated for a kitchen, additional budgets may be hard to come by. It is better to have standby equipment on hand. Another explanation for excessive equipment is that most professional kitchen planners are paid a percentage of the total cost of the kitchen; for the unscrupulous, the higher the cost, the greater the fee.

Professional kitchen planners in the past have tended to be associated with restaurant equipment houses. The larger equipment firms

employ layout specialists who are called upon to plan new kitchens, their services being included in the contract for the purchase of the kitchen equipment.

Following World War II, a few foodservice consultants set themselves up in business, offering their kitchen planning skills for a fee. In the 1950s a group of the independent consultants formed the Food Facilities Engineering Society. Another group, including both independent consultants and kitchen planners employed by equipment houses, formed the International Society of Food Service Consultants. The two groups are now merged into one.

Because the number of possible arrangements in any given kitchen is astronomical, no two kitchen consultants plan a kitchen alike. Each has developed patterns which are preferred and which have been observed as working satisfactorily over the years.

The Scientific Approach

The attempt to make kitchen planning more scientific and exact goes back to Count Rumford and Alexis Soyer. In 1945 the book,

Figure 9-6 *The layout of the McDonald's kitchens has evolved over the years. The kitchen is compact and highly efficient. Hamburger patties are grilled on the large griddle and garnished on the rotary table that is across the aisle from the griddle.*

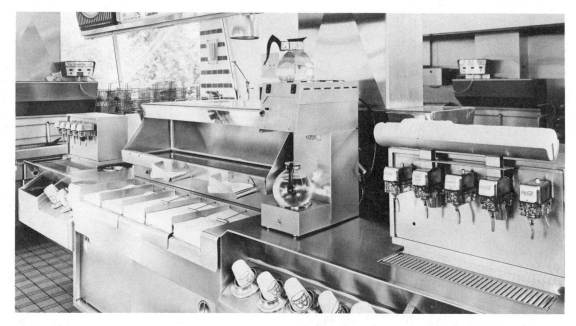

Figure 9-7 *Another section of the McDonald's kitchen showing how the paper service is arranged for most efficient use. Hamburgers are bagged and held up to ten minutes. If after ten minutes they are not sold, they are discarded. Paper cups are separated by size and held upside-down for use.*

Kitchen Planning for Quantity Food Service, by Arthur W. Dana was published. It was the first systematic attempt to state principles of kitchen design and to describe kinds of problems encountered and types of equipment available for kitchen use.[2]

In 1962 the American Gas Association published *Commerical Kitchens.*[3] The book is a general statement of kitchen planning and quite naturally emphasizes the use of gas cooking equipment. The competitive situation being what it is between the electric and gas utility companies, the kitchen planner is beset by claims of superiority for gas on the one hand and electricity on the other.

Since most chefs have learned the trade using gas equipment, the tendency is for them to favor gas as a cooking fuel. Gas, they feel, as used for top-of-the-stove cooking is more controllable than the electric heating element. The gas flame responds instantaneously to a turn of the knob and can be seen.

The electric utility companies point out that burning gas consumes oxygen from a kitchen, and if there is not a constant source of fresh air, the carbon monoxide level in a kitchen can rise dangerously. The electric people contend that the use of electric fuel in a kitchen results in a cleaner kitchen—a debatable contention. Proportionately more institutional kitchens use electric cooking equipment than commercial eating places.

The cost of cooking fuel is a major consideration for the operator. The American Gas Association readily admits that one BTU of electricity is equivalent to 1.6 BTU of gas for cooking. The reason is that much of the heat produced by gas is carried out the ventilation system along with the noxious fumes produced by gas combustion. But, say the gas people, even applying the appropriate gas and electric rate to this ratio, electric cooking costs in typical cities in the United States are from two to ten times as much as gas. (In a few areas where hydroelectric power is cheap, electricity for cooking is cheaper than gas.) The gas people also argue that their product is more fail-safe in that the gas supply is not likely to break down, as happens periodically with an electric supply.

The gas versus electricity decision need not be made in favor of one or the other but in terms of specific pieces of cooking equipment. Either gas or electricity can be used to produce the hot

2. Arthur W. Dana, *Kitchen Planning for Quantity Food Service* (New York: Harper's, 1945).

3. *Commercial Kitchens* (Arlington, Va.: American Gas Assn., 1962).

air needed in ovens, stove-top temperatures of 3000°F or more, steam, and infrared energy.

Electricity must be used for the microwave ovens. Gas broilers seem to be more effective than electric ones; electric deep fryers, in which the heating units are immersed in the fat, seem to be more effective than gas fryers, where the heat is concentrated on the bottom of the kettle; some electric equipment in the past has been more attractive in appearance and better insulated than comparable gas equipment. In my opinion, gas is more hazardous than electric fuel because of its combustibility. Regarding the fail-safe feature, the kitchen operators can protect themselves by having a combination of gas and electric equipment.

The arrangement of all the cooking equipment in an island in the center of the room is used in some institutional kitchens. Institutional kitchens are not likely to be as departmentalized as commercial kitchens. Placing the equipment in the island permits all of it to be placed under one exhaust hood, which can draw off the hot air and vapors created by the equipment.

The tendency in recent years has been to place the dishwashing section away from the kitchen or to entirely close it off from the kitchen. The scullery is a noisy, hot, and humid area. It belongs near a kitchen only because in the past waiters, waitresses, or busboys have had to drop off soiled ware and pick up clean ware there.

Conveyors and subveyors can deliver soiled ware to a dishroom in almost any location and also deliver the washed ware to the point of use. In some large installations, the dishroom is placed on a lower level, on a floor separate from the kitchen.

Debatable Areas in Kitchen Planning

Points of debate in planning a kitchen revolve around whether serving personnel should enter the kitchen, and what they should do if they do enter. Some operators require waiting personnel to make salads and toast and do other pantry work. Other operators believe that the less time the waiting personnel are in the kitchen, the better. They arrange for soiled ware to be carried into the kitchen via conveyor belt. Another way to move soiled ware is to install a merry-go-round type of dishmachine with part of the rotary rack system extended into the dining room where soiled ware can be directly loaded onto the dishmachine racks.

The answer to the question of how much time waiting personnel should spend in the kitchen is partly determined by the speed of the dining room. If breakfast and lunch are relatively slow, waiting personnel might well be used in the pantry and elsewhere in the kitchen. If there is a fast turnover in the dining room, waiting personnel can be more efficiently used in the dining room than in the kitchen when they are supported by specialized personnel in the kitchen.

Kitchen floors are characteristically covered with quarry tile that is easy to clean, relatively impervious to water, and durable. Quarry tile is also extremely slippery when wet, which is probably the greatest cause of accidents in the hospitality business. Whoever has experienced a fall on tile, hitting his or her head on the floor, will never forget it—or perhaps he or she will.

A few kitchens have installed carpets. A Washington, D.C., cafeteria operator provides each employee with a small rag rug for his or her station and finds both safety and cleanliness increased. Quarry tile is inefficient, varicose vein-forming, and tiring; it should be replaced with mats or carpets.

Duckboards are often laid behind cooking equipment. They can be taken up and cleaned in the dishmachine, and refuse can collect between the slats without interfering with the cooks' work. On the other hand, some cooks may feel as though they have been working out on a trampoline after a day on the slats.

The Display Kitchen

Many of the theme or specialty restaurants that have been developed since the 1950s incorporate display kitchens in the dining room. In the Charlie Brown restaurants, the chef and his supporting equipment are installed in the dining room. Display kitchens either must be supported by an auxiliary kitchen elsewhere or must use an extremely limited menu. The Rib Rooms are built around a limited menu featuring roast beef, baked potatoes, and tossed salads. Some of the Japanese-style restaurants operate with the guests sitting around a large griddle, and the wait personnel acting as both cook and server.

Among the most efficient restaurant operations are the Friendly Ice Cream Shops located in New England. All food preparation is done on an island surrounded by counters and stools. The menu is limited to sandwiches, soup, and ice cream so that every employee may be a grill operator as well as a waiter or waitress. The Chock Full O' Nuts, headquartered in New York City, has a similar style of operation with minimal need for preparation skills and personnel training time. The distance between preparation area and serving area is a matter of a few steps. Most of the food is pre-prepared. The wait personnel merely hand it to the customer across a counter.

The value of color in a kitchen is becoming recognized. Instead of the customary antiseptic white, walls and ceilings can be painted peach and yellow, colors that have been found to be "appetizing." Adequate lighting is especially

Figure 9-8 *Locke-Ober's, long a noted Boston restaurant, has retained the same style over several decades, maintaining the atmosphere characteristic of fine restaurants in this country at the turn of the century. Note the weighted covers that are suspended over the silver holding dishes.*

needed at the pick-up area of the dishmachine and at food preparation work stations. Lighting must be bright enough so that the employee can see whether the dishes are clean and in the case of cooks, see the results of their handiwork in garnishment and plate arrangement.

According to Arthur Avery, a well-known foodservice consultant, the dishroom should have twenty to thirty footcandles. At the clean end of the dishwasher, lighting should be raised to forty to fifty footcandles. Egg white and white cereal residues are hard to see without enough light. The dishroom can be "cooled," from a psychological standpoint, by the use of cool blue and blue green colors on the wall.

The kitchen is usually much too noisy, especially the dishroom. Plastic racks reduce clatter. Coating the underside of dish tables with a mastic material or the use of plastic or rubber mats on the tables decreases decibels. Acoustic tile on the walls and ceilings also helps. Acoustic paint can be used, or a honeycomb system of baffles hung from the ceiling. Air conditioning a kitchen or sink room increases human productivity by 10 to 15 percent. It also reduces accidents and improves quality control.

Sinks in kitchens are almost always too low for workers; having to bend too low to work in the sink can create back problems. Someday sinks will be adjustable to fit the height of the worker. Aisles are often too narrow or too wide. The industrial engineer tells us that aisle space should be at least 30 inches; 36 to 38 inches when the person has to get something from under a counter; 45 inches if one must kneel at work. When two employees work on either side of an aisle, 48 inches should be allowed. Dials should be at eye level so that they can be read easily.

More Precision in Cooking

Cooking is growing more precise as more technical knowledge about the cooking process becomes known. The fisherman's platter, combining a fillet of fish, scallops, oysters, and french fries, is not likely to be cooked all at once, as it has been in the past. Each item requires a different cooking time; if they are all dumped into the deep fryer at once, some are overcooked and some are underdone.

Richard Keating of Chicago tells us that though all parts of a chicken are usually cooked at 350°F, actual cooking time and temperature should be something different. At 350°F, the leg and wing require ten minutes to be cooked to complete doneness; the breast of the same chicken, a 2¾ pounder, requires twelve minutes; the thigh, thirteen minutes. This means that if the chicken parts are all placed in a fry basket at the same time, the leg and wing will be 30 percent overcooked. Shrinkage and flavor loss is the result. The next time you order fried chicken, see if the leg does not look as though it came from a smaller chicken.

With microwave cooking, timing is even more exact; seconds count. The cook today needs more than skill with a knife to cook well. Slicing onions may not have to be done at all, if dehydrated onions are used, which are lower in cost, require less labor, and, for many dishes, are just as tasty as the fresh onion.

The quality of instant potatoes varies widely, and the cook must be somewhat of an analyst to determine which are best from a cost and quality standpoint. The cook will take on some of the character of a food technologist, and understand a little food chemistry and a little physics as related to cooking.

Computer Assistance in Kitchen Planning

It had to come—computer-assisted kitchen planning. The optimal arrangement of equipment in a kitchen may appear to be a fairly simple problem. The mathematics of the problem, however, are formidable. A kitchen can be thought of as a system of interacting components.

A major problem in kitchen design is to arrange the work stations so as to minimize the steps taken between stations, equipment, and storage areas. George Conrade has estimated that if there were ten stations in a kitchen, the calculations required to arrive at the best possible layout would require three years. With a computer, the calculations can be made in a matter of minutes.

Burger King, the Miami-based fast-food chain, uses the computer to project sales levels at which kitchen counters need to be extended, and point of sales terminals and fry stations added. The computer-assisted analysis has reduced labor costs by 1.5 percent.

Information needed to feed into the computer were customer arrival patterns, manning strategies, customer/cashier interactions, ordering characteristics, production time standards, stocking rules, and inventory. The goal was to continue to serve the customer within three minutes and to utilize personnel and equipment to the maximum.

A computer model is used to evaluate the number of employees needed to handle any given sales volume based on the layout of the kitchen, the sales mix, and the percentage of drive-through customers. The model also suggests the most effective positioning of employees. By reference to charts developed from the computer model, managers know when to shift employees to overloaded stations such as cash registers, the preparation board, or drink stations.

This computer-assisted analysis resulted in lengthening the drive-in wait area and adding a second drive-through window.

It was found that as sales reached a certain level service declined and remodeling was necessary. Burger King is able to keep labor costs to 16 percent of sales. The computer analysis is credited with helping to make this possible.

Point of Sales Terminals

Is it a cash register, a mini-computer, or part of a computer system? The point of sales terminal can be all three, and is being installed in a number of restaurants, especially chain operations. As commonly used, service personnel punch ordered items in on a small console containing a number of keys. Each key represents a menu item. The information is kept in that machine, or, if the machine is part of a larger system, transferred electronically to a "master" computer. The master can be in another electronic cash register or in another location (perhaps miles away). As part of the larger system and tied to a "master," the individual terminal is called a "slave."

In some systems as information is introduced by waiters or waitresses, kitchen printers type out the order. Drink orders appear simultaneously in the bar. The order appears on a guest check and is totaled by the machine. This saves time and avoids errors.

Information captured at the point of sale can be "called up" in the form of daily, weekly, and monthly sales. The machine will tally the number of each menu item sold, which is valuable information to use in deciding if an item should be dropped because of low sales.

Some systems eliminate the need to reconcile duplicate checks, a time-consuming practice in common use. The system can track each waitperson's sales and allow management to evaluate his or her sales performance. The system speeds seat turnover by speeding the delivery system. Because drink orders are relayed electronically to the bar, waitpersons can pick up their drink orders when entering the bar. Service personnel need not enter the kitchen until the order is ready.

On the negative side, the system is fairly expensive and is vulnerable to electrical power fluctuations. Electrical power brownouts and blackouts can cause mini-computers to lose parts of their memories and important information is irretrievably lost.

TO PRODUCE FOOD BY COMMISSARY?

Instead of operating a number of kitchens, some managements centralize food preparation into one or several central foodservice commissaries. Under such an arrangement much or all of the food preparation for a multi-unit foodservice is done in a central production kitchen rather than in each foodservice establishment. The objective is to systematize and industrialize the food preparation, thereby reducing costs and increasing quality control.

By centralization, economies of scale are made possible. Serving units require no food preparation equipment. All purchases are made by a specialized food purchaser. Warehousing can be made more efficient with the use of forklifts and conveyor belts. Jobs can be specialized and simplified. Heavy-duty and more productive food preparation equipment can be purchased. A better qualified, more highly paid supervisor can be employed as a commissary manager, and better supervision and quality control can be effected.

Over the years some commissaries have been highly effective; others have not. Foodservice specialists disagree as to the merits of centralization. Some ardently favor it; others are vehemently opposed. Those who favor the commissary point to the value of operating the kitchen like a factory, using standardized recipes and labor-saving equipment. They recommend operating the commissary very much like a food processing plant.

Those who oppose the commissary maintain that the intricacies of relating the commissary to the unit are overly complicated. Food produced in the commissary and finally delivered to the unit foodservice, they say, is of a less desirable quality than can be produced in the unit itself.

It should be kept in mind that whenever food is prepared in one location and delivered to another, energy costs are involved, and there is a strong possibility of quality loss in the food. Inflight food service is a good example. The food must be refrigerated (chilled), kept heated at relatively low temperatures, or frozen. In the plane the food must be brought up to serving temperature. Almost everyone concerned with inflight food service agrees that under the circumstances it is most difficult to produce a meal on the passenger's tray that measures up to the quality of a meal produced from scratch in a restaurant and served immediately. If they are honest with themselves food experts almost unanimously agree that the best food is that prepared from scratch and served at once. Quality inevitably declines the longer food is held from its fresh state. Of course it is quite possible to become accustomed to any type of food, preferring margarine over butter, chicory over coffee, skim milk over whole milk, and perhaps frozen entrees over food prepared and served at once.

The palate is originally educated in the home and by the local culture to prefer particular textures, odors, and tastes. It can be reconditioned to different foods. For example, persons with high blood pressure can learn to enjoy foods with little or no salt. Taste can be acquired, even for such bitter beverages as Guiness Stout.

Holding food in any form after it is cooked requires energy—energy to chill it or freeze it and energy to "reconstitute" (reheat) the food.

Convenience food can be of top quality, for example, powdered potatoes, frozen rolls, and a few other prepared foods. Once heat is applied to finish cooking these items and the item is cooked, quality usually declines the longer it is held.

The debate over using commissaries is particularly relevant to college and university food-services since most of the larger schools have a number of houses or dining commons and have the option of centralizing part or all of the food-service preparation. Smith College has some thirty houses, each with its own kitchen and preparation team. The college administration recognizes that centralization would reduce costs. They are willing to pay extra for food prepared in each kitchen. Michigan State University operates from a central commissary, as do a number of other universities.

CENTRALIZATION IN SCHOOL LUNCH

Centralization of the school lunch program was begun in the late 1950s, and in the 1960s many school systems centralized school food preparation. Food is prepared by industrial methods and machinery, then distributed by truck to the individual school for service. With a centralized kitchen, fewer employees are needed than when each school operates its own kitchen. Part of the savings in labor, however, is offset by the cost of transporting the food from the centralized kitchen to the individual schools.

Centralized commissaries for commercial restaurants go back at least to the 1890s when the John R. Thompson Company of Chicago operated a central commissary for three restaurants and later distributed prepared food to the individual units by electrically driven vans. The Marriott Corporation began commissary operation in the early 1930s by centralizing some of the food preparation in one store, distributing the prepared food to the other stores.

In 1941 a large centralized commissary building and headquarters was built. This has been enlarged several times, and in 1967 a completely new commissary building was completed. The new commissary in Prince Georges County, Maryland, covers 285,000 square feet. It is one of the largest in operation today for serving restaurants. Food is sent as far west as Chicago and Texas, north to Albany. The Marriott operations in California are served by a separate commissary.

The Marriott operation is one of the most automated of any in the business. Purchase orders from the individual stores are telephoned into the commissary via data-phone. This system does not use words as the language of ordering but relies on a communication code. The order is relayed by long distance phone by inserting a properly punched card; the order is transmitted via a code. A computer at the receiving end compiles the orders and prints them out.

The Howard Johnson Company is another of the large companies to make extensive use of the commissary. As early as 1952 much of the Howard Johnson menu was prepared in Miami and in a location near Boston, for freezing and delivery by trailer van trucks. Miami serviced Howard Johnson stores as far away as Texas with frozen entrees. In 1969 there were twenty-two central commissaries and distribution centers that prepared 700 items.

A number of companies have elected to produce foods selectively in their commissaries, producing only those foods where economies of scale are involved and foods produced are as good or better in quality than produced on premise or purchased from a supplier. Items like soups, chili, dressings, teriyaki sauce, and barbecue sauce can be made in a commissary and distributed without any loss in quality.

FACTOR OF GEOGRAPHICAL SPREAD

Whether or not the central commissary is economical and effective depends on its design, the menu it produces, the number of units it serves, and the geographical spread of the units. If an individual unit has a high enough volume of sales, it can, in effect, operate its own food processing plant on premise. If the individual unit is large enough to achieve the economy of scale, there is no need to turn to another commissary to produce the same thing and transport it to the unit.

A large dining commons in a university serving 5,000 meals a day can probably produce some of its food on the premises as economically as can a commissary. Even so, in the future the "economies of scale" of any individual unit—no matter how large—will be compared with the economies of scale of the large industrial "meal" manufacturer, companies like Swift, Sexton, Armour, and Campbell Soup Company.

The commissary style of operation is well suited to the large multi-unit organization that has a fairly small range of menu items. These items can be produced in quantities of thousands on a production line basis. For example, the coconut cake served by the Howard Johnson Company is mass-produced day after day, using the same equipment and the same personnel.

The question arises as to whether or not the food for the individual unit should be purchased from a mass producer of food such as Campbell Soup Company or Armour and Company. The answer must be in terms of cost accounting, a comparison of the cost of the item produced by the individual organization versus what it costs from a food manufacturer. Also important, of course, is the comparative quality of the products available. Most food experts agree that food prepared and served at once is superior in flavor and texture than that cooked and held in any way, chilled, frozen, or warm.

According to Woodrow Marriott, Marriott's canned foods are necessarily less desirable in quality than frozen foods because of the high temperature and long cooking time used in canning foods by conventional methods. A few foods, such as baked beans and cream of tomato soup, are as good or better in the can than the same product commissary-prepared and frozen. The new high-temperature-short-time method of canning may overcome some of the objections raised by Marriott's study.

Another factor in the operation of a commissary is the distance involved in transporting the food from the commissary to the individual unit. At some point it becomes necessary to introduce another commissary or to produce locally because of transportation costs. The Teamsters union has been another factor in driving up transportation costs.

When food is produced centrally and distributed, there is the problem of maintaining the quality of the food from the time it is prepared until the time it is served. Freezing has been one answer; heated containers provide another.

Nearly every large hospital, in effect, has a centralized commissary. Food is prepared in a central kitchen and distributed throughout the building or buildings.

Commissaries have not always been successful. It is reported that the Horn and Hardart Baking Company of Philadelphia installed a multi-million dollar commissary only to find that its capacity was much too great for the volume of food that could be sold in the individual units. Other companies have tried commissaries and abandoned them.

Many small chains of restaurants have compromised on the commissary concept by having a central bakery and doing the heavy meat roasting, sauce making, and soup making at a central kitchen. Salad making and all frying is done on the premises of the unit store.

HOW TO HOLD PREPARED FOOD?

In setting up a centralized commissary, the administrator has several alternatives among the methods of food preparation, the amount of preparation done at the commissary, and the amount to be prepared at the unit where the food is served. A tough administrative decision relates to whether the food should be held and transported frozen, refrigerated, or hot. This is a major decision that if unwisely made can bankrupt a company.

A pioneering effort in a commercial restaurant in New York City had the food being prepared in the basement of the restaurant, frozen, and carried to the street level where it was heated and served to the customer. Obviously, there was no need to freeze the food since it was being served on the next level. There was also no need to refrigerate it; it could have been carried hot to the next level.

An industrial foodservice operation in Long Island made a similar dramatic mistake; they prepared food in a central kitchen, froze it, and then carried it to a nearby outlet where it was reheated and served.

Chilling Rather than Freezing

It costs money to freeze and to reheat, and it is not necessary to freeze if the food does not have to be held over extended periods. Ford Motor Company refrigerates much of its food for service in its employee foodservices. The more solid foods can be refrigerated to as low as

28°F, which is not freezing for them. The food holds for several days.

A large, hospital contract foodservice company refrigerates cooked food in five-portion quantities in vacuum sealed bags. Their system is based on the Swedish Nacka food system, named after the Nacka hospitals in Stockholm where it originated. The food is packaged and processed at various stages of doneness. Stewed items, such as meat or chicken pot pie are completely cooked. Broiled items, such as chopped sirloin steak, are grilled just long enough to give surface color. Other foods are packaged raw and completely cooked within the pouch.

The food is portioned and packaged under vacuum. It is then cooked to doneness in a water bath. Quick chilling is done in cold water, and the food is stored in the refrigerator. Shelf life, it is said, is at least sixty days for such foods. When the food is to be heated for serving, it is placed in a hot water bath for thirty to forty minutes, until it reaches an internal temperature of 160°F. It is then plated and placed briefly in a microwave oven before service.

Using this low temperature cooking, meat shrinkage is reduced as much as 20 percent. An advantage of the system is that seven-day requirements can be produced in a five-day, forty-hour week. Batching of production, producing a number of the same items at one time, permits greater efficiency in foodservice.

Many times food need not be refrigerated at all if the temperature can be held at 140°F or higher without damaging the quality of the food. A chain of cafeterias in Georgia transports round ribs of beef from a central commissary some fifty miles to various service cafeterias. Some cooking takes place during transportation, but the food is undercooked initially, and the holding merely finishes off the cooking process.

Items like soups, sauces, gravies, and heavy roasts can be held for forty-eight hours or longer at temperatures that will not permit bacterial growth. A few items actually improve with holding but most lose quality in terms of flavor. It is true that some people prefer cold chicken to hot, but they usually add mayonnaise or other condiment to increase flavor.

A flat statement can be made about fried items: their quality falls off rapidly, and none

should be held for more than about fifteen minutes before serving. Salad greens can be prepared and held for several hours, if held in a moist, cool environment. Salad dressings, however, cannot be added until just before serving without severe quality loss. Salads, with or without dressings, cannot be held on the cafeteria line for more than a few minutes without quality deterioration.

ENERGY CONSERVATION

Energy costs in the kitchen have been important, but little attention was given to them until the energy crisis, beginning in 1973, when those costs doubled in some areas. Since the typical kitchen consumes 40 percent or more of the total energy used in the restaurant, the National Restaurant Association, the American Hotel and Motel Association, and several hospitality chains began to examine ways to reduce the costs of heating water for dishwashing, pot and pan washing, cooking, and heating and cooling the kitchen. Among the more intensive studies conducted was that by Sambo's Restaurants, a chain of coffee shops, in cooperation with Elster's, a kitchen planning and equipment firm. The Sambo's restaurant in Calabasas, California, was used as a research unit, and several energy-saving systems were installed and studied. The exhaust ducts over the cooking equipment were lined with tubes carrying water that collected heat being exhausted from the cooking equipment. The heated water was carried to a heat exchanger, a 3,000-gallon water tank outside the building. Here the heat, collected from the cooking equipment and carried through the tubing, heats the tap water.

In the usual kitchen, a large flow of air moves from the dining room into the kitchen and out the exhaust ducts over the cooking equipment, all of which costs money. In the Sambo's research unit only a small, negative pressure was maintained in the ducts, so that only about 20 percent of the make-up air from the kitchen was exhausted.

Heat generated by the compressors operating air conditioning units and refrigeration units is usually exhausted into the building or to the outside. In the Calabasas unit that heat was also captured and transferred to the 3,000-

gallon tank where it was absorbed by the water. The water in the tank was further heated by the sun, through solar radiation picked up by a glycol solution in the tubing on the roof and carried to the water tank. If more heat input is needed for the stored water, it is provided by gas. With study, it was found that a 1,000-gallon heat exchanger would supply the needs of the restaurant. With these and other energy-saving devices the use of natural gas for cooking, heating water, and heating the building was reduced 59 percent; electricity consumption was reduced by about 80 percent.

Other ideas for conserving energy include: constructing thick walls on the western and southern exposures of a restaurant, planning windows for 20 percent or less of the floor space, using fluorescent lighting in areas other than in dining spaces, installing devices to control electrical equipment to reduce peak electricity load at any one time (rates for electricity are based on maximum consumption for a fifteen-minute period plus the total amount consumed), and installing heat recovery devices as wrap-arounds on incinerator stacks and using the hot air generated for heating purposes.

The Heating, Ventilation, and Air-Conditioning System (HVAC) in a Restaurant

The workings of the HVAC system in a restaurant are usually not well understood by restaurant operators. Understandably, their efforts are directed more to operation, and seldom do they have much interest in engineering. Nevertheless, it is helpful to know in a general way how the restaurant is heated and cooled so that the system can be maintained and repaired or modified if necessary.

Ordinarily the kitchen HVAC system should operate independently of the other rooms. Exhaust fumes and odors must be exhausted through separate filters and by means of exhaust fans directly to the outdoors. Fans draw air through filters that trap grease and fumes and force it to the outside. The kitchen is kept under a slight negative pressure so that air will not move from the kitchen into the dining room. As a result there is a slight air movement from the dining and other rooms into the kitch-

en and out the exhaust ducts over the cooking and dishwashing equipment.

Since air is continually being exhausted out of the ducts, "make-up" air is often pumped directly into the kitchen, which helps to cool the kitchen in the summer. If necesssary the make-up air can be heated during cold periods.

Air pressure for the entire restaurant must be slightly positive, meaning that the amount of fresh or make-up air should be slightly greater than the amount exhausted. When doors and windows are opened, air gently flows out; outside air does not rush in.

Some HVAC systems for restaurants distribute air through the ducts at the temperature needed by the room with the greatest cooling requirement—the main dining room. For other rooms small heaters inside the ducts reheat the air as required. The duct heaters are operated by thermostats within each room. During the winter, air is distributed through the ducts at an intermediate temperature. The duct heaters then heat the air as needed for each individual room. These systems are known as *terminal reheat systems*.

Variable volume systems deliver the same temperature air to each room where dampers inside the ducts, operated by room thermostats, regulate the amount of air delivered in the room.

While most restaurant operators will never engineer an HVAC system they should look into how the system works, by following out the ducts from where the air is taken in to where it is exhausted. They should know the location of each blower, heater, and chiller.

In its *Guide to Energy Conservation for Foodservice* the Federal Energy Administration includes a number of simplified drawings showing how kitchen equipment and HVAC systems operate. Figure 9–9 is taken from that publication.

THE EVOLVING KITCHEN

The hotel and restaurant kitchen has been changing for some time from a production "from scratch" processing plant to a finish-and-assembly station. Grilling, broiling, and frying processes will probably remain a part of most kitchens for some time; so, too, with the salad station. Most pre-preparation has al-

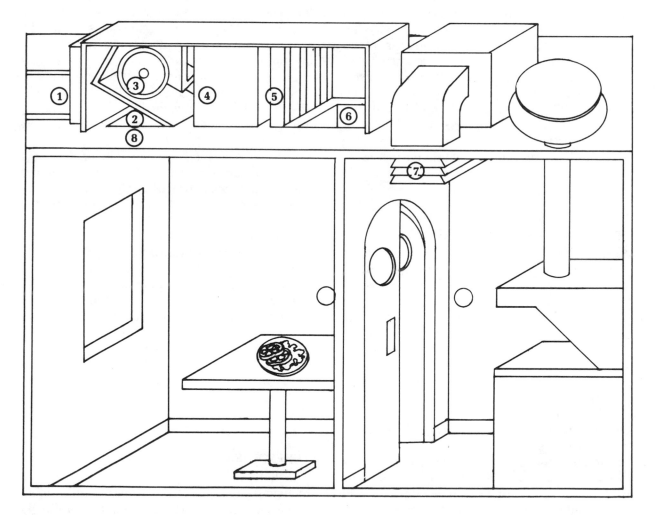

Figure 9-9 *A "typical" central HVAC system and kitchen make-up unit.*

ready left the kitchen and is being done in the industrialized food processing plant. The romantic image of the kitchen with its gleaming copper pans and kettles is already a part of nostalgia for the past.

As research finally comes to the kitchen, specific pieces of cooking equipment will be seen to be effective for special use. The microwave oven, for example, begins to be seen as a limited heating device, one essentially for boiling the water found within food materials.

Today's kitchen has become cooler, cleaner, and more technically precise. Much of the mystique and expertise has already been moved back to the food manufacturing plant. The traditional kitchen is likely to remain much longer in Europe and in a few expensive restaurants and clubs here. The fast-food restaurant has defrocked the high priest of cooking and replaced him with food warmers and mini-wage teenage assemblers. Who is to say if this is progress?

Questions

1. Name three pieces of kitchen equipment used in an ancient Roman kitchen and the colonial kitchen of the United States.

2. What is the name of a prestige restaurant that operated before 1900 in New York City?

3. Count Rumford, a gentleman who was born in Massachusetts, achieved some fame as a kitchen inventor. Can you name one of his inventions?

4. Who is the famous chef given credit for first organizing the kitchen into departments?

5. Why is a kitchen called a food processing plant?

6. The tilting skillet (or braising pan) can be used to cook several ways. Name three such ways.

7. Fires in the kitchen before about 1950 were frequently caused by overheated fat used in frying. What device has helped to limit such fires?

8. How is a forced convection oven different from the conventional oven?

9. What is the advantage of pulsing the heat source in an oven?

10. Define a magnetron and its use in the kitchen.

11. Name three advantages and the three disadvantages of microwave cooking.

12. Define a salamander.

13. What is the advantage of using a grooved griddle over the flat griddle?

14. Define bain marie.

15. Dishmachines that use a rotary table have what advantage over a flight-type machine?

16. Is it necessary to place a dishwashing room close to the dining room? Explain.

17. Why is it necessary to use 1.6 BTU of gas to accomplish the same cooking action as 1 BTU of electricity?

18. What is the great disadvantage of using gas over electricity?

19. Is there one best way to plan a kitchen? Explain.

20. Kitchen floors are normally covered with quarry tile. What is the advantage of quarry tile and what is a big disadvantage?

21. Define convenience food and describe its origin.

22. Why is it not a good idea to fry all parts of the chicken at the same time in a deep fry kettle?

23. Name three advantages of using a central commissary to prepare school lunches for a number of schools. Name a major disadvantage.

24. Name three or four items that can be easily prepared in a commissary and distributed without loss of quality.

25. Name two food items that are difficult to prepare in a commissary and distribute without loss of quality.

26. Name a major disadvantage of freezing prepared food before distributing it.

27. Energy management is being considered by a number of restaurant operators. Name

three ideas that can be incorporated into a restaurant to reduce energy demand.

28. Air pressure in a restaurant dining room must be slightly positive. Why?

29. Which uses less energy, fluorescent lighting or incandescent lighting?

30. Why not use fluorescent lighting throughout a restaurant?

31. Why is it so important to spread out the demand for electricity as much as possible throughout a day?

32. Suppose you installed solar collectors on the roof of your restaurant. How would the heat collected in them be transferred and used in the restaurant?

Discussion Questions

1. What will the kitchen be like in the year 2000?

2. Will the highly trained chef become more and more valuable? Or will he or she fade in importance because of equipment and systems advances?

GEORGES AUGUSTE ESCOFFIER (1846–1935)* ⸺⸺⸺⸺

*Information adapted from *George Auguste Escoffier,* Eugene Herbodeau and Paul Thalamas; *Pupils and Literary Executors of Maitre Escoffier* (London: Practical Press, 1955); and *The Master Chefs,* Edward B. Page and P. W. Kingsford (London: Edward Arnold, 1970).

Georges Auguste Escoffier, called "King of Chefs, Chef to Kings," was the most respected culinary personality of our times, and was almost a cult figure among chefs.

Only a few chefs have known international fame: Vatel, Maitre d'hotel to the Prince de Conde; Alexis Soyer, Master Chef to The Reform Club in London; and Antonine Careme, also a writer and chef to kings. To become internationally known, a chef must use the media, and before television and radio, the literary route was the most effective, unless like Vatel you gained immortality by committing suicide when the fish did not arrive in time for the royal banquet. (A dubious distinction at best.)

To become outstanding in any metier usually requires tremendous devotion and energy; Escoffier had these in abundance. Although married, Escoffier lived most of his off-working hours in hotel apartments by himself in London and Paris while his wife lived in Monaco. They had no children. Every day (except Sundays) for the better part of seventy-five years was concentrated on his work. His day typically started with breakfast in his office, after which he would walk around the kitchen supervising personnel and overseeing food preparation. No detail was overlooked, including personal behavior (no indulgence in alcohol, smoking, vulgarity, or fits of temper).

At 11 A.M., he joined the restaurant manager and the head waiters where together they discussed the likes and dislikes of the VIPs coming for the day's meals.

During lunch he tasted and supervised food preparation, and after lunch went for a walk, taking the same route every day. So well known did he become on his walks that friendly police stopped traffic for him to cross the street, whereupon with great deliberation, Escoffier would reward the gesture with a six-pence. A brief nap followed, and then he went back to the kitchen at 6 P.M., where he worked until 9:00. Like many illustrious chefs, he eschewed the rich foods of the trade, preferring a little rice and fruit for supper. The day ended at midnight where he oversaw the collection of leftovers, which were given to a religious organization for distribution to charity.

Perhaps Escoffier's greatest achievement was his book *Le Guide Culinaire,* prepared in collaboration with several of his friends, also culinary experts. The book has been called "the new testament of contemporary cookery," but of course, food and cookery research has been extensive since 1902 and Escoffier's book (available in this country as the Escoffier Cookbook) should be looked on as a collection of the best cooking knowledge at the turn of the century. A collection of his menus appeared in Le Livre des Menus, a complement to Le Guide Culinaire.

The Guide was an attempt to end the age of empiricism in cooking, with cooks following the practice of a pinch of that and a spoonful of this. Escoffier's cookbook prescribed exact weights and measures, and set the stage for modern cookbook writing.

Much of Escoffier's effectiveness can be traced to his association with Ritz, as executive chef of the famous Ritz-managed hotels. Madame Ritz said of the Ritz/Escoffier association: "The collaboration of Ritz and Escoffier must be counted as one of the most fortunate events of their lives." Escoffier held forth in the back of the house with a brigade of some sixty or more cooks, while Ritz managed the front of the house. Both men were perfectionists, complementing each other.

Artistically sensitive and creative, it was only natural that Escoffier would bend his talents to pleasing the great patrons of the day—the rich, the powerful, and those in the entertainment world. He was particularly successful with opera stars. As an opera devotee, several of his more famous dishes were created especially for opera stars. Escoffier was probably only partly joking when he said, "My success comes from the fact that my best dishes were created for ladies."

Great chefs are expected to produce works of art as well as cook, and Escoffier excelled at producing baskets of flowers and birds from wax and icing sugar, and swans from huge blocks of ice.

His Peches Eugenie is an example of his artistry: Monreuil peaches, stones and skins removed, placed on a silver dish, interspersed with wild strawberries and the whole sprinkled with sugar, Kirsch, and maraschino. Just before serving, the peaches are covered with iced champagne-flavored sabayon (the wine-custard dessert).

His associates always thought of him as kindly, thoughtful, and helpful. His personal life was one of order and simplicity. He is credited with bringing new status to the vocation of chef, insisting that the cooks and chefs change to respectable street clothing when leaving the kitchen for home. In the kitchen he demanded discipline and a curb on temper. The rush hour he said was not the signal for a rush of words, and under his management the L'Aboyeur who barked out the orders from the dining room gave way to the L'Announceur who called them out.

He has been called the father of the modern menu and the creator of the kitchen system as we know it today. A contemporary of Frederick Winslow Taylor, the efficiency expert, Escoffier was similarly interested in quality and speed of service. The French kitchen had been departmentalized before Escoffier but he integrated and coordinated it. Under Escoffier each order from a customer was taken in triplicate, one copy going to the cashier, one to the kitchen, and one kept by the waiter. The guest's name was written on the check so that Escoffier could include in the dishes any refinements of which he knew the guest was particularly fond. The announcer called the order in the kitchen and the chef of each department or "partie" began the preparation of that part of the meal for which he was responsible. When the entire course was ready it was brought to a hot plate where Escoffier reviewed it before being sent to the customer. Escoffier reduced the number of items on the menu and simplified preparation wherever possible.

Before canonizing Escoffier, remember that he was subject to the same temptations of other executive chefs who purchase with other people's money. According to David Ogilvy, one of the chefs who worked under Escoffier at The Savoy Hotel in London saw Escoffier signing receipts for cartloads of beef that were then delivered to his brother Robert's sauce factory in the Tottenham Court Road.[2] Escoffier grew rich and, in Ogilvy's view, looked in his later years like a Victorian banker.

It is doubtful if in this day of chain restaurants and highly standardized menus any one

2. David Ogilvy, *Blood, Brains and Beer* (New York: Atheneum, 1978), p. 46.

chef can ever emulate Escoffier in international acclaim. There are too many excellent television food commentators, home economists, and others showing homemakers how to cook, and too many food entertainers and cookbook writers for any one person to be needed to perform the kind of culinary overview that Escoffier accomplished.

Of all national groups, the French probably respect fine food preparation and service the most, and it was not surprising when the French government gave public recognition to Escoffier's genius. This was done when Escoffier was awarded the Legion of Honor and later made an officer in that honorable company.

10 Fast Food and Franchising

What single factor created the greatest change in the hotel and restaurant business in the 1960s? The answer is undoubtedly the franchise. It is a method of operation that has permitted hundreds of small businesspeople to enter the hotel and restaurant business equipped with a prepackaged product, a format, an image, a system of operation, a market plan, and a scheme of finance.

It has greatly reduced the chances of failure in the hotel and restaurant business. It has produced products and services that are generally superior to what would have been produced by businesspeople on their own. It has excited the imagination of: (1) persons producing the franchise, (2) the franchisor, (3) the individual buying it (the franchisee), and (4) the general public.

From the individual investor's viewpoint, the fast-food franchise boom of the 1960s had faded somewhat by the middle 1970s. The reason is that several of the really successful franchise companies that had accumulated capital had shifted policy sharply. Several had stopped selling franchises and were busy buying back the properties that were successful. Also, a large number of franchisees have failed, as have several franchisors.

In 1980, according to the U.S. Department of Commerce, franchised restaurants totaled 63,000. Total sales were about $28 billion. Those selling hamburgers, frankfurters, and roast beef had the most sales. Chicken franchised restaurants were next. Other franchised restaurants sold pizza, tacos, seafood, pancakes and waffles, steaks, and other types of sandwiches. McDonald's sales in 1981 exceeded $6 billion, Kentucky Fried Chicken $2 billion, and a number of similar fast-food companies had sales exceeding $100 million annually. Franchised restaurant sales constituted about 42 percent of the eating place market.

The word *franchise* comes from the old French "francer," meaning "to free." The word was used during the Middle Ages in connection with franchises granted by the Catholic Church to friendly persons who served as tax collectors taking a sizeable cut for themselves and sending the rest to the Pope. Franchising appeared in the United States just after the Civil War, franchises being offered to Singer Sewing Machine dealers. Toward the end of the century, auto makers, soft drink manufacturers, brewers, and the oil people spread the franchise concept. Following World War II, soft ice cream outlets numbered about 100, but by 1969 "Frostee Freeze" alone had 2,600 franchise stands. In 1945 a total of 3,500 fast-food outlets existed.[1]

Fast-food franchising goes back to the late 1920s and 1930s when A & W Root Beer and Howard Johnson's franchised some of their units, but the field had little momentum until hundreds of soft ice cream stores appeared in the 1950s. The number of franchisors expanded rapidly in the 1960s, cashing in on general prosperity and the opportunity for an individual to own his or her own business with a relatively small investment.

In the later 1960s, fast-food franchising took a new turn, with major food manufacturing

---

1. Boas and Chain, *Big Mac, The Unauthorized Story of McDonald's* (New York: E. P. Dutton, 1976), p. 147.

companies buying established chains or building their own. Between 1967 and 1969 Pillsbury Company acquired Burger King; General Foods, Burger Chef; Consolidated Foods Corporation, Chicken Delight and Big Boy Restaurants; Ralston-Purina, Jack-in-the-Box; Pet Milk Company, Stuckeys; and AMK Corporation's United Fruit Company, A & W Root Beer. Others that have entered the picture include Pepsi Cola Co., General Mills, and Green Giant. These companies, with their access to large capital and people resources, give the franchise business a new stability.

According to a Commerce Department survey, franchise restaurants employed close to 900,000 people in 1976, about 27 percent of the total number of eating and drinking place employees. About half of them featured hamburgers, frankfurters, or roast beef, with seafood outlets growing rapidly. About half of the 60,000 franchise outlets were franchised or directly controlled by eleven companies.

In 1975 California led the states in numbers of franchise restaurants, followed by Texas, Ohio, Illinois, and Michigan. Outside of

the United States, Canada had 940 such units; the United Kingdom, 408; and Japan, 311.[2]

By the mid-1960s, the franchise had affected the entire hotel and restaurant business, stimulating it, upsetting old ways of doing business, and accelerating change. Coincidentally, it was in part responsible for making millionaires of a number of franchisors and at least small fortunes for hundreds of small entrepreneurs.

Technically, a franchise as used in the hotel and restaurant business is an agreement between one party, the franchisor, and another party, the franchisee. The franchisor grants the franchisee the right to market certain goods and services under prescribed conditions and within a certain territory. What those goods and services are can be seen on every highway: Howard Johnson Restaurants, McDonald's, A & W Restaurants, Holiday Inns, and Hilton Inns.

Through franchising, small businesspeople acquire an instant image, extend their economic power, and gain relative assurance of success. The franchise combines the managerial knowhow of big business with the personal incentive of the individual owner. Cost controls, promotional plans, buying advice, and, usually, tested operating methods are sold as part of the package.

Most motel franchise agreements require that the franchisee construct a building to certain specifications. Usually the franchisee also agrees to buy and erect a particular sign and to follow a list of operational practices. In many cases the restaurant franchisee has been expected to buy certain foods and kitchen equipment from the franchiser and follow particular procedures. Under some agreements the franchisee can buy foods where he or she likes but must follow purchase specifications laid down by the franchisor.

Figure 10-1 *One section of the dining room of the Wedgwood Inn, St. Petersburg, Florida. Charles Creighton, the owner, was one of the first to create atmosphere restaurants in Florida. Note the green palm and other tropical plantings, and the large amount of window space that looks out on a beautiful garden. A cage on the right contains exotic birds. The name of the room comes from the fact that many pieces of Wedgwood china are permanently displayed.*

THE FAST-FOOD FRANCHISE

Fast-food franchisees may expect to pay:

1. An initial franchise fee
2. Continuing royalty fees ranging from 5 to 7 percent of the unit's gross sales; advertis-

2. *Franchising in the Economy*, 1975–77, U.S. Department of Commerce.

TYPICAL RESTAURANT FRANCHISE COMPANIES

BONANZA INTERNATIONAL, INC., Dallas, TX
Appeals to 30 to 50 year olds. Steak house menu, also has fish and sandwiches; beer and wine in some stores.
Franchise Fee: $10,000: minimum cash required $25,000 to $100,000; $90,000 equipment package; 3% of sales for local advertising; 4.8% royalty.

BURGER CHEF SYSTEMS, INC., Tarrytown, N.Y.
Appeals to young families: 18 to 35 year olds. Limited menu features hamburgers.
Minimum Franchise Requirements: $25,000 franchise fee; $50,000 to $75,000 cash; $65,000 equipment package; $130,000 for building (plus site development); 4% royalty; 4% for advertising (includes national, regional, and local).

BURGER KING CORPORATION, Miami, FLA
Appeals to 18 to 49 year olds. Fast food menu: hamburgers, fish sandwich, fries, shakes.
Minimum Franchise Requirements: $150,000 net worth (including $75,000 liquid assets).
Franchise Fee: $30,500.

CHURCHES FRIED CHICKEN, San Antonio, TX
Appeals to 20 to 38 year olds. Limited menu: chicken, french fries, cole slaw.
Minimum Franchise Requirements: $175,000 total per store.
Franchise Fee: $7,500; royalty: 4% of sales; 2% advertising program.

DUNKIN' DONUTS OF AMERICA, Randolph, MA
Appeals to 18 to 55 year olds. Limited menu features donuts and coffee.
Minimum Franchise Requirements: $20,000 to $30,000 cash; good health and financial history.
Franchise Fee: $27,000 in east, $22,000 southeast and west. One-third discount if franchise develops own realty.

INTERNATIONAL DAIRY QUEEN, INC., Minneapolis, MINN
Appeals to young families; fast food menu combines sandwiches and soft ice creams.
Minimum Franchise Requirements: $35,000 cash.
Franchise Fee: $15,000.

KFC CORPORATION, Louisville, KY
Appeals to all age groups. Menu limited to: fried chicken and related products. Also ribs.

Minimum Franchise Requirements: initial equity. This includes franchise fee, working capital of $25,000, and 20% down payment on equipment. Franchisee must personally participate in the business.
Franchise Fee: $4,000.

LONG JOHN SILVER'S, Lexington, KY
Appeals to all ages. Seafood menus; also chicken, hush puppies, corn on the cob, pecan tarts. Beer where available. Prospective franchisee needs financial ability for development of 5 or more stores.
Franchise Fee: $10,000 plus royalty of 5% of sales.

MCDONALD'S SYSTEMS, INC., Oakbrook, ILL
Appeals to young families. Expanded menu includes some breakfast items, hamburgers, fries, shakes.
Minimum Franchise Requirements: Vary from $85,000 to $100,000; includes $20,000 equipment package.
Franchise Fee: $10,000.

THE PIZZA INN, INC., Dallas, TX
Appeals to 14 to 35 year olds. Menu is limited: pizza, spaghetti, Italian sandwiches. Beer and wine ok.
Minimum Franchise Requirements: initial unit: $40,000 cash plus ability to finance (mortgage or lease) approximately $200,000 for land, building, equipment package.
Franchise Fee: $10,000 for first unit; $5,000 for additional unit.

PONDEROSA SYSTEM, INC., Dayton, OH
Menu is "full meal" oriented and includes meat, potatoes, salad, and desserts.
Franchise Fee: $20,000, capital needed for franchise investment is $75,000 to $80,000.

SIZZLER FAMILY STEAKHOUSES, INC., Los Angeles, CA
Appeals to 18 to 39 year olds. Limited menu: steak, seafood, and fish sandwiches; beer and wine in some stores.
Franchise Requirements: minimum $80,000 cash.
Franchise Fee: $20,000. National advertising program requires 5% of sales; local advertising 3%. No equipment package.

Source: Food and Lodging Hospitality, December 1975.

ing assessments of about 1.3 to 4 percent of gross sales

3. Equipment purchase price or rental cost

4. Rent

Cash requirements to launch a franchise restaurant run from $10,000 to $15,000 for a small pizza or seafood place, up to more than $400,000 for the more profitable hamburger or chicken outlets.

The chart on page 321 lists representative foodservice franchises, and gives an idea of the investment needed and the kind of advertising required by the franchisor.

The majority of the chains are categorized as fast food establishments and have these characteristics:

High-speed service, mostly to walk-up customers

Immediate service of food or assignment of an in-turn number for pick-up

High customer turnover per hour

Limited menu

Low check average

Assembly line food production

Strict purchasing and portion control

Throw-away plates, cups, and utensils

Special training programs for managers and workers

Franchise operators know the value of market research and promotion, and spend up to 7 percent of their gross sales on TV and other media ads and promotional gimmicks. The McDonald Corporation has the record for an advertising budget—more than $200 million a year. One chain spent a million dollars on an eight-week ad to publicize only its french-fried potatoes.

WHAT FRANCHISEES GET

For fees paid, the franchisee can expect from a reputable and established franchisor an image and an established brand name, maintained by advertising, and generally a complete promotion package including roadside pylons, a logo or a signature on take-out boxes, bags, coffee cups, napkins, match books, and just about everything else that the customer sees.

The franchisee can also expect quality control in purchasing and operations, a control which the franchisee sometimes resents and resists. Perhaps most important of all, if the franchisor is not overly hungry for new franchisees, the franchisee gets careful location analysis and a certain amount of financial advice (and even help in financing in some cases). Eventually it can be expected that many franchise plans will include central accounting as part of the service offered.

Nearly all franchisors provide some kind of initial training at a Hamburger University, a Mr. Donut College, or a similar training center. Following the initial training, the franchisee and the operation are watched over by an area supervisor or field coordinator. The franchisee's books are set up and audited by the franchisor in one way or another to assure that the correct franchise fee is paid. Most franchise fees are based on sales together with other fees.

A prospective franchise buyer has a wide range of choices in either lodging or restaurant franchises, according to the cash he or she can raise and the style and size of operation one desires. A relatively small amount of cash is needed for some of the smaller restaurants; several hundred thousand dollars in cash is necessary for franchising one of the larger motor lodges or inns. Among franchised restaurants, the buyer has a choice ranging from a relatively small and simple operation like Burger Chef to a large, relatively complicated restaurant coffee shop.

The franchisor is the big winner in that business can be expanded straight across the country by merely signing up hundreds of franchisees. The franchisee is then almost always largely or totally responsible for raising the necessary capital to start the business. The franchisor can expand as rapidly as the franchisees buy. The two principal problems of the franchisor are: (1) to maintain the quality and the standard of the product and services franchised, and (2) to see to it that few if any of the franchisees fail.

COMPARATIVE COSTS AND SALES

Each fast-food franchise has developed its own menu and unit layout so that food and labor costs vary widely. Capital costs per stores and

TABLE 10-1   Franchise Chains

	Sales/Unit	Capital Cost Per Store	Food & Paper Cost %Sales	Labor Cost %Sales
Burger King	$463,000	$347,000	40%	21%
Chart House	665,000	750,000	43	18
Cork 'n Cleaver	517,000	550,000	44	17
Denny's	594,000	600,000	33	34
Friendly	312,000	290,500	47	20
Jerrico (LJS)	299,000	200,000	38	14
McDonald's	727,000	502,000	40	22
Pizza Hut	179,000	240,000	30	24
Sambo's	505,000	450,000	35	23
Victoria Station	1,560,000	925,000	43	19
Wendy's	463,000	280,000	42	15

Source: Harvard Business School, 1976.

sales also vary widely. Table 10-1 suggests these wide differences.

The fast-food figures—Burger King, Friendly's, Jerrico, McDonald's, and Wendy's —can be compared with dinner house figures—Chart House, Cork n' Cleaver, and Victoria Station. Compare also the coffee shops (Sambo's and Denny's) with the numbers involved with the other two restaurant formats, and with the pizza chain, Pizza Hut.

FRANCHISE SUCCESS

McDonald's, the most successful of the restaurant franchisors, has had a failure rate of less than 2 percent. For those franchised units that do fail, the franchise company either works with the franchisee to make the unit successful after negotiation or buys it back. However, by 1969 some franchised units were being allowed to lapse.

The Howard Johnson Company and Denny's have decided to buy back a number of their franchised stores with the thought that standards can be more easily maintained if stores are company operated (or that the parent company can make greater profits operating than franchising). Where the franchise involves primarily the use of a name, as is the case with the Sheraton Hotel franchise, the parent company may quietly nullify the agreement, take back its sign, and remove the hotel or motel from the list of Sheraton Hotels that take part in the Sheraton referral system.

From the viewpoint of the franchisee, the agreement is generally restrictive with regard to the style of operation, the product, and services offered. No room is left for imagination or for changes in menu, decor, furnishings, or equipment. Neither is there room for regional differences in taste or other customer preference. Some of the franchise fees add up to 15 percent of the gross sales, and more; this can be a burden especially during slow periods.

The franchise favors the franchisor. The terms of a franchise agreement are drawn up by the franchisor; the franchisee is free to buy the franchise or reject it. Ordinarily the agreement is fixed. Most franchise agreements contain clauses that permit the franchisor to buy back the franchise, or to cancel it, should the franchisee fail to live up to the terms of the agreement.

When the franchisor acquires capital or when the franchised units are particularly profitable, the franchisor is tempted to buy it back. Chock Full O'Nuts, a New York City restaurant and franchise company, apparently faced such a temptation. In May of 1969, ten franchisees picketed the headquarters of Chock Full O'Nuts, stormed the building, and threatened to stay all night unless they could see William Black, the company president. The franchisees protested what they called company harassment of those who did not want to sell their franchises back to the company. Moreover, they stated that they received no supervision, and that the prices of frankfurters, hamburgers, and soups charged to the franchisee by the parent company had been raised arbitrarily.

The franchised restaurant was first seen when A & W Root Beer opened a stand in Lodi, California, in 1919. In the 1920s, an A & W franchise was sold to J. Willard Marriott. Bill Marriott had been a student at the University of Utah and had observed another early franchisee A & W Root Beer stand doing an exceptionally large business across the street from the campus. This was in 1926.

In 1927 Howard D. Johnson began franchising his stores and the name Howard Johnson was to become a household word on the East Coast. Later, the company expanded its operation into the Midwest and, in the middle 1960s, into California. In 1973 the Howard Johnson Company included more than 900 restaurants and more than 450 motor lodges.

The most colorful of the franchise stories involves the originator of Kentucky Fried Chicken, "Colonel" Harland Sanders. He had been a farm hand, carriage painter, soldier, railroad fireman, blacksmith, streetcar conductor, Justice of the Peace, salesman, and service station operator. At the age of sixty-five, he was operating his own restaurant-motel in Kentucky but found himself without business because a new interstate highway had by-passed his establishment seven miles away. His only income was a social security check of $105 per month.

While in the restaurant business he had experimented with frying chicken and found that cooking it in a home-size pressure cooker produced an especially tender product. He had also assembled a zesty coating for the chicken. He set off on a trip around the country selling restaurant operators a franchise to produce Kentucky Fried Chicken (KFC). Since it was a promotion package and a procedure for cooking chicken, the franchise could be used in any existing restaurant. The initial investment was low, only enough to buy a few needed pieces of cooking equipment.

With his first franchisee, Pete Harmon, he put on a television cooking show in Salt Lake City. To add some color he decided to change into a full-fledged Kentucky Colonel with a pure white suit and Kentucky colonel goatee. "You got to remember," he said, "I didn't have no money for advertising and promoting, so I had to do the best I could." The Colonel's thoughts on marketing: "If you have something good, a certain number of people will beat a path to your doorstep; the rest you have to go and get."[3]

The franchisee paid the Colonel 5¢ for every order of fried chicken served. According to Sanders, he would stop at a restaurant, demonstrate his frying process, stay on a few days without pay until the customers began to react to the chicken, then move on. He traveled from city to city, often sleeping rolled up in a blanket in his car.

Within three years, restaurant operators were coming to him to procure a franchise. But it was a twenty-nine-year-old lawyer/promoter who put KFC on the map and incidentally made multimillions for himself. John Brown, Jr., was the kind of person who made $500 a weekend selling encyclopedias while attending the University of Kentucky. He and an associate changed the chicken shop into a standard red-and-white building and streamlined the operations. A $5,000 investment in KFC stock in 1964 was worth $3.5 million five years later. (Brown later married a national beauty queen contest winner and became governor of Kentucky.)

The Colonel who had received $2 million in cash and KFC franchises in Canada was hired as a public relations image-builder under contract. His "finger-lickin' good" recipes were changed so that in the Colonel's words they became "slop." KFC was bought by Heublein, a liquor company, in 1971 for a reported $267 million. In 1974 Sanders filed a $222 million suit against Heublein for trying to interfere with his plans to develop a new franchise operation. An out of court settlement resulted.

Kentucky Fried Chicken is the number one chicken franchisor. By 1977 sales exceeded $2 billion. Two buildings were offered, the more popular being a 24- by 65-foot unit. The recommended location is a 126- by 125-foot lot, pref-

---

3. Colonel Harland D. Sanders, *Finger Lickin' Good* (Carol Stream, Ill.: Creation House, 1974).

erably on a corner or on a "going home" side of the road. Traffic that goes by the site should total at least 16,000 cars a day, according to their estimates.

Unlike many of the franchisors who insist that their units be in sizeable population centers, KFC executives state that their operations can gross up to $250,000 in communities of 10,000 population.

As a representative for Heublein, the current owner of KFC, the Colonel, dressed all in white with the country Colonel black-string tie, white mustache, and goatee, made television and other appearances.

Always a tither, the Colonel became a devout Christian after conversion at an evangelistic meeting when he was seventy-nine years old. In trying to live up to his new standards his hardest problem he said was to give up cussing, a practice at which he had few peers. God, he says, was responsible for curing him of what looked on x-rays like malignant cancer of the colon. Always generous, he became a philanthropist. One of his gifts was unusual. All of his stock in Colonel Sanders Kentucky Fried Chicken of Canada, Ltd., was given to a foundation established in Toronto. After expenses of operation, all profit goes to charity. Each Canadian franchisee is allocated a portion of the profit for which he or she names the charities that shall receive that franchisee's share. As for the Colonel, his personal charities included churches, the Salvation Army, a city Mission, and a number of schools.

Of all the people who have received the Horatio Alger Award, few deserved it more than the Colonel. Few people have experienced more vicissitudes in a lifetime and overcome more circumstances. His pressure fried chicken seasoned with eleven secret herbs and spices is seen in almost every community in this country and in dozens of other countries around the world. Like Ellsworth Statler, Sanders was forced to drop out of school at an early age to help support his family. Like Statler he had the indomitable will to succeed and luckily the stamina, perseverance, and ability to do so. He happened to be a good friend of Ray Kroc, the founder of McDonald's, and it is easy to see why. Sanders died in 1980 at the age of ninety, well-respected, and an ornament to the food service industry.

"NAME" FRANCHISORS

In the late 1960s, a number of franchisors assembled a restaurant franchise package, gave it the name of a prominent sports or entertainment figure, made a public offering of stock, and sailed off into business with little or no practical restaurant experience represented in the organization. The general public, at that time eager for any stock with a franchise restaurant label, gobbled up the stock offering the day it was offered.

It has been relatively easy to offer stock to the general public through an underwriter, especially if the stock offering amounts to $300,000 or less. The Securities Exchange Commission permits such an offering, without a proven record of experience, if the offering does not exceed the $300,000 figure. Much larger stock offerings are possible, but the application for approval from the SEC is more detailed and requires a longer time for approval.

New stock issues had two fertile seasons in the 1960s. Large numbers were offered in 1960–1961, but the number fell following the 1962 stock market recession. The really big growth came in 1968 and extended through the summer of 1969. Over 200 restaurant companies went public or filed to do so in 1968.

Typically, a franchisor would offer 100,000 shares of stock to the general public at $3 per share. The stock offering would represent perhaps 15 or 20 percent of the total voting stock of the newly formed company. The nationally known sports or entertainment personality who was affiliated with the company might be given as much as 20 percent of the total stock for the use of his or her name. Of course, the personality involved knew little or nothing about the restaurant business and probably never did anything more than sample food in a few of the franchise operations.

Restaurant franchises during this period were being aggressively sold. The July 10, 1969 *Wall Street Journal* carried ads for Chefs International, Sea Host, Li'l Abner (owned by Longchamps), London Beef House, Hardee's, Mr. Pizza, Circus Wagon (burgers, hotdogs, roast beef, chicken, shakes, soda, cotton candy, peanuts, popcorn), and Zuider Zee Fish 'n Puppies. Capital required for these franchises, according to the ads, ranged from $16,000 to $35,000.

By August 1969 the stock of most of the fast-food franchisors had suffered sharp losses. Broadway Joe's, Inc., stock plunged from 17 to 1. According to *New York Magazine*, Broadway Joe's lost $243,978 on revenues of $667,952 in the eight months ending July 31, 1970—something of a record. Joe Namath, who obviously knows more about football than food, having performed at openings of new stores and posing for photographs, got out fast. Al Hirt's, which came out at 10½, was at 5. Mickey Mantle's dropped from 15 to 9. Minnie Pearl's Chicken system, which reached 70 at one time, had dropped to 7 and, by 1974, was no longer in operation.

CONTROLS HAVE BEEN INTRODUCED

Franchisors in the past have promised prospective franchisees the moon and it was a case of "caveat emptor"—let the buyer beware.

Controls began to be introduced. In June of 1969, the Attorney General of the state of New York ordered Dutch Inns of America Incorporated to stop selling franchises within the state without first complying with the state's Real Estate Syndicate Act, part of the securities laws.[4] Dutch Inns, based in Miami, was selling motel franchises and, according to the Attorney General's office, had "extended financial commitments, inadequate funds to meet these commitments, and, in fact was using the franchise fees for its own working capital." Since then other states have acted to restrict what franchisors can demand of the franchisee.

Franchising offers one of the safest and easiest routes for a hotel or restaurant chain to go international. Special problems found in any particular area can be better solved by the franchise owner on the scene who is wise socially and politically. In many instances the franchise holder is already a foodservice or lodging operator who knows the ropes locally and has an established organization.

A major disadvantage to the franchisee exists if he or she is not given territorial protection, the legal assurance that the company itself will not move in with a store and will guarantee that new franchisees will not be sold within a certain distance of the franchise holder. Potential franchisees also may not be aware of the long hours that may be required for success.

FRANCHISING INTERNATIONAL

Intercontinental Hotels Corporation led the way in operating hotels abroad and was soon followed by Hilton International. The soft ice cream franchisors, Tastee Freez and International Dairy Queen, have the largest number of units abroad, 460 and 386 respectively (1969). In 1977 Holiday Inns had franchised some 200 inns around the world. A number of other restaurant and lodging franchisors are abroad in a small way, and a great many more are considering such a move. It is no longer surprising to see Kentucky Fried Chicken in Acapulco.

DANGERS OF OVER-FRANCHISING

Franchising makes it easy for a husband and wife to get into the restaurant business—perhaps too easy. In some areas too many franchised food outlets have appeared; so many, in fact, that few can achieve a satisfactory sales volume. In Nashville, home of Kentucky Fried Chicken, when Minnie Pearl Chicken was also in operation, there were nineteen fried chicken stores.

Another reason for caution in rapid expansion of franchising is the rise in land values. A site that might have leased for $8,000 a year in 1963 cost $12,000 to $20,000 in 1969. Many of the franchisors lacked food experience and have failed. General Foods, parent company for Burger Chef for a time, "was shutting down Burger Chefs all over the country."[5]

FRANCHISING HERE TO STAY

Among the franchisors who are successful, there is a current trend toward increasing the number of company-owned units. The management of Denny's, for example, no longer franchise their stores, and are buying back units so as to better control menus, prices, and opera-

---

4. *The Wall Street Journal*, June 5, 1969.

5. *Barrons*, September 15, 1969.

tions. Reason: if the chain is successful, more profits for the parent company.

While the franchised food outlets showed hamburgers the favorite specialty at 35 percent of total dollar values, followed by fried chicken and ice cream (20 percent each), many of the franchisors were elaborating the menu and decor to tantalize the public into eating more, and to eating out more often. Food companies like Pillsbury's (Burger King), General Foods (Burger Chef and Rix Roast Beef), and Green Giant have deeply involved themselves in the franchise business.

By 1979 it was clear that single units of a franchise operation located some distance from similar franchised units were at a disadvantage in promotion and advertising. Franchise restaurants were growing more like the retail grocery market business, highly standardized, and highly competitive. The single unit did not have enough advertising and promotion money to compete with chain units advertising as a group. As a consequence, some franchise companies would not sell less than five units, clustering units so that mass newspaper advertising and television time could be purchased. Franchisees, unless family operations, needed three or more units to be competitive in profits and in promotion and advertising.

Another trend in franchising appeared that could be called "standardized flexibility," a concept that permits some flexibility in menu building and operations. The Lums restaurant corporation offered franchisees optional packages A, B, and C, or combinations of the three options. The franchisee could use the exterior of Plan A with the interior of the B plan or of the C plan. Standardized flexibility had to be controlled to maintain the overall image that the franchisor needed to maintain identity and quality.

Another trend became apparent when a major franchise company such as McDonalds introduced a new concept and the others were quick to follow suit or at least to take advantage of the change. When McDonald's began promoting breakfast sales, breakfast sales increased in other restaurants as well because the consumer was conditioned by the advertising and the experience of eating breakfast out.

Federal and state legislation has been enacted to supervise more closely the sale and franchise and the post-contract relationship between franchisor and franchisee. Several states regulate the conditions under which a franchisee may terminate or fail to renew a franchise, and a number of states can more closely regulate registration and disclosure of information pertinent to the purchase of franchises.

Questions

1. Someone states that fast-food restaurants have never grossed as much as a million dollars in sales in one particular unit. What is your reply?

2. As a franchisee of McDonald's you would be paying what percentage of your gross revenue for rent?

3. Who originated the McDonald's concept of restaurant operation?

4. One of the keys to the success of the fast-food franchise is to have a standardized format. Looking at the development of McDonald's design, would you say that design should be fixed and never changed?

5. As an owner of McDonald's Company stock would you expect much in the way of a yield on your investment?

6. Someone says "With a franchise you completely avoid a chance of failure in a fast-food restaurant." What is your response?

7. Name at least three of the top ten fast-food franchisors in this country.

8. Give at least three advantages for an individual in buying a franchise over operating from a private format.

9. Give at least three disadvantages of franchised operation as compared with independent operation.

10. Restaurants generally spend less than 2 percent of their sales for advertising; fast-food restaurants, however, spend about what percent of sales for advertising and promotion?

11. One of the more colorful characters in the fast-food business was Colonel Harland Sanders who put together what franchising chain?

12. Two individuals who have been highly successful in the fast-food franchising did not get into the business until they were over fifty. Can you name them?

13. Some of the franchisors sell only groups of franchises—a state or a large area. What does this have to do with advertising and promotion?

Discussion Questions

1. Fast-food restaurants have been adding menu items. Will they eventually become coffeeshop in nature? Give reasons for your answer.

2. Supermarkets and twenty-four hour mini-markets are adding deli sections and even snack bars. How much of a threat are they to the fast-food restaurant?

RAY KROC (1902–　　　)*

Of all hospitality entrepreneurs none have been more financially successful than Ray Kroc. In 1982 he was senior chairman of the Board of McDonald's, an organization intent upon covering

*Most information based on a personal interview and on the books, *Grinding It Out, The Making of McDonald's,* by Ray Kroc with Robert Anderson (Chicago: Regnery Co., 1976) and *Big Mac, The Unauthorized Story Of McDonald's,* by Max Boas and Steve Chain (New York: E. P. Dutton, 1976).

the earth with hamburgers. Among the remarkable things about Kroc is that it was not until the age of fifty-two that he even embarked on the royal road to fame and fortune.

The hospitality business has seen many millionaires like Howard Johnson and Conrad Hilton but no one has approached the financial pinnacle reached by Kroc. What makes the accomplishment the more astounding is that Kroc invented nothing new. In fact, the McDonald's concept was leased from two brothers from New Hampshire who had set up an octagonal-shaped fastfood hamburgatorium in San Bernadino, California.

Kroc was impressed with the golden arches, the McDonald's sign lighting up the sky at night, and the cleanliness and the simplicity of the operation. Even more fascinating was the long waiting line of customers. The two owners, the McDonald brothers, were not interested in expanding, being quite content to live near their restaurant and drive their Cadillacs.

Kroc's genius came in organizational skill, perseverance sparked with enthusiasm, and an incredible talent for marketing. His talent extended to selecting close associates who were equally dedicated and who added financial, analytical, and managerial skills to the enterprise. Kroc remains the spark-plug and master merchandiser.

At age seventy-six he held one-fifth of the forty million shares of the McDonald's Company stock, worth well over $400 million. He is busy giving it away to employees, hospitals, and the Marshall Field Museum and distributing it through his own Kroc Foundation. Perhaps more importantly, he has probably made more millionaires than any other person in modern times. Since the average McDonald's in 1981 grossed about $1.1 million, and net earnings to the operation easily exceeded 10 percent of sales, it is not hard to see how franchisees could become millionaires especially when they have several stores.

A would-be franchisee needs about $100,000 in cash and a credit line for another $100,000. For this he or she gets a twenty-year license and a site plus a complete McDonald's store put together by the company. Rent is 8.5 percent of gross revenues. A 3 percent annual franchise fee is additional.

The McDonald's Corporation is the projected image of Ray Kroc, entrepreneur par excellence, who believes with a passion that business means competition, dedication, and drive. The McDonald's empire was built in part as a result of his arch competitiveness best illustrated by his reply to a question. "Is the restaurant business a dog eat dog business?" His reply was "No, it's a rat eat rat business."

Some of the operational guidelines developed by Kroc include the concept of KISS—Keep It Simple Stupid—a concept that lends itself beautifully to the fast-food operation and to the franchise business, and QSC&V—Quality, Service, Cleanliness, and Value. McDonald's menu well illustrates the simplicity concept. The original McDonald's menu comprised hamburger (containing one-tenth of a pound of meat) at 15¢, a slice of cheese on it at 4¢ more, soft drinks at 10¢, 16-ounce milkshakes at 20¢, and coffee at 5¢. French-fried potatoes were also a big seller and long-profit item, as they are today. Any changes in menu came slowly and only after much experimentation and market testing. Changes in restaurant design and layout also came only after much study and consultation.

It takes fifty seconds at a McDonald's to serve a hamburger, shake, and french fries. Precise specifications for everything: a 3½ inch bun, one-quarter ounce of onions, etc. A 385-page operations manual details it all.

Never be idle a moment is Kroc's motto. What pleases Kroc as much as anything else is to see a crew in a McDonald's working together at fever pitch, tied together by the rhythm and flow of business and careful kitchen layout.

Kroc has a fierce determination to maintain a family image for McDonald's. He allows no jukeboxes, no vending machines, and no pay telephones in any McDonald's restaurants; such items create unproductive traffic and encourage loitering. "McDonald's," says Kroc, "is kind of synonymous with Sunday School, the Girl Scouts, and the YMCA."

What could be more American than hamburger, french fries, apple pie, and milkshakes—the heart of the McDonald menu. Attempts at sophisticating the McDonald's menu have failed. A hulaburger, two slices of cheese with a slice of grilled pineapple on a toasted bun, was a giant flop. As one customer said "I like the hula, but where is the burger?" Filet-O-Fish did work and so did the breakfast sandwich. The sandwich is an egg fried in a teflon circle with yolk broken and dressed with a slice of cheese and slice of grilled Canadian bacon placed open faced on a toasted, buttered English muffin. It changed the breakfast business not only for McDonald's but brought in breakfast trade from competing restaurants as well.

Other restaurant concepts failed; a Pie-Shop and Raymonds, a high-style hamburger shop, proved to be too sophisticated. Pancakes are working, but are a special case because they cannot be held (as other McDonald's items can for a few minutes).

When McDonald's first appeared and standardized everything, including the red and white building and golden arches, it was following principles of success already laid down by Howard Johnson with white buildings and orange roofs. Identity and visibility were essential. The American public is sanitation conscious. The public was pleased to accept uniformity in exchange for immunity from salmonella and staphylococci. Also, the price was right. McDonald's, however, does not stand still. Building design was switched to a brick and mansard-roofed building with inside seating.

The downtown McDonald's of today would not be recognized by the patron of the sixties. Some of the units provide saddles for little people on which to ride the range while eating hamburgers. There are hamburger manikins in the shape of a policeman. On the walls may be pictures of an old Spanish mission as at San Juan Capistrano. At Port Hueneme a stylized surfboard graces the wall flanked by beach scenes. In Chula Vista a tree is reminiscent of the Wizard of Oz. On Wilshire Boulevard a fountain sparkles not with water but with lights. McDonald's has jumped on the Disneyland bandwagon with a vengeance. Inside the prestigious water tower complex hamburgers are a grilling in McDonald's and the place is jumping. Anything a franchisee wants within certain parameters is now acceptable to the design department.

Kroc believes in running a lean team with a minimum number of staff executives and levels between himself and unit management. He also believes in owner participation in operation. A favorite saying, "McDonald's is for the needy, not the greedy" means that he wants no investors as such, only active franchisees who show up everyday at the store and provide leadership. Kroc says that he could be overwhelmed with absentee investors but will have none of them.

Arch defender of private enterprise, Kroc believes that doing what one enjoys is the way to be happy. "Find out where your talents lie and then do whatever you are doing better than anybody else. But be willing to pay the price of accomplishment." A story he tells to illustrate the point is about the woman who approached the great pianist and said, "I would give anything to be able to play like you!" The great pianist replied, "No you wouldn't." The point is that few people will pay the price of excellence.

There is no doubt about the quality of McDonald's products. Extensive research has resulted in a quality product and innovative equipment with which to prepare and serve it. Fish purchased is of the highest specification. The control on the fry basket for frying the fish is keyed to the weight of the fish—more weight, longer cooking time. And it is true that a hamburger held more than ten minutes is thrown out. The patty itself is 19 percent fat; the french fries are cut small so as to absorb a lot of oil, meeting the teenager taste. The buns have a little sugar, and a great deal of loving attention has gone into their formula. Meat patties are frozen both for convenience of handling and to hold down bacteria count.

Kroc has always been interested in placing McDonald's in the right locations that are less subject to loitering or becoming hangouts. To find such a location Kroc would rent a plane and fly over a community looking for schools and church steeples. After getting a general picture from the air he would follow up with a site survey. The company now uses one of its five helicopters for the same purpose. A computer in Oakbrook, McDonald's Headquarters, is programmed to make real estate printouts, but in the last analysis the top executives make their own judgments about the desirability of a location by driving around in a car, going to the corner saloon, and into the neighborhood supermarket. "Mingling with the people" says Mr. Kroc, tells him what he needs to know about how well a McDonald's store will do there.

In starting out, Kroc was not above checking out the garbage cans of competitors and counting wrappers to estimate their sales volume. Today he calls himself "the location and griddle man." Like so many men of great determination, Kroc was blessed with endurance and he surrounded himself with enduring people, himself averaging not more than six hours sleep a night. Many times,

says Kroc, he got four hours or less. "But I slept as hard as I worked." He does not believe that intelligence necessarily makes for restaurant success; rather, it is application, dedication, and hard work.

Investors in McDonald's stock have not done well except for those who knew when to get out. The stock came out at $22.50 a share in 1964, shot up to $30.00 before the trading day ended, then rose to $50.00 a share before the end of the month. It was one of the several glamor growth stocks of the late sixties, spurred upward by the hope that it would go even higher along with other "growth" stocks. It is hard to fathom why investors would drive a stock up in price to fifty and more times the dollar earnings per year when the company was not paying a dividend. In other words, the investor hoped that somebody else would pay even more for the stock. Those who owned the stock and were wise enough to sell did extremely well. Those who held on to the stock saw it decline precipitously; in 1977 the stock was selling at $48. Investors have become dividend conscious, and the company now pays a tiny dividend which, says Kroc, will be increased substantially each year.

What are the keys of McDonald's success, an organization that in 1981 exceeded $6 billion in sales and had over 4,000 outlets? They are the system, simplicity of format, sanitation and cleanliness, attractive architecture, and simplicity of menu and correct menu choice. How then is McDonald's any different from any other hamburger chain? What unique contribution did Kroc bring to the enterprise?

Enterprises like McDonald's are not built without the dedication, some would say fanaticism, of at least one person. Kroc as a promoter and salesman, fired with daring unquenchable ambition and confidence in the American future, was a hard combination to beat. His guiding principles are sound ones for any merchandising effort—give quality and value in pleasant surroundings not the least of which are pleasant people. Giving quality has been an abiding principle. As Kroc puts it, "We had principles when we were poor."

Even these are not enough without marketing and advertising, in which Kroc fervently believes. The name McDonald's itself is significant. Kroc believed that name had more advertising appeal than his own name. As a result, his name is relatively unknown to the general public, while the name McDonald's is a household word. Television advertising, over $100 million worth a year, has been remarkably effective. "We do it all for you," the wholesome, beaming teenagers eager to serve, corny, catchy names of the product, "Big

Mac," "Egg McMuffin," and "McFeast" have proved spectacularly effective in getting the under-thirty crowd to move en masse toward the nearest McDonald's. And don't forget ever-friendly Ronald McDonald.

A major difference between McDonald's and many of the fast-food franchise companies, a difference that adds tremendous value to the McDonald's Corporation, is that McDonald's owns the land and the buildings of many of the units. The capital investment required to purchase the land and construct the buildings runs into the multimillions and keeps the earnings of the company relatively low. At the same time, the market value, the real equity position of the company, becomes stronger. Moreover the well-located sites continue to appreciate in value.

In the restaurant business once the break-even point has been passed, profits accelerate at a greater rate than sales. McDonald's units in 1978 were averaging over $900,000 in annual sales volume. In the more than one hundred stores in Canada, sales exceeded a million-dollar average. In 1979 a few stores were approaching the $3 million mark.

Like most restaurant chains, McDonald's paid no dividends until 1976, and then only 2.5 cents per share. The dividend policy, according to Mr. Kroc, will be to double dividend payments each year for a number of years.

Critics of Kroc say that he made millions by working teenagers hard at the lowest possible wage. "Assistant managers" (teenagers themselves) get a little more, but not much. Health faddists say that Kroc pushes high-caloric, junk food on the American public, especially on unsuspecting children. French-fried potatoes are low in protein, high in fat. Soft drinks offer nothing but empty calories in the form of sugar, waste, and flavorings. Self-appointed critics throw up their dainty hands certain that anything as simple to make as a hamburger, a milkshake, or a french fry must be undermining the American culture. It must be pointed out that meat, milk, potatoes, and bread are nutritious foods by any reasonable standard and that young people need calories (but not to the exclusion of vitamins).

Kroc is a five-foot, eight-inch dynamo. Part of the reason for his exuberance no doubt is that like many very rich people he can do pretty much as he pleases. A personal assistant travels with him and acts as a chauffeur, valet, and assistant. A $4.5 million jet that will seat seventeen passengers is ready when Kroc is. He is flown from his La Jolla home to his ranch near Solvang, northwest of Santa Barbara. People eagerly respond to his wishes both because of his power and prestige and because most of the time he comes across as a very likeable person—a person who loves what he is doing.

11 The Private Club

The urge to join a club probably goes back to the days of primitive beings or their predecessors, the hunting apes. When the upright apes left the forest they found it necessary to band together to survive. Mutual protection, common interests, and social and economic advantages were and are still reasons for people gathering together to form clubs. We feel safer, more secure, and comfortable being with people of similar background, social status, and interests. Membership in some clubs brings prestige and perhaps a sense of accomplishment.

Practical reasons for the existence of clubs are several. A family of middle income can belong to a luxurious country club with part ownership in an olympic-sized pool, an eighteen-hole golf course, tennis courts, a fine restaurant, and bar. A chemist can join a club whose members are also chemists. The sports-minded can join an athletic club, a tennis club, even a curling club. The person with a yacht, and no place to park it, can dock at a yacht club slip paying by the foot for the privilege. There are fraternal clubs, religious clubs, and service clubs.

Country clubs are given several concessions, without which they probably could not exist. In many states the nonprofit club is granted a liquor license at no cost. Clubs without liquor licenses are few and far between. The real property of the golf club is taxed at a much lower rate than similar, privately owned land. In California the rate is about one-quarter that of comparable private land. A third concession is seen in that clubs are charged a much lower water rate than, for example, industry. (Golf

courses in most parts of the United States require heavy sprinkling.) Usually the rate is regressive; the more used, the less cost per unit.

If the club is large enough or has enough facilities, employees and a manager are needed. Food and drink are the common denominators of most clubs, and this makes them a part of the hospitality business.

Starting a golf course clubhouse for a country club is not cheap. About 160 acres of land are required for the course. The National Golf Foundation notes that there were 4,770 private club courses and 1,586 municipal courses in 1976. Graduates of hotel and restaurant schools do not rush into the club field immediately following graduation even though starting salaries tend to be higher than for trainee positions in motels and restaurant chains. Later in their careers, however, many do shift over to the club field, finding it less stressful and, in many instances, more lucrative.

Membership in a city club can confer a certain cachet, a place to relax over a meal. Food and food service is usually a cut above and lower priced than that offered by the better commercial restaurants in the area. The club offers a less hurried, less cluttered atmosphere, greater personal attention, and a good setting for discussing sports and business. Often the initiation fee and the monthly dues are borne not by the individual but by the business the member works for or owns. Business entertainment at the club is a fringe benefit and tax deductible. Membership gives access to like-minded members, usually the business and social elite of the community or profession.

CLUB MANAGERS' ASSOCIATION OF AMERICA

The term *club* is broadly defined and could refer to a stamp club, a bowling club, a bridge club, or the Cosa Nostra. What is usually referred to by the club business are those clubs known as private city, country, and military clubs. The Club Managers' Association of America, CMAA, the professional organization of club managers, has about 3,000 members who manage most of the important city and country clubs in the United States and Canada. A number of CMAA members manage military clubs. The CMAA defines the private club as a made-up group of people who select their fellow members, pay annual dues, and usually have permanent facilities for serving food and beverages to their members.

In 1977 the Club Managers' Association of America estimated that nineteen million Americans belonged to 12,000 private clubs in the United States. The club industry, said the Association, employed almost 600,000 persons with an annual payroll of $2.5 billion. Beverage sales alone exceeded $1 billion dollars in that year.[1]

Since the late nineteenth century, city and country clubs have been a sizeable part of the hospitality business in the United States. Clubs probably employ more top chefs than do hotels and restaurants. Few restaurants serve food in the style and of the quality found in the better clubs. A majority both of the managers and the food and beverage managers in clubs have been a part of the hotel and restaurant field, as students, employees, or managers.

Let us trace the development of clubs through the years and then examine club management as a specialized area of management within the hospitality business.

Our clubs are mostly developments of English city and sporting clubs. The Royal and Ancient Golf Club of St. Andrews, Scotland, founded in 1758, is known as the home of golf and is the ancestor of our country clubs. The precursor of the city club dates back to the early fifteenth century when a club called "La Court de Bonne Campagnie," or Club of Good Companions, was formed. Sir Walter Raleigh is credited with founding the Mermaid Club, which made its headquarters at the Mermaid Tavern in London and included such notables as Shakespeare and Kit Marlowe among its membership. Ben Jonson founded a club that held forth at The Devil, another of the Fleet Street taverns in London in the early seventeenth century. These early clubs were vehicles for people of like interest to associate together, sharing food, drink, and expenses. This is how the word *club* probably came to have its present meaning, "to share," or divide, expenses.

EARLY ENGLISH CLUBS

The early English club, especially those that flourished in the late seventeenth and early eighteenth centuries, usually met in one of the taverns or coffee houses of the day. White's Club, one of the most exclusive of today's London clubs, was originally a coffee house. The owner, Francesco Bianco, an Italian immigrant who anglicized his name to White, raised the admission fee from an English penny to a sixpence, which assured him an exclusive clientele.

Gambling was also a part of the appeal and many of the English clubs retain that appeal. Play ran high. Lord Carlisle lost $10,000 at a cast of hazard. The members could bet on anything. Horace Walpole records that when a man fell down, apparently dead, at the door of the club, he was carried inside, and the members at once made bets on whether he was dead or not; "and when they were going to bleed him, the wagerers for his death interfered and said it would affect the fairness of the bet." Quarrels at gaming tables frequently resulted in duels. In 1751 the gambling salons employed a captain, "who is to fight any gentleman who is peevish at losing his money."[2] In 1736, the customers took over from White and established the practice of admitting no one except those who had been voted on by an admissions committee. Membership became a "social credential of definite significance and practical value," and many clubs still offer prestige as a primary appeal. The practice of black-balling, the right of any member to drop a black ball into a box thus excluding an applicant from membership, has long been a source of snobbery in clubs, making them especially attractive to the social climber.

1. *Club Management*, Club Managers' Association of America, Washington, D.C., 1977.

2. James Laver, *Age of Illusion* (New York: McKay, 1972).

Some of the early clubs accepted only members of a particular political stamp. The Reform Club is perhaps the best known of the English political clubs. Our own political clubs have had less stability.

One reason for the fame of the Reform Club was its chef, Alexis Soyer, who was with the club during the 1830s and 1840s. Soyer, a flamboyant genius, ranks with Careme and Escoffier in the culinary world. As an innovator, he devised a 40- by 110-foot kitchen which included a cold meat larder, a sauce larder, a pastry room, a butler's pantry, and a game larder. He equipped the kitchen with pickling tubs, slate wells for soaking ham, marble slabs, tin-lined drawers, steam drawers, steam boilers, gas stoves, and bain-maries.

The word *club*, especially as used in England, connotes exclusiveness and snobbishness as revealed in the comment of a French nobleman about a century ago. He said, "The club will ever remain a resort—tranquil, elegant, and exclusive—forbidden to the humble and insignificant." Snob appeal is a great attraction—perhaps the strongest—for members in many clubs. By the end of the nineteenth century, there were about one hundred clubs in Britain with a membership of only 80,000, but this exclusiveness was not to last.

The YMCA was formed in Britain as a place for people to enjoy recreation without the necessity of drink. The Rev. Henry Solly, a Unitarian, founded the first "workingman's" club in 1862. Today, there are more than 3,700 workingmen's clubs in Britain "providing food, drink, entertainment, gaming, and, incidentally, camaraderie—women included."

EARLY CLUBS IN THE UNITED STATES

The earliest clubs in the United States date from before 1800. The Hoboken Turtle Club was founded in 1792. Boston had a Sans Souci (without a care) club in 1785. The Somerset Club was formed in 1817 (but under a different name). The Chilton (ladies only) came along about a decade later.

The Bread and Cheese Club, noted by James Fenimore Cooper, was said to be the first private membership club with rooms of its own in New York City. Founded in 1836, it met in The City Hotel. New York City had a Union Club in 1836. The need to support the Civil War led to the founding of Union League Clubs in New York, Philadelphia, and San Francisco (later the Pacific-Union Club). Some of the finest food in the country is today served at the Union League Club of Philadelphia.

The first country clubs in the United States appeared outside Philadelphia, the Foxborough (1887) and the St. Andrews Country Club of Westchester (1888).

MILITARY CLUBS

Military clubs had their antecedents in the Spartan messes of 200 B.C., and earlier, and in the "sodalitas" of Roman soldiers. The Battle of Waterloo was the immediate predecessor of the present military club and was responsible for some of the character of city clubs today. The London club, as an institution with a large and elaborate clubhouse of its own, did not really arrive until about 1815. The Guards Club and the Royal Navy Club already existed, but officers in Wellington's Army, accustomed to eating "in the mess," founded the United Service Club in 1815. "With the exception of a sleeping room, he may live at his club with a degree of state and profuse luxury that nothing but a princely fortune could otherwise command, not to mention the enjoyment without the expense of constant society."[3]

After Napoleon was defeated, many unemployed British officers lived on slender pensions and "clubbed" together for purposes of association and economy in housing and eating. Professional people and members of the clergy soon followed suit and established their own clubs.

In 1975 London had some forty-two gentlemen's clubs. Many are still snobbish, still stuffy, and many are nearly empty except for a few senior citizens. Many are fading because of the squeeze between declining membership and the necessary money to maintain the old spit and polish. Typical is the United Service Club. Built by John Nash in 1823, its huge building is mostly quiet. Opened originally only to senior army officers, it has necessarily "lowered its standards."

About twenty-five years ago, a high-ranking army officer strolled through the palatial rooms on Pall Mall and paused beneath the portrait of a marshal of the Royal Air Force, resplendent in a bemedaled dress uniform.

3. Laver, *Age of Illusion.*

"When you start letting chaps like that in," grumbled the general to the club secretary, "it's the beginning of the end."

White's, one of the most famous gentlemen's clubs, still has a seven-year waiting list, mainly of sons of present members.

A good reason for maintaining membership is the fact that members at most clubs can get meals at about 50 percent or less than they would in a quality restaurant, and wine by the bottle is especially inexpensive.[4]

Military clubs today are operated much like private city clubs, divided into those for officers and those for enlisted personnel.

In the past most of these 5,000 or more clubs were managed by officers (officers' clubs) or by noncommissioned officers (enlisted men's clubs). Today, the larger ones—both "O" clubs and "EM" clubs—are likely to be managed by civilians who report to a member of the military designated as club officer. Military club managers who are in the service are eligible for membership in CMAA after four years of experience as manager.

FRATERNAL CLUBS

In this country almost anyone can be a club member. If you are a veteran, you have only to join the local post of the American Legion or the Veterans of Foreign Wars. You can be an Elk, an Eagle, or an Odd Fellow, a Knight of Columbus, or a Son of Italy. You can be one of the more than a million Moose in this country. You can join the local branch of the American Polish Club, the YWCA, or the YMCA.

A bit further up the social ladder, you may be a Mason, wear your fez and regalia, and proudly display your Shriner ring or lapel pin. It is often a distinction of sorts to belong to the local Women's Club, and one must have the right ancestors to be a Daughter of the American Revolution or a member of the Cincinnatus Club.

SERVICE CLUBS

Service clubs are slightly different in appeal and activity. Rotarians, Kiwanis, Optimists, or one of several other such clubs are made up of business and professional people who support one or more charities. They usually own no property but meet for lunch once a week at a local hotel or restaurant.

COUNTRY CLUBS

According to some commentators, the prime motive in joining a club is status-seeking; no doubt this is true for some prestige clubs. Status-seeking, however, accounts for only part of the fact that clubs are growing at the rate of more than 200 a year.

Most of these new clubs are a part of land developments. The developer well knows that the presence of a fine country club increases the value of the land nearby, and in many developments club membership comes with the purchase of the building lot or a condominium. Several of the old clubs, such as the Dallas Country Club and the Chevy Chase Country Club in Washington, D.C., are now surrounded by city. Their land is extremely valuable.

In suburbia, the country club offers a relatively inexpensive way of gaining access to a fine golf course, a swimming pool, and a higher type of cuisine than can otherwise be had in the community. In the 1970s tennis courts, indoors and out, became a major draw for club membership. In the mid-1970s racquetball clubs became popular, one reason being the relatively small amount of land required. Most country club members are athletically and socially minded, but in the prestige city clubs the average age of the membership exceeds forty-five years, and the athletic facilities are more symbolic than used.

UNIVERSITY CLUBS

The larger cities have University clubs which anyone who has been to college may join. Yale, Harvard, Cornell, and a few other universities have their own clubs in a few cities. The Oxford Club in London may not be representative of the prosperity of such clubs; its furniture is becoming unglued, and the place has the musty smell of an enterprise that is not doing well. The University Club of Philadelphia has passed away. It may be that attendance at a university no longer stamps one as a member of the elite.

COMPANY CLUBS

Some of the most thriving clubs are subsidized by companies for their own employees; IBM has

---

4. *Los Angeles Times*, December 15, 1974.

its own club. In England, the most vigorous of the new clubs may not have a former guards sergeant as a doorman or claim a few dukes as members, but they are more in tune with the times. Probably the most dynamic of the London clubs is the Managing Directors Club—any managing director (president) of a business, no matter how large or small, can be a member.

PROFESSIONAL CLUBS

Engineers, parachutists, chemists, and a variety of other groups with the same professional interests have formed clubs in major cities, some of the club facilities being impressive and well done. The Washington Press Club and the Petroleum Club of Houston are examples of such clubs.

KEY CLUBS

A new type of drink-and-sex club has appeared; typical are the Playboy and Gaslight clubs. These are operated for profit. They are not bona fide clubs in the usually accepted sense.

The Playboy clubs are part of the Hugh Hefner enterprises, which are tied together with a bright red ribbon of sophisticated sex and a fast-stepping style of life. Of the nineteen Playboy clubs in 1969, fifteen were owned by Playboy International; the others were franchised.

The average Playboy Club keyholder is a forty-two-year-old businessman in management or in one of the professions. Eighty-five percent are college graduates. The some 500,000 playboys apparently like to be close to beautiful, undraped females, ounce-and-a-half drinks, and sprightly shows. Some playboys are more equal than others, for there are VIP rooms where the meal cost is higher per person, and drinks cost extra. Little difficulty is experienced in securing the bunny waitresses, for their average income is said to be well above $20,000 a year.

CLUB STATISTICS

A 1980 study of clubs by Pannell Kerr Forster showed that the usual country club took in about $1,000 in dues and guest fees from each member, and another $1,127 in food and bever-

The 1980 Country Club Income Dollar... And Where It Went

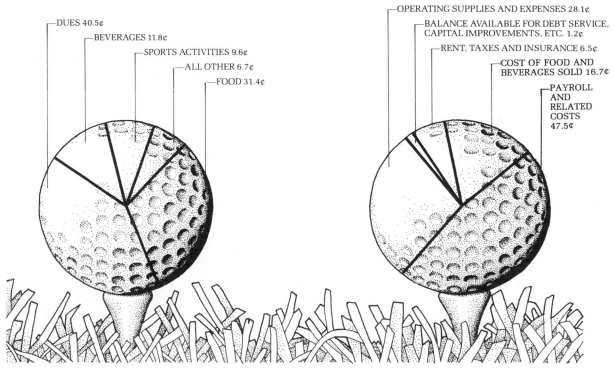

DUES 40.5¢
BEVERAGES 11.8¢
SPORTS ACTIVITIES 9.6¢
ALL OTHER 6.7¢
FOOD 31.4¢

OPERATING SUPPLIES AND EXPENSES 28.1¢
BALANCE AVAILABLE FOR DEBT SERVICE, CAPITAL IMPROVEMENTS, ETC. 1.2¢
RENT, TAXES AND INSURANCE 6.5¢
COST OF FOOD AND BEVERAGES SOLD 16.7¢
PAYROLL AND RELATED COSTS 47.5¢

PREPARED BY PANNELL KERR FORSTER

Figure 11-1

The 1980 City Club Income Dollar...   # And Where It Went

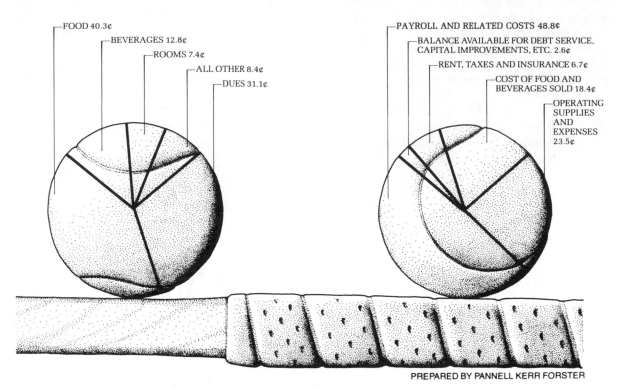

FOOD 40.3¢
BEVERAGES 12.8¢
ROOMS 7.4¢
ALL OTHER 8.4¢
DUES 31.1¢

PAYROLL AND RELATED COSTS 48.8¢
BALANCE AVAILABLE FOR DEBT SERVICE, CAPITAL IMPROVEMENTS, ETC. 2.6¢
RENT, TAXES AND INSURANCE 6.7¢
COST OF FOOD AND BEVERAGES SOLD 18.4¢
OPERATING SUPPLIES AND EXPENSES 23.5¢

PREPARED BY PANNELL KERR FORSTER

Figure 11-2

age sales, plus "other sales," for a total of about $2,600 per member (see Figure 11-1).[5] The cost of food consumed in a club runs much higher than in the usual commercial restaurant for the simple reason that the member expects lower menu prices—a loss that is made up in the form of dues. The cost of food runs about 47.2 percent of sales, allowing about 5.2 percent for employees' meals. Beverage cost was also higher than found in a commercial restaurant, close to 28 percent of sales. Total club payroll and related costs ran a whopping 79.8 percent of total sales and income, excluding dues. Without the income of dues, the clubs would fold overnight.

In the city clubs surveyed, each member paid $366 dues and guest fees, and spent an-

other $624 in food and beverage in the club (see Figure 11-2). Food costs ran about the same as for country clubs.

THE CLUB MANAGER'S JOB

What about the job of club manager? It is somewhat different from that of a hotel or restaurant manager. The primary purpose of the club manager is to satisfy the club member; the hotel and restaurant is operated primarily for profit. The club manager usually reports to a house committee or the club president; a hotel or restaurant manager usually reports to a corporation executive or an owner.

The job of club manager is more demanding in the area of human relations. The hotel or restaurant manager tries to satisfy the patron or the guest; the club manager's reason for existence is to please the member, and, in the smaller clubs, there is much more face-to-face

5. "Clubs in Town and Country," 1980, Pannell Kerr Forster and Co., 420 Lexington Avenue, New York, NY, 1981.

contact with the member than the hotel or restaurant manager usually has with guests.

In the hotel and restaurant business, ownership or top executives change from time to time. In the club, the change is more frequent; at least some of the officers and committee members change annually. A major responsibility for the club manager is to orient himself to the new officers and at the same time orient them to their new responsibilities.

Because club members often think of themselves as part of the social elite, and because they may pay an initiation fee of as high as $75,000 plus annual dues, they may expect the same deference from the manager as from a servant. The wise manager rejects this.

The manager tries instead to maintain a social relationship that is somewhere between that of a business manager reporting to a board of directors, a friend of the family, and a professional hotel or restaurant manager dealing with patrons. To make life more interesting for the manager, many members expect to pay less for the food and beverages they buy at the club, expect a higher quality than they would find in a first-class restaurant or hotel, and expect service at odd hours.

The club manager should be a technical expert, and be better informed and experienced in the operation of the club than any of the members, no matter how rich or expert they may be in other fields. The tactful and knowledgeable manager can shape the nature of the club, help in great part to set a proper tone, and act as a leader for the governing board, the members, and the employees.

Club managers' hours are dictated by the peak periods of activity at the club—weekends in the country club, and luncheon periods in the city clubs. Many club managers work long hours at a stretch, particularly in the busy season, and then go for weeks or even months with little to do.

Starting and average salaries for club managers are considerably higher than for comparable positions in restaurants and hotels. Salaries go as high as $75,000 a year, plus food and, often, bonuses and other fringe benefits. In 1975 the average member of the Club Managers' Association received about $35,000 a year (including fringe benefits such as meals, car allowances, travel, etc.). According to a study conducted by the Club Managers' Association (from which many of the statistics in this section are drawn), the average manager received a salary of 3.2 percent of the club's annual revenue from all sources.

Club managers must dress well and appropriately and drive a respectable car. It also helps if their family is socially attractive. They are usually highly intelligent individuals with more than their share of social poise and ability. They should be "au courant" on manners and social niceties. Good health, being well informed, and possessing an interest in people are assets. They must be discreet and above suspicion if they are to survive among the various factions that abound in the club atmosphere.

A few club managers retire from the same club where they started. Typically, however, the manager moves every three to five years, having grown tired of the same old faces. The job can call for a great amount of imagination or for hidebound routine, depending upon the age and attitudes of the club members.

Food and Beverage Knowledge

After the human relations skills required on the job, those connected with planning and producing interesting and varied food and parties are paramount. Managers need not be skilled cooks, but they should be aware of what is fashionable and impressive in the way of hors d'oeuvres, buffets, and foodservice generally. Some club experts recommend that food and beverage experience be acquired before entering the club field.

The club manager must "fit" the club's membership. A club manager who is highly successful in a middle-class club, where aggressiveness might stand him in good stead, could find this trait completely out of place in an old, quiet, prestigious club. Personal appearance must also fit and manners must be what the members feel to be acceptable. A new, growing club needs one kind of manager; an old, established club prefers another, more subtle type. The dynamic manager of a new club may find that he is developing himself right out of a job after the club has reached a certain level of style and size.

Managers may be confronted with divided loyalties on the part of some of their employees. Older employees are likely to have developed personal relationships with influential club members and to relate themselves more directly to the particular members than to the manager. One fine Southwestern club had a porter who reputedly was worth $2 million and received about $300 a day in tips. It can be seen that such an employee might not be too responsive to the wishes of the manager. Once in a while the manager finds that he is in the position of throwing down the gauntlet over whether *he* goes or one of the employees who refuses to cooperate is discharged.

The manager is well advised to find a powerful sponsor or sponsors within the club membership who will stand by him when the inevitable storms appear and the boat begins to rock. Of course, the manager cannot openly favor one member over another, but the knowledgeable, honest, and reasonably diplomatic person can survive for at least a few years.

A source of friction between private clubs and hotels and restaurants has been the practice of many nonprofit clubs of soliciting parties. Restaurant and hotel owners feel this is unfair competition because the nonprofit clubs pay no income tax.

The problem has apparently been settled by the Internal Revenue Service, which has ruled that private clubs may do no more than 5 percent of their total food and beverage business with patrons other than club members.

Alcohol Creates Problems

Another major problem in clubs centers around alcohol. Most clubs cannot survive without it, and many owe their existence to the fact that the club has a special political concession for serving liquor in a "dry" community. When for some reason liquor is not permitted in the club, the club is likely to die, as was recently the case of a British club in the Moslem community of Kuwait where liquor privileges suddenly ended. Overnight the club was deserted.

Many clubs in dry communities, as in parts of the deep South, rely heavily on the fact that they can serve liquor in a social setting. The same is true of many of the American Legion and Veterans of Foreign Wars clubs around the country.

It is no easy problem to handle the member who has had that extra martini and is criticizing the food, a waitress, or the manager. Evi-

dence that the job of club manager is no bed of roses is the fact that each year, according to the CMAA, one of every six managers changes jobs, and 25 percent of these leave the field permanently. Yet few club managers want long-term job contracts; apparently they want to be free to change jobs at short notice. One manager put it pointedly, "I live very closely with my members—too close. I want no strings attached. I want to be able to move quickly whenever I get sick of them, or they of me."

It was not long ago that the club manager was considered a high-class servant or steward. As recently as 1914, the manager of the Harvard Club in Boston had to insist that his title remain club manager and not steward. It was not until 1927 that the Club Managers' Association of America was formed. In 1946 there were only 623 members. By 1956 the number had increased only to 916. Today, CMAA has several thousand members managing clubs in the United States, Canada, and abroad. The official journal of CMAA is *Club Management.*

Challenge of Management

Club management is a particularly challenging field that calls for social skills, poise, leadership, and good taste. In addition to being a manager and all that term implies, the club manager must also be respected by members and be

Figure 11–3 *The Jonathan Club of Los Angeles, one of the prestige city clubs on the West Coast.*

a person with whom they enjoy dealing. Clubs, both nonprofit and operated-for-a-profit, are growing in number and sophistication. They are part of our English heritage, offering millions of Americans amenities and associations that would be difficult to enjoy without the club.

The exclusive clubs are centers of wealth and influence, according to Ferdinand Lundberg in the book *The Rich and the Super-Rich.*[6] Private clubs, he avers, are societal control centers of the elite. Each major city has at least one club for the wealthy, either an imitation or extension of earlier clubs in Boston, New York, Philadelphia, and Baltimore. Those, in turn, were imitations of English clubs. The most important, he says, are in New York City, where the greatest fortunes are centered. The leading New York clubs include among their members the wealthiest of the out-of-towners and many foreigners.

The Chicago Club, the Cleveland Club, the Jonathan Club of Los Angeles (Figure 11–3), the Houston Petroleum Club, and the Duquesne

6. Ferdinand Lundberg and Lyle Stuart, *The Rich and the Super-Rich* (New York: Bantam, 1969).

Figure 11–4

Figure 11–5

Club of Pittsburgh are such centers of wealth and influence. At the top of the social rating, says Lundberg, is the Links in New York, followed closely by the Knickerbocker, the Metropolitan, the Racquet and Tennis Club, the Brook, the Union, and the Union League.

Some of the other prestige clubs include the Philadelphia Club and Union League Club in Philadelphia, the Somerset Club in Boston (naturally, the oldest), the Algonquin in Boston, the Houston Club, the Lake Shore, Standard, and Chicago Clubs of Chicago, the California Club of Los Angeles, the Bohemian Club of San Francisco, and the Chevy Chase Club in Washington, D.C. Yacht clubs also tend to be exclusive since not everyone owns a yacht.

Cleveland Amory, another commentator on the American social scene, writing in the book, *Who Killed Society?* rates clubs by quoting a club man who says, "At the Metropolitan or the Union League or the University, you might do a ten thousand deal but you'd use a Knickerbocker or the Union or the Racquet for a hundred thousand dollars, and then for one million dollars you would move on to the Brook or the Links."

CLUBS INFLUENCE POLITICS

There is little doubt that many of the clubs are aristocratic and privileged. No doubt many great financial deals are concocted "at the

Figures 11-4, 11-5, and 11-6 *Lake Arrowhead Country Club offers this area as a focal point for guest activity. Overlooking a magnificent wooded area, the lobby soars to forty feet and is flooded with light from the continuous skylight at the apex of the A-frame. The Country Club, with an eighteen-hole golf course, was the first of the supporting facilities constructed at Bella Vista Village, north of Fayetteville, Arkansas. Membership is made up primarily of home owners in the Village. The majority are senior citizens, and furnishings for the lounge are selected with their requirements in mind. The clubhouse is built on the side of a hill and arranged so that the large public spaces face the golf course and the view across the valley.*

club." I believe that the more important clubs also greatly influence politics. Once a party line has been reached, the clubs present a solid front. Views are invariably expressed in the light of property interest. They are the most intense partisans of freedom—their freedom—in the world today. To control or influence public policy, one is better placed if one has a strong voice in an important club than if one has a strong voice in the Senate of the United States. Amory writes that the leading freedom of the top clubs is the freedom to be anti-democratic and pro-aristocratic. In the earlier days, he says, they would have been Federalists. Clubs were no partisans of the New Deal. They feared and hated Franklin D. Roosevelt. Their heroes were Harding, Coolidge, and Hoover. They showed little enthusiasm for Eisenhower, much less for Kennedy, but were inclined to favor Lyndon B. Johnson who was a big depletion allowance man after their own hearts.

Many clubs are pretty boring places; nevertheless, membership in some of them is the ultimate mark of status for most businesspeople of the area. The exclusive clubs want to remain that way. An applicant for the Racquet and Tennis club in New York, for example, must be proposed in writing by a member, procure a seconding letter and six supporting letters, then meet individually with at least eight members of the Board of Managers. Club waiting lists can run as long as ten years, and some clubs even have waiting lists for their waiting lists.[7]

Members of the Jewish faith are excluded from many of the prestige clubs. A 450-page report in 1969, published by the American Jewish Committee, concluded that Jewish executives are deprived of opportunities because of exclusion from important clubs.[8] Of some 1,800 downtown men's clubs, roughly 80 percent have no Jewish members, according to a survey made by the same committee.[9] In most cities the Jewish community has countered such exclusion by building clubs of its own, often the most lavish in the area.

The importance of the private country and city club in social and political power has not been explored in any depth. That the club is a focal center of such power is highly likely. If some clubs are suspicious of ethnic or religious groups dissimilar to themselves, many have also been suspicious of women, forbidding them entrance to parts of the club or allowing them in only at certain times of the day, or even the year. This is no longer legal.

7. "The Blooming Clubs of Business," *Dun's Review,* July 1969.

8. Ibid.

9. *The Wall Street Journal,* September 10, 1969.

The Yale Club of New York City, which for seventy-two years had prided itself on its all-male tradition, in 1969 met to decide if female graduates of the University would be admitted. The decision was whether or not they would be admitted on the same basis as wives of members and lady guests of members. They would not be allowed in many of the twenty-two story building's rooms, nor allowed to use any athletic facilities, or eat in three of the club's dining rooms. They would, however, be allowed to eat in the roof dining room, to stay in boarding rooms, and to walk in the especially designated "women's lobby" on the ground floor. Such restrictions can no longer be enforced.

At first the Harvard Club allowed Radcliffe College graduates to sign for food and beverages but denied them most other privileges. However, the Harvard Club is now fully open to Radcliffe College alumnae. Cornell University's club allowed women graduates to be associate members, which meant they could not vote. The women countered by establishing exclusive clubs of their own in some cities.

Pressure for pushing open the doors to clubs always existed and is increasing. In Maine a club dispensing food and liquor legally cannot exclude anyone on the basis of race or religion. The Union League Club of Chicago admitted its first black member in 1969, and the eighty-seven-year-old Detroit Club accepted a Jewish businessman.

PROFIT-MAKING CLUBS

As noted previously, the word *club* originally meant to divide expenses; most were not in any way concerned with operating for a profit. It is true, however, that some of the early clubs operated in conjunction with a coffee house, and the owner, of course, did operate for a profit.

Some of the gambling clubs of Britain and elsewhere are profit-making organizations, to be sure, and numerous city and country clubs are being operated for profit. Club Corporation of America alone operates 130 clubs in this country and abroad. The Hathaway family of Los Angeles are prominent among clubs-for-profit operators, owning and operating the Los Angeles Athletic Club with some 6,000 members, a country club, and a yacht club. The La Jolla Beach and Tennis Club is another well-known club, presently owned by the Kellog family. The average club, however, is nonprofit in nature and is so treated by the Internal Revenue Service. Any surplus that the club might accumulate is not distributed to members but is plowed back into the club, usually in the form of improvements and additions.

The IRS states that a club qualifies for federal income tax exemption as a club organized exclusively for pleasure, recreation, and other nonprofitable purposes. No part of the net earnings may go to private shareholders. May a club get most of its revenue from the gambling of its members and their guests? Yes, says the IRS, since gambling supplies those elements of diversion that are commonly accepted as pleasure and recreation. Oddly enough, illegality of gaming devices under local law has no effect on the club's exempt status.[10]

Privately owned clubs must offer food, beverage, and facilities at prices to compete with nonprofit clubs and restaurants in the area. Sometimes the profit comes mainly from land appreciation. For example, Riviera Country Club in Pacific Palisades, California, sits on 150 acres of prime residential land, which in 1977 was worth about $10 million and continues to appreciate.

Slot machines in a club can make the financial life of the club easy. For many years, the officers' clubs in the military took in huge sums of money from slot machines. This enabled many military clubs to build luxurious quarters and provide food and beverages at prices only a little above cost.

A PART OF MIDDLE AND UPPER-CLASS AMERICANA

The club, which started in this country on the East Coast, patterned after the English golf and city club, has spread across the country and is a part of suburban and town life. Some of the older downtown clubs will fade, to be replaced by new ones.

Retirement communities, "new" towns, resort communities, and the ever-expanding suburbs will continue to create clubs as a part of the American way of life. Many clubs will be forced to lower their membership bars; others

10. *Washington Report*, National Restaurant Association, March 24, 1969.

will no doubt arrange to raise theirs higher. Social segregation will probably continue because most of us feel more comfortable associating with people whose values, beliefs—and prejudices—support our own. Regardless of social segregation there will continue to be economic segregation. The job of the club manager will continue to be one of challenge, calling for tact, diplomacy, and a considerable amount of specialized expertise.

Questions

1. Approximately how many private clubs are there in this country?

2. Would you say that a large percentage of graduates of hotel and restaurant management degree programs move directly into club management?

3. Our clubs have as their origin clubs located in what country?

4. Clubs often restrict membership by black-balling, or by other means. What is the origin of the term *black-balling*?

5. The military clubs of today date from what period in what country?

6. Can you name four different kinds of clubs?

7. The cost of food as a percentage of sales runs much higher in private clubs than is true in commercial restaurants. Explain why.

8. Name three advantages of being a club manager as compared with being a hotel manager; and name three disadvantages.

9. Would you say that the job of club manager has high job security; in other words do club managers tend to stay at the same club for long periods of time?

10. It is often said that a manager can manage anything. Is this true for different kinds of clubs?

11. Why in some cases are restaurant managers and owners antagonistic to private clubs?

12. Do some private clubs wield political influence? Explain.

13. In your opinion will clubs ever be completely democratic in their membership selection?

14. Is it possible to set up a club as a private enterprise and run it as any other business, paying income taxes and operating for a profit? Explain.

15. The fact that clubs are often part of land development schemes will have what impact on the club business in the future?

Discussion Questions

1. Private clubs have been called "bastions of privilege." Is this true? If it is true, is this necessarily bad?

2. What is the future of private profit-making clubs in this country?

JAMES A. COLLINS (1926–)

The magnates of the hospitality business have appeared in a variety of shapes, size, and appearance. Conrad Hilton was Mr. Suave. Ray Kroc is the fiesty little fighter. Ellsworth Statler was a small dynamo. Jim Collins at age fifty-five looks like the All-American boy, Jack Armstrong, as an adult. "The world out there is Okay and I'm going to make it better." Clearly he is not the scheming driver out to get his, and then some. The world is not a rat race. It is a place in which to achieve, have fun, and enjoy.

Like most hospitality industry winners, Collins paid his dues. At age twenty-five his first fast-food restaurant, "Hamburger Handout," called for sixteen-hour days, seven days a week. His first restaurant format was patterned after the original McDonald Brothers' "hamburger, french fries, and milkshake" operation; hamburgers for 19¢, 11¢ french fries, and 20¢ shakes. Marketing, especially advertising and promotion, is one of Collins's fortes. "Two-for-ones" and half-price specials were used to attract new customers and let them sample the product. An innovator, he changed the budget steak house into a semi-dinner house, adding lobster, shrimp, salad bars, and beer and wine, but he retained the semi-self service concept. He also ran with the franchise concept, both as the major franchisee and franchisor.

His career story is that of the All-American boy: college at UCLA, a strong interest in sports, especially field and track, and a major in civil engineering and two years of work in that field. At age twenty-five a strong determination to be in business for himself found expression in a self-service drive-in. His huge sales enabled him to open three smaller stores, "Hamburger Handout Jrs." The year 1960 was a turning point in that he met Colonel Sanders and began selling Kentucky Fried Chicken. Two years later, the Colonel assigned Jim all of southern California.

Another major turning point came in 1967 when Jim and some associates bought the Sizzler Family Steak Houses for $899,000. A year later the Sizzler and Kentucky Fried Chicken restaurants (33 KFCs and 156 franchised Sizzlers) were taken public. Some 300,000 shares were sold at $18 a share.

In 1983 there were over 500 Sizzlers in thirty-nine states and franchised operations in Japan, Guam, Kuwait, and Saudi Arabia. Some 240 KFC units are under the Collins Foods International banner, headquartered in Los Angeles. About half are in southern California, the others are in Florida, Illinois, Oregon, Texas, and Queensland, Australia.

Five distribution centers assure franchised and franchisee stores a reliable supply source of uniform food quality.

Three words have loomed large in the lexicon of fast-food success—timing, marketing, and value. The era of fast food was in the 1950s to 1975. Good restaurant locations were available to serve ready markets. Good sites could be purchased or leased, a condition that changed as markets were saturated and land and building prices soared. Fast-food marketing became highly effective with the use of TV advertising. Fast food served in attractive, clean surroundings offered value for the money, low prices made possible by teenage labor at minimum wages, excellent distribution, and sales systems. Children, teenagers, and young families constituted new markets that did not patronize the coffee shop or the traditional table service restaurant. Collins capitalized on trends using mass marketing techniques and always keeping the price/value concept before the public.

The All-American boy image continues today. In his mid-fifties Collins jogs six miles a day and looks and acts like a man in his thirties. Other rich men in the hospitality business give millions for good causes, but always near the end of their careers. Collins has been a donor and a fund raiser for a number of years. He has raised multiple millions, some of it from his own pocket, for UCLA, the YMCA, and the Center for Hospitality Management at Cal Poly Pomona. Unlike most hospitality magnates who are too busy or too individualistic to take part in the hospitality trade organizations, Collins has taken a very active role in both the California Restaurant Association and the National Restaurant Association.

Sitting in a meeting chaired by Collins, the observer sees a highly integrated and highly organized person, a man with definite, well planned goals, in action. Meetings are on time, brief, to the point, and effective. Obviously he is a person who thrives on challenge. The beauty of this man is that many of the challenges he takes on are for the benefit of the industry and society as a whole. If he is the adult version of the All-American boy, it is only to be hoped that others will emulate him.

Bibliography

American Gas Association. *Commercial Kitchens.* Arlington, Va.: The Association, 1962.

American Heritage Book of the Revolution. New York: Simon and Schuster, 1958.

American Hotel and Motel Association. *The Hubbart Formula.*

American Hotel and Motel Association and School of Hotel, Restaurant, and Institutional Management. *Commercial Lodging Market, Phase Two.* East Lansing: Michigan State University, 1968.

Baum, Vicki. *Grand Hotel.* New York: Doubleday, 1931.

_____. *Hotel Berlin.* New York: Doubleday, 1944.

Bemelmans, Ludwig. *Hotel Splendide.* New York: Viking, 1941.

Bennett, Arnold. *Imperial Palace.* New York: Doubleday, 1931.

Boorstin, Daniel A. *The American National Experience.* New York: Random House, 1965.

Cella, Francis R. *Retail Site Selection.* Unpublished manuscript.

Dabney, Thomas E. *The Man Who Bought the Waldorf.* Duell, Sloane and Pearce, 1950.

Dana, Arthur W. *Kitchen Planning for Quantity Food Service.* New York: Harpers, 1945.

Dean, Edward B. "The Miami Beach Hotel Strike." *Cornell Hotel and Restaurant Administration Quarterly* (May 1962).

Deiss, Joseph J. *Herculaneum, Italy's Buried Treasure.* New York: Thomas R. Crowell, 1969.

Dyer, Dewey A. *So You Want to Start a Restaurant?* Boston: CBI, 1981.

Hailey, Arthur. *Hotel.* New York: Doubleday, 1965.

Handbook of Nantucket. Nantucket: Island Review Office, 1874.

Hayes, William A. *An Economic Analysis of the American Hotel Industry.* A dissertation, The Catholic University of America, 1952.

Hayner, Norman S. *Hotel Life.* Chapel Hill: University of North Carolina, 1936.

Henderson, Ernest. *The World of Mr. Sheraton.* New York: Popular Library, 1962.

Hilton, Conrad. *Be My Guest.* New York: Prentice-Hall, 1957.

"Hotel Food and Beverage Management." *Cornell Hotel and Restaurant Administration Quarterly* (November 1966).

Josephson, Matthew. *Union House, Union Bar.* New York: Random House, 1956.

King, Doris. "The Community Hotel." *The SFA Economist,* Dept. of Business Administration, Austin State College, Vol. 4, No. 2 (Spring 1960).

_____. *Explanations in Entrepreneurial History.* Harvard Research Center in Entrepreneurial History, February, 1956.

Lansing and Blood. *The Changing Travel Market.* Ann Arbor: University of Michigan, Research Center, 1964.

Lately, Thomas. *Delmonico's, A Century of Splendor.* New York: Houghton-Mifflin, 1967.

Lattin, Gerald W. *Modern Hotel and Motel Management.* San Francisco: W. H. Freeman and Co., 1968.

Laventhol & Horwath. *U.S. Lodging Industry.* New York: 1975.

_____. *Financing the Lodging Industry: A Survey of Lender Attitudes.* New York: 1975.

Laventhol and Horwath. "U.S. Lodging Industry," Philadelphia. Published annually.

_____. *Uniform System of Accounts for Restaurants.* Rev. Ed. Chicago: Cahners Books, 1968.

Laver, James. *Age of Illusion.* New York: McKay, 1972.

Lewis, Sinclair. *Work of Art.* New York: Doubleday, 1934.

Lundberg, Donald E. *Inside Innkeeping.* Dubuque, Iowa: Wm. C. Brown Co., Inc., 1956.

_____, and Armatas, James P. *The Management of People in Hotels, Restaurants and Clubs.* Rev. Ed. Chapter on "The Harris, Kerr, Forster Payroll Cost System." Dubuque, Iowa: Wm. C. Brown Co., Inc., 1980.

_____, and Kotschevar, Lendal. *Understanding Cooking*. Amherst: Marcus Printing Co. 20 Appleton St. Holyoke, Mass. 01040, 1970.

_____, and Kudrley, A. E. "Special Report on Puerto Rico." *Hotel Management Review* (July 1963).

Lundberg, Ferdinand. *The Rich and Super-Rich*. Secaucus, N.J.: Lyle Stuart, Inc., 1968.

Luxton, Howard. *Pompeii and Herculaneum*. London: Spring Books, 1966.

Miller, Floyd. *America's Extraordinary Hotelman*. The Statler Foundation, 1968.

Mitchell, Harold. *Caribbean Patterns*. London: Chambers, Ltd., 1967.

"Motels." *Architectural Record*, August, 1966.

"The 1968 Study of Puerto Rico Hotel Operations." *The Accountant* (LKHH) Vol. 48, No. 4 (1969).

Pannell Kerr Forster. *Funds in the Hotel Industry*. 16800 Imperial Valley Drive, Houston. Published annually.

Podd, George O., and Lesure, John D. *Planning and Operating Motels and Motor Hotels*, Rochelle Park, N.J.: Hayden Book Co., Inc., 1964.

Powers, Thomas F. "The Competitive Structure of the Hotel/Motel Market." A paper presented to the Council on Hotel, Restaurant and Institutional Education, 1969.

"The Quest for Identification." *Cornell Hotel and Restaurant Administration Quarterly* (February 1968).

Ranhofer, Charles, and Ranhofer, R. *The Epicurean*. New York: Dover, 1971.

"Restaurants and Catering." *Small Business Bibliography* (July 1965).

Ritz, Marie Louise, *Cesar Ritz, Host to the World*. New York: Lippincott, 1938.

Robel, James L. "How Much Is Your Motel Worth?" *Transcript* (January 1964).

Today's Commercial Lodging Market: Target Opportunity. Ann Arbor: Bureau of Business and Economic Research, Michigan State University, 1968.

Travel Trends in the United States and Canada. Boulder: Business Research Div., University of Colorado, 1975.

U.S. Government Printing Office. *Directory of National Trade Associations of Businessmen*. Washington, D.C.: Government Printing Office.

U.S. Travel Data Center. *The Importance of Tourism to the U.S. Economy*. Washington, D.C., 1975.

University of Massachusetts, *Statler Lectures*, 1971, 1972, 1973, Amherst.

_____. *Education Directory*. Washington, D.C.: Government Printing Office.

"Using Break-Even Analysis in Food Service Establishments." *Food Management Program Leaflet No. 13*, College of Agriculture, University of Massachusetts.

Vallen, Jerome, J. *Art and Science of Modern Innkeeping*. Rochelle Park, N.J.: Ahrens Publishing Co., 1968.

Watts, Stephen. *The Ritz*. London: The Bodley Head, 1963.

Whyte, William Foote. *Human Relations in the Restaurant Industry*. New York: McGraw-Hill, 1948.

_____, Hamilton, E. L., and Wiley, M. C. *Action Research for Management*.

Williamson, Jefferson. *American Hotel: An Anecdoted History*. New York: Alfred Knopf, 1930.

Younger, William. *Gods, Men and Wine*. London: The Wine and Food Society, 1966.

Index

NOTES

NOTES

NOTES

NOTES

NOTES

NOTES

NOTES